SPEAK LEBANESE

SPEAK LEBANESE

THE BASICS OF THE
LEBANESE LANGUAGE
GRAMMAR, DICTIONARY AND DIALOGUE TIPS

WALID SHAMMAS

Copyright Information

ISBN-10: 0994062117
ISBN-13: 978-0994062116

Cover Photo by Khaled Nahra.

Contents

Preface

The Lebanese language is only a spoken language. Lebanese people use the Arabic language for official written communication. However, Lebanese is different from Arabic due to its different path of evolution from the Aramaic and Syriac roots. If someone is skilled in the written Arabic language but not in Lebanese, she will not be able to carry on a casual conversation with Lebanese speakers. Other Arabic languages share similarities with the Lebanese language, like Syrian, Palestinian and Egyptian, for instance. Nevertheless, each spoken language is its own entity and has variances that shape it and differentiate it from its sister languages.

Being able to speak Lebanese gives you the advantage of being able to communicate verbally with people from the Arabic world, as the written Arabic language is never used in daily life. Once you adapt your ears to the Lebanese language, you will find that the other languages of the Arabic world will not be difficult to speak or understand. Furthermore, with some extreme exceptions, if you speak enough Lebanese you will be understood everywhere in the Arabic world.

You will notice that different Lebanese speakers will have different ways of pronunciation and even different choice of words as the language may change from area to area and from person to person. This doesn't mean that there is right and wrong, it all depends on the speakers' personal preference. The material in this book is not meant to be a representation of all variants of the Lebanese language, but rather to provide content that is understandable to all Lebanese speakers.

The grammar rules that you will find in this book for the spoken Lebanese language have not been written before and they are not written in stone. My goal is to offer a tool for those who prefer to learn by grammar and rules rather than by memory.

GRAMMAR

Alphabet

- Subscripted letters in this book indicate very rapid vowels. Shorten the emphasis on these vowels but don't eliminate them, they help expressing the proper pronunciation.

- An (') apostrophe represents a stop and a re-start (sounds like - AH or EH but the H is silent). If it is at the beginning or the end of the word, it is an abrupt-loud stop.

- For the Ď, Ŝ, Ť, and Ž, to achieve a heavy sound, it is suggested that you place the tip of your tongue further back on the upper palate than you would for the regular D, S, T, and Z.

Ä= Augh in bought	Ď= a heavy D	É= like A in Bay	G= G in beige	ĥ= like an H with smaller air passage	I= I as in ink	Ḱ= like ch in Irish loch
O= O as in home	OO= as in boots	R= roll the rrr	Ť= a heavy T	Ř= like a French R (gargle it)	Ŝ= a heavy S	Ž= a heavy Z

The letters used in this book	Way of pronunciation	Lebanese example	Meaning of the example
A	A as in apple	Alb	Heart
Ǎ (Doesn't exist in English)	Like the *augh* in daughter or the *ough* in bought (stress this letter).	Ǎain	Eye
B	B as in Bear	B_arrd	Cold
D	D as in Dear	D_ibb	Bear
Ď (Doesn't exist in English)	* Like a heavy D	Ďow (Ďa-ow)	Light
É	É like the "A" in **Ba**y, **Sa**y, plane	Lsén	Tongue
EE	Like EA or EE in the middle of a word: as in s**ea**l or st**ee**l.	Kbeer	Large
F	F as in Free	F_ard	Gun
G	G as in the second **G** in Garage, or the **G** in beige (pronounced more like the French G)	Gabal	Mountain
H	H as in Hotel	Hon	Here
Ĥ (Doesn't exist in English)	H (like an "H" but tighten your throat so less air can go through)	ĥ_abl	Rope
I	I as in **I**nn	Sin	Tooth
K	K as in as**k**	K_alb	Dog
Ḱ (Doesn't exist in English)	Like the "**ch**" in the Irish Loch	Ḱass	Lettuce
L	L as in Last	Laimoon	Lemon/ Orange
M	M as in Moon	Mikinsé	Broom
N	N as in Night	Naĥlé	Bee
O	O as in home	Lon	Color
OO	OO as in boot	Ĥoot	Whale
R	R like rrr.. (Should be rolled)	Reeshé	Feather
Ř (Doesn't exist in English)	The R must be rolled in the back of the tongue like a French R (as if gargling)	Ř_areeb	Strange/ stranger
S	S as in slow	Sy-yara	Car
Ŝ (Doesn't exist in English)	* Like a heavy S	Ŝoor_ah	Picture/ Photo
Sh	Sh as in She	Shmél	North
T	T as in tree	Teen	Figs
Ť (Doesn't exist in English)	* Like a heavy T	Ť_ablé	Drum
W	W as in West	W_ar'_ah	Paper/Leaf
Y	Like Y in the beginning of a word: as in **Y**ard	Yaum	Paper/Leaf
Z	Z as in Zoo	Z_alméh	Man
Ž (Doesn't exist in English)	* Like a heavy Z (very rarely used in Lebanese, often replaced by a regular Z)	Žir-bén	Skunk

Ǎ= Augh in bought	**Ď**= a heavy D	**É**= like A in Bay	**G**= G in beige	**ĥ**= like an H with smaller air passage	**I**= I as in ink	**Ḱ**= like ch in Irish loch
O= O as in home	**OO**= as in boots	**R**= roll the rrr	**Ť**= a heavy T	**Ř**= like a French R (gargle it)	**Ŝ**= a heavy S	**Ž**= a heavy Z

<u>The following letters are to be introduced to the English alphabet in order to cover all the Lebanese letters:</u>

Ř = This letter is a **must learn**. Many words require this letter and it can not be replaced by another letter.

Ḱ = If you replace this letter by the regular letter "K" you will still be understood by Lebanese people

Ŝ = If you replace this letter by the regular letter "S" you will still be understood by Lebanese people

Ď = If you replace this letter by the regular letter "D" you will still be understood by Lebanese people

Ť = If you replace this letter by the regular letter "T" you will still be understood by Lebanese people

Ž = If you replace this letter by the regular letter "Z" you will still be understood by Lebanese people

Ă = It is **preferred to learn** this letter, however if you replace it with a regular "A" you will usually be understood

Ĥ = It is **preferred to learn** this letter, however if you replace it with a regular "H" you will usually be understood

Ă= Augh in bought	Ď= a heavy D	É= like A in Bay	G= G in beige	ĥ= like an H with smaller air passage	I= I as in ink	Ḱ= like ch in Irish loch
O= O as in home	OO= as in boots	R= roll the rrr	Ť= a heavy T	Ř= like a French R (gargle it)	Ŝ= a heavy S	Ž= a heavy Z

| Ă= Augh in bought | Ď= a heavy D | É= like A in Bay | G= G in beige | ḥ= like an H with smaller air passage | I= I as in ink | Ḱ= like ch in Irish loch |
| O= O as in home | OO= as in boots | R= roll the rrr | Ť= a heavy T | Ř= like a French R (gargle it) | Ṣ= a heavy S | Ž= a heavy Z |

Please study the alphabet very well as they will be the basis of the rest of this book.

Articles
Definite/Indefinite

Words that start with: A, Ă, B, É, F, G, H, Ĥ, I, K, Ќ, L, M, Ř, K, W, Y or ' (apostrophe) take the letter "L" in front of them when you need to use the definite article "the". "L" is used in Lebanese for "The".

Words that start with: Sh, D, Ď, N, R, S, Ŝ, T, Ť, Z and Ž don't take the letter "L" when you need to put "The". Instead, you just stress the first letter.

Stressing the first letter will be shown in this book by doubling the first lettet in the word.

Ă= Augh in bought	Ď= a heavy D	É= like A in Bay	G= G in beige	ĥ= like an H with smaller air passage	I= I as in ink	Ќ= like ch in Irish loch
O= O as in home	OO= as in boots	R= roll the rrr	Ť= a heavy T	Ř= like a French R (gargle it)	Ŝ= a heavy S	Ž= a heavy Z

If you make a mistake you will still be understood as the difference might not be noticeable. You may go by how easy it is for you to pronounce the "L" in front of each letter and when it is hard to be pronounced just stress the first letter.

Example:

Két₍ₑ₎b	Writer
L-Két₍ₑ₎b	The writer
Dibb	Bear
Ḍdibb	The bear
Am₍ₐ₎r	Moon
L-Am₍ₐ₎r	The moon
Sirr	Secret
Ṣsirr	The secret

In Lebanese, there is no indefinite article. It is just skipped all together.
Remember also that the definite article "L" can not be added to names.)

Ã= Augh in bought	Ḍ= a heavy D	É= like A in Bay	G= G in beige	ḥ= like an H with smaller air passage	I= I as in ink	Ķ= like ch in Irish loch
O= O as in home	OO= as in boots	R= roll the rrr	Ṭ= a heavy T	Ř= like a French R (gargle it)	Ṣ= a heavy S	Ž= a heavy Z

Prepositions

At (someone's place)	Ăₐnd		In	Bi
At (the table)	Ăla (also Ăa)		About (talking about)	Ăₐn
At (the church)	Bi		But	Bₐss
On	Ăla (also Ăa)		Underneath	Tₐĥt
To	Ăla (also Ăa)		In front of	'iddém
To (when used before "where" or the prepositions in red)	Lₐ		Behind	Wₐrₐ
From	Min		Near	Ĥₐd
With	mₐĂ		Inside/Indoor	Goowₐ
Almost	Ăa shwₐy – Ăa nitfé		Outside/Outdoor	Barrₐ
Of	Min		Over/Above	Fo'

Example:

1) I'm at Patrick's = ana Ăₐnd Patrick
2) I'm sitting at the table = ana 'aĂéd Ăa ttawla
3) I'm at the church = ana bi L-kneesé
4) There are apples on the table = fee tifféĥ Ăa ttawla
5) He is going to work = Hoowé rayéĥ Ăa sh-shiŘl
6) (to) where are you going? = lₐ wén rayéĥ ?
7) I'm from Canada = ana min Canada
8) She is going with Peter = heeyé rayĥa mₐĂ Peter
9) I almost fell = Ăa shwₐy w'aĂt
10) Give me five of these please = ĂŤeené Ќamsé min ĥawdé

please

11) Put the toys in the box = ĥiŤ L-liĂab bi ŜŜanĎoo'
12) We are talking about Katie = naĥna Ăam niĥnké Ăₐn Katie
13) I'm young but smart = ana ŜŘeer bₐss zaké

Ă= Augh in bought	Ď= a heavy D	É= like A in Bay	G= G in beige	ĥ= like an H with smaller air passage	I= I as in ink	Ќ= like ch in Irish loch
O= O as in home	OO= as in boots	R= roll the rrr	Ť= a heavy T	Ř= like a French R (gargle it)	Ŝ= a heavy S	Ž= a heavy Z

Conjunctions

And	Woo (also pronounced as "wi" when followed by the definite article and is linked to the following letter.	Or	A₀w

Example:

1) The boy and his mother   =   ŜŜabé woo immoo
2) The king and the queen   =   L-malak wi-L-malaké
3) Fries or salad?   =   baŤaŤa a₀w salaŤa

Ǎ= Augh in bought	Ď= a heavy D	É= like A in Bay	G= G in beige	ĥ= like an H with smaller air passage	I= I as in ink	Ǩ= like ch in Irish loch
O= O as in home	OO= as in boots	R= roll the rrr	Ť= a heavy T	Ř= like a French R (gargle it)	Ŝ= a heavy S	Ž= a heavy Z

Demonstrative adjectives

This (Masculine)	Hayda	That (Masculine)	Haydék
This (Feminine)	Haydé	That (Feminine)	Haydeek
These	Hawdé	Those	Hawdeek

- Verb "to be" is not required in Lebanese after demonstrative adjectives. "haydé seeyara" literally translates to "this car" but means "this is a car". To say "this car", you will be specifying a certain car which requires you to use the definite article "L" when appropriate or double the first letter if "L" isn't appropriate, eg: "haydé sseeyara" which translates literally to "this the car" but means "this car".

Ă= Augh in bought	Ď= a heavy D	É= like A in Bay	G= G in beige	ḥ= like an H with smaller air passage	I= I as in ink	Ḱ= like ch in Irish loch
O= O as in home	OO= as in boots	R= roll the rrr	Ť= a heavy T	Ř= like a French R (gargle it)	Ŝ= a heavy S	Ž= a heavy Z

You might find some Lebanese speakers using words like "Ha", "Hé" or "How" to replace the demonstrative adjectives above. Be aware that they are used but try to avoid them till you are comfortable using the original ones (from the table) as these can be used in all situations unlike their substitutes.

Relative adjectives

There is one Lebanese term that can fill for: that, who, which and whom. This term is: "Yalli". You can also minimize it to just "lli"

Possessive Pronouns:

Mine	TabaĂé	Ours	TabaĂna
Yours (masculine)	TabaĂak	His	TabaĂo
Yours (feminine)	TabaĂik	Hers	TabaĂa
Yours (plural)	TabaĂkon	Theirs	TabaĂon

OR

Mine	Ilé	Ours	Ilna
Yours (masculine)	Ilak	His	Ilo
Yours (feminine)	Ilik	Hers	Ila
Yours (plural)	Ilkon	Theirs	Ilon

Both above sets of possessive pronouns are used. You may chose only one of them to learn and use but be aware of the other set so that you understand it if you hear someone else using it.

Example:

Hayda L-ktéb TabaĂé	This book is mine	Hayda L-ktéb Ilé	This book is mine
Hayda ddaftar TabaĂak	This notebook is yours (masculin)	Hayda ddaftar Ilak	This notebook is yours (masculin)
Haydé L-kirsé TabaĂik	This chair is yours (female)	Haydé L-kirsé Ilik	This chair is yours (female)
Hawdé ssyyarat TabaĂkon	These cars are yours (plural)	Hawdé ssyyarat Ilkon	These cars are yours (plural)
Haydé L-madrasé TabaĂna	This school is ours	Haydé L-madrasé Ilna	This school is ours
Haydé shhanta TabaĂo	This suitcase is his	Haydé shhanta Ilo	This suitcase is his
Haydé L-Řirfé TabaĂa	This room is hers	Haydé L-Řirfé Ila	This room is hers
Hawdé L-byoot TabaĂon	These houses are theirs	Hawdé L-byoot Ilon	These houses are theirs

Ă= Augh in bought	**Ď**= a heavy D	**É**= like A in Bay	**G**= G in beige	**ĥ**= like an H with smaller air passage	**I**= I as in ink	**Ǩ**= like ch in Irish loch
O= O as in home	**OO**= as in boots	**R**= roll the rrr	**Ť**= a heavy T	**Ř**= like a French R (gargle it)	**Š**= a heavy S	**Ž**= a heavy Z

Possession Suffixes:

These suffixes are added to the end of the word and are to replace the English Possessive Adjectives.

Used with Masculine objects		Used with Feminine objects	
My	É	My	Té (for singular objects) – é (for plural objects)
Your (M)	Ak	Your (M)	Tak (for singular objects) – ak (for plural objects)
Your (F)	Ik	Your (F)	Tik (for singular objects) – ik (for plural objects)
His	OO	His	To (for singular objects) – o (for plural objects)
Her	A	Her	Ta (for singular objects) – a (for plural objects)
Our	Na	Our	Itna (for singular objects) – na (for plural objects)
Your (plural)	Kon	Your (Plural)	Itkon (for singular objects) - kon (for plural objects)
Their	On	Their	Iton (for singular objects) – on (for plural objects)

Example:

My husband	Zawgé	My wife	Marté
Your dog *(your-Masculin)*	Kalbak	Your wife *(your-Masculin)*	Martak
Your husband *(your-Feminine)*	Zawgik	Your cat *(your-Feminine)*	Bséntik
His dog	Kalboo	His wife	Marto
Her husband	Zawga	Her cat	Bsénta
Our husbands	Azwégna	Our cats	Bseinétna
Your husbands *(your-plural)*	Azwégkon	Your cats *(your-plural)*	Bseinétkon
Their husbands	Azwégon	Their cats	Bseinéton

Ă= Augh in bought	Ď= a heavy D	É= like A in Bay	G= G in beige	ḥ= like an H with smaller air passage	I= I as in ink	Ḱ= like ch in Irish loch
O= O as in home	OO= as in boots	R= roll the rrr	Ť= a heavy T	Ř= like a French R (gargle it)	Ŝ= a heavy S	Ž= a heavy Z

There is another way to express possession and that's by forming the sentence in a certain way.

Example (1): "Ăain L-bsén" translates literally to "eye the cat" but means "the cat's eye".

Example (2): "seeyarit zzalamé" translates literally to "car the man" but means "the man's car"

Example (3) to say Peter's car you say "seeyarit Peter" and to say Peter's eye you say "Ăain Peter".

- In Lebanese you don't need to add "the = L" to the word "eye" in example (1) because the word "cat" has "the = L" which makes both the cat and its eye identified by the same definite article.

- If the first word is feminine (ending with "é" or "a" – with some exceptions) then you have to eliminate the last vowel and replace it by the sound "it" eg: seeyara becomes seeyarit (example 2).

- If you are using a propper noun instead of a noun you will not have to add the definite article "L" as we don't add "L" to propper nouns in Lebanese, (see example 3).

Ă= Augh in bought	Ď= a heavy D	É= like A in Bay	G= G in beige	ĥ= like an H with smaller air passage	I= I as in ink	Ќ= like ch in Irish loch
O= O as in home	OO= as in boots	R= roll the rrr	Ť= a heavy T	Ř= like a French R (gargle it)	Ŝ= a heavy S	Ž= a heavy Z

Interrogative Pronouns/ Adjectives/Adverbs:

Who	Meen		How much	addésh
Whom	Meen		How many	K$_a$m
Why	Lésh		For what	Mishén shoo
When	'émta		Whose / for whom	Lameen / _also_ / lmeen
What	Shoo			
Where	Wén			
Which	Ay-ya			
How	Keef			

Object Suffixes:

These suffixes are added to the end of the verb in any tense to replace the object in the sentence.

Add these to the end of the verb to replace an object	
Me	Né
You (M)	Ak
You (F)	Ik
Him	Oo (ee if the subject is you-feminine)
Her	Ha (the H is very light)
Us	Na
You (plural)	Kon
Them	Hon (the H is very light)

Example:

He carries Heidi	Hoowé byiĥmél Heidi
He carries her	Howwé byiĥmélha

1) He loves me *(me-feminine)*: Hoowé biĥibbné
2) He loves you *(you-masculine)*: Hoowé biĥibbak
3) He loves you *(you-feminine)*: Hoowé biĥibbik
4) He loves him: Hoowé biĥibboo
5) He loves her: Hoowé biĥibbha
6) He loves us: Hoowé biĥibbna
7) He loves you *(you-plurel)*: Hoowé biĥibbkon
8) He loves them: Hoowé biĥibbhon
9) She saw me *(me-masculine)*: Heeyé shéfitné
10) They ate it *(it being feminine - her)*: hinné aklooha
11) I ate it *(it being masculine - him)*: ana akaltoo
12) They ate it *(it being masculine – him)*: hinné akalooo (notice that as the original verb included two O's at the end, and as the suffix consists of two Os, you just add one O to the verb to emphasize the stretch of the O sound.)
13) You (f) tickled him: inté zakzaktee

Ă= Augh in bought	Ď= a heavy D	É= like A in Bay	G= G in beige	ĥ= like an H with smaller air passage	I= I as in ink	Ḱ= like ch in Irish loch
O= O as in home	OO= as in boots	R= roll the rrr	Ť= a heavy T	Ř= like a French R (gargle it)	Ŝ= a heavy S	Ž= a heavy Z

The exceptions are:

A) You (masculin) = AK: is used with all forms of verbs except when the subject is in the first person plural or third person plural.

Example:
Normally: I saw you(m): ana shift**ak**
Exception: we saw you(m): naĥna shif**nék** - & - they saw you: hinné shéf**ook**

B) You (feminin): IK is used with all forms of verbs except when the subject is in the first person plural or third person plural.

Example:
Normally: I saw you(f): ana shift**ik**
Exception: we saw you: naĥna shif**néké** - & - they saw you: hinné shéf**ooké**

Notice that in the first person plural the last vowel in the verb was removed and replaced by the suffix. In all other forms the suffix is added without modifying the original verb.

Ă= Augh in bought	Ď= a heavy D	É= like A in Bay	G= G in beige	ĥ= like an H with smaller air passage	I= I as in ink	Ḱ= like ch in Irish loch
O= O as in home	OO= as in boots	R= roll the rrr	Ť= a heavy T	Ř= like a French R (gargle it)	Ŝ= a heavy S	Ž= a heavy Z

Other Suffixes:

The suffix "T$_a$" is used before verbs sometimes to give the meaning of the English "to do".

When "T$_a$" is added, it replaces the suffixes that normally fall before the verb in both the present and the past tenses.

In Lebanese you don't have to put "to" before a verb unless if the first verb in the phrase justifies or rationalizes the occurance of the second verb.

Example:

I went to school to learn: Riĥt Ăa L-madrasé T$_a$ 'ItĂallam
(Riĥt=went – Ăal=to – L=the – madrasé=school – T$_a$=to – 'itĂallam=study)

Learning (the second verb) justifies and rationalizes going to school (the first verb).

Ă= Augh in bought	Đ= a heavy D	É= like A in Bay	G= G in beige	ĥ= like an H with smaller air passage	I= I as in ink	Ќ= like ch in Irish loch
O= O as in home	OO= as in boots	R= roll the rrr	Ť= a heavy T	Ř= like a French R (gargle it)	Ŝ= a heavy S	Ž= a heavy Z

Can / May:

Can and May in Lebanese are used in the same way they are used in the Englisg language. You can use them to be polite when asking for a favour or you can use them to form a question. The table below shows the conjugation of Can/May.

Can / May	
Ana	Feené
Inta	Feek
Inté	Feeké
Hoowé	Fee
Heeyé	Feeya
Naĥna	Feena
Intoo	Feekon
Hinné	Feeyon

Example:

I can eat	Ana feené 'ékol	She can't play	Heeyé ma feeya tilĂab
Can you(m) drink?	Inta feek tishranb?	We can't drive	Naĥna ma feena nsoo'
Can you(f) walk?	Inté feeké timshé?	You(plural)can't sleep	Intoo ma feekon tnémoo
He may go	Hoowé fee yrooĥ	Can't they help?	Ma feeyon yséĂdoo?

Ă= Augh in bought	Ď= a heavy D	É= like A in Bay	G= G in beige	ĥ= like an H with smaller air passage	I= I as in ink	Ķ= like ch in Irish loch
O= O as in home	OO= as in boots	R= roll the rrr	Ť= a heavy T	Ř= like a French R (gargle it)	Ŝ= a heavy S	Ž= a heavy Z

Ā= Augh in bought	Ď= a heavy D	É= like A in Bay	G= G in beige	ĥ= like an H with smaller air passage	I= I as in ink	Ḱ= like ch in Irish loch
O= O as in home	OO= as in boots	R= roll the rrr	Ť= a heavy T	Ř= like a French R (gargle it)	Ŝ= a heavy S	Ž= a heavy Z

When can/may are used infront of a verb you should drop the first letter of the suffix.

Pronouns:

I = Ana	We = Naĥna
You (Male) = Inta	You (Plural) = Intoo
You (Female) = Inté	
He = Hoowé	They = Hinné
She = Heeyé	

Ă= Augh in bought	Ď= a heavy D	É= like A in Bay	G= G in beige	ĥ= like an H with smaller air passage	I= I as in ink	Ќ= like ch in Irish loch
O= O as in home	OO= as in boots	R= roll the rrr	Ť= a heavy T	Ř= like a French R (gargle it)	Ŝ= a heavy S	Ž= a heavy Z

Verbs

Ǎ= Augh in bought	Ď= a heavy D	É= like A in Bay	G= G in beige	ĥ= like an H with smaller air passage	I= I as in ink	Ḱ= like ch in Irish loch
O= O as in home	OO= as in boots	R= roll the rrr	Ť= a heavy T	Ř= like a French R (gargle it)	Ṡ= a heavy S	Ž= a heavy Z

- This tense is used in Lebanese to state facts, example: I eat vegetables. If you want to say that you are eating vegetables right now then you will be using the present continuous form.

Use the suffixes in green when the verb in the first person singular starts with a consonant after the b

I = ana b	We = naĥna mn
You (male) = Inta bt	You (plural) = intoo bt
You (Female) = Inté bt	
He = Hoowé bi	They = hinné bi
She = heeyé bt	

Use the suffixes in blue when the verb in the first person singular starts with a vowel after the b

I = ana b	We = naĥna mn(i/é)
You (male) = Inta bt(i/é)	You (plural) = intoo bt(i/é)
You (Female) = Inté bt(i/é)	
He = Hoowé by(i/é)	They = hinné by(i/é)
She = heeyé bt(i/é)	

Ă= Augh in bought	Ď= a heavy D	É= like A in Bay	G= G in beige	ĥ= like an H with smaller air passage	I= I as in ink	Ķ= like ch in Irish loch
O= O as in home	OO= as in boots	R= roll the rrr	Ť= a heavy T	Ř= like a French R (gargle it)	Ŝ= a heavy S	Ž= a heavy Z

Verb to want (present)

I want = ana baddéh	We want = naĥna baddna
You (male) want = Inta baddak	You (plural) want = intoo badkon
You (Female) want = Inté baddik	
He wants = Hoowé baddoo	They want = hinné baddon
She wants = heeyé badda	

Verb to travel (present)

I = ana bséfér	We = naĥna mnséfér
You (male) = Inta btséfér	You (plural) = intoo btséfroo
You (Female) = Inté btséfré	
He = Hoowé biséfér	They = hinné biséfroo
She = heeyé btséfér	

Verb to eat (present)

I = ana békol	We = naĥna mnékol
You (male) = Inta btékol	You (plural) = intoo btékloo
You (Female) = Inté btéklé	
He = Hoowé byékol	They = hinné byékloo
She = heeyé btékol	

Verb to sleep (present)

I = ana bném	We = naĥna mn-ném
You (male) = Inta btném	You (plural) = intoo btnémoo
You (Female) = Inté btnémé	
He = Hoowé biném	They = hinné binémoo
She = heeyé btném	

Verb to drink (present)

I = ana bishrab	We = naĥna mnishrab
You (male) = Inta btishrab	You (plural) = intoo btishraboo
You (Female) = Inté btishrabé	
He = Hoowé byishrab	They = hinné byishraboo
She = heeyé btishrab	

Verb to go (present)

I = ana brooĥ	We = naĥna mnrooĥ
You (male) = Inta btrooĥ	You (plural) = intoo btrooĥoo
You (Female) = Inté btrooĥé	
He = Hoowé birooĥ	They = hinné birooĥoo
She = heeyé btrooĥ	

Ă= Augh in bought	Ď= a heavy D	É= like A in Bay	G= G in beige	ĥ= like an H with smaller air passage	I= I as in ink	Ќ= like ch in Irish loch
O= O as in home	OO= as in boots	R= roll the rrr	Ť= a heavy T	Ř= like a French R (gargle it)	Ŝ= a heavy S	Ž= a heavy Z

Verb to see (present)

I = ana bshoof	We want = naĥna mnshoof
You (male) = Inta btshoof	You (plural) = intoo btshoofoo
You (Female) = Inté btshoofé	
He = Hoowé bishoof	They = hinné bishoofoo
She = heeyé btshoof	

Verb to walk (present)

I = ana bimshé	• We want = naĥna mnimshé
You (male) = Inta btimshé	You (plural) = intoo btimshoo
You (Female) = Inté btimshé	
He = Hoowé byimshé	They = hinné byimshoo
She = heeyé btimshé	

Verb to wear (present)

I = ana bilbéss	We want = naĥna mnilbéss
You (male) = Inta btilbéss	You (plural) = intoo btilbsoo
You (Female) = Inté btilbsé	
He = Hoowé byilbéss	They = hinné byilbsoo
She = heeyé btilbéss	

Ă= Augh in bought	Ď= a heavy D	É= like A in Bay	G= G in beige	ĥ= like an H with smaller air passage	I= I as in ink	Ќ= like ch in Irish loch
O= O as in home	OO= as in boots	R= roll the rrr	Ť= a heavy T	Ř= like a French R (gargle it)	Ŝ= a heavy S	Ž= a heavy Z

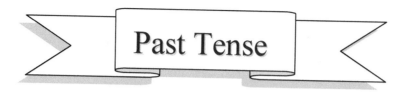

Past Tense

Verb to want (past) (exception)

I wanted = ana kint baddé	We wanted = naĥna kinna baddna
You (male) wanted = Inta kint baddak	You (plural) wanted = intoo kintoo badkon
You (Female) wanted = Inté kinté baddik	
He wanted = Hoowé kén baddoo	They wanted = hinné kénoo baddon
She wanted = heeyé kénét badda	

- Notice the addition of the auxiliary "kint" which is equivalent in English to the past tense of "verb to be" and tends to mean "used to".

- Verb "to want" doesn't have a simple past form in Lebanese and that is why the auxiliary "kint" is added to form the past continuous as an exception.

- This auxiliary can be used with any other verb in the present tense to give the meaning that "one used to do" or was doing something when another action took place (see past continuous)

Verb to travel (past)

I = ana séf$_a$rt	We = naĥna séf$_a$rna
You (male) = Inta séf$_a$rt	You (plural) = intoo séf$_a$rtoo
You (Female) = Inté séf$_a$rté	
He = Hoowé séf$_a$r	They = hinné séf$_a$roo
She = heeyé séf$_a$rét	

Verb to eat (past)

I = ana ak$_a$lt	We = naĥna ak$_a$lna
You (male) = Inta ak$_a$lt	You (plural) = intoo ak$_a$ltoo
You (Female) = Inté ak$_a$lté	
He = Hoowé ak$_a$l	They = hinné ak$_a$loo
She = heeyé aklét	

Verb to sleep (past)

I = ana nimt	We = naĥna nimna
You (male) = Inta nimt	You (plural) = intoo nimtoo
You (Female) = Inté nimté	
He = Hoowé nem	They = hinné némoo
She = heeyé némét	

Ă= Augh in bought	Đ= a heavy D	É= like A in Bay	G= G in beige	ĥ= like an H with smaller air passage	I= I as in ink	Ќ= like ch in Irish loch
O= O as in home	OO= as in boots	R= roll the rrr	Ť= a heavy T	Ř= like a French R (gargle it)	Ŝ= a heavy S	Ž= a heavy Z

Verb to drink (past)

I = ana shribt	We = naĥna shribna
You (male) = Inta shribt	You (plural) = intoo shribtoo
You (Female) = Inté shribté	
He = Hoowé shiréb	They = hinné shirboo
She = heeyé shirbét	

Verb to go (past)

I = ana riĥt	We = naĥna riĥna
You (male) = Inta riĥt	You (plural) = intoo riĥtoo
You (Female) = Inté riĥté	
He = Hoowé raĥ	They = hinné raĥoo
She = heeyé raĥét	

Verb to see (past)

I = ana shift	We want = naĥna shifna
You (male) = Inta shift	You (plural) = intoo shiftoo
You (Female) = Inté shifté	
He = Hoowé shéf	They = hinné shéfoo
She = heeyé shéfét	

Verb to walk (past)

I = ana msheet	We want = naĥna msheena
You (male) = Inta msheet	You (plural) = intoo msheetoo
You (Female) = Inté msheeté	
He = Hoowé mishé	They = hinné mishyoo
She = heeyé mishyét	

Verb to wear (past)

I = ana lbist	We want = naĥna lbisna
You (male) = Inta lbist	You (plural) = intoo lbistoo
You (Female) = Inté lbisté	
He = Hoowé libés	They = hinné libsoo
She = heeyé libsét	

Ă= Augh in bought	Ď= a heavy D	É= like A in Bay	G= G in beige	ĥ= like an H with smaller air passage	I= I as in ink	Ǩ= like ch in Irish loch
O= O as in home	OO= as in boots	R= roll the rrr	Ť= a heavy T	Ř= like a French R (gargle it)	Š= a heavy S	Ž= a heavy Z

Present Continuous

- This tense is used in Lebanese when the action is happening at this very moment. The auxiliary *Ăam* is added before the present tense of the verb to form the present continuous. Try to liaison (link) the Ăam with the first letter of the following verb.

- You will also notice that most of the verbs have an alternative way to conjugate the present continuous. For the alternative conjugation there is no actual English translation and it can be difficult to understand. With this form, the sentences don't require verbs at all because a noun (that is derived from the verb) describes the action. When you become more fluent in Lebanese, you will start differentiating more between these two different ways. As for now it is practical to assume that both ways are used in the same way.

Verb to want (pc)

I am wanting = ana baddé	We are wanting = nahna baddna
You (male) are wanting = Inta baddak	You (plural) are wanting = intoo badkon
You (Female) are wanting = Inté baddik	
He is wanting = Hoowé baddoo	They are wanting = hinné baddon
She is wanting = heeyé badda	

- This verb remains the same in the present tense and the present continuous forms.

Verb to travel (pc)

I = ana Ăam bséfér (also ana mséfar/mséfra)	We = nahna Ăam mnséfér (also nahna mséfreen)
You (male) = Inta Ăam btséfér (also inta mséfar)	You (plural) = intoo Ăam btséfroo (also intoo mséfreen)
You (Female) = Inté Ăam btséfré (also inté mséfra)	
He = Hoowé Ăam biséfér (also hoowé mséfar)	They = hinné Ăam biséfroo (also hinné mséfreen)
She = heeyé Ăam btséfér (also heeyé mséfra)	

Ă= Augh in bought	**Ď**= a heavy D	**É**= like A in Bay	**G**= G in beige	**ĥ**= like an H with smaller air passage	**I**= I as in ink	**Ḱ**= like ch in Irish loch
O= O as in home	**OO**= as in boots	**R**= roll the rrr	**Ť**= a heavy T	**Ř**= like a French R (gargle it)	**Ŝ**= a heavy S	**Ž**= a heavy Z

Verb to eat (pc)

I = ana Ăam békol	We = naĥna Ăam mnékol
You (male) = Inta Ăam btékol	You (plural) = intoo Ăam btékloo
You (Female) = Inté Ăam btéklé	
He = Hoowé Ăam byékol	They = hinné Ăam byékloo
She = heeyé Ăam btékol	

Verb to sleep (pc)

I = ana Ăam bném (also ana néyém/néymé)	We = naĥna Ăam mn-ném (also naĥna néymeen)
You (male) = Inta Ăam btném (also inta néyém)	You (plural) = intoo btnémoo (also intoo néymeen)
You (Female) = Inté Ăam btnémé (also inté néymé)	
He = Hoowé Ăam biném (also hoowé néyém)	They = hinné Ăam binémoo (also hinné néymeen)
She = heeyé Ăam btném (also heeyé néymé)	

Verb to drink (pc)

I = ana Ăam bishrab	We = naĥna Ăam mnishrab
You (male) = Inta Ăam btishrab	You (plural) = intoo Ăam btishraboo
You (Female) = Inté Ăam btishrabé	
He = Hoowé Ăam byishrab	They = hinné Ăam byishraboo
She = heeyé Ăam btishrab	

Verb to go (pc)

I = ana Ăam brooĥ (also ana rayéĥ/rayĥa)	We = naĥna Ăam mnrooĥ (also naĥna rayheen)
You (male) = inta Ăam btrooĥ (also Inta rayéĥ)	You (plural) = intoo Ăam btroohoo (also intoo rayheen)
You (Female) = inté Ăam btroohé (also Inté rayĥa)	
He = howwé Ăam birooĥ (also Hoowé rayéĥ)	They = hinné Ăam biroohoo (also hinné rayheen)
She = heeyé Ăam btrooĥ (also heeyé rayĥa)	

Ă= Augh in bought	Đ= a heavy D	É= like A in Bay	G= G in beige	ĥ= like an H with smaller air passage	I= I as in ink	Ķ= like ch in Irish loch
O= O as in home	OO= as in boots	R= roll the rrr	Ť= a heavy T	Ř= like a French R (gargle it)	Ŝ= a heavy S	Ž= a heavy Z

Verb to see (pc)

I = ana Ăam bshoof (also ana shéyéf/shéyfé)	We want = naĥna Ăam mnshoof (also naĥna shéyfeen)
You (male) = Inta Ăam btshoof (also inta shéyéf)	You (plural) = intoo Ăam btshoofoo (also intoo shéyfeen)
You (Female) = Inté Ăam btshoofé (also inté shéyfé)	
He = Hoowé Ăam bishoof (also hoowé shéyéf)	They = hinné Ăam bishoofoo (also hinné shéyfeen)
She = heeyé Ăam btshoof (also heeyé shéyfé)	

Verb to walk (pc)

I = ana Ăam bimshé (also ana méshé/méshyé)	We want = naĥna Ăam mnimshé (also naĥna méshyeen)
You (male) = Inta Ăam btimshé (also inta méshé)	You (plural) = intoo Ăam btimshoo (also intoo méshyeen)
You (Female) = Inté Ăam btimshé (also inté méshyé)	
He = Hoowé Ăam byimshé (also hoowé méshé)	They = hinné Ăam byimshoo (also hinné méshyeen)
She = heeyé Ăam btimshé (also heeyé méshyé)	

Verb to wear (pc)

I = ana Ăam bilbéss (ending can also be "oss") (also ana lébés/lébsé)	We want = naĥna Ăam mnilbéss (also naĥna lébseen)
You (male) = Inta Ăam btilbéss (also inta lébés)	You (plural) = intoo Ăam btilbsoo (also intoo lébseen)
You (Female) = Inté Ăam btilbsé (also inté lébsé)	
He = Hoowé Ăam byilbéss (also hoowé lébés)	They = hinné Ăam byilbsoo (also hinné lébseen)
She = heeyé Ăam btilbéss (also heeyé lébsé)	

Ă= Augh in bought	**Ď**= a heavy D	**É**= like A in Bay	**G**= G in beige	**ĥ**= like an H with smaller air passage	**I**= I as in ink	**Ḱ**= like ch in Irish loch
O= O as in home	**OO**= as in boots	**R**= roll the rrr	**Ť**= a heavy T	**Ř**= like a French R (gargle it)	**Ṧ**= a heavy S	**Ž**= a heavy Z

Past Continuous

- This tense is used in Lebanese to describe an action that was happening in the past when another action took place at the same time. The auxiliary kint is added before Ăam to form the past continuous. You will notice that an alternative conjugation is given for some of the verbs below, please pay more attention to the first (main) way of conjugation as the alternative option will be easier to learn later on.

- The auxiliary Kint is similar to the past tense of the verb "to be" in English. However, Kint doesn't exist in other tenses. This auxiliary is used to form the past continuous of almost all verbs and it is used exceptionally to form the simple past for some verbs (eg. Verb to want in the past tense).

- For the past continuous it is crucial to know how to conjugate the auxiliary kint.

The Auxiliary Kint	
Ana	Kint
Inta	Kint
Inté	Kinté
Hoowé	Kén
Heeyé	Kénét
Nahna	Kinna
Intoo	Kintoo
Hinné	Kénoo

- Like the alternative conjugation of the present continuous, the alternative conjugation of the past continuous has no actual English translation and it can be difficult to understand. With this form, the sentences don't require verbs at all because a noun (that is derived from the verb) describes the action. The auxiliary kint (respecting gender & number) must be added after the pronoun to form the alternative conjugation of the past continuous. When you become more fluent in Lebanese, you will start differentiating more between the two different ways of conjugation. As for now it is practical to assume that both ways are used in the same way.

Ă= Augh in bought	Ď= a heavy D	É= like A in Bay	G= G in beige	ĥ= like an H with smaller air passage	I= I as in ink	Ќ= like ch in Irish loch
O= O as in home	OO= as in boots	R= roll the rrr	Ť= a heavy T	Ř= like a French R (gargle it)	Ŝ= a heavy S	Ž= a heavy Z

Grammar

Verb to want (past c.)

I was wanting = ana kint baddé	We were wanting = naĥna kinna baddna
You (male) were wanting = Inta kint baddak	You (plural) were wanting = intoo kintoo badkon
You (Female) were wanting = Inté kinté baddik	
He was wanting = Hoowé kén baddoo	They were wanting = hinné kénoo baddon
She was wanting = heeyé kénét badda	

This verb remains the same in the past tense and the past continuous forms.

Verb to travel (past c.)

I = ana kint Ăam bséfér (also ana kint mséfar)	We = naĥna kinna Ăam mnséfér (also naĥna kinna mséfreen)
You (male) = Inta kint Ăam btséfér (also inta kint mséfar)	You (plural) = intoo kintoo Ăam btséfroo (also intoo kintoo mséfreen)
You (Female) = Inté kinté Ăam btséfré (also inté kinté mséfra)	
He = Hoowé kén Ăam biséfér (also hoowé kén mséfar)	They = hinné kénoo Ăam biséfroo (also hinné kénoo mséfreen)
She = heeyé kénét Ăam btséfér (also heeyé kénét mséfra)	

Verb to eat (past c.)

I = ana kint Ăam békol	We = naĥna kinna Ăam mnékol
You (male) = Inta kint Ăam btékol	You (plural) = intoo kintoo Ăam btékloo
You (Female) = Inté kinté Ăam btéklé	
He = Hoowé kén Ăam byékol	They = hinné kénoo Ăam byékloo
She = heeyé kénét Ăam btékol	

Verb to sleep (past c.)

I = ana kint Ăam bném	We = naĥna kinna Ăam mn-ném
You (male) = Inta kint Ăam btném	You (plural) = intoo kintoo btnémoo
You (Female) = Inté kinté Ăam btnémé	
He = Hoowé kén Ăam biném	They = hinné kénoo Ăam binémoo
She = heeyé kénét Ăam btném	

Verb to drink (past c.)

I = ana kint Ăam bishrab	We = naĥna kinna Ăam mnishrab
You (male) = Inta kint Ăam btishrab	You (plural) = intoo kintoo Ăam btishraboo
You (Female) = Inté kinté Ăam btishrabé	
He = Hoowé kén Ăam byishrab	They = hinné kénoo Ăam byshraboo
She = heeyé kénét Ăam btishrab	

Ă= Augh in bought	Ď= a heavy D	É= like A in Bay	G= G in beige	ĥ= like an H with smaller air passage	I= I as in ink	Ќ= like ch in Irish loch
O= O as in home	OO= as in boots	R= roll the rrr	Ť= a heavy T	Ř= like a French R (gargle it)	Ŝ= a heavy S	Ž= a heavy Z

Verb to go (past c.)

I = ana kint Ăam brooĥ (also ana kint rayéĥ)	We = naĥna kinna Ăam mnrooĥ (also naĥna kinna rayheen)
You (male) = Inta kint Ăam btrooĥ (also inta kint rayéĥ)	You (plural) = intoo kintoo Ăam btrooĥoo (also intoo kintoo rayheen)
You (Female) = Inté kinté Ăam btrooĥé (also inté kinté rayĥa)	
He = Hoowé kén Ăam birooĥ (also hoowé kén rayéĥ)	They = hinné kénoo Ăam birooĥoo (also hinné kénoo rayheen)
She = heeyé kénét Ăam btrooĥ (also heeyé kénét rayéĥa)	

Verb to see (past c.)

I = ana kint Ăam bshoof (also ana kint shéyéf)	We want = naĥna kinna Ăam mnshoof (also naĥna shéyfeen)
You (male) = Inta kint Ăam btshoof (also inta kint shéyéf)	You (plural) = intoo kintoo Ăam btshoofoo (also intoo kintoo shéyfeen)
You (Female) = Inté kinté Ăam btshoofé (also inté kinté shéyfé)	
He = Hoowé kén Ăam bishoof (also hoowé kén shéyéf)	They = hinné kénoo Ăam bishoofoo (also hinné kénoo shéyfeen)
She = heeyé kénét Ăam btshoof (also heeyé kénét shéyfé)	

Verb to walk (past c.)

I = ana kint Ăam bimshé (also ana kint méshé)	We want = naĥna kinna Ăam mnimshé (also naĥna kinna méshyeen)
You (male) = Inta kint Ăam btimshé (also inta kint méshé)	You (plural) = intoo kintoo Ăam btimshoo (also intoo kintoo méshyeen)
You (Female) = Inté kinté Ăam btimshé (also inté kinté méshyé)	
He = Hoowé kén Ăam byimshé (also hoowé kén méshé)	They = hinné kénoo Ăam byimshoo (also hinné kénoo méshyeen)
She = heeyé kénét Ăam btimshé (also heeyé kénét méshyé)	

Ă= Augh in bought	**Ď**= a heavy D	**É**= like A in Bay	**G**= G in beige	**ĥ**= like an H with smaller air passage	**I**= I as in ink	**Ǩ**= like ch in Irish loch
O= O as in home	**OO**= as in boots	**R**= roll the rrr	**Ť**= a heavy T	**Ř**= like a French R (gargle it)	**Ŝ**= a heavy S	**Ž**= a heavy Z

Verb to wear (past c.)

I = ana kint Ăam bilbéss (ending can also be "oss") (also ana kint lébés)	We want = naĥna kinna Ăam mnilbéss (also naĥna kinna lébseen)
You (male) = Inta kint Ăam btilbéss (also inta kint lébés)	You (plural) = intoo kintoo Ăam btilbsoo (also intoo kintoo lébseen)
You (Female) = Inté kinté Ăam btilbsé (also inté kinté lébsé)	
He = Hoowé kén Ăam byilbéss (also hoowé kén lébés)	They = hinné kénoo Ăam byilbsoo (also hinné kénoo lébseen)
She = heeyé kénét Ăam btilbéss (also heeyé kénét lébsé)	

Ă= Augh in bought	Ď= a heavy D	É= like A in Bay	G= G in beige	ĥ= like an H with smaller air passage	I= I as in ink	Ќ= like ch in Irish loch
O= O as in home	OO= as in boots	R= roll the rrr	Ť= a heavy T	Ř= like a French R (gargle it)	Š= a heavy S	Ž= a heavy Z

Future

- This tense is used in Lebanese to describe an act that will take place in the future. The auxiliary laĥ is added before the present form of the verb. Some people keep the suffixes as is before the present verb and they just add the auxiliary laĥ. Other people strip the verb from a part of the preceding suffix. If you prefer to use the easier way where you just add the auxiliary laĥ to the present form you will still be well understood (review the present form and just add laĥ between the verb and the pronoun). The examples below show only the second way were the suffixes change (this way is considered more modern). Please see the pattern.

- Notice that in the first person singular, if the verb starts with a vowel then an apostrophe (') is added before the verb to give a start to the vowel.

Verb to want (future) (exception)

I will want = ana laĥ ykoon baddé	We will want = naĥna laĥ ykoon baddna
You (male) will want = Inta laĥ ykoon baddak	You (plural) will want = intoo laĥ ykoon badkon
You (Female) will want = Inté laĥ ykoon baddik	
He will want = Hoowé laĥ ykoon baddoo	They will want = hinné laĥ ykoon baddon
She will want = heeyé laĥ ykoon badda	

Verb to travel (future)

I = ana laĥ séfér	We = naĥna laĥ nséfér
You (male) = Inta laĥ tséfér	You (plural) = intoo laĥ tséfroo
You (Female) = Inté laĥ tséfré	
He = Hoowé laĥ yséfér	They = hinné laĥ yséfroo
She = heeyé laĥ tséfér	

Verb to eat (future)

I = ana laĥ 'ékol	We = naĥna laĥ nékol
You (male) = Inta laĥ tékol	You (plural) = intoo laĥ tékloo
You (Female) = Inté laĥ téklé	
He = Hoowé laĥ yékol	They = hinné laĥ yékloo
She = heeyé laĥ tékol	

Ă= Augh in bought	Ď= a heavy D	É= like A in Bay	G= G in beige	ĥ= like an H with smaller air passage	I= I as in ink	Ќ= like ch in Irish loch
O= O as in home	OO= as in boots	R= roll the rrr	Ť= a heavy T	Ř= like a French R (gargle it)	Ŝ= a heavy S	Ž= a heavy Z

Verb to sleep (future)

I = ana laĥ ném	We = naĥna laĥ n-ném
You (male) = Inta laĥ tném	
You (Female) = Inté laĥ tnémé	You (plural) = intoo laĥ tnémoo
He = Hoowé laĥ yném	
She = heeyé laĥ yném	They = hinné laĥ ynémoo

Verb to drink (future)

I = ana laĥ 'ishrab	We = naĥna laĥ nishrab
You (male) = Inta laĥ tishrab	
You (Female) = Inté laĥ tishrabé	You (plural) = intoo laĥ tishraboo
He = Hoowé laĥ yishrab	
She = heeyé laĥ tishrab	They = hinné laĥ yishraboo

Verb to go (future)

I = ana laĥ rooĥ	We = naĥna laĥ nrooĥ
You (male) = Inta laĥ trooĥ	
You (Female) = Inté laĥ trooĥé	You (plural) = intoo laĥ trooĥoo
He = Hoowé laĥ yrooĥ	
She = heeyé laĥ trooĥ	They = hinné laĥ yrooĥoo

Verb to see (future)

I = ana laĥ shoof	We want = naĥna laĥ nshoof
You (male) = Inta laĥ tshoof	
You (Female) = Inté laĥ tshoofé	You (plural) = intoo laĥ tshoofoo
He = Hoowé laĥ yshoof	
She = heeyé laĥ tshoof	They = hinné laĥ yshoofoo

Verb to walk (future)

I = ana laĥ 'imshé	We want = naĥna laĥ nimshé
You (male) = Inta laĥ timshé	
You (Female) = Inté laĥ timshé	You (plural) = intoo laĥ timshoo
He = Hoowé laĥ yimshé	
She = heeyé laĥ timshé	They = hinné laĥ yimshoo

Verb to wear (future)

I = ana laĥ 'ilbéss	We want = naĥna laĥ nilbéss
You (male) = Inta laĥ tilbéss	
You (Female) = Inté laĥ tilbsé	You (plural) = intoo laĥ tilbsoo
He = Hoowé laĥ yilbéss	
She = heeyé laĥ tilbéss	They = hinné laĥ yilbsoo

Ă= Augh in bought	Ď= a heavy D	É= like A in Bay	G= G in beige	ĥ= like an H with smaller air passage	Ĭ= I as in ink	Ќ= like ch in Irish loch
O= O as in home	OO= as in boots	R= roll the rrr	Ť= a heavy T	Ř= like a French R (gargle it)	Ŝ= a heavy S	Ž= a heavy Z

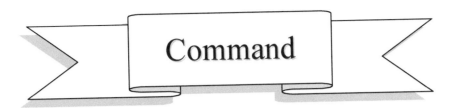

Command

- This form is equivalent to the imperative mood in English grammar. It exists as positive or negative. In a positive command, take the original present tense of the verb and strip it entirely of its suffix. In a negative command, add "ma" and strip the verb suffix of the letter "B" only.

Verb to travel (command)

You (male) = séfér	You (plural) = séfroo
You (Female) = séfré	
You (male) = ma tséfér	You (plural) = ma tséfroo
You (Female) = ma tséfré	

Verb to eat (command)

You (male) = kol	You (plural) = kilo
You (Female) = kilé	
You (male) = ma tékol	You (plural) = ma tékloo
You (Female) = ma téklé	

Verb to sleep (command)

You (male) = ném	You (plural) = némoo
You (Female) = némé	
You (male) = ma tném	You (plural) = ma tnémoo
You (Female) = ma tnémé	

Verb to drink (command)

You (male) = shrab	You (plural) = shraboo
You (Female) = shrabé	
You (male) = ma tishrab	You (plural) = ma tishraboo
You (Female) = ma tishrabé	

Verb to go (command)

You (male) = rooĥ	You (plural) = rooĥoo
You (Female) = rooĥé	
You (male) = ma trooĥ	You (plural) = ma trooĥoo
You (Female) = ma trooĥé	

Ă= Augh in bought	Ď= a heavy D	É= like A in Bay	G= G in beige	ĥ= like an H with smaller air passage	I= I as in ink	Ќ= like ch in Irish loch
O= O as in home	OO= as in boots	R= roll the rrr	Ť= a heavy T	Ř= like a French R (gargle it)	Š= a heavy S	Ž= a heavy Z

Verb to see (command)

You (male) = shoof	You (plural) = shoofoo
You (Female) = shoofé	
You (male) = ma tshoof	You (plural) = ma tshoofoo
You (Female) = ma tshoofé	

Verb to walk (command)

You (male) = mshee	You (plural) = mshoo
You (Female) = mshee	
You (male) = ma timshé	You (plural) = ma timshoo
You (Female) = ma timshé	

Verb to wear (command)

You (male) = lbéss	You (plural) = lbisoo (exception)
You (Female) = lbᵢsé (exception)	
You (male) = ma tilbéss	You (plural) = ma tilbsoo
You (Female) = ma tilbsé	

Ă= Augh in bought	Ď= a heavy D	É= like A in Bay	G= G in beige	ĥ= like an H with smaller air passage	I= I as in ink	Ќ= like ch in Irish loch
O= O as in home	OO= as in boots	R= roll the rrr	Ť= a heavy T	Ř= like a French R (gargle it)	Ŝ= a heavy S	Ž= a heavy Z

Adjectives:

- Adjectives in Lebanese follow the gender and number of the subject. Adjectives usually come after the subject in the sentence.

- Adjectives can sometimes take: "L" meaning "the". To understand how to use the definite article "L" please read the examples below:

Example:

1. The boy is big: ŜŜabé kbeer.
2. The woman is young: L-mara ŜŘeeré

In the above example the word Ŝabé means boy and the word kbeer means big. The Ŝ is doubled for Ŝabé as this is one of the letters that behave by doubling instead of adding the definite article "L" (review the definite article section). As verb "to be" doesn't exist in Lebanese in the present form, you can follow the subject by the adjective right away.

Example:

1. The big boy: ŜŜabé L-kbeer.
2. The young woman: L-mara ŜŜŘeeré

In the above examples you will find that each of the word Ŝabé (boy) and the adjective kbeer (big) received an indefinite article. This is because the sentence is not based on this subject and its adjective. Instead they both serve as the subject.

Ă= Augh in bought	Ď= a heavy D	É= like A in Bay	G= G in beige	ĥ= like an H with smaller air passage	I= I as in ink	Ḱ= like ch in Irish loch
O= O as in home	OO= as in boots	R= roll the rrr	Ť= a heavy T	Ř= like a French R (gargle it)	Ŝ= a heavy S	Ž= a heavy Z

Here's a list of some conjugated adjectives. See the pattern and apply it to all other adjectives.

	Small/Young	Tasty/Delicious	Tall / Long	Ugly
Ana	ŜŘeer/ ŜŘeeré	Ťayéb/Ťaybé	Ťaweel/ Ťaweelé	bisheĂ/ bishĂa
Inta	ŜŘeer	Ťayéb	Ťaweel	bisheĂ
Inté	ŜŘeeré	Ťaybé	Ťaweel	bishĂa
Hoowé	ŜŘeer	Ťayéb	Ťaweelé	bishĂa
Heeyé	ŜŘeeré	Ťaybé	Ťaweel	bisheĂ
Naĥna	ŜŘar	Ťaybeen	Ťwal	bisheĂ
Intoo	ŜŘar	Ťaybeen	Ťwal	bishĂeen
Hinné	ŜŘar	Ťaybeen	Ťwal	bishĂeen

	Disgusting	Good	Old/Big	Pretty
Ana	Mi'réf/mi'irfé	Mneeĥ/ Mneeĥa	Kbeer/kbeeré	ĥiloo/ ĥilwé
Inta	Mi'réf	Mneeĥ	Kbeer	ĥiloo
Inté	mi'irfé	Mneeĥa	Kbeeré	ĥilwé
Hoowé	Mi'réf	Mneeĥ	Kbeer	ĥiloo
Heeyé	mi'irfé	Mneeĥa	Kbeeré	ĥilwé
Naĥna	mi'irfeen	Mnéĥ	Kbar	ĥilween
Intoo	mi'irfeen	Mnéĥ	Kbar	ĥilween
Hinné	mi'irfeen	Mnéĥ	kbar	ĥilween

Ă= Augh in bought	Ď= a heavy D	É= like A in Bay	G= G in beige	ĥ= like an H with smaller air passage	I= I as in ink	Ḱ= like ch in Irish loch
O= O as in home	OO= as in boots	R= roll the rrr	Ť= a heavy T	Ř= like a French R (gargle it)	Ŝ= a heavy S	Ž= a heavy Z

DIALOGUE
TIPS

Useful Tables

Conversation / ĥadees

Yes (if arguing)	Mb$_a$l$_a$
No	L$_a$' / or / la
Yes(if answering a question)	Éh (not formal)
Yes(if answering a question)	NaĂam (formal)
If	Iza
Of course	ŤabĂan
For sure	Akeed
Can you?	Feek?
Must*	Léz$_é$m*
Because	Li'annoo
Anyways	Ă$_a$ kill ĥal
Never	Ab$_a$d$_a$n
No way	Mish m$_a$Ă'ool
Usually / Normally	Ăad$_a$t$_a$n
Stop it	Ḱalas / B$_a$ss
There is	Fee
When (not interrogative)	Lamma
Like this	Hék

* When "léz$_é$m" is used, the verb that follows it should
be stripped of the first letter of its suffix.

Quantity - kammyyé

Many / Very	Kteer
A little / few	Shway / nitfé
Some	Shway / nitfé
so so	Hék hék
Enough	Bizyédé / Bikaffé

Ă= Augh in bought	Ď= a heavy D	É= like A in Bay	G= G in beige	ĥ= like an H with smaller air passage	I= I as in ink	Ḱ= like ch in Irish loch
O= O as in home	OO= as in boots	R= roll the rrr	Ť= a heavy T	Ř= like a French R (gargle it)	Ŝ= a heavy S	Ž= a heavy Z

Salutation - salém

Question / soo'él	
How are you?	Keefak(m) / keefik(f) / keefkon(p)
How is it going?	Keef L-ĥal
How is the health?	Keef ŜŜaĥĥa
What's up?	Shoo fee ma fee
What's new?	Shoo LAK̂bar? / shoo fee gdeed?

Answer / gawéb	
Congratulations	Mₐbrook
Good	Mneeĥ (m) / Mneeĥa (f)
Good bye	(use French or English)
Good evening	Masa L-K̂ér
Good morning	Sabaĥ L-K̂ér
Hello	(use French or English)
Hello	Marĥaba
Let's go	Yalla
Not bad	Meshé Lĥal
Please	(use French or English)
Please	Laow sₐmₐht
Say hi to/pass my regards	**Sallimlé (m)/ Sallmeelé (f)**
Thank you	(use French or English)
Thank you	Shₒₒkrₐn
Welcome	Ahla

Ā= Augh in bought	Ď= a heavy D	É= like A in Bay	G= G in beige	ĥ= like an H with smaller air passage	I= I as in ink	Ќ= like ch in Irish loch
O= O as in home	OO= as in boots	R= roll the rrr	Ť= a heavy T	Ř= like a French R (gargle it)	Ŝ= a heavy S	Ž= a heavy Z

The Time - Lwa't

Afternoon	baĂd ĎĎihr
Day	Yom
Daytime	Nhar
Evening	Masa
Midnight	niŜ L-lél
Night	Lél
Noon	Ďihr
Today	L-yom
Tomorrow	Bookra
Tonight	L-laylé
Yesterday	Mbereĥ
Always	Déyman
Always	ĂaTool
Before	Abl
Every time	Kil marr_a
Later	B_aĂdén
Previously	séb_i'_an
Quickly	BsirĂa
Right now	H_all_a'
Slowly	Ăa L-hada / Ăa mahl
Slowly	Shway shway

The Clock – SséĂa

9:00 O'clock	sséĂa tisĂa
9:05	tisĂa w – Ќamsé
9:10	tisĂa w – Ăashra
9:15	tisĂa w – ribĂ
9:20	tisĂa w – tilt
9:25	tisĂa w – niŜ illa Ќamsé
9:30	tisĂa w – niŜŜ
9:35	tisĂa w – niŜŜ w - Ќamsé
9:40	Ăashra illa tilt / tisĂa - arbĂeen d'ee'a
9:45	Ăashra illa ribĂ
9:50	Ăashra illa Ăashra
9:55	Ăashra illa Ќamsé
Quarter	ribĂ
Half	niŜŜ
20 minutes (one third)	Tilt
Ten after one	Wiĥdé w Ăashra *(literally: one and ten)*
Ten to one	Wiĥdé illa Ăashra *(literally: one minus ten)*

Ă= Augh in bought	**Ď**= a heavy D	**É**= like A in Bay	**G**= G in beige	**ĥ**= like an H with smaller air passage	**I**= I as in ink	**Ќ**= like ch in Irish loch
O= O as in home	**OO**= as in boots	**R**= roll the rrr	**Ť**= a heavy T	**Ř**= like a French R (gargle it)	**Ŝ**= a heavy S	**Ž**= a heavy Z

Family (Ăailé)

Father	Bay	Uncle (father's side)	Ăammo	Father's brother's son	Ibn Ăammé
Mother	Im	Uncle (mother's side)	Ḱalo	Father's sister's son	Ibn Ăamté
Brother	Ḱay	Aunt (father's side)	Ăamté (or tante)	Mother's brother's son	Ibn Ḱalé
Sister	iḰt	Aunt (mother's side)	Ḱalté (or tante)	Mother's sister's son	Ibn Ḱalté
Grandfather	Gid	Son	Ibn	Father's brother's daughter	Bint Ăammé
Grandmother	Sit	Daughter	Bint	Father's sister's daughter	Bint Ăamté
				Mother's brother's daughter	Bint Ḱalé
				Mother's sister's daughter	Bint Ḱalté

Fruits - fawéké
(singular / plural – when applicable)

Apple	Tifféḣa / tifféḣ
Apricot	Mishmshé / mishmosh
Banana	Mowzé / moz
Berry	Tooté / toot
Cantalope	Ăaggoora / Ăaggor
Cherry	K$_a$rzé / ka$_{ra}$z
Date (soft)	T$_a$mr$_a$ / t$_a$mr
Date (hard)	B$_{al}$ḣ$_a$ / b$_{al}$aḣ
Fig	Teen
Grapes	Ăinab
Kiwi	Kiwi
Lemon	Léimooné ḣamĎ$_a$
Orange	Léimooné / léimoon
Peach	Dirra'a / dirra'
Pear	NgaŠa / ngaŠ
Pineapple	Ananas
Plum	ḰawḰa / ḰoḰ
Strawberry	Fraise
Watermelon	B$_a$Ṫ̌TeeḰa / b$_a$Ṫ̌TeeḰ

Ă= Augh in bought	Ď= a heavy D	É= like A in Bay	G= G in beige	ḣ= like an H with smaller air passage	I= I as in ink	Ḱ= like ch in Irish loch
O= O as in home	OO= as in boots	R= roll the rrr	Ṫ= a heavy T	Ř= like a French R (gargle it)	Š= a heavy S	Ž= a heavy Z

Spices – bharat

Pepper	Bhar
Salt	Milĥ

Vegetables and herbs - ḰiĎra w ĥashé'ésh
(singular / plural – when applicable)

Basil	ĥₐbₐ'
Bean	FaŜoolya
Beet	Shmandar
Cabbage	Ras malfoof / malfoof
Carrot	Gₐzra / gₐzₐr
Corn (cob of corn)	Ăarnoos dₐrₐ / dₐrₐ
Cucumber	Ḱyara / Ḱyar
Eggplant	Batingéné / batingén
Garlic	HirŜ toom / toom
Hot peppers	Arn fléflé ĥarra / fléflé ĥarra
Lettuce	Ras Ḱₐss / Ḱass
Mint	Bé'ét naĂnaĂ / naĂnaĂ
Mushroom	Fᵢtr
Olive	Ĥabbét zaitoon / zaitoon
Onion	bₐŜlé / bₐŜal
Oregano	Z₀₀béĂ
Parsley	Bé'ét Ba'doonés / Ba'doonés
Pea	Bazéllₐ
Pepper	Arn fléflé / Fléflé
Pickle	kₐbeese / kₐbees
Potato	ĥirŜ bₐŤaŤa / bₐŤaŤa
Radish	Figlé / figil
Salad	Salad / sₐlₐtₐ
Thyme	ZaĂtar
Tomato	ĥirŜ banadoora / banadoora
Turnip	Ras lift / lifté
Zucchini	Koosₑyé / koosa

Ă= Augh in bought	Ď= a heavy D	É= like A in Bay	G= G in beige	ĥ= like an H with smaller air passage	I= I as in ink	Ḱ= like ch in Irish loch
O= O as in home	OO= as in boots	R= roll the rrr	Ť= a heavy T	Ř= like a French R (gargle it)	Ŝ= a heavy S	Ž= a heavy Z

Colors - alwén

(Masculine / Feminine – when applicable)

Black	Ass$_w$$_a$d	/s$_a$wda
Blue	Azr$_a$'	/z$_a$r'a
Brown	Binné	/binneeyé
Dark Blue	kiĥlé	/kiĥleeyé
Gold	D$_a$h$_a$bé	/d$_a$h$_a$beeyé
Green	AḰD$_a$r	/Ḱ$_a$Ďra
Grey	Rmédé	/rmédeeyé
Orange	Orange	
Pink	Z$_a$hré	/z$_a$hreeyé
Purple	B$_a$n$_a$fs$_a$gé	
Red	Aĥm$_a$r	/ ĥ$_a$mra
Silver	FiĎé	/fiĎeeyé
Wine	Nbeedé	/nbeedeeyé
White	Aby$_a$Ď	/b$_a$yda
Yellow	AŜf$_a$r	/Ŝ$_a$fra

Ǎ= Augh in bought	**Ď**= a heavy D	**É**= like A in Bay	**G**= G in beige	**ĥ**= like an H with smaller air passage	**I**= I as in ink	**Ḱ**= like ch in Irish loch
O= O as in home	**OO**= as in boots	**R**= roll the rrr	**Ť**= a heavy T	**Ř**= like a French R (gargle it)	**Ŝ**= a heavy S	**Ž**= a heavy Z

Animals – ĥayawénét
(Masculine / Feminine / PLURAL– when applicable)

Bat	WᵢŤwaŤ / WŤAWEEŤ
Bear	dᵢbb / dᵢbbé /DIBAB
Bird	Ăₐsfoor / Ăₐsfoora / ĂSAFEER
Camel	Gₐmₐl
Cat	Bsén / bséiné /BSÉINÉTt
Chameleon	Gₐmₐl élyéhood
Chicken	Dgégé / DGÉG
Cow	Ba'rₐ / tor / Bₐ'ₐR
Crocodile	Timséĥ / timséĥa / TMÉSEEĥ
Dear	Řₐzél / ŘIZLÉN
Dog	kₐlb / kₐlbé /KLÉB
Donkcy	Îlmar / ĥmara / ĤAMEER
Duck	bₐŤŤₐ /BAŤ
Elephant	Feel / FYOOLÉ
Fish	Sₐmké /SₐMₐK
Fox	sₐĂlₐb / SₐĂₐLᵉ́B
Frog	ĎᵢfĎₐĂ / ĎᵢfĎĂₐ / ĎFADᵉ́Ă
Giraffe	Zₐrafé / ZₐRₐFÉT
Goat	MiĂzéyé / MIĂZÉ
Goose	Wₐzzé / WₐZZ
Groundhog	Řrér
Horse	ĤŜan / faras / 'ĤSNÉ
Hyena	ĎabĂ /ĎbéĂ
Lamb	Ar'oor / 'RA'EER
Lion	asₐd / lₐbwé /'SOODÉ
Lizard ?	Simballé
Mice	Far / fara / FEERAN
Monkey	siĂdén / siĂdéné / SĂÉDEEN
Mule	BₐŘl / baŘlé / BŘAL
Ostrich	NₐĂamé
Peacock	Ťawoos / ŤWAWEES
Pig	Ќanzeer / ЌanzEEra / ЌNÉZEER
Rats	Gₐrdoon / GRADEEN
Rhinocerous	Wₐĥeed él'ₐrn
Rooster	Deek / DYOOK
Sheep	Ќaroof / ЌWᵉ́REEF
Skunk	Žirbén
Snake	Ĥayé / HAYÉT or ĥYÉYA
Squirrel	Singéb / SNÉGEEB
Tiger	Nimr / NMOORₐ
Turkey	Deek ĥₐbₐsh / DYOOK ĥₐBₐSH
Turtle	Zilĥₐfé / ZLÉĥᵉ́F
Wolf	Deeb / DYÉB
Zebra	Zebra

Ă= Augh in bought	Ď= a heavy D	É= like A in Bay	G= G in beige	ĥ= like an H with smaller air passage	I= I as in ink	Ќ= like ch in Irish loch
O= O as in home	OO= as in boots	R= roll the rrr	Ť= a heavy T	Ř= like a French R (gargle it)	Ŝ= a heavy S	Ž= a heavy Z

Insects - ĥₐshₐrat

(Singular/ *PLURAL*– when applicable)

Ant	Nₐmlé / *NₐML*
Bee	Nₐĥlé / *NₐĥL*
Beetle	Ќinfsé / *ЌNÉFÉS*
Butterfly	Fₐrashé / *FₐRₐSHÉT*
Cockroach	ŜₐrŜoor / *ŚRₐŚEER*
Cricket	Zeez
Earwig	Ăa'oos ézzabra
Flea	BₐrŘoota / *BRₐŘEET*
Fly	Dibbéné / *DIBBÉN*
Grasshopper	AbbooŤ / *'BABEEŤ*
Hornet	Dabboor / *DBÉBEER*
Lady bug	Coccinnelle
Louse	Amlé / *AML*
Mosquito	BₐriŘshé / *BₐRŘₐSH*
Moth	Bishhayra
Praying mantis	Garadé / *GARAD*
Wasp	Ziliʼta / *ZLAʼÉT*
Spider	Ăₐnkₐboot or 'irtaylé
Tick	Baʼʼₐ / *Bₐ'*
Scorpion	Ăₐʼrₐbé / *Ăʼaréb*
Worm	Doodé / *DOOD*

Months (ash-hor)

January	*Kénoon tténé*	July	*Tammooz*
February	*ShbaŤ*	August	*'éb*
March	*'édar*	September	*Ailool*
April	*Neesén*	October	*Tishreen L-awwal*
May	*Iyyar*	November	*Tishreen tténé*
June	*Ħzayran*	December	*Kénoon L-awwal*

Ă= Augh in bought	Ď= a heavy D	É= like A in Bay	G= G in beige	ĥ= like an H with smaller air passage	I= I as in ink	Ќ= like ch in Irish loch
O= O as in home	OO= as in boots	R= roll the rrr	Ť= a heavy T	Ř= like a French R (gargle it)	Ŝ= a heavy S	Ž= a heavy Z

Days of the week ('yyém L-isbooĂ)

Sunday	L-aĥad
Monday	Ttanén
Tuesday	Ttaléta
Wednesday	L-arbĂa
Thursday	L-Ḱamees
Friday	L-gimĂa
Saturday	Ssabbit

please notice that the definit article "the"
is added in front of all the week days

Transportation (moowaŜalét)

Airplane	Ťyyara(s) Ťyyarat(p)
Bicycle	(same as English or French)
Bridge	Gisr(s) gsoora(p)
Boat	shaḰtoor(s) shḰateer(p)
Bus	baŜ(s) baŜét(p)
Car	Syyara(s) syyarat(p)
Flight/Trip	Riĥle(s) rihlét(p)
Highway	Highway /also/ Autostrad
Motorcycle	(same as English or French)
Port	Marfa'(s)marafé'(p)
Railway	Sikkit L-hadeed (s-p)
Road	Ťaree'(s) Ťooro'(p)
Scooter	(same as English or French)
Sea	Baĥr(s) bĥoor(p)
Ship	béḰra(s) bawéḰér(p)
Street	shéréĂ(s) shwéréĂ(p)
Taxi	Taxi(s) taxésé(p)
Traffic circle	Moostadeera(s) moostadeerat(p)
Traffic jam	Ăag'it sér
Traffic light	Isharét ssér(s) isharat ssér(p)
Train	Trén(s-p)
Tunnel	Nafa'(s) anfé'(p)
Water	Maay

Geography (giŘrafya)

Border	*Ḣdood(s-p)*
Capital (city)	*ĂaŜmé(s) ĂawaŜém(p)*
City	*Madeené(s) midon(p)*
Cliff	*Mihwar(s) mhéweer(p)*
Desert	*Ŝaĥra(s) Ŝaĥaré(p)*
Forest	*Řabé(s) Řabét(p)*
Hill	*Tallé(s) tlél(p)*
Lake	*Booĥayra(s) booĥayrat(p)*
Land	*arĎ(s) araĎé(p)*
Mountain	*Gabal(s) gbél(p)*
Ocean	*mooheeŤ(s) mooheeŤat(p)*
Pond	*Birké(s) birak(p)*
River	*Nahr(s) anhar(p)*
Sea	*Baĥr(s)bĥoor(p)*
Spring	*nabĂ(s) yanébeeĂ(p)*
Town/village	*ĎaiAa(s) ĎeeyaĂ(p)*
Valley	*Wédé(s) widyén(p)*

Garden (gnayné)

Branch	*farĂ(s) frooĂ(p)*
Cedar	*arzé(s) arz(p)*
Chemical fertilizer	*Keeméwé(s-p)*
Farm	*mazrĂa(s) mazéréĂ(p)*
Flower	*Zahra(s) zhoor(p)*
Garden	*Gnainé(s) gnainét(p)*
Hose	*Nabreesh(s) nbéreesh(p)*
Leaf	*War'a(s) wara'(p)*
Manure	*Zibil(s-p)*
Palm tree	*Balĥa(s) balaĥ(p)*
Pine tree	*Ŝnoobra(s) Ŝnoobar(p)*
Plant	*Nabté(s) nabét(p)*
Rock	*ŜaḰra(s) ŜaḰr(p)*
Root	*Shilsh(s) shloosh(p)*
Rose	*Wardé(s) ward(p)*
Sand	*Raml(s-p)*
Seed	*Bizré(s) bizr(p)*
Shovel	*Rabsh(s) rbooshé(p)*
Soil	*Trab(s-p)*
Stem	*gizĂ(s) gzooĂ(p)*
Sunflower	*Dwwar sh-shamis(s-p)*
Tree	*Shagra(s) shagar(p)*

Ă= Augh in bought	**Ď**= a heavy D	**É**= like A in Bay	**G**= G in beige	**ĥ**= like an H with smaller air passage	**I**= I as in ink	**Ḱ**= like ch in Irish loch
O= O as in home	**OO**= as in boots	**R**= roll the rrr	**Ť**= a heavy T	**Ř**= like a French R (gargle it)	**Ŝ**= a heavy S	**Ž**= a heavy Z

Counting

1 (M)	Waĥad /or/ wéĥéd	29	TisĂa w-Ăishreen	58	Tméné w-Ḱamseen	87	SabĂa w-tméneen
1 (F)	Wiĥdé	30	Tléteen	59	TisĂa w-Ḱamseen	88	Tméné w-tméneen
2	Tnén	31	Wéhéd w-tléteen	60	Sitteen	89	TisĂaaa w-tméneen
3	Tlété	32	Tnén w-tléteen	61	Wéhéd w-sittéen	90	TisĂeen
4	ArbĂa	33	Tlété w-tléteen	62	Tnén w-sitteen	91	Wéhéd w-TisĂeen
5	Ḱamsé	34	ArbĂa w-tléteen	63	Tlété w-sitteen	92	Tnén w-TisĂeen
6	Sitté	35	Ḱamsé w-tléteen	64	ArbĂa w-sitteen	93	Tlété w-TisĂeen
7	sabĂa	36	Sitté w-tléteen	65	Ḱamsé w-sitteen	94	ArbĂa w-TisĂeen
8	Tméné	37	SabĂa w-tléteen	66	Sitté w-sitteen	95	Ḱamsé w-TisĂeen
9	TisĂa	38	Tméné w-tléteen	67	SabĂa w-sitteen	96	Sitté w-TisĂeen
10	Ăashra	39	TisĂa w-tléteen	68	Tménc w-sittccn	97	SabĂa w-TisĂeen
11	ĥdaĂsh	40	ArbĂeen	69	TisĂa w-sitteen	98	Tméné w-TisĂeen
12	TnaĂsh	41	Wéhéd w-arbĂeen	70	SabĂeen	99	TisĂa w-TisĂeen
13	Tlat-taĂsh	42	Tnén w-arbĂeen	71	Wéhéd w-SabĂeen	100	Mee-yé
14	ArbaĂ-taĂsh	43	Tlété w-arbĂeen	72	Tnén w-SabĂeen	101	Meeyé w-wéhéd
15	Ḱams-taĂsh	44	ArbĂa w-arbĂeen	73	Tlété w-SabĂeen	102	Meeyé w-tnén
16	Sit-taĂsh	45	Ḱamsé w-arbĂeen	74	ArbĂa w-SabĂeen	103	Meeyé w-tlété
17	SabĂ-taĂsh	46	Sitté w-arbĂeen	75	Ḱamsé w-SabĂeen	104	Meeyé w-arbĂa
18	Tmin-taĂsh	47	SabĂa w-arbĂeen	76	Sitté w-SabĂeen	105	Meeyé w-Ḱamsé
19	TisĂ-taĂsh	48	Tméné w-arbĂeen	77	SabĂa w-SabĂeen	106	Meeyé w-sitté
20	Ăishreen	49	TisĂa w-arbĂeen	78	Tméné w-SabĂeen	107	Meeyé w-sabĂa
21	Wéhéd w-Ăishreen	50	Ḱamseen	79	TisĂa w-SabĂeen	108	Meeyé w-tméné
22	Tnén w- Ăishreen	51	Wéhéd w-Ḱamseen	80	Tméneen	109	Meeyé w-tisĂa
23	Tlété w- Ăishreen	52	Tnén w-Ḱamseen	81	Wéhéd w-tméneen	110	Meeyé w-Ăashra
24	ArbĂa w-Ăishreen	53	Tlété w-Ḱamseen	82	Tnén w-tméneen	111	Meeyé w-ĥdaĂsh
25	Ḱamsé w-Ăishreen	54	ArbĂa w-Ḱamseen	83	Tlété w-tméneen	112	Meeyé w-tnaĂsh
26	Sitté w- Ăishreen	55	Ḱamsé w-Ḱamseen	84	ArbĂa w-tméneen	113	Meeyé w-tlattaĂsh
27	SabĂa w-Ăishreen	56	Sitté w-Ḱamseen	85	Ḱamsé w-tméneen	120	Meeyé w-Ăishreen
28	Tméné w-Ăishreen	57	SabĂa w-Ḱamseen	86	Sitté w-tméneen		Etc...

Ă= Augh in bought	Ď= a heavy D	É= like A in Bay	G= G in beige	ĥ= like an H with smaller air passage	I= I as in ink	Ḱ= like ch in Irish loch
O= O as in home	OO= as in boots	R= roll the rrr	Ť= a heavy T	Ř= like a French R (gargle it)	Ŝ= a heavy S	Ž= a heavy Z

CONJUGATION
LIBRARY

To abbreviate

Present

Ana	BiḰtiŜir
Inta	BtiḰtiŜir
Inté	BtiḰtiŜré
Hoowé	ByiḰtiŜir
Heeyé	BtiḰtiŜir
Naḣna	MniḰtiŜir
Intoo	BtiḰtiŜroo
Hinné	ByiḰtiŜroo

Present Continuous

Ana	Ăam	BiḰtiŜir
Inta	Ăam	BtiḰtiŜir
Inté	Ăam	BtiḰtiŜré
Hoowé	Ăam	ByiḰtiŜir
Heeyé	Ăam	BtiḰtiŜir
Naḣna	Ăam	MniḰtiŜir
Intoo	Ăam	BtiḰtiŜroo
Hinné	Ăam	ByiḰtiŜroo

Past

Ana	ḰtaŜart
Inta	ḰtaŜart
Inté	ḰtaŜarté
Hoowé	ḰtaŜar
Heeyé	ḰtaŜarét
Naḣna	ḰtaŜarna
Intoo	ḰtaŜartoo
Hinné	ḰtaŜaroo

Past Continuous

Ana	Kint Ăam	BiḰtiŜir
Inta	Kint Ăam	BtiḰtiŜir
Inté	Kinté Ăam	BtiḰtiŜré
Hoowé	Kén Ăam	ByiḰtiŜir
Heeyé	Kénét Ăam	BtiḰtiŜir
Naḣna	Kinna Ăam	MniḰtiŜir
Intoo	Kintoo Ăam	BtiḰtiŜroo
Hinné	Kénoo Ăam	ByiḰtiŜroo

Future

Ana	Laḣ	iḰtiŜir
Inta	Laḣ	tiḰtiŜir
Inté	Laḣ	tiḰtiŜré
Hoowé	Laḣ	yiḰtiŜir
Heeyé	Laḣ	tiḰtiŜir
Naḣna	Laḣ	niḰtiŜir
Intoo	Laḣ	tiḰtiŜroo
Hinné	Laḣ	yiḰtiŜroo

Command

Inta	ḰtiŜir
Inté	ḰtiŜré
Intoo	ḰtiŜroo
Inta	Ma tḰtiŜir
Inté	Ma tḰtiŜré
Intoo	Ma tḰtiŜroo

To act (in theatre)

Present

Ana	Bmassél
Inta	Btmassél
Inté	Btmasslé
Hoowé	Bimassél
Heeyé	Btmassél
Naḣna	Mnmassél
Intoo	Btmassloo
Hinné	Bimassloo

Present Continuous

Ana	Ăam	Bmassél
Inta	Ăam	Btmassél
Inté	Ăam	Btmasslé
Hoowé	Ăam	Bimassél
Heeyé	Ăam	Btmassél
Naḣna	Ăam	Mnmassél
Intoo	Ăam	Btmassloo
Hinné	Ăam	Bimassloo

Past

Ana	Massalt
Inta	Massalt
Inté	Masslté
Hoowé	Massal
Heeyé	Massalét
Naḣna	Massalna
Intoo	Massaltoo
Hinné	Massaloo

Past Continuous

Ana	Kint Ăam	Bmassél
Inta	Kint Ăam	Btmassél
Inté	Kinté Ăam	Btmasslé
Hoowé	Kén Ăam	Bimassél
Heeyé	Kénét Ăam	Btmassél
Naḣna	Kinna Ăam	Mnmassél
Intoo	Kintoo Ăam	Btmassloo
Hinné	Kénoo Ăam	Bimassloo

Future

Ana	Laḣ	Massél
Inta	Laḣ	tmassél
Inté	Laḣ	tmasslé
Hoowé	Laḣ	ymassél
Heeyé	Laḣ	tmassél
Naḣna	Laḣ	nmassél
Intoo	Laḣ	tmassloo
Hinné	Laḣ	ymassloo

Command

Inta	Massél
Inté	Masslé
Intoo	Massloo
Inta	Ma tmassél
Inté	Ma tmasslé
Intoo	Ma tmassloo

Ă= Augh in bought	Ď= a heavy D	É= like A in Bay	G= G in beige	ḣ= like an H with smaller air passage	I= I as in ink	Ḱ= like ch in Irish loch
O= O as in home	OO= as in boots	R= roll the rrr	Ť= a heavy T	Ř= like a French R (gargle it)	Ŝ= a heavy S	Ž= a heavy Z

To accompany

Present

Ana	Brafé'
Inta	Btrafé'
Inté	Btraf'é
Hoowé	Birafé'
Heeyé	Btrafé'
Nahna	Mnrafé'
Intoo	Btraf'oo
Hinné	Biraf'oo

Present Continuous

Ana	Ăam	Brafé'
Inta	Ăam	Btrafé'
Inté	Ăam	Btraf'é
Hoowé	Ăam	Birafé'
Heeyé	Ăam	Btrafé'
Nahna	Ăam	Mnrafé'
Intoo	Ăam	Btraf'oo
Hinné	Ăam	Biraf'oo

Past

Ana	Rafa't
Inta	Rafa't
Inté	Rafa'té
Hoowé	Rafa'
Heeyé	Rafa'ét
Nahna	Rafa'na
Intoo	Rafa'too
Hinné	Rafa'oo

Past Continuous

Ana	Kint Ăam	Brafé'
Inta	Kint Ăam	Btrafé'
Inté	Kinté Ăam	Btraf'é
Hoowé	Kén Ăam	Birafé'
Heeyé	Kénét Ăam	Btrafé'
Nahna	Kinna Ăam	Mnrafé'
Intoo	Kintoo Ăam	Btraf'oo
Hinné	Kénoo Ăam	Biraf'oo

Future

Ana	Laĥ	rafé'
Inta	Laĥ	trafé'
Inté	Laĥ	traf'é
Hoowé	Laĥ	yrafé'
Heeyé	Laĥ	trafé'
Nahna	Laĥ	nrafé'
Intoo	Laĥ	traf'oo
Hinné	Laĥ	yraf'oo

Command

Inta	Rafé'
Inté	Raf'é
Intoo	Raf'oo
Inta	Ma trafé'
Inté	Ma traf'é
Intoo	Ma traf'oo

To adapt

Present

Ana	Bit'aklam
Inta	Btit'aklam
Inté	Btit'aklamé
Hoowé	Byit'aklam
Heeyé	Btit'aklam
Nahna	mnit'aklam
Intoo	Btit'aklamoo
Hinné	Byit'aklamoo

Present Continuous

Ana	Ăam	Bit'aklam
Inta	Ăam	Btit'aklam
Inté	Ăam	Btit'aklamé
Hoowé	Ăam	Byit'aklam
Heeyé	Ăam	Btit'aklam
Nahna	Ăam	mnit'aklam
Intoo	Ăam	Btit'aklamoo
Hinné	Ăam	Byit'aklamoo

Past

Ana	T'aklamt
Inta	T'aklamt
Inté	T'aklamté
Hoowé	T'aklam
Heeyé	T'aklamét
Nahna	T'aklamna
Intoo	T'aklamtoo
Hinné	T'aklamoo

Past Continuous

Ana	Kint Ăam	Bit'aklam
Inta	Kint Ăam	Btit'aklam
Inté	Kinté Ăam	Btit'aklamé
Hoowé	Kén Ăam	Byit'aklam
Heeyé	Kénét Ăam	Btit'aklam
Nahna	Kinna Ăam	mnit'aklam
Intoo	Kintoo Ăam	Btit'aklamoo
Hinné	Kénoo Ăam	Byit'aklamoo

Future

Ana	Laĥ	it'aklam
Inta	Laĥ	tit'aklam
Inté	Laĥ	tit'aklamé
Hoowé	Laĥ	yit'aklam
Heeyé	Laĥ	tit'aklam
Nahna	Laĥ	nit'aklam
Intoo	Laĥ	tit'aklamoo
Hinné	Laĥ	yit'aklamoo

Command

Inta	T'aklam
Inté	T'aklamé
Intoo	T'aklamoo
Inta	Ma tt'aklam
Inté	Ma tt'aklamé
Intoo	Ma tt'alamoo

Ă= Augh in bought	Ď= a heavy D	É= like A in Bay	G= G in beige	ĥ= like an H with smaller air passage	I= I as in ink	Ķ= like ch in Irish loch
O= O as in home	OO= as in boots	R= roll the rrr	Ť= a heavy T	Ř= like a French R (gargle it)	Š= a heavy S	Ž= a heavy Z

To add

Present	
Ana	Bzeed
Inta	Btzeed
Inté	Btzeedé
Hoowé	Bizeed
Heeyé	Btzeed
Naĥna	Mnzeed
Intoo	Btzeedoo
Hinné	Bizeedoo

Present Continuous		
Ana	Ăam	Bzeed
Inta	Ăam	Btzeed
Inté	Ăam	Btzeedé
Hoowé	Ăam	Bizeed
Heeyé	Ăam	Btzeed
Naĥna	Ăam	Mnzeed
Intoo	Ăam	Btzeedoo
Hinné	Ăam	Bizeedoo

Past	
Ana	Zidt
Inta	Zidt
Inté	Zidté
Hoowé	Zéd
Heeyé	Zédét
Naĥna	Zidna
Intoo	Zidtoo
Hinné	Zédoo

Past Continuous		
Ana	Kint Ăam	Bzeed
Inta	Kint Ăam	Btzeed
Inté	Kinté Ăam	Btzeedé
Hoowé	Kén Ăam	Bizeed
Heeyé	Kénét Ăam	Btzeed
Naĥna	Kinna Ăam	Mnzeed
Intoo	Kintoo Ăam	Btzeedoo
Hinné	Kénoo Ăam	Bizeedoo

Future		
Ana	Laĥ	zeed
Inta	Laĥ	tzeed
Inté	Laĥ	tzeedé
Hoowé	Laĥ	yzeed
Heeyé	Laĥ	tzeed
Naĥna	Laĥ	nzeed
Intoo	Laĥ	tzeedoo
Hinné	Laĥ	yzeedoo

Command	
Inta	Zeed
Inté	Zeedé
Intoo	Zeedoo
Inta	Ma tzeed
Inté	Ma tzeedé
Intoo	Ma tzeedoo

To admire

Present	
Ana	Biĥtirém
Inta	Btiĥtirém
Inté	Btiĥtirmé
Hoowé	Byiĥtirém
Heeyé	Btiĥtirém
Naĥna	Mniĥtirém
Intoo	Btiĥtirmoo
Hinné	Byiĥtirmoo

Present Continuous		
Ana	Ăam	Biĥtirém
Inta	Ăam	Btiĥtirém
Inté	Ăam	Btiĥtirmé
Hoowé	Ăam	Byiĥtirém
Heeyé	Ăam	Btiĥtirém
Naĥna	Ăam	Mniĥtirém
Intoo	Ăam	Btiĥtirmoo
Hinné	Ăam	Byiĥtirmoo

Past	
Ana	Ĥtaramt
Inta	Ĥtaramt
Inté	Ĥtaramté
Hoowé	Ĥtaram
Heeyé	Ĥtaramét
Naĥna	Ĥtaramna
Intoo	Ĥtaramtoo
Hinné	Ĥtaramoo

Past Continuous		
Ana	Kint Ăam	Biĥtirém
Inta	Kint Ăam	Btiĥtirém
Inté	Kinté Ăam	Btiĥtirmé
Hoowé	Kén Ăam	Byiĥtirém
Heeyé	Kénét Ăam	Btiĥtirém
Naĥna	Kinna Ăam	Mniĥtirém
Intoo	Kintoo Ăam	Btiĥtirmoo
Hinné	Kénoo Ăam	Byiĥtirmoo

Future		
Ana	Laĥ	iĥtirém
Inta	Laĥ	tiĥtirém
Inté	Laĥ	tiĥtirmé
Hoowé	Laĥ	yiĥtirém
Heeyé	Laĥ	tiĥtirém
Naĥna	Laĥ	niĥtirém
Intoo	Laĥ	tiĥtirmoo
Hinné	Laĥ	yiĥtirmoo

Command	
Inta	Ĥtirim
Inté	Ĥtitmé
Intoo	Ĥtirmoo
Inta	Ma tĥtirim
Inté	Ma tĥtirmé
Intoo	Ma tĥtirmoo

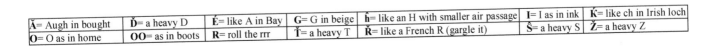

Ă= Augh in bought	Ď= a heavy D	É= like A in Bay	G= G in beige	ĥ= like an H with smaller air passage	I= I as in ink	Ќ= like ch in Irish loch
O= O as in home	OO= as in boots	R= roll the rrr	Ť= a heavy T	Ř= like a French R (gargle it)	Ŝ= a heavy S	Ž= a heavy Z

To admit

Present	
Ana	biĂtiréf
Inta	btiĂtiréf
Inté	btiĂtirfé
Hoowé	byiĂtiréf
Heeyé	btiĂtiréf
Naĥna	mniĂtiréf
Intoo	btiĂtirfoo
Hinné	byiĂtiréfoo

Present Continuous		
Ana	Ăam	biĂtiréf
Inta	Ăam	btiĂtiréf
Inté	Ăam	btiĂtirfé
Hoowé	Ăam	byiĂtiréf
Heeyé	Ăam	btiĂtiréf
Naĥna	Ăam	mniĂtiréf
Intoo	Ăam	btiĂtirfoo
Hinné	Ăam	byiĂtiréfoo

Past	
Ana	Ătaraft
Inta	Ătaraft
Inté	Ătarafté
Hoowé	Ătaraf
Heeyé	Ătarafét
Naĥna	Ătarafna
Intoo	Ătaraftoo
Hinné	Ătarafoo

Past Continuous		
Ana	Kint Ăam	biĂtiréf
Inta	Kint Ăam	btiĂtiréf
Inté	Kinté Ăam	btiĂtirfé
Hoowé	Kén Ăam	byiĂtiréf
Heeyé	Kénét Ăam	btiĂtiréf
Naĥna	Kinna Ăam	mniĂtiréf
Intoo	Kintoo Ăam	btiĂtirfoo
Hinné	Kénoo Ăam	byiĂtiréfoo

Future		
Ana	Laĥ	iĂtiréf
Inta	Laĥ	tiĂtiréf
Inté	Laĥ	tiĂtirfé
Hoowé	Laĥ	yiĂtiréf
Heeyé	Laĥ	tiĂtiréf
Naĥna	Laĥ	niĂtiréf
Intoo	Laĥ	tiĂtirfoo
Hinné	Laĥ	yiĂtirfoo

Command	
Inta	Ătiréf
Inté	Ătirfé
Intoo	Ătirfoo
Inta	Ma tĂtiréf
Inté	Ma tĂtirfé
Intoo	Ma tĂtirfoo

To adopt

Present	
Ana	Bitbanna
Inta	Btitbanna
Inté	Btitbanné
Hoowé	Byitbanna
Heeyé	Btitbanna
Naĥna	Mnitbanna
Intoo	Btitbannoo
Hinné	Byitbannoo

Present Continuous		
Ana	Ăam	Bitbanna
Inta	Ăam	Btitbanna
Inté	Ăam	Btitbanné
Hoowé	Ăam	Byitbanna
Heeyé	Ăam	Btitbanna
Naĥna	Ăam	Mnitbanna
Intoo	Ăam	Btitbannoo
Hinné	Ăam	Byitbannoo

Past	
Ana	Tbannét
Inta	Tbannét
Inté	Tbannaité
Hoowé	Tbanna
Heeyé	Tbannét
Naĥna	Tbannaina
Intoo	Tbannaitoo
Hinné	Tbannoo

Past Continuous		
Ana	Kint Ăam	Bitbanna
Inta	Kint Ăam	Btitbanna
Inté	Kinté Ăam	Btitbanné
Hoowé	Kén Ăam	Byitbanna
Heeyé	Kénét Ăam	Btitbanna
Naĥna	Kinna Ăam	Mnitbanna
Intoo	Kintoo Ăam	Btitbannoo
Hinné	Kénoo Ăam	Byitbannoo

Future		
Ana	Laĥ	Itbanna
Inta	Laĥ	Titbanna
Inté	Laĥ	Titbanné
Hoowé	Laĥ	Yitbanna
Heeyé	Laĥ	Titbanna
Naĥna	Laĥ	Nitbanna
Intoo	Laĥ	Titbannoo
Hinné	Laĥ	Yitbannoo

Command	
Inta	Tbanna
Inté	Tbanné
Intoo	Tbannoo
Inta	Ma ttbanna
Inté	Ma ttbanné
Intoo	Ma ttbannoo

Ă= Augh in bought	Ď= a heavy D	É= like A in Bay	G= G in beige	ĥ= like an H with smaller air passage	I= I as in ink	Ќ= like ch in Irish loch
O= O as in home	OO= as in boots	R= roll the rrr	Ť= a heavy T	Ř= like a French R (gargle it)	Ŝ= a heavy S	Ž= a heavy Z

To advise

Present	
Ana	binŜaĥ
Inta	btinŜaĥ
Inté	btinŜaĥé
Hoowé	byinŜaĥ
Heeyé	btinŜaĥ
Naĥna	mninŜaĥ
Intoo	btinŜaĥoo
Hinné	byinŜaĥoo

Present Continuous		
Ana	Ăam	binŜaĥ
Inta	Ăam	btinŜaĥ
Inté	Ăam	btinŜaĥé
Hoowé	Ăam	byinŜaĥ
Heeyé	Ăam	btinŜaĥ
Naĥna	Ăam	mninŜaĥ
Intoo	Ăam	btinŜaĥoo
Hinné	Ăam	byinŜaĥoo

Past	
Ana	naŜaĥt
Inta	naŜaĥt
Inté	naŜaĥté
Hoowé	naŜaĥ
Heeyé	naŜaĥét
Naĥna	naŜaĥna
Intoo	naŜaĥtoo
Hinné	naŜaĥoo

Past Continuous		
Ana	Kint Ăam	binŜaĥ
Inta	Kint Ăam	btinŜaĥ
Inté	Kinté Ăam	btinŜaĥé
Hoowé	Kén Ăam	byinŜaĥ
Heeyé	Kénét Ăam	btinŜaĥ
Naĥna	Kinna Ăam	mninŜaĥ
Intoo	Kintoo Ăam	btinŜaĥoo
Hinné	Kénoo Ăam	byinŜaĥoo

Future		
Ana	Laĥ	inŜaĥ
Inta	Laĥ	tinŜaĥ
Inté	Laĥ	tinŜaĥé
Hoowé	Laĥ	yinŜaĥ
Heeyé	Laĥ	tinŜaĥ
Naĥna	Laĥ	ninŜaĥ
Intoo	Laĥ	tinŜaĥoo
Hinné	Laĥ	yinŜaĥoo

Command	
Inta	nŜaĥ
Inté	nŜaĥé
Intoo	nŜaĥoo
Inta	Ma tnŜaĥ
Inté	Ma tnŜaĥé
Intoo	Ma tnŜaĥoo

To agree

Present	
Ana	Bwéfé'
Inta	Btwéfé'
Inté	Btwéf'é'
Hoowé	Biwéfé'
Heeyé	Btwéfé'
Naĥna	Mnwéfé'
Intoo	Btwéf'oo
Hinné	Biwéf'oo

Present Continuous			
Ana	Ăam	Bwéfé'	(mwéfa'/mwéf'a)
Inta	Ăam	Btwéfé'	(mwéfa')
Inté	Ăam	Btwéf'é'	(mwéf'a)
Hoowé	Ăam	Biwéfé'	(mwéfa')
Heeyé	Ăam	Btwéfé'	(mwéf'a)
Naĥna	Ăam	Mnwéfé'	(mwéf'een)
Intoo	Ăam	Btwéf'oo	(mwéf'een)
Hinné	Ăam	Biwéf'oo	(mwéf'een)

Past	
Ana	Wéfa't
Inta	Wéfa't
Inté	Wéfa'té
Hoowé	Wéfa'
Heeyé	Wéfa'ét
Naĥna	Wéfa'na
Intoo	Wéfa'too
Hinné	Wéfa'oo

Past Continuous				
Ana	Kint Ăam	Bwéfé'	(kint	mwéfa'/mwéf'a)
Inta	Kint Ăam	Btwéfé'	(Kint	mwéfa')
Inté	Kinté Ăam	Btwéf'é'	(Kinté	mwéf'a)
Hoowé	Kén Ăam	Biwéfé'	(Kén	mwéfa')
Heeyé	Kénét Ăam	Btwéfé'	(Kénét	mwéf'a)
Naĥna	Kinna Ăam	Mnwéfé'	(Kinna	mwéf'een)
Intoo	Kintoo Ăam	Btwéf'oo	(Kintoo	mwéf'een)
Hinné	Kénoo Ăam	Biwéf'oo	(Kénoo	mwéf'een)

Future		
Ana	Laĥ	wéfé'
Inta	Laĥ	Twéfé'
Inté	Laĥ	twéf'é'
Hoowé	Laĥ	ywéfé'
Heeyé	Laĥ	Twéfé'
Naĥna	Laĥ	nwéfé'
Intoo	Laĥ	twéf'oo
Hinné	Laĥ	ywéf'oo

Command	
Inta	Wéfé'
Inté	Wéf'é
Intoo	Wéf'oo
Inta	Ma twéfé'
Inté	Ma twéf'é
Intoo	Ma twef'oo

To aim

Present	
Ana	bŜawwéb
Inta	btŜawwéb
Inté	btŜawwbé
Hoowé	biŜawwéb
Heeyé	btŜawwéb
Naĥna	mnŜawwéb
Intoo	btŜawwboo
Hinné	biŜawwboo

Present Continuous		
Ana	Ăam	bŜawwéb
Inta	Ăam	btŜawwéb
Inté	Ăam	btŜawwbé
Hoowé	Ăam	biŜawwéb
Heeyé	Ăam	btŜawwéb
Naĥna	Ăam	mnŜawwéb
Intoo	Ăam	btŜawwboo
Hinné	Ăam	biŜawwboo

Past	
Ana	Ŝawwabt
Inta	Ŝawwabt
Inté	Ŝawwabté
Hoowé	Ŝawwab
Heeyé	Ŝawwabét
Naĥna	Ŝawwabna
Intoo	Ŝawwabtoo
Hinné	Ŝawwaboo

Past Continuous		
Ana	Kint Ăam	bŜawwéb
Inta	Kint Ăam	btŜawwéb
Inté	Kinté Ăam	btŜawwbé
Hoowé	Kén Ăam	biŜawwéb
Heeyé	Kénét Ăam	btŜawwéb
Naĥna	Kinna Ăam	mnŜawwéb
Intoo	Kintoo Ăam	btŜawwboo
Hinné	Kénoo Ăam	biŜawwboo

Future		
Ana	Laĥ	Ŝawwéb
Inta	Laĥ	tŜawwéb
Inté	Laĥ	tŜawwbé
Hoowé	Laĥ	yŜawwéb
Heeyé	Laĥ	tŜawwéb
Naĥna	Laĥ	nŜawwéb
Intoo	Laĥ	tŜawwboo
Hinné	Laĥ	yŜawwboo

Command	
Inta	Ŝawwéb
Inté	Ŝawwbé
Intoo	Ŝawwboo
Inta	Ma tŜawwéb
Inté	Ma tŜawwbé
Intoo	Ma tŜawwboo

To allow

Present	
Ana	Bisamĥ
Inta	Btisamĥ
Inté	Btisamĥé
Hoowé	Byisamĥ
Heeyé	Btisamĥ
Naĥna	Mnisamĥ
Intoo	Btisamĥoo
Hinné	Byisamĥoo

Present Continuous			
Ana	Ăam	Bisamĥ	(séméĥ/sémĥa)
Inta	Ăam	Btisamĥ	(séméĥ)
Inté	Ăam	Btisamĥé	(sémĥa)
Hoowé	Ăam	Byisamĥ	(séméĥ)
Heeyé	Ăam	Btisamĥ	(sémĥa)
Naĥna	Ăam	Mnisamĥ	(sémĥeen)
Intoo	Ăam	Btisamĥoo	(sémĥeen)
Hinné	Ăam	Byisamĥoo	(sémĥeen)

Past	
Ana	Samaĥt
Inta	Samaĥt
Inté	Samaĥté
Hoowé	Samaĥ
Heeyé	Samaĥét
Naĥna	Samaĥna
Intoo	Samaĥtoo
Hinné	Samaĥoo

Past Continuous			
Ana	Kint Ăam	Bisamĥ	(kint séméĥ/sémĥa
Inta	Kint Ăam	Btisamĥ	(Kint séméĥ)
Inté	Kinté Ăam	Btisamĥé	(Kinté sémĥa)
Hoowé	Kén Ăam	Byisamĥ	(Kén séméĥ)
Heeyé	Kénét Ăam	Btisamĥ	(Kénét sémĥa)
Naĥna	Kinna Ăam	Mnisamĥ	(Kinna sémĥeen)
Intoo	Kintoo Ăam	Btisamĥoo	(Kintoo sémĥeen)
Hinné	Kénoo Ăam	Byisamĥoo	(Kénoo sémĥeen)

Future		
Ana	Laĥ	Isamĥ
Inta	Laĥ	tisamĥ
Inté	Laĥ	tisamĥé
Hoowé	Laĥ	yisamĥ
Heeyé	Laĥ	tisamĥ
Naĥna	Laĥ	nisamĥ
Intoo	Laĥ	tisamĥoo
Hinné	Laĥ	yisamĥoo

Command	
Inta	Smaĥ
Inté	Smaĥé
Intoo	Smaĥoo
Inta	Ma tsmaĥ
Inté	Ma tsmaĥé
Intoo	Ma tsmaĥoo

Ă= Augh in bought	Đ= a heavy D	É= like A in Bay	G= G in beige	ĥ= like an H with smaller air passage	I= I as in ink	Ќ= like ch in Irish loch
O= O as in home	OO= as in boots	R= roll the rrr	Ŧ= a heavy T	Ř= like a French R (gargle it)	Ŝ= a heavy S	Ž= a heavy Z

A

To analyze

Present	
Ana	Bḣallil
Inta	Btḣallil
Inté	Btḣallilé
Hoowé	Biḣallil
Heeyé	Btḣallil
Naḣna	Mnḣallil
Intoo	Btḣalliloo
Hinné	Biḣalliloo

Present Continuous		
Ana	Ăam	Bḣallil
Inta	Ăam	Btḣallil
Inté	Ăam	Btḣallilé
Hoowé	Ăam	Biḣallil
Heeyé	Ăam	Btḣallil
Naḣna	Ăam	Mnḣallil
Intoo	Ăam	Btḣalliloo
Hinné	Ăam	Biḣalliloo

Past	
Ana	Ḣallalt
Inta	Ḣallalt
Inté	Ḣallalté
Hoowé	Ḣallal
Heeyé	Ḣallalét
Naḣna	Ḣallalna
Intoo	Ḣallaltoo
Hinné	Ḣallaloo

Past Continuous		
Ana	Kint Ăam	Bḣallil
Inta	Kint Ăam	Btḣallil
Inté	Kinté Ăam	Btḣallilé
Hoowé	Kén Ăam	Biḣallil
Heeyé	Kénét Ăam	Btḣallil
Naḣna	Kinna Ăam	Mnḣallil
Intoo	Kintoo Ăam	Btḣalliloo
Hinné	Kénoo Ăam	Biḣalliloo

Future		
Ana	Laḣ	ḣallil
Inta	Laḣ	tḣallil
Inté	Laḣ	tḣallilé
Hoowé	Laḣ	yḣallil
Heeyé	Laḣ	tḣallil
Naḣna	Laḣ	nḣallil
Intoo	Laḣ	tḣalliloo
Hinné	Laḣ	yḣalliloo

Command	
Inta	Ḣallil
Inté	Ḣallilé
Intoo	Ḣalliloo
Inta	Ma tḣallil
Inté	Ma tḣallilé
Intoo	Ma tḣalliloo

A

To annoy

Present	
Ana	bizĂag
Inta	btizĂag
Inté	btizĂagé
Hoowé	byizĂag
Heeyé	btizĂag
Naḣna	mnizĂag
Intoo	btizĂagoo
Hinné	byizĂagoo

Present Continuous		
Ana	Ăam	bizĂag
Inta	Ăam	btizĂag
Inté	Ăam	btizĂagé
Hoowé	Ăam	byizĂag
Heeyé	Ăam	btizĂag
Naḣna	Ăam	mnizĂag
Intoo	Ăam	btizĂagoo
Hinné	Ăam	byizĂagoo

Past	
Ana	zaĂagt
Inta	zaĂagt
Inté	zaĂagté
Hoowé	zaĂag
Heeyé	zaĂagét
Naḣna	zaĂagna
Intoo	zaĂagtoo
Hinné	zaĂagoo

Past Continuous		
Ana	Kint Ăam	bizĂag
Inta	Kint Ăam	btizĂag
Inté	Kinté Ăam	btizĂagé
Hoowé	Kén Ăam	byizĂag
Heeyé	Kénét Ăam	btizĂag
Naḣna	Kinna Ăam	mnizĂag
Intoo	Kintoo Ăam	btizĂagoo
Hinné	Kénoo Ăam	byizĂagoo

Future		
Ana	Laḣ	izĂag
Inta	Laḣ	tizĂag
Inté	Laḣ	tizĂagé
Hoowé	Laḣ	yizĂag
Heeyé	Laḣ	tizĂag
Naḣna	Laḣ	nizĂag
Intoo	Laḣ	tizĂagoo
Hinné	Laḣ	yizĂagoo

Command	
Inta	zĂag
Inté	zĂagé
Intoo	zĂagoo
Inta	Ma tzĂag
Inté	Ma tzĂagé
Intoo	Ma tzĂagoo

Ă= Augh in bought	Ď= a heavy D	É= like A in Bay	G= G in beige	ḣ= like an H with smaller air passage	I= I as in ink	Ќ= like ch in Irish loch
O= O as in home	OO= as in boots	R= roll the rrr	Ť= a heavy T	Ř= like a French R (gargle it)	Ŝ= a heavy S	Ž= a heavy Z

To be annoyed

Present	
Ana	binziĂég
Inta	btinziĂég
Inté	btinziĂgé
Hoowé	byinziĂég
Heeyé	btinziĂég
Naȟna	mninziĂég
Intoo	btinziĂgoo
Hinné	byinziĂgoo

Present Continuous		
Ana	Ăam	binziĂég
Inta	Ăam	btinziĂég
Inté	Ăam	btinziĂgé
Hoowé	Ăam	byinziĂég
Heeyé	Ăam	btinziĂég
Naȟna	Ăam	mninziĂég
Intoo	Ăam	btinziĂgoo
Hinné	Ăam	byinziĂgoo

Past	
Ana	nzaĂagt
Inta	nzaĂagt
Inté	nzaĂagté
Hoowé	nzaĂag
Heeyé	nzaĂagét
Naȟna	nzaĂagna
Intoo	nzaĂagtoo
Hinné	nzaĂagoo

Past Continuous		
Ana	Kint Ăam	binziĂég
Inta	Kint Ăam	btinziĂég
Inté	Kinté Ăam	btinziĂgé
Hoowé	Kén Ăam	byinziĂég
Heeyé	Kénét Ăam	btinziĂég
Naȟna	Kinna Ăam	mninziĂég
Intoo	Kintoo Ăam	btinziĂgoo
Hinné	Kénoo Ăam	byinziĂgoo

Future		
Ana	Laȟ	inziĂég
Inta	Laȟ	tinziĂég
Inté	Laȟ	tinziĂgé
Hoowé	Laȟ	yinziĂég
Heeyé	Laȟ	tinziĂég
Naȟna	Laȟ	ninziĂég
Intoo	Laȟ	tinziĂgoo
Hinné	Laȟ	yinziĂgoo

Command	
Inta	nziĂég
Inté	nziĂgé
Intoo	naiĂgoo
Inta	Ma tnziĂég
Inté	Ma tnziĂgé
Intoo	Ma tnziĂgoo

To apply

Present	
Ana	bŤabbé'
Inta	btŤabbé'
Inté	btŤabb'é
Hoowé	biŤabbé'
Heeyé	btŤabbé'
Naȟna	mnŤabbé'
Intoo	btŤabb'oo
Hinné	biŤabb'oo

Present Continuous		
Ana	Ăam	bŤabbé'
Inta	Ăam	btŤabbé'
Inté	Ăam	btŤabb'é
Hoowé	Ăam	biŤabbé'
Heeyé	Ăam	btŤabbé'
Naȟna	Ăam	mnŤabbé'
Intoo	Ăam	btŤabb'oo
Hinné	Ăam	biŤabb'oo

Past	
Ana	Ťabba't
Inta	Ťabba't
Inté	Ťabba'té
Hoowé	Ťabba'
Heeyé	Ťabba'ét
Naȟna	Ťabba'na
Intoo	Ťabba'too
Hinné	Ťabba'oo

Past Continuous		
Ana	Kint Ăam	bŤabbé'
Inta	Kint Ăam	btŤabbé'
Inté	Kinté Ăam	btŤabb'é
Hoowé	Kén Ăam	biŤabbé'
Heeyé	Kénét Ăam	btŤabbé'
Naȟna	Kinna Ăam	mnŤabbé'
Intoo	Kintoo Ăam	btŤabb'oo
Hinné	Kénoo Ăam	biŤabb'oo

Future		
Ana	Laȟ	Ťabbé'
Inta	Laȟ	tŤabbé'
Inté	Laȟ	tŤabb'é
Hoowé	Laȟ	yŤabbé'
Heeyé	Laȟ	tŤabbé'
Naȟna	Laȟ	nŤabbé'
Intoo	Laȟ	tŤabb'oo
Hinné	Laȟ	yŤabb'oo

Command	
Inta	Ťabbé'
Inté	Ťabb'é
Intoo	Ťabb'oo
Inta	Ma tŤabbé'
Inté	Ma tŤabb'é
Intoo	Ma tŤabb'oo

Ă= Augh in bought	Ď= a heavy D	É= like A in Bay	G= G in beige	ȟ= like an H with smaller air passage	I= I as in ink	Ќ= like ch in Irish loch
O= O as in home	OO= as in boots	R= roll the rrr	Ť= a heavy T	Ř= like a French R (gargle it)	Ŝ= a heavy S	Ž= a heavy Z

To approve

Present	
Ana	Bwéfé'
Inta	Btwéfé'
Inté	Btwéf'é'
Hoowé	Biwéfé'
Heeyé	Btwéfé'
Nahna	Mnwéfé'
Intoo	Btwéf'oo
Hinné	Biwéf'oo

Present Continuous		
Ana	Ăam Bwéfé'	(mwéfa'/mwéf'a)
Inta	Ăam Btwéfé'	(mwéfa')
Inté	Ăam Btwéf'é'	(mwéf'a)
Hoowé	Ăam Biwéfé'	(mwéfa')
Heeyé	Ăam Btwéfé'	(mwéf'a)
Nahna	Ăam Mnwéfé'	(mwéf'een)
Intoo	Ăam Btwéf'oo	(mwéf'een)
Hinné	Ăam Biwéf'oo	(mwéf'een)

Past	
Ana	Wéfa't
Inta	Wéfa't
Inté	Wéfa'té
Hoowé	Wéfa'
Heeyé	Wéfa'ét
Nahna	Wéfa'na
Intoo	Wéfa'too
Hinné	Wéfa'oo

Past Continuous		
Ana	Kint Ăam Bwéfé'	(kint mwéfa'/mwéf'a)
Inta	Kint Ăam Btwéfé'	(Kint mwéfa')
Inté	Kinté Ăam Btwéf'é'	(Kinté mwéf'a)
Hoowé	Kén Ăam Biwéfé'	(Kén mwéfa')
Heeyé	Kénét Ăam Btwéfé'	(Kénét mwéf'a)
Nahna	Kinna Ăam Mnwéfé'	(Kinna mwéf'een)
Intoo	Kintoo Ăam Btwéf'oo	(Kintoo mwéf'een)
Hinné	Kénoo Ăam Biwéf'oo	(Kénoo mwéf'een)

Future	
Ana	Laĥ wéfé'
Inta	Laĥ Twéfé'
Inté	Laĥ twéf'é'
Hoowé	Laĥ ywéfé'
Heeyé	Laĥ Twéfé'
Nahna	Laĥ nwéfé'
Intoo	Laĥ twéf'oo
Hinné	Laĥ ywéf'oo

Command	
Inta	Wéfé'
Inté	Wéf'é
Intoo	Wéf'oo
Inta	Ma twéfé'
Inté	Ma twéf'é
Intoo	Ma twef'oo

To argue

Present	
Ana	bshéréĂ
Inta	btshéréĂ
Inté	btshérĂe
Hoowé	bishéréĂ
Heeyé	btshéréĂ
Nahna	mnshéréĂ
Intoo	btshérĂoo
Hinné	bishérĂoo

Present Continuous		
Ana	Ăam	bshéréĂ
Inta	Ăam	btshéréĂ
Inté	Ăam	btshérĂe
Hoowé	Ăam	bishéréĂ
Heeyé	Ăam	btshéréĂ
Nahna	Ăam	mnshéréĂ
Intoo	Ăam	btshérĂoo
Hinné	Ăam	bishérĂoo

Past	
Ana	shéraĂt
Inta	shéraĂt
Inté	shéraĂté
Hoowé	shéraĂ
Heeyé	shéraĂét
Nahna	shéraĂna
Intoo	shéraĂtoo
Hinné	shéraĂoo

Past Continuous		
Ana	Kint Ăam	bshéréĂ
Inta	Kint Ăam	btshéréĂ
Inté	Kinté Ăam	btshérĂe
Hoowé	Kén Ăam	bishéréĂ
Heeyé	Kénét Ăam	btshéréĂ
Nahna	Kinna Ăam	mnshéréĂ
Intoo	Kintoo Ăam	btshérĂoo
Hinné	Kénoo Ăam	bishérĂoo

Future	
Ana	Laĥ shéréĂ
Inta	Laĥ tshéréĂ
Inté	Laĥ tshérĂe
Hoowé	Laĥ yshéréĂ
Heeyé	Laĥ tshéréĂ
Nahna	Laĥ nshéréĂ
Intoo	Laĥ tshérĂoo
Hinné	Laĥ yshérĂoo

Command	
Inta	shéréĂ
Inté	shérĂe
Intoo	shérĂoo
Inta	Ma tshéréĂ
Inté	Ma tshérĂe
Intoo	Ma tshérĂoo

Ă= Augh in bought	Đ= a heavy D	É= like A in Bay	G= G in beige	ĥ= like an H with smaller air passage	I= I as in ink	Ќ= like ch in Irish loch
O= O as in home	OO= as in boots	R= roll the rrr	Ť= a heavy T	Ř= like a French R (gargle it)	Ŝ= a heavy S	Ž= a heavy Z

To arrange

Present

Ana	bnaŽŽém
Inta	btnaŽŽém
Inté	btnaŽŽmé
Hoowé	binaŽŽém
Heeyé	btnaŽŽém
Naĥna	mnnaŽŽém
Intoo	btnaŽŽmoo
Hinné	binaŽŽmoo

Present Continuous

Ana	Ăam	bnaŽŽém	(mnaŽŽam/mnaŽŽmé)
Inta	Ăam	btnaŽŽém	(mnaŽŽam)
Inté	Ăam	btnaŽŽmé	(mnaŽŽmé)
Hoowé	Ăam	binaŽŽém	(mnaŽŽém)
Heeyé	Ăam	btnaŽŽém	(mnaŽŽmé)
Naĥna	Ăam	mnnaŽŽém	(mnaŽŽmeen)
Intoo	Ăam	btnaŽŽmoo	(mnaŽŽmeen)
Hinné	Ăam	binaŽŽmoo	(mnaŽŽmeen)

Past

Ana	naŽŽamt
Inta	naŽŽamt
Inté	naŽŽamté
Hoowé	naŽŽam
Heeyé	naŽŽamét
Naĥna	naŽŽamna
Intoo	naŽŽamtoo
Hinné	naŽŽamoo

Past Continuous

Ana	Kint Ăam	bnaŽŽém	(kint	mnaŽŽam/mnaŽŽmé)
Inta	Kint Ăam	btnaŽŽém	(Kint	mnaŽŽam)
Inté	Kinté Ăam	btnaŽŽmé	(Kinté	mnaŽŽmé)
Hoowé	Kén Ăam	binaŽŽém	(Kén	mnaŽŽém)
Heeyé	Kénét Ăam	btnaŽŽém	(Kénét	mnaŽŽmé)
Naĥna	Kinna Ăam	mnnaŽŽém	(Kinna	mnaŽŽmeen)
Intoo	Kintoo Ăam	btnaŽŽmoo	(Kintoo	mnaŽŽmeen)
Hinné	Kénoo Ăam	binaŽŽmoo	(Kénoo	mnaŽŽmeen)

Future

Ana	Laĥ	naŽŽém
Inta	Laĥ	tnaŽŽém
Inté	Laĥ	tnaŽŽmé
Hoowé	Laĥ	ynaŽŽém
Heeyé	Laĥ	tnaŽŽém
Naĥna	Laĥ	nnaŽŽém
Intoo	Laĥ	tnaŽŽmoo
Hinné	Laĥ	ynaŽŽmoo

Command

Inta	naŽŽém
Inté	naŽŽmé
Intoo	naŽŽmoo
Inta	Ma tnaŽŽém
Inté	Ma tnaŽŽmé
Intoo	Ma tnaŽŽmoo

To ascend

Present

Ana	BiŤlaĂ
Inta	BtiŤlaĂ
Inté	BtiŤlaĂé
Hoowé	ByiŤlaĂ
Heeyé	BtiŤlaĂ
Naĥna	MniŤlaĂ
Intoo	BtiŤlaĂoo
Hinné	ByiŤlaĂoo

Present Continuous

Ana	Ăam biŤlaĂ (or ana ŤaléĂ/ŤalĂa)
Inta	Ăam btiŤlaĂ (or ŤaléĂ)
Inté	Ăam btiŤlaĂé (or ŤalĂa)
Hoowé	Ăam byiŤlaĂ (or ŤaléĂ)
Heeyé	Ăam btiŤlaĂ (or ŤalĂa)
Naĥna	Ăam mnilaĂ (or ŤalĂeen)
Intoo	Ăam btiŤlaĂoo (or ŤalĂeen)
Hinné	Ăam byiŤlaĂoo (or ŤalĂeen)

Past

Ana	ŤlaĂt
Inta	ŤlaĂt
Inté	ŤlaĂté
Hoowé	ŤileĂ
Heeyé	ŤilĂét
Naĥna	ŤlaĂna
Intoo	ŤlaĂtoo
Hinné	ŤilĂoo

Past Continuous

Ana	Kint Ăam biŤlaĂ (or kint ŤaléĂ/ŤalĂa)
Inta	Kint Ăam btiŤlaĂ (or kint ŤaléĂ)
Inté	Kinté Ăam btiŤlaĂé (or kinté ŤalĂa)
Hoowé	Kén Ăam byiŤlaĂ (or kén ŤaléĂ)
Heeyé	Kénét Ăam btiŤlaĂ (or kénét ŤalĂa)
Naĥna	Kinna Ăam mniŤlaĂ (or kinna ŤalĂeen)
Intoo	Kintoo Ăam btiŤlaĂoo (kintoo ŤalĂeen)
Hinné	Kénoo Ăam byiŤlaĂoo (or kénoo ŤalĂeen)

Future

Ana	Laĥ	'iŤlaĂ
Inta	Laĥ	tiŤlaĂ
Inté	Laĥ	tiŤlaĂé
Hoowé	Laĥ	yiŤlaĂ
Heeyé	Laĥ	tiŤlaĂ
Naĥna	Laĥ	niŤlaĂ
Intoo	Laĥ	tiŤlaĂoo
Hinné	Laĥ	yiŤlaĂoo

Command

Inta	ŤlaĂ
Inté	ŤlaĂé
Intoo	ŤlaĂoo
Inta	Ma tŤlaĂ
Inté	Ma tŤlaĂé
Intoo	Ma tŤlaĂoo

Ă= Augh in bought	Ď= a heavy D	É= like A in Bay	G= G in beige	ĥ= like an H with smaller air passage	I= I as in ink	Ќ= like ch in Irish loch
O= O as in home	OO= as in boots	R= roll the rrr	Ť= a heavy T	Ř= like a French R (gargle it)	Š= a heavy S	Ž= a heavy Z

A   A

To ask

Present

Ana	Bis'al
Inta	Btis'al
Inté	Btis'alé
Hoowé	Byis'al
Heeyé	Btis'al
Nahna	mnis'al
Intoo	Btis'aloo
Hinné	Byis'aloo

Present Continuous

Ana	Ăam	Bis'al
Inta	Ăam	Btis'al
Inté	Ăam	Btis'alé
Hoowé	Ăam	Byis'al
Heeyé	Ăam	Btis'al
Nahna	Ăam	mnis'al
Intoo	Ăam	Btis'aloo
Hinné	Ăam	Byis'aloo

Past

Ana	Sa'alt
Inta	Sa'alt
Inté	Sa'alté
Hoowé	Sa'al
Heeyé	Sa'lét
Nahna	S'alna
Intoo	S'altoo
Hinné	Sa'loo

Past Continuous

Ana	Kint Ăam	Bis'al
Inta	Kint Ăam	Btis'al
Inté	Kinté Ăam	Btis'alé
Hoowé	Kén Ăam	Byis'al
Heeyé	Kénét Ăam	Btis'al
Nahna	Kinna Ăam	mnis'al
Intoo	Kintoo Ăam	Btis'aloo
Hinné	Kénoo Ăam	Byis'aloo

Future

Ana	Laĥ	Is'al
Inta	Laĥ	Tis'al
Inté	Laĥ	Tis'alé
Hoowé	Laĥ	yis'al
Heeyé	Laĥ	Tis'al
Nahna	Laĥ	nis'al
Intoo	Laĥ	Tis'aloo
Hinné	Laĥ	yis'aloo

Command

Inta	S'al
Inté	S'alé
Intoo	S'aloo
Inta	Ma ts'al
Inté	Ma ts'alé
Intoo	Ma ts'aloo

To assemble

Present

Ana	Brakkéb
Inta	Brakkéb
Inté	Brakkbé
Hoowé	Birakkéb
Heeyé	Btrakkéb
Nahna	Mnrakkéb
Intoo	Btrakkboo
Hinné	Birakkboo

Present Continuous

Ana	Ăam	Brakkéb
Inta	Ăam	Brakkéb
Inté	Ăam	Brakkbé
Hoowé	Ăam	Birakkéb
Heeyé	Ăam	Btrakkéb
Nahna	Ăam	Mnrakkéb
Intoo	Ăam	Btrakkboo
Hinné	Ăam	Birakkboo

Past

Ana	Rakkabt
Inta	Rakkabt
Inté	Rakkabté
Hoowé	Rakkab
Heeyé	Rakkabét
Nahna	Rakkabna
Intoo	Rakkabtoo
Hinné	Rakkaboo

Past Continuous

Ana	Kint Ăam	Brakkéb
Inta	Kint Ăam	Brakkéb
Inté	Kinté Ăam	Brakkbé
Hoowé	Kén Ăam	Birakkéb
Heeyé	Kénét Ăam	Btrakkéb
Nahna	Kinna Ăam	Mnrakkéb
Intoo	Kintoo Ăam	Btrakkboo
Hinné	Kénoo Ăam	Birakkboo

Future

Ana	Laĥ	rakkéb
Inta	Laĥ	rakkéb
Inté	Laĥ	rakkbé
Hoowé	Laĥ	yrakkéb
Heeyé	Laĥ	trakkéb
Nahna	Laĥ	nrakkéb
Intoo	Laĥ	trakkboo
Hinné	Laĥ	yrakkboo

Command

Inta	Rakkéb
Inté	Rakkbé
Intoo	Rakboo
Inta	Ma trakkéb
Inté	Ma trakkbé
Intoo	Ma trakkboo

Ă= Augh in bought	Đ= a heavy D	É= like A in Bay	G= G in beige	ĥ= like an H with smaller air passage	I= I as in ink	Ḱ= like ch in Irish loch
O= O as in home	OO= as in boots	R= roll the rrr	Ť= a heavy T	Ř= like a French R (gargle it)	Ŝ= a heavy S	Ž= a heavy Z

To attack

Present	
Ana	Bihgom
Inta	Btihgom
Inté	Btihgmé
Hoowé	Byihgom
Heeyé	Btihgom
Naĥna	Mnihgom
Intoo	Btihgmoo
Hinné	Byihgmoo

Present Continuous		
Ana	Ăam Bihgom	(hégém/hégmé)
Inta	Ăam Btihgom	(hégém)
Inté	Ăam Btihgmé	(hégmé)
Hoowé	Ăam Byihgom	(hégém)
Heeyé	Ăam Btihgom	(hégmé)
Naĥna	Ăam Mnihgom	(hégmeen)
Intoo	Ăam Btihgmoo	(hégmeen)
Hinné	Ăam Byihgmoo	(hégmeen)

Past	
Ana	Hagamt
Inta	Hagamt
Inté	Hagamté
Hoowé	Hagam
Heeyé	Hagamét
Naĥna	Hagamna
Intoo	Hagamtoo
Hinné	Hagamoo

Past Continuous			
Ana	Kint Ăam	Bihgom	(kint hégém/hégmé)
Inta	Kint Ăam	Btihgom	(Kint hégém)
Inté	Kinté Ăam	Btihgmé	(Kinté hégmé)
Hoowé	Kén Ăam	Byihgom	(Kén hégém)
Heeyé	Kénét Ăam	Btihgom	(Kénét hégmé)
Naĥna	Kinna Ăam	Mnihgom	(Kinna hégmeen)
Intoo	Kintoo Ăam	Btihgmoo	(Kintoo hégmeen)
Hinné	Kénoo Ăam	Byihgmoo	(Kénoo hégmeen)

Future		
Ana	Laĥ	Ihgom
Inta	Laĥ	tihgom
Inté	Laĥ	tihgmé
Hoowé	Laĥ	yihgom
Heeyé	Laĥ	tihgom
Naĥna	Laĥ	nihgom
Intoo	Laĥ	tihgmoo
Hinné	Laĥ	yihgmoo

Command	
Inta	Hgom
Inté	Hgimé
Intoo	Hgimoo
Inta	Ma thgom
Inté	Ma thgmé
Intoo	Ma thgmoo

To attract

Present	
Ana	Bigzob
Inta	Btigzob
Inté	Btigzbé
Hoowé	Byigzob
Heeyé	Btigzob
Naĥna	Mnigzob
Intoo	Btigzboo
Hinné	Byigzboo

Present Continuous	
Ana	Ăam Bigzob
Inta	Ăam Btigzob
Inté	Ăam Btigzbé
Hoowé	Ăam Byigzob
Heeyé	Ăam Btigzob
Naĥna	Ăam Mnigzob
Intoo	Ăam Btigzboo
Hinné	Ăam Byigzboo

Past	
Ana	Gazabt
Inta	Gazabt
Inté	Gazabté
Hoowé	Gazab
Heeyé	Gazabét
Naĥna	Gazabna
Intoo	Gazabtoo
Hinné	Gazaboo

Past Continuous		
Ana	Kint Ăam	Bigzob
Inta	Kint Ăam	Btigzob
Inté	Kinté Ăam	Btigzbé
Hoowé	Kén Ăam	Byigzob
Heeyé	Kénét Ăam	Btigzob
Naĥna	Kinna Ăam	Mnigzob
Intoo	Kintoo Ăam	Btigzboo
Hinné	Kénoo Ăam	Byigzboo

Future		
Ana	Laĥ	igzob
Inta	Laĥ	tigzob
Inté	Laĥ	tigzbé
Hoowé	Laĥ	yigzob
Heeyé	Laĥ	tigzob
Naĥna	Laĥ	nigzob
Intoo	Laĥ	tigzboo
Hinné	Laĥ	yigzboo

Command	
Inta	Gzob
Inté	Gzibé
Intoo	Gziboo
Inta	Ma tgzob
Inté	Ma tgzbé
Intoo	Ma tgzboo

Ă= Augh in bought	Ď= a heavy D	É= like A in Bay	G= G in beige	ĥ= like an H with smaller air passage	I= I as in ink	Ќ= like ch in Irish loch
O= O as in home	OO= as in boots	R= roll the rrr	Ť= a heavy T	Ř= like a French R (gargle it)	Ŝ= a heavy S	Ž= a heavy Z

A

B

To avoid

Present

Ana	Bitféda
Inta	Btitféda
Inté	Btitfédé
Hoowé	Byitféda
Heeyé	Btitféda
Naħna	Mnitféda
Intoo	Btitfédoo
Hinné	Byitfédoo

Present Continuous

Ana	Ăam	Bitféda
Inta	Ăam	Btitféda
Inté	Ăam	Btitfédé
Hoowé	Ăam	Byitféda
Heeyé	Ăam	Btitféda
Naħna	Ăam	Mnitféda
Intoo	Ăam	Btitfédoo
Hinné	Ăam	Byitfédoo

Past

Ana	Tfédét
Inta	Tfédét
Inté	Tfédaité
Hoowé	Tféda
Heeyé	Tfédét
Naħna	Tfédaina
Intoo	Tfédaitoo
Hinné	Tfédoo

Past Continuous

Ana	Kint Ăam	Bitféda
Inta	Kint Ăam	Btitféda
Inté	Kinté Ăam	Btitfédé
Hoowé	Kén Ăam	Byitféda
Heeyé	Kénét Ăam	Btitféda
Naħna	Kinna Ăam	Mnitféda
Intoo	Kintoo Ăam	Btitfédoo
Hinné	Kénoo Ăam	Byitfédoo

Future

Ana	Laħ	itféda
Inta	Laħ	titféda
Inté	Laħ	titfédé
Hoowé	Laħ	yitféda
Heeyé	Laħ	titféda
Naħna	Laħ	nitféda
Intoo	Laħ	titfédoo
Hinné	Laħ	yitfédoo

Command

Inta	Tféda
Inté	Tfédé
Intoo	Tfédoo
Inta	Ma ttféda
Inté	Ma ttfédé
Intoo	Ma ttfédoo

To bark

Present

Ana	Binbaħ
Inta	Btinbaħ
Inté	Btinbaħé
Hoowé	Byinbaħ
Heeyé	Btinbaħ
Naħna	Mninbaħ
Intoo	Btinbaħoo
Hinné	Byinbaħoo

Present Continuous

Ana	Ăam	Binbaħ
Inta	Ăam	Btinbaħ
Inté	Ăam	Btinbaħé
Hoowé	Ăam	Byinbaħ
Heeyé	Ăam	Btinbaħ
Naħna	Ăam	Mninbaħ
Intoo	Ăam	Btinbaħoo
Hinné	Ăam	Byinbaħoo

Past

Ana	Nabaħt
Inta	Nabaħt
Inté	Nabaħté
Hoowé	Nabaħ
Heeyé	Nabaħét
Naħna	Nabaħna
Intoo	Nabaħtoo
Hinné	Nabaħoo

Past Continuous

Ana	Kint Ăam	Binbaħ
Inta	Kint Ăam	Btinbaħ
Inté	Kinté Ăam	Btinbaħé
Hoowé	Kén Ăam	Byinbaħ
Heeyé	Kénét Ăam	Btinbaħ
Naħna	Kinna Ăam	Mninbaħ
Intoo	Kintoo Ăam	Btinbaħoo
Hinné	Kénoo Ăam	Byinbaħoo

Future

Ana	Laħ	Inbaħ
Inta	Laħ	Tinbaħ
Inté	Laħ	Tinbaħé
Hoowé	Laħ	Yinbaħ
Heeyé	Laħ	Tinbaħ
Naħna	Laħ	Ninbaħ
Intoo	Laħ	Tinbaħoo
Hinné	Laħ	Yinbaħoo

Command

Inta	Nbaħ
Inté	Nbaħé
Intoo	Nbaħoo
Inta	Ma tnbaħ
Inté	Ma tnbaħé
Intoo	Ma tnbaħoo

Ă= Augh in bought	Ď= a heavy D	É= like A in Bay	G= G in beige	ħ= like an H with smaller air passage	I= I as in ink	Ќ= like ch in Irish loch
O= O as in home	OO= as in boots	R= roll the rrr	Ť= a heavy T	Ř= like a French R (gargle it)	Ŝ= a heavy S	Ž= a heavy Z

B   B

To become

Present	
Ana	BŜeer
Inta	BtŜeer
Inté	BtŜeeré
Hoowé	BiŜeer
Heeyé	BtŜeer
Nahna	MnŜeer
Intoo	BitŜeeroo
Hinné	BiŜeeroo

Present Continuous	
Ana	Ăam bŜeer (or ana Ŝayér/Ŝayra)
Inta	Ăam btŜeer (or Ŝayér)
Inté	Ăam btŜeeré (or Ŝayra)
Hoowé	Ăam biŜeer (or Ŝayér)
Heeyé	Ăam btŜeer (or Ŝayra)
Nahna	Ăam mnŜeer (or Ŝayreen)
Intoo	Ăam bitŜeeroo (or Ŝayreen)
Hinné	Ăam biŜeeroo (or Ŝayreen)

Past	
Ana	Ŝirt
Inta	Ŝirt
Inté	Ŝirté
Hoowé	Ŝar
Heeyé	Ŝarét
Nahna	Ŝirna
Intoo	Ŝirtoo
Hinné	Ŝaroo

Past Continuous	
Ana	Kint Ăam bŜeer (or ana kint Ŝayér/Ŝayra)
Inta	Kint Ăam btŜeer (or kint Ŝayér)
Inté	Kinté Ăam btŜeeré (or kinté Ŝayra)
Hoowé	Kén Ăam biŜeer (or kén Ŝayer)
Heeyé	Kénét Ăam btŜeer (or kénét Ŝaira)
Nahna	Kinna Ăam mnŜeer (or kinna Ŝaireen)
Intoo	Kintoo Ăam bitŜeeroo (or kintoo Ŝaireen)
Hinné	Kénoo Ăam biŜeeroo (or kénoo Ŝaireen)

Future	
Ana	Laĥ Ŝeer
Inta	Laĥ tŜeer
Inté	Laĥ tŜeeré
Hoowé	Laĥ yŜeer
Heeyé	Laĥ tŜeer
Nahna	Laĥ nŜeer
Intoo	Laĥ tŜeeroo
Hinné	Laĥ yŜeeroo

Command	
Inta	Ŝeer
Inté	Ŝeeré
Intoo	Ŝeeroo
Inta	Ma tŜeer
Inté	Ma tŜeeré
Intoo	Ma tŜeeroo

To beg (for forgivness)

Present	
Ana	Bitragga
Inta	Btitragga
Inté	Btitraggé
Hoowé	Byitragga
Heeyé	Btitragga
Nahna	Mnitragga
Intoo	Btitraggoo
Hinné	Byitraggoo

Present Continuous		
Ana	Ăam	Bitragga
Inta	Ăam	Btitragga
Inté	Ăam	Btitraggé
Hoowé	Ăam	Byitragga
Heeyé	Ăam	Btitragga
Nahna	Ăam	Mnitragga
Intoo	Ăam	Btitraggoo
Hinné	Ăam	Byitraggoo

Past	
Ana	traggét
Inta	traggét
Inté	Traggaité
Hoowé	Tragga
Heeyé	traggét
Nahna	Traggaina
Intoo	Traggaitoo
Hinné	traggoo

Past Continuous		
Ana	Kint Ăam	Bitragga
Inta	Kint Ăam	Btitragga
Inté	Kinté Ăam	Btitraggé
Hoowé	Kén Ăam	Byitragga
Heeyé	Kénét Ăam	Btitragga
Nahna	Kinna Ăam	Mnitragga
Intoo	Kintoo Ăam	Btitraggoo
Hinné	Kénoo Ăam	Byitraggoo

Future		
Ana	Laĥ	Itragga
Inta	Laĥ	Titragga
Inté	Laĥ	Titraggé
Hoowé	Laĥ	Yitragga
Heeyé	Laĥ	Titragga
Nahna	Laĥ	Nitragga
Intoo	Laĥ	Titraggoo
Hinné	Laĥ	Yitraggoo

Command	
Inta	Tragga
Inté	Traggé
Intoo	Traggoo
Inta	Ma ttragga
Inté	Ma ttraggé
Intoo	Ma ttraggoo

Ă= Augh in bought	Ď= a heavy D	É= like A in Bay	G= G in beige	ĥ= like an H with smaller air passage	I= I as in ink	Ќ= like ch in Irish loch
O= O as in home	OO= as in boots	R= roll the rrr	Ť= a heavy T	Ř= like a French R (gargle it)	Ŝ= a heavy S	Ž= a heavy Z

B

B

To beg (on the streets)

Present		
Ana	Bishȟad	
Inta	Btishȟad	
Inté	Bitshȟadé	
Hoowé	Byishȟad	
Heeyé	Btishȟad	
Naȟna	Mnishȟad	
Intoo	Btishȟadoo	
Hinné	Byishȟadoo	

Present Continuous		
Ana	Ăam	Bishȟad
Inta	Ăam	Btishȟad
Inté	Ăam	Bitshȟadé
Hoowé	Ăam	Byishȟad
Heeyé	Ăam	Btishȟad
Naȟna	Ăam	Mnishȟad
Intoo	Ăam	Btishȟadoo
Hinné	Ăam	Byishȟadoo

Past		
Ana	Shaȟadt	
Inta	Shaȟadt	
Inté	Shaȟadté	
Hoowé	Shaȟad	
Heeyé	Shaȟadét	
Naȟna	Shaȟadna	
Intoo	Shaȟadtoo	
Hinné	Shaȟadoo	

Past Continuous		
Ana	Kint Ăam	Bishȟad
Inta	Kint Ăam	Btishȟad
Inté	Kinté Ăam	Bitshȟadé
Hoowé	Kén Ăam	Byishȟad
Heeyé	Kénét Ăam	Btishȟad
Naȟna	Kinna Ăam	Mnishȟad
Intoo	Kintoo Ăam	Btishȟadoo
Hinné	Kénoo Ăam	Byishȟadoo

Future		
Ana	Laȟ	Ishȟad
Inta	Laȟ	Tishȟad
Inté	Laȟ	Itshȟadé
Hoowé	Laȟ	Yishȟad
Heeyé	Laȟ	Tishȟad
Naȟna	Laȟ	Nishȟad
Intoo	Laȟ	Tishȟadoo
Hinné	Laȟ	Yishȟadoo

Command		
Inta	Shȟad	
Inté	Shȟadé	
Intoo	shHadoo	
Inta	Ma tshȟad	
Inté	Ma tshȟadé	
Intoo	Ma tshȟadoo	

To betray

Present		
Ana	bḰoon	
Inta	btḰoon	
Inté	btḰooné	
Hoowé	biḰoon	
Heeyé	btḰoon	
Naȟna	mnḰoon	
Intoo	btḰoonoo	
Hinné	biḰoonoo	

Present Continuous		
Ana	Ăam	bḰoon
Inta	Ăam	btḰoon
Inté	Ăam	btḰooné
Hoowé	Ăam	biḰoon
Heeyé	Ăam	btḰoon
Naȟna	Ăam	mnḰoon
Intoo	Ăam	btḰoonoo
Hinné	Ăam	biḰoonoo

Past		
Ana	Ḱint	
Inta	Ḱint	
Inté	Ḱinté	
Hoowé	Ḱan	
Heeyé	Ḱanit	
Naȟna	Ḱinna	
Intoo	Ḱintoo	
Hinné	Ḱanoo	

Past Continuous		
Ana	Kint Ăam	bḰoon
Inta	Kint Ăam	btḰoon
Inté	Kinté Ăam	btḰooné
Hoowé	Kén Ăam	biḰoon
Heeyé	Kénét Ăam	btḰoon
Naȟna	Kinna Ăam	mnḰoon
Intoo	Kintoo Ăam	btḰoonoo
Hinné	Kénoo Ăam	biḰoonoo

Future		
Ana	Laȟ	Ḱoon
Inta	Laȟ	tḰoon
Inté	Laȟ	tḰooné
Hoowé	Laȟ	yḰoon
Heeyé	Laȟ	tḰoon
Naȟna	Laȟ	nḰoon
Intoo	Laȟ	tḰoonoo
Hinné	Laȟ	yḰoonoo

Command		
Inta	Ḱoon	
Inté	Ḱooné	
Intoo	Ḱoonoo	
Inta	Ma tḰoon	
Inté	Ma tḰooné	
Intoo	Ma tḰoonoo	

Ă= Augh in bought	Ď= a heavy D	É= like A in Bay	G= G in beige	ȟ= like an H with smaller air passage	I= I as in ink	Ḱ= like ch in Irish loch
O= O as in home	OO= as in boots	R= roll the rrr	Ť= a heavy T	Ř= like a French R (gargle it)	Ŝ= a heavy S	Ž= a heavy Z

B

B

To bite

Present	
Ana	bĂaĎĎ
Inta	btĂaĎĎ
Inté	btĂaĎĎé
Hoowé	biĂaĎĎ
Heeyé	btĂaĎĎ
Naĥna	mnĂaĎĎ
Intoo	btĂaĎĎoo
Hinné	biĂaĎĎoo

Present Continuous		
Ana	Ăam	bĂaĎĎ
Inta	Ăam	btĂaĎĎ
Inté	Ăam	btĂaĎĎé
Hoowé	Ăam	biĂaĎĎ
Heeyé	Ăam	btĂaĎĎ
Naĥna	Ăam	mnĂaĎĎ
Intoo	Ăam	btĂaĎĎoo
Hinné	Ăam	biĂaĎĎoo

Past	
Ana	ĂaĎĎét
Inta	ĂaĎĎét
Inté	ĂaĎĎaité
Hoowé	ĂaĎĎ
Heeyé	ĂaĎĎét
Naĥna	ĂaĎĎaina
Intoo	ĂaĎĎaitoo
Hinné	ĂaĎĎoo

Past Continuous		
Ana	Kint Ăam	bĂaĎĎ
Inta	Kint Ăam	btĂaĎĎ
Inté	Kinté Ăam	btĂaĎĎé
Hoowé	Kén Ăam	biĂaĎĎ
Heeyé	Kénét Ăam	btĂaĎĎ
Naĥna	Kinna Ăam	mnĂaĎĎ
Intoo	Kintoo Ăam	btĂaĎĎoo
Hinné	Kénoo Ăam	biĂaĎĎoo

Future		
Ana	Laĥ	ĂaĎĎ
Inta	Laĥ	tĂaĎĎ
Inté	Laĥ	tĂaĎĎé
Hoowé	Laĥ	yĂaĎĎ
Heeyé	Laĥ	tĂaĎĎ
Naĥna	Laĥ	nĂaĎĎ
Intoo	Laĥ	tĂaĎĎoo
Hinné	Laĥ	yĂaĎĎoo

Command	
Inta	ĂaĎĎ
Inté	ĂaĎĎé
Intoo	ĂaĎĎoo
Inta	Ma tĂaĎĎ
Inté	Ma tĂaĎĎé
Intoo	Ma tĂaĎĎoo

To blame

Present	
Ana	Bloom
Inta	Btloom
Inté	Btloomé
Hoowé	Biloom
Heeyé	Btloom
Naĥna	Mnloom
Intoo	Btloomoo
Hinné	Biloomoo

Present Continuous		
Ana	Ăam	Bloom
Inta	Ăam	Btloom
Inté	Ăam	Btloomé
Hoowé	Ăam	Biloom
Heeyé	Ăam	Btloom
Naĥna	Ăam	Mnloom
Intoo	Ăam	Btloomoo
Hinné	Ăam	Biloomoo

Past	
Ana	limt
Inta	limt
Inté	Limté
Hoowé	Lém
Heeyé	lémét
Naĥna	Limna
Intoo	Limtoo
Hinné	Lémoo

Past Continuous		
Ana	Kint Ăam	Bloom
Inta	Kint Ăam	Btloom
Inté	Kinté Ăam	Btloomé
Hoowé	Kén Ăam	Biloom
Heeyé	Kénét Ăam	Btloom
Naĥna	Kinna Ăam	Mnloom
Intoo	Kintoo Ăam	Btloomoo
Hinné	Kénoo Ăam	Biloomoo

Future		
Ana	Laĥ	Loom
Inta	Laĥ	Tloom
Inté	Laĥ	Tloomé
Hoowé	Laĥ	Yloom
Heeyé	Laĥ	Tloom
Naĥna	Laĥ	Nloom
Intoo	Laĥ	Tloomoo
Hinné	Laĥ	Yloomoo

Command	
Inta	Loom
Inté	Loomé
Intoo	Loomoo
Inta	Ma tloom
Inté	Ma tloomé
Intoo	Ma tloomoo

Ă= Augh in bought	Ď= a heavy D	É= like A in Bay	G= G in beige	ĥ= like an H with smaller air passage	I= I as in ink	Ќ= like ch in Irish loch
O= O as in home	OO= as in boots	R= roll the rrr	Ť= a heavy T	Ř= like a French R (gargle it)	Ŝ= a heavy S	Ž= a heavy Z

<u>B</u>   # <u>B</u>

To bleed

Present

Ana	Binzof
Inta	Btinzof
Inté	Btinzfé
Hoowé	Byinzof
Heeyé	Btinzof
Nahna	Mninzof
Intoo	Btinzfoo
Hinné	Byinzfoo

Present Continuous

Ana	Ăam	Binzof
Inta	Ăam	Btinzof
Inté	Ăam	Btinzfé
Hoowé	Ăam	Byinzof
Heeyé	Ăam	Btinzof
Nahna	Ăam	Mninzof
Intoo	Ăam	Btinzfoo
Hinné	Ăam	Byinzfoo

Past

Ana	Nazaft
Inta	Nazaft
Inté	Nazafté
Hoowé	Nazaf
Heeyé	Nazafét
Nahna	Nazafna
Intoo	Nazaftoo
Hinné	Nazafoo

Past Continuous

Ana	Kint Ăam	Binzof
Inta	Kint Ăam	Btinzof
Inté	Kinté Ăam	Btinzfé
Hoowé	Kén Ăam	Byinzof
Heeyé	Kénét Ăam	Btinzof
Nahna	Kinna Ăam	Mninzof
Intoo	Kintoo Ăam	Btinzfoo
Hinné	Kénoo Ăam	Byinzfoo

Future

Ana	Laĥ	Inzof
Inta	Laĥ	Tinzof
Inté	Laĥ	Tinzfé
Hoowé	Laĥ	Yinzof
Heeyé	Laĥ	Tinzof
Nahna	Laĥ	Ninzof
Intoo	Laĥ	Tinzfoo
Hinné	Laĥ	Yinzfoo

Command

Inta	Nzof
Inté	Nzifé
Intoo	Nzifoo
Inta	Ma tnzof
Inté	Ma tnzfé
Intoo	Ma tnzfoo

To blend

Present

Ana	Bimzog
Inta	Btimzog
Inté	Btimzgé
Hoowé	Byimzog
Heeyé	Btimzog
Nahna	Mnimzog
Intoo	Btimzgoo
Hinné	Byimzgoo

Present Continuous

Ana	Ăam	Bimzog
Inta	Ăam	Btimzog
Inté	Ăam	Btimzgé
Hoowé	Ăam	Byimzog
Heeyé	Ăam	Btimzog
Nahna	Ăam	Mnimzog
Intoo	Ăam	Btimzgoo
Hinné	Ăam	Byimzgoo

Past

Ana	Mazagt
Inta	Mazagt
Inté	Mazagté
Hoowé	Mazag
Heeyé	Mazagét
Nahna	Mazagna
Intoo	Mazagtoo
Hinné	Mazagoo

Past Continuous

Ana	Kint Ăam	Bimzog
Inta	Kint Ăam	Btimzog
Inté	Kinté Ăam	Btimzgé
Hoowé	Kén Ăam	Byimzog
Heeyé	Kénét Ăam	Btimzog
Nahna	Kinna Ăam	Mnimzog
Intoo	Kintoo Ăam	Btimzgoo
Hinné	Kénoo Ăam	Byimzgoo

Future

Ana	Laĥ	Imzog
Inta	Laĥ	Timzog
Inté	Laĥ	Timzgé
Hoowé	Laĥ	Yimzog
Heeyé	Laĥ	Timzog
Nahna	Laĥ	Nimzog
Intoo	Laĥ	Timzgoo
Hinné	Laĥ	Yimzgoo

Command

Inta	Mzog
Inté	Mzigé
Intoo	Mzigoo
Inta	Ma tmzog
Inté	Ma tmzgé
Intoo	Ma tmzgoo

Ă= Augh in bought	Ď= a heavy D	É= like A in Bay	G= G in beige	ĥ= like an H with smaller air passage	I= I as in ink	Ќ= like ch in Irish loch
O= O as in home	OO= as in boots	R= roll the rrr	Ť= a heavy T	Ř= like a French R (gargle it)	Ŝ= a heavy S	Ž= a heavy Z

B

B

To block

Present

Ana	Bsidd
Inta	Btsidd
Inté	Btsiddé
Hoowé	Bisidd
Heeyé	Btsidd
Nahna	Mnsidd
Intoo	Bstiddoo
Hinné	Bisiddoo

Present Continuous

Ana	Ăam	Bsidd
Inta	Ăam	Btsidd
Inté	Ăam	Btsiddé
Hoowé	Ăam	Bisidd
Heeyé	Ăam	Btsidd
Nahna	Ăam	Mnsidd
Intoo	Ăam	Bstiddoo
Hinné	Ăam	Bisiddoo

Past

Ana	Saddét
Inta	Saddét
Inté	Saddaité
Hoowé	Sadd
Heeyé	Saddét
Nahna	Saddaina
Intoo	Saddaitoo
Hinné	Saddoo

Past Continuous

Ana	Kint Ăam	Bsidd
Inta	Kint Ăam	Btsidd
Inté	Kinté Ăam	Btsiddé
Hoowé	Kén Ăam	Bisidd
Heeyé	Kénét Ăam	Btsidd
Nahna	Kinna Ăam	Mnsidd
Intoo	Kintoo Ăam	Bstiddoo
Hinné	Kénoo Ăam	Bisiddoo

Future

Ana	Laĥ	Sidd
Inta	Laĥ	Tsidd
Inté	Laĥ	Tsiddé
Hoowé	Laĥ	Ysidd
Heeyé	Laĥ	Tsidd
Nahna	Laĥ	Nsidd
Intoo	Laĥ	Stiddoo
Hinné	Laĥ	Ysiddoo

Command

Inta	Sidd
Inté	Siddé
Intoo	Siddoo
Inta	Ma tsidd
Inté	Ma tsiddé
Intoo	Ma tsiddoo

To blow

Present

Ana	binfoḰ
Inta	btinfoḰ
Inté	btinfḰé
Hoowé	byinfoḰ
Heeyé	btinfoḰ
Nahna	mninfoḰ
Intoo	btinfḰoo
Hinné	byinfoḰoo

Present Continuous

Ana	Ăam	binfoḰ
Inta	Ăam	btinfoḰ
Inté	Ăam	btinfḰé
Hoowé	Ăam	byinfoḰ
Heeyé	Ăam	btinfoḰ
Nahna	Ăam	mninfoḰ
Intoo	Ăam	btinfḰoo
Hinné	Ăam	byinfoḰoo

Past

Ana	nafaḰt
Inta	nafaḰt
Inté	nafaḰté
Hoowé	nafaḰ
Heeyé	nafaḰét
Nahna	nafaḰna
Intoo	nafaḰtoo
Hinné	nafaḰoo

Past Continuous

Ana	Kint Ăam	binfoḰ
Inta	Kint Ăam	btinfoḰ
Inté	Kinté Ăam	btinfḰé
Hoowé	Kén Ăam	byinfoḰ
Heeyé	Kénét Ăam	btinfoḰ
Nahna	Kinna Ăam	mninfoḰ
Intoo	Kintoo Ăam	btinfḰoo
Hinné	Kénoo Ăam	byinfoḰoo

Future

Ana	Laĥ	infoḰ
Inta	Laĥ	tinfoḰ
Inté	Laĥ	tinfḰé
Hoowé	Laĥ	yinfoḰ
Heeyé	Laĥ	tinfoḰ
Nahna	Laĥ	ninfoḰ
Intoo	Laĥ	tinfḰoo
Hinné	Laĥ	yinfoḰoo

Command

Inta	nfoḰ
Inté	nfiḰé
Intoo	nfiḰoo
Inta	Ma tnfoḰ
Inté	Ma tnfḰé
Intoo	Ma tnfḰoo

Ă= Augh in bought	Ď= a heavy D	É= like A in Bay	G= G in beige	ĥ= like an H with smaller air passage	I= I as in ink	Ḱ= like ch in Irish loch
O= O as in home	OO= as in boots	R= roll the rrr	Ť= a heavy T	Ř= like a French R (gargle it)	Ŝ= a heavy S	Ž= a heavy Z

B

B

To boil

Present	
Ana	biŘlé
Inta	btiŘlé
Inté	btiŘlé
Hoowé	byiŘlé
Heeyé	btiŘlé
Nahna	mniŘlé
Intoo	btiŘloo
Hinné	byiŘloo

Present Continuous		
Ana	Ăam	biŘlé
Inta	Ăam	btiŘlé
Inté	Ăam	btiŘlé
Hoowé	Ăam	byiŘlé
Heeyé	Ăam	btiŘlé
Nahna	Ăam	mniŘlé
Intoo	Ăam	btiŘloo
Hinné	Ăam	byiŘloo

Past	
Ana	Řleet
Inta	Řleet
Inté	Řleeté
Hoowé	Řilé
Heeyé	Řilyét
Nahna	Řleena
Intoo	Řleetoo
Hinné	Řilyoo

Past Continuous		
Ana	Kint Ăam	biŘlé
Inta	Kint Ăam	btiŘlé
Inté	Kinté Ăam	btiŘlé
Hoowé	Kén Ăam	byiŘlé
Heeyé	Kénét Ăam	btiŘlé
Nahna	Kinna Ăam	mniŘlé
Intoo	Kintoo Ăam	btiŘloo
Hinné	Kénoo Ăam	byiŘloo

Future		
Ana	Laĥ	iŘlé
Inta	Laĥ	tiŘlé
Inté	Laĥ	tiŘlé
Hoowé	Laĥ	yiŘlé
Heeyé	Laĥ	tiŘlé
Nahna	Laĥ	niŘlé
Intoo	Laĥ	tiŘloo
Hinné	Laĥ	yiŘloo

Command	
Inta	Řlee
Inté	Řlee
Intoo	Řloo
Inta	Ma tŘlé
Inté	Ma tŘlé
Intoo	Ma tŘloo

To be born

Present	
Ana	biḰla'
Inta	btiḰla'
Inté	btiḰla'é
Hoowé	byiḰla'
Heeyé	btiḰla'
Nahna	mniḰla'
Intoo	btiḰla'oo
Hinné	byiḰla'oo

Present Continuous		
Ana	Ăam	biḰla'
Inta	Ăam	btiḰla'
Inté	Ăam	btiḰla'é
Hoowé	Ăam	byiḰla'
Heeyé	Ăam	btiḰla'
Nahna	Ăam	mniḰla'
Intoo	Ăam	btiḰla'oo
Hinné	Ăam	byiḰla'oo

Past	
Ana	Ḱli't
Inta	Ḱli't
Inté	Ḱli'té
Hoowé	Ḱili'
Heeyé	Ḱil'ét
Nahna	Ḱli'na
Intoo	Ḱli'too
Hinné	Ḱil'oo

Past Continuous		
Ana	Kint Ăam	biḰla'
Inta	Kint Ăam	btiḰla'
Inté	Kinté Ăam	btiḰla'é
Hoowé	Kén Ăam	byiḰla'
Heeyé	Kénét Ăam	btiḰla'
Nahna	Kinna Ăam	mniḰla'
Intoo	Kintoo Ăam	btiḰla'oo
Hinné	Kénoo Ăam	byiḰla'oo

Future		
Ana	Laĥ	iḰla'
Inta	Laĥ	tiḰla'
Inté	Laĥ	tiḰla'é
Hoowé	Laĥ	yiḰla'
Heeyé	Laĥ	tiḰla'
Nahna	Laĥ	niḰla'
Intoo	Laĥ	tiḰla'oo
Hinné	Laĥ	yiḰla'oo

Command	
Inta	Ḱla'
Inté	Ḱla'é
Intoo	Ḱla'oo
Inta	Ma tḰla'
Inté	Ma tḰla'é
Intoo	Ma tḰla'oo

Ă= Augh in bought	Đ= a heavy D	É= like A in Bay	G= G in beige	ĥ= like an H with smaller air passage	I= I as in ink	Ḱ= like ch in Irish loch
O= O as in home	OO= as in boots	R= roll the rrr	Ť= a heavy T	Ř= like a French R (gargle it)	Ŝ= a heavy S	Ž= a heavy Z

B   B

To bounce

Present	
Ana	bŤigg
Inta	btŤigg
Inté	btŤiggé
Hoowé	biŤigg
Heeyé	btŤigg
Naĥna	mnŤigg
Intoo	btŤiggoo
Hinné	biŤiggoo

Present Continuous		
Ana	Ăam	bŤigg
Inta	Ăam	btŤigg
Inté	Ăam	btŤiggé
Hoowé	Ăam	biŤigg
Heeyé	Ăam	btŤigg
Naĥna	Ăam	mnŤigg
Intoo	Ăam	btŤiggoo
Hinné	Ăam	biŤiggoo

Past	
Ana	Ťaggét
Inta	Ťaggét
Inté	Ťaggaité
Hoowé	Ťagg
Heeyé	Ťaggét
Naĥna	Ťaggaina
Intoo	Ťaggaitoo
Hinné	Ťaggoo

Past Continuous		
Ana	Kint Ăam	bŤigg
Inta	Kint Ăam	btŤigg
Inté	Kinté Ăam	btŤiggé
Hoowé	Kén Ăam	biŤigg
Heeyé	Kénét Ăam	btŤigg
Naĥna	Kinna Ăam	mnŤigg
Intoo	Kintoo Ăam	btŤiggoo
Hinné	Kénoo Ăam	biŤiggoo

Future		
Ana	Laĥ	Ťigg
Inta	Laĥ	tŤigg
Inté	Laĥ	tŤiggé
Hoowé	Laĥ	yŤigg
Heeyé	Laĥ	tŤigg
Naĥna	Laĥ	nŤigg
Intoo	Laĥ	tŤiggoo
Hinné	Laĥ	yŤiggoo

Command	
Inta	Ťigg
Inté	Ťiggé
Intoo	Ťiggoo
Inta	Ma tŤigg
Inté	Ma tŤiggé
Intoo	Ma tŤiggoo

To branch

Present	
Ana	bitfarraĂ
Inta	btitfarraĂ
Inté	btitfarraĂé
Hoowé	byitfarraĂ
Heeyé	btitfarraĂ
Naĥna	mnitfarraĂ
Intoo	btitfarraĂoo
Hinné	byitfarraĂoo

Present Continuous		
Ana	Ăam	bitfarraĂ
Inta	Ăam	btitfarraĂ
Inté	Ăam	btitfarraĂé
Hoowé	Ăam	byitfarraĂ
Heeyé	Ăam	btitfarraĂ
Naĥna	Ăam	mnitfarraĂ
Intoo	Ăam	btitfarraĂoo
Hinné	Ăam	byitfarraĂoo

Past	
Ana	tfarraĂt
Inta	tfarraĂt
Inté	tfarraĂté
Hoowé	tfarraĂ
Heeyé	tfarraĂét
Naĥna	tfarraĂna
Intoo	tfarraĂtoo
Hinné	tfarraĂoo

Past Continuous		
Ana	Kint Ăam	bitfarraĂ
Inta	Kint Ăam	btitfarraĂ
Inté	Kinté Ăam	btitfarraĂé
Hoowé	Kén Ăam	byitfarraĂ
Heeyé	Kénét Ăam	btitfarraĂ
Naĥna	Kinna Ăam	mnitfarraĂ
Intoo	Kintoo Ăam	btitfarraĂoo
Hinné	Kénoo Ăam	byitfarraĂoo

Future		
Ana	Laĥ	itfarraĂ
Inta	Laĥ	titfarraĂ
Inté	Laĥ	titfarraĂé
Hoowé	Laĥ	yitfarraĂ
Heeyé	Laĥ	titfarraĂ
Naĥna	Laĥ	nitfarraĂ
Intoo	Laĥ	titfarraĂoo
Hinné	Laĥ	yitfarraĂoo

Command	
Inta	tfarraĂ
Inté	tfarrĂé
Intoo	tfarrĂoo
Inta	Ma ttfarraĂ
Inté	Ma ttfarraĂé
Intoo	Ma ttfarraĂoo

Ă= Augh in bought	Đ= a heavy D	É= like A in Bay	G= G in beige	ĥ= like an H with smaller air passage	I= I as in ink	Ǩ= like ch in Irish loch
O= O as in home	OO= as in boots	R= roll the rrr	Ť= a heavy T	Ř= like a French R (gargle it)	Ŝ= a heavy S	Ž= a heavy Z

B

B

To break

To breath

Present

Ana	Biksor
Inta	Btiksor
Inté	Btiksré
Hoowé	Byiksor
Heeyé	Btiksor
Naĥna	Mniksor
Intoo	Btiksroo
Hinné	Byiksroo

Present

Ana	Bitnaffas
Inta	Btitnaffas
Inté	Btitnaffasé
Hoowé	Byitnaffas
Heeyé	Btitnaffas
Naĥna	Mnitnaffas
Intoo	Btitnaffasoo
Hinné	Byitnaffasoo

Present Continuous

Ana	Ăam	Biksor
Inta	Ăam	Btiksor
Inté	Ăam	Btiksré
Hoowé	Ăam	Byiksor
Heeyé	Ăam	Btiksor
Naĥna	Ăam	Mniksor
Intoo	Ăam	Btiksroo
Hinné	Ăam	Byiksroo

Present Continuous

Ana	Ăam	Bitnaffas
Inta	Ăam	Btitnaffas
Inté	Ăam	Btitnaffasé
Hoowé	Ăam	Byitnaffas
Heeyé	Ăam	Btitnaffas
Naĥna	Ăam	Mnitnaffas
Intoo	Ăam	Btitnaffasoo
Hinné	Ăam	Byitnaffasoo

Past

Ana	Kasart
Inta	Kasart
Inté	Kasarté
Hoowé	Kasar
Heeyé	Kasarét
Naĥna	Kasarna
Intoo	Kasartoo
Hinné	Kasaroo

Past

Ana	Tnaffast
Inta	Tnaffast
Inté	Tnaffasté
Hoowé	Tnaffas
Heeyé	Tnaffasét
Naĥna	Tnaffasna
Intoo	Tnaffastoo
Hinné	Tnaffasoo

Past Continuous

Ana	Kint Ăam	Biksor
Inta	Kint Ăam	Btiksor
Inté	Kinté Ăam	Btiksré
Hoowé	Kén Ăam	Byiksor
Heeyé	Kénét Ăam	Btiksor
Naĥna	Kinna Ăam	Mniksor
Intoo	Kintoo Ăam	Btiksroo
Hinné	Kénoo Ăam	Byiksroo

Past Continuous

Ana	Kint Ăam	Bitnaffas
Inta	Kint Ăam	Btitnaffas
Inté	Kinté Ăam	Btitnaffasé
Hoowé	Kén Ăam	Byitnaffas
Heeyé	Kénét Ăam	Btitnaffas
Naĥna	Kinna Ăam	Mnitnaffas
Intoo	Kintoo Ăam	Btitnaffasoo
Hinné	Kénoo Ăam	Byitnaffasoo

Future

Ana	Laĥ	Iksor
Inta	Laĥ	Tiksor
Inté	Laĥ	Tiksré
Hoowé	Laĥ	Yiksor
Heeyé	Laĥ	Tiksor
Naĥna	Laĥ	Niksor
Intoo	Laĥ	Tiksroo
Hinné	Laĥ	Yiksroo

Future

Ana	Laĥ	Itnaffas
Inta	Laĥ	Titnaffas
Inté	Laĥ	Titnaffasé
Hoowé	Laĥ	Yitnaffas
Heeyé	Laĥ	Titnaffas
Naĥna	Laĥ	Nitnaffas
Intoo	Laĥ	Titnaffasoo
Hinné	Laĥ	Yitnaffasoo

Command

Inta	Ksor
Inté	Ksiré
Intoo	Ksiroo
Inta	Ma tksor
Inté	Ma tksré
Intoo	Ma tksroo

Command

Inta	Tnaffas
Inté	Tnaffasé
Intoo	Tnaffasoo
Inta	Ma ttnaffas
Inté	Ma ttnaffasé
Intoo	Ma ttnaffasoo

Ă= Augh in bought	Ď= a heavy D	É= like A in Bay	G= G in beige	ĥ= like an H with smaller air passage	I= I as in ink	Ḱ= like ch in Irish loch
O= O as in home	OO= as in boots	R= roll the rrr	Ť= a heavy T	Ř= like a French R (gargle it)	Ŝ= a heavy S	Ž= a heavy Z

B

B

To bring

Present	
Ana	Bjeeb
Inta	Btjeeb
Inté	Btjeebé
Hoowé	Bijeeb
Heeyé	Btjeeb
Naĥna	Mnjeeb
Intoo	Btjeeboo
Hinné	Bijeeboo

Present Continuous		
Ana	Ăam	Bgeeb	(géyéb / Géybé)
Inta	Ăam	Btgeeb	(géyéb)
Inté	Ăam	Btgeebé	(géyéb)
Hoowé	Ăam	Bigeeb	(géyéb)
Heeyé	Ăam	Btgeeb	(géyéb)
Naĥna	Ăam	Mngeeb	(Géybeen)
Intoo	Ăam	Btgeeboo	(Géybeen)
Hinné	Ăam	Bigeeboo	(Géybeen)

Past	
Ana	Gibt
Inta	Gibt
Inté	Gibté
Hoowé	Géb
Heeyé	Gébét
Naĥna	Gibna
Intoo	Gibtoo
Hinné	Géboo

Past Continuous			
Ana	Kint Ăam	Bgeeb	(kint Géyéb/géybé)
Inta	Kint Ăam	Btgeeb	(Kint Géyéb)
Inté	Kinté Ăam	Btgeebé	(Kinté Géybé)
Hoowé	Kén Ăam	Bigeeb	(Kén Géyéb)
Heeyé	Kénét Ăam	Btgeeb	(Kénét Géyéb)
Naĥna	Kinna Ăam	Mngeeb	(Kinna Géybeen)
Intoo	Kintoo Ăam	Btgeeboo	(Kintoo Géybeen)
Hinné	Kénoo Ăam	Bigeeboo	(Kénoo Géybeen)

Future		
Ana	Laĥ	Geeb
Inta	Laĥ	Tgeeb
Inté	Laĥ	Tgeebé
Hoowé	Laĥ	Ygeeb
Heeyé	Laĥ	Tgeeb
Naĥna	Laĥ	Ngeeb
Intoo	Laĥ	Tgeeboo
Hinné	Laĥ	Ygeeboo

Command	
Inta	Geeb
Inté	Geebé
Intoo	Geeboo
Inta	Ma tgeeb
Inté	Ma tgeebé
Intoo	Ma tgeeboo

To brush

Present	
Ana	Bfarshé
Inta	Btfarshé
Inté	Btfarshé
Hoowé	Bifarshé
Heeyé	Btfarshé
Naĥna	Mnfarshé
Intoo	Btfarshoo
Hinné	Bifarshoo

Present Continuous		
Ana	Ăam	Bfarshé
Inta	Ăam	Btfarshé
Inté	Ăam	Btfarshé
Hoowé	Ăam	Bifarshé
Heeyé	Ăam	Btfarshé
Naĥna	Ăam	Mnfarshé
Intoo	Ăam	Btfarshoo
Hinné	Ăam	Bifarshoo

Past	
Ana	Farshét
Inta	Farshét
Inté	Farshaité
Hoowé	Farsha
Heeyé	Farshét
Naĥna	Farshaina
Intoo	Farshaitoo
Hinné	Farshoo

Past Continuous		
Ana	Kint Ăam	Bfarshé
Inta	Kint Ăam	Btfarshé
Inté	Kinté Ăam	Btfarshé
Hoowé	Kén Ăam	Bifarshé
Heeyé	Kénét Ăam	Btfarshé
Naĥna	Kinna Ăam	Mnfarshé
Intoo	Kintoo Ăam	Btfarshoo
Hinné	Kénoo Ăam	Bifarshoo

Future		
Ana	Laĥ	Farshé
Inta	Laĥ	Tfarshé
Inté	Laĥ	Tfarshé
Hoowé	Laĥ	Yfarshé
Heeyé	Laĥ	Tfarshé
Naĥna	Laĥ	Nfarshé
Intoo	Laĥ	Tfarshoo
Hinné	Laĥ	Yfarshoo

Command	
Inta	Farshé
Inté	Farshé
Intoo	Farshoo
Inta	Ma tfarshé
Inté	Ma tfarshé
Intoo	Ma tfarshoo

Ă= Augh in bought	Ď= a heavy D	É= like A in Bay	G= G in beige	ĥ= like an H with smaller air passage	I= I as in ink	Ķ= like ch in Irish loch
O= O as in home	OO= as in boots	R= roll the rrr	Ť= a heavy T	Ř= like a French R (gargle it)	Š= a heavy S	Ž= a heavy Z

B   B

To build / To construct

To build / To construct

Present	
Ana	Bibné
Inta	Btibné
Inté	Btibné
Hoowé	Byibné
Heeyé	Btibné
Nahna	mnibné
Intoo	Btibnoo
Hinné	Byibnoo

Present Continuous		
Ana	Ăam	Bibné
Inta	Ăam	Btibné
Inté	Ăam	Btibné
Hoowé	Ăam	Byibné
Heeyé	Ăam	Btibné
Nahna	Ăam	mnibné
Intoo	Ăam	Btibnoo
Hinné	Ăam	Byibnoo

Past	
Ana	Bneet
Inta	Bneet
Inté	Bneeté
Hoowé	Biné
Heeyé	Binyét
Nahna	Bneena
Intoo	Bneetoo
Hinné	Binyoo

Past Continuous		
Ana	Kint Ăam	Bibné
Inta	Kint Ăam	Btibné
Inté	Kinté Ăam	Btibné
Hoowé	Kén Ăam	Byibné
Heeyé	Kénét Ăam	Btibné
Nahna	Kinna Ăam	mnibné
Intoo	Kintoo Ăam	Btibnoo
Hinné	Kénoo Ăam	Byibnoo

Future		
Ana	Laĥ	ibné
Inta	Laĥ	tibné
Inté	Laĥ	tibné
Hoowé	Laĥ	yibné
Heeyé	Laĥ	tibné
Nahna	Laĥ	nibné
Intoo	Laĥ	Tibnoo
Hinné	Laĥ	Yibnoo

Command	
Inta	Bnee
Inté	Bnee
Intoo	Bnoo
Inta	Ma tbné
Inté	Ma tbné
Intoo	Ma tbnoo

To buy

Present	
Ana	Bishtré
Inta	Btishtré
Inté	Btishtré
Hoowé	Biyshtré
Heeyé	Btishtré
Nahna	Mnishtré
Intoo	Btishtroo
Hinné	Byishtroo

Present Continuous			
Ana	Ăam	Bishtré	(shéré / shéryé)
Inta	Ăam	Btishtré	(shéré)
Inté	Ăam	Btishtré	(shéryé)
Hoowé	Ăam	Biyshtré	(shéré)
Heeyé	Ăam	Btishtré	(shéryé)
Nahna	Ăam	mnishtré	(shéryeen)
Intoo	Ăam	Btishtroo	(shéryeen)
Hinné	Ăam	Byishtroo	(shéryeen)

Past	
Ana	Shtarét
Inta	Shtarét
Inté	Shtaraité
Hoowé	Shtara
Heeyé	Shtaryét
Nahna	Shtaraina
Intoo	Shtaraitoo
Hinné	Shtarioo

Past Continuous			
Ana	Kint Ăam	Bishtré	(kint Shéré/ shéryé
Inta	Kint Ăam	Btishtré	(Kint Shéré)
Inté	Kinté Ăam	Btishtré	(Kinté shéryé)
Hoowé	Kén Ăam	Biyshtré	(Kén Shéré)
Heeyé	Kénét Ăam	Btishtré	(Kénét shéryé)
Nahna	Kinna Ăam	mnishtré	(Kinna shéryeen)
Intoo	Kintoo Ăam	Btishtroo	(Kintoo shéryeen)
Hinné	Kénoo Ăam	Byishtroo	(Kénoo shéryeen)

Future		
Ana	Laĥ	Ishtré
Inta	Laĥ	Tishtré
Inté	Laĥ	Tishtré
Hoowé	Laĥ	Yishtré
Heeyé	Laĥ	Tishtré
Nahna	Laĥ	Nishtré
Intoo	Laĥ	Tishtroo
Hinné	Laĥ	Yishtroo

Command	
Inta	Shtiré
Inté	Shtiré
Intoo	Shtiroo
Inta	Ma tshtiré
Inté	Ma tshtiré
Intoo	Ma tshtiroo

Ă= Augh in bought	Đ= a heavy D	É= like A in Bay	G= G in beige	ĥ= like an H with smaller air passage	I= I as in ink	Ḱ= like ch in Irish loch
O= O as in home	OO= as in boots	R= roll the rrr	Ť= a heavy T	Ř= like a French R (gargle it)	Ŝ= a heavy S	Ž= a heavy Z

C   C

To calculate

Present	
Ana	Biĥsob
Inta	Btiĥsob
Inté	Btiĥsbé
Hoowé	Byiĥsob
Heeyé	Btiĥsob
Naĥna	Mniĥsob
Intoo	Btiĥsboo
Hinné	Byiĥsboo

Present Continuous		
Ana	Ăam Biĥsob	(Ĥéséb/ĥésbé)
Inta	Ăam Btiĥsob	(Ĥéséb)
Inté	Ăam Btiĥsbé	(Ĥésbé)
Hoowé	Ăam Byiĥsob	(Ĥéséb)
Heeyé	Ăam Btiĥsob	(Ĥésbeen)
Naĥna	Ăam Mniĥsob	(Ĥésbeen)
Intoo	Ăam Btiĥsboo	(Ĥésbeen)
Hinné	Ăam Byiĥsboo	(Ĥésbeen)

Past	
Ana	Ĥasabt
Inta	Ĥasabt
Inté	Ĥasabté
Hoowé	Ĥasab
Heeyé	Ĥasabét
Naĥna	Ĥsabna
Intoo	Ĥsabtoo
Hinné	Ĥasaboo

Past Continuous			
Ana	Kint Ăam Biĥsob	(kint	Ĥéséb/hésbé)
Inta	Kint Ăam Btiĥsob	(Kint	Ĥéséb)
Inté	Kinté Ăam Btiĥsbé	(Kinté	Ĥéséb)
Hoowé	Kén Ăam Byiĥsob	(Kén	Ĥéséb)
Heeyé	Kénét Ăam Btiĥsob	(Kénét	Ĥésbé)
Naĥna	Kinna Ăam Mniĥsob	(Kinna	Ĥésbeen)
Intoo	Kintoo Ăam Btiĥsboo	(Kintoo	Ĥésbeen)
Hinné	Kénoo Ăam Byiĥsboo	(Kénoo	Ĥésbeen)

Future		
Ana	Laĥ	Iĥsob
Inta	Laĥ	Tiĥsob
Inté	Laĥ	Tiĥsob
Hoowé	Laĥ	Yiĥsob
Heeyé	Laĥ	Tiĥsob
Naĥna	Laĥ	Niĥsob
Intoo	Laĥ	Tiĥsboo
Hinné	Laĥ	yiĥsboo

Command	
Inta	Ĥsob
Inté	Ĥsibé
Intoo	Ĥsiboo
Inta	Ma tĥsob
Inté	Ma tĥsbé
Intoo	Ma tĥsboo

To call / To phone

Present	
Ana	Btalfén
Inta	bittalfen
Inté	Bittalfné
Hoowé	Bitalfén
Heeyé	Bittalfén
Naĥna	Mntalfén
Intoo	Bittalfnoo
Hinné	Bitalfnoo

Present Continuous		
Ana	Ăam	Btalfén
Inta	Ăam	bittalfen
Inté	Ăam	Bittalfné
Hoowé	Ăam	Bitalfén
Heeyé	Ăam	Bittalfén
Naĥna	Ăam	Mntalfén
Intoo	Ăam	Bittalfnoo
Hinné	Ăam	Bitalfnoo

Past	
Ana	Talfant
Inta	Talfant
Inté	Talfanté
Hoowé	Talfan
Heeyé	Talfanét
Naĥna	Talfanna
Intoo	Talfantoo
Hinné	Talfanoo

Past Continuous		
Ana	Kint Ăam	Btalfén
Inta	Kint Ăam	bittalfen
Inté	Kinté Ăam	Bittalfné
Hoowé	Kén Ăam	Bitalfén
Heeyé	Kénét Ăam	Bittalfén
Naĥna	Kinna Ăam	Mntalfén
Intoo	Kintoo Ăam	Bittalfnoo
Hinné	Kénoo Ăam	Bitalfnoo

Future		
Ana	Laĥ	talfén
Inta	Laĥ	ttalfén
Inté	Laĥ	ttalfné
Hoowé	Laĥ	ytalfén
Heeyé	Laĥ	ttalfén
Naĥna	Laĥ	ntalfén
Intoo	Laĥ	Ttalfnoo
Hinné	Laĥ	Ytalfnoo

Command	
Inta	Talfén
Inté	Talfné
Intoo	Talfnoo
Inta	Ma ttalfen
Inté	Ma ttalfné
Intoo	Ma ttalfnoo

Ă= Augh in bought	Ď= a heavy D	É= like A in Bay	G= G in beige	ĥ= like an H with smaller air passage	I= I as in ink	Ќ= like ch in Irish loch
O= O as in home	OO= as in boots	R= roll the rrr	Ť= a heavy T	Ř= like a French R (gargle it)	Ŝ= a heavy S	Ž= a heavy Z

C

C

To call

Present

Ana	Bindah
Inta	Btindah
Inté	Btindahé
Hoowé	Byindah
Heeyé	Btindah
Naĥna	Mnindah
Intoo	Btindahoo
Hinné	Byindahoo

Present Continuous

Ana	Ăam	Bindah
Inta	Ăam	Btindah
Inté	Ăam	Btindahé
Hoowé	Ăam	Byindah
Heeyé	Ăam	Btindah
Naĥna	Ăam	Mnindah
Intoo	Ăam	Btindahoo
Hinné	Ăam	Byindahoo

Past

Ana	Nadaht
Inta	Nadaht
Inté	Nadahté
Hoowé	Nadah
Heeyé	Nadahét
Naĥna	Nadahna
Intoo	Nadahtoo
Hinné	Nadahoo

Past Continuous

Ana	Kint Ăam	Bindah
Inta	Kint Ăam	Btindah
Inté	Kinté Ăam	Btindahé
Hoowé	Kén Ăam	Byindah
Heeyé	Kénét Ăam	Btindah
Naĥna	Kinna Ăam	Mnindah
Intoo	Kintoo Ăam	Btindahoo
Hinné	Kénoo Ăam	Byindahoo

Future

Ana	Laĥ	Indah
Inta	Laĥ	tindah
Inté	Laĥ	Tindahé
Hoowé	Laĥ	yindah
Heeyé	Laĥ	tindah
Naĥna	Laĥ	nindah
Intoo	Laĥ	Tindahoo
Hinné	Laĥ	Yindahoo

Command

Inta	Ndah
Inté	Ndahé
Intoo	Ndahoo
Inta	Ma tndah
Inté	Ma tndahé
Intoo	Ma tndahoo

To cancel

Present

Ana	bilŘé
Inta	btilŘé
Inté	btilŘé
Hoowé	byilŘé
Heeyé	btilŘé
Naĥna	mnilŘé
Intoo	btilŘoo
Hinné	byilŘoo

Present Continuous

Ana	Ăam	bilŘé
Inta	Ăam	btilŘé
Inté	Ăam	btilŘé
Hoowé	Ăam	byilŘé
Heeyé	Ăam	btilŘé
Naĥna	Ăam	mnilŘé
Intoo	Ăam	btilŘoo
Hinné	Ăam	byilŘoo

Past

Ana	lŘeet
Inta	lŘeet
Inté	lŘeet
Hoowé	liŘé
Heeyé	liŘyét
Naĥna	lŘeena
Intoo	lŘeetoo
Hinné	liŘyoo

Past Continuous

Ana	Kint Ăam	bilŘé
Inta	Kint Ăam	btilŘé
Inté	Kinté Ăam	btilŘé
Hoowé	Kén Ăam	byilŘé
Heeyé	Kénét Ăam	btilŘé
Naĥna	Kinna Ăam	mnilŘé
Intoo	Kintoo Ăam	btilŘoo
Hinné	Kénoo Ăam	byilŘoo

Future

Ana	Laĥ	ilŘé
Inta	Laĥ	tilŘé
Inté	Laĥ	tilŘé
Hoowé	Laĥ	yilŘé
Heeyé	Laĥ	tilŘé
Naĥna	Laĥ	nilŘé
Intoo	Laĥ	tilŘoo
Hinné	Laĥ	yilŘoo

Command

Inta	LŘee
Inté	LRee
Intoo	LŘoo
Inta	Ma tlŘé
Inté	Ma tlŘé
Intoo	Ma tlŘoo

Ă= Augh in bought	Ď= a heavy D	É= like A in Bay	G= G in beige	ĥ= like an H with smaller air passage	I= I as in ink	Ḱ= like ch in Irish loch
O= O as in home	OO= as in boots	R= roll the rrr	Ť= a heavy T	Ř= like a French R (gargle it)	Ŝ= a heavy S	Ž= a heavy Z

C

C

To care

Present

Ana	Biĥtamm
Inta	Btiĥtamm
Inté	Btiĥtammé
Hoowé	Byiĥtamm
Heeyé	Btiĥtamm
Naĥna	Mniĥtamm
Intoo	Btiĥtammoo
Hinné	Byiĥtammoo

Present Continuous

Ana	Ăam	Biĥtamm	(miĥtamm/miĥtammé)
Inta	Ăam	Btiĥtamm	(miĥtamm)
Inté	Ăam	Btiĥtammé	(miĥtammé)
Hoowé	Ăam	Byiĥtamm	(miĥtamm)
Heeyé	Ăam	Btiĥtamm	(miĥtammé)
Naĥna	Ăam	Mniĥtamm	(miĥtammeen)
Intoo	Ăam	Btiĥtammoo	(miĥtammeen)
Hinné	Ăam	Byiĥtammoo	(miĥtammeen)

Past

Ana	Ĥtammét
Inta	Ĥtammét
Inté	Ĥtammaité
Hoowé	Ĥtamm
Heeyé	Ĥtammét
Naĥna	Ĥtammaina
Intoo	Ĥtammaitoo
Hinné	Ĥtammoo

Past Continuous

Ana	Kint Ăam	Biĥtamm	(kint miĥtamm/miĥtammé)
Inta	Kint Ăam	Btiĥtamm	(Kint miĥtamm)
Inté	Kinté Ăam	Btiĥtammé	(Kinté miĥtammé)
Hoowé	Kén Ăam	Byiĥtamm	(Kén miĥtamm)
Heeyé	Kénét Ăam	Btiĥtamm	(Kénét miĥtammé)
Naĥna	Kinna Ăam	Mniĥtamm	(Kinna miĥtammeen)
Intoo	Kintoo Ăam	Btiĥtammoo	(Kintoo miĥtammeen)
Hinné	Kénoo Ăam	Byiĥtammoo	(Kénoo miĥtammeen)

Future

Ana	Laĥ	Iĥtamm
Inta	Laĥ	Tiĥtamm
Inté	Laĥ	Tiĥtammé
Hoowé	Laĥ	Yiĥtamm
Heeyé	Laĥ	Tiĥtamm
Naĥna	Laĥ	Niĥtamm
Intoo	Laĥ	Tiĥtammoo
Hinné	Laĥ	Yiĥtammoo

Command

Inta	Ĥtamm
Inté	Ĥtammé
Intoo	Ĥtammoo
Inta	Ma thtamm
Inté	Ma thtammé
Intoo	Ma thtammoo

To carry

Present

Ana	Biĥmél
Inta	Btĥmél
Inté	Btĥmlé
Hoowé	Byiĥmél
Heeyé	Btiĥmél
Naĥna	Mniĥmél
Intoo	Btiĥmloo
Hinné	Byiĥmloo

Present Continuous

Ana	Ăam Biĥmél (ĥémél/ĥémlé)
Inta	Ăam Btĥmél (ĥémél)
Inté	Ăam Btĥmlé (ĥémlé)
Hoowé	Ăam Byiĥmél (ĥémél)
Heeyé	Ăam Btiĥmél (ĥémlé)
Naĥna	Ăam Mniĥmél (ĥemleen)
Intoo	Ăam Btiĥmloo (ĥemleen)
Hinné	Ăam Byiĥmloo (ĥemleen)

Past

Ana	Ĥmilit
Inta	Ĥmilit
Inté	Ĥmilté
Hoowé	Ĥimil
Heeyé	Ĥimlét
Naĥna	Ĥmilna
Intoo	Ĥmiltoo
Hinné	Ĥimloo

Past Continuous

Ana	Kint Ăam Biĥmél (kint Hémél/ĥémlé)
Inta	Kint Ăam Btĥmél (kint Hémél)
Inté	Kinté Ăam Btĥmlé (kinté ĥémlé)
Hoowé	Kén Ăam Byiĥmél (kén Hémél)
Heeyé	Kénét Ăam Btiĥmél (kénét ĥémél)
Naĥna	Kinna Ăam Mniĥmél (kinna ĥémleen)
Intoo	Kintoo Ăam Btiĥmloo (kintoo ĥémleen)
Hinné	Kénoo Ăam Byiĥmloo (kénoo ĥémleen)

Future

Ana	Laĥ iĥmél
Inta	Laĥ tiĥmél
Inté	Laĥ tiĥmlé
Hoowé	Laĥ yiHmél
Heeyé	Laĥ tiĥmél
Naĥna	Laĥ niĥmél
Intoo	Laĥ tiĥmloo
Hinné	Laĥ yiĥmloo

Command

Inta	Ĥmél (also ĥmol)
Inté	Ĥmilé
Intoo	Ĥmiloo
Inta	Ma tiĥmél (also tiĥmol)
Inté	Ma tiĥmlé
Intoo	Ma tiĥmloo

Ă= Augh in bought	Ď= a heavy D	É= like A in Bay	G= G in beige	ĥ= like an H with smaller air passage	I= I as in ink	Ќ= like ch in Irish loch
O= O as in home	OO= as in boots	R= roll the rrr	Ť= a heavy T	Ř= like a French R (gargle it)	Ŝ= a heavy S	Ž= a heavy Z

C

C

To catch

Present

Ana	Bimsok
Inta	Btimsok
Inté	Btimské
Hoowé	Byimsok
Heeyé	Btimsok
Naĥna	Mnimsok
Intoo	Btimskoo
Hinné	Byimskoo

Present Continuous

Ana	Ăam	Bimsok	(mésék/méské)
Inta	Ăam	Btimsok	(mésék)
Inté	Ăam	Btimské	(méské)
Hoowé	Ăam	Byimsok	(mésék)
Heeyé	Ăam	Btimsok	(méské)
Naĥna	Ăam	Mnimsok	(méskeen)
Intoo	Ăam	Btimskoo	(méskeen)
Hinné	Ăam	Byimskoo	(méskeen)

Past

Ana	Masakt
Inta	Masakt
Inté	Masakté
Hoowé	Masak
Heeyé	Masakét
Naĥna	Masakna
Intoo	Masaktoo
Hinné	Masakoo

Past Continuous

Ana	Kint Ăam	Bimsok	(kint	mésék/mésské)
Inta	Kint Ăam	Btimsok	(Kint	mésék)
Inté	Kinté Ăam	Btimské	(Kinté	méské)
Hoowé	Kén Ăam	Byimsok	(Kén	mésék)
Heeyé	Kénét Ăam	Btimsok	(Kénét	méské)
Naĥna	Kinna Ăam	Mnimsok	(Kinna	méskeen)
Intoo	Kintoo Ăam	Btimskoo	(Kintoo	méskeen)
Hinné	Kénoo Ăam	Byimskoo	(Kénoo	méskeen)

Future

Ana	Laĥ	Imsok
Inta	Laĥ	Timsok
Inté	Laĥ	Timské
Hoowé	Laĥ	Yimsok
Heeyé	Laĥ	Timsok
Naĥna	Laĥ	Nimsok
Intoo	Laĥ	Timskoo
Hinné	Laĥ	Yimskoo

Command

Inta	Msok
Inté	Msiké
Intoo	Msikoo
Inta	Ma tmsok
Inté	Ma tmské
Intoo	Ma tmskoo

To cause

Present

Ana	Bsabbib
Inta	Btsabbib
Inté	Btsabbibé
Hoowé	Bisabbib
Heeyé	Btsabbib
Naĥna	Mnsabbib
Intoo	Btsabbiboo
Hinné	Bisabbiboo

Present Continuous

Ana	Ăam	Bsabbib
Inta	Ăam	Btsabbib
Inté	Ăam	Btsabbibé
Hoowé	Ăam	Bisabbib
Heeyé	Ăam	Btsabbib
Naĥna	Ăam	Mnsabbib
Intoo	Ăam	Btsabbiboo
Hinné	Ăam	Bisabbiboo

Past

Ana	Sabbabt
Inta	Sabbabt
Inté	Sabbabté
Hoowé	Sabbab
Heeyé	Sabbabét
Naĥna	Sabbabna
Intoo	Sabbabtoo
Hinné	Sabbaboo

Past Continuous

Ana	Kint Ăam	Bsabbib
Inta	Kint Ăam	Btsabbib
Inté	Kinté Ăam	Btsabbibé
Hoowé	Kén Ăam	Bisabbib
Heeyé	Kénét Ăam	Btsabbib
Naĥna	Kinna Ăam	Mnsabbib
Intoo	Kintoo Ăam	Btsabbiboo
Hinné	Kénoo Ăam	Bisabbiboo

Future

Ana	Laĥ	sabbib
Inta	Laĥ	tsabbib
Inté	Laĥ	tsabbibé
Hoowé	Laĥ	ysabbib
Heeyé	Laĥ	tsabbib
Naĥna	Laĥ	nsabbib
Intoo	Laĥ	tsabbiboo
Hinné	Laĥ	ysabbiboo

Command

Inta	Sabbib
Inté	Sabbibé
Intoo	Sabbiboo
Inta	Ma tsabbib
Inté	Ma tsabbibé
Intoo	Ma tsabbiboo

Ă= Augh in bought	Ď= a heavy D	É= like A in Bay	G= G in beige	ĥ= like an H with smaller air passage	I= I as in ink	Ќ= like ch in Irish loch
O= O as in home	OO= as in boots	R= roll the rrr	Ť= a heavy T	Ř= like a French R (gargle it)	Ŝ= a heavy S	Ž= a heavy Z

C   C

To clean

Present

Ana	bnaĎĎéf
Inta	btnaĎĎéf
Inté	btnaĎĎfé
Hoowé	binaĎĎéf
Heeyé	btnaĎĎéf
Naḣna	mnnaĎĎéf
Intoo	btnaĎĎfoo
Hinné	binaĎĎfoo

Present Continuous

Ana	Ăam	bnaĎĎéf
Inta	Ăam	btnaĎĎéf
Inté	Ăam	btnaĎĎfé
Hoowé	Ăam	binaĎĎéf
Heeyé	Ăam	btnaĎĎéf
Naḣna	Ăam	mnnaĎĎéf
Intoo	Ăam	btnaĎĎfoo
Hinné	Ăam	binaĎĎfoo

Past

Ana	naĎĎaft
Inta	naĎĎaft
Inté	naĎĎafté
Hoowé	naĎĎaf
Heeyé	naĎĎafét
Naḣna	naĎĎafna
Intoo	naĎĎaftoo
Hinné	naĎĎafoo

Past Continuous

Ana	Kint Ăam	bnaĎĎéf
Inta	Kint Ăam	btnaĎĎéf
Inté	Kinté Ăam	btnaĎĎfé
Hoowé	Kén Ăam	binaĎĎéf
Heeyé	Kénét Ăam	btnaĎĎéf
Naḣna	Kinna Ăam	mnnaĎĎéf
Intoo	Kintoo Ăam	btnaĎĎfoo
Hinné	Kénoo Ăam	binaĎĎfoo

Future

Ana	Laḣ	naĎĎéf
Inta	Laḣ	tnaĎĎéf
Inté	Laḣ	tnaĎĎfé
Hoowé	Laḣ	ynaĎĎéf
Heeyé	Laḣ	tnaĎĎéf
Naḣna	Laḣ	nnaĎĎéf
Intoo	Laḣ	tnaĎĎfoo
Hinné	Laḣ	ynaĎĎfoo

Command

Inta	NaĎĎéf
Inté	NaĎĎfé
Intoo	NaĎĎfoo
Inta	Ma TnaĎĎéf
Inté	Ma TnaĎĎfé
Intoo	Ma tnaĎĎfoo

To change

Present

Ana	bŘayér
Inta	btŘayér
Inté	btŘayré
Hoowé	biŘayér
Heeyé	btŘayér
Naḣna	mnŘayér
Intoo	btŘayroo
Hinné	biŘayroo

Present Continuous

Ana	Ăam	bŘayér	(mŘayar/mŘayra)
Inta	Ăam	btŘayér	(mŘayar)
Inté	Ăam	btŘayré	(mŘayra)
Hoowé	Ăam	biŘayér	(mŘayar)
Heeyé	Ăam	btŘayér	(mŘayra)
Naḣna	Ăam	mnŘayér	(mŘayreen)
Intoo	Ăam	btŘayroo	(mŘayreen)
Hinné	Ăam	biŘayroo	(mŘayreen)

Past

Ana	Řayart
Inta	Řayart
Inté	Řayarté
Hoowé	Řayar
Heeyé	Řayarét
Naḣna	Řayarna
Intoo	Řayartoo
Hinné	Řayaroo

Past Continuous

Ana	Kint Ăam	bŘayér	(kint mŘayar/mŘayra)
Inta	Kint Ăam	btŘayér	(Kint mŘayar)
Inté	Kinté Ăam	btŘayré	(Kinté mŘayra)
Hoowé	Kén Ăam	biŘayér	(Kén mŘayar)
Heeyé	Kénét Ăam	btŘayér	(Kénét mŘayra)
Naḣna	Kinna Ăam	mnŘayér	(Kinna mŘayreen)
Intoo	Kintoo Ăam	btŘayroo	(Kintoo mŘayreen)
Hinné	Kénoo Ăam	biŘayroo	(Kénoo mŘayreen)

Future

Ana	Laḣ	Řayér
Inta	Laḣ	tŘayér
Inté	Laḣ	tŘayré
Hoowé	Laḣ	yŘayér
Heeyé	Laḣ	tŘayér
Naḣna	Laḣ	nŘayér
Intoo	Laḣ	tŘayroo
Hinné	Laḣ	yŘayroo

Command

Inta	Řayér
Inté	Řayré
Intoo	Řayroo
Inta	Ma tŘayér
Inté	Ma tŘayré
Intoo	Ma tŘayroo

Ă= Augh in bought	Ď= a heavy D	É= like A in Bay	G= G in beige	ḣ= like an H with smaller air passage	I= I as in ink	Ḱ= like ch in Irish loch
O= O as in home	OO= as in boots	R= roll the rrr	Ť= a heavy T	Ř= like a French R (gargle it)	Ŝ= a heavy S	Ž= a heavy Z

C

C

To chew

Present	
Ana	blaĂwés
Inta	btlaĂwés
Inté	btlaĂwsé
Hoowé	bilaĂwés
Heeyé	btlaĂwés
Nahna	mnlaĂwés
Intoo	btlaĂwsoo
Hinné	bilaĂwsoo

Present Continuous		
Ana	Ăam	blaĂwés
Inta	Ăam	btlaĂwés
Inté	Ăam	btlaĂwsé
Hoowé	Ăam	bilaĂwés
Heeyé	Ăam	btlaĂwés
Nahna	Ăam	mnlaĂwés
Intoo	Ăam	btlaĂwsoo
Hinné	Ăam	bilaĂwsoo

Past	
Ana	laĂwast
Inta	laĂwast
Inté	laĂwasté
Hoowé	laĂwas
Heeyé	laĂwasét
Nahna	laĂwasna
Intoo	laĂwastoo
Hinné	laĂwasoo

Past Continuous		
Ana	Kint Ăam	blaĂwés
Inta	Kint Ăam	btlaĂwés
Inté	Kinté Ăam	btlaĂwsé
Hoowé	Kén Ăam	bilaĂwés
Heeyé	Kénét Ăam	btlaĂwés
Nahna	Kinna Ăam	mnlaĂwés
Intoo	Kintoo Ăam	btlaĂwsoo
Hinné	Kénoo Ăam	bilaĂwsoo

Future		
Ana	Laĥ	laĂwés
Inta	Laĥ	tlaĂwés
Inté	Laĥ	tlaĂwsé
Hoowé	Laĥ	ylaĂwés
Heeyé	Laĥ	tlaĂwés
Nahna	Laĥ	nlaĂwés
Intoo	Laĥ	tlaĂwsoo
Hinné	Laĥ	ylaĂwsoo

Command	
Inta	laĂwés
Inté	laĂwsé
Intoo	laĂwsoo
Inta	Ma tlaĂwés
Inté	Ma tlaĂwsé
Intoo	Ma tlaĂwsoo

To choke

Present	
Ana	biKtini'
Inta	btiKtini'
Inté	btiKtin'é
Hoowé	byiKtini'
Heeyé	btiKtini'
Nahna	mniKtini'
Intoo	btiKtin'oo
Hinné	byiKtin'oo

Present Continuous		
Ana	Ăam	biKtini'
Inta	Ăam	btiKtini'
Inté	Ăam	btiKtin'é
Hoowé	Ăam	byiKtini'
Heeyé	Ăam	btiKtini'
Nahna	Ăam	mniKtini'
Intoo	Ăam	btiKtin'oo
Hinné	Ăam	byiKtin'oo

Past	
Ana	Ktana't
Inta	Ktana't
Inté	Ktana'té
Hoowé	Ktana'
Heeyé	Ktana'ét
Nahna	Ktana'na
Intoo	Ktana'too
Hinné	Ktana'oo

Past Continuous		
Ana	Kint Ăam	biKtini'
Inta	Kint Ăam	btiKtini'
Inté	Kinté Ăam	btiKtin'é
Hoowé	Kén Ăam	byiKtini'
Heeyé	Kénét Ăam	btiKtini'
Nahna	Kinna Ăam	mniKtini'
Intoo	Kintoo Ăam	btiKtin'oo
Hinné	Kénoo Ăam	byiKtin'oo

Future		
Ana	Laĥ	iKtini'
Inta	Laĥ	tiKtini'
Inté	Laĥ	tiKtin'é
Hoowé	Laĥ	yiKtini'
Heeyé	Laĥ	tiKtini'
Nahna	Laĥ	niKtini'
Intoo	Laĥ	tiKtin'oo
Hinné	Laĥ	yiKtin'oo

Command	
Inta	Ktini'
Inté	Ktin'é
Intoo	Ktin'oo
Inta	Ma tKtini'
Inté	Ma tKtin'é
Intoo	Ma tKtin'oo

Ă= Augh in bought	**Đ**= a heavy D	**É**= like A in Bay	**G**= G in beige	**ĥ**= like an H with smaller air passage	**I**= I as in ink	**Ḱ**= like ch in Irish loch
O= O as in home	**OO**= as in boots	**R**= roll the rrr	**Ť**= a heavy T	**Ř**= like a French R (gargle it)	**Ŝ**= a heavy S	**Ž**= a heavy Z

C   C

To climb

Present	
Ana	bĂarbésh
Inta	btĂarbésh
Inté	btĂarbshé
Hoowé	biĂarbésh
Heeyé	btĂarbésh
Nahna	mnĂarbésh
Intoo	btĂarbshoo
Hinné	biĂarbshoo

Present Continuous			
Ana	Ăam	bĂarbésh	(mĂarbash)
Inta	Ăam	btĂarbésh	(mĂarbash)
Inté	Ăam	btĂarbshé	(mĂarbashé)
Hoowé	Ăam	biĂarbésh	(mĂarbash)
Heeyé	Ăam	btĂarbésh	(mĂarbashé)
Nahna	Ăam	mnĂarbésh	(mĂarbasheen)
Intoo	Ăam	btĂarbshoo	(mĂarbasheen)
Hinné	Ăam	biĂarbshoo	(mĂarbasheen)

Past	
Ana	Ăarbasht
Inta	Ăarbasht
Inté	Ăarbashté
Hoowé	Ăarbash
Heeyé	Ăarbashét
Nahna	Ăarbashna
Intoo	Ăarbashtoo
Hinné	Ăarbashoo

Past Continuous				
Ana	Kint Ăam	bĂarbésh	(kint	mĂarbash/mĂarbasheen)
Inta	Kint Ăam	btĂarbésh	(Kint	mĂarbash)
Inté	Kinté Ăam	btĂarbshé	(Kinté	mĂarbashé)
Hoowé	Kén Ăam	biĂarbésh	(Kén	mĂarbash)
Heeyé	Kénét Ăam	btĂarbésh	(Kénét	mĂarbashé)
Nahna	Kinna Ăam	mnĂarbésh	(Kinna	mĂarbasheen)
Intoo	Kintoo Ăam	btĂarbshoo	(Kintoo	(mĂarbasheen)
Hinné	Kénoo Ăam	biĂarbshoo	(Kénoo	mĂarbasheen)

Future		
Ana	Laĥ	Ăarbésh
Inta	Laĥ	tĂarbésh
Inté	Laĥ	tĂarbshé
Hoowé	Laĥ	yĂarbésh
Heeyé	Laĥ	tĂarbésh
Nahna	Laĥ	nĂarbésh
Intoo	Laĥ	tĂarbshoo
Hinné	Laĥ	yĂarbshoo

Command	
Inta	Ăarbésh
Inté	Ărbshé
Intoo	Ăarbshoo
Inta	Ma tĂarbésh
Inté	Ma tĂarbshé
Intoo	Ma tĂarbshoo

To close

Present	
Ana	bsakkér
Inta	btsakkér
Inté	Btsakkré
Hoowé	bisakkér
Heeyé	btsakkér
Nahna	mnsakkér
Intoo	Btsakkroo
Hinné	bisakkroo

Present Continuous			
Ana	Ăam	bsakkér	(msakkar/msakkra)
Inta	Ăam	btsakkér	(msakkar)
Inté	Ăam	Btsakkré	(msakkra)
Hoowé	Ăam	bisakkér	(msakkar)
Heeyé	Ăam	btsakkér	(msakkra)
Nahna	Ăam	mnsakkér	(msakkreen)
Intoo	Ăam	Btsakkroo	(msakkreen)
Hinné	Ăam	bisakkroo	(msakkreen)

Past	
Ana	Sakkart
Inta	Sakkart
Inté	Sakkarté
Hoowé	Sakkar
Heeyé	Sakkarét
Nahna	Sakkarna
Intoo	Sakkartoo
Hinné	Sakkaroo

Past Continuous				
Ana	Kint Ăam	bsakkér	(kint	msakkar/msakkra)
Inta	Kint Ăam	btsakkér	(Kint	msakkar)
Inté	Kinté Ăam	Btsakkré	(Kinté	msakkra)
Hoowé	Kén Ăam	bisakkér	(Kén	msakkar)
Heeyé	Kénét Ăam	btsakkér	(Kénét	msakkra)
Nahna	Kinna Ăam	mnsakkér	(Kinna	msakkreen)
Intoo	Kintoo Ăam	Btsakkroo	(Kintoo	msakkreen)
Hinné	Kénoo Ăam	bisakkroo	(Kénoo	msakkreen)

Future		
Ana	Laĥ	sakkér
Inta	Laĥ	tsakkér
Inté	Laĥ	tsakkré
Hoowé	Laĥ	ysakkér
Heeyé	Laĥ	tsakkér
Nahna	Laĥ	nsakkér
Intoo	Laĥ	tsakkroo
Hinné	Laĥ	ysakkroo

Command	
Inta	Sakkér
Inté	Sakkré
Intoo	Sakkroo
Inta	Ma tsakkér
Inté	Ma tsakkré
Intoo	Ma tsakkroo

Ă= Augh in bought	Ď= a heavy D	É= like A in Bay	G= G in beige	ĥ= like an H with smaller air passage	I= I as in ink	Ќ= like ch in Irish loch
O= O as in home	OO= as in boots	R= roll the rrr	Ť= a heavy T	Ř= like a French R (gargle it)	Ŝ= a heavy S	Ž= a heavy Z

C   C

To collect/add

Present

Ana	bigmaĂ
Inta	btigmaĂ
Inté	btigmaĂé
Hoowé	byigmaĂ
Heeyé	btigmaĂ
Naḥna	mnigmaĂ
Intoo	btigmaĂoo
Hinné	byigmaĂoo

Present Continuous

Ana	Ăam	bigmaĂ	(géméĂ/gémĂa)
Inta	Ăam	btigmaĂ	(géméĂ)
Inté	Ăam	btigmaĂé	(gémĂa)
Hoowé	Ăam	byigmaĂ	(géméĂ)
Heeyé	Ăam	btigmaĂ	(gémĂa)
Naḥna	Ăam	mnigmaĂ	(gémĂeen)
Intoo	Ăam	btigmaĂoo	(gémĂeen)
Hinné	Ăam	byigmaĂoo	(gémĂeen)

Past

Ana	gamaĂt
Inta	gamaĂt
Inté	gamaĂté
Hoowé	gamaĂ
Heeyé	gamaĂét
Naḥna	gamaĂna
Intoo	gamaĂtoo
Hinné	gamaĂoo

Past Continuous

Ana	Kint Ăam	bigmaĂ	(kint	géméĂ/gémĂa)
Inta	Kint Ăam	btigmaĂ	(Kint	géméĂ)
Inté	Kinté Ăam	btigmaĂé	(Kinté	gémĂa)
Hoowé	Kén Ăam	byigmaĂ	(Kén	géméĂ)
Heeyé	Kénét Ăam	btigmaĂ	(Kénét	gémĂa)
Naḥna	Kinna Ăam	mnigmaĂ	(Kinna	gémĂeen)
Intoo	Kintoo Ăam	btigmaĂoo	(Kintoo	gémĂeen)
Hinné	Kénoo Ăam	byigmaĂoo	(Kénoo	gémĂeen)

Future

Ana	Laḥ	igmaĂ
Inta	Laḥ	tigmaĂ
Inté	Laḥ	tigmaĂé
Hoowé	Laḥ	yigmaĂ
Heeyé	Laḥ	tigmaĂ
Naḥna	Laḥ	nigmaĂ
Intoo	Laḥ	tigmaĂoo
Hinné	Laḥ	yigmaĂoo

Command

Inta	gmaĂ
Inté	gmaĂé
Intoo	gmaĂoo
Inta	Ma tgmaĂ
Inté	Ma tgmaĂé
Intoo	Ma tgmaĂoo

To comb

Present

Ana	bmashéṪ
Inta	btmashéṪ
Inté	mnmashéṪ
Hoowé	bimashéṪ
Heeyé	btmashéṪ
Naḥna	mnmashéṪ
Intoo	btmashṪoo
Hinné	bimashṪoo

Present Continuous

Ana	Ăam	bmashéṪ
Inta	Ăam	btmashéṪ
Inté	Ăam	mnmashéṪ
Hoowé	Ăam	bimashéṪ
Heeyé	Ăam	btmashéṪ
Naḥna	Ăam	mnmashéṪ
Intoo	Ăam	btmashṪoo
Hinné	Ăam	bimashṪoo

Past

Ana	mashaṪt
Inta	mashaṪt
Inté	mashaṪté
Hoowé	mashaṪ
Heeyé	mashaṪét
Naḥna	mashaṪna
Intoo	mashaṪtoo
Hinné	mashaṪoo

Past Continuous

Ana	Kint Ăam	bmashéṪ
Inta	Kint Ăam	btmashéṪ
Inté	Kinté Ăam	mnmashéṪ
Hoowé	Kén Ăam	bimashéṪ
Heeyé	Kénét Ăam	btmashéṪ
Naḥna	Kinna Ăam	mnmashéṪ
Intoo	Kintoo Ăam	btmashṪoo
Hinné	Kénoo Ăam	bimashṪoo

Future

Ana	Laḥ	mashéṪ
Inta	Laḥ	tmashéṪ
Inté	Laḥ	nmashéṪ
Hoowé	Laḥ	ymashéṪ
Heeyé	Laḥ	tmashéṪ
Naḥna	Laḥ	nmashéṪ
Intoo	Laḥ	tmashṪoo
Hinné	Laḥ	ymashṪoo

Command

Inta	mashéṪ
Inté	mashṪé
Intoo	mashṪoo
Inta	Ma tmashéṪ
Inté	Ma tmashṪoo
Intoo	Ma tmashṪé

Ă= Augh in bought	Ď= a heavy D	É= like A in Bay	G= G in beige	ḥ= like an H with smaller air passage	I= I as in ink	Ќ= like ch in Irish loch
O= O as in home	OO= as in boots	R= roll the rrr	Ṫ= a heavy T	Ř= like a French R (gargle it)	Ŝ= a heavy S	Ž= a heavy Z

C   C

To come

Present

Ana	Bige
Inta	Btigé
Inté	Btige
Hoowé	Byigé
Heeyé	Btige
Naȟna	Mnigé
Intoo	Btigoo
Hinné	Byigoo

Present Continuous

Ana	Ăam bigé (or ana géyé)
Inta	Ăam btigé (or géyé)
Inté	Ăam btigé (or géyé)
Hoowé	Ăam byigé (or géyé)
Heeyé	Ăam btigé (or géyé)
Naȟna	Ăam mnigé (or géyeen)
Intoo	Ăam btigoo (or géyeen)
Hinné	Ăam byigoo (or géyeen)

Past

Ana	Geet
Inta	Geet
Inté	Geeté
Hoowé	'iga
Heeyé	'igét
Naȟna	Geena
Intoo	Geetoo
Hinné	'igoo

Past Continuous

Ana	Kint Ăam bigé (or ana kint géyé)
Inta	Kint Ăam btigé (or kint géyé)
Inté	Kinté Ăam btigé (or kinté géyé)
Hoowé	Kén Ăam byigé (or kén géyé)
Heeyé	Kénét Ăam btigé (or kénét géyé)
Naȟna	Kinna Ăam mnigé (or kinna géyeen)
Intoo	Kintoo Ăam btigoo (or kintoo géyeen)
Hinné	Kénoo Ăam byigoo (or kénoo géyeen)

Future

Ana	Laȟ	'igé
Inta	Laȟ	tigé
Inté	Laȟ	tigé
Hoowé	Laȟ	yigé
Heeyé	Laȟ	tigé
Naȟna	Laȟ	nigé
Intoo	Laȟ	tigoo
Hinné	Laȟ	yigoo

Command

Inta	t_aĂa
Inté	t_aĂe
Intoo	t_aĂoo
Inta	Ma tigé
Inté	Ma tigé
Intoo	Ma tigoo

To command

Present

Ana	Bi'mor
Inta	Bti'mor
Inté	Bti'mré
Hoowé	Byi'mor
Heeyé	Bti'mor
Naȟna	Mni'mor
Intoo	Bti'mroo
Hinné	Byi'mroo

Present Continuous

Ana	Ăam	Bi'mor
Inta	Ăam	Bti'mor
Inté	Ăam	Bti'mré
Hoowé	Ăam	Byi'mor
Heeyé	Ăam	Bti'mor
Naȟna	Ăam	Mni'mor
Intoo	Ăam	Bti'mroo
Hinné	Ăam	Byi'mroo

Past

Ana	Amart
Inta	Amart
Inté	Amarté
Hoowé	Amar
Heeyé	Amarét
Naȟna	Amarna
Intoo	Amartoo
Hinné	Amaroo

Past Continuous

Ana	Kint Ăam	Bi'mor
Inta	Kint Ăam	Bti'mor
Inté	Kinté Ăam	Bti'mré
Hoowé	Kén Ăam	Byi'mor
Heeyé	Kénét Ăam	Bti'mor
Naȟna	Kinna Ăam	Mni'mor
Intoo	Kintoo Ăam	Bti'mroo
Hinné	Kénoo Ăam	Byi'mroo

Future

Ana	Laȟ	i'mor
Inta	Laȟ	ti'mor
Inté	Laȟ	ti'mré
Hoowé	Laȟ	yi'mor
Heeyé	Laȟ	ti'mor
Naȟna	Laȟ	ni'mor
Intoo	Laȟ	ti'mroo
Hinné	Laȟ	yi'mroo

Command

Inta	'mor
Inté	'miré
Intoo	'miroo
Inta	Ma t'mor
Inté	Ma t'mré
Intoo	Ma t'mroo

Ă= Augh in bought	Ď= a heavy D	É= like A in Bay	G= G in beige	ȟ= like an H with smaller air passage	I= I as in ink	Ǩ= like ch in Irish loch
O= O as in home	OO= as in boots	R= roll the rrr	Ť= a heavy T	Ř= like a French R (gargle it)	Ŝ= a heavy S	Ž= a heavy Z

C

C

To complete

Present	
Ana	Bkammél
Inta	Btkammél
Inté	Btkammlé
Hoowé	Bikammél
Heeyé	Btkammél
Nahna	Mnkammél
Intoo	Btkammloo
Hinné	Bikammloo

Present Continuous		
Ana	Ăam	Bkammél
Inta	Ăam	Btkammél
Inté	Ăam	Btkammlé
Hoowé	Ăam	Bikammél
Heeyé	Ăam	Btkammél
Nahna	Ăam	Mnkammél
Intoo	Ăam	Btkammloo
Hinné	Ăam	Bikammloo

Past	
Ana	Kammalt
Inta	Kammalt
Inté	Kammalté
Hoowé	Kammal
Heeyé	Kammalét
Nahna	Kammalna
Intoo	Kammaltoo
Hinné	Kammaloo

Past Continuous		
Ana	Kint Ăam	Bkammél
Inta	Kint Ăam	Btkammél
Inté	Kinté Ăam	Btkammlé
Hoowé	Kén Ăam	Bikammél
Heeyé	Kénét Ăam	Btkammél
Nahna	Kinna Ăam	Mnkammél
Intoo	Kintoo Ăam	Btkammloo
Hinné	Kénoo Ăam	Bikammloo

Future		
Ana	Lah	Kammél
Inta	Lah	Tkammél
Inté	Lah	Tkammlé
Hoowé	Lah	Ykammél
Heeyé	Lah	Tkammél
Nahna	Lah	Nkammél
Intoo	Lah	Tkammloo
Hinné	Lah	Ykammloo

Command	
Inta	Kammél
Inté	Kammlé
Intoo	Kammloo
Inta	Ma tkammél
Inté	Ma tkammlé
Intoo	Ma tkammloo

To complain

Present	
Ana	Bishké
Inta	Btishké
Inté	Btishké
Hoowé	Byishké
Heeyé	Btishké
Nahna	Mnishké
Intoo	Btishkoo
Hinné	Byishkoo

Present Continuous		
Ana	Ăam	Bishké
Inta	Ăam	Btishké
Inté	Ăam	Btishké
Hoowé	Ăam	Byishké
Heeyé	Ăam	Btishké
Nahna	Ăam	Mnishké
Intoo	Ăam	Btishkoo
Hinné	Ăam	Byishkoo

Past	
Ana	Shkeet
Inta	Shkeet
Inté	Shkeeté
Hoowé	Shiké
Heeyé	Shikyét
Nahna	Shkeena
Intoo	Shkeetoo
Hinné	Shikyoo

Past Continuous		
Ana	Kint Ăam	Bishké
Inta	Kint Ăam	Btishké
Inté	Kinté Ăam	Btishké
Hoowé	Kén Ăam	Byishké
Heeyé	Kénét Ăam	Btishké
Nahna	Kinna Ăam	Mnishké
Intoo	Kintoo Ăam	Btishkoo
Hinné	Kénoo Ăam	Byishkoo

Future		
Ana	Lah	Ishké
Inta	Lah	Tishké
Inté	Lah	Tishké
Hoowé	Lah	Yishké
Heeyé	Lah	Tishké
Nahna	Lah	Nishké
Intoo	Lah	Tishkoo
Hinné	Lah	Yishkoo

Command	
Inta	Shkee
Inté	Shkee
Intoo	Shkoo
Inta	Ma tshké
Inté	Ma tshké
Intoo	Ma tshkoo

Ă= Augh in bought	Ď= a heavy D	É= like A in Bay	G= G in beige	ĥ= like an H with smaller air passage	I= I as in ink	Ķ= like ch in Irish loch
O= O as in home	OO= as in boots	R= roll the rrr	Ť= a heavy T	Ř= like a French R (gargle it)	Ŝ= a heavy S	Ž= a heavy Z

C   C

To complicate   To compose music

Present	
Ana	bĂa''éd
Inta	btĂa''éd
Inté	btĂa''dé
Hoowé	biĂa''éd
Heeyé	btĂa''éd
Nahna	mnĂa''éd
Intoo	btĂa''doo
Hinné	biĂa''doo

Present Continuous		
Ana	Ăam	bĂa''éd
Inta	Ăam	btĂa''éd
Inté	Ăam	btĂa''dé
Hoowé	Ăam	biĂa''éd
Heeyé	Ăam	btĂa''éd
Nahna	Ăam	mnĂa''éd
Intoo	Ăam	btĂa''doo
Hinné	Ăam	biĂa''doo

Past	
Ana	Ăa'adt
Inta	Ăa'adt
Inté	Ăa'adté
Hoowé	Ăa'ad
Heeyé	Ăa'adét
Nahna	Ăa'adna
Intoo	Ăa'adtoo
Hinné	Ăa'adoo

Past Continuous		
Ana	Kint Ăam	bĂa''éd
Inta	Kint Ăam	btĂa''éd
Inté	Kinté Ăam	btĂa''dé
Hoowé	Kén Ăam	biĂa''éd
Heeyé	Kénét Ăam	btĂa''éd
Nahna	Kinna Ăam	mnĂa''éd
Intoo	Kintoo Ăam	btĂa''doo
Hinné	Kénoo Ăam	biĂa''doo

Future		
Ana	Laĥ	Ăa''éd
Inta	Laĥ	tĂa''éd
Inté	Laĥ	tĂa''dé
Hoowé	Laĥ	yĂa''éd
Heeyé	Laĥ	tĂa''éd
Nahna	Laĥ	nĂa''éd
Intoo	Laĥ	tĂa''doo
Hinné	Laĥ	yĂa''doo

Command	
Inta	Ăa''éd
Inté	Ăa'dé
Intoo	Ăa'doo
Inta	Ma tĂa'éd
Inté	Ma tĂa'dé
Intoo	Ma tĂa'doo

Present	
Ana	Blaĥĥén
Inta	Btlaĥĥén
Inté	Btlaĥĥné
Hoowé	Bilaĥĥén
Heeyé	Btlaĥĥén
Nahna	Mnlaĥĥén
Intoo	Btlaĥĥnoo
Hinné	Bilaĥĥnoo

Present Continuous			
Ana	Ăam	Blaĥĥén	(mlaĥĥan/mlaĥĥné)
Inta	Ăam	Btlaĥĥén	(mlaĥĥan)
Inté	Ăam	Btlaĥĥné	(mlaĥĥné)
Hoowé	Ăam	Bilaĥĥén	(mlaĥĥan)
Heeyé	Ăam	Btlaĥĥén	(mlaĥĥné)
Nahna	Ăam	Mnlaĥĥén	(mlaĥĥneen)
Intoo	Ăam	Btlaĥĥnoo	(mlaĥĥneen)
Hinné	Ăam	Bilaĥĥnoo	(mlaĥĥneen)

Past	
Ana	Laĥĥant
Inta	Laĥĥant
Inté	Laĥĥanté
Hoowé	Laĥĥan
Heeyé	Laĥĥanét
Nahna	Laĥĥanna
Intoo	Laĥĥantoo
Hinné	Laĥĥanoo

Past Continuous			
Ana	Kint Ăam	Blaĥĥén	(kint (mlaĥĥan/mlaĥĥné)
Inta	Kint Ăam	Btlaĥĥén	(Kint (mlaĥĥan)
Inté	Kinté Ăam	Btlaĥĥné	(Kinté (mlaĥĥné)
Hoowé	Kén Ăam	Bilaĥĥén	(Kén (mlaĥĥan)
Heeyé	Kénét Ăam	Btlaĥĥén	(Kénét (mlaĥĥné)
Nahna	Kinna Ăam	Mnlaĥĥén	(Kinna (mlaĥĥneen)
Intoo	Kintoo Ăam	Btlaĥĥnoo	(Kintoo (mlaĥĥneen)
Hinné	Kénoo Ăam	Bilaĥĥnoo	(Kénoo (mlaĥĥneen)

Future		
Ana	Laĥ	laĥĥén
Inta	Laĥ	tlaĥĥén
Inté	Laĥ	tlaĥĥné
Hoowé	Laĥ	ylaĥĥén
Heeyé	Laĥ	tlaĥĥén
Nahna	Laĥ	nlaĥĥén
Intoo	Laĥ	tlaĥĥnoo
Hinné	Laĥ	ylaĥĥnoo

Command	
Inta	Laĥĥén
Inté	Laĥĥné
Intoo	Laĥĥnoo
Inta	Ma tlaĥĥén
Inté	Ma tlaĥĥné
Intoo	Ma tlaĥĥnoo

Ă= Augh in bought	Ď= a heavy D	É= like A in Bay	G= G in beige	ĥ= like an H with smaller air passage		I= I as in ink	Ќ= like ch in Irish loch
O= O as in home	OO= as in boots	R= roll the rrr	Ť= a heavy T	Ř= like a French R (gargle it)		Ŝ= a heavy S	Ž= a heavy Z

C   C

To compose a book

Present

Ana	B'alléf
Inta	Bt'alléf
Inté	Bt'allfé
Hoowé	Bi'alléf
Heeyé	Bt'alléf
Naĥna	Mn'alléf
Intoo	Bt'allfoo
Hinné	Bi'allfoo

Present Continuous

Ana	Ăam	B'alléf	(m'allaf/m'allfé)
Inta	Ăam	Bt'alléf	(m'allaf)
Inté	Ăam	Bt'allfé	(m'allfé)
Hoowé	Ăam	Bi'alléf	(m'allaf)
Heeyé	Ăam	Bt'alléf	(m'allfé)
Naĥna	Ăam	Mn'alléf	(m'allfeen)
Intoo	Ăam	Bt'allfoo	(m'allfeen)
Hinné	Ăam	Bi'allfoo	(m'allfeen)

Past

Ana	Allaft
Inta	Allaft
Inté	Allafté
Hoowé	Allaf
Heeyé	Allafét
Naĥna	Allafna
Intoo	Allafto
Hinné	Allafoo

Past Continuous

Ana	Kint Ăam	B'alléf	(kint	m'allaf/m'allfé)
Inta	Kint Ăam	Bt'alléf	(Kint	m'allaf)
Inté	Kinté Ăam	Bt'allfé	(Kinté	m'allfé)
Hoowé	Kén Ăam	Bi'alléf	(Kén	m'allaf)
Heeyé	Kénét Ăam	Bt'alléf	(Kénét	m'allfé)
Naĥna	Kinna Ăam	Mn'alléf	(Kinna	m'allfeen)
Intoo	Kintoo Ăam	Bt'allfoo	(Kintoo	m'allfeen)
Hinné	Kénoo Ăam	Bi'allfoo	(Kénoo	m'allfeen)

Future

Ana	Laĥ	Alléf
Inta	Laĥ	T'alléf
Inté	Laĥ	t'allfé
Hoowé	Laĥ	Y'alléf
Heeyé	Laĥ	T'alléf
Naĥna	Laĥ	N'alléf
Intoo	Laĥ	T'allfoo
Hinné	Laĥ	Y'allfoo

Command

Inta	Alléf
Inté	Allfé
Intoo	Allfoo
Inta	Ma t'alléf
Inté	Ma t'allfé
Intoo	Ma t'allfoo

To confront/face

Present

Ana	Bwégéh
Inta	Btwégéh
Inté	Btwéghé
Hoowé	Biwégéh
Heeyé	Btwégéh
Naĥna	Mnwégéh
Intoo	Btwéghoo
Hinné	Biwéghoo

Present Continuous

Ana	Ăam	Bwégéh
Inta	Ăam	Btwégéh
Inté	Ăam	Btwéghé
Hoowé	Ăam	Biwégéh
Heeyé	Ăam	Btwégéh
Naĥna	Ăam	Mnwégéh
Intoo	Ăam	Btwéghoo
Hinné	Ăam	Biwéghoo

Past

Ana	Wégaht
Inta	Wégaht
Inté	Wégahté
Hoowé	Wégah
Heeyé	Wégahét
Naĥna	Wégahna
Intoo	Wégahtoo
Hinné	Wégahoo

Past Continuous

Ana	Kint Ăam	Bwégéh
Inta	Kint Ăam	Btwégéh
Inté	Kinté Ăam	Btwéghé
Hoowé	Kén Ăam	Biwégéh
Heeyé	Kénét Ăam	Btwégéh
Naĥna	Kinna Ăam	Mnwégéh
Intoo	Kintoo Ăam	Btwéghoo
Hinné	Kénoo Ăam	Biwéghoo

Future

Ana	Laĥ	wégéh
Inta	Laĥ	twégéh
Inté	Laĥ	twéghé
Hoowé	Laĥ	ywégéh
Heeyé	Laĥ	twégéh
Naĥna	Laĥ	nwégéh
Intoo	Laĥ	twéghoo
Hinné	Laĥ	ywéghoo

Command

Inta	Wégéh
Inté	Wéghé
Intoo	Wéghoo
Inta	Ma twégéh
Inté	Ma twéghé
Intoo	Ma twéghoo

Ă= Augh in bought	Ď= a heavy D	É= like A in Bay	G= G in beige	ĥ= like an H with smaller air passage	I= I as in ink	Ќ= like ch in Irish loch
O= O as in home	OO= as in boots	R= roll the rrr	Ť= a heavy T	Ř= like a French R (gargle it)	Ŝ= a heavy S	Ž= a heavy Z

C   C

To connect   To consider

To connect

Present	
Ana	booŜol
Inta	btooŜol
Inté	btooŜlé
Hoowé	byooŜol
Heeyé	btooŜol
Naĥna	mnooŜol
Intoo	btooŜloo
Hinné	byooŜloo

Present Continuous		
Ana	Ăam	booŜol
Inta	Ăam	btooŜol
Inté	Ăam	btooŜlé
Hoowé	Ăam	byooŜol
Heeyé	Ăam	btooŜol
Naĥna	Ăam	mnooŜol
Intoo	Ăam	btooŜloo
Hinné	Ăam	byooŜloo

Past	
Ana	waŜalt
Inta	waŜalt
Inté	waŜalté
Hoowé	waŜal
Heeyé	waŜalét
Naĥna	waŜalna
Intoo	waŜaltoo
Hinné	waŜaloo

Past Continuous		
Ana	Kint Ăam	booŜol
Inta	Kint Ăam	btooŜol
Inté	Kinté Ăam	btooŜlé
Hoowé	Kén Ăam	byooŜol
Heeyé	Kénét Ăam	btooŜol
Naĥna	Kinna Ăam	mnooŜol
Intoo	Kintoo Ăam	btooŜloo
Hinné	Kénoo Ăam	byooŜloo

Future		
Ana	Laĥ	'ooŜol
Inta	Laĥ	tooŜol
Inté	Laĥ	tooŜlé
Hoowé	Laĥ	yooŜol
Heeyé	Laĥ	tooŜol
Naĥna	Laĥ	nooŜol
Intoo	Laĥ	tooŜloo
Hinné	Laĥ	yooŜloo

Command	
Inta	wŜol
Inté	wŜilé
Intoo	wŜiloo
Inta	Ma tooŜol
Inté	Ma tooŜlé
Intoo	Ma tooŜloo

To consider

Present	
Ana	biĂtibér
Inta	btiĂtibér
Inté	btiĂtibré
Hoowé	byiĂtibér
Heeyé	btiĂtibér
Naĥna	mniĂtibér
Intoo	btiĂtibroo
Hinné	byiĂtibroo

Present Continuous			
Ana	Ăam	biĂtibér	(miĂtibér/miĂtibra)
Inta	Ăam	btiĂtibér	(miĂtibér)
Inté	Ăam	btiĂtibré	(miĂtibra)
Hoowé	Ăam	byiĂtibér	(miĂtibér)
Heeyé	Ăam	btiĂtibér	(miĂtibra)
Naĥna	Ăam	mniĂtibér	(miĂtibreen)
Intoo	Ăam	btiĂtibroo	(miĂtibreen)
Hinné	Ăam	byiĂtibroo	(miĂtibreen)

Past	
Ana	Ătabart
Inta	Ătabart
Inté	Ătabarté
Hoowé	Ătabar
Heeyé	Ătabarét
Naĥna	Ătabarna
Intoo	Ătabartoo
Hinné	Ătabaroo

Past Continuous			
Ana	Kint Ăam	biĂtibér	(kint miĂtibér/mi Ătibra)
Inta	Kint Ăam	btiĂtibér	(Kint miĂtibér)
Inté	Kinté Ăam	btiĂtibré	(Kinté miĂtibra)
Hoowé	Kén Ăam	byiĂtibér	(Kén miĂtibér)
Heeyé	Kénét Ăam	btiĂtibér	(Kénét miĂtibra)
Naĥna	Kinna Ăam	mniĂtibér	(Kinna miĂtibreen)
Intoo	Kintoo Ăam	btiĂtibroo	(Kintoo miĂtibreen)
Hinné	Kénoo Ăam	byiĂtibroo	(Kénoo miĂtibreen)

Future		
Ana	Laĥ	iĂtibér
Inta	Laĥ	tiĂtibér
Inté	Laĥ	tiĂtibré
Hoowé	Laĥ	yiĂtibér
Heeyé	Laĥ	tiĂtibér
Naĥna	Laĥ	niĂtibér
Intoo	Laĥ	tiĂtibroo
Hinné	Laĥ	yiĂtibroo

Command	
Inta	Ătibér
Inté	Ătibré
Intoo	Ătibroo
Inta	Ma tĂtibér
Inté	Ma tĂtibré
Intoo	Ma tĂtibroo

Ă= Augh in bought	Đ= a heavy D	É= like A in Bay	G= G in beige	ĥ= like an H with smaller air passage	I= I as in ink	Ќ= like ch in Irish loch
O= O as in home	OO= as in boots	R= roll the rrr	Ť= a heavy T	Ř= like a French R (gargle it)	Ŝ= a heavy S	Ž= a heavy Z

C

C

To construct

Present	
Ana	Bibné
Inta	Btibné
Inté	Btibné
Hoowé	Byibné
Heeyé	Btibné
Naḣna	Mnibné
Intoo	Btibnoo
Hinné	Byibnoo

Present Continuous		
Ana	Ăam	Bibné
Inta	Ăam	Btibné
Inté	Ăam	Btibné
Hoowé	Ăam	Byibné
Heeyé	Ăam	Btibné
Naḣna	Ăam	Mnibné
Intoo	Ăam	Btibnoo
Hinné	Ăam	Byibnoo

Past	
Ana	Bneet
Inta	Bneet
Inté	Bneeté
Hoowé	Biné
Heeyé	Binyet
Naḣna	Bneena
Intoo	Bneetoo
Hinné	Binyoo

Past Continuous		
Ana	Kint Ăam	Bibné
Inta	Kint Ăam	Btibné
Inté	Kinté Ăam	Btibné
Hoowé	Kén Ăam	Byibné
Heeyé	Kénét Ăam	Btibné
Naḣna	Kinna Ăam	Mnibné
Intoo	Kintoo Ăam	Btibnoo
Hinné	Kénoo Ăam	Byibnoo

Future		
Ana	Laḣ	Ibné
Inta	Laḣ	Tibné
Inté	Laḣ	Tibné
Hoowé	Laḣ	Yibné
Heeyé	Laḣ	Tibné
Naḣna	Laḣ	Nibné
Intoo	Laḣ	Tibnoo
Hinné	Laḣ	Yibnoo

Command	
Inta	Bnee
Inté	Bnee
Intoo	Bnoo
Inta	Ma tbné
Inté	Ma tbné
Intoo	Ma tbnoo

To construct / to build

Present	
Ana	bĂammér
Inta	btĂammér
Inté	btĂammré
Hoowé	biĂammér
Heeyé	btĂammér
Naḣna	mnĂammér
Intoo	btĂammroo
Hinné	biĂammroo

Present Continuous		
Ana	Ăam	bĂammér
Inta	Ăam	btĂammér
Inté	Ăam	btĂammré
Hoowé	Ăam	biĂammér
Heeyé	Ăam	btĂammér
Naḣna	Ăam	mnĂammér
Intoo	Ăam	btĂammroo
Hinné	Ăam	biĂammroo

Past	
Ana	Ăammart
Inta	Ăammart
Inté	Ăammarté
Hoowé	Ăammar
Heeyé	Ăammarét
Naḣna	Ăammarna
Intoo	Ăammartoo
Hinné	Ăammaroo

Past Continuous		
Ana	Kint Ăam	bĂammér
Inta	Kint Ăam	btĂammér
Inté	Kinté Ăam	btĂammré
Hoowé	Kén Ăam	biĂammér
Heeyé	Kénét Ăam	btĂammér
Naḣna	Kinna Ăam	mnĂammér
Intoo	Kintoo Ăam	btĂammroo
Hinné	Kénoo Ăam	biĂammroo

Future		
Ana	Laḣ	Ăammér
Inta	Laḣ	tĂammér
Inté	Laḣ	tĂammré
Hoowé	Laḣ	yĂammér
Heeyé	Laḣ	tĂammér
Naḣna	Laḣ	nĂammér
Intoo	Laḣ	tĂammroo
Hinné	Laḣ	yĂammroo

Command	
Inta	Ăammér
Inté	Ăammré
Intoo	Ăammroo
Inta	Ma tĂammér
Inté	Ma Ăammré
Intoo	Ma Ăammroo

Ă= Augh in bought	Ď= a heavy D	É= like A in Bay	G= G in beige	ḣ= like an H with smaller air passage	I= I as in ink	Ќ= like ch in Irish loch
O= O as in home	OO= as in boots	R= roll the rrr	Ť= a heavy T	Ř= like a French R (gargle it)	Š= a heavy S	Ž= a heavy Z

C

C

To consume

Present	
Ana	Bistahlék
Inta	Btistahlék
Inté	Btistahlké
Hoowé	Byistahlék
Heeyé	Btistahlék
Nahna	Mnistahlék
Intoo	Btistahlkoo
Hinné	Byistahlkoo

Present Continuous		
Ana	Ăam	Bistahlék
Inta	Ăam	Btistahlék
Inté	Ăam	Btistahlké
Hoowé	Ăam	Byistahlék
Heeyé	Ăam	Btistahlék
Nahna	Ăam	Mnistahlék
Intoo	Ăam	Btistahlkoo
Hinné	Ăam	Byistahlkoo

Past	
Ana	Stahlakt
Inta	Stahlakt
Inté	Stahlakté
Hoowé	Stahlak
Heeyé	Stahlakét
Nahna	Stahlakna
Intoo	Stahlaktoo
Hinné	Stahlakoo

Past Continuous		
Ana	Kint Ăam	Bistahlék
Inta	Kint Ăam	Btistahlék
Inté	Kinté Ăam	Btistahlké
Hoowé	Kén Ăam	Byistahlék
Heeyé	Kénét Ăam	Btistahlék
Nahna	Kinna Ăam	Mnistahlék
Intoo	Kintoo Ăam	Btistahlkoo
Hinné	Kénoo Ăam	Byistahlkoo

Future		
Ana	Laĥ	Istahlék
Inta	Laĥ	Tistahlék
Inté	Laĥ	Tistahlké
Hoowé	Laĥ	Yistahlék
Heeyé	Laĥ	Tistahlék
Nahna	Laĥ	Nistahlék
Intoo	Laĥ	Tistahlkoo
Hinné	Laĥ	Yistahlkoo

Command	
Inta	Stahlék
Inté	Stahlké
Intoo	Stahlkoo
Inta	Ma tstahlék
Inté	Ma tstahlké
Intoo	Ma tstahlkoo

To contain

Present	
Ana	Biĥwé
Inta	Btiĥwé
Inté	Btiĥwé
Hoowé	Byiĥwé
Heeyé	Btiĥwé
Nahna	Mniĥwé
Intoo	Btiĥwoo
Hinné	Byiĥwoo

Present Continuous		
Ana	Ăam	Biĥwé
Inta	Ăam	Btiĥwé
Inté	Ăam	Btiĥwé
Hoowé	Ăam	Byiĥwé
Heeyé	Ăam	Btiĥwé
Nahna	Ăam	Mniĥwé
Intoo	Ăam	Btiĥwoo
Hinné	Ăam	Byiĥwoo

Past	
Ana	ĥawét
Inta	ĥawét
Inté	Ĥawaité
Hoowé	Ĥawa
Heeyé	ĥawét
Nahna	Ĥawaina
Intoo	Ĥawaitoo
Hinné	Ĥawoo

Past Continuous		
Ana	Kint Ăam	Biĥwé
Inta	Kint Ăam	Btiĥwé
Inté	Kinté Ăam	Btiĥwé
Hoowé	Kén Ăam	Byiĥwé
Heeyé	Kénét Ăam	Btiĥwé
Nahna	Kinna Ăam	Mniĥwé
Intoo	Kintoo Ăam	Btiĥwoo
Hinné	Kénoo Ăam	Byiĥwoo

Future		
Ana	Laĥ	Iĥwé
Inta	Laĥ	Tiĥwé
Inté	Laĥ	Tiĥwé
Hoowé	Laĥ	Yiĥwé
Heeyé	Laĥ	Tiĥwé
Nahna	Laĥ	Niĥwé
Intoo	Laĥ	Tiĥwoo
Hinné	Laĥ	Yiĥwoo

Command	
Inta	Ĥwee
Inté	Ĥwee
Intoo	Ĥwoo
Inta	Ma tĥwé
Inté	Ma tĥwé
Intoo	Ma tĥwoo

Ă= Augh in bought	**Đ**= a heavy D	**É**= like A in Bay	**G**= G in beige	**ĥ**= like an H with smaller air passage	**I**= I as in ink	**Ќ**= like ch in Irish loch
O= O as in home	**OO**= as in boots	**R**= roll the rrr	**Ť**= a heavy T	**Ř**= like a French R (gargle it)	**Ŝ**= a heavy S	**Ž**= a heavy Z

C

C

To control

Present

Ana	Bitĥakkam
Inta	Btitĥakkam
Inté	Btitĥakkamé
Hoowé	Byitĥakkam
Heeyé	Btitĥakkam
Naĥna	Mnitĥakkam
Intoo	Btitĥakkamoo
Hinné	Byitĥakkamoo

Present Continuous

Ana	Ăam	Bitĥakkam
Inta	Ăam	Btitĥakkam
Inté	Ăam	Btitĥakkamé
Hoowé	Ăam	Byitĥakkam
Heeyé	Ăam	Btitĥakkam
Naĥna	Ăam	Mnitĥakkam
Intoo	Ăam	Btitĥakkamoo
Hinné	Ăam	Byitĥakkamoo

Past

Ana	Tĥakkamt
Inta	Tĥakkamt
Inté	Tĥakkamté
Hoowé	Tĥakkam
Heeyé	Tĥakkamét
Naĥna	Tĥakkamna
Intoo	Tĥakkamtoo
Hinné	Tĥakkamoo

Past Continuous

Ana	Kint Ăam	Bitĥakkam
Inta	Kint Ăam	Btitĥakkam
Inté	Kinté Ăam	Btitĥakkamé
Hoowé	Kén Ăam	Byitĥakkam
Heeyé	Kénét Ăam	Btitĥakkam
Naĥna	Kinna Ăam	Mnitĥakkam
Intoo	Kintoo Ăam	Btitĥakkamoo
Hinné	Kénoo Ăam	Byitĥakkamoo

Future

Ana	Laĥ	Itĥakkam
Inta	Laĥ	Titĥakkam
Inté	Laĥ	Titĥakkamé
Hoowé	Laĥ	Yitĥakkam
Heeyé	Laĥ	Titĥakkam
Naĥna	Laĥ	Nitĥakkam
Intoo	Laĥ	Titĥakkamoo
Hinné	Laĥ	Yitĥakkamoo

Command

Inta	Tĥakkam
Inté	Tĥakkamé
Intoo	Tĥakkamoo
Inta	Ma tthakkam
Inté	Ma tthakkamé
Intoo	Ma tthakkamoo

To cook

Present

Ana	biŤboǨ
Inta	btiŤboǨ
Inté	btiŤbǨé
Hoowé	byiŤboǨ
Heeyé	btiŤboǨ
Naĥna	mniŤboǨ
Intoo	btiŤbǨoo
Hinné	byiŤbǨoo

Present Continuous

Ana	Ăam	biŤboǨ	(ŤabéǨ/ŤabKa)
Inta	Ăam	btiŤboǨ	(ŤabéǨ)
Inté	Ăam	btiŤbǨé	(ŤabKa)
Hoowé	Ăam	byiŤboǨ	(ŤabéǨ)
Heeyé	Ăam	btiŤboǨ	(ŤabKa)
Naĥna	Ăam	mniŤboǨ	(ŤabKeen)
Intoo	Ăam	btiŤbǨoo	(ŤabKeen)
Hinné	Ăam	byiŤbǨoo	(ŤabKeen)

Past

Ana	ŤabaǨt
Inta	ŤabaǨt
Inté	ŤabaǨté
Hoowé	ŤabaǨ
Heeyé	ŤabaǨét
Naĥna	ŤabaǨna
Intoo	ŤabaǨtoo
Hinné	ŤabaǨoo

Past Continuous

Ana	Kint Ăam	biŤboǨ	(kint ŤabéǨ/ŤabǨa)
Inta	Kint Ăam	btiŤboǨ	(Kint ŤabéǨ)
Inté	Kinté Ăam	btiŤbǨé	(Kinté ŤabKa)
Hoowé	Kén Ăam	byiŤboǨ	(Kén ŤabéǨ)
Heeyé	Kénét Ăam	btiŤboǨ	(Kénét ŤabKa)
Naĥna	Kinna Ăam	mniŤboǨ	(Kinna ŤabKeen)
Intoo	Kintoo Ăam	btiŤbǨoo	(Kintoo ŤabKeen)
Hinné	Kénoo Ăam	byiŤbǨoo	(Kénoo ŤabKeen)

Future

Ana	Laĥ	iŤboǨ
Inta	Laĥ	tiŤboǨ
Inté	Laĥ	tiŤbǨé
Hoowé	Laĥ	yiŤboǨ
Heeyé	Laĥ	tiŤboǨ
Naĥna	Laĥ	niŤboǨ
Intoo	Laĥ	tiŤbǨoo
Hinné	Laĥ	yiŤbǨoo

Command

Inta	ŤboǨ
Inté	ŤbiǨé
Intoo	ŤbiǨoo
Inta	Ma tŤboǨ
Inté	Ma tŤbǨé
Intoo	Ma tŤbǨoo

Ă= Augh in bought	Ď= a heavy D	É= like A in Bay	G= G in beige	ĥ= like an H with smaller air passage	I= I as in ink	Ǩ= like ch in Irish loch
O= O as in home	OO= as in boots	R= roll the rrr	Ť= a heavy T	Ř= like a French R (gargle it)	Ŝ= a heavy S	Ž= a heavy Z

<u>C</u>   <u>C</u>

To cool

Present	
Ana	Bbarréd
Inta	Btbarréd
Inté	Btbarrdé
Hoowé	Bibarréd
Heeyé	Btbarréd
Nahna	Mnbarréd
Intoo	Btbarrdoo
Hinné	Bibarrdoo

Present Continuous		
Ana	Ăam	Bbarréd
Inta	Ăam	Btbarréd
Inté	Ăam	Btbarrdé
Hoowé	Ăam	Bibarréd
Heeyé	Ăam	Btbarréd
Nahna	Ăam	Mnbarréd
Intoo	Ăam	Btbarrdoo
Hinné	Ăam	Bibarrdoo

Past	
Ana	Barradt
Inta	Barradt
Inté	Barradté
Hoowé	Barrad
Heeyé	Barradét
Nahna	Barradna
Intoo	Barradtoo
Hinné	Barradoo

Past Continuous		
Ana	Kint Ăam	Bbarréd
Inta	Kint Ăam	Btbarréd
Inté	Kinté Ăam	Btbarrdé
Hoowé	Kén Ăam	Bibarréd
Heeyé	Kénét Ăam	Btbarréd
Nahna	Kinna Ăam	Mnbarréd
Intoo	Kintoo Ăam	Btbarrdoo
Hinné	Kénoo Ăam	Bibarrdoo

Future		
Ana	Laĥ	barréd
Inta	Laĥ	tbarréd
Inté	Laĥ	tbarrdé
Hoowé	Laĥ	ybarréd
Heeyé	Laĥ	tbarréd
Nahna	Laĥ	nbarréd
Intoo	Laĥ	tbarrdoo
Hinné	Laĥ	ybarrdoo

Command	
Inta	Barréd
Inté	Barrdé
Intoo	Barrdoo
Inta	Ma tbarréd
Inté	Ma tbarrdé
Intoo	Ma tbarrdoo

To copy/photograph

Present	
Ana	bŜawwér
Inta	btŜawwér
Inté	btŜawwré
Hoowé	biŜawwér
Heeyé	btŜawwér
Nahna	mnŜawwér
Intoo	btŜawwroo
Hinné	biŜawwroo

Present Continuous		
Ana	Ăam	bŜawwér
Inta	Ăam	btŜawwér
Inté	Ăam	btŜawwré
Hoowé	Ăam	biŜawwér
Heeyé	Ăam	btŜawwér
Nahna	Ăam	mnŜawwér
Intoo	Ăam	btŜawwroo
Hinné	Ăam	biŜawwroo

Past	
Ana	Ŝawwart
Inta	Ŝawwart
Inté	Ŝawwarté
Hoowé	Ŝawwar
Heeyé	Ŝawwarét
Nahna	Ŝawwarna
Intoo	Ŝawwartoo
Hinné	Ŝawwaroo

Past Continuous		
Ana	Kint Ăam	bŜawwér
Inta	Kint Ăam	btŜawwér
Inté	Kinté Ăam	btŜawwré
Hoowé	Kén Ăam	biŜawwér
Heeyé	Kénét Ăam	btŜawwér
Nahna	Kinna Ăam	mnŜawwér
Intoo	Kintoo Ăam	btŜawwroo
Hinné	Kénoo Ăam	biŜawwroo

Future		
Ana	Laĥ	Ŝawwér
Inta	Laĥ	tŜawwér
Inté	Laĥ	tŜawwré
Hoowé	Laĥ	yŜawwér
Heeyé	Laĥ	tŜawwér
Nahna	Laĥ	nŜawwér
Intoo	Laĥ	tŜawwroo
Hinné	Laĥ	yŜawwroo

Command	
Inta	Ŝawwér
Inté	Ŝawwré
Intoo	Ŝawwroo
Inta	Ma tŜawwér
Inté	Ma tŜawwré
Intoo	Ma tŜawwroo

Ă= Augh in bought	Đ= a heavy D	É= like A in Bay	G= G in beige	ĥ= like an H with smaller air passage	I= I as in ink	Ќ= like ch in Irish loch
O= O as in home	OO= as in boots	R= roll the rrr	Ŧ= a heavy T	Ř= like a French R (gargle it)	Ŝ= a heavy S	Ž= a heavy Z

C

C

To count

Present

Ana	bĂidd
Inta	btĂidd
Inté	btĂiddé
Hoowé	biĂidd
Heeyé	btĂidd
Naĥna	mnĂidd
Intoo	btĂiddoo
Hinné	biĂiddoo

Present Continuous

Ana	Ăam	bĂidd
Inta	Ăam	btĂidd
Inté	Ăam	btĂiddé
Hoowé	Ăam	biĂidd
Heeyé	Ăam	btĂidd
Naĥna	Ăam	mnĂidd
Intoo	Ăam	btĂiddoo
Hinné	Ăam	biĂiddoo

Past

Ana	Ăaddét
Inta	Ăaddét
Inté	Ăaddaité
Hoowé	Ăadd
Heeyé	Ăaddét
Naĥna	Ăaddaina
Intoo	Ăaddaitoo
Hinné	Ăaddoo

Past Continuous

Ana	Kint Ăam	bĂidd
Inta	Kint Ăam	btĂidd
Inté	Kinté Ăam	btĂiddé
Hoowé	Kén Ăam	biĂidd
Heeyé	Kénét Ăam	btĂidd
Naĥna	Kinna Ăam	mnĂidd
Intoo	Kintoo Ăam	btĂiddoo
Hinné	Kénoo Ăam	biĂiddoo

Future

Ana	Laĥ	Ăidd
Inta	Laĥ	tĂidd
Inté	Laĥ	tĂiddé
Hoowé	Laĥ	yĂidd
Heeyé	Laĥ	tĂidd
Naĥna	Laĥ	nĂidd
Intoo	Laĥ	tĂiddoo
Hinné	Laĥ	yĂiddoo

Command

Inta	Ăidd
Inté	Ăiddé
Intoo	Ăiddoo
Inta	Ma tĂidd
Inté	Ma tĂiddé
Intoo	Ma tAiddoo

To cover

Present

Ana	bŘaŤté
Inta	btŘaŤté
Inté	btŘaŤté
Hoowé	biŘaŤté
Heeyé	btŘaŤté
Naĥna	mnŘaŤté
Intoo	btŘaŤtoo
Hinné	biŘaŤtoo

Present Continuous

Ana	Ăam	bŘaŤté
Inta	Ăam	btŘaŤté
Inté	Ăam	btŘaŤté
Hoowé	Ăam	biŘaŤté
Heeyé	Ăam	btŘaŤté
Naĥna	Ăam	mnŘaŤté
Intoo	Ăam	btŘaŤtoo
Hinné	Ăam	biŘaŤtoo

Past

Ana	ŘaŤtét
Inta	ŘaŤtét
Inté	ŘaŤtaité
Hoowé	ŘaŤta
Heeyé	ŘaŤtét
Naĥna	ŘaŤtaina
Intoo	ŘaŤtaitoo
Hinné	ŘaŤtoo

Past Continuous

Ana	Kint Ăam	bŘaŤté
Inta	Kint Ăam	btŘaŤté
Inté	Kinté Ăam	btŘaŤté
Hoowé	Kén Ăam	biŘaŤté
Heeyé	Kénét Ăam	btŘaŤté
Naĥna	Kinna Ăam	mnŘaŤté
Intoo	Kintoo Ăam	btŘaŤtoo
Hinné	Kénoo Ăam	biŘaŤtoo

Future

Ana	Laĥ	ŘaŤté
Inta	Laĥ	tŘaŤté
Inté	Laĥ	tŘaŤté
Hoowé	Laĥ	yŘaŤté
Heeyé	Laĥ	tŘaŤté
Naĥna	Laĥ	nŘaŤté
Intoo	Laĥ	tŘaŤtoo
Hinné	Laĥ	yŘaŤtoo

Command

Inta	ŘaŤté
Inté	ŘaŤté
Intoo	ŘaŤtoo
Inta	Ma tŘaŤté
Inté	Ma tŘaŤté
Intoo	Ma tŘaŤtoo

Ă= Augh in bought	Ď= a heavy D	É= like A in Bay	G= G in beige	ĥ= like an H with smaller air passage	I= I as in ink	Ḱ= like ch in Irish loch
O= O as in home	OO= as in boots	R= roll the rrr	Ť= a heavy T	Ř= like a French R (gargle it)	Š= a heavy S	Ž= a heavy Z

C   C

To crawl

Present	
Ana	Bdabdib
Inta	Btdabdib
Inté	Btdabdbé
Hoowé	Bidabdib
Heeyé	Btdabdib
Nahna	Mndabdib
Intoo	Btdabdboo
Hinné	Bidabdboo

Present Continuous		
Ana	Ăam	Bdabdib
Inta	Ăam	Btdabdib
Inté	Ăam	Btdabdbé
Hoowé	Ăam	Bidabdib
Heeyé	Ăam	Btdabdib
Nahna	Ăam	Mndabdib
Intoo	Ăam	Btdabdboo
Hinné	Ăam	Bidabdboo

Past	
Ana	Dabdabt
Inta	Dabdabt
Inté	Dabdabté
Hoowé	Dabdab
Heeyé	Dabdabét
Nahna	Dabdabna
Intoo	Dabdabtoo
Hinné	Dabdaboo

Past Continuous		
Ana	Kint Ăam	Bdabdib
Inta	Kint Ăam	Btdabdib
Inté	Kinté Ăam	Btdabdbé
Hoowé	Kén Ăam	Bidabdib
Heeyé	Kénét Ăam	Btdabdib
Nahna	Kinna Ăam	Mndabdib
Intoo	Kintoo Ăam	Btdabdboo
Hinné	Kénoo Ăam	Bidabdboo

Future		
Ana	Laĥ	Dabdib
Inta	Laĥ	Tdabdib
Inté	Laĥ	Tdabdbé
Hoowé	Laĥ	Ydabdib
Heeyé	Laĥ	Tdabdib
Nahna	Laĥ	Ndabdib
Intoo	Laĥ	Tdabdboo
Hinné	Laĥ	Ydabdboo

Command	
Inta	Dabdib
Inté	Dabdbé
Intoo	Dabdboo
Inta	Ma tdabdib
Inté	Ma tdabdbé
Intoo	Ma tdabdboo

To create

Present	
Ana	biḰlo'
Inta	btiḰlo'
Inté	btiḰl'é
Hoowé	byiḰlo'
Heeyé	btiḰlo'
Nahna	mniḰlo'
Intoo	btiḰl'oo
Hinné	byiḰl'oo

Present Continuous		
Ana	Ăam	biḰlo'
Inta	Ăam	btiḰlo'
Inté	Ăam	btiḰl'é
Hoowé	Ăam	byiḰlo'
Heeyé	Ăam	btiḰlo'
Nahna	Ăam	mniḰlo'
Intoo	Ăam	btiḰl'oo
Hinné	Ăam	byiḰl'oo

Past	
Ana	Ḱala't
Inta	Ḱala't
Inté	Ḱala'té
Hoowé	Ḱala'
Heeyé	Ḱala'ét
Nahna	Ḱala'na
Intoo	Ḱala'too
Hinné	Ḱala'oo

Past Continuous		
Ana	Kint Ăam	biḰlo'
Inta	Kint Ăam	btiḰlo'
Inté	Kinté Ăam	btiḰl'é
Hoowé	Kén Ăam	byiḰlo'
Heeyé	Kénét Ăam	btiḰlo'
Nahna	Kinna Ăam	mniḰlo'
Intoo	Kintoo Ăam	btiḰl'oo
Hinné	Kénoo Ăam	byiḰl'oo

Future		
Ana	Laĥ	iḰlo'
Inta	Laĥ	tiḰlo'
Inté	Laĥ	tiḰl'é
Hoowé	Laĥ	yiḰlo'
Heeyé	Laĥ	tiḰlo'
Nahna	Laĥ	niḰlo'
Intoo	Laĥ	tiḰl'oo
Hinné	Laĥ	yiḰl'oo

Command	
Inta	Ḱlo'
Inté	Ḱli'é
Intoo	Ḱli'oo
Inta	Ma tḰlo'
Inté	Ma tḰl'é
Intoo	Ma tḰl'oo

Ă= Augh in bought	Ď= a heavy D	É= like A in Bay	G= G in beige	ĥ= like an H with smaller air passage	I= I as in ink	Ḱ= like ch in Irish loch
O= O as in home	OO= as in boots	R= roll the rrr	Ť= a heavy T	Ř= like a French R (gargle it)	Š= a heavy S	Ž= a heavy Z

C

C

To cry

Present

Ana	Bibké
Inta	btibké
Inté	btibké
Hoowé	byibké
Heeyé	btibké
Nahna	mnibké
Intoo	Btibkoo
Hinné	Byibkoo

Present Continuous

Ana	Ăam	bibké	(béké/békyé)
Inta	Ăam	btibké	(béké)
Inté	Ăam	btibké	(békyé)
Hoowé	Ăam	byibké	(béké)
Heeyé	Ăam	btibké	(békyé)
Nahna	Ăam	mnibké	(békyeen)
Intoo	Ăam	Btibkoo	(békyeen)
Hinné	Ăam	Byibkoo	(békyeen)

Past

Ana	Bkeet
Inta	Bkeet
Inté	Bkeeté
Hoowé	Biké
Heeyé	Bikyét
Nahna	Bkeena
Intoo	Bkeetoo
Hinné	Bikyoo

Past Continuous

Ana	Kint Ăam	bibké	(kint béké/békyé)
Inta	Kint Ăam	btibké	(Kint béké)
Inté	Kinté Ăam	btibké	(Kinté békyé)
Hoowé	Kén Ăam	byibké	(Kén béké)
Heeyé	Kénét Ăam	btibké	(Kénét békyé)
Nahna	Kinna Ăam	mnibké	(Kinna békyeen)
Intoo	Kintoo Ăam	Btibkoo	(Kintoo békyeen)
Hinné	Kénoo Ăam	Byibkoo	(Kénoo békyeen)

Future

Ana	Lah	Ibké
Inta	Lah	Tibké
Inté	Lah	Tibké
Hoowé	Lah	Yibké
Heeyé	Lah	Tibké
Nahna	Lah	Nibké
Intoo	Lah	Tibkoo
Hinné	Lah	Yibkoo

Command

Inta	Bkee
Inté	Bkee
Intoo	Bkoo
Inta	Ma tbké
Inté	Ma tbké
Intoo	Ma tbkoo

To cut / To trim

Present

Ana	B'iŜŜ
Inta	Bt'iŜŜ
Inté	Bt'iŜŜé
Hoowé	Bi'iŜŜ
Heeyé	Bt'iŜŜ
Nahna	Mn'iŜŜ
Intoo	Bt'iŜŜoo
Hinné	Bi'iŜŜoo

Present Continuous

Ana	Ăam	B'iŜŜ
Inta	Ăam	Bt'iŜŜ
Inté	Ăam	Bt'iŜŜé
Hoowé	Ăam	Bi'iŜŜ
Heeyé	Ăam	Bt'iŜŜ
Nahna	Ăam	Mn'iŜŜ
Intoo	Ăam	Bt'iŜŜoo
Hinné	Ăam	Bi'iŜŜoo

Past

Ana	aŜŜét
Inta	aŜŜét
Inté	aŜŜaité
Hoowé	aŜŜ
Heeyé	aŜŜét
Nahna	aŜŜaina
Intoo	aŜŜaitoo
Hinné	aŜŜoo

Past Continuous

Ana	Kint Ăam	B'iŜŜ
Inta	Kint Ăam	Bt'iŜŜ
Inté	Kinté Ăam	Bt'iŜŜé
Hoowé	Kén Ăam	Bi'iŜŜ
Heeyé	Kénét Ăam	Bt'iŜŜ
Nahna	Kinna Ăam	Mn'iŜŜ
Intoo	Kintoo Ăam	Bt'iŜŜoo
Hinné	Kénoo Ăam	Bi'iŜŜoo

Future

Ana	Lah	'iŜŜ
Inta	Lah	T'iŜŜ
Inté	Lah	T'iŜŜé
Hoowé	Lah	Y'iŜŜ
Heeyé	Lah	T'iŜŜ
Nahna	Lah	N'iŜŜ
Intoo	Lah	T'iŜŜoo
Hinné	Lah	Y'iŜŜoo

Command

Inta	'iŜŜ
Inté	'iŜŜé
Intoo	'iŜŜoo
Inta	Ma t'iŜŜ
Inté	Ma t'iŜŜé
Intoo	Ma t'iŜŜoo

Ă= Augh in bought	Ď= a heavy D	É= like A in Bay	G= G in beige	h̄= like an H with smaller air passage	I= I as in ink	Ќ= like ch in Irish loch
O= O as in home	OO= as in boots	R= roll the rrr	Ť= a heavy T	Ř= like a French R (gargle it)	Ŝ= a heavy S	Ž= a heavy Z

D   D

To damn   To dance

To damn

Present	
Ana	bilĂan
Inta	btilĂan
Inté	btilĂané
Hoowé	byilĂan
Heeyé	btilĂan
Naĥna	mnilĂan
Intoo	btilĂanoo
Hinné	byilĂanoo

Present Continuous		
Ana	Ăam	bilĂan
Inta	Ăam	btilĂan
Inté	Ăam	btilĂané
Hoowé	Ăam	byilĂan
Heeyé	Ăam	btilĂan
Naĥna	Ăam	mnilĂan
Intoo	Ăam	btilĂanoo
Hinné	Ăam	byilĂanoo

Past	
Ana	laĂant
Inta	laĂant
Inté	laĂanté
Hoowé	laĂan
Heeyé	laĂanét
Naĥna	laĂanna
Intoo	laĂantoo
Hinné	laĂanoo

Past Continuous		
Ana	Kint Ăam	bilĂan
Inta	Kint Ăam	btilĂan
Inté	Kinté Ăam	btilĂané
Hoowé	Kén Ăam	byilĂan
Heeyé	Kénét Ăam	btilĂan
Naĥna	Kinna Ăam	mnilĂan
Intoo	Kintoo Ăam	btilĂanoo
Hinné	Kénoo Ăam	byilĂanoo

Future		
Ana	Laĥ	ilĂan
Inta	Laĥ	tilĂan
Inté	Laĥ	tilĂané
Hoowé	Laĥ	yilĂan
Heeyé	Laĥ	tilĂan
Naĥna	Laĥ	nilĂan
Intoo	Laĥ	tilĂanoo
Hinné	Laĥ	yilĂanoo

Command	
Inta	lĂan
Inté	lĂané
Intoo	lĂanoo
Inta	Ma tlĂan
Inté	Ma tlĂané
Intoo	Ma tlAanoo

To dance

Present	
Ana	Bir'oŜ
Inta	Btir'oŜ
Inté	Btir'Ŝé
Hoowé	Byir'oŜ
Heeyé	Btir'oŜ
Naĥna	Mnir'oŜ
Intoo	Btir'Ŝoo
Hinné	Byir'Ŝoo

Present Continuous		
Ana	Ăam	Bir'oŜ
Inta	Ăam	Btir'oŜ
Inté	Ăam	Btir'Ŝé
Hoowé	Ăam	Byir'oŜ
Heeyé	Ăam	Btir'oŜ
Naĥna	Ăam	Mnir'oŜ
Intoo	Ăam	Btir'Ŝoo
Hinné	Ăam	Byir'Ŝoo

Past	
Ana	Ra'aŜt
Inta	Ra'aŜt
Inté	Ra'aŜté
Hoowé	Ra'aŜ
Heeyé	Ra'aŜét
Naĥna	Ra'aŜna
Intoo	Ra'aŜtoo
Hinné	Ra'aŜoo

Past Continuous		
Ana	Kint Ăam	Bir'oŜ
Inta	Kint Ăam	Btir'oŜ
Inté	Kinté Ăam	Btir'Ŝé
Hoowé	Kén Ăam	Byir'oŜ
Heeyé	Kénét Ăam	Btir'oŜ
Naĥna	Kinna Ăam	Mnir'oŜ
Intoo	Kintoo Ăam	Btir'Ŝoo
Hinné	Kénoo Ăam	Byir'Ŝoo

Future		
Ana	Laĥ	ir'oŜ
Inta	Laĥ	tir'oŜ
Inté	Laĥ	tir'Ŝé
Hoowé	Laĥ	yir'oŜ
Heeyé	Laĥ	tir'oŜ
Naĥna	Laĥ	nir'oŜ
Intoo	Laĥ	tir'Ŝoo
Hinné	Laĥ	yir'Ŝoo

Command	
Inta	R'oŜ
Inté	R'iŜé
Intoo	R'iŜoo
Inta	Ma tr'oŜ
Inté	Ma tr'Ŝé
Intoo	Ma tr'Ŝoo

Ă= Augh in bought	Ď= a heavy D	É= like A in Bay	G= G in beige	ĥ= like an H with smaller air passage	I= I as in ink	Ќ= like ch in Irish loch
O= O as in home	OO= as in boots	R= roll the rrr	Ť= a heavy T	Ř= like a French R (gargle it)	Ŝ= a heavy S	Ž= a heavy Z

D   D

To Dare / To challange

Present	
Ana	Bithadda
Inta	Btithadda
Inté	Btithaddé
Hoowé	Byithadda
Heeyé	Btithadda
Nahna	Mnithadda
Intoo	Btithaddoo
Hinné	Byithaddoo

Present Continuous		
Ana	Ăam	Bithadda
Inta	Ăam	Btithadda
Inté	Ăam	Btithaddé
Hoowé	Ăam	Byithadda
Heeyé	Ăam	Btithadda
Nahna	Ăam	Mnithadda
Intoo	Ăam	Btithaddoo
Hinné	Ăam	Byithaddoo

Past	
Ana	thadét
Inta	thadét
Inté	Thadaité
Hoowé	Thada
Heeyé	thadét
Nahna	Thadaina
Intoo	Thadaitoo
Hinné	thadoo

Past Continuous		
Ana	Kint Ăam	Bithadda
Inta	Kint Ăam	Btithadda
Inté	Kinté Ăam	Btithaddé
Hoowé	Kén Ăam	Byithadda
Heeyé	Kénét Ăam	Btithadda
Nahna	Kinna Ăam	Mnithadda
Intoo	Kintoo Ăam	Btithaddoo
Hinné	Kénoo Ăam	Byithaddoo

Future		
Ana	Lah	ithadda
Inta	Lah	tithadda
Inté	Lah	tithaddé
Hoowé	Lah	yithadda
Heeyé	Lah	tithadda
Nahna	Lah	nithadda
Intoo	Lah	tithaddoo
Hinné	Lah	yithaddoo

Command	
Inta	Thadda
Inté	Thaddé
Intoo	Thaddoo
Inta	Ma tthadda
Inté	Ma tthaddé
Intoo	Ma tthadoo

To decide

Present	
Ana	B'arrir
Inta	Bt'arrir
Inté	Bt'arriré
Hoowé	Bi'arrir
Heeyé	Bt'arrir
Nahna	Mn'arrir
Intoo	Bt'arriroo
Hinné	Bi'arriroo

Present Continuous			
Ana	Ăam	B'arrir	(m'arrar/m'arrara)
Inta	Ăam	Bt'arrir	(m'arrar)
Inté	Ăam	Bt'arriré	(m'arrara)
Hoowé	Ăam	Bi'arrir	(m'arrar)
Heeyé	Ăam	Bt'arrir	(m'arrara)
Nahna	Ăam	Mn'arrir	(m'arrareen)
Intoo	Ăam	Bt'arriroo	(m'arrareen)
Hinné	Ăam	Bi'arriroo	(m'arrarenn)

Past	
Ana	Arrart
Inta	Arrart
Inté	Arrarté
Hoowé	Arrar
Heeyé	Arrarét
Nahna	Arrarna
Intoo	Arrartoo
Hinné	Arraroo

Past Continuous				
Ana	Kint Ăam	B'arrir	(kint	m'arrar/m'arrara)
Inta	Kint Ăam	Bt'arrir	(Kint	m'arrar)
Inté	Kinté Ăam	Bt'arriré	(Kinté	m'arrara)
Hoowé	Kén Ăam	Bi'arrir	(Kén	m'arrar)
Heeyé	Kénét Ăam	Bt'arrir	(Kénét	m'arrara)
Nahna	Kinna Ăam	Mn'arrir	(Kinna	m'arrareen)
Intoo	Kintoo Ăam	Bt'arriroo	(Kintoo	m'arrareen)
Hinné	Kénoo Ăam	Bi'arriroo	(Kénoo	m'arrarenn)

Future		
Ana	Lah	arrir
Inta	Lah	t'arrir
Inté	Lah	t'arriré
Hoowé	Lah	Y'arrir
Heeyé	Lah	t'arrir
Nahna	Lah	n'arrir
Intoo	Lah	t'arriroo
Hinné	Lah	Y'arriroo

Command	
Inta	Arrir
Inté	Arriré
Intoo	Arriroo
Inta	Ma t'arrir
Inté	Ma t'arriré
Intoo	Ma t'arriroo

Ă= Augh in bought	Ď= a heavy D	É= like A in Bay	G= G in beige	ĥ= like an H with smaller air passage	I= I as in ink	Ќ= like ch in Irish loch
O= O as in home	OO= as in boots	R= roll the rrr	Ť= a heavy T	Ř= like a French R (gargle it)	Ŝ= a heavy S	Ž= a heavy Z

D

D

To decrease

Present

Ana	B'allil
Inta	Bt'allil
Inté	Bt'allilé
Hoowé	Bi'allil
Heeyé	Bt'allil
Nahna	Mn'allil
Intoo	Bt'alliloo
Hinné	Bi'alliloo

Present Continuous

Ana	Ăam	B'allil	(m'allal/m'allalé)
Inta	Ăam	Bt'allil	(m'allal)
Inté	Ăam	Bt'allilé	(m'allalé)
Hoowé	Ăam	Bi'allil	(m'allal)
Heeyé	Ăam	Bt'allil	(m'allalé)
Nahna	Ăam	Mn'allil	(m'allaleen)
Intoo	Ăam	Bt'alliloo	(m'allaleen)
Hinné	Ăam	Bi'alliloo	(m'allaleen)

Past

Ana	Allalt
Inta	Allalt
Inté	Allalté
Hoowé	Allal
Heeyé	Allalét
Nahna	Allalna
Intoo	Allaltoo
Hinné	Allaloo

Past Continuous

Ana	Kint Ăam	B'allil	(kint m'allal/m'allalé)
Inta	Kint Ăam	Bt'allil	(Kint m'allal)
Inté	Kinté Ăam	Bt'allilé	(Kinté m'allalé)
Hoowé	Kén Ăam	Bi'allil	(Kén m'allal)
Heeyé	Kénét Ăam	Bt'allil	(Kénét m'allalé)
Nahna	Kinna Ăam	Mn'allil	(Kinna m'allaleen)
Intoo	Kintoo Ăam	Bt'alliloo	(Kintoo m'allaleen)
Hinné	Kénoo Ăam	Bi'alliloo	(Kénoo m'allaleen)

Future

Ana	Lah	'allil
Inta	Lah	t'allil
Inté	Lah	t'allilé
Hoowé	Lah	Y'allil
Heeyé	Lah	t'allil
Nahna	Lah	n'allil
Intoo	Lah	t'alliloo
Hinné	Lah	Y'alliloo

Command

Inta	Allil
Inté	Allilé
Intoo	Alliloo
Inta	Ma t'allil
Inté	Ma t'allilé
Intoo	Ma t'alliloo

To decorate

Present

Ana	Bzayén
Inta	Btzayén
Inté	Btzayné
Hoowé	Bizayén
Heeyé	Btzayén
Nahna	Mnzayén
Intoo	Btzaynoo
Hinné	Bizaynoo

Present Continuous

Ana	Ăam	Bzayén
Inta	Ăam	Btzayén
Inté	Ăam	Btzayné
Hoowé	Ăam	Bizayén
Heeyé	Ăam	Btzayén
Nahna	Ăam	Mnzayén
Intoo	Ăam	Btzaynoo
Hinné	Ăam	Bizaynoo

Past

Ana	Zayyant
Inta	Zayyant
Inté	Zayyanté
Hoowé	Zayyan
Heeyé	Zayyanét
Nahna	Zayyanna
Intoo	Zayyantoo
Hinné	Zayyanoo

Past Continuous

Ana	Kint Ăam	Bzayén
Inta	Kint Ăam	Btzayén
Inté	Kinté Ăam	Btzayné
Hoowé	Kén Ăam	Bizayén
Heeyé	Kénét Ăam	Btzayén
Nahna	Kinna Ăam	Mnzayén
Intoo	Kintoo Ăam	Btzaynoo
Hinné	Kénoo Ăam	Bizaynoo

Future

Ana	Lah	zayén
Inta	Lah	tzayén
Inté	Lah	tzayné
Hoowé	Lah	yzayén
Heeyé	Lah	tzayén
Nahna	Lah	nzayén
Intoo	Lah	tzaynoo
Hinné	Lah	yzaynoo

Command

Inta	Zayyant
Inté	Zayyanté
Intoo	Zayyantoo
Inta	Ma tzayyén
Inté	Ma tzayyné
Intoo	Ma tzayynoo

Ă= Augh in bought	Ď= a heavy D	É= like A in Bay	G= G in beige	h̆= like an H with smaller air passage	I= I as in ink	Ќ= like ch in Irish loch
O= O as in home	OO= as in boots	R= roll the rrr	Ť= a heavy T	Ř= like a French R (gargle it)	Ŝ= a heavy S	Ž= a heavy Z

D   D

To delay

Present

Ana	B'aḰḰér
Inta	Bt'aḰḰér
Inté	Bt'aḰḰré
Hoowé	Bi'aḰḰér
Heeyé	Bt'aḰḰér
Naḥna	Mn'aḰḰér
Intoo	Bt'aḰḰroo
Hinné	Bi'aḰḰroo

Present Continuous

Ana	Ăam	B'aḰḰer
Inta	Ăam	Bt'aḰḰer
Inté	Ăam	Bt'aḰḰré
Hoowé	Ăam	Bi'aḰḰer
Heeyé	Ăam	Bt'aḰḰer
Naḥna	Ăam	Mn'aḰḰer
Intoo	Ăam	Bt'aḰḰroo
Hinné	Ăam	Bi'aḰḰroo

Past

Ana	aḰḰart
Inta	aḰḰart
Inté	aḰḰarté
Hoowé	aḰḰar
Heeyé	aḰḰarét
Naḥna	aḰḰarna
Intoo	aḰḰartoo
Hinné	aḰḰaroo

Past Continuous

Ana	Kint Ăam	B'aḰḰer	
Inta	Kint Ăam	Bt'aḰḰer	
Inté	Kinté Ăam	Bt'aḰḰré	
Hoowé	Kén Ăam	Bi'aḰḰer	
Heeyé	Kénét Ăam	Bt'aḰḰer	
Naḥna	Kinna Ăam	Mn'aḰḰer	
Intoo	Kintoo Ăam	Bt'aḰḰroo	
Hinné	Kénoo Ăam	Bi'aḰḰroo	

Future

Ana	Laḥ	aḰḰér
Inta	Laḥ	t'aḰḰér
Inté	Laḥ	t'aḰḰré
Hoowé	Laḥ	Y'aḰḰér
Heeyé	Laḥ	t'aḰḰér
Naḥna	Laḥ	n'aḰḰér
Intoo	Laḥ	t'aḰḰroo
Hinné	Laḥ	y'aḰḰroo

Command

Inta	AḰḰér
Inté	AḰḰré
Intoo	AḰḰroo
Inta	Ma t'aḰḰér
Inté	Ma t'aḰḰré
Intoo	Ma t'aḰḰroo

To be delayed

Present

Ana	Bit'aḰḰér
Inta	Btit'aḰḰér
Inté	Btit'aḰḰré
Hoowé	Byit'aḰḰér
Heeyé	Btit'aḰḰér
Naḥna	Mnit'aḰḰér
Intoo	Btit'aḰḰroo
Hinné	Byit'aḰḰroo

Present Continuous

Ana	Ăam	Bit'aḰḰér	(m'aḰḰar/m'aḰḰra)
Inta	Ăam	Btit'aḰḰér	(m'aḰḰar)
Inté	Ăam	Btit'aḰḰré	(m'aḰḰra)
Hoowé	Ăam	Byit'aḰḰér	(m'aḰḰar)
Heeyé	Ăam	Btit'aḰḰér	(m'aḰḰra)
Naḥna	Ăam	Mnit'aḰḰér	(M'aḰḰreen)
Intoo	Ăam	Btit'aḰḰroo	(m'aḰḰreen)
Hinné	Ăam	Byit'aḰḰroo	(m'aḰḰreen)

Past

Ana	T'aḰḰart
Inta	T'aḰḰart
Inté	T'aḰḰarté
Hoowé	T'aḰḰar
Heeyé	T'aḰḰarét
Naḥna	T'aḰḰarna
Intoo	T'aḰḰartoo
Hinné	T'aḰḰaroo

Past Continuous

Ana	Kint Ăam	Bit'aḰḰér	(kint	m'aḰḰar/m'aḰḰra)
Inta	Kint Ăam	Btit'aḰḰér	(Kint	m'aḰḰar)
Inté	Kinté Ăam	Btit'aḰḰré	(Kinté	m'aḰḰra)
Hoowé	Kén Ăam	Byit'aḰḰér	(Kén	m'aḰḰar)
Heeyé	Kénét Ăam	Btit'aḰḰér	(Kénét	m'aḰḰra)
Naḥna	Kinna Ăam	Mnit'aḰḰér	(Kinna	M'aḰḰreen)
Intoo	Kintoo Ăam	Btit'aḰḰroo	(Kintoo	m'aḰḰreen)
Hinné	Kénoo Ăam	Byit'aḰḰroo	(Kénoo	m'aḰḰreen)

Future

Ana	Laḥ	it'aḰḰér
Inta	Laḥ	tit'aḰḰér
Inté	Laḥ	tit'aḰḰré
Hoowé	Laḥ	yit'aḰḰér
Heeyé	Laḥ	tit'aḰḰér
Naḥna	Laḥ	nit'aḰḰér
Intoo	Laḥ	tit'aḰḰroo
Hinné	Laḥ	yit'aḰḰroo

Command

Inta	T'aḰḰar
Inté	T'aḰḰaré
Intoo	T'aḰḰaroo
Inta	Ma tt'aḰḰar
Inté	Ma tt'aḰḰaré
Intoo	Ma tt'aḰḰaroo

Ă= Augh in bought	**Ď**= a heavy D	**É**= like A in Bay	**G**= G in beige	**ḥ**= like an H with smaller air passage	**I**= I as in ink	**Ḱ**= like ch in Irish loch
O= O as in home	**OO**= as in boots	**R**= roll the rrr	**Ť**= a heavy T	**Ř**= like a French R (gargle it)	**Ŝ**= a heavy S	**Ž**= a heavy Z

D   D

To demand

Present

Ana	biŤlob
Inta	btiŤlob
Inté	btiŤlbé
Hoowé	byiŤlob
Heeyé	btiŤlob
Naĥna	mniŤlob
Intoo	btiŤlboo
Hinné	byiŤlboo

Present Continuous

Ana	Ăam	biŤlob	(Ťaléb/Ťalbé)
Inta	Ăam	btiŤlob	(Ťaléb)
Inté	Ăam	btiŤlbé	(Ťalbé)
Hoowé	Ăam	byiŤlob	(Ťaléb)
Heeyé	Ăam	btiŤlob	(Ťalbé)
Naĥna	Ăam	mniŤlob	(Ťalbeen)
Intoo	Ăam	btiŤlboo	(Ťalbeen)
Hinné	Ăam	byiŤlboo	(Ťalbeen)

Past

Ana	Ťalabt
Inta	Ťalabt
Inté	Ťalabté
Hoowé	Ťalab
Heeyé	Ťalabét
Naĥna	Ťalabna
Intoo	Ťalabtoo
Hinné	Ťalaboo

Past Continuous

Ana	Kint Ăam	biŤlob	(kint Ťaléb/Ťalbé)
Inta	Kint Ăam	btiŤlob	(Kint Ťaléb)
Inté	Kinté Ăam	btiŤlbé	(Kinté Ťalbé)
Hoowé	Kén Ăam	byiŤlob	(Kén Ťaléb)
Heeyé	Kénét Ăam	btiŤlob	(Kénét Ťalbé)
Naĥna	Kinna Ăam	mniŤlob	(Kinna Ťalbeen)
Intoo	Kintoo Ăam	btiŤlboo	(Kintoo Ťalbeen)
Hinné	Kénoo Ăam	byiŤlboo	(Kénoo Ťalbeen)

Future

Ana	Laĥ	iŤlob
Inta	Laĥ	tiŤlob
Inté	Laĥ	tiŤlbé
Hoowé	Laĥ	yiŤlob
Heeyé	Laĥ	tiŤlob
Naĥna	Laĥ	niŤlob
Intoo	Laĥ	tiŤlboo
Hinné	Laĥ	yiŤlboo

Command

Inta	Ťlob
Inté	Ťlibé
Intoo	Ťliboo
Inta	Ma tŤlob
Inté	Ma tŤlbé
Intoo	Ma tŤlboo

To deny

Present

Ana	Binkor
Inta	Btinkor
Inté	Btinkré
Hoowé	Byinkor
Heeyé	Btinkor
Naĥna	Mninkor
Intoo	Btinkroo
Hinné	Byinkroo

Present Continuous

Ana	Ăam	Binkor
Inta	Ăam	Btinkor
Inté	Ăam	Btinkré
Hoowé	Ăam	Byinkor
Heeyé	Ăam	Btinkor
Naĥna	Ăam	Mninkor
Intoo	Ăam	Btinkroo
Hinné	Ăam	Byinkroo

Past

Ana	Nakart
Inta	Nakart
Inté	Nakarté
Hoowé	Nakar
Heeyé	Nakarét
Naĥna	Nakarna
Intoo	Nakartoo
Hinné	Nakaroo

Past Continuous

Ana	Kint Ăam	Binkor
Inta	Kint Ăam	Btinkor
Inté	Kinté Ăam	Btinkré
Hoowé	Kén Ăam	Byinkor
Heeyé	Kénét Ăam	Btinkor
Naĥna	Kinna Ăam	Mninkor
Intoo	Kintoo Ăam	Btinkroo
Hinné	Kénoo Ăam	Byinkroo

Future

Ana	Laĥ	inkor
Inta	Laĥ	tinkor
Inté	Laĥ	tinkré
Hoowé	Laĥ	yinkor
Heeyé	Laĥ	tinkor
Naĥna	Laĥ	ninkor
Intoo	Laĥ	tinkroo
Hinné	Laĥ	yinkroo

Command

Inta	Nkor
Inté	Nkiré
Intoo	Nkiroo
Inta	Ma tnkor
Inté	Ma tnkré
Intoo	Ma tnkroo

Ă= Augh in bought	Đ= a heavy D	É= like A in Bay	G= G in beige	ĥ= like an H with smaller air passage	I= I as in ink	Ḱ= like ch in Irish loch
O= O as in home	OO= as in boots	R= roll the rrr	Ť= a heavy T	Ř= like a French R (gargle it)	Ŝ= a heavy S	Ž= a heavy Z

D

D

To descend

Present

Ana	Binzal
Inta	Btinzal
Inté	Btinzalé
Hoowé	Byinzal
Heeyé	Btinzal
Naẖna	Mninzal
Intoo	Btinzaloo
Hinné	Byinzaloo

Present Continuous

Ana	Ăam binzal (or ana nézél/nézlé)
Inta	Ăam btinzal (or nézél)
Inté	Ăam btinzalé (or nézlé)
Hoowé	Ăam byinzal (or nézél)
Heeyé	Ăam btinzal (or nézlé)
Naẖna	Ăam mninzal (or nézleen)
Intoo	Ăam btinzaloo (or nézleen)
Hinné	Ăam byinzaloo (or nézleen)

Past

Ana	Nzilt
Inta	Nzilt
Inté	Nzilté
Hoowé	Nizél
Heeyé	Nizlét
Naẖna	Nzilna
Intoo	Nziltoo
Hinné	Nizloo

Past Continuous

Ana	Kint Ăam binzal (or ana kint nézél/nézlé)
Inta	Kint Ăam btinzal (or kint nézél)
Inté	Kinté Ăam btinzalé (or kinté nézlé)
Hoowé	Kén Ăam byinzal (or kén nézél)
Heeyé	Kénét Ăam btinzal (or kénét nézlé)
Naẖna	Kinna Ăam mninzal (or kinna nézleen)
Intoo	Kintoo Ăam btinzaloo (or kintoo nézleen)
Hinné	Kénoo Ăam byinzaloo (or kénoo nézleen)

Future

Ana	Laẖ 'inzal
Inta	Laẖ tinzal
Inté	Laẖ tinzalé
Hoowé	Laẖ yinzal
Heeyé	Laẖ tinzal
Naẖna	Laẖ ninzal
Intoo	Laẖ tinzaloo
Hinné	Laẖ yinzaloo

Command

Inta	Nzalé
Inté	Nzal
Intoo	Nzaloo
Inta	Ma tinzal
Inté	Ma tinzalé
Intoo	Ma tinzaloo

To design

Present

Ana	bŜammim
Inta	btŜammim
Inté	btŜammimé
Hoowé	biŜammim
Heeyé	btŜammim
Naẖna	mnŜammim
Intoo	btŜammimoo
Hinné	biŜammimoo

Present Continuous

Ana	Ăam	bŜammim
Inta	Ăam	btŜammim
Inté	Ăam	btŜammimé
Hoowé	Ăam	biŜammim
Heeyé	Ăam	btŜammim
Naẖna	Ăam	mnŜammim
Intoo	Ăam	btŜammimoo
Hinné	Ăam	biŜammimoo

Past

Ana	Ŝammamt
Inta	Ŝammamt
Inté	Ŝammamté
Hoowé	Ŝammam
Heeyé	Ŝammamét
Naẖna	Ŝammamna
Intoo	Ŝammamtoo
Hinné	Ŝammamoo

Past Continuous

Ana	Kint Ăam	bŜammim
Inta	Kint Ăam	btŜammim
Inté	Kinté Ăam	btŜammimé
Hoowé	Kén Ăam	biŜammim
Heeyé	Kénét Ăam	btŜammim
Naẖna	Kinna Ăam	mnŜammim
Intoo	Kintoo Ăam	btŜammimoo
Hinné	Kénoo Ăam	biŜammimoo

Future

Ana	Laẖ	Ŝammim
Inta	Laẖ	tŜammim
Inté	Laẖ	tŜammimé
Hoowé	Laẖ	yŜammim
Heeyé	Laẖ	tŜammim
Naẖna	Laẖ	nŜammim
Intoo	Laẖ	tŜammimoo
Hinné	Laẖ	yŜammimoo

Command

Inta	Ŝammim
Inté	Ŝammimé
Intoo	Ŝammimoo
Inta	Ma tŜammim
Inté	Ma tŜammimé
Intoo	Ma tŜammimoo

Ă= Augh in bought	Ď= a heavy D	É= like A in Bay	G= G in beige	ẖ= like an H with smaller air passage	I= I as in ink	Ќ= like ch in Irish loch
O= O as in home	OO= as in boots	R= roll the rrr	Ť= a heavy T	Ř= like a French R (gargle it)	Ŝ= a heavy S	Ž= a heavy Z

D

D

to destroy

Present	
Ana	Bdammér
Inta	Btdammér
Inté	Btdammré
Hoowé	Bidammér
Heeyé	Btdammér
Nahna	Mndammér
Intoo	Btdammroo
Hinné	Bidammroo

Present Continuous		
Ana	Ăam	Bdammér
Inta	Ăam	Btdammér
Inté	Ăam	Btdammré
Hoowé	Ăam	Bidammér
Heeyé	Ăam	Btdammér
Nahna	Ăam	Mndammér
Intoo	Ăam	Btdammroo
Hinné	Ăam	Bidammroo

Past	
Ana	Dammart
Inta	Dammart
Inté	Dammarté
Hoowé	Dammar
Heeyé	Dammarét
Nahna	Dammarna
Intoo	Dammartoo
Hinné	Dammaroo

Past Continuous		
Ana	Kint Ăam	Bdammér
Inta	Kint Ăam	Btdammér
Inté	Kinté Ăam	Btdammré
Hoowé	Kén Ăam	Bidammér
Heeyé	Kénét Ăam	Btdammér
Nahna	Kinna Ăam	Mndammér
Intoo	Kintoo Ăam	Btdammroo
Hinné	Kénoo Ăam	Bidammroo

Future		
Ana	Laĥ	dammér
Inta	Laĥ	tdammér
Inté	Laĥ	tdammré
Hoowé	Laĥ	ydammér
Heeyé	Laĥ	tdammér
Nahna	Laĥ	ndammér
Intoo	Laĥ	tdammroo
Hinné	Laĥ	ydammroo

Command	
Inta	Dammér
Inté	Dammré
Intoo	Dammroo
Inta	Ma tdammér
Inté	Ma tdammré
Intoo	Ma tdammroo

To develop

Present	
Ana	bŤawwér
Inta	btŤawwér
Inté	btŤawwré
Hoowé	biŤawwér
Heeyé	btŤawwér
Nahna	mnŤawwér
Intoo	btŤawwroo
Hinné	biŤawwroo

Present Continuous		
Ana	Ăam	bŤawwér
Inta	Ăam	btŤawwér
Inté	Ăam	btŤawwré
Hoowé	Ăam	biŤawwér
Heeyé	Ăam	btŤawwér
Nahna	Ăam	mnŤawwér
Intoo	Ăam	btŤawwroo
Hinné	Ăam	biŤawwroo

Past	
Ana	Ťawwart
Inta	Ťawwart
Inté	Ťawwarté
Hoowé	Ťawwar
Heeyé	Ťawwarét
Nahna	Ťawwarna
Intoo	Ťawwartoo
Hinné	Ťawwaroo

Past Continuous		
Ana	Kint Ăam	bŤawwér
Inta	Kint Ăam	btŤawwér
Inté	Kinté Ăam	btŤawwré
Hoowé	Kén Ăam	biŤawwér
Heeyé	Kénét Ăam	btŤawwér
Nahna	Kinna Ăam	mnŤawwér
Intoo	Kintoo Ăam	btŤawwroo
Hinné	Kénoo Ăam	biŤawwroo

Future		
Ana	Laĥ	Ťawwér
Inta	Laĥ	tŤawwér
Inté	Laĥ	tŤawwré
Hoowé	Laĥ	yŤawwér
Heeyé	Laĥ	tŤawwér
Nahna	Laĥ	nŤawwér
Intoo	Laĥ	tŤawwroo
Hinné	Laĥ	yŤawwroo

Command	
Inta	Ťawwér
Inté	Ťawwré
Intoo	Ťawroo
Inta	Ma tŤawwér
Inté	Ma tŤawwré
Intoo	Ma tŤawroo

Ă= Augh in bought	Ď= a heavy D	É= like A in Bay	G= G in beige	ĥ= like an H with smaller air passage	I= I as in ink	Ќ= like ch in Irish loch
O= O as in home	OO= as in boots	R= roll the rrr	Ť= a heavy T	Ř= like a French R (gargle it)	Ŝ= a heavy S	Ž= a heavy Z

D

D

To die

Present

Ana	Bmoot
Inta	Btmoot
Inté	Btmooté
Hoowé	Bimoot
Heeyé	Btmoot
Nahna	Mnmoot
Intoo	Btmootoo
Hinné	Bimootoo

Present Continuous

Ana	Ăam	Bmoot	(mayét/mayté)
Inta	Ăam	Btmoot	(mayét)
Inté	Ăam	Btmooté	(mayté)
Hoowé	Ăam	Bimoot	(mayét)
Heeyé	Ăam	Btmoot	(mayté)
Nahna	Ăam	Mnmoot	(mayteen)
Intoo	Ăam	Btmootoo	(mayteen)
Hinné	Ăam	Bimootoo	(mayteen)

Past

Ana	Mitit
Inta	Mitit
Inté	Mitté
Hoowé	Mét
Heeyé	Métét
Nahna	Mittna
Intoo	Mittoo
Hinné	Métoo

Past Continuous

Ana	Kint Ăam	Bmoot	(kint mayét/mayté)
Inta	Kint Ăam	Btmoot	(Kint mayét)
Inté	Kinté Ăam	Btmooté	(Kinté mayté)
Hoowé	Kén Ăam	Bimoot	(Kén mayét)
Heeyé	Kénét Ăam	Btmoot	(Kénét mayté)
Nahna	Kinna Ăam	Mnmoot	(Kinna mayteen)
Intoo	Kintoo Ăam	Btmootoo	(Kintoo mayteen)
Hinné	Kénoo Ăam	Bimootoo	(Kénoo mayteen)

Future

Ana	Laĥ	Moot
Inta	Laĥ	Tmoot
Inté	Laĥ	tmooté
Hoowé	Laĥ	ymoot
Heeyé	Laĥ	Tmoot
Nahna	Laĥ	nmoot
Intoo	Laĥ	tmootoo
Hinné	Laĥ	ymootoo

Command

Inta	Moot
Inté	Mooté
Intoo	Mootoo
Inta	Ma tmoot
Inté	Ma tmooté
Intoo	Ma tmootoo

To differ/ To disagree

Present

Ana	biḰtilif
Inta	btiḰtilif
Inté	btiḰtilfé
Hoowé	byiḰtilif
Heeyé	btiḰtilif
Nahna	mniḰtilif
Intoo	btiḰtilfoo
Hinné	byiḰtilfoo

Present Continuous

Ana	Ăam	biḰtilif	(miḰtilif/miḰtilfé)
Inta	Ăam	btiḰtilif	(miḰtilif)
Inté	Ăam	btiḰtilfé	(miḰtilfé)
Hoowé	Ăam	byiḰtilif	(miḰtilif)
Heeyé	Ăam	btiḰtilif	(miḰtilfé)
Nahna	Ăam	mniḰtilif	(miḰtilfeen)
Intoo	Ăam	btiḰtilfoo	(miḰtilfeen)
Hinné	Ăam	byiḰtilfoo	(miḰtilfeen)

Past

Ana	Ḱtalaft
Inta	Ḱtalaft
Inté	Ḱtalafté
Hoowé	Ḱtalaf
Heeyé	Ḱtalafét
Nahna	Ḱtalafna
Intoo	Ḱtalaftoo
Hinné	Ḱtalafoo

Past Continuous

Ana	Kint Ăam	biḰtilif	(kint miḰtilif/miḰtilfé)
Inta	Kint Ăam	btiḰtilif	(Kint miḰtilif)
Inté	Kinté Ăam	btiḰtilfé	(Kinté miḰtilfé)
Hoowé	Kén Ăam	byiḰtilif	(Kén miḰtilif)
Heeyé	Kénét Ăam	btiḰtilif	(Kénét miḰtilfé)
Nahna	Kinna Ăam	mniḰtilif	(Kinna miḰtilfeen)
Intoo	Kintoo Ăam	btiḰtilfoo	(Kintoo miḰtilfeen)
Hinné	Kénoo Ăam	byiḰtilfoo	(Kénoo miḰtilfeen)

Future

Ana	Laĥ	iḰtilif
Inta	Laĥ	tiḰtilif
Inté	Laĥ	tiḰtilfé
Hoowé	Laĥ	yiḰtilif
Heeyé	Laĥ	tiḰtilif
Nahna	Laĥ	niḰtilif
Intoo	Laĥ	tiḰtilfoo
Hinné	Laĥ	yiḰtilfoo

Command

Inta	Ḱtilif
Inté	Ḱtilfé
Intoo	Ḱtilfoo
Inta	Ma tḰtilif
Inté	Ma tḰtilfé
Intoo	Ma tḰtilfoo

D

D

To differentiate

Present	
Ana	Bfarré'
Inta	Btfarré'
Inté	Btfarr'é
Hoowé	Bifarré'
Heeyé	Btfarré'
Naĥna	Mnfarré'
Intoo	Btfarr'oo
Hinné	Bifarr'oo

Present Continuous		
Ana	Ăam	Bfarré'
Inta	Ăam	Btfarré'
Inté	Ăam	Btfarr'é
Hoowé	Ăam	Bifarré'
Heeyé	Ăam	Btfarré'
Naĥna	Ăam	Mnfarré'
Intoo	Ăam	Btfarr'oo
Hinné	Ăam	Bifarr'oo

Past	
Ana	Farra't
Inta	Farra't
Inté	Farra'té
Hoowé	Farra'
Heeyé	Farra'ét
Naĥna	Farra'na
Intoo	Farra'too
Hinné	Farra'oo

Past Continuous		
Ana	Kint Ăam	Bfarré'
Inta	Kint Ăam	Btfarré'
Inté	Kinté Ăam	Btfarr'é
Hoowé	Kén Ăam	Bifarré'
Heeyé	Kénét Ăam	Btfarré'
Naĥna	Kinna Ăam	Mnfarré'
Intoo	Kintoo Ăam	Btfarr'oo
Hinné	Kénoo Ăam	Bifarr'oo

Future		
Ana	Laĥ	farré'
Inta	Laĥ	tfarré'
Inté	Laĥ	tfarr'é
Hoowé	Laĥ	yifarré'
Heeyé	Laĥ	tfarré'
Naĥna	Laĥ	nfarré'
Intoo	Laĥ	tfarr'oo
Hinné	Laĥ	yfarr'oo

Command	
Inta	Farré'
Inté	Farr'é
Intoo	Farr'oo
Inta	Ma tfarré'
Inté	Ma tfarr'é
Intoo	Ma tfarr'oo

To dig

Present	
Ana	Biĥfor
Inta	Btiĥfor
Inté	Btiĥfré
Hoowé	Byiĥfor
Heeyé	Btiĥfor
Naĥna	Mniĥfor
Intoo	Btiĥfroo
Hinné	Byiĥfroo

Present Continuous		
Ana	Ăam	Biĥfor
Inta	Ăam	Btiĥfor
Inté	Ăam	Btiĥfré
Hoowé	Ăam	Byiĥfor
Heeyé	Ăam	Btiĥfor
Naĥna	Ăam	Mniĥfor
Intoo	Ăam	Btiĥfroo
Hinné	Ăam	Byiĥfroo

Past	
Ana	Ĥafart
Inta	Ĥafart
Inté	Ĥafarté
Hoowé	Ĥafar
Heeyé	Ĥafarét
Naĥna	Ĥafarna
Intoo	Ĥafartoo
Hinné	Ĥafaroo

Past Continuous		
Ana	Kint Ăam	Biĥfor
Inta	Kint Ăam	Btiĥfor
Inté	Kinté Ăam	Btiĥfré
Hoowé	Kén Ăam	Byiĥfor
Heeyé	Kénét Ăam	Btiĥfor
Naĥna	Kinna Ăam	Mniĥfor
Intoo	Kintoo Ăam	Btiĥfroo
Hinné	Kénoo Ăam	Byiĥfroo

Future		
Ana	Laĥ	iĥfor
Inta	Laĥ	tiĥfor
Inté	Laĥ	tiĥfré
Hoowé	Laĥ	yiĥfor
Heeyé	Laĥ	tiĥfor
Naĥna	Laĥ	niĥfor
Intoo	Laĥ	tiĥfroo
Hinné	Laĥ	yiĥfroo

Command	
Inta	Ĥfor
Inté	Ĥfiré
Intoo	Ĥfiroo
Inta	Ma tĥfor
Inté	Ma tĥfré
Intoo	Ma tĥfroo

Ă= Augh in bought	Ď= a heavy D	É= like A in Bay	G= G in beige	ĥ= like an H with smaller air passage	I= I as in ink	Ќ= like ch in Irish loch
O= O as in home	OO= as in boots	R= roll the rrr	Ṫ= a heavy T	Ř= like a French R (gargle it)	Ŝ= a heavy S	Ž= a heavy Z

D   D

To digest

Present

Ana	bihĎom
Inta	btihĎom
Inté	btihĎmé
Hoowé	byihĎom
Heeyé	btihĎom
Nahna	mnihĎom
Intoo	btihĎmoo
Hinné	byihĎmoo

Present Continuous

Ana	Ăam	bihĎom
Inta	Ăam	btihĎom
Inté	Ăam	btihĎmé
Hoowé	Ăam	byihĎom
Heeyé	Ăam	btihĎom
Nahna	Ăam	mnihĎom
Intoo	Ăam	btihĎmoo
Hinné	Ăam	byihĎmoo

Past

Ana	haĎamt
Inta	haĎamt
Inté	haĎamté
Hoowé	haĎam
Heeyé	haĎamét
Nahna	haĎamna
Intoo	haĎamtoo
Hinné	haĎamoo

Past Continuous

Ana	Kint Ăam	bihĎom
Inta	Kint Ăam	btihĎom
Inté	Kinté Ăam	btihĎmé
Hoowé	Kén Ăam	byihĎom
Heeyé	Kénét Ăam	btihĎom
Nahna	Kinna Ăam	mnihĎom
Intoo	Kintoo Ăam	btihĎmoo
Hinné	Kénoo Ăam	byihĎmoo

Future

Ana	Laĥ	ihĎom
Inta	Laĥ	tihĎom
Inté	Laĥ	tihĎmé
Hoowé	Laĥ	yihĎom
Heeyé	Laĥ	tihĎom
Nahna	Laĥ	nihĎom
Intoo	Laĥ	tihĎmoo
Hinné	Laĥ	yihĎmoo

Command

Inta	hĎom
Inté	hĎimé
Intoo	hĎimoo
Inta	Ma thĎom
Inté	Ma thĎmé
Intoo	Ma thĎmoo

To dilute / To lighten

Present

Ana	bЌaffif
Inta	btЌaffif
Inté	btЌaffifé
Hoowé	biЌaffif
Heeyé	btЌaffif
Nahna	mnЌaffif
Intoo	btЌaffifoo
Hinné	biЌaffifoo

Present Continuous

Ana	Ăam	bЌaffif	(mЌaffaf/mЌaffafé)
Inta	Ăam	btЌaffif	(mЌaffaf)
Inté	Ăam	btЌaffifé	(mЌaffafé)
Hoowé	Ăam	biЌaffif	(mЌaffaf)
Heeyé	Ăam	btЌaffif	(mЌaffafé)
Nahna	Ăam	mnЌaffif	(mЌaffafeen)
Intoo	Ăam	btЌaffifoo	(mЌaffafeen)
Hinné	Ăam	biЌaffifoo	(mЌaffafeen)

Past

Ana	Ќaffaft
Inta	Ќaffaft
Inté	Ќaffafté
Hoowé	Ќaffaf
Heeyé	Ќaffafét
Nahna	Ќaffafna
Intoo	Ќaffaftoo
Hinné	Ќaffafoo

Past Continuous

Ana	Kint Ăam	bЌaffif	(kint	mЌaffaf/mЌaffafé)
Inta	Kint Ăam	btЌaffif	(Kint	mЌaffaf)
Inté	Kinté Ăam	btЌaffifé	(Kinté	mЌaffafé)
Hoowé	Kén Ăam	biЌaffif	(Kén	mЌaffaf)
Heeyé	Kénét Ăam	btЌaffif	(Kénét	mЌaffafé)
Nahna	Kinna Ăam	mnЌaffif	(Kinna	mЌaffafeen)
Intoo	Kintoo Ăam	btЌaffifoo	(Kintoo	mЌaffafeen)
Hinné	Kénoo Ăam	biЌaffifoo	(Kénoo	mЌaffafeen)

Future

Ana	Laĥ	Ќaffif
Inta	Laĥ	tЌaffif
Inté	Laĥ	tЌaffifé
Hoowé	Laĥ	yЌaffif
Heeyé	Laĥ	tЌaffif
Nahna	Laĥ	nЌaffif
Intoo	Laĥ	tЌaffifoo
Hinné	Laĥ	yЌaffifoo

Command

Inta	Ќaffif
Inté	Ќaffifé
Intoo	Ќaffifoo
Inta	Ma tЌaffif
Inté	Ma tЌaffifé
Intoo	Ma tЌaffifoo

Ă= Augh in bought	Ď= a heavy D	É= like A in Bay	G= G in beige	ĥ= like an H with smaller air passage	I= I as in ink	Ќ= like ch in Irish loch
O= O as in home	OO= as in boots	R= roll the rrr	Ť= a heavy T	Ř= like a French R (gargle it)	Ŝ= a heavy S	Ž= a heavy Z

D   D

To dip / (also To land)   To direct

Present	
Ana	bŘiŤŤ
Inta	btŘiŤŤ
Inté	btŘiŤŤé
Hoowé	biŘiŤŤ
Heeyé	btŘiŤŤ
Naḥna	mnŘiŤŤ
Intoo	btŘiŤŤoo
Hinné	biŘiŤŤoo

Present Continuous			
Ana	Ăam	bŘiŤŤ	(ŘaŤét/ŘaŤŤa)
Inta	Ăam	btŘiŤŤ	(ŘaŤét)
Inté	Ăam	btŘiŤŤé	(ŘaŤŤa)
Hoowé	Ăam	biŘiŤŤ	(ŘaŤŤét)
Heeyé	Ăam	btŘiŤŤ	(ŘaŤŤa)
Naḥna	Ăam	mnŘiŤŤ	(ŘaŤŤeen)
Intoo	Ăam	btŘiŤŤoo	(ŘaŤŤeen)
Hinné	Ăam	biŘiŤŤoo	(ŘaŤŤeen)

Past	
Ana	ŘaŤŤét
Inta	ŘaŤŤét
Inté	ŘaŤŤaité
Hoowé	ŘaŤŤ
Heeyé	ŘaŤŤét
Naḥna	ŘaŤŤaina
Intoo	ŘaŤŤaitoo
Hinné	ŘaŤŤoo

Past Continuous				
Ana	Kint Ăam	bŘiŤŤ	(kint	ŘaŤét/ŘaŤŤa)
Inta	Kint Ăam	btŘiŤŤ	(Kint	ŘaŤét)
Inté	Kinté Ăam	btŘiŤŤé	(Kinté	ŘaŤŤa)
Hoowé	Kén Ăam	biŘiŤŤ	(Kén	ŘaŤŤét)
Heeyé	Kénét Ăam	btŘiŤŤ	(Kénét	ŘaŤŤa)
Naḥna	Kinna Ăam	mnŘiŤŤ	(Kinna	ŘaŤŤeen)
Intoo	Kintoo Ăam	btŘiŤŤoo	(Kintoo	ŘaŤŤeen)
Hinné	Kénoo Ăam	biŘiŤŤoo	(Kénoo	ŘaŤŤeen)

Future		
Ana	Laḥ	ŘiŤŤ
Inta	Laḥ	tŘiŤŤ
Inté	Laḥ	tŘiŤŤé
Hoowé	Laḥ	yŘiŤŤ
Heeyé	Laḥ	tŘiŤŤ
Naḥna	Laḥ	nŘiŤŤ
Intoo	Laḥ	tŘiŤŤoo
Hinné	Laḥ	yŘiŤŤoo

Command	
Inta	ŘiŤŤ
Inté	ŘiŤŤé
Intoo	ŘiŤŤoo
Inta	Ma tŘiŤŤ
Inté	Ma tŘiŤŤé
Intoo	Ma tŘiŤŤoo

Present	
Ana	Bwaggéh
Inta	Btwaggéh
Inté	Btwagghé
Hoowé	Biwaggéh
Heeyé	Btwaggéh
Naḥna	Mnwaggéh
Intoo	Btwagghoo
Hinné	Biwagghoo

Present Continuous			
Ana	Ăam	Bwaggéh	(mwaggah/mwaggha)
Inta	Ăam	Btwaggéh	(mwaggah)
Inté	Ăam	Btwagghé	(mwaggha)
Hoowé	Ăam	Biwaggéh	(mwaggah)
Heeyé	Ăam	Btwaggéh	(mwaggha)
Naḥna	Ăam	Mnwaggéh	(mwaggheen)
Intoo	Ăam	Btwagghoo	(mwaggheen)
Hinné	Ăam	Biwagghoo	(mwaggheen)

Past	
Ana	Waggaht
Inta	Waggaht
Inté	Waggahté
Hoowé	Waggah
Heeyé	Waggahét
Naḥna	Waggahna
Intoo	Waggahtoo
Hinné	Waggahoo

Past Continuous				
Ana	Kint Ăam	Bwaggéh	(kint	mwaggah/mwaggha)
Inta	Kint Ăam	Btwaggéh	(Kint	mwaggah)
Inté	Kinté Ăam	Btwagghé	(Kinté	mwaggha)
Hoowé	Kén Ăam	Biwaggéh	(Kén	mwaggah)
Heeyé	Kénét Ăam	Btwaggéh	(Kénét	mwaggha)
Naḥna	Kinna Ăam	Mnwaggéh	(Kinna	mwaggheen)
Intoo	Kintoo Ăam	Btwagghoo	(Kintoo	mwaggheen)
Hinné	Kénoo Ăam	Biwagghoo	(Kénoo	mwaggheen)

Future		
Ana	Laḥ	Waggéh
Inta	Laḥ	twaggéh
Inté	Laḥ	twagghé
Hoowé	Laḥ	ywaggéh
Heeyé	Laḥ	twaggéh
Naḥna	Laḥ	nwaggéh
Intoo	Laḥ	twagghoo
Hinné	Laḥ	ywagghoo

Command	
Inta	Waggéh
Inté	Wagghé
Intoo	Wagghoo
Inta	Ma twaggéh
Inté	Ma twagghé
Intoo	Ma twagghoo

Ă= Augh in bought	Ď= a heavy D	É= like A in Bay	G= G in beige	ḥ= like an H with smaller air passage	I= I as in ink	Ķ= like ch in Irish loch
O= O as in home	OO= as in boots	R= roll the rrr	Ť= a heavy T	Ř= like a French R (gargle it)	Ŝ= a heavy S	Ž= a heavy Z

D   D

To dirty / To soil

Present	
Ana	bwasséK̇
Inta	btwasséK̇
Inté	btwassK̇é
Hoowé	biwasséK̇
Heeyé	btwasséK̇
Nahna	mnwasséK̇
Intoo	btwassK̇oo
Hinné	biwassK̇oo

Present Continuous			
Ana	Ăam	bwasséK̇	(mwassaK̇/mwassK̇a)
Inta	Ăam	btwasséK̇	(mwassaK̇)
Inté	Ăam	btwassK̇ó	(mwassK̇a)
Hoowé	Ăam	biwasséK̇	(mwassaK̇)
Heeyé	Ăam	btwasséK̇	(mwassK̇a)
Nahna	Ăam	mnwasséK̇	(mwassK̇een)
Intoo	Ăam	btwassK̇oo	(mwassK̇een)
Hinné	Ăam	biwassK̇oo	(mwassK̇een)

Past	
Ana	wassaK̇t
Inta	wassaK̇t
Inté	wassaK̇té
Hoowé	wassaK̇
Heeyé	wassaK̇ét
Nahna	wassaK̇na
Intoo	wassaK̇too
Hinné	wassaK̇oo

Past Continuous			
Ana	Kint Ăam	bwasséK̇	(kint mwassaK̇/mwassK̇a)
Inta	Kint Ăam	btwasséK̇	(Kint mwassaK̇)
Inté	Kinté Ăam	btwassK̇é	(Kinté mwassK̇a)
Hoowé	Kén Ăam	biwasséK̇	(Kén mwassaK̇)
Heeyé	Kénét Ăam	btwasséK̇	(Kénét mwassK̇a)
Nahna	Kinna Ăam	mnwasséK̇	(Kinna mwassK̇een)
Intoo	Kintoo Ăam	btwassK̇oo	(Kintoo mwassK̇een)
Hinné	Kénoo Ăam	biwassK̇oo	(Kénoo mwassK̇een)

Future		
Ana	Laĥ	wasséK̇
Inta	Laĥ	twasséK̇
Inté	Laĥ	twassK̇é
Hoowé	Laĥ	ywasséK̇
Heeyé	Laĥ	twasséK̇
Nahna	Laĥ	nwasséK̇
Intoo	Laĥ	twassK̇oo
Hinné	Laĥ	ywassK̇oo

Command	
Inta	wasséK̇
Inté	Wasské̇
Intoo	wassK̇oo
Inta	Ma twasséK̇
Inté	Ma twassK̇é
Intoo	Ma twassK̇oo

To dirty / To soil

Present	
Ana	Bigwé
Inta	Btigwé
Inté	Btigwé
Hoowé	Byigwé
Heeyé	Btigwé
Nahna	Mnigwé
Intoo	Btigwoo
Hinné	Byigwoo

Present Continuous			
Ana	Ăam	Bigwé	(géwé/géwyé)
Inta	Ăam	Btigwé	(géwé)
Inté	Ăam	Btigwé	(géwyé)
Hoowé	Ăam	Byigwé	(géwé)
Heeyé	Ăam	Btigwé	(géwyé)
Nahna	Ăam	Mnigwé	(géwyeen)
Intoo	Ăam	Btigwoo	(gewyeen)
Hinné	Ăam	Byigwoo	(gewyeen)

Past	
Ana	Gweet
Inta	Gweet
Inté	Gweeté
Hoowé	Giwé
Heeyé	Géwyét
Nahna	Gweena
Intoo	Gweetoo
Hinné	Gwyoo

Past Continuous			
Ana	Kint Ăam	Bigwé	(kint géwé/géwyé)
Inta	Kint Ăam	Btigwé	(Kint géwé)
Inté	Kinté Ăam	Btigwé	(Kinté géwyé)
Hoowé	Kén Ăam	Byigwé	(Kén géwé)
Heeyé	Kénét Ăam	Btigwé	(Kénét géwyé)
Nahna	Kinna Ăam	Mnigwé	(Kinna géwyeen)
Intoo	Kintoo Ăam	Btigwoo	(Kintoo gewyeen)
Hinné	Kénoo Ăam	Byigwoo	(Kénoo gewyeen)

Future		
Ana	Laĥ	igwé
Inta	Laĥ	tigwé
Inté	Laĥ	tigwé
Hoowé	Laĥ	yigwé
Heeyé	Laĥ	tigwé
Nahna	Laĥ	nigwé
Intoo	Laĥ	tigwoo
Hinné	Laĥ	yigwoo

Command	
Inta	Gwee
Inté	Gwee
Intoo	Gwoo
Inta	Ma tgwé
Inté	Ma tgwé
Intoo	Ma tgwoo

Ă= Augh in bought	Ď= a heavy D	É= like A in Bay	G= G in beige	ĥ= like an H with smaller air passage	I= I as in ink	K̇= like ch in Irish loch
O= O as in home	OO= as in boots	R= roll the rrr	Ť= a heavy T	Ř= like a French R (gargle it)	Ŝ= a heavy S	Ž= a heavy Z

D   D

To discipline   To discover

Present	
Ana	Bhazzéb
Inta	Bthazzéb
Inté	Bthazzbé
Hoowé	Bihazzéb
Heeyé	Bthazzéb
Naḥna	Mnhazzéb
Intoo	Bthazzboo
Hinné	Bihazzboo

Present Continuous		
Ana	Ăam	Bhazzéb
Inta	Ăam	Bthazzéb
Inté	Ăam	Bthazzbé
Hoowé	Ăam	Bihazzéb
Heeyé	Ăam	Bthazzéb
Naḥna	Ăam	Mnhazzéb
Intoo	Ăam	Bthazzboo
Hinné	Ăam	Bihazzboo

Past	
Ana	Hazzabt
Inta	Hazzabt
Inté	Hazzabté
Hoowé	Hazzab
Heeyé	Hazzabét
Naḥna	Hazzabna
Intoo	Hazzabtoo
Hinné	Hazzaboo

Past Continuous		
Ana	Kint Ăam	Bhazzéb
Inta	Kint Ăam	Bthazzéb
Inté	Kinté Ăam	Bthazzbé
Hoowé	Kén Ăam	Bihazzéb
Heeyé	Kénét Ăam	Bthazzéb
Naḥna	Kinna Ăam	Mnhazzéb
Intoo	Kintoo Ăam	Bthazzboo
Hinné	Kénoo Ăam	Bihazzboo

Future		
Ana	Laḥ	Hazzéb
Inta	Laḥ	Thazzéb
Inté	Laḥ	Thazzbé
Hoowé	Laḥ	yhazzéb
Heeyé	Laḥ	Thazzéb
Naḥna	Laḥ	nhazzéb
Intoo	Laḥ	thazzboo
Hinné	Laḥ	yhazzboo

Command	
Inta	Hazzéb
Inté	Hazzbé
Intoo	Hazzboo
Inta	Ma thazzéb
Inté	Ma thazzbé
Intoo	Ma thazzboo

Present	
Ana	Biktishif
Inta	Btiktishif
Inté	Btiktishfé
Hoowé	Byiktishif
Heeyé	Btiktishif
Naḥna	Mniktishif
Intoo	Btiktishfoo
Hinné	Byiktishfoo

Present Continuous		
Ana	Ăam	Biktishif
Inta	Ăam	Btiktishif
Inté	Ăam	Btiktishfé
Hoowé	Ăam	Byiktishif
Heeyé	Ăam	Btiktishif
Naḥna	Ăam	Mniktishif
Intoo	Ăam	Btiktishfoo
Hinné	Ăam	Byiktishfoo

Past	
Ana	Ktashaft
Inta	Ktashaft
Inté	Ktashafté
Hoowé	Ktashaf
Heeyé	Ktashafét
Naḥna	Ktashafna
Intoo	Ktashaftoo
Hinné	Ktashafoo

Past Continuous		
Ana	Kint Ăam	Biktishif
Inta	Kint Ăam	Btiktishif
Inté	Kinté Ăam	Btiktishfé
Hoowé	Kén Ăam	Byiktishif
Heeyé	Kénét Ăam	Btiktishif
Naḥna	Kinna Ăam	Mniktishif
Intoo	Kintoo Ăam	Btiktishfoo
Hinné	Kénoo Ăam	Byiktishfoo

Future		
Ana	Laḥ	Iktishif
Inta	Laḥ	Tiktishif
Inté	Laḥ	Tiktishfé
Hoowé	Laḥ	Yiktishif
Heeyé	Laḥ	Tiktishif
Naḥna	Laḥ	Niktishif
Intoo	Laḥ	Tiktishfoo
Hinné	Laḥ	Yiktishfoo

Command	
Inta	Ktishif
Inté	Ktishfé
Intoo	Ktishfoo
Inta	Ma tktishif
Inté	Ma tktishfé
Intoo	Ma tktishfoo

Ă= Augh in bought	Ď= a heavy D	É= like A in Bay	G= G in beige	ḥ= like an H with smaller air passage	I= I as in ink	Ǩ= like ch in Irish loch
O= O as in home	OO= as in boots	R= roll the rrr	Ť= a heavy T	Ř= like a French R (gargle it)	Š= a heavy S	Ž= a heavy Z

D

D

To diguise

Present

Ana	Bitnakkar
Inta	Btitnakkar
Inté	Btitnakkaré
Hoowé	Byitnakkar
Heeyé	Btitnakkar
Nahna	Mnitnakkar
Intoo	Btitnakkaroo
Hinné	Byitnakkaroo

Present Continuous

Ana	Ăam Bitnakkar	(mtnakkar/mtnakkara)
Inta	Ăam Btitnakkar	(mtnakkar)
Inté	Ăam Btitnakkaré	(mtnakkara)
Hoowé	Ăam Byitnakkar	(mtnakkar)
Heeyé	Ăam Btitnakkar	(mtnakkara)
Nahna	Ăam Mnitnakkar	(mtnakkareen)
Intoo	Ăam Btitnakkaroo	(mtnakkareen)
Hinné	Ăam Byitnakkaroo	(mtnakkareen)

Past

Ana	Tnakkart
Inta	Tnakkart
Inté	Tnakkarté
Hoowé	Tnakkar
Heeyé	Tnakkarét
Nahna	Tnakkarna
Intoo	Tnakkartoo
Hinné	Tnakkaroo

Past Continuous

Ana	Kint Ăam	Bitnakkar	(kint	mtnakkar/mtnakkara)
Inta	Kint Ăam	Btitnakkar	(Kint	mtnakkar)
Inté	Kinté Ăam	Btitnakkaré	(Kinté	mtnakkara)
Hoowé	Kén Ăam	Byitnakkar	(Kén	mtnakkar)
Heeyé	Kénét Ăam	Btitnakkar	(Kénét	mtnakkara)
Nahna	Kinna Ăam	Mnitnakkar	(Kinna	mtnakkareen)
Intoo	Kintoo Ăam	Btitnakkaroo	(Kintoo	mtnakkareen)
Hinné	Kénoo Ăam	Byitnakkaroo	(Kénoo	mtnakkareen)

Future

Ana	Lah	Itnakkar
Inta	Lah	Titnakkar
Inté	Lah	Titnakkaré
Hoowé	Lah	Yitnakkar
Heeyé	Lah	Titnakkar
Nahna	Lah	Nitnakkar
Intoo	Lah	Titnakkaroo
Hinné	Lah	Yitnakkaroo

Command

Inta	Tnakkar
Inté	Tnakkaré
Intoo	Tnakkaroo
Inta	Ma ttnakkar
Inté	Ma ttnakkaré
Intoo	Ma ttnakkaroo

To distribute

Present

Ana	bwazzéĂ
Inta	btwazzéĂ
Inté	btwazzĂé
Hoowé	biwazzéĂ
Heeyé	btwazzéĂ
Nahna	mnwazzéĂ
Intoo	btwazzĂoo
Hinné	biwazzĂoo

Present Continuous

Ana	Ăam	bwazzéĂ
Inta	Ăam	btwazzéĂ
Inté	Ăam	btwazzĂé
Hoowé	Ăam	biwazzéĂ
Heeyé	Ăam	btwazzéĂ
Nahna	Ăam	mnwazzéĂ
Intoo	Ăam	btwazzĂoo
Hinné	Ăam	biwazzĂoo

Past

Ana	wazzzaĂt
Inta	wazzzaĂt
Inté	wazzzaĂté
Hoowé	wazzzaĂ
Heeyé	wazzzaĂét
Nahna	wazzzaĂna
Intoo	wazzzaĂtoo
Hinné	WazzzaĂoo

Past Continuous

Ana	Kint Ăam	bwazzéĂ
Inta	Kint Ăam	btwazzéĂ
Inté	Kinté Ăam	btwazzĂé
Hoowé	Kén Ăam	biwazzéĂ
Heeyé	Kénét Ăam	btwazzéĂ
Nahna	Kinna Ăam	mnwazzéĂ
Intoo	Kintoo Ăam	btwazzĂoo
Hinné	Kénoo Ăam	biwazzĂoo

Future

Ana	Lah	wazzéĂ
Inta	Lah	twazzéĂ
Inté	Lah	twazzĂé
Hoowé	Lah	ywazzéĂ
Heeyé	Lah	twazzéĂ
Nahna	Lah	nwazzéĂ
Intoo	Lah	twazzĂoo
Hinné	Lah	ywazzĂoo

Command

Inta	wazzéĂ
Inté	wazzĂé
Intoo	wazzĂoo
Inta	Ma twazzéĂ
Inté	Ma twazzĂé
Intoo	Ma twazzĂoo

Ă= Augh in bought	Ď= a heavy D	É= like A in Bay	G= G in beige	ĥ= like an H with smaller air passage	I= I as in ink	Ḱ= like ch in Irish loch
O= O as in home	OO= as in boots	R= roll the rrr	Ť= a heavy T	Ř= like a French R (gargle it)	Ŝ= a heavy S	Ž= a heavy Z

D   D

To dive

Present

Ana	biŘŤoŠ
Inta	btiŘŤoŠ
Inté	btiŘŤŠé
Hoowé	byiŘŤoŠ
Heeyé	btiŘŤoŠ
Naĥna	mniŘŤoŠ
Intoo	btiŘŤŠoo
Hinné	byiŘŤŠoo

Present Continuous

Ana	Ăam	biŘŤoŠ
Inta	Ăam	btiŘŤoŠ
Inté	Ăam	btiŘŤŠé
Hoowé	Ăam	byiŘŤoŠ
Heeyé	Ăam	btiŘŤoŠ
Naĥna	Ăam	mniŘŤoŠ
Intoo	Ăam	btiŘŤŠoo
Hinné	Ăam	byiŘŤŠoo

Past

Ana	ŘaŤaŠt
Inta	ŘaŤaŠt
Inté	ŘaŤaŠté
Hoowé	ŘaŤaŠ
Heeyé	ŘaŤaŠét
Naĥna	ŘaŤaŠna
Intoo	ŘaŤaŠtoo
Hinné	ŘaŤaŠoo

Past Continuous

Ana	Kint Ăam	biŘŤoŠ
Inta	Kint Ăam	btiŘŤoŠ
Inté	Kinté Ăam	btiŘŤŠé
Hoowé	Kén Ăam	byiŘŤoŠ
Heeyé	Kénét Ăam	btiŘŤoŠ
Naĥna	Kinna Ăam	mniŘŤoŠ
Intoo	Kintoo Ăam	btiŘŤŠoo
Hinné	Kénoo Ăam	byiŘŤŠoo

Future

Ana	Laĥ	iŘŤoŠ
Inta	Laĥ	tiŘŤoŠ
Inté	Laĥ	tiŘŤŠé
Hoowé	Laĥ	yiŘŤoŠ
Heeyé	Laĥ	tiŘŤoŠ
Naĥna	Laĥ	niŘŤoŠ
Intoo	Laĥ	tiŘŤŠoo
Hinné	Laĥ	yiŘŤŠoo

Command

Inta	ŘŤoŠ
Inté	ŘŤiŠé
Intoo	ŘŤiŠoo
Inta	Ma tŘŤoŠ
Inté	Ma tŘŤŠé
Intoo	Ma tŘŤŠoo

To divide

Present

Ana	Bi'Šom
Inta	Bti'Šom
Inté	Bti'Šmé
Hoowé	Byi'Šom
Heeyé	Bti'Šom
Naĥna	Mni'Šom
Intoo	Bti'Šmoo
Hinné	Byi'Šmoo

Present Continuous

Ana	Ăam	Bi'Šom
Inta	Ăam	Bti'Šom
Inté	Ăam	Bti'Šmé
Hoowé	Ăam	Byi'Šom
Heeyé	Ăam	Bti'Šom
Naĥna	Ăam	Mni'Šom
Intoo	Ăam	Bti'Šmoo
Hinné	Ăam	Byi'Šmoo

Past

Ana	aŠamt
Inta	aŠamt
Inté	aŠamté
Hoowé	aŠam
Heeyé	aŠamét
Naĥna	aŠamna
Intoo	aŠamtoo
Hinné	aŠamoo

Past Continuous

Ana	Kint Ăam	Bi'Šom
Inta	Kint Ăam	Bti'Šom
Inté	Kinté Ăam	Bti'Šmé
Hoowé	Kén Ăam	Byi'Šom
Heeyé	Kénét Ăam	Bti'Šom
Naĥna	Kinna Ăam	Mni'Šom
Intoo	Kintoo Ăam	Bti'Šmoo
Hinné	Kénoo Ăam	Byi'Šmoo

Future

Ana	Laĥ	i'Šom
Inta	Laĥ	ti'Šom
Inté	Laĥ	ti'Šmé
Hoowé	Laĥ	yi'Šom
Heeyé	Laĥ	ti'Šom
Naĥna	Laĥ	ni'Šom
Intoo	Laĥ	ti'Šmoo
Hinné	Laĥ	yi'Šmoo

Command

Inta	'Šom
Inté	'Šimé
Intoo	'Šimoo
Inta	Ma t'Šom
Inté	Ma t'Šmé
Intoo	Ma t'Šmoo

Ă= Augh in bought	Ď= a heavy D	É= like A in Bay	G= G in beige	ĥ= like an H with smaller air passage	I= I as in ink	Ќ= like ch in Irish loch
O= O as in home	OO= as in boots	R= roll the rrr	Ť= a heavy T	Ř= like a French R (gargle it)	Š= a heavy S	Ž= a heavy Z

D

D

To donate

Present	
Ana	Bimnaĥ
Inta	Btimnaĥ
Inté	Btimnahé
Hoowé	Byimnaĥ
Heeyé	Btimnaĥ
Naĥna	Mnimnaĥ
Intoo	Btimnaĥoo
Hinné	Byimnaĥoo

Present Continuous		
Ana	Ăam	Bimnaĥ
Inta	Ăam	Btimnaĥ
Inté	Ăam	Btimnahé
Hoowé	Ăam	Byimnaĥ
Heeyé	Ăam	Btimnaĥ
Naĥna	Ăam	Mnimnaĥ
Intoo	Ăam	Btimnaĥoo
Hinné	Ăam	Byimnaĥoo

Past	
Ana	Manaĥt
Inta	Manaĥt
Inté	Manaĥté
Hoowé	Manaĥ
Heeyé	Manaĥét
Naĥna	Manaĥna
Intoo	Manaĥtoo
Hinné	Manaĥoo

Past Continuous		
Ana	Kint Ăam	Bimnaĥ
Inta	Kint Ăam	Btimnaĥ
Inté	Kinté Ăam	Btimnahé
Hoowé	Kén Ăam	Byimnaĥ
Heeyé	Kénét Ăam	Btimnaĥ
Naĥna	Kinna Ăam	Mnimnaĥ
Intoo	Kintoo Ăam	Btimnaĥoo
Hinné	Kénoo Ăam	Byimnaĥoo

Future		
Ana	Laĥ	Imnaĥ
Inta	Laĥ	Timnaĥ
Inté	Laĥ	Timnahé
Hoowé	Laĥ	Yimnaĥ
Heeyé	Laĥ	Timnaĥ
Naĥna	Laĥ	Nimnaĥ
Intoo	Laĥ	Timnaĥoo
Hinné	Laĥ	Yimnaĥoo

Command	
Inta	Mnaĥ
Inté	Mnahé
Intoo	Mnaĥoo
Inta	Ma tmnaĥ
Inté	Ma tmnahé
Intoo	Ma tmnaĥoo

To doubt

Present	
Ana	Bshikk
Inta	Btshikk
Inté	Btshikké
Hoowé	Bishikk
Heeyé	Btshikk
Naĥna	Mnshikk
Intoo	Btshikkoo
Hinné	Bishikkoo

Present Continuous			
Ana	Ăam	Bshikk	(shékék/shékké)
Inta	Ăam	Btshikk	(shékék)
Inté	Ăam	Btshikké	(shékké)
Hoowé	Ăam	Bishikk	(shékék)
Heeyé	Ăam	Btshikk	(shékké)
Naĥna	Ăam	Mnshikk	(shékeen)
Intoo	Ăam	Btshikkoo	(shékeen)
Hinné	Ăam	Bishikkoo	(shékeen)

Past	
Ana	Shakkét
Inta	Shakkét
Inté	Shakkaité
Hoowé	Shakk
Heeyé	Shakkét
Naĥna	Shakkaina
Intoo	Shakkaitoo
Hinné	Shakkoo

Past Continuous			
Ana	Kint Ăam	Bshikk	(kint shékék/shékké)
Inta	Kint Ăam	Btshikk	(Kint shékék)
Inté	Kinté Ăam	Btshikké	(Kinté shékké)
Hoowé	Kén Ăam	Bishikk	(Kén shékék)
Heeyé	Kénét Ăam	Btshikk	(Kénét shékké)
Naĥna	Kinna Ăam	Mnshikk	(Kinna shékeen)
Intoo	Kintoo Ăam	Btshikkoo	(Kintoo shékeen)
Hinné	Kénoo Ăam	Bishikkoo	(Kénoo shékeen)

Future		
Ana	Laĥ	shikk
Inta	Laĥ	tshikk
Inté	Laĥ	tshikké
Hoowé	Laĥ	yshikk
Heeyé	Laĥ	tshikk
Naĥna	Laĥ	nshikk
Intoo	Laĥ	tshikkoo
Hinné	Laĥ	yshikkoo

Command	
Inta	Shikk
Inté	Shikké
Intoo	Shikkoo
Inta	Ma tshikk
Inté	Ma tshikké
Intoo	Ma tshikkoo

Ă= Augh in bought	Đ= a heavy D	É= like A in Bay	G= G in beige	ĥ= like an H with smaller air passage	I= I as in ink	Ķ= like ch in Irish loch
O= O as in home	OO= as in boots	R= roll the rrr	Ť= a heavy T	Ř= like a French R (gargle it)	Ŝ= a heavy S	Ž= a heavy Z

D   D

To drag

Present	
Ana	Bgirr
Inta	Btgirr
Inté	Btgirré
Hoowé	Bigirr
Heeyé	Btgirr
Nahna	Mngirr
Intoo	Btgirroo
Hinné	Bigirroo

Present Continuous		
Ana	Ăam Bgirr	(gérér/gérra)
Inta	Ăam Btgirr	(gérér)
Inté	Ăam Btgirré	(gérra)
Hoowé	Ăam Bigirr	(gérér)
Heeyé	Ăam Btgirr	(gerra)
Nahna	Ăam Mngirr	(gérreen)
Intoo	Ăam Btgirroo	(gérreen)
Hinné	Ăam Bigirroo	(gérreen)

Past	
Ana	Garrét
Inta	Garrét
Inté	Garraité
Hoowé	Garr
Heeyé	Garrét
Nahna	Garraina
Intoo	Garraitoo
Hinné	Garroo

Past Continuous		
Ana	Kint Ăam Bgirr	(kint gérér/gérra)
Inta	Kint Ăam Btgirr	(Kint gérér)
Inté	Kinté Ăam Btgirré	(Kinté gérra)
Hoowé	Kén Ăam Bigirr	(Kén gérér)
Heeyé	Kénét Ăam Btgirr	(Kénét gerra)
Nahna	Kinna Ăam Mngirr	(Kinna gérreen)
Intoo	Kintoo Ăam Btgirroo	(Kintoo gérreen)
Hinné	Kénoo Ăam Bigirroo	(Kénoo gérreen)

Future		
Ana	Lah	Girr
Inta	Lah	Tgirr
Inté	Lah	Tgirré
Hoowé	Lah	Ygirr
Heeyé	Lah	Tgirr
Nahna	Lah	Ngirr
Intoo	Lah	Tgirroo
Hinné	Lah	Ygirroo

Command	
Inta	Girr
Inté	Girré
Intoo	Girroo
Inta	Ma tgirr
Inté	Ma tgirré
Intoo	Ma tgirroo

To draw

Present	
Ana	Birsom
Inta	Btirsom
Inté	Btirsmé
Hoowé	Byirsom
Heeyé	Btirsom
Nahna	Mnirsom
Intoo	Btirsmoo
Hinné	Byirsmoo

Present Continuous	
Ana	Ăam Birsom
Inta	Ăam Btirsom
Inté	Ăam Btirsmé
Hoowé	Ăam Byirsom
Heeyé	Ăam Btirsom
Nahna	Ăam Mnirsom
Intoo	Ăam Btirsmoo
Hinné	Ăam Byirsmoo

Past	
Ana	Rasamt
Inta	Rasamt
Inté	Sarasmté
Hoowé	Rasam
Heeyé	Rasamét
Nahna	Rasamna
Intoo	Rasamtoo
Hinné	Rasamoo

Past Continuous	
Ana	Kint Ăam Birsom
Inta	Kint Ăam Btirsom
Inté	Kinté Ăam Btirsmé
Hoowé	Kén Ăam Byirsom
Heeyé	Kénét Ăam Btirsom
Nahna	Kinna Ăam Mnirsom
Intoo	Kintoo Ăam Btirsmoo
Hinné	Kénoo Ăam Byirsmoo

Future		
Ana	Lah	Irsom
Inta	Lah	Tirsom
Inté	Lah	Tirmé
Hoowé	Lah	Yirsom
Heeyé	Lah	Tirsom
Nahna	Lah	Nirsom
Intoo	Lah	Tirsmoo
Hinné	Lah	Yirsmoo

Command	
Inta	Rsom
Inté	Rsimé
Intoo	Rsimoo
Inta	Ma trsom
Inté	Ma trsmé
Intoo	Ma trsmoo

Ă= Augh in bought	Ď= a heavy D	É= like A in Bay	G= G in beige	ĥ= like an H with smaller air passage	I= I as in ink	Ķ= like ch in Irish loch
O= O as in home	OO= as in boots	R= roll the rrr	Ť= a heavy T	Ř= like a French R (gargle it)	Š= a heavy S	Ž= a heavy Z

D

D

To dream

Present

Ana	Biĥlam
Inta	Btiĥlam
Inté	Btiĥlamé
Hoowé	Byiĥlam
Heeyé	Btiĥlam
Naĥna	Mniĥlam
Intoo	Btiĥlamoo
Hinné	Byiĥlamoo

Present Continuous

Ana	Ăam	Biĥlam	(ĥélém/ĥélmé)
Inta	Ăam	Btiĥlam	(ĥélém)
Inté	Ăam	Btiĥlamé	(ĥélmé)
Hoowé	Ăam	Byiĥlam	(ĥélém)
Heeyé	Ăam	Btiĥlam	(ĥélmé)
Naĥna	Ăam	Mniĥlam	(ĥélmeen)
Intoo	Ăam	Btiĥlamoo	(ĥélmeen)
Hinné	Ăam	Byiĥlamoo	(ĥélmeen)

Past

Ana	Ĥlimt
Inta	Ĥlimt
Inté	Ĥlimté
Hoowé	Ĥilim
Heeyé	Ĥilmét
Naĥna	Ĥlimna
Intoo	Ĥlimtoo
Hinné	Ĥlimoo

Past Continuous

Ana	Kint Ăam	Biĥlam	(kint ĥélém/ĥélmé)
Inta	Kint Ăam	Btiĥlam	(Kint ĥélém)
Inté	Kinté Ăam	Btiĥlamé	(Kinté ĥélmé)
Hoowé	Kén Ăam	Byiĥlam	(Kén ĥélém)
Heeyé	Kénét Ăam	Btiĥlam	(Kénét ĥélmé)
Naĥna	Kinna Ăam	Mniĥlam	(Kinna ĥélmeen)
Intoo	Kintoo Ăam	Btiĥlamoo	(Kintoo ĥélmeen)
Hinné	Kénoo Ăam	Byiĥlamoo	(Kénoo ĥélmeen)

Future

Ana	Laĥ	Iĥlam
Inta	Laĥ	Tiĥlam
Inté	Laĥ	Tiĥlamé
Hoowé	Laĥ	Yiĥlam
Heeyé	Laĥ	Tiĥlam
Naĥna	Laĥ	Niĥlam
Intoo	Laĥ	Tiĥlamoo
Hinné	Laĥ	Yiĥlamoo

Command

Inta	Ĥlam
Inté	ĥlamé
Intoo	Ĥlimtoo
Inta	Ma tĥlam
Inté	Ma tĥlamé
Intoo	Ma tĥlamoo

To drink

Present

Ana	Bishrab
Inta	Btishrab
Inté	Btishrabé
Hoowé	Byishrab
Heeyé	Btishrab
Naĥna	Mnishrab
Intoo	Btishraboo
Hinné	Byishraboo

Present Continuous

Ana	Ăam	Bishrab	(shéréb/shérbé)
Inta	Ăam	Btishrab	(shéréb)
Inté	Ăam	Btishrabé	(shérbé)
Hoowé	Ăam	Byishrab	(shéréb)
Heeyé	Ăam	Btishrab	(shérbé)
Naĥna	Ăam	Mnishrab	(shérbeen)
Intoo	Ăam	Btishraboo	(shérbeen)
Hinné	Ăam	Byishraboo	(shérbeen)

Past

Ana	Shribt
Inta	Shribt
Inté	Shribté
Hoowé	Shiréb
Heeyé	Shirbét
Naĥna	Shribna
Intoo	Shribtoo
Hinné	Shirboo

Past Continuous

Ana	Kint Ăam	Bishrab	(kint shéréb/shérbé)
Inta	Kint Ăam	Btishrab	(Kint shéréb)
Inté	Kinté Ăam	Btishrabé	(Kinté shérbé)
Hoowé	Kén Ăam	Byishrab	(Kén shéréb)
Heeyé	Kénét Ăam	Btishrab	(Kénét shérbé)
Naĥna	Kinna Ăam	Mnishrab	(Kinna shérbeen)
Intoo	Kintoo Ăam	Btishraboo	(Kintoo shérbeen)
Hinné	Kénoo Ăam	Byishraboo	(Kénoo shérbeen)

Future

Ana	Laĥ	Ishrab
Inta	Laĥ	Tishrab
Inté	Laĥ	Tishrabé
Hoowé	Laĥ	Yishrab
Heeyé	Laĥ	Tishrab
Naĥna	Laĥ	Nishrab
Intoo	Laĥ	Tishraboo
Hinné	Laĥ	Yishraboo

Command

Inta	Shrab
Inté	Shrabé
Intoo	Shraboo
Inta	Ma tshrab
Inté	Ma tshrabé
Intoo	Ma tshraboo

Ă= Augh in bought	Đ= a heavy D	É= like A in Bay	G= G in beige	ĥ= like an H with smaller air passage	I= I as in ink	Ḱ= like ch in Irish loch
O= O as in home	OO= as in boots	R= roll the rrr	Ť= a heavy T	Ř= like a French R (gargle it)	Ŝ= a heavy S	Ž= a heavy Z

D

D

To drive

Present	
Ana	Bsoo'
Inta	Btsoo'
Inté	Btsoo'é
Hoowé	Bisoo'
Heeyé	Btsoo'
Nahna	Mnsoo'
Intoo	Btsoo'oo
Hinné	Bisoo'oo

Present Continuous			
Ana	Ăam	Bsoo'	(séyé'/séy'a)
Inta	Ăam	Btsoo'	(séyé')
Inté	Ăam	Btsoo'é	(séy'a)
Hoowé	Ăam	Bisoo'	(séyé')
Heeyé	Ăam	Btsoo'	(séy'a)
Nahna	Ăam	Mnsoo'	(séy'een)
Intoo	Ăam	Btsoo'oo	(séy'een)
Hinné	Ăam	Bisoo'oo	(séy'een)

Past	
Ana	Si't
Inta	Si't
Inté	Si'té
Hoowé	Sé'
Heeyé	Se'ét
Nahna	Si'na
Intoo	Si'too
Hinné	Sé'oo

Past Continuous			
Ana	Kint Ăam	Bsoo'	(kint séyé'/séy'a)
Inta	Kint Ăam	Btsoo'	(Kint séyé')
Inté	Kinté Ăam	Btsoo'é	(Kinté séy'a)
Hoowé	Kén Ăam	Bisoo'	(Kén séyé')
Heeyé	Kénét Ăam	Btsoo'	(Kénét séy'a)
Nahna	Kinna Ăam	Mnsoo'	(Kinna séy'een)
Intoo	Kintoo Ăam	Btsoo'oo	(Kintoo séy'een)
Hinné	Kénoo Ăam	Bisoo'oo	(Kénoo séy'een)

Future		
Ana	Lah	Soo'
Inta	Lah	Tsoo'
Inté	Lah	Tsoo'é
Hoowé	Lah	Ysoo'
Heeyé	Lah	Tsoo'
Nahna	Lah	Nsoo'
Intoo	Lah	Tsoo'oo
Hinné	Lah	Ysoo'oo

Command	
Inta	Soo'
Inté	Soo'é
Intoo	Soo'oo
Inta	Ma tsoo'
Inté	Ma tsoo'é
Intoo	Ma tsoo'oo

To drop

Present	
Ana	Bwa''éĂ
Inta	Btwa''éĂ
Inté	Btwa''Ăé
Hoowé	Biwa''éĂ
Heeyé	Btwa''éĂ
Nahna	Mnwa''éĂ
Intoo	Btwa''Ăoo
Hinné	Biwa''Ăoo

Present Continuous		
Ana	Ăam	Bwa''éĂ
Inta	Ăam	Btwa''éĂ
Inté	Ăam	Btwa''Ăé
Hoowé	Ăam	Biwa''éĂ
Heeyé	Ăam	Btwa''éĂ
Nahna	Ăam	Mnwa''éĂ
Intoo	Ăam	Btwa''Ăoo
Hinné	Ăam	Biwa''Ăoo

Past	
Ana	Wa''aĂt
Inta	Wa''aĂt
Inté	Wa''aĂté
Hoowé	Wa''aĂ
Heeyé	Wa''aĂét
Nahna	Wa''aĂna
Intoo	Wa''aĂtoo
Hinné	Wa''aĂoo

Past Continuous		
Ana	Kint Ăam	Bwa''éĂ
Inta	Kint Ăam	Btwa''éĂ
Inté	Kinté Ăam	Btwa''Ăé
Hoowé	Kén Ăam	Biwa''éĂ
Heeyé	Kénét Ăam	Btwa''éĂ
Nahna	Kinna Ăam	Mnwa''éĂ
Intoo	Kintoo Ăam	Btwa''Ăoo
Hinné	Kénoo Ăam	Biwa''Ăoo

Future		
Ana	Lah	wa''éĂ
Inta	Lah	twa''éĂ
Inté	Lah	twa''Ăé
Hoowé	Lah	ywa''éĂ
Heeyé	Lah	twa''éĂ
Nahna	Lah	Nwa''éĂ
Intoo	Lah	twa''Ăoo
Hinné	Lah	Ywa''Ăoo

Command	
Inta	Wa''éĂ
Inté	Wa''Ăé
Intoo	Wa''Ăoo
Inta	Ma twa''éĂ
Inté	Ma twa''Ăé
Intoo	Ma twa''Ăoo

Ă= Augh in bought	Ď= a heavy D	É= like A in Bay	G= G in beige	ĥ= like an H with smaller air passage	I= I as in ink	Ќ= like ch in Irish loch
O= O as in home	OO= as in boots	R= roll the rrr	Ť= a heavy T	Ř= like a French R (gargle it)	Ŝ= a heavy S	Ž= a heavy Z

D   D

To drown / To sink

Present

Ana	biǓra'
Inta	btiǓra'
Inté	btiǓra'é
Hoowé	byiǓra'
Heeyé	btiǓra'
Nahna	mniǓra'
Intoo	btiǓra'oo
Hinné	byiǓra'oo

Present Continuous

Ana	Ăam	biǓra'	(Ǔir'an/Ǔir'ané)
Inta	Ăam	btiǓra'	(Ǔir'an)
Inté	Ăam	btiǓra'é	(Ǔir'ané)
Hoowé	Ăam	byiǓra'	(Ǔir'an)
Heeyé	Ăam	btiǓra'	(Ǔir'ané)
Nahna	Ăam	mniǓra'	(Ǔir'aneen)
Intoo	Ăam	btiǓra'oo	(Ǔir'aneen)
Hinné	Ăam	byiǓra'oo	(Ǔir'aneen)

Past

Ana	Ǔri't
Inta	Ǔri't
Inté	Ǔri'té
Hoowé	Ǔiri'
Heeyé	Ǔiri'ét
Nahna	Ǔri'na
Intoo	Ǔri'too
Hinné	Ǔri'oo

Past Continuous

Ana	Kint Ăam	biǓra'	(kint	(Ǔir'an/Ǔir'ané)
Inta	Kint Ăam	btiǓra'	(Kint	(Ǔir'an)
Inté	Kinté Ăam	btiǓra'é	(Kinté	(Ǔir'ané)
Hoowé	Kén Ăam	byiǓra'	(Kén	(Ǔir'an)
Heeyé	Kénét Ăam	btiǓra'	(Kénét	(Ǔir'ané)
Nahna	Kinna Ăam	mniǓra'	(Kinna	(Ǔir'aneen)
Intoo	Kintoo Ăam	btiǓra'oo	(Kintoo	(Ǔir'aneen)
Hinné	Kénoo Ăam	byiǓra'oo	(Kénoo	(Ǔir'aneen)

Future

Ana	Laĥ	iǓra'
Inta	Laĥ	tiǓra'
Inté	Laĥ	tiǓra'é
Hoowé	Laĥ	yiǓra'
Heeyé	Laĥ	tiǓra'
Nahna	Laĥ	niǓra'
Intoo	Laĥ	tiǓra'oo
Hinné	Laĥ	yiǓra'oo

Command

Inta	Ǔra'
Inté	Ǔra'é
Intoo	Ǔra'oo
Inta	Ma tǓra'
Inté	Ma tǓra'é
Intoo	Ma tǓra'oo

To dry

Present

Ana	Bnashéf
Inta	Btnashéf
Inté	Btnashfé
Hoowé	Binashéf
Heeyé	Btnashéf
Nahna	Mnnashéf
Intoo	Btnashfoo
Hinné	Binashfoo

Present Continuous

Ana	Ăam	Bnashéf
Inta	Ăam	Btnashéf
Inté	Ăam	Btnashfé
Hoowé	Ăam	Binashéf
Heeyé	Ăam	Btnashéf
Nahna	Ăam	Mnnashéf
Intoo	Ăam	Btnashfoo
Hinné	Ăam	Binashfoo

Past

Ana	Nashaft
Inta	Nashaft
Inté	Nashafté
Hoowé	Nashaf
Heeyé	Nashafét
Nahna	Nashafna
Intoo	Nashaftoo
Hinné	Nashafoo

Past Continuous

Ana	Kint Ăam	Bnashéf
Inta	Kint Ăam	Btnashéf
Inté	Kinté Ăam	Btnashfé
Hoowé	Kén Ăam	Binashéf
Heeyé	Kénét Ăam	Btnashéf
Nahna	Kinna Ăam	Mnnashéf
Intoo	Kintoo Ăam	Btnashfoo
Hinné	Kénoo Ăam	Binashfoo

Future

Ana	Laĥ	nashéf
Inta	Laĥ	tnashéf
Inté	Laĥ	tnashfé
Hoowé	Laĥ	ynashéf
Heeyé	Laĥ	tnashéf
Nahna	Laĥ	nnashéf
Intoo	Laĥ	tnashfoo
Hinné	Laĥ	ynashfoo

Command

Inta	Nashéf
Inté	Nashfé
Intoo	Nashfoo
Inta	Ma tnashéf
Inté	Ma tnashfé
Intoo	Ma tnashfoo

Ă= Augh in bought	Đ= a heavy D	É= like A in Bay	G= G in beige	ĥ= like an H with smaller air passage	I= I as in ink	Ḱ= like ch in Irish loch
O= O as in home	OO= as in boots	R= roll the rrr	Ť= a heavy T	Ǔ= like a French R (gargle it)	Ŝ= a heavy S	Ž= a heavy Z

D

E

To dye

Present	
Ana	biŠboŘ
Inta	btiŠboŘ
Inté	btiŠbŘé
Hoowé	byiŠboŘ
Heeyé	btiŠboŘ
Naĥna	mniŠboŘ
Intoo	btiŠbŘoo
Hinné	byiŠbŘoo

Present Continuous		
Ana	Ăam	biŠboŘ
Inta	Ăam	btiŠboŘ
Inté	Ăam	btiŠbŘé
Hoowé	Ăam	byiŠboŘ
Heeyé	Ăam	btiŠboŘ
Naĥna	Ăam	mniŠboŘ
Intoo	Ăam	btiŠbŘoo
Hinné	Ăam	byiŠbŘoo

Past	
Ana	ŠabaŘt
Inta	ŠabaŘt
Inté	ŠabaŘté
Hoowé	ŠabaŘ
Heeyé	ŠabaŘét
Naĥna	ŠabaŘna
Intoo	ŠabaŘtoo
Hinné	ŠabaŘoo

Past Continuous		
Ana	Kint Ăam	biŠboŘ
Inta	Kint Ăam	btiŠboŘ
Inté	Kinté Ăam	btiŠbŘé
Hoowé	Kén Ăam	byiŠboŘ
Heeyé	Kénét Ăam	btiŠboŘ
Naĥna	Kinna Ăam	mniŠboŘ
Intoo	Kintoo Ăam	btiŠbŘoo
Hinné	Kénoo Ăam	byiŠbŘoo

Future		
Ana	Laĥ	iŠboŘ
Inta	Laĥ	tiŠboŘ
Inté	Laĥ	tiŠbŘé
Hoowé	Laĥ	yiŠboŘ
Heeyé	Laĥ	tiŠboŘ
Naĥna	Laĥ	niŠboŘ
Intoo	Laĥ	tiŠbŘoo
Hinné	Laĥ	yiŠbŘoo

Command	
Inta	ŠboŘ
Inté	ŠbiŘé
Intoo	ŠbiŘoo
Inta	Ma tŠboŘ
Inté	Ma tŠbRé
Intoo	Ma tŠbŘoo

To eat

Present	
Ana	Békol
Inta	Btékol
Inté	Btéklé
Hoowé	Byékol
Heeyé	Btékol
Naĥna	Mnékol
Intoo	Btékloo
Hinné	Byékloo

Present Continuous		
Ana	Ăam	Békol	('ékél/'éklé)
Inta	Ăam	Btékol	('ékél)
Inté	Ăam	Btéklé	('éklé)
Hoowé	Ăam	Byékol	('ékél)
Heeyé	Ăam	Btékol	('éklé)
Naĥna	Ăam	Mnékol	('ékleen)
Intoo	Ăam	Btékloo	('ékleen)
Hinné	Ăam	Byékloo	('ékleen)

Past	
Ana	Akalt
Inta	Akalt
Inté	Akalté
Hoowé	Akal
Heeyé	Akalét
Naĥna	Akalna
Intoo	Akaltoo
Hinné	Akaloo

Past Continuous			
Ana	Kint Ăam	Békol	(kint ('ékél/'éklé)
Inta	Kint Ăam	Btékol	(Kint ('ékél)
Inté	Kinté Ăam	Btéklé	(Kinté ('éklé)
Hoowé	Kén Ăam	Byékol	(Kén ('ékél)
Heeyé	Kénét Ăam	Btékol	(Kénét ('éklé)
Naĥna	Kinna Ăam	Mnékol	(Kinna ('ékleen)
Intoo	Kintoo Ăam	Btékloo	(Kintoo ('ékleen)
Hinné	Kénoo Ăam	Byékloo	(Kénoo ('ékleen)

Future		
Ana	Laĥ	'ékol
Inta	Laĥ	tékol
Inté	Laĥ	téklé
Hoowé	Laĥ	yékol
Heeyé	Laĥ	tékol
Naĥna	Laĥ	nékol
Intoo	Laĥ	tékloo
Hinné	Laĥ	yékloo

Command	
Inta	Kol
Inté	Kilé
Intoo	Kiloo
Inta	Ma tékol
Inté	Ma téklé
Intoo	Ma tékloo

Ă= Augh in bought	**Ď**= a heavy D	**É**= like A in Bay	**G**= G in beige	**ĥ**= like an H with smaller air passage	**I**= I as in ink	**Ǩ**= like ch in Irish loch
O= O as in home	**OO**= as in boots	**R**= roll the rrr	**Ť**= a heavy T	**Ř**= like a French R (gargle it)	**Š**= a heavy S	**Ž**= a heavy Z

E

E

To have breakfast

Present

Ana	Bitrawwa'
Inta	Btitrawwa'
Inté	Btitrawwa'é
Hoowé	Byitrawwa'
Heeyé	Btitrawwa'
Nahna	Mnitrawwa'
Intoo	Btitrawwa'oo
Hinné	Byitrawwa'oo

Present Continuous

Ana	Ăam	Bitrawwa'	(mitrawwa'/mitraww'a)
Inta	Ăam	Btitrawwa'	(mitrawwa')
Inté	Ăam	Btitrawwa'é	(mitraww'a)
Hoowé	Ăam	Byitrawwa'	(mitrawwa')
Heeyé	Ăam	Btitrawwa'	(mitraww'a)
Nahna	Ăam	Mnitrawwa'	(mitraww'een)
Intoo	Ăam	Btitrawwa'oo	(mitraww'een)
Hinné	Ăam	Byitrawwa'oo	(mitraww'een)

Past

Ana	Trawwa't
Inta	Trawwa't
Inté	Trawwa'té
Hoowé	Trawwa'
Heeyé	Trawwa'ét
Nahna	Trawwa'na
Intoo	Trawwa'too
Hinné	Trawwa'oo

Past Continuous

Ana	Kint Ăam	Bitrawwa'	(kint	mitrawwa'/mit raww'a)
Inta	Kint Ăam	Btitrawwa'	(Kint	mitrawwa')
Inté	Kinté Ăam	Btitrawwa'é	(Kinté	mitraww'a)
Hoowé	Kén Ăam	Byitrawwa'	(Kén	mitrawwa')
Heeyé	Kénét Ăam	Btitrawwa'	(Kénét	mitraww'a)
Nahna	Kinna Ăam	Mnitrawwa'	(Kinna	mitraww'een)
Intoo	Kintoo Ăam	Btitrawwa'oo	(Kintoo	mitraww'een)
Hinné	Kénoo Ăam	Byitrawwa'oo	(Kénoo	mitraww'een)

Future

Ana	Laĥ	Itrawwa'
Inta	Laĥ	Titrawwa'
Inté	Laĥ	Titrawwa'é
Hoowé	Laĥ	Yitrawwa'
Heeyé	Laĥ	Titrawwa'
Nahna	Laĥ	Nitrawwa'
Intoo	Laĥ	Titrawwa'oo
Hinné	Laĥ	Yitrawwa'oo

Command

Inta	Trawwa'
Inté	Trawwa'é
Intoo	Trawwa'oo
Inta	Ma ttrawwa'
Inté	Ma ttrawwa'é
Intoo	Ma ttrawwa'oo

To have lunch

Present

Ana	BitŘadda
Inta	BtitŘadda
Inté	BtitŘaddé
Hoowé	ByitŘadda
Heeyé	BtitŘadda
Nahna	MnitŘadda
Intoo	BtitŘaddoo
Hinné	ByitŘaddoo

Present Continuous

Ana	Ăam	BitŘadda	(mitŘadda/mitŘiddéyeen
Inta	Ăam	BtitŘadda	(mitŘadda)
Inté	Ăam	BtitŘaddé	(mitŘiddéyé)
Hoowé	Ăam	ByitŘadda	(mitŘadda)
Heeyé	Ăam	BtitŘadda	(mitŘiddéyé)
Nahna	Ăam	MnitŘadda	(mitŘiddéyeen)
Intoo	Ăam	BtitŘaddoo	(mitŘiddéyeen)
Hinné	Ăam	ByitŘaddoo	(mitŘiddéyeen)

Past

Ana	ŤŘaddét
Inta	ŤŘaddét
Inté	ŤŘaddaité
Hoowé	ŤŘadda
Heeyé	ŤŘaddét
Nahna	ŤŘaddaina
Intoo	ŤŘaddaitoo
Hinné	ŤŘaddoo

Past Continuous

Ana	Kint Ăam	BitŘadda	(kint	mitŘadda/mit Řiddéyeen)
Inta	Kint Ăam	BtitŘadda	(Kint	mitŘadda)
Inté	Kinté Ăam	BtitŘaddé	(Kinté	mitŘiddéyé)
Hoowé	Kén Ăam	ByitŘadda	(Kén	mitŘadda)
Heeyé	Kénét Ăam	BtitŘadda	(Kénét	mitŘiddéyé)
Nahna	Kinna Ăam	MnitŘadda	(Kinna	mitŘiddéyeen)
Intoo	Kintoo Ăam	BtitŘaddoo	(Kintoo	mitŘiddéyeen)
Hinné	Kénoo Ăam	ByitŘaddoo	(Kénoo	mitŘiddéyeen)

Future

Ana	Laĥ	itŘadda
Inta	Laĥ	titŘadda
Inté	Laĥ	titŘaddé
Hoowé	Laĥ	yitŘadda
Heeyé	Laĥ	titŘadda
Nahna	Laĥ	nitŘadda
Intoo	Laĥ	titŘaddoo
Hinné	Laĥ	yitŘaddoo

Command

Inta	tŘadda
Inté	tŘaddé
Intoo	tŘaddoo
Inta	Ma ttŘadda
Inté	Ma ttŘaddé
Intoo	Ma ttŘaddoo

Ă= Augh in bought	Đ= a heavy D	É= like A in Bay	G= G in beige	ĥ= like an H with smaller air passage	I= I as in ink	Ḱ= like ch in Irish loch
O= O as in home	OO= as in boots	R= roll the rrr	Ť= a heavy T	Ř= like a French R (gargle it)	Ŝ= a heavy S	Ž= a heavy Z

E

E

To have supper

Present	
Ana	bitĂasha
Inta	btitĂasha
Inté	btitĂashé
Hoowé	byitĂasha
Heeyé	btitĂasha
Nahna	mnitĂasha
Intoo	btitĂashoo
Hinné	byitĂashoo

Present Continuous			
Ana	Ăam	bitĂasha	(mitĂasha/mitĂishéyeen)
Inta	Ăam	btitĂasha	(mitĂasha)
Inté	Ăam	btitĂashé	(mitĂishéyé)
Hoowé	Ăam	byitĂasha	(mitĂasha)
Heeyé	Ăam	btitĂasha	(mitĂishéyé)
Nahna	Ăam	mnitĂasha	(mitĂishéyeen)
Intoo	Ăam	btitĂashoo	(mitĂishéyeen)
Hinné	Ăam	byitĂashoo	(mitĂishéyeen)

Past	
Ana	tĂashét
Inta	tĂashét
Inté	tĂashaité
Hoowé	tĂasha
Heeyé	tĂashét
Nahna	tĂashaina
Intoo	tĂashaitoo
Hinné	tĂashoo

Past Continuous				
Ana	Kint Ăam	bitĂasha	(kint	mitĂasha/mit Ăishéyeen)
Inta	Kint Ăam	btitĂasha	(Kint	mitĂasha)
Inté	Kinté Ăam	btitĂashé	(Kinté	mitĂishéyé)
Hoowé	Kén Ăam	byitĂasha	(Kén	mitĂasha)
Heeyé	Kénét Ăam	btitĂasha	(Kénét	mitĂishéyé)
Nahna	Kinna Ăam	mnitĂasha	(Kinna	mitĂishéyeen)
Intoo	Kintoo Ăam	btitĂashoo	(Kintoo	mitĂishéyeen)
Hinné	Kénoo Ăam	byitĂashoo	(Kénoo	mitĂishéyeen)

Future		
Ana	Laĥ	itĂasha
Inta	Laĥ	titĂasha
Inté	Laĥ	titĂashé
Hoowé	Laĥ	yitĂasha
Heeyé	Laĥ	titĂasha
Nahna	Laĥ	nitĂasha
Intoo	Laĥ	titĂashoo
Hinné	Laĥ	yitĂashoo

Command		
Inta	tĂasha	
Inté	tĂashé	
Intoo	tĂashoo	
Inta	Ma ttĂasha	
Inté	Ma ttĂashé	
Intoo	Ma ttĂashoo	

To empty

Present	
Ana	bfaĎĎé
Inta	btfaĎĎé
Inté	btfaĎĎé
Hoowé	bifaĎĎé
Heeyé	btfaĎĎé
Nahna	mnfaĎĎé
Intoo	btfaĎĎoo
Hinné	bifaĎĎoo

Present Continuous		
Ana	Ăam	bfaĎĎé
Inta	Ăam	btfaĎĎé
Inté	Ăam	btfaĎĎé
Hoowé	Ăam	bifaĎĎé
Heeyé	Ăam	btfaĎĎé
Nahna	Ăam	mnfaĎĎé
Intoo	Ăam	btfaĎĎoo
Hinné	Ăam	bifaĎĎoo

Past	
Ana	faĎĎét
Inta	faĎĎét
Inté	faĎĎaité
Hoowé	faĎĎa
Heeyé	faĎĎét
Nahna	faĎĎaina
Intoo	faĎĎaitoo
Hinné	faĎĎoo

Past Continuous		
Ana	Kint Ăam	bfaĎĎé
Inta	Kint Ăam	btfaĎĎé
Inté	Kinté Ăam	btfaĎĎé
Hoowé	Kén Ăam	bifaĎĎé
Heeyé	Kénét Ăam	btfaĎĎé
Nahna	Kinna Ăam	mnfaĎĎé
Intoo	Kintoo Ăam	btfaĎĎoo
Hinné	Kénoo Ăam	bifaĎĎoo

Future		
Ana	Laĥ	faĎĎé
Inta	Laĥ	tfaĎĎé
Inté	Laĥ	tfaĎĎé
Hoowé	Laĥ	yfaĎĎé
Heeyé	Laĥ	tfaĎĎé
Nahna	Laĥ	nfaĎĎé
Intoo	Laĥ	tfaĎĎoo
Hinné	Laĥ	yfaĎĎoo

Command	
Inta	faĎĎé
Inté	faĎĎé
Intoo	faĎĎoo
Inta	Ma tfaĎĎé
Inté	Ma tfaĎĎé
Intoo	Ma tfaĎĎoo

Ă= Augh in bought	Ď= a heavy D	É= like A in Bay	G= G in beige	ĥ= like an H with smaller air passage	I= I as in ink	Ķ= like ch in Irish loch
O= O as in home	OO= as in boots	R= roll the rrr	Ť= a heavy T	Ř= like a French R (gargle it)	Š= a heavy S	Ž= a heavy Z

E E

To engrave

Present

Ana	Bin'osh
Inta	Btin'osh
Inté	Btin'shé
Hoowé	Byin'osh
Heeyé	Btin'osh
Nahna	Mnin'osh
Intoo	Btin'shoo
Hinné	Byin'shoo

Present Continuous

Ana	Ăam	Bin'osh
Inta	Ăam	Btin'osh
Inté	Ăam	Btin'shé
Hoowé	Ăam	Byin'osh
Heeyé	Ăam	Btin'osh
Nahna	Ăam	Mnin'osh
Intoo	Ăam	Btin'shoo
Hinné	Ăam	Byin'shoo

Past

Ana	Na'asht
Inta	Na'asht
Inté	Na'ashté
Hoowé	Na'ash
Heeyé	Na'ashét
Nahna	Na'ashna
Intoo	Na'ashtoo
Hinné	Na'ashoo

Past Continuous

Ana	Kint Ăam	Bin'osh
Inta	Kint Ăam	Btin'osh
Inté	Kinté Ăam	Btin'shé
Hoowé	Kén Ăam	Byin'osh
Heeyé	Kénét Ăam	Btin'osh
Nahna	Kinna Ăam	Mnin'osh
Intoo	Kintoo Ăam	Btin'shoo
Hinné	Kénoo Ăam	Byin'shoo

Future

Ana	Laĥ	in'osh
Inta	Laĥ	tin'osh
Inté	Laĥ	tin'shé
Hoowé	Laĥ	yin'osh
Heeyé	Laĥ	tin'osh
Nahna	Laĥ	nin'osh
Intoo	Laĥ	tin'shoo
Hinné	Laĥ	yin'shoo

Command

Inta	N'osh
Inté	N'ishé
Intoo	N'ishoo
Inta	Ma tn'osh
Inté	Ma tn'shé
Intoo	Ma tn'shoo

To enlarge

Present

Ana	Bkabbér
Inta	Btkabbér
Inté	Btkabbré
Hoowé	Bikabbér
Heeyé	Btkabbér
Nahna	Mnkabbér
Intoo	Btkabbroo
Hinné	Bikabbroo

Present Continuous

Ana	Ăam	Bkabbér
Inta	Ăam	Btkabbér
Inté	Ăam	Btkabbré
Hoowé	Ăam	Bikabbér
Heeyé	Ăam	Btkabbér
Nahna	Ăam	Mnkabbér
Intoo	Ăam	Btkabbroo
Hinné	Ăam	Bikabbroo

Past

Ana	Kabbart
Inta	Kabbart
Inté	Kabbarté
Hoowé	Kabbar
Heeyé	Kabbarét
Nahna	Kabbarna
Intoo	Kabbartoo
Hinné	Kabbaroo

Past Continuous

Ana	Kint Ăam	Bkabbér
Inta	Kint Ăam	Btkabbér
Inté	Kinté Ăam	Btkabbré
Hoowé	Kén Ăam	Bikabbér
Heeyé	Kénét Ăam	Btkabbér
Nahna	Kinna Ăam	Mnkabbér
Intoo	Kintoo Ăam	Btkabbroo
Hinné	Kénoo Ăam	Bikabbroo

Future

Ana	Laĥ	Kabbér
Inta	Laĥ	Tkabbér
Inté	Laĥ	Tkabbré
Hoowé	Laĥ	Ykabbér
Heeyé	Laĥ	Tkabbér
Nahna	Laĥ	Nkabbér
Intoo	Laĥ	Tkabbroo
Hinné	Laĥ	Ykabbroo

Command

Inta	Kabbér
Inté	Kabbré
Intoo	Kabbroo
Inta	Ma tkabbér
Inté	Ma tkabbré
Intoo	Ma tkabbroo

Ă= Augh in bought	Ď= a heavy D	É= like A in Bay	G= G in beige	ĥ= like an H with smaller air passage	I= I as in ink	Ḱ= like ch in Irish loch
O= O as in home	OO= as in boots	R= roll the rrr	Ť= a heavy T	Ř= like a French R (gargle it)	Ŝ= a heavy S	Ž= a heavy Z

E   E

To enlighten

Present	
Ana	Bnawwér
Inta	Btnawwér
Inté	Btnawwré
Hoowé	Binawwér
Heeyé	Btnawwér
Naĥna	Mnnawwér
Intoo	Btnawwroo
Hinné	Binawwroo

Present Continuous		
Ana	Ăam	Bnawwér
Inta	Ăam	Btnawwér
Inté	Ăam	Btnawwré
Hoowé	Ăam	Binawwér
Heeyé	Ăam	Btnawwér
Naĥna	Ăam	Mnnawwér
Intoo	Ăam	Btnawwroo
Hinné	Ăam	Binawwroo

Past	
Ana	Nawwart
Inta	Nawwart
Inté	Nawwarté
Hoowé	Nawwar
Heeyé	Nawwarét
Naĥna	Nawwarna
Intoo	Nawwartoo
Hinné	Nawwaroo

Past Continuous		
Ana	Kint Ăam	Bnawwér
Inta	Kint Ăam	Btnawwér
Inté	Kinté Ăam	Btnawwré
Hoowé	Kén Ăam	Binawwér
Heeyé	Kénét Ăam	Btnawwér
Naĥna	Kinna Ăam	Mnnawwér
Intoo	Kintoo Ăam	Btnawwroo
Hinné	Kénoo Ăam	Binawwroo

Future		
Ana	Laĥ	Nawwér
Inta	Laĥ	Tnawwér
Inté	Laĥ	Tnawwré
Hoowé	Laĥ	Ynawwér
Heeyé	Laĥ	Tnawwér
Naĥna	Laĥ	Nnawwér
Intoo	Laĥ	Tnawwroo
Hinné	Laĥ	Ynawwroo

Command	
Inta	Nawwér
Inté	Nawwré
Intoo	Nawwroo
Inta	Ma tnawwér
Inté	Ma tnawwré
Intoo	Ma tnawwroo

To enter

Present	
Ana	bidḰol
Inta	btidḰol
Inté	btidḰlé
Hoowé	byidḰol
Heeyé	btidḰol
Naĥna	mnidḰol
Intoo	btidḰloo
Hinné	byidḰloo

Present Continuous			
Ana	Ăam	bidḰol	(déḰél/déḰlé)
Inta	Ăam	btidḰol	(déḰél)
Inté	Ăam	btidḰlé	(déḰlé)
Hoowé	Ăam	byidḰol	(déḰél)
Heeyé	Ăam	btidḰol	(déḰlé)
Naĥna	Ăam	mnidḰol	(déḰleen)
Intoo	Ăam	btidḰloo	(déḰleen)
Hinné	Ăam	byidḰloo	(déḰleen)

Past	
Ana	daḰalt
Inta	daḰalt
Inté	daḰalté
Hoowé	daḰal
Heeyé	daḰalét
Naĥna	daḰalna
Intoo	daḰaltoo
Hinné	daḰaloo

Past Continuous			
Ana	Kint Ăam	bidḰol	(kint déḰél/déḰlé)
Inta	Kint Ăam	btidḰol	(Kint déḰél)
Inté	Kinté Ăam	btidḰlé	(Kinté déḰlé)
Hoowé	Kén Ăam	byidḰol	(Kén déḰél)
Heeyé	Kénét Ăam	btidḰol	(Kénét déḰlé)
Naĥna	Kinna Ăam	mnidḰol	(Kinna déḰleen)
Intoo	Kintoo Ăam	btidḰloo	(Kintoo déḰleen)
Hinné	Kénoo Ăam	byidḰloo	(Kénoo déḰleen)

Future		
Ana	Laĥ	idḰol
Inta	Laĥ	tidḰol
Inté	Laĥ	tidḰlé
Hoowé	Laĥ	yidḰol
Heeyé	Laĥ	tidḰol
Naĥna	Laĥ	nidḰol
Intoo	Laĥ	tidḰloo
Hinné	Laĥ	yidḰloo

Command	
Inta	dḰol
Inté	dḰilé
Intoo	dḰiloo
Inta	Ma tdḰol
Inté	Ma tdklé
Intoo	Ma tdḰloo

Ă= Augh in bought	Ď= a heavy D	É= like A in Bay	G= G in beige	ĥ= like an H with smaller air passage	I= I as in ink	Ḱ= like ch in Irish loch
O= O as in home	OO= as in boots	R= roll the rrr	Ť= a heavy T	Ř= like a French R (gargle it)	Ŝ= a heavy S	Ž= a heavy Z

E

E

To entertain

Present

Ana	Bsallé
Inta	Btsallé
Inté	Btsallé
Hoowé	Bisallé
Heeyé	Btsallé
Nahna	Mnsallé
Intoo	Btsalloo
Hinné	Bisalloo

Present Continuous

Ana	Ăam	Bsallé
Inta	Ăam	Btsallé
Inté	Ăam	Btsallé
Hoowé	Ăam	Bisallé
Heeyé	Ăam	Btsallé
Nahna	Ăam	Mnsallé
Intoo	Ăam	Btsalloo
Hinné	Ăam	Bisalloo

Past

Ana	Sallét
Inta	Sallét
Inté	Sallaité
Hoowé	Salla
Heeyé	Sallét
Nahna	Sallaina
Intoo	Sallaitoo
Hinné	Salloo

Past Continuous

Ana	Kint Ăam	Bsallé
Inta	Kint Ăam	Btsallé
Inté	Kinté Ăam	Btsallé
Hoowé	Kén Ăam	Bisallé
Heeyé	Kénét Ăam	Btsallé
Nahna	Kinna Ăam	Mnsallé
Intoo	Kintoo Ăam	Btsalloo
Hinné	Kénoo Ăam	Bisalloo

Future

Ana	Lah	Sallé
Inta	Lah	Tsallé
Inté	Lah	Tsallé
Hoowé	Lah	Ysallé
Heeyé	Lah	Tsallé
Nahna	Lah	Nsallé
Intoo	Lah	Tsalloo
Hinné	Lah	Ysalloo

Command

Inta	Sallé
Inté	Sallé
Intoo	Salloo
Inta	Ma tsallé
Inté	Ma tsallé
Intoo	Ma tsalloo

To be entertained

Present

Ana	Bitsalla
Inta	Btitsalla
Inté	Btitsallé
Hoowé	Byitsalla
Heeyé	Btitsalla
Nahna	Mnitsalla
Intoo	Btitsalloo
Hinné	Byitsalloo

Present Continuous

Ana	Ăam	Bitsalla	(mitsalla/mitsilléyé)
Inta	Ăam	Btitsalla	(mitssalla)
Inté	Ăam	Btitsallé	(mitsilléyé)
Hoowé	Ăam	Byitsalla	(mitsalla)
Heeyé	Ăam	Btitsalla	(mitsilléyé)
Nahna	Ăam	Mnitsalla	(mitsilléyeen)
Intoo	Ăam	Btitsalloo	(mitsilléyeen)
Hinné	Ăam	Byitsalloo	(mitsilléyeen)

Past

Ana	Sallét
Inta	Sallét
Inté	Sallaité
Hoowé	Salla
Heeyé	Sallét
Nahna	Sallaina
Intoo	Sallaitoo
Hinné	Salloo

Past Continuous

Ana	Kint Ăam	Bitsalla	(kint	mitsalla/mitsilléyé)
Inta	Kint Ăam	Btitsalla	(Kint	mitssalla)
Inté	Kinté Ăam	Btitsallé	(Kinté	mitsilléyé)
Hoowé	Kén Ăam	Byitsalla	(Kén	mitsalla)
Heeyé	Kénét Ăam	Btitsalla	(Kénét	mitsilléyé)
Nahna	Kinna Ăam	Mnitsalla	(Kinna	mitsilléyeen)
Intoo	Kintoo Ăam	Btitsalloo	(Kintoo	mitsilléyeen)
Hinné	Kénoo Ăam	Byitsalloo	(Kénoo	mitsilléyeen)

Future

Ana	Lah	Itsalla
Inta	Lah	Titsalla
Inté	Lah	Titsallé
Hoowé	Lah	Yitsalla
Heeyé	Lah	Titsalla
Nahna	Lah	Nitsalla
Intoo	Lah	Titsalloo
Hinné	Lah	Yitsalloo

Command

Inta	Tsall
Inté	Tsallé
Intoo	Tsalloo
Inta	Ma ttsalla
Inté	Ma ttsallé
Intoo	Ma ttsalloo

Ă= Augh in bought	Ď= a heavy D	É= like A in Bay	G= G in beige	ĥ= like an H with smaller air passage	I= I as in ink	Ќ= like ch in Irish loch
O= O as in home	OO= as in boots	R= roll the rrr	Ť= a heavy T	Ř= like a French R (gargle it)	Ŝ= a heavy S	Ž= a heavy Z

E

E

To erase

Present

Ana	Bimḣé
Inta	Btimḣé
Inté	Btimḣé
Hoowé	Byimḣé
Heeyé	Btimḣé
Naḣna	Mnimḣé
Intoo	Btimḣoo
Hinné	Byimḣoo

Present Continuous

Ana	Ăam	Bimḣé
Inta	Ăam	Btimḣé
Inté	Ăam	Btimḣé
Hoowé	Ăam	Byimḣé
Heeyé	Ăam	Btimḣé
Naḣna	Ăam	Mnimḣé
Intoo	Ăam	Btimḣoo
Hinné	Ăam	Byimḣoo

Past

Ana	maḣét
Inta	maḣét
Inté	Maḣaité
Hoowé	Maḣa
Heeyé	maḣét
Naḣna	Maḣaina
Intoo	Maḣaitoo
Hinné	maḣoo

Past Continuous

Ana	Kint Ăam	Bimḣé
Inta	Kint Ăam	Btimḣé
Inté	Kinté Ăam	Btimḣé
Hoowé	Kén Ăam	Byimḣé
Heeyé	Kénét Ăam	Btimḣé
Naḣna	Kinna Ăam	Mnimḣé
Intoo	Kintoo Ăam	Btimḣoo
Hinné	Kénoo Ăam	Byimḣoo

Future

Ana	Laḣ	Imḣé
Inta	Laḣ	Timḣé
Inté	Laḣ	Timḣé
Hoowé	Laḣ	Yimḣé
Heeyé	Laḣ	Timḣé
Naḣna	Laḣ	Nimḣé
Intoo	Laḣ	Timḣoo
Hinné	Laḣ	Yimḣoo

Command

Inta	Mḣee
Inté	Mḣee
Intoo	Mḣoo
Inta	Ma tmḣé
Inté	Ma tmḣé
Intoo	Ma tmḣoo

To estimate

Present

Ana	B'addér
Inta	Bt'addér
Inté	Bt'addré
Hoowé	Bi'addér
Heeyé	Bt'addér
Naḣna	Mn'addér
Intoo	Bt'addroo
Hinné	Bi'addroo

Present Continuous

Ana	Ăam	B'addér
Inta	Ăam	Bt'addér
Inté	Ăam	Bt'addré
Hoowé	Ăam	Bi'addér
Heeyé	Ăam	Bt'addér
Naḣna	Ăam	Mn'addér
Intoo	Ăam	Bt'addroo
Hinné	Ăam	Bi'addroo

Past

Ana	Addart
Inta	Addart
Inté	Addarté
Hoowé	Addar
Heeyé	Addarét
Naḣna	Addarna
Intoo	Addartoo
Hinné	Addaroo

Past Continuous

Ana	Kint Ăam	B'addér
Inta	Kint Ăam	Bt'addér
Inté	Kinté Ăam	Bt'addré
Hoowé	Kén Ăam	Bi'addér
Heeyé	Kénét Ăam	Bt'addér
Naḣna	Kinna Ăam	Mn'addér
Intoo	Kintoo Ăam	Bt'addroo
Hinné	Kénoo Ăam	Bi'addroo

Future

Ana	Laḣ	Addér
Inta	Laḣ	t'addér
Inté	Laḣ	t'addré
Hoowé	Laḣ	Y'addér
Heeyé	Laḣ	t'addér
Naḣna	Laḣ	n'addér
Intoo	Laḣ	t'addroo
Hinné	Laḣ	Y'addroo

Command

Inta	Addér
Inté	Addré
Intoo	Addroo
Inta	Ma t'addér
Inté	Ma t'addré
Intoo	Ma t'addroo

Ă= Augh in bought	**Ď**= a heavy D	**É**= like A in Bay	**G**= G in beige	**ḣ**= like an H with smaller air passage	**I**= I as in ink	**Ķ**= like ch in Irish loch
O= O as in home	**OO**= as in boots	**R**= roll the rrr	**Ť**= a heavy T	**Ř**= like a French R (gargle it)	**Ŝ**= a heavy S	**Ž**= a heavy Z

E E

To examin

Present

Ana	Bimtiĥin
Inta	Btimtiĥin
Inté	Btimtiĥné
Hoowé	Byimtiĥin
Heeyé	Btimtiĥin
Naĥna	Mnimtiĥin
Intoo	Btimtiĥnoo
Hinné	Byimtiĥnoo

Present Continuous

Ana	Ăam	Bimtiĥin
Inta	Ăam	Btimtiĥin
Inté	Ăam	Btimtiĥné
Hoowé	Ăam	Byimtiĥin
Heeyé	Ăam	Btimtiĥin
Naĥna	Ăam	Mnimtiĥin
Intoo	Ăam	Btimtiĥnoo
Hinné	Ăam	Byimtiĥnoo

Past

Ana	Mtaĥant
Inta	Mtaĥant
Inté	Mtaĥanté
Hoowé	Mtaĥan
Heeyé	Mtaĥanét
Naĥna	Mtaĥanna
Intoo	Mtaĥantoo
Hinné	Mtaĥanoo

Past Continuous

Ana	Kint Ăam	Bimtiĥin
Inta	Kint Ăam	Btimtiĥin
Inté	Kinté Ăam	Btimtiĥné
Hoowé	Kén Ăam	Byimtiĥin
Heeyé	Kénét Ăam	Btimtiĥin
Naĥna	Kinna Ăam	Mnimtiĥin
Intoo	Kintoo Ăam	Btimtiĥnoo
Hinné	Kénoo Ăam	Byimtiĥnoo

Future

Ana	Laĥ	Imtiĥin
Inta	Laĥ	Timtiĥin
Inté	Laĥ	Timtiĥné
Hoowé	Laĥ	Yimtiĥin
Heeyé	Laĥ	Timtiĥin
Naĥna	Laĥ	Nimtiĥin
Intoo	Laĥ	Timtiĥnoo
Hinné	Laĥ	Yimtiĥnoo

Command

Inta	Mtiĥén
Inté	Mtiĥné
Intoo	Mtiĥnoo
Inta	Ma tmtiĥén
Inté	Ma tmtiĥné
Intoo	Ma tmtiĥnoo

To exchange

Present

Ana	bŜarréf
Inta	btŜarréf
Inté	btŜarrfé
Hoowé	biŜarréf
Heeyé	btŜarréf
Naĥna	mnŜarréf
Intoo	btŜarrfoo
Hinné	biŜarrfoo

Present Continuous

Ana	Ăam	bŜarréf
Inta	Ăam	btŜarréf
Inté	Ăam	btŜarrfé
Hoowé	Ăam	biŜarréf
Heeyé	Ăam	btŜarréf
Naĥna	Ăam	mnŜarréf
Intoo	Ăam	btŜarrfoo
Hinné	Ăam	biŜarrfoo

Past

Ana	Ŝarraft
Inta	Ŝarraft
Inté	Ŝarrafté
Hoowé	Ŝarraf
Heeyé	Ŝarrafét
Naĥna	Ŝarrafna
Intoo	Ŝarraftoo
Hinné	Ŝarrafoo

Past Continuous

Ana	Kint Ăam	bŜarréf
Inta	Kint Ăam	btŜarréf
Inté	Kinté Ăam	btŜarrfé
Hoowé	Kén Ăam	biŜarréf
Heeyé	Kénét Ăam	btŜarréf
Naĥna	Kinna Ăam	mnŜarréf
Intoo	Kintoo Ăam	btŜarrfoo
Hinné	Kénoo Ăam	biŜarrfoo

Future

Ana	Laĥ	Ŝarréf
Inta	Laĥ	tŜarréf
Inté	Laĥ	tŜarrfé
Hoowé	Laĥ	yŜarréf
Heeyé	Laĥ	tŜarréf
Naĥna	Laĥ	nŜarréf
Intoo	Laĥ	tŜarrfoo
Hinné	Laĥ	yŜarrfoo

Command

Inta	Ŝarréf
Inté	Ŝarrfé
Intoo	Ŝarrfoo
Inta	Ma tŜarréf
Inté	Ma tŜarrfé
Intoo	Ma tŜarfoo

Ă= Augh in bought	Đ= a heavy D	É= like A in Bay	G= G in beige	ĥ= like an H with smaller air passage	I= I as in ink	Ḱ= like ch in Irish loch
O= O as in home	OO= as in boots	R= roll the rrr	Ť= a heavy T	Ř= like a French R (gargle it)	Ŝ= a heavy S	Ž= a heavy Z

E

E

To exhibit

Present	
Ana	biĂroĎ
Inta	btiĂroĎ
Inté	btiĂrĎé
Hoowé	byiĂroĎ
Heeyé	btiĂroĎ
Naĥna	mniĂroĎ
Intoo	btiĂrĎoo
Hinné	byiĂrĎoo

Present Continuous		
Ana	Ăam biĂroĎ	(ĂaréĎ/ĂarĎa)
Inta	Ăam btiĂroĎ	(ĂaréĎ)
Inté	Ăam btiĂrĎé	(ĂarĎa)
Hoowé	Ăam byiĂroĎ	(ĂaréĎ)
Heeyé	Ăam btiĂroĎ	(ĂarĎa)
Naĥna	Ăam mniĂroĎ	(ĂarĎeen)
Intoo	Ăam btiĂrĎoo	(ĂarĎeen)
Hinné	Ăam byiĂrĎoo	(ĂarĎeen)

Past	
Ana	ĂaraĎt
Inta	ĂaraĎt
Inté	ĂaraĎté
Hoowé	ĂaraĎ
Heeyé	ĂaraĎét
Naĥna	ĂaraĎna
Intoo	ĂaraĎtoo
Hinné	ĂaraĎoo

Past Continuous		
Ana	Kint Ăam biĂroĎ	(kint ĂaréĎ/ĂarĎa)
Inta	Kint Ăam btiĂroĎ	(Kint ĂaréĎ)
Inté	Kinté Ăam btiĂrĎé	(Kinté ĂarĎa)
Hoowé	Kén Ăam byiĂroĎ	(Kén ĂaréĎ)
Heeyé	Kénét Ăam btiĂroĎ	(Kénét ĂarĎa)
Naĥna	Kinna Ăam mniĂroĎ	(Kinna ĂarĎeen)
Intoo	Kintoo Ăam btiĂrĎoo	(Kintoo ĂarĎeen)
Hinné	Kénoo Ăam byiĂrĎoo	(Kénoo ĂarĎeen)

Future		
Ana	Laĥ	iĂroĎ
Inta	Laĥ	tiĂroĎ
Inté	Laĥ	tiĂrĎé
Hoowé	Laĥ	yiĂroĎ
Heeyé	Laĥ	tiĂroĎ
Naĥna	Laĥ	niĂroĎ
Intoo	Laĥ	tiĂrĎoo
Hinné	Laĥ	yiĂrĎoo

Command	
Inta	ĂroĎ
Inté	ĂriĎé
Intoo	ĂriĎoo
Inta	Ma tĂroĎ
Inté	Ma tĂrdé
Intoo	Ma tĂrdoo

To exit

Present	
Ana	BiŤlaĂ
Inta	BtiŤlaĂ
Inté	BtiŤlaĂé
Hoowé	ByiŤlaĂ
Heeyé	BtiŤlaĂ
Naĥna	MniŤlaĂ
Intoo	BtiŤlaĂoo
Hinné	ByiŤlaĂoo

Present Continuous	
Ana	Ăam biŤlaĂ (or ana ŤaléĂ/ŤalĂa)
Inta	Ăam btiŤlaĂ (or ŤaléĂ)
Inté	Ăam btiŤlaĂé (or ŤalĂa)
Hoowé	Ăam byiŤlaĂ (or ŤaléĂ)
Heeyé	Ăam btiŤlaĂ (or ŤalĂa)
Naĥna	Ăam mnilaĂ (or ŤalĂeen)
Intoo	Ăam btiŤlaĂoo (or ŤalĂeen)
Hinné	Ăam byiŤlaĂoo (or ŤalĂeen)

Past	
Ana	ŤlaĂt
Inta	ŤlaĂt
Inté	ŤlaĂté
Hoowé	ŤileĂ
Heeyé	ŤilĂét
Naĥna	ŤlaĂna
Intoo	ŤlaĂtoo
Hinné	ŤilĂoo

Past Continuous	
Ana	Kint Ăam biŤlaĂ (or kint ŤaléĂ/TalĂa)
Inta	Kint Ăam btiŤlaĂ (or kint ŤaléĂ)
Inté	Kinté Ăam btiŤlaĂé (or kinté ŤalĂa)
Hoowé	Kén Ăam byiŤlaĂ (or kén ŤaléĂ)
Heeyé	Kénét Ăam btiŤlaĂ (or kénét ŤalĂa)
Naĥna	Kinna Ăam mniŤlaĂ (or kinna ŤalĂeen)
Intoo	Kintoo Ăam btiŤlaĂoo (kintoo ŤalĂeen)
Hinné	Kénoo Ăam byiŤlaĂoo (or kénoo ŤalĂeen)

Future		
Ana	Laĥ	'iŤlaĂ
Inta	Laĥ	tiŤlaĂ
Inté	Laĥ	tiŤlaĂé
Hoowé	Laĥ	yiŤlaĂ
Heeyé	Laĥ	tiŤlaĂ
Naĥna	Laĥ	niŤlaĂ
Intoo	Laĥ	tiŤlaĂoo
Hinné	Laĥ	yiŤlaĂoo

Command	
Inta	ŤlaĂ
Inté	ŤlaĂé
Intoo	ŤlaĂoo
Inta	Ma tŤlaĂ
Inté	Ma tŤlaĂé
Intoo	Ma tŤlaĂoo

Ă= Augh in bought	Ď= a heavy D	É= like A in Bay	G= G in beige	ĥ= like an H with smaller air passage	I= I as in ink	Ќ= like ch in Irish loch
O= O as in home	OO= as in boots	R= roll the rrr	Ť= a heavy T	Ř= like a French R (gargle it)	Ŝ= a heavy S	Ž= a heavy Z

E̲

To expand

Present

Ana	bitwassaĂ
Inta	btitwassaĂ
Inté	btitwassaĂé
Hoowé	byitwassaĂ
Heeyé	btitwassaĂ
Naĥna	mnitwassaĂ
Intoo	btitwassaĂoo
Hinné	byitwassaĂoo

Present Continuous

Ana	Ăam	bitwassaĂ
Inta	Ăam	btitwassaĂ
Inté	Ăam	btitwassaĂé
Hoowé	Ăam	byitwassaĂ
Heeyé	Ăam	btitwassaĂ
Naĥna	Ăam	mnitwassaĂ
Intoo	Ăam	btitwassaĂoo
Hinné	Ăam	byitwassaĂoo

Past

Ana	twassaĂt
Inta	twassaĂt
Inté	twassaĂté
Hoowé	twassaĂ
Heeyé	twassaĂét
Naĥna	twassaĂna
Intoo	twassaĂtoo
Hinné	twassaĂoo

Past Continuous

Ana	Kint Ăam	bitwassaĂ
Inta	Kint Ăam	btitwassaĂ
Inté	Kinté Ăam	btitwassaĂé
Hoowé	Kén Ăam	byitwassaĂ
Heeyé	Kénét Ăam	btitwassaĂ
Naĥna	Kinna Ăam	mnitwassaĂ
Intoo	Kintoo Ăam	btitwassaĂoo
Hinné	Kénoo Ăam	byitwassaĂoo

Future

Ana	Laĥ	itwassaĂ
Inta	Laĥ	titwassaĂ
Inté	Laĥ	titwassaĂé
Hoowé	Laĥ	yitwassaĂ
Heeyé	Laĥ	titwassaĂ
Naĥna	Laĥ	nitwassaĂ
Intoo	Laĥ	titwassaĂoo
Hinné	Laĥ	yitwassaĂoo

Command

Inta	twassaĂ
Inté	twassaĂé
Intoo	twassaĂoo
Inta	Ma ttwassaĂ
Inté	Ma ttwassaĂé
Intoo	Ma ttwassaĂoo

E̲

To expect

Present

Ana	Bitwa''aĂ
Inta	Btitwa''aĂ
Inté	Btitwa''aĂé
Hoowé	Byitwa''aĂ
Heeyé	Btitwa''aĂ
Naĥna	Mnitwa''aĂ
Intoo	Btitwa''aĂoo
Hinné	Byitwa''aĂoo

Present Continuous

Ana	Ăam Bitwa''aĂ	(mitwa''aĂ/mitwa''Ăa)
Inta	Ăam Btitwa''aĂ	(mitwa''aĂ)
Inté	Ăam Btitwa''aĂé	(mitwa''aĂa)
Hoowé	Ăam Byitwa''aĂ	(mitwa''aĂ)
Heeyé	Ăam Btitwa''aĂ	(mitwa''aĂa)
Naĥna	Ăam Mnitwa''aĂ	(mitwa''Ăeen)
Intoo	Ăam Btitwa''aĂoo	(mitwa''Ăeen)
Hinné	Ăam Byitwa''aĂoo	(mitwa''Ăeen)

Past

Ana	Twa''aĂt
Inta	Twa''aĂt
Inté	Twa''aĂté
Hoowé	Twa''aĂ
Heeyé	Twa''aĂét
Naĥna	Twa''aĂna
Intoo	Twa''aĂtoo
Hinné	Twa''aĂoo

Past Continuous

Ana	Kint Ăam	Bitwa''aĂ	(kint mitwa''aĂ/mitwa''Ăa)
Inta	Kint Ăam	Btitwa''aĂ	(Kint mitwa''aĂ)
Inté	Kinté Ăam	Btitwa''aĂé	(Kinté mitwa''aĂa)
Hoowé	Kén Ăam	Byitwa''aĂ	(Kén mitwa''aĂ)
Heeyé	Kénét Ăam	Btitwa''aĂ	(Kénét mitwa''aĂa)
Naĥna	Kinna Ăam	Mnitwa''aĂ	(Kinna mitwa''Ăeen)
Intoo	Kintoo Ăam	Btitwa''aĂoo	(Kintoo mitwa''Ăeen)
Hinné	Kénoo Ăam	Byitwa''aĂoo	(Kénoo mitwa''Ăeen)

Future

Ana	Laĥ	itwa''aĂ
Inta	Laĥ	titwa''aĂ
Inté	Laĥ	titwa''aĂé
Hoowé	Laĥ	yitwa''aĂ
Heeyé	Laĥ	titwa''aĂ
Naĥna	Laĥ	nitwa''aĂ
Intoo	Laĥ	titwa''aĂoo
Hinné	Laĥ	yitwa''aĂoo

Command

Inta	Twa''aĂ
Inté	Twa''aĂé
Intoo	Twa''aĂoo
Inta	Ma ttwa''aĂ
Inté	Ma ttwa''aĂé
Intoo	Ma ttwa''aĂoo

Ă= Augh in bought	Ď= a heavy D	É= like A in Bay	G= G in beige	ĥ= like an H with smaller air passage	I= I as in ink	Ḱ= like ch in Irish loch
O= O as in home	OO= as in boots	R= roll the rrr	Ť= a heavy T	Ř= like a French R (gargle it)	Ŝ= a heavy S	Ž= a heavy Z

E   F

To explain   To fall

Present	
Ana	Bfassér
Inta	Btfassér
Inté	Btfassré
Hoowé	Bifassér
Heeyé	Btfassér
Naĥna	Mnfassér
Intoo	Btfassroo
Hinné	Bifassroo

Present Continuous		
Ana	Ăam	Bfassér
Inta	Ăam	Btfassér
Inté	Ăam	Btfassré
Hoowé	Ăam	Bifassér
Heeyé	Ăam	Btfassér
Naĥna	Ăam	Mnfassér
Intoo	Ăam	Btfassroo
Hinné	Ăam	Bifassroo

Past	
Ana	Fassart
Inta	Fassart
Inté	Fassarté
Hoowé	Fassar
Heeyé	Fassarét
Naĥna	Fassarna
Intoo	Fassartoo
Hinné	Fassaroo

Past Continuous		
Ana	Kint Ăam	Bfassér
Inta	Kint Ăam	Btfassér
Inté	Kinté Ăam	Btfassré
Hoowé	Kén Ăam	Bifassér
Heeyé	Kénét Ăam	Btfassér
Naĥna	Kinna Ăam	Mnfassér
Intoo	Kintoo Ăam	Btfassroo
Hinné	Kénoo Ăam	Bifassroo

Future		
Ana	Laĥ	Fassér
Inta	Laĥ	Tfassér
Inté	Laĥ	Tfassré
Hoowé	Laĥ	Yfassér
Heeyé	Laĥ	Tfassér
Naĥna	Laĥ	Nfassér
Intoo	Laĥ	Tfassroo
Hinné	Laĥ	Yfassroo

Command	
Inta	Fassér
Inté	Fassré
Intoo	Fassroo
Inta	Ma tfassér
Inté	Ma tfassré
Intoo	Ma tfassroo

Present	
Ana	Boo'aĂ
Inta	Btoo'aĂ
Inté	Btoo'aĂé
Hoowé	Byoo'aĂ
Heeyé	Btoo'aĂ
Naĥna	Mnoo'aĂ
Intoo	Btoo'aĂoo
Hinné	Byoo'aĂoo

Present Continuous			
Ana	Ăam	Boo'aĂ	(wé'éĂ/wé'Ăa)
Inta	Ăam	Btoo'aĂ	(wé'éĂ)
Inté	Ăam	Btoo'aĂé	(wé'Ăa)
Hoowé	Ăam	Byoo'aĂ	(wé'éĂ)
Heeyé	Ăam	Btoo'aĂ	(wé'Ăa)
Naĥna	Ăam	Mnoo'aĂ	(wé'Ăeen)
Intoo	Ăam	Btoo'aĂoo	(wé'Ăeen)
Hinné	Ăam	Byoo'aĂoo	(wé'Ăeen)

Past	
Ana	Wa'aĂt
Inta	Wa'aĂt
Inté	Wa'aĂté
Hoowé	Wa'aĂ
Heeyé	Wa'aĂét
Naĥna	Wa'aĂna
Intoo	Wa'aĂtoo
Hinné	Wa'aĂoo

Past Continuous			
Ana	Kint Ăam	Boo'aĂ	(kint wé'éĂ/wé'Ăa)
Inta	Kint Ăam	Btoo'aĂ	(Kint wé'éĂ)
Inté	Kinté Ăam	Btoo'aĂé	(Kinté wé'Ăa)
Hoowé	Kén Ăam	Byoo'aĂ	(Kén wé'éĂ)
Heeyé	Kénét Ăam	Btoo'aĂ	(Kénét wé'Ăa)
Naĥna	Kinna Ăam	Mnoo'aĂ	(Kinna wé'Ăeen)
Intoo	Kintoo Ăam	Btoo'aĂoo	(Kintoo wé'Ăeen)
Hinné	Kénoo Ăam	Byoo'aĂoo	(Kénoo wé'Ăeen)

Future		
Ana	Laĥ	Oo'aĂ
Inta	Laĥ	Too'aĂ
Inté	Laĥ	Too'aĂé
Hoowé	Laĥ	Yoo'aĂ
Heeyé	Laĥ	Too'aĂ
Naĥna	Laĥ	Noo'aĂ
Intoo	Laĥ	Too'aĂoo
Hinné	Laĥ	Yoo'aĂoo

Command	
Inta	W'aĂ
Inté	W'aĂé
Intoo	W'aĂoo
Inta	Ma too'aĂ
Inté	Ma too'aĂé
Intoo	Ma too'aĂé

Ă= Augh in bought	Đ= a heavy D	É= like A in Bay	G= G in beige	ĥ= like an H with smaller air passage	I= I as in ink	Ќ= like ch in Irish loch
O= O as in home	OO= as in boots	R= roll the rrr	Ŧ= a heavy T	Ř= like a French R (gargle it)	Ŝ= a heavy S	Ž= a heavy Z

F̲   F̲

To fail (a test)

Present	
Ana	Bis'oŤ
Inta	Btis'oŤ
Inté	Btis'Ťé
Hoowé	Byis'oŤ
Heeyé	Btis'oŤ
Naḣna	Mnis'oŤ
Intoo	Btis'Ťoo
Hinné	Byis'Ťoo

Present Continuous		
Ana	Ăam Bis'oŤ	(sa'éŤ/sa'Ťa)
Inta	Ăam Btis'oŤ	(sa'éŤ)
Inté	Ăam Btis'Ťé	(sa'Ťa)
Hoowé	Ăam Byis'oŤ	(sa'éŤ)
Heeyé	Ăam Btis'oŤ	(sa'Ťa)
Naḣna	Ăam Mnis'oŤ	(sa'Ťeen)
Intoo	Ăam Btis'Ťoo	(sa'Ťeen)
Hinné	Ăam Byis'Ťoo	(sa'Ťeen)

Past	
Ana	Sa'aŤt
Inta	Sa'aŤt
Inté	Sa'aŤté
Hoowé	Sa'aŤ
Heeyé	Sa'aŤét
Naḣna	Sa'aŤna
Intoo	Sa'aŤtoo
Hinné	Sa'aŤoo

Past Continuous		
Ana	Kint Ăam Bis'oŤ	(kint sa'éŤ/sa'Ťa)
Inta	Kint Ăam Btis'oŤ	(Kint sa'éŤ)
Inté	Kinté Ăam Btis'Ťé	(Kinté sa'Ťa)
Hoowé	Kén Ăam Byis'oŤ	(Kén sa'éŤ)
Heeyé	Kénét Ăam Btis'oŤ	(Kénét sa'Ťa)
Naḣna	Kinna Ăam Mnis'oŤ	(Kinna sa'Ťeen)
Intoo	Kintoo Ăam Btis'Ťoo	(Kintoo sa'Ťeen)
Hinné	Kénoo Ăam Byis'Ťoo	(Kénoo sa'Ťeen)

Future		
Ana	Laḣ	is'oŤ
Inta	Laḣ	tis'oŤ
Inté	Laḣ	tis'Ťé
Hoowé	Laḣ	yis'oŤ
Heeyé	Laḣ	tis'oŤ
Naḣna	Laḣ	nis'oŤ
Intoo	Laḣ	tis'Ťoo
Hinné	Laḣ	yis'Ťoo

Command	
Inta	S'oŤ
Inté	S'iŤé
Intoo	S'iŤoo
Inta	Ma ts'oŤ
Inté	Ma ts'Ťé
Intoo	Ma ts'Ťoo

To fail (a project)

Present	
Ana	Bifshal
Inta	Btifshal
Inté	Btifshalé
Hoowé	Byifshal
Heeyé	Btifshal
Naḣna	Mnifshal
Intoo	Btifshaloo
Hinné	Byifshaloo

Present Continuous		
Ana	Ăam	Bifshal
Inta	Ăam	Btifshal
Inté	Ăam	Btifshalé
Hoowé	Ăam	Byifshal
Heeyé	Ăam	Btifshal
Naḣna	Ăam	Mnifshal
Intoo	Ăam	Btifshaloo
Hinné	Ăam	Byifshaloo

Past	
Ana	Fashalt
Inta	Fashalt
Inté	Fashalté
Hoowé	Fashal
Heeyé	Fashalét
Naḣna	Fashalna
Intoo	Fashaltoo
Hinné	Fashaloo

Past Continuous		
Ana	Kint Ăam	Bifshal
Inta	Kint Ăam	Btifshal
Inté	Kinté Ăam	Btifshalé
Hoowé	Kén Ăam	Byifshal
Heeyé	Kénét Ăam	Btifshal
Naḣna	Kinna Ăam	Mnifshal
Intoo	Kintoo Ăam	Btifshaloo
Hinné	Kénoo Ăam	Byifshaloo

Future		
Ana	Laḣ	Ifshal
Inta	Laḣ	Tifshal
Inté	Laḣ	Tifshalé
Hoowé	Laḣ	Yifshal
Heeyé	Laḣ	Tifshal
Naḣna	Laḣ	Nifshal
Intoo	Laḣ	Tifshaloo
Hinné	Laḣ	Yifshaloo

Command	
Inta	Fshél
Inté	Fshalé
Intoo	Fshaloo
Inta	Ma tfshal
Inté	Ma tfshalé
Intoo	Ma tfshaloo

Ă= Augh in bought	Ď= a heavy D	É= like A in Bay	G= G in beige	ḣ= like an H with smaller air passage	I= I as in ink	Ǩ= like ch in Irish loch
O= O as in home	OO= as in boots	R= roll the rrr	Ť= a heavy T	Ř= like a French R (gargle it)	Ŝ= a heavy S	Ž= a heavy Z

F   F

To fear

Present

Ana	bḰaf
Inta	btḰaf
Inté	btḰafé
Hoowé	biḰaf
Heeyé	btḰaf
Nahna	mnḰaf
Intoo	btḰafoo
Hinné	biḰafoo

Present Continuous

Ana	Ăam	bḰaf	(Ḱayéf/Kayfé)
Inta	Ăam	btḰaf	(Ḱayéf)
Inté	Ăam	btḰafé	(Ḱayfé)
Hoowé	Ăam	biḰaf	(Ḱayéf)
Heeyé	Ăam	btḰaf	(Ḱayfé)
Nahna	Ăam	mnḰaf	(Ḱayfeen)
Intoo	Ăam	btḰafoo	(Ḱayfeen)
Hinné	Ăam	biḰafoo	(Ḱayfeen)

Past

Ana	Ḱift
Inta	Ḱift
Inté	Ḱifté
Hoowé	Ḱaf
Heeyé	Ḱafét
Nahna	Ḱifna
Intoo	Ḱiftoo
Hinné	Ḱafoo

Past Continuous

Ana	Kint Ăam	bḰaf	(kint Ḱayéf/Kayfé)
Inta	Kint Ăam	btḰaf	(Kint Ḱayéf)
Inté	Kinté Ăam	btḰafé	(Kinté Ḱayfé)
Hoowé	Kén Ăam	biḰaf	(Kén Ḱayéf)
Heeyé	Kénét Ăam	btḰaf	(Kénét Ḱayfé)
Nahna	Kinna Ăam	mnḰaf	(Kinna Ḱayfeen)
Intoo	Kintoo Ăam	btḰafoo	(Kintoo Ḱayfeen)
Hinné	Kénoo Ăam	biḰafoo	(Kénoo Ḱayfeen)

Future

Ana	Laĥ	Ḱaf
Inta	Laĥ	tḰaf
Inté	Laĥ	tḰafé
Hoowé	Laĥ	yḰaf
Heeyé	Laĥ	tḰaf
Nahna	Laĥ	nḰaf
Intoo	Laĥ	tḰafoo
Hinné	Laĥ	yḰafoo

Command

Inta	Ḱaf
Inté	Ḱafé
Intoo	Ḱafoo
Inta	Ma tḰaf
Inté	Ma tḰafé
Intoo	Ma tḰafoo

To feed

Present

Ana	bȚaĂmé
Inta	btȚaĂmé
Inté	btȚaĂmé
Hoowé	biȚaĂmé
Heeyé	btȚaĂmé
Nahna	mnȚaĂmé
Intoo	btȚaĂmoo
Hinné	biȚaĂmoo

Present Continuous

Ana	Ăam	bȚaĂmé
Inta	Ăam	btȚaĂmé
Inté	Ăam	btȚaĂmé
Hoowé	Ăam	biȚaĂmé
Heeyé	Ăam	btȚaĂmé
Nahna	Ăam	mnȚaĂmé
Intoo	Ăam	btȚaĂmoo
Hinné	Ăam	biȚaĂmoo

Past

Ana	ȚaĂmét
Inta	ȚaĂmét
Inté	ȚaĂmaité
Hoowé	ȚaĂma
Heeyé	ȚaĂmét
Nahna	ȚaĂmaina
Intoo	ȚaĂmaitoo
Hinné	ȚaĂmoo

Past Continuous

Ana	Kint Ăam	bȚaĂmé
Inta	Kint Ăam	btȚaĂmé
Inté	Kinté Ăam	btȚaĂmé
Hoowé	Kén Ăam	biȚaĂmé
Heeyé	Kénét Ăam	btȚaĂmé
Nahna	Kinna Ăam	mnȚaĂmé
Intoo	Kintoo Ăam	btȚaĂmoo
Hinné	Kénoo Ăam	biȚaĂmoo

Future

Ana	Laĥ	ȚaĂmé
Inta	Laĥ	tȚaĂmé
Inté	Laĥ	tȚaĂmé
Hoowé	Laĥ	yȚaĂmé
Heeyé	Laĥ	tȚaĂmé
Nahna	Laĥ	nȚaĂmé
Intoo	Laĥ	tȚaĂmoo
Hinné	Laĥ	yȚaĂmoo

Command

Inta	ȚaĂmé
Inté	ȚaĂmé
Intoo	ȚaĂmoo
Inta	Ma tȚaĂmé
Inté	Ma tȚaĂmé
Intoo	Ma tȚaĂmoo

Ă= Augh in bought	Ď= a heavy D	É= like A in Bay	G= G in beige	ĥ= like an H with smaller air passage	I= I as in ink	Ḱ= like ch in Irish loch
O= O as in home	OO= as in boots	R= roll the rrr	Ț= a heavy T	Ř= like a French R (gargle it)	Ŝ= a heavy S	Ž= a heavy Z

F

F

To feel

Present

Ana	B̂hiss
Inta	Bthiss
Inté	Bthissé
Hoowé	Bihiss
Heeyé	Bthiss
Naĥna	Mnĥiss
Intoo	Bthissoo
Hinné	Bihissoo

Present Continuous

Ana	Ăam	B̂hiss	(ĥésés/ĥéssé)
Inta	Ăam	Bthiss	(ĥésés)
Inté	Ăam	Bthissé	(ĥéssé)
Hoowé	Ăam	Bihiss	(ĥésés)
Heeyé	Ăam	Bthiss	(ĥéssé)
Naĥna	Ăam	Mnĥiss	(ĥésseen)
Intoo	Ăam	Bthissoo	(ĥésseen)
Hinné	Ăam	Bihissoo	(ĥésseen)

Past

Ana	Ĥassét
Inta	Ĥassét
Inté	Ĥassaité
Hoowé	Ĥass
Heeyé	Ĥassét
Naĥna	Ĥassaina
Intoo	Ĥassaitoo
Hinné	Ĥassoo

Past Continuous

Ana	Kint Ăam	B̂hiss	(kint ĥésés/ĥéssé)
Inta	Kint Ăam	Bthiss	(Kint ĥésés)
Inté	Kinté Ăam	Bthissé	(Kinté ĥéssé)
Hoowé	Kén Ăam	Bihiss	(Kén ĥésés)
Heeyé	Kénét Ăam	Bthiss	(Kénét ĥéssé)
Naĥna	Kinna Ăam	Mnĥiss	(Kinna ĥésseen)
Intoo	Kintoo Ăam	Bthissoo	(Kintoo ĥésseen)
Hinné	Kénoo Ăam	Bihissoo	(Kénoo ĥésseen)

Future

Ana	Laĥ	ĥiss
Inta	Laĥ	thiss
Inté	Laĥ	Thissé
Hoowé	Laĥ	yĥiss
Heeyé	Laĥ	thiss
Naĥna	Laĥ	nĥiss
Intoo	Laĥ	Thissoo
Hinné	Laĥ	Yĥissoo

Command

Inta	Ĥiss
Inté	Ĥissé
Intoo	Ĥissoo
Inta	Ma thiss
Inté	Ma thissé
Intoo	Ma thissoo

To fight

Present

Ana	biĂla'
Inta	btiĂla'
Inté	btiĂla'é
Hoowé	byiĂla'
Heeyé	btiĂla'
Naĥna	mniĂla'
Intoo	btiĂla'oo
Hinné	byiĂla'oo

Present Continuous

Ana	Ăam	biĂla'	(Ăélé'/Ăél'a)
Inta	Ăam	btiĂla'	(Ăélé')
Inté	Ăam	btiĂla'é	(Ăél'a)
Hoowé	Ăam	byiĂla'	(Ăélé')
Heeyé	Ăam	btiĂla'	(Ăél'a)
Naĥna	Ăam	mniĂla'	(Ăél'een)
Intoo	Ăam	btiĂla'oo	(Ăél'een)
Hinné	Ăam	byiĂla'oo	(Ăél'een)

Past

Ana	Ăli't
Inta	Ăli't
Inté	Ăli'té
Hoowé	Ăili'
Heeyé	Ăil'ét
Naĥna	Ăli'na
Intoo	Ăli'too
Hinné	Ăil'oo

Past Continuous

Ana	Kint Ăam	biĂla'	(kint Ăélé'/Ăél'a)
Inta	Kint Ăam	btiĂla'	(Kint Ăélé')
Inté	Kinté Ăam	btiĂla'é	(Kinté Ăél'a)
Hoowé	Kén Ăam	byiĂla'	(Kén Ăélé')
Heeyé	Kénét Ăam	btiĂla'	(Kénét Ăél'a)
Naĥna	Kinna Ăam	mniĂla'	(Kinna Ăél'een)
Intoo	Kintoo Ăam	btiĂla'oo	(Kintoo Ăél'een)
Hinné	Kénoo Ăam	byiĂla'oo	(Kénoo Ăél'een)

Future

Ana	Laĥ	iĂla'
Inta	Laĥ	tiĂla'
Inté	Laĥ	tiĂla'é
Hoowé	Laĥ	yiĂla'
Heeyé	Laĥ	tiĂla'
Naĥna	Laĥ	niĂla'
Intoo	Laĥ	tiĂla'oo
Hinné	Laĥ	yiĂla'oo

Command

Inta	Ăla'
Inté	Ăla'é
Intoo	Ăla'oo
Inta	Ma tĂla'
Inté	Ma tĂla'é
Intoo	Ma tĂla'oo

Ă= Augh in bought	Ď= a heavy D	É= like A in Bay	G= G in beige	ĥ= like an H with smaller air passage	I= I as in ink	Ḱ= like ch in Irish loch
O= O as in home	OO= as in boots	R= roll the rrr	Ť= a heavy T	Ř= like a French R (gargle it)	Ŝ= a heavy S	Ž= a heavy Z

F

F

To fill

Present	
Ana	bĂabbé
Inta	btĂabbé
Inté	btĂabbé
Hoowé	biĂabbé
Heeyé	btĂabbé
Naĥna	mnĂabbé
Intoo	btĂabboo
Hinné	biĂabboo

Present Continuous		
Ana	Ăam	bĂabbé
Inta	Ăam	btĂabbé
Inté	Ăam	btĂabbé
Hoowé	Ăam	biĂabbé
Heeyé	Ăam	btĂabbé
Naĥna	Ăam	mnĂabbé
Intoo	Ăam	btĂabboo
Hinné	Ăam	biĂabboo

Past	
Ana	Ăabbét
Inta	Ăabbét
Inté	Ăabbaité
Hoowé	Ăabba
Heeyé	Ăabbét
Naĥna	Ăabbaina
Intoo	Ăabbaitoo
Hinné	Ăabboo

Past Continuous		
Ana	Kint Ăam	bĂabbé
Inta	Kint Ăam	btĂabbé
Inté	Kinté Ăam	btĂabbé
Hoowé	Kén Ăam	biĂabbé
Heeyé	Kénét Ăam	btĂabbé
Naĥna	Kinna Ăam	mnĂabbé
Intoo	Kintoo Ăam	btĂabboo
Hinné	Kénoo Ăam	biĂabboo

Future		
Ana	Laĥ	Ăabbé
Inta	Laĥ	tĂabbé
Inté	Laĥ	tĂabbé
Hoowé	Laĥ	yĂabbé
Heeyé	Laĥ	tĂabbé
Naĥna	Laĥ	nĂabbé
Intoo	Laĥ	tĂabboo
Hinné	Laĥ	yĂabboo

Command	
Inta	Ăabbé
Inté	Ăabbé
Intoo	Ăabboo
Inta	Ma tĂabbé
Inté	Ma tĂabbé
Intoo	Ma tĂabboo

To filter / To purify

Present	
Ana	bŜaffé
Inta	btŜaffé
Inté	btŜaffé
Hoowé	biŜaffé
Heeyé	btŜaffé
Naĥna	mnŜaffé
Intoo	btŜaffoo
Hinné	biŜaffoo

Present Continuous		
Ana	Ăam	bŜaffé
Inta	Ăam	btŜaffé
Inté	Ăam	btŜaffé
Hoowé	Ăam	biŜaffé
Heeyé	Ăam	btŜaffé
Naĥna	Ăam	mnŜaffé
Intoo	Ăam	btŜaffoo
Hinné	Ăam	biŜaffoo

Past	
Ana	Ŝaffét
Inta	Ŝaffét
Inté	Ŝaffaité
Hoowé	Ŝaffa
Heeyé	Ŝaffét
Naĥna	Ŝaffaina
Intoo	Ŝaffaitoo
Hinné	Ŝaffoo

Past Continuous		
Ana	Kint Ăam	bŜaffé
Inta	Kint Ăam	btŜaffé
Inté	Kinté Ăam	btŜaffé
Hoowé	Kén Ăam	biŜaffé
Heeyé	Kénét Ăam	btŜaffé
Naĥna	Kinna Ăam	mnŜaffé
Intoo	Kintoo Ăam	btŜaffoo
Hinné	Kénoo Ăam	biŜaffoo

Future		
Ana	Laĥ	Ŝaffé
Inta	Laĥ	tŜaffé
Inté	Laĥ	tŜaffé
Hoowé	Laĥ	yŜaffé
Heeyé	Laĥ	tŜaffé
Naĥna	Laĥ	nŜaffé
Intoo	Laĥ	tŜaffoo
Hinné	Laĥ	yŜaffoo

Command	
Inta	Ŝaffé
Inté	Ŝaffé
Intoo	Ŝaffoo
Inta	Ma tŜaffé
Inté	Ma tŜaffé
Intoo	Ma tŜaffoo

Ă= Augh in bought	Ď= a heavy D	É= like A in Bay	G= G in beige	ĥ= like an H with smaller air passage	I= I as in ink	Ќ= like ch in Irish loch
O= O as in home	OO= as in boots	R= roll the rrr	Ŧ= a heavy T	Ř= like a French R (gargle it)	Ŝ= a heavy S	Ž= a heavy Z

F   F

To find

Present

Ana	Blé'é
Inta	Btlé'é
Inté	Btlé'é
Hoowé	Bilé'é
Heeyé	Btlé'é
Naĥna	Mnlé'é
Intoo	Btlé'oo
Hinné	Bilé'oo

Present Continuous

Ana	Ăam	Blé'é
Inta	Ăam	Btlé'é
Inté	Ăam	Btlé'é
Hoowé	Ăam	Bilé'é
Heeyé	Ăam	Btlé'é
Naĥna	Ăam	Mnlé'é
Intoo	Ăam	Btlé'oo
Hinné	Ăam	Bilé'oo

Past

Ana	La'ét
Inta	La'ét
Inté	La'aité
Hoowé	La'a
Heeyé	La'yét
Naĥna	La'yna
Intoo	La'ytoo
Hinné	La'yoo

Past Continuous

Ana	Kint Ăam	Blé'é
Inta	Kint Ăam	Btlé'é
Inté	Kinté Ăam	Btlé'é
Hoowé	Kén Ăam	Bilé'é
Heeyé	Kénét Ăam	Btlé'é
Naĥna	Kinna Ăam	Mnlé'é
Intoo	Kintoo Ăam	Btlé'oo
Hinné	Kénoo Ăam	Bilé'oo

Future

Ana	Laĥ	Lé'é
Inta	Laĥ	Tlé'é
Inté	Laĥ	Tlé'é
Hoowé	Laĥ	Ylé'é
Heeyé	Laĥ	Tlé'é
Naĥna	Laĥ	Nlé'é
Intoo	Laĥ	Tlé'oo
Hinné	Laĥ	Ylé'oo

Command

Inta	Lé'é
Inté	Lé'é
Intoo	Lé'oo
Inta	Ma tlé'é
Inté	Ma tlé'é
Intoo	Ma tlé'oo

To finish

Present

Ana	bḰalléŜ
Inta	btḰalléŜ
Inté	btḰallSé
Hoowé	biḰalléŜ
Heeyé	btḰalléŜ
Naĥna	mnḰalléŜ
Intoo	btḰallŜoo
Hinné	biḰallŜoo

Present Continuous

Ana	Ăam	bḰalléŜ	(mḰallaŜ/mḰallŜa)
Inta	Ăam	btḰalléŜ	(mḰallaŜ)
Inté	Ăam	btḰallSé	(mḰallŜa)
Hoowé	Ăam	biḰalléŜ	(mḰallaŜ)
Heeyé	Ăam	btḰalléŜ	(mḰallŜa)
Naĥna	Ăam	mnḰalléŜ	(mḰallŜeen)
Intoo	Ăam	btḰallŜoo	(mḰallŜeen)
Hinné	Ăam	biḰallŜoo	(mḰallŜeen)

Past

Ana	ḰallaŜt
Inta	ḰallaŜt
Inté	ḰallaŜté
Hoowé	ḰallaŜ
Heeyé	ḰallaŜét
Naĥna	ḰallaŜna
Intoo	ḰallaŜtoo
Hinné	ḰallaŜoo

Past Continuous

Ana	Kint Ăam	bḰalléŜ	(kint	mḰallaŜ/mḰallŜa)
Inta	Kint Ăam	btḰalléŜ	(Kint	mḰallaŜ)
Inté	Kinté Ăam	btḰallSé	(Kinté	mḰallŜa)
Hoowé	Kén Ăam	biḰalléŜ	(Kén	mḰallaŜ)
Heeyé	Kénét Ăam	btḰalléŜ	(Kénét	mḰallŜa)
Naĥna	Kinna Ăam	mnḰalléŜ	(Kinna	mḰallŜeen)
Intoo	Kintoo Ăam	btḰallŜoo	(Kintoo	mḰallŜeen)
Hinné	Kénoo Ăam	biḰallŜoo	(Kénoo	mḰallŜeen)

Future

Ana	Laĥ	ḰalléŜ
Inta	Laĥ	tḰalléŜ
Inté	Laĥ	tḰallSé
Hoowé	Laĥ	yḰalléŜ
Heeyé	Laĥ	tḰalléŜ
Naĥna	Laĥ	nḰalléŜ
Intoo	Laĥ	tḰallŜoo
Hinné	Laĥ	ḰallaŜoo

Command

Inta	ḰalléŜ
Inté	ḰallaŜté
Intoo	ḰallaŜtoo
Inta	Ma tḰalleŜ
Inté	Ma tḰallSé
Intoo	Ma tḰallŜoo

Ă= Augh in bought	Ď= a heavy D	É= like A in Bay	G= G in beige	ĥ= like an H with smaller air passage	I= I as in ink	Ḱ= like ch in Irish loch
O= O as in home	OO= as in boots	R= roll the rrr	Ť= a heavy T	Ř= like a French R (gargle it)	Ŝ= a heavy S	Ž= a heavy Z

F   F

To fire / To kickout

Present

Ana	Bikḣash
Inta	Btikḣash
Inté	Btikḣashé
Hoowé	Byikḣash
Heeyé	Btikḣash
Naḣna	Mnikḣash
Intoo	Btikḣashoo
Hinné	Byikḣashoo

Present Continuous

Ana	Ăam	Bikḣash
Inta	Ăam	Btikḣash
Inté	Ăam	Btikḣashé
Hoowé	Ăam	Byikḣash
Heeyé	Ăam	Btikḣash
Naḣna	Ăam	Mnikḣash
Intoo	Ăam	Btikḣashoo
Hinné	Ăam	Byikḣashoo

Past

Ana	Kaḣasht
Inta	Kaḣasht
Inté	Kaḣashté
Hoowé	Kaḣash
Heeyé	Kaḣashét
Naḣna	Kaḣashna
Intoo	Kaḣashtoo
Hinné	Kaḣashoo

Past Continuous

Ana	Kint Ăam	Bikḣash
Inta	Kint Ăam	Btikḣash
Inté	Kinté Ăam	Btikḣashé
Hoowé	Kén Ăam	Byikḣash
Heeyé	Kénét Ăam	Btikḣash
Naḣna	Kinna Ăam	Mnikḣash
Intoo	Kintoo Ăam	Btikḣashoo
Hinné	Kénoo Ăam	Byikḣashoo

Future

Ana	Laḣ	Ikḣash
Inta	Laḣ	Tikḣash
Inté	Laḣ	Tikḣashé
Hoowé	Laḣ	Yikḣash
Heeyé	Laḣ	Tikḣash
Naḣna	Laḣ	Nikḣash
Intoo	Laḣ	Tikḣashoo
Hinné	Laḣ	Yikḣashoo

Command

Inta	Kḣash
Inté	Kḣashé
Intoo	Kḣashoo
Inta	Ma tkḣash
Inté	Ma tkḣashé
Intoo	Ma tkḣashoo

To fix

Present

Ana	bŜalléḣ
Inta	btŜalléḣ
Inté	btŜallhé
Hoowé	biŜalléḣ
Heeyé	btŜalléḣ
Naḣna	mnŜalléḣ
Intoo	btŜallhoo
Hinné	biŜallhoo

Present Continuous

Ana	Ăam	bŜalléḣ
Inta	Ăam	btŜalléḣ
Inté	Ăam	btŜallhé
Hoowé	Ăam	biŜalléḣ
Heeyé	Ăam	btŜalléḣ
Naḣna	Ăam	mnŜalléḣ
Intoo	Ăam	btŜallhoo
Hinné	Ăam	biŜallhoo

Past

Ana	Ŝallaḣt
Inta	Ŝallaḣt
Inté	Ŝallaḣté
Hoowé	Ŝallaḣ
Heeyé	Ŝallaḣét
Naḣna	Ŝallaḣna
Intoo	Ŝallaḣtoo
Hinné	Ŝallaḣoo

Past Continuous

Ana	Kint Ăam	bŜalléḣ
Inta	Kint Ăam	btŜalléḣ
Inté	Kinté Ăam	btŜallhé
Hoowé	Kén Ăam	biŜalléḣ
Heeyé	Kénét Ăam	btŜalléḣ
Naḣna	Kinna Ăam	mnŜalléḣ
Intoo	Kintoo Ăam	btŜallhoo
Hinné	Kénoo Ăam	biŜallhoo

Future

Ana	Laḣ	Ŝalléḣ
Inta	Laḣ	tŜalléḣ
Inté	Laḣ	tŜallhé
Hoowé	Laḣ	yŜalléḣ
Heeyé	Laḣ	tŜalléḣ
Naḣna	Laḣ	nŜalléḣ
Intoo	Laḣ	tŜallhoo
Hinné	Laḣ	yŜallhoo

Command

Inta	Ŝallaḣt
Inté	Ŝallaḣté
Intoo	Ŝallaḣtoo
Inta	Ma tŜalléḣ
Inté	Ma tŜllhé
Intoo	Ma tŜallhoo

F̲   F̲

To flee

Present		
Ana	Bihrob	
Inta	Btihrob	
Inté	Btihrbé	
Hoowé	Byihrob	
Heeyé	Btihrob	
Naḣna	Mnihrob	
Intoo	Btihrboo	
Hinné	Byihrboo	

Present Continuous			
Ana	Ăam	Bihrob	(hirbén/hirbéné)
Inta	Ăam	Btihrob	(hirbén)
Inté	Ăam	Btihrbé	(hirbéné)
Hoowé	Ăam	Byihrob	(hirbén)
Heeyé	Ăam	Btihrob	(hirbéné)
Naḣna	Ăam	Mnihrob	(hirbéneen)
Intoo	Ăam	Btihrboo	(hirbéneen)
Hinné	Ăam	Byihrboo	(hirbéneen)

Past		
Ana	Hribit	
Inta	Hribit	
Inté	Hribtè	
Hoowé	Hirib	
Heeyé	Hirbét	
Naḣna	Hribna	
Intoo	Hribtoo	
Hinné	Hirboo	

Past Continuous				
Ana	Kint Ăam	Bihrob	(kint	hirbén/hirbéné)
Inta	Kint Ăam	Btihrob	(Kint	hirbén)
Inté	Kinté Ăam	Btihrbé	(Kinté	hirbéné)
Hoowé	Kén Ăam	Byihrob	(Kén	hirbén)
Heeyé	Kénét Ăam	Btihrob	(Kénét	hirbéné)
Naḣna	Kinna Ăam	Mnihrob	(Kinna	hirbéneen)
Intoo	Kintoo Ăam	Btihrboo	(Kintoo	hirbéneen)
Hinné	Kénoo Ăam	Byihrboo	(Kénoo	hirbéneen)

Future		
Ana	Laḣ	Ihrob
Inta	Laḣ	Tihrob
Inté	Laḣ	Tihrbé
Hoowé	Laḣ	Yihrob
Heeyé	Laḣ	Tihrob
Naḣna	Laḣ	Nihrob
Intoo	Laḣ	Tihrboo
Hinné	Laḣ	Yihrboo

Command	
Inta	Hrob
Inté	Hribé
Intoo	Hriboo
Inta	Ma throb
Inté	Ma thrbé
Intoo	Ma thrboo

To fly

Present	
Ana	bŤeer
Inta	btŤeer
Inté	btŤeeré
Hoowé	biŤeer
Heeyé	btŤeer
Naḣna	mnŤeer
Intoo	btŤeeroo
Hinné	biŤeeroo

Present Continuous			
Ana	Ăam	bŤeer	(Ťayér/Ťayra)
Inta	Ăam	btŤeer	(Ťayér)
Inté	Ăam	btŤeeré	(Ťayra)
Hoowé	Ăam	biŤeer	(Ťayér)
Heeyé	Ăam	btŤeer	(Ťayra)
Naḣna	Ăam	mnŤeer	(Ťayreen)
Intoo	Ăam	btŤeeroo	(Ťayreen)
Hinné	Ăam	biŤeeroo	(Ťayreen)

Past	
Ana	Ťirt
Inta	Ťirt
Inté	Ťirté
Hoowé	Ťar
Heeyé	Ťarit
Naḣna	Ťirna
Intoo	Ťirtoo
Hinné	Ťaroo

Past Continuous				
Ana	Kint Ăam	bŤeer	(kint	Ťayér/Ťayra)
Inta	Kint Ăam	btŤeer	(Kint	Ťayér)
Inté	Kinté Ăam	btŤeeré	(Kinté	Ťayra)
Hoowé	Kén Ăam	biŤeer	(Kén	Ťayér)
Heeyé	Kénét Ăam	btŤeer	(Kénét	Ťayra)
Naḣna	Kinna Ăam	mnŤeer	(Kinna	Ťayreen)
Intoo	Kintoo Ăam	btŤeeroo	(Kintoo	Ťayreen)
Hinné	Kénoo Ăam	biŤeeroo	(Kénoo	Ťayreen)

Future		
Ana	Laḣ	Ťeer
Inta	Laḣ	tŤeer
Inté	Laḣ	tŤeeré
Hoowé	Laḣ	yŤeer
Heeyé	Laḣ	tŤeer
Naḣna	Laḣ	nŤeer
Intoo	Laḣ	tŤeeroo
Hinné	Laḣ	yŤeeroo

Command	
Inta	Ťeer
Inté	Ťeeré
Intoo	Ťeeroo
Inta	Ma tŤeer
Inté	Ma tŤeeré
Intoo	Ma tŤeeroo

Ă= Augh in bought	Ď= a heavy D	É= like A in Bay	G= G in beige	ḣ= like an H with smaller air passage	I= I as in ink	Ḱ= like ch in Irish loch
O= O as in home	OO= as in boots	R= roll the rrr	Ť= a heavy T	Ř= like a French R (gargle it)	Ŝ= a heavy S	Ž= a heavy Z

F　　　　　　　　　F

To follow

Present

Ana	Bilha'
Inta	Btilha'
Inté	Btilha'é
Hoowé	Byilha'
Heeyé	Btilha'
Nahna	Mnilha'
Intoo	Btilha'oo
Hinné	Byilha'oo

Present Continuous

Ana	Ăam	Bilha'	(léhé'/léĥ'a)
Inta	Ăam	Btilha'	(léhé')
Inté	Ăam	Btilha'é	(léĥ'a)
Hoowé	Ăam	Byilha'	(léhé')
Heeyé	Ăam	Btilha'	(léĥ'a)
Nahna	Ăam	Mnilha'	(léĥ'een)
Intoo	Ăam	Btilha'oo	(léĥ'een)
Hinné	Ăam	Byilha'oo	(léĥ'een)

Past

Ana	Laha't
Inta	Laha't
Inté	Laha'té
Hoowé	Laha'
Heeyé	Laha'ét
Nahna	Laha'na
Intoo	Laha'too
Hinné	Laha'oo

Past Continuous

Ana	Kint Ăam	Bilha'	(kint léhé'/léĥ'a)
Inta	Kint Ăam	Btilha'	(Kint léhé')
Inté	Kinté Ăam	Btilha'é	(Kinté léĥ'a)
Hoowé	Kén Ăam	Byilha'	(Kén léhé')
Heeyé	Kénét Ăam	Btilha'	(Kénét léĥ'a)
Nahna	Kinna Ăam	Mnilha'	(Kinna léĥ'een)
Intoo	Kintoo Ăam	Btilha'oo	(Kintoo léĥ'een)
Hinné	Kénoo Ăam	Byilha'oo	(Kénoo léĥ'een)

Future

Ana	Laĥ	Ilha'
Inta	Laĥ	Tilha'
Inté	Laĥ	Tilha'é
Hoowé	Laĥ	Yilha'
Heeyé	Laĥ	Tilha'
Nahna	Laĥ	Nilha'
Intoo	Laĥ	Tilha'oo
Hinné	Laĥ	Yilha'oo

Command

Inta	Lha'
Inté	Lha'é
Intoo	Lha'oo
Inta	Ma tlha'
Inté	Ma tlha'é
Intoo	Ma tlha'oo

To forbid

Present

Ana	bimnaĂ
Inta	btimnaĂ
Inté	btimnaĂé
Hoowé	byimnaĂ
Heeyé	btimnaĂ
Nahna	mnimnaĂ
Intoo	btimnaĂoo
Hinné	byimnaĂoo

Present Continuous

Ana	Ăam	bimnaĂ
Inta	Ăam	btimnaĂ
Inté	Ăam	btimnaĂé
Hoowé	Ăam	byimnaĂ
Heeyé	Ăam	btimnaĂ
Nahna	Ăam	mnimnaĂ
Intoo	Ăam	btimnaĂoo
Hinné	Ăam	byimnaĂoo

Past

Ana	manaĂt
Inta	manaĂt
Inté	manaĂté
Hoowé	manaĂ
Heeyé	manaĂét
Nahna	manaĂna
Intoo	manaĂtoo
Hinné	manaĂoo

Past Continuous

Ana	Kint Ăam	bimnaĂ
Inta	Kint Ăam	btimnaĂ
Inté	Kinté Ăam	btimnaĂé
Hoowé	Kén Ăam	byimnaĂ
Heeyé	Kénét Ăam	btimnaĂ
Nahna	Kinna Ăam	mnimnaĂ
Intoo	Kintoo Ăam	btimnaĂoo
Hinné	Kénoo Ăam	byimnaĂoo

Future

Ana	Laĥ	imnaĂ
Inta	Laĥ	timnaĂ
Inté	Laĥ	timnaĂé
Hoowé	Laĥ	yimnaĂ
Heeyé	Laĥ	timnaĂ
Nahna	Laĥ	nimnaĂ
Intoo	Laĥ	timnaĂoo
Hinné	Laĥ	yimnaĂoo

Command

Inta	mnaĂ
Inté	mnaĂé
Intoo	mnaĂoo
Inta	Ma tmnaĂ
Inté	Ma tmnaĂé
Intoo	Ma tmnaĂoo

Ă= Augh in bought	Ď= a heavy D	É= like A in Bay	G= G in beige	ĥ= like an H with smaller air passage	I= I as in ink	Ķ= like ch in Irish loch
O= O as in home	OO= as in boots	R= roll the rrr	Ť= a heavy T	Ř= like a French R (gargle it)	Ŝ= a heavy S	Ž= a heavy Z

F̲   F̲

To forget

Present

Ana	Binsa
Inta	Btinsa
Inté	Btinsé
Hoowé	Byinsa
Heeyé	Btinsa
Naḥna	Mninsa
Intoo	Btinsoo
Hinné	Byinsoo

Present Continuous

Ana	Ăam	Binsa	(nésé/nésyé)
Inta	Ăam	Btinsa	(nésé)
Inté	Ăam	Btinsé	(nésyé)
Hoowé	Ăam	Byinsa	(nésé)
Heeyé	Ăam	Btinsa	(nésyé)
Naḥna	Ăam	Mninsa	(nésyeen)
Intoo	Ăam	Btinsoo	(nésyeen)
Hinné	Ăam	Byinsoo	(nésyeen)

Past

Ana	Nseet
Inta	Nseet
Inté	Nseeté
Hoowé	Nisé
Heeyé	Nisyét
Naḥna	Nseena
Intoo	Nseetoo
Hinné	Nisyoo

Past Continuous

Ana	Kint Ăam	Binsa	(kint nésé/nésyé)
Inta	Kint Ăam	Btinsa	(Kint nésé)
Inté	Kinté Ăam	Btinsé	(Kinté nésyé)
Hoowé	Kén Ăam	Byinsa	(Kén nésé)
Heeyé	Kénét Ăam	Btinsa	(Kénét nésyé)
Naḥna	Kinna Ăam	Mninsa	(Kinna nésyeen)
Intoo	Kintoo Ăam	Btinsoo	(Kintoo nésyeen)
Hinné	Kénoo Ăam	Byinsoo	(Kénoo nésyeen)

Future

Ana	Laḥ	Insa
Inta	Laḥ	Tinsa
Inté	Laḥ	Tinsé
Hoowé	Laḥ	Yinsa
Heeyé	Laḥ	Tinsa
Naḥna	Laḥ	Ninsa
Intoo	Laḥ	Tinsoo
Hinné	Laḥ	Yinsoo

Command

Inta	Nsee
Inté	Nsee
Intoo	Nsoo
Inta	Ma tnsa
Inté	Ma tnsé
Intoo	Ma tnsoo

To forgive

Present

Ana	biŘfor
Inta	btiŘfor
Inté	btiŘfré
Hoowé	byiŘfor
Heeyé	btiŘfor
Naḥna	mniŘfor
Intoo	btiŘfroo
Hinné	byiŘfroo

Present Continuous

Ana	Ăam	biŘfor
Inta	Ăam	btiŘfor
Inté	Ăam	btiŘfré
Hoowé	Ăam	byiŘfor
Heeyé	Ăam	btiŘfor
Naḥna	Ăam	mniŘfor
Intoo	Ăam	btiŘfroo
Hinné	Ăam	byiŘfroo

Past

Ana	Řafart
Inta	Řafart
Inté	Řafarté
Hoowé	Řafar
Heeyé	Řafarét
Naḥna	Řafarna
Intoo	Řafartoo
Hinné	Řafaroo

Past Continuous

Ana	Kint Ăam	biŘfor
Inta	Kint Ăam	btiŘfor
Inté	Kinté Ăam	btiŘfré
Hoowé	Kén Ăam	byiŘfor
Heeyé	Kénét Ăam	btiŘfor
Naḥna	Kinna Ăam	mniŘfor
Intoo	Kintoo Ăam	btiŘfroo
Hinné	Kénoo Ăam	byiŘfroo

Future

Ana	Laḥ	iŘfor
Inta	Laḥ	tiŘfor
Inté	Laḥ	tiŘfré
Hoowé	Laḥ	yiŘfor
Heeyé	Laḥ	tiŘfor
Naḥna	Laḥ	niŘfor
Intoo	Laḥ	tiŘfroo
Hinné	Laḥ	yiŘfroo

Command

Inta	Řfor
Inté	Řfiré
Intoo	Řfiroo
Inta	Ma tiŘfor
Inté	Ma tiŘfré
Intoo	Ma tiŘfroo

Ă= Augh in bought	Ď= a heavy D	É= like A in Bay	G= G in beige	ḥ= like an H with smaller air passage	I= I as in ink	Ḱ= like ch in Irish loch
O= O as in home	OO= as in boots	R= roll the rrr	Ť= a heavy T	Ř= like a French R (gargle it)	Š= a heavy S	Ž= a heavy Z

<u>F</u>　　　　<u>F</u>

To freeze

Present

Ana	Bgalléd
Inta	Btgalléd
Inté	Btgalldé
Hoowé	Bigalléd
Heeyé	Btgalléd
Naḣna	Mngalléd
Intoo	Btgalldoo
Hinné	Bigalldoo

Present Continuous

Ana	Ăam	Bgalléd	(mgallad/mgalldé)
Inta	Ăam	Btgalléd	(mgallad)
Inté	Ăam	Btgalldé	(mgalldé)
Hoowé	Ăam	Bigalléd	(mgallad)
Heeyé	Ăam	Btgalléd	(mgalldé)
Naḣna	Ăam	Mngalléd	(mgalldeen)
Intoo	Ăam	Btgalldoo	(mgalldeen)
Hinné	Ăam	Bigalldoo	(mgalldeen)

Past

Ana	Galladt
Inta	Galladt
Inté	Galladté
Hoowé	Gallad
Heeyé	Galladét
Naḣna	Galladna
Intoo	Galladtoo
Hinné	Galladoo

Past Continuous

Ana	Kint Ăam	Bgalléd	(kint	mgallad/mgalldé)
Inta	Kint Ăam	Btgalléd	(Kint	mgallad)
Inté	Kinté Ăam	Btgalldé	(Kinté	mgalldé)
Hoowé	Kén Ăam	Bigalléd	(Kén	mgallad)
Heeyé	Kénét Ăam	Btgalléd	(Kénét	mgalldé)
Naḣna	Kinna Ăam	Mngalléd	(Kinna	mgalldeen)
Intoo	Kintoo Ăam	Btgalldoo	(Kintoo	mgalldeen)
Hinné	Kénoo Ăam	Bigalldoo	(Kénoo	mgalldeen)

Future

Ana	Laḣ	Galléd
Inta	Laḣ	Tgalléd
Inté	Laḣ	Tgalldé
Hoowé	Laḣ	Ygalléd
Heeyé	Laḣ	Tgalléd
Naḣna	Laḣ	Ngalléd
Intoo	Laḣ	Tgalldoo
Hinné	Laḣ	Ygalldoo

Command

Inta	Galléd
Inté	Galldé
Intoo	Galldoo
Inta	Ma tgalléd
Inté	Ma tgalldé
Intoo	Ma tgalldoo

To fry

Present

Ana	Bi'lé
Inta	Bti'lé
Inté	Bti'lé
Hoowé	Byi'lé
Heeyé	Bti'lé
Naḣna	Mni'lé
Intoo	Bti'loo
Hinné	Byi'loo

Present Continuous

Ana	Ăam	Bi'lé
Inta	Ăam	Bti'lé
Inté	Ăam	Bti'lé
Hoowé	Ăam	Byi'lé
Heeyé	Ăam	Bti'lé
Naḣna	Ăam	Mni'lé
Intoo	Ăam	Bti'loo
Hinné	Ăam	Byi'loo

Past

Ana	'alét
Inta	'alét
Inté	'alaité
Hoowé	'ala
Heeyé	'alyét
Naḣna	'alaina
Intoo	'alaitoo
Hinné	'alyoo

Past Continuous

Ana	Kint Ăam	Bi'lé
Inta	Kint Ăam	Bti'lé
Inté	Kinté Ăam	Bti'lé
Hoowé	Kén Ăam	Byi'lé
Heeyé	Kénét Ăam	Bti'lé
Naḣna	Kinna Ăam	Mni'lé
Intoo	Kintoo Ăam	Bti'loo
Hinné	Kénoo Ăam	Byi'loo

Future

Ana	Laḣ	I'lé
Inta	Laḣ	Ti'lé
Inté	Laḣ	Ti'lé
Hoowé	Laḣ	Yi'lé
Heeyé	Laḣ	Ti'lé
Naḣna	Laḣ	Ni'lé
Intoo	Laḣ	Ti'loo
Hinné	Laḣ	Yi'loo

Command

Inta	'lee
Inté	'lee
Intoo	'loo
Inta	Ma t'lé
Inté	Ma t'lé
Intoo	Ma t'loo

Ă= Augh in bought	Ď= a heavy D	É= like A in Bay	G= G in beige	ḣ= like an H with smaller air passage	I= I as in ink	Ḱ= like ch in Irish loch
O= O as in home	OO= as in boots	R= roll the rrr	Ť= a heavy T	Ř= like a French R (gargle it)	Ŝ= a heavy S	Ž= a heavy Z

G   G

To gain weight

Present

Ana	binŜaĥ
Inta	btinŜaĥ
Inté	btinŜahé
Hoowé	byinŜaĥ
Heeyé	btinŜaĥ
Nahna	mninŜaĥ
Intoo	btinŜahoo
Hinné	byinŜahoo

Present Continuous

Ana	Ăam	binŜaĥ	(niŜhan/niŜhané)
Inta	Ăam	btinŜaĥ	(niŜhan)
Inté	Ăam	btinŜahé	(niŜhané)
Hoowé	Ăam	byinŜaĥ	(niŜhan)
Heeyé	Ăam	btinŜaĥ	(niŜhané)
Nahna	Ăam	mninŜaĥ	(niŜhaneen)
Intoo	Ăam	btinŜahoo	(niŜhaneen)
Hinné	Ăam	byinŜahoo	(niŜhaneen)

Past

Ana	nŜaht
Inta	nŜaht
Inté	nŜahté
Hoowé	niŜéĥ
Heeyé	niŜhét
Nahna	nŜahna
Intoo	nŜahtoo
Hinné	naŜhoo

Past Continuous

Ana	Kint Ăam	binŜaĥ	(kint	niŜhan/niŜhané)
Inta	Kint Ăam	btinŜaĥ	(Kint	niŜhan)
Inté	Kinté Ăam	btinŜahé	(Kinté	niŜhané)
Hoowé	Kén Ăam	byinŜaĥ	(Kén	niŜhan)
Heeyé	Kénét Ăam	btinŜaĥ	(Kénét	niŜhané)
Nahna	Kinna Ăam	mninŜaĥ	(Kinna	niŜhaneen)
Intoo	Kintoo Ăam	btinŜahoo	(Kintoo	niŜhaneen)
Hinné	Kénoo Ăam	byinŜahoo	(Kénoo	niŜhaneen)

Future

Ana	Laĥ	inŜaĥ
Inta	Laĥ	tinŜaĥ
Inté	Laĥ	tinŜahé
Hoowé	Laĥ	yinŜaĥ
Heeyé	Laĥ	tinŜaĥ
Nahna	Laĥ	ninŜaĥ
Intoo	Laĥ	tinŜahoo
Hinné	Laĥ	yinŜahoo

Command

Inta	nŜaĥ
Inté	nŜahé
Intoo	nŜahoo
Inta	Ma tnŜaĥ
Inté	Ma tnŜahé
Intoo	Ma tnŜahoo

To gargle

Present

Ana	bmaЌméĎ
Inta	btmaЌméĎ
Inté	btmaЌmĎé
Hoowé	bimaЌméĎ
Heeyé	btmaЌméĎ
Nahna	mnmaЌméĎ
Intoo	btmaЌmĎoo
Hinné	bimaЌmĎoo

Present Continuous

Ana	Ăam	bmaЌméĎ
Inta	Ăam	btmaЌméĎ
Inté	Ăam	btmaЌmĎé
Hoowé	Ăam	bimaЌméĎ
Heeyé	Ăam	btmaЌméĎ
Nahna	Ăam	mnmaЌméĎ
Intoo	Ăam	btmaЌmĎoo
Hinné	Ăam	bimaЌmĎoo

Past

Ana	maЌmaĎt
Inta	maЌmaĎt
Inté	maЌmaĎté
Hoowé	maЌmaĎ
Heeyé	maЌmaĎét
Nahna	maЌmaĎna
Intoo	maЌmaĎtoo
Hinné	maЌmaĎtoo

Past Continuous

Ana	Kint Ăam	bmaЌméĎ
Inta	Kint Ăam	btmaЌméĎ
Inté	Kinté Ăam	btmaЌmĎé
Hoowé	Kén Ăam	bimaЌméĎ
Heeyé	Kénét Ăam	btmaЌméĎ
Nahna	Kinna Ăam	mnmaЌméĎ
Intoo	Kintoo Ăam	btmaЌmĎoo
Hinné	Kénoo Ăam	bimaЌmĎoo

Future

Ana	Laĥ	maЌméĎ
Inta	Laĥ	tmaЌméĎ
Inté	Laĥ	tmaЌmĎé
Hoowé	Laĥ	ymaЌméĎ
Heeyé	Laĥ	tmaЌméĎ
Nahna	Laĥ	nmaЌméĎ
Intoo	Laĥ	tmaЌmĎoo
Hinné	Laĥ	ymaЌmĎoo

Command

Inta	maЌméĎ
Inté	maЌmĎé
Intoo	maЌmĎoo
Inta	Ma tmaЌméĎ
Inté	Ma tmaЌmĎé
Intoo	Ma tmaЌmĎoo

Ă= Augh in bought	**Ď**= a heavy D	**É**= like A in Bay	**G**= G in beige	**ĥ**= like an H with smaller air passage	**I**= I as in ink	**Ќ**= like ch in Irish loch
O= O as in home	**OO**= as in boots	**R**= roll the rrr	**Ť**= a heavy T	**Ř**= like a French R (gargle it)	**Ŝ**= a heavy S	**Ž**= a heavy Z

G   G

To give

Present

Ana	baĂŤé
Inta	btaĂŤé
Inté	btaĂŤé
Hoowé	byaĂŤé
Heeyé	btaĂŤé
Nahna	mnaĂŤé
Intoo	btaĂŤoo
Hinné	byaĂŤoo

Present Continuous

Ana	Ăam	baĂŤé
Inta	Ăam	btaĂŤé
Inté	Ăam	btaĂŤé
Hoowé	Ăam	byaĂŤé
Heeyé	Ăam	btaĂŤé
Nahna	Ăam	mnaĂŤé
Intoo	Ăam	btaĂŤoo
Hinné	Ăam	byaĂŤoo

Past

Ana	ĂaŤét
Inta	ĂaŤét
Inté	ĂaŤaité
Hoowé	ĂaŤa
Heeyé	ĂaŤyét
Nahna	ĂaŤaina
Intoo	ĂaŤaitoo
Hinné	ĂaŤoo

Past Continuous

Ana	Kint Ăam	baĂŤé
Inta	Kint Ăam	btaĂŤé
Inté	Kinté Ăam	btaĂŤé
Hoowé	Kén Ăam	byaĂŤé
Heeyé	Kénét Ăam	btaĂŤé
Nahna	Kinna Ăam	mnaĂŤé
Intoo	Kintoo Ăam	btaĂŤoo
Hinné	Kénoo Ăam	byaĂŤoo

Future

Ana	Laĥ	aĂŤé
Inta	Laĥ	taĂŤé
Inté	Laĥ	taĂŤé
Hoowé	Laĥ	yaĂŤé
Heeyé	Laĥ	taĂŤé
Nahna	Laĥ	naĂŤé
Intoo	Laĥ	taĂŤoo
Hinné	Laĥ	yaĂŤoo

Command

Inta	ĂŤee
Inté	ĂŤee
Intoo	ĂŤoo
Inta	Ma taĂŤé
Inté	Ma taĂŤé
Intoo	Ma taĂŤoo

To go

Present

Ana	Brooĥ
Inta	Btrooĥ
Inté	Btrooĥé
Hoowé	Birooĥ
Heeyé	Btrooĥ
Nahna	Mnrooĥ
Intoo	Btroohoo
Hinné	Birooĥ

Present Continuous

Ana	Ăam	Brooĥ	(rayéĥ/rayĥa)
Inta	Ăam	Btrooĥ	(rayéĥ)
Inté	Ăam	Btrooĥé	(rayĥa)
Hoowé	Ăam	Birooĥ	(rayéĥ)
Heeyé	Ăam	Btrooĥ	(rayĥa)
Nahna	Ăam	Mnrooĥ	(rayĥeen)
Intoo	Ăam	Btroohoo	(rayĥeen)
Hinné	Ăam	Birooĥ	(rayĥeen)

Past

Ana	Riĥt
Inta	Riĥt
Inté	Riĥté
Hoowé	Raĥ
Heeyé	Raĥét
Nahna	Riĥna
Intoo	Riĥtoo
Hinné	Raĥoo

Past Continuous

Ana	Kint Ăam	Brooĥ	(kint rayéĥ/rayĥa)
Inta	Kint Ăam	Btrooĥ	(Kint rayéĥ)
Inté	Kinté Ăam	Btrooĥé	(Kinté rayĥa)
Hoowé	Kén Ăam	Birooĥ	(Kén rayéĥ)
Heeyé	Kénét Ăam	Btrooĥ	(Kénét rayĥa)
Nahna	Kinna Ăam	Mnrooĥ	(Kinna rayĥeen)
Intoo	Kintoo Ăam	Btroohoo	(Kintoo rayĥeen)
Hinné	Kénoo Ăam	Birooĥ	(Kénoo rayĥeen)

Future

Ana	Laĥ	Rooĥ
Inta	Laĥ	Trooĥ
Inté	Laĥ	Trooĥé
Hoowé	Laĥ	Yrooĥ
Heeyé	Laĥ	Trooĥ
Nahna	Laĥ	Nrooĥ
Intoo	Laĥ	Troohoo
Hinné	Laĥ	Yrooĥ

Command

Inta	Rooĥ
Inté	Roohé
Intoo	Roohoo
Inta	Ma trooĥ
Inté	Ma troohé
Intoo	Ma troohoo

Ă= Augh in bought	Ď= a heavy D	É= like A in Bay	G= G in beige	ĥ= like an H with smaller air passage	I= I as in ink	Ќ= like ch in Irish loch
O= O as in home	OO= as in boots	R= roll the rrr	Ť= a heavy T	Ř= like a French R (gargle it)	Ŝ= a heavy S	Ž= a heavy Z

G

G

To grow

Present	
Ana	bikbar
Inta	btikbar
Inté	Btikbaré
Hoowé	byikbar
Heeyé	btikbar
Naĥna	mnikbar
Intoo	Btikbaroo
Hinné	byikbaroo

Present Continuous		
Ana	Ăam	Bikbar
Inta	Ăam	Btikbar
Inté	Ăam	Btikbaré
Hoowé	Ăam	byikbar
Heeyé	Ăam	btikbar
Naĥna	Ăam	mnikbar
Intoo	Ăam	Btikbaroo
Hinné	Ăam	byikbaroo

Past	
Ana	kbirt
Inta	kbirt
Inté	Kbirté
Hoowé	Kibér
Heeyé	kibrét
Naĥna	Kbirna
Intoo	Kbirtoo
Hinné	Kbiroo

Past Continuous		
Ana	Kint Ăam	bikbar
Inta	Kint Ăam	btikbar
Inté	Kinté Ăam	Btikbaré
Hoowé	Kén Ăam	byikbar
Heeyé	Kénét Ăam	btikbar
Naĥna	Kinna Ăam	mnikbar
Intoo	Kintoo Ăam	Btikbaroo
Hinné	Kénoo Ăam	byikbaroo

Future		
Ana	Laĥ	ikbar
Inta	Laĥ	tikbar
Inté	Laĥ	tikbaré
Hoowé	Laĥ	yikbar
Heeyé	Laĥ	tikbar
Naĥna	Laĥ	nikbar
Intoo	Laĥ	tikbaroo
Hinné	Laĥ	yikbaroo

Command	
Inta	Kbar
Inté	Kbaré
Intoo	Kbaroo
Inta	Ma tkbar
Inté	Ma tkbaré
Intoo	Ma tkbaroo

To guard

Present	
Ana	Biĥros
Inta	Btiĥros
Inté	Btiĥrsé
Hoowé	Byiĥros
Heeyé	Btiĥros
Naĥna	Mniĥros
Intoo	Btiĥrsoo
Hinné	Byiĥrsoo

Present Continuous		
Ana	Ăam Biĥros	(Hérés/ĥérsé)
Inta	Ăam Btiĥros	(ĥérés)
Inté	Ăam Btiĥrsé	(ĥérsé)
Hoowé	Ăam Byiĥros	(ĥérés)
Heeyé	Ăam Btiĥros	(ĥérsé)
Naĥna	Ăam Mniĥros	(ĥérseen)
Intoo	Ăam Btiĥrsoo	(ĥérseen)
Hinné	Ăam Byiĥrsoo	(ĥérseen)

Past	
Ana	Ĥarast
Inta	Ĥarast
Inté	Ĥarasté
Hoowé	Ĥaras
Heeyé	Ĥarasét
Naĥna	Ĥarasna
Intoo	Ĥarastoo
Hinné	Ĥarasoo

Past Continuous		
Ana	Kint Ăam Biĥros	(kint Hérés/ĥérsé)
Inta	Kint Ăam Btiĥros	(Kint ĥérés)
Inté	Kinté Ăam Btiĥrsé	(Kinté ĥérsé)
Hoowé	Kén Ăam Byiĥros	(Kén ĥérés)
Heeyé	Kénét Ăam Btiĥros	(Kénét ĥérsé)
Naĥna	Kinna Ăam Mniĥros	(Kinna ĥérseen)
Intoo	Kintoo Ăam Btiĥrsoo	(Kintoo ĥérseen)
Hinné	Kénoo Ăam Byiĥrsoo	(Kénoo ĥérseen)

Future		
Ana	Laĥ	iĥros
Inta	Laĥ	tiĥros
Inté	Laĥ	tiĥrsé
Hoowé	Laĥ	yiĥros
Heeyé	Laĥ	tiĥros
Naĥna	Laĥ	niĥros
Intoo	Laĥ	tiĥrsoo
Hinné	Laĥ	yiĥrsoo

Command	
Inta	Ĥros
Inté	Ĥrisé
Intoo	Ĥrisoo
Inta	Ma tĥros
Inté	Ma tĥrsé
Intoo	Ma tĥrsoo

Ă= Augh in bought	Ď= a heavy D	É= like A in Bay	G= G in beige	ĥ= like an H with smaller air passage	I= I as in ink	Ḱ= like ch in Irish loch
O= O as in home	OO= as in boots	R= roll the rrr	Ť= a heavy T	Ř= like a French R (gargle it)	Ŝ= a heavy S	Ž= a heavy Z

G   G

To guess

Present

Ana	biĥzar
Inta	btiĥzar
Inté	Btiĥzaré
Hoowé	byiĥzar
Heeyé	btiĥzar
Naĥna	mniĥzar
Intoo	Btiĥzaroo
Hinné	byiĥzaroo

Present Continuous

Ana	Ăam	biĥzar
Inta	Ăam	btiĥzar
Inté	Ăam	Btiĥzaré
Hoowé	Ăam	byiĥzar
Heeyé	Ăam	btiĥzar
Naĥna	Ăam	mniĥzar
Intoo	Ăam	Btiĥzaroo
Hinné	Ăam	byiĥzaroo

Past

Ana	Ĥzirt
Inta	Ĥzirt
Inté	Ĥzirté
Hoowé	Ĥizér
Heeyé	Ĥizrét
Naĥna	Ĥzirna
Intoo	Ĥzirtoo
Hinné	Ĥziroo

Past Continuous

Ana	Kint Ăam	biĥzar
Inta	Kint Ăam	btiĥzar
Inté	Kinté Ăam	Btiĥzaré
Hoowé	Kén Ăam	byiĥzar
Heeyé	Kénét Ăam	btiĥzar
Naĥna	Kinna Ăam	mniĥzar
Intoo	Kintoo Ăam	Btiĥzaroo
Hinné	Kénoo Ăam	byiĥzaroo

Future

Ana	Laĥ	iĥzar
Inta	Laĥ	tiĥzar
Inté	Laĥ	tiĥzaré
Hoowé	Laĥ	yiĥzar
Heeyé	Laĥ	tiĥzar
Naĥna	Laĥ	niĥzar
Intoo	Laĥ	tiĥzaroo
Hinné	Laĥ	yiĥzaroo

Command

Inta	Ĥzar
Inté	Ĥzaré
Intoo	Ĥzaroo
Inta	Ma tĥzar
Inté	Ma tĥzaré
Intoo	Ma tĥzaroo

To guide / to point at

Present

Ana	bdallé
Inta	btdallé
Inté	btdallé
Hoowé	bidallé
Heeyé	btdallé
Naĥna	mndallé
Intoo	Btdalloo
Hinné	bidalloo

Present Continuous

Ana	Ăam	bdallé
Inta	Ăam	btdallé
Inté	Ăam	btdallé
Hoowé	Ăam	bidallé
Heeyé	Ăam	btdallé
Naĥna	Ăam	mndallé
Intoo	Ăam	Btdalloo
Hinné	Ăam	bidalloo

Past

Ana	dallét
Inta	dallét
Inté	Dallaité
Hoowé	Dalla
Heeyé	dallét
Naĥna	Dallaina
Intoo	Dallaitoo
Hinné	dalloo

Past Continuous

Ana	Kint Ăam	bdallé
Inta	Kint Ăam	btdallé
Inté	Kinté Ăam	btdallé
Hoowé	Kén Ăam	bidallé
Heeyé	Kénét Ăam	btdallé
Naĥna	Kinna Ăam	mndallé
Intoo	Kintoo Ăam	Btdalloo
Hinné	Kénoo Ăam	bidalloo

Future

Ana	Laĥ	Dallé
Inta	Laĥ	tdallé
Inté	Laĥ	tdallé
Hoowé	Laĥ	ydallé
Heeyé	Laĥ	tdallé
Naĥna	Laĥ	ndallé
Intoo	Laĥ	tdalloo
Hinné	Laĥ	ydalloo

Command

Inta	Dallé
Inté	Dallé
Intoo	Dalloo
Inta	Ma tdallé
Inté	Ma tdallé
Intoo	Ma tdalloo

Ă= Augh in bought	Ď= a heavy D	É= like A in Bay	G= G in beige	ĥ= like an H with smaller air passage	I= I as in ink	Ǩ= like ch in Irish loch
O= O as in home	OO= as in boots	R= roll the rrr	Ť= a heavy T	Ř= like a French R (gargle it)	Š= a heavy S	Ž= a heavy Z

H   H

To hang a thing

Present

Ana	bĂallé'
Inta	btĂallé'
Inté	btĂall'é
Hoowé	biĂallé'
Heeyé	btĂallé'
Naĥna	mnĂallé'
Intoo	btĂall'oo
Hinné	biĂall'oo

Present Continuous

Ana	Ăam	bĂallé'
Inta	Ăam	btĂallé'
Inté	Ăam	btĂall'é
Hoowé	Ăam	biĂallé'
Heeyé	Ăam	btĂallé'
Naĥna	Ăam	mnĂallé'
Intoo	Ăam	btĂall'oo
Hinné	Ăam	biĂall'oo

Past

Ana	Ăalla't
Inta	Ăalla't
Inté	Ăalla'té
Hoowé	Ăalla'
Heeyé	Ăalla'ét
Naĥna	Ăalla'na
Intoo	Ăalla'too
Hinné	Ăalla'oo

Past Continuous

Ana	Kint Ăam	bĂallé'
Inta	Kint Ăam	btĂallé'
Inté	Kinté Ăam	btĂall'é
Hoowé	Kén Ăam	biĂallé'
Heeyé	Kénét Ăam	btĂallé'
Naĥna	Kinna Ăam	mnĂallé'
Intoo	Kintoo Ăam	btĂall'oo
Hinné	Kénoo Ăam	biĂall'oo

Future

Ana	Laĥ	Ăallé'
Inta	Laĥ	tĂallé'
Inté	Laĥ	tĂall'é
Hoowé	Laĥ	yĂallé'
Heeyé	Laĥ	tĂallé'
Naĥna	Laĥ	nĂallé'
Intoo	Laĥ	tĂall'oo
Hinné	Laĥ	yĂall'oo

Command

Inta	Ăallé'
Inté	Aall'é
Intoo	Aall'oo
Inta	Ma tĂallé'
Inté	Ma tĂall'é
Intoo	Ma tĂall'oo

To hang (people)

Present

Ana	Bishno'
Inta	Btishno'
Inté	Btishn'é
Hoowé	Byishno'
Heeyé	Btishno'
Naĥna	Mnishno'
Intoo	Btishn'oo
Hinné	Byishn'oo

Present Continuous

Ana	Ăam	Bishno'
Inta	Ăam	Btishno'
Inté	Ăam	Btishn'é
Hoowé	Ăam	Byishno'
Heeyé	Ăam	Btishno'
Naĥna	Ăam	Mnishno'
Intoo	Ăam	Btishn'oo
Hinné	Ăam	Byishn'oo

Past

Ana	Shana't
Inta	Shana't
Inté	Shana'té
Hoowé	Shana'
Heeyé	Shana'ét
Naĥna	Shana'na
Intoo	Shana'too
Hinné	Shana'oo

Past Continuous

Ana	Kint Ăam	Bishno'
Inta	Kint Ăam	Btishno'
Inté	Kinté Ăam	Btishn'é
Hoowé	Kén Ăam	Byishno'
Heeyé	Kénét Ăam	Btishno'
Naĥna	Kinna Ăam	Mnishno'
Intoo	Kintoo Ăam	Btishn'oo
Hinné	Kénoo Ăam	Byishn'oo

Future

Ana	Laĥ	Ishno'
Inta	Laĥ	tishno'
Inté	Laĥ	Tishn'é
Hoowé	Laĥ	yishno'
Heeyé	Laĥ	tishno'
Naĥna	Laĥ	nishno'
Intoo	Laĥ	Tishn'oo
Hinné	Laĥ	Yishn'oo

Command

Inta	Shno'
Inté	Shni'é
Intoo	Shni'oo
Inta	Ma tshno'
Inté	Ma tshn'é
Intoo	Ma tshn'oo

Ă= Augh in bought	Ď= a heavy D	É= like A in Bay	G= G in beige	ĥ= like an H with smaller air passage	I= I as in ink	Ќ= like ch in Irish loch
O= O as in home	OO= as in boots	R= roll the rrr	Ť= a heavy T	Ř= like a French R (gargle it)	Ŝ= a heavy S	Ž= a heavy Z

H   H

To hate

Present

Ana	Bikrah
Inta	Btikrah
Inté	Btikrahé
Hoowé	Byikrah
Heeyé	Btikrah
Naĥna	Mnikrah
Intoo	Btikrahoo
Hinné	Byikrahoo

Present Continuous

Ana	Ăam bikrah (or ana kirhan/kirhané)
Inta	Ăam btikrah (or kirhan)
Inté	Ăam btikrahé (or kirhané)
Hoowé	Ăam byikrah (or kirhan)
Heeyé	Ăam btikrah (or kirhané)
Naĥna	Ăam mnikrah (or kirhaneen)
Intoo	Ăam btikrahoo (or kirhaneen)
Hinné	Ăam byikrahoo (or kirhaneen)

Past

Ana	Karaht
Inta	Karaht
Inté	Karahté
Hoowé	Karah
Heeyé	Karahét
Naĥna	Karahna
Intoo	Karahtoo
Hinné	Karahoo

Past Continuous

Ana	Kint Ăam bikrah (or ana kint kirhan/kirhané)
Inta	Kint Ăam btikrah (or kint kirhan)
Inté	Kinté Ăam btikrahé (or kinté kirhané)
Hoowé	Kén Ăam byikrah (or kén kirhan)
Heeyé	Kénét Ăam btikrah (or kénét kirhané)
Naĥna	Kinna Ăam mnikrah (or kinna kirhaneen)
Intoo	Kintoo Ăam btikrahoo (or kintoo kirhaneen)
Hinné	Kénoo Ăam byikrahoo (or kénoo kirhaneen)

Future

Ana	Laĥ 'ikrah
Inta	Laĥ tikrah
Inté	Laĥ tikrahé
Hoowé	Laĥ yikrah
Heeyé	Laĥ tikrah
Naĥna	Laĥ nikrah
Intoo	Laĥ tikrahoo
Hinné	Laĥ yikrahoo

Command

Inta	Krah
Inté	Krahé
Intoo	Krahoo
Inta	Ma tikrah
Inté	Ma tikrahé
Intoo	Ma tikrahoo

To haunt

Present

Ana	birŜod
Inta	btirŜod
Inté	btirŜdé
Hoowé	byirŜod
Heeyé	btirŜod
Naĥna	mnirŜod
Intoo	btirŜdoo
Hinné	byirŜdoo

Present Continuous

Ana	Ăam	birŜod
Inta	Ăam	btirŜod
Inté	Ăam	btirŜdé
Hoowé	Ăam	byirŜod
Heeyé	Ăam	btirŜod
Naĥna	Ăam	mnirŜod
Intoo	Ăam	btirŜdoo
Hinné	Ăam	byirŜdoo

Past

Ana	raŜadt
Inta	raŜadt
Inté	raŜadté
Hoowé	raŜad
Heeyé	raŜadét
Naĥna	raŜadna
Intoo	raŜadtoo
Hinné	raŜadoo

Past Continuous

Ana	Kint Ăam	birŜod
Inta	Kint Ăam	btirŜod
Inté	Kinté Ăam	btirŜdé
Hoowé	Kén Ăam	byirŜod
Heeyé	Kénét Ăam	btirŜod
Naĥna	Kinna Ăam	mnirŜod
Intoo	Kintoo Ăam	btirŜdoo
Hinné	Kénoo Ăam	byirŜdoo

Future

Ana	Laĥ	irŜod
Inta	Laĥ	tirŜod
Inté	Laĥ	tirŜdé
Hoowé	Laĥ	yirŜod
Heeyé	Laĥ	tirŜod
Naĥna	Laĥ	nirŜod
Intoo	Laĥ	tirŜdoo
Hinné	Laĥ	yirŜdoo

Command

Inta	rŜod
Inté	rŜidé
Intoo	rŜidoo
Inta	Ma trŜod
Inté	Ma trŜdé
Intoo	Ma trŜdoo

Ă= Augh in bought	**Ď**= a heavy D	**É**= like A in Bay	**G**= G in beige	**ĥ**= like an H with smaller air passage	**I**= I as in ink	**Ќ**= like ch in Irish loch
O= O as in home	**OO**= as in boots	**R**= roll the rrr	**Ť**= a heavy T	**Ř**= like a French R (gargle it)	**Ŝ**= a heavy S	**Ž**= a heavy Z

H H

To have

Present

Ana	Ăandé
Inta	Ăandak
Inté	Ăandeek
Hoowé	Ăandoo
Heeyé	Ăanda
Naḥna	Ăanna
Intoo	Ăandkon
Hinné	Aandon

Present Continuous (exception)

Ana	Ăandé
Inta	Ăandak
Inté	Ăandeek
Hoowé	Ăandoo
Heeyé	Ăanda
Naḥna	Ăanna
Intoo	Ăandkon
Hinné	Aandon

Past

Ana	Kint Ăandé
Inta	Kint Ăandak
Inté	Kinté Ăandeek
Hoowé	Kén Ăandoo
Heeyé	Kénét Ăanda
Naḥna	Kinna Ăanna
Intoo	Kintoo Ăandkon
Hinné	Kénoo Aandon

Past Continuous (exception)

Ana	Kint Ăandé
Inta	Kint Ăandak
Inté	Kinté Ăandeek
Hoowé	Kén Ăandoo
Heeyé	Kénét Ăanda
Naḥna	Kinna Ăanna
Intoo	Kintoo Ăandkon
Hinné	Kénoo Aandon

Future (exception)

Ana	Laḥ ykoon Ăandé
Inta	Laḥ ykoon Ăandak
Inté	Laḥ ykoon Ăandeek
Hoowé	Laḥ ykoon Ăandoo
Heeyé	Laḥ ykoon Ăanda
Naḥna	Laḥ ykoon Ăanna
Intoo	Laḥ ykoon Ăandkon
Hinné	Laḥ ykoon Aandon

Command

Inta	n/a
Inté	n/a
Intoo	n/a
Inta	n/a
Inté	n/a
Intoo	n/a

To hear/listen

Present

Ana	BismaĂ
Inta	BtismaĂ
Inté	BtismaĂé
Hoowé	ByismaĂ
Heeyé	BtismaĂ
Naḥna	MnismaĂ
Intoo	BtismaĂoo
Hinné	ByismaĂoo

Present Continuous

Ana	Ăam bismaĂ (or ana séméĂ/sémĂa)
Inta	Ăam btismaĂ (or séméĂ)
Inté	Ăam btismaĂé (or sémĂa)
Hoowé	Ăam byismaĂ (or séméĂ)
Heeyé	Ăam btismaĂ (or sémĂa)
Naḥna	Ăam mnismaĂ (or sémĂeen)
Intoo	Ăam btismaĂoo (or sémĂeen)
Hinné	Ăam byismaĂoo (or sémĂeen)

Past

Ana	smaĂt
Inta	smaĂt
Inté	smaĂté
Hoowé	siméĂ
Heeyé	simĂét
Naḥna	smiĂna
Intoo	smiĂtoo
Hinné	simĂoo

Past Continuous

Ana	Kint Ăam bismaĂ (or ana kint séméĂ/sémĂa)
Inta	Kint Ăam btismaĂ (or kint séméĂ)
Inté	Kinté Ăam btismaĂé (or kinté sémĂa)
Hoowé	Kén Ăam byismaĂ (or kén séméĂ)
Heeyé	Kénét Ăam btismaĂ (or Kénét sémĂa)
Naḥna	Kinna Ăam mnismaĂ (or kinna sémĂeen)
Intoo	Kintoo Ăam btismaĂoo (or kintoo sémĂeen)
Hinné	Kénoo Ăam byismaĂoo (or kénoo sémĂeen)

Future

Ana	Laḥ 'ismaĂ
Inta	Laḥ tismaĂ
Inté	Laḥ tismaĂé
Hoowé	Laḥ yismaĂ
Heeyé	Laḥ tismaĂ
Naḥna	Laḥ nismaĂ
Intoo	Laḥ tismaĂoo
Hinné	Laḥ yismaĂoo

Command

Inta	sméĂ
Inté	smaĂé
Intoo	smaĂoo
Inta	Ma tismaĂ
Inté	Ma tismaĂé
Intoo	Ma tismaĂoo

Ă= Augh in bought	Ď= a heavy D	É= like A in Bay	G= G in beige	ḣ= like an H with smaller air passage	I= I as in ink	Ḱ= like ch in Irish loch
O= O as in home	OO= as in boots	R= roll the rrr	Ť= a heavy T	Ř= like a French R (gargle it)	Ŝ= a heavy S	Ž= a heavy Z

To heat

Present	
Ana	bsaḰḰén
Inta	btsaḰḰén
Inté	btsaḰḰné
Hoowé	bisaḰḰén
Heeyé	btsaḰḰén
Naħna	mnsaḰḰén
Intoo	btsaḰḰnoo
Hinné	bisaḰḰnoo

Present Continuous		
Ana	Ăam	bsaḰḰén
Inta	Ăam	btsaḰḰén
Inté	Ăam	btsaḰḰné
Hoowé	Ăam	bisaḰḰén
Heeyé	Ăam	btsaḰḰén
Naħna	Ăam	mnsaḰḰén
Intoo	Ăam	btsaḰḰnoo
Hinné	Ăam	bisaḰḰnoo

Past	
Ana	saḰḰant
Inta	saḰḰant
Inté	saḰḰanté
Hoowé	saḰḰan
Heeyé	saḰḰanét
Naħna	saḰḰanna
Intoo	saḰḰantoo
Hinné	saḰḰanoo

Past Continuous		
Ana	Kint Ăam	bsaḰḰén
Inta	Kint Ăam	btsaḰḰén
Inté	Kinté Ăam	btsaḰḰné
Hoowé	Kén Ăam	bisaḰḰén
Heeyé	Kénét Ăam	btsaḰḰén
Naħna	Kinna Ăam	mnsaḰḰén
Intoo	Kintoo Ăam	btsaḰḰnoo
Hinné	Kénoo Ăam	bisaḰḰnoo

Future		
Ana	Laħ	saḰḰén
Inta	Laħ	tsaḰḰén
Inté	Laħ	tsaḰḰné
Hoowé	Laħ	ysaḰḰén
Heeyé	Laħ	tsaḰḰén
Naħna	Laħ	nsaḰḰén
Intoo	Laħ	tsaḰḰnoo
Hinné	Laħ	ysaḰḰnoo

Command	
Inta	saḰḰén
Inté	saḰḰné
Intoo	saḰḰnoo
Inta	Ma tsaḰḰén
Inté	Ma tsaḰḰné
Intoo	Ma tsaḰḰnoo

To help

Present	
Ana	bséĂéd
Inta	btséĂéd
Inté	btséĂdé
Hoowé	biséĂéd
Heeyé	btséĂéd
Naħna	mnséĂéd
Intoo	btséĂdoo
Hinné	biséĂdoo

Present Continuous		
Ana	Ăam	bséĂéd
Inta	Ăam	btséĂéd
Inté	Ăam	btséĂdé
Hoowé	Ăam	biséĂéd
Heeyé	Ăam	btséĂéd
Naħna	Ăam	mnséĂéd
Intoo	Ăam	btséĂdoo
Hinné	Ăam	biséĂdoo

Past	
Ana	séĂadt
Inta	séĂadt
Inté	séĂadté
Hoowé	séĂad
Heeyé	séĂadét
Naħna	séĂadna
Intoo	séĂadtoo
Hinné	séĂadoo

Past Continuous		
Ana	Kint Ăam	bséĂéd
Inta	Kint Ăam	btséĂéd
Inté	Kinté Ăam	btséĂdé
Hoowé	Kén Ăam	biséĂéd
Heeyé	Kénét Ăam	btséĂéd
Naħna	Kinna Ăam	mnséĂéd
Intoo	Kintoo Ăam	btséĂdoo
Hinné	Kénoo Ăam	biséĂdoo

Future		
Ana	Laħ	séĂéd
Inta	Laħ	tséĂéd
Inté	Laħ	tséĂdé
Hoowé	Laħ	yséĂéd
Heeyé	Laħ	tséĂéd
Naħna	Laħ	nséĂéd
Intoo	Laħ	tséĂdoo
Hinné	Laħ	yséĂdoo

Command	
Inta	séĂéd
Inté	séĂdé
Intoo	séĂdoo
Inta	Ma tséĂéd
Inté	Ma tséĂdé
Intoo	Ma tséĂdoo

Ă= Augh in bought	Ď= a heavy D	É= like A in Bay	G= G in beige	ĥ= like an H with smaller air passage	I= I as in ink	Ḱ= like ch in Irish loch
O= O as in home	OO= as in boots	R= roll the rrr	Ť= a heavy T	Ř= like a French R (gargle it)	Ŝ= a heavy S	Ž= a heavy Z

H H

To hide

Present

Ana	bitK̆abba
Inta	btitK̆abba
Inté	btitK̆abbé
Hoowé	byitK̆abba
Heeyé	btitK̆abba
Naĥna	mnitK̆abba
Intoo	btitK̆abboo
Hinné	byitK̆abboo

Present Continuous

Ana	Ăam	bitK̆abba	(mitK̆abba/mitKibbéyé)
Inta	Ăam	btitK̆abba	(mitK̆abba)
Inté	Ăam	btitK̆abbé	(mitKibbéyé)
Hoowé	Ăam	byitK̆abba	(mitK̆abba)
Heeyé	Ăam	btitK̆abba	(mitKibbéyé)
Naĥna	Ăam	mnitK̆abba	(mitKibbéyeen)
Intoo	Ăam	btitK̆abboo	(mitKibbéyeen)
Hinné	Ăam	byitK̆abboo	(mitKibbéyeen)

Past

Ana	tK̆abbét
Inta	tK̆abbét
Inté	tK̆abbaité
Hoowé	tK̆abba
Heeyé	tK̆abbét
Naĥna	tK̆abbaina
Intoo	tK̆abbaitoo
Hinné	tK̆abboo

Past Continuous

Ana	Kint Ăam	bitK̆abba	(kint mitK̆abba/mitKibbéyé)
Inta	Kint Ăam	btitK̆abba	(Kint mitK̆abba)
Inté	Kinté Ăam	btitK̆abbé	(Kinté mitKibbéyé)
Hoowé	Kén Ăam	byitK̆abba	(Kén mitK̆abba)
Heeyé	Kénét Ăam	btitK̆abba	(Kénét mitKibbéyé)
Naĥna	Kinna Ăam	mnitK̆abba	(Kinna mitKibbéyeen)
Intoo	Kintoo Ăam	btitK̆abboo	(Kintoo mitKibbéyeen)
Hinné	Kénoo Ăam	byitK̆abboo	(Kénoo mitKibbéyeen)

Future

Ana	Laĥ	itK̆abba
Inta	Laĥ	titK̆abba
Inté	Laĥ	titK̆abbé
Hoowé	Laĥ	yitK̆abba
Heeyé	Laĥ	titK̆abba
Naĥna	Laĥ	nitK̆abba
Intoo	Laĥ	titK̆abboo
Hinné	Laĥ	yitK̆abboo

Command

Inta	tK̆abba
Inté	tK̆abbé
Intoo	tK̆abboo
Inta	Ma ttK̆abba
Inté	Ma ttK̆abbé
Intoo	Ma ttK̆abboo

To hit

Present

Ana	biĎrob
Inta	btiĎrob
Inté	btiĎrbé
Hoowé	byiĎrob
Heeyé	btiĎrob
Naĥna	mniĎrob
Intoo	btiĎrboo
Hinné	byiĎrboo

Present Continuous

Ana	Ăam	biĎrob
Inta	Ăam	btiĎrob
Inté	Ăam	btiĎrbé
Hoowé	Ăam	byiĎrob
Heeyé	Ăam	btiĎrob
Naĥna	Ăam	mniĎrob
Intoo	Ăam	btiĎrboo
Hinné	Ăam	byiĎrboo

Past

Ana	Ďarabt
Inta	Ďarabt
Inté	Ďarabté
Hoowé	Ďarab
Heeyé	Ďarbét
Naĥna	Ďarabna
Intoo	Ďarabtoo
Hinné	Ďaraboo

Past Continuous

Ana	Kint Ăam	biĎrob
Inta	Kint Ăam	btiĎrob
Inté	Kinté Ăam	btiĎrbé
Hoowé	Kén Ăam	byiĎrob
Heeyé	Kénét Ăam	btiĎrob
Naĥna	Kinna Ăam	mniĎrob
Intoo	Kintoo Ăam	btiĎrboo
Hinné	Kénoo Ăam	byiĎrboo

Future

Ana	Laĥ	iĎrob
Inta	Laĥ	tiĎrob
Inté	Laĥ	tiĎrbé
Hoowé	Laĥ	yiĎrob
Heeyé	Laĥ	tiĎrob
Naĥna	Laĥ	niĎrob
Intoo	Laĥ	tiĎrboo
Hinné	Laĥ	yiĎrboo

Command

Inta	Ďrob
Inté	Ďribé
Intoo	Ďriboo
Inta	Ma tĎrob
Inté	Ma tiĎrbé
Intoo	Ma tĎrboo

Ă= Augh in bought	Ď= a heavy D	É= like A in Bay	G= G in beige	ĥ= like an H with smaller air passage	I= I as in ink	K̆= like ch in Irish loch
O= O as in home	OO= as in boots	R= roll the rrr	Ť= a heavy T	Ř= like a French R (gargle it)	Š= a heavy S	Ž= a heavy Z

To hold

Present	
Ana	Bimsék
Inta	Btimsék
Inté	Btimské
Hoowé	Byimsékl
Heeyé	Btimsék
Nahna	Mnimsék
Intoo	Btimskoo
Hinné	Byimskoo

Present Continuous	
Ana	Ăam Bimsék (mésék/méské)
Inta	Ăam Btimsék (késék)
Inté	Ăam Btimské (méské)
Hoowé	Ăam Byimsék (mésék)
Heeyé	Ăam Btimsék (méské)
Nahna	Ăam Mnimsék (méskeen)
Intoo	Ăam Btimskoo (méskeen)
Hinné	Ăam Byimskoo (méskeen)

Past	
Ana	Masakt
Inta	Masakt
Inté	Masakté
Hoowé	Masak
Heeyé	Maskét
Nahna	Masakna
Intoo	Masaktoo
Hinné	Maskoo

Past Continuous	
Ana	Kint Ăam Bimsék (kint mésék/méské)
Inta	Kint Ăam Btimsék (kint mésék)
Inté	Kinté Ăam Btimsék (kinté méské)
Hoowé	Kén Ăam Byimsék (kén mésék)
Heeyé	Kénét Ăam Btimsék (kénét méské)
Nahna	Kinna Ăam Mnimsék (kinna méskeen)
Intoo	Kintoo Ăam Btimskoo (kintoo méskeen)
Hinné	Kénoo Ăam Byimskoo (kénoo méskeen)

Future	
Ana	Laĥ imsék
Inta	Laĥ timsék
Inté	Laĥ timské
Hoowé	Laĥ yimsék
Heeyé	Laĥ timsék
Nahna	Laĥ nimsék
Intoo	Laĥ timskoo
Hinné	Laĥ yimskoo

Command	
Inta	msék (also msok)
Inté	Msiké
Intoo	Msikoo
Inta	Ma timsék (also timsok)
Inté	Ma timské
Intoo	Ma timskoo

To honk

Present		
Ana	Bzammér	
Inta	Btzammér	
Inté	Btzammré	
Hoowé	Bizammér	
Heeyé	Btzammér	
Nahna	Mnzammér	
Intoo	Btzammroo	
Hinné	Bizammroo	

Present Continuous		
Ana	Ăam	Bzammér
Inta	Ăam	Btzammér
Inté	Ăam	Btzammré
Hoowé	Ăam	Bizammér
Heeyé	Ăam	Btzammér
Nahna	Ăam	Mnzammér
Intoo	Ăam	Btzammroo
Hinné	Ăam	Bizammroo

Past		
Ana	Zammart	
Inta	Zammart	
Inté	Zammarté	
Hoowé	Zammar	
Heeyé	Zammarét	
Nahna	Zammarna	
Intoo	Zammartoo	
Hinné	Zammaroo	

Past Continuous		
Ana	Kint Ăam	Bzammér
Inta	Kint Ăam	Btzammér
Inté	Kinté Ăam	Btzammré
Hoowé	Kén Ăam	Bizammér
Heeyé	Kénét Ăam	Btzammér
Nahna	Kinna Ăam	Mnzammér
Intoo	Kintoo Ăam	Btzammroo
Hinné	Kénoo Ăam	Bizammroo

Future		
Ana	Laĥ	Zammér
Inta	Laĥ	Tzammér
Inté	Laĥ	Tzammré
Hoowé	Laĥ	Yzammér
Heeyé	Laĥ	Tzammér
Nahna	Laĥ	Nzammér
Intoo	Laĥ	Tzammroo
Hinné	Laĥ	Yzammroo

Command	
Inta	Zammér
Inté	Zammré
Intoo	Zammroo
Inta	Ma tzammér
Inté	Ma tzammré
Intoo	Ma tzammroo

Ă= Augh in bought	Ď= a heavy D	É= like A in Bay	G= G in beige	ĥ= like an H with smaller air passage	I= I as in ink	Ķ= like ch in Irish loch
O= O as in home	OO= as in boots	R= roll the rrr	Ť= a heavy T	Ř= like a French R (gargle it)	Ŝ= a heavy S	Ž= a heavy Z

To honour

Present

Ana	Bkarrém
Inta	Btkarrém
Inté	Btkarrmé
Hoowé	Bikarrém
Heeyé	Bkarrém
Nahna	Mnkarrém
Intoo	Btkarrmoo
Hinné	Bikarrmoo

Present Continuous

Ana	Ăam	Bkarrém
Inta	Ăam	Btkarrém
Inté	Ăam	Btkarrmé
Hoowé	Ăam	Bikarrém
Heeyé	Ăam	Bkarrém
Nahna	Ăam	Mnkarrém
Intoo	Ăam	Btkarrmoo
Hinné	Ăam	Bikarrmoo

Past

Ana	Karramt
Inta	Karramt
Inté	Karramté
Hoowé	Karram
Heeyé	Karramét
Nahna	Karramna
Intoo	Karramtoo
Hinné	Karramoo

Past Continuous

Ana	Kint Ăam	Bkarrém
Inta	Kint Ăam	Btkarrém
Inté	Kinté Ăam	Btkarrmé
Hoowé	Kén Ăam	Bikarrém
Heeyé	Kénét Ăam	Bkarrém
Nahna	Kinna Ăam	Mnkarrém
Intoo	Kintoo Ăam	Btkarrmoo
Hinné	Kénoo Ăam	Bikarrmoo

Future

Ana	Lah	Karrém
Inta	Lah	Tkarrém
Inté	Lah	Tkarrmé
Hoowé	Lah	Ykarrém
Heeyé	Lah	Karrém
Nahna	Lah	Nkarrém
Intoo	Lah	Tkarrmoo
Hinné	Lah	Ykarrmoo

Command

Inta	Karrém
Inté	Karrmé
Intoo	Karrmoo
Inta	Ma tkarrém
Inté	Ma tkarrmé
Intoo	Ma tkarmoo

To hope

Present

Ana	Bt'ammal
Inta	Btit'ammal
Inté	Btit'ammlé
Hoowé	Byit'ammal
Heeyé	Btit'ammal
Nahna	mnt'ammal
Intoo	Btit'ammloo
Hinné	Byit'ammloo

Present Continuous

Ana	Ăam	Bt'ammal	(mit'ammal/mit'ammlé)
Inta	Ăam	Btit'ammal	(mit'ammal)
Inté	Ăam	Btit'ammlé	(mit'ammlé)
Hoowé	Ăam	Byit'ammal	(mit'ammal)
Heeyé	Ăam	Btit'ammal	(mit'ammlé)
Nahna	Ăam	mnt'ammal	(mt'ammleen)
Intoo	Ăam	Btit'ammloo	(mt'ammleen)
Hinné	Ăam	Byit'ammloo	(mt'ammleen)

Past

Ana	t'ammalt
Inta	t'ammalt
Inté	t'ammalté
Hoowé	t'ammalt
Heeyé	t'ammalét
Nahna	t'ammalna
Intoo	t'ammaltoo
Hinné	t'ammaloo

Past Continuous

Ana	Kint Ăam	Bt'ammal	(kint mit'ammal/mit'ammlé)
Inta	Kint Ăam	Btit'ammal	(Kint mit'ammal)
Inté	Kinté Ăam	Btit'ammlé	(Kinté mit'ammlé)
Hoowé	Kén Ăam	Byit'ammal	(Kén mit'ammal)
Heeyé	Kénét Ăam	Btit'ammal	(Kénét mit'ammlé)
Nahna	Kinna Ăam	mnt'ammal	(Kinna mt'ammleen)
Intoo	Kintoo Ăam	Btit'ammloo	(Kintoo mt'ammleen)
Hinné	Kénoo Ăam	Byit'ammloo	(Kénoo mt'ammleen)

Future

Ana	Lah	it'ammal
Inta	Lah	tit'ammal
Inté	Lah	tit'ammlé
Hoowé	Lah	yit'ammal
Heeyé	Lah	tit'ammal
Nahna	Lah	nit'ammal
Intoo	Lah	tit'ammloo
Hinné	Lah	yit'ammloo

Command

Inta	T'ammal
Inté	T'ammlé
Intoo	T'ammloo
Inta	Ma tit'ammal
Inté	Ma tit'ammlé
Intoo	Ma tit'ammloo

Ă= Augh in bought	Ď= a heavy D	É= like A in Bay	G= G in beige	h= like an H with smaller air passage	I= I as in ink	Ќ= like ch in Irish loch
O= O as in home	OO= as in boots	R= roll the rrr	Ť= a heavy T	Ř= like a French R (gargle it)	Ŝ= a heavy S	Ž= a heavy Z

H H

To humiliate

Present

Ana	Bheen
Inta	Btheen
Inté	Btheené
Hoowé	Biheen
Heeyé	Btheen
Naĥna	Mnheen
Intoo	Btheenoo
Hinné	Biheenoo

Present Continuous

Ana	Ăam	Bheen
Inta	Ăam	Btheen
Inté	Ăam	Btheené
Hoowé	Ăam	Biheen
Heeyé	Ăam	Btheen
Naĥna	Ăam	Mnheen
Intoo	Ăam	Btheenoo
Hinné	Ăam	Biheenoo

Past

Ana	Hint
Inta	Hint
Inté	Hinté
Hoowé	Hén
Heeyé	Hénét
Naĥna	Hinna
Intoo	Hinntoo
Hinné	Hénoo

Past Continuous

Ana	Kint Ăam	Bheen
Inta	Kint Ăam	Btheen
Inté	Kinté Ăam	Btheené
Hoowé	Kén Ăam	Biheen
Heeyé	Kénét Ăam	Btheen
Naĥna	Kinna Ăam	Mnheen
Intoo	Kintoo Ăam	Btheenoo
Hinné	Kénoo Ăam	Biheenoo

Future

Ana	Laĥ	Heen
Inta	Laĥ	Theen
Inté	Laĥ	Theené
Hoowé	Laĥ	Yheen
Heeyé	Laĥ	Theen
Naĥna	Laĥ	Nheen
Intoo	Laĥ	Theenoo
Hinné	Laĥ	Yheenoo

Command

Inta	Heen
Inté	Heené
Intoo	Heenoo
Inta	Ma theen
Inté	Ma theené
Intoo	Ma theenoo

To hunt

Present

Ana	bitŜayad
Inta	btitŜayad
Inté	btitŜayadé
Hoowé	byitŜayad
Heeyé	btitŜayad
Naĥna	mnitŜayad
Intoo	btitŜayadoo
Hinné	byitŜayadoo

Present Continuous

Ana	Ăam	bitŜayad
Inta	Ăam	btitŜayad
Inté	Ăam	btitŜayadé
Hoowé	Ăam	byitŜayad
Heeyé	Ăam	btitŜayad
Naĥna	Ăam	mnitŜayad
Intoo	Ăam	btitŜayadoo
Hinné	Ăam	byitŜayadoo

Past

Ana	tŜayadt
Inta	tŜayadt
Inté	tŜayadté
Hoowé	tŜayad
Heeyé	tŜayadét
Naĥna	tŜayadna
Intoo	tŜayadtoo
Hinné	tŜayadoo

Past Continuous

Ana	Kint Ăam	bitŜayad
Inta	Kint Ăam	btitŜayad
Inté	Kinté Ăam	btitŜayadé
Hoowé	Kén Ăam	byitŜayad
Heeyé	Kénét Ăam	btitŜayad
Naĥna	Kinna Ăam	mnitŜayad
Intoo	Kintoo Ăam	btitŜayadoo
Hinné	Kénoo Ăam	byitŜayadoo

Future

Ana	Laĥ	itŜayad
Inta	Laĥ	titŜayad
Inté	Laĥ	titŜayadé
Hoowé	Laĥ	yitŜayad
Heeyé	Laĥ	titŜayad
Naĥna	Laĥ	nitŜayad
Intoo	Laĥ	titŜayadoo
Hinné	Laĥ	yitŜayadoo

Command

Inta	tŜayad
Inté	tŜaydé
Intoo	tŜaydoo
Inta	Ma ttŜayad
Inté	Ma ttŜayadé
Intoo	Ma ttŜayadoo

Ă= Augh in bought	Ď= a heavy D	É= like A in Bay	G= G in beige	ĥ= like an H with smaller air passage	I= I as in ink	Ḱ= like ch in Irish loch
O= O as in home	OO= as in boots	R= roll the rrr	Ť= a heavy T	Ř= like a French R (gargle it)	Ŝ= a heavy S	Ž= a heavy Z

H I

To hurt

Present

Ana	Bi'zé
Inta	Bti'zé
Inté	Bti'zé
Hoowé	Byi'zé
Heeyé	Bti'zé
Naḥna	Mni'zé
Intoo	Bti'zoo
Hinné	Byi'zoo

Present Continuous

Ana	Ăam	Bi'zé
Inta	Ăam	Bti'zé
Inté	Ăam	Bti'zé
Hoowé	Ăam	Byi'zé
Heeyé	Ăam	Bti'zé
Naḥna	Ăam	Mni'zé
Intoo	Ăam	Bti'zoo
Hinné	Ăam	Byi'zoo

Past

Ana	Azét
Inta	Azét
Inté	Azité
Hoowé	Aza
Heeyé	Azét
Naḥna	Azaina
Intoo	Azaitoo
Hinné	azoo

Past Continuous

Ana	Kint Ăam	Bi'zé
Inta	Kint Ăam	Bti'zé
Inté	Kinté Ăam	Bti'zé
Hoowé	Kén Ăam	Byi'zé
Heeyé	Kénét Ăam	Bti'zé
Naḥna	Kinna Ăam	Mni'zé
Intoo	Kintoo Ăam	Bti'zoo
Hinné	Kénoo Ăam	Byi'zoo

Future

Ana	Laḥ	I'zé
Inta	Laḥ	Ti'zé
Inté	Laḥ	Ti'zé
Hoowé	Laḥ	yi'zé
Heeyé	Laḥ	Ti'zé
Naḥna	Laḥ	ni'zé
Intoo	Laḥ	Ti'zoo
Hinné	Laḥ	yi'zoo

Command

Inta	'zee
Inté	'zee
Intoo	'zoo
Inta	Ma t'zé
Inté	Ma t'zé
Intoo	Ma t'zoo

To immitate

Present

Ana	B'alléd
Inta	Bt'alléd
Inté	Bt'alldé
Hoowé	Bi'alléd
Heeyé	Bt'alléd
Naḥna	Mn'alléd
Intoo	Bt'alldoo
Hinné	Bi'alldoo

Present Continuous

Ana	Ăam	B'alléd
Inta	Ăam	Bt'alléd
Inté	Ăam	Bt'alldé
Hoowé	Ăam	Bi'alléd
Heeyé	Ăam	Bt'alléd
Naḥna	Ăam	Mn'alléd
Intoo	Ăam	Bt'alldoo
Hinné	Ăam	Bi'alldoo

Past

Ana	'alladt
Inta	'alladt
Inté	'alladté
Hoowé	'allad
Heeyé	'alladét
Naḥna	'alladna
Intoo	'alladtoo
Hinné	'alladoo

Past Continuous

Ana	Kint Ăam	B'alléd
Inta	Kint Ăam	Bt'alléd
Inté	Kinté Ăam	Bt'alldé
Hoowé	Kén Ăam	Bi'alléd
Heeyé	Kénét Ăam	Bt'alléd
Naḥna	Kinna Ăam	Mn'alléd
Intoo	Kintoo Ăam	Bt'alldoo
Hinné	Kénoo Ăam	Bi'alldoo

Future

Ana	Laḥ	'alléd
Inta	Laḥ	T'alléd
Inté	Laḥ	T'alldé
Hoowé	Laḥ	Y'alléd
Heeyé	Laḥ	T'alléd
Naḥna	Laḥ	N'alléd
Intoo	Laḥ	T'alldoo
Hinné	Laḥ	Y'alldoo

Command

Inta	'alléd
Inté	'alldé
Intoo	'alldoo
Inta	Ma t'alléd
Inté	Ma t'alldé
Intoo	Ma t'alldoo

Ă= Augh in bought	Ď= a heavy D	É= like A in Bay	G= G in beige	ḥ= like an H with smaller air passage	I= I as in ink	Ḱ= like ch in Irish loch
O= O as in home	OO= as in boots	R= roll the rrr	Ť= a heavy T	Ř= like a French R (gargle it)	Ŝ= a heavy S	Ž= a heavy Z

I

I

To improve

Present

Ana	Bḥassén
Inta	Btḥassén
Inté	Btḥassné
Hoowé	Biḥassén
Heeyé	Btḥassén
Naḥna	Mnḥassén
Intoo	Btḥassnoo
Hinné	Biḥassnoo

Present Continuous

Ana	Ăam	Bḥassén
Inta	Ăam	Btḥassén
Inté	Ăam	Btḥassné
Hoowé	Ăam	Biḥassén
Heeyé	Ăam	Btḥassén
Naḥna	Ăam	Mnḥassén
Intoo	Ăam	Btḥassnoo
Hinné	Ăam	Biḥassnoo

Past

Ana	Ḥassant
Inta	Ḥassant
Inté	Ḥassanté
Hoowé	Ḥassan
Heeyé	Ḥassanét
Naḥna	Ḥassanna
Intoo	Ḥassantoo
Hinné	Ḥassanoo

Past Continuous

Ana	Kint Ăam	Bḥassén
Inta	Kint Ăam	Btḥassén
Inté	Kinté Ăam	Btḥassné
Hoowé	Kén Ăam	Biḥassén
Heeyé	Kénét Ăam	Btḥassén
Naḥna	Kinna Ăam	Mnḥassén
Intoo	Kintoo Ăam	Btḥassnoo
Hinné	Kénoo Ăam	Biḥassnoo

Future

Ana	Laḥ	Ḥassén
Inta	Laḥ	Tḥassén
Inté	Laḥ	Tḥassné
Hoowé	Laḥ	Yḥassén
Heeyé	Laḥ	Tḥassén
Naḥna	Laḥ	Nḥassén
Intoo	Laḥ	Tḥassnoo
Hinné	Laḥ	Yḥassnoo

Command

Inta	Ḥassén
Inté	Ḥassné
Intoo	Ḥassnoo
Inta	Ma tḥassén
Inté	Ma tḥassné
Intoo	Ma tḥassnoo

To include

Present

Ana	bDĭmm
Inta	btDĭmm
Inté	btDĭmmé
Hoowé	biDĭmm
Heeyé	btDĭmm
Naḥna	mnDĭmm
Intoo	btDĭmmoo
Hinné	biDĭmmoo

Present Continuous

Ana	Ăam	bDĭmm
Inta	Ăam	btDĭmm
Inté	Ăam	btDĭmmé
Hoowé	Ăam	biDĭmm
Heeyé	Ăam	btDĭmm
Naḥna	Ăam	mnDĭmm
Intoo	Ăam	btDĭmmoo
Hinné	Ăam	biDĭmmoo

Past

Ana	Dammét
Inta	Dammét
Inté	Dammaité
Hoowé	Damm
Heeyé	Dammét
Naḥna	Dammaina
Intoo	Dammaitoo
Hinné	Dammoo

Past Continuous

Ana	Kint Ăam	bDĭmm
Inta	Kint Ăam	btDĭmm
Inté	Kinté Ăam	btDĭmmé
Hoowé	Kén Ăam	biDĭmm
Heeyé	Kénét Ăam	btDĭmm
Naḥna	Kinna Ăam	mnDĭmm
Intoo	Kintoo Ăam	btDĭmmoo
Hinné	Kénoo Ăam	biDĭmmoo

Future

Ana	Laḥ	Dĭmm
Inta	Laḥ	tDĭmm
Inté	Laḥ	tDĭmmé
Hoowé	Laḥ	yDĭmm
Heeyé	Laḥ	tDĭmm
Naḥna	Laḥ	nDĭmm
Intoo	Laḥ	tDĭmmoo
Hinné	Laḥ	yDĭmmoo

Command

Inta	Dĭmm
Inté	Dĭmmé
Intoo	Dĭmmoo
Inta	Ma tDĭmm
Inté	Ma tDĭmmé
Intoo	Ma tDĭmmoo

Ă= Augh in bought	Ď= a heavy D	É= like A in Bay	G= G in beige	ḥ= like an H with smaller air passage	I= I as in ink	Ќ= like ch in Irish loch
O= O as in home	OO= as in boots	R= roll the rrr	Ť= a heavy T	Ř= like a French R (gargle it)	Ŝ= a heavy S	Ž= a heavy Z

I   I

To increase

Present	
Ana	Bzeed
Inta	Btzeed
Inté	Btzeedé
Hoowé	Bizeed
Heeyé	Btzeed
Naĥna	Mnzeed
Intoo	Btzeedoo
Hinné	Bizeedoo

Present Continuous			
Ana	Ăam	Bzeed	(zéyéd/zéydé))
Inta	Ăam	Btzeed	(zéyéd)
Inté	Ăam	Btzeedé	(zéydé)
Hoowé	Ăam	Bizeed	(zéyéd)
Heeyé	Ăam	Btzeed	(zéydé)
Naĥna	Ăam	Mnzeed	(zéydeen)
Intoo	Ăam	Btzeedoo	(zéydeen)
Hinné	Ăam	Bizeedoo	(zéydeen)

Past	
Ana	Zidt
Inta	Zidt
Inté	Zidté
Hoowé	Zéd
Heeyé	Zédét
Naĥna	Zidna
Intoo	Zidtoo
Hinné	Zédoo

Past Continuous			
Ana	Kint Ăam	Bzeed	(kint zéyéd/zéydé)
Inta	Kint Ăam	Btzeed	(Kint zéyéd)
Inté	Kinté Ăam	Btzeedé	(Kinté zéydé)
Hoowé	Kén Ăam	Bizeed	(Kén zéyéd)
Heeyé	Kénét Ăam	Btzeed	(Kénét zéydé)
Naĥna	Kinna Ăam	Mnzeed	(Kinna zéydeen)
Intoo	Kintoo Ăam	Btzeedoo	(Kintoo zéydeen)
Hinné	Kénoo Ăam	Bizeedoo	(Kénoo zéydeen)

Future		
Ana	Laĥ	Zeed
Inta	Laĥ	Tzeed
Inté	Laĥ	Tzeedé
Hoowé	Laĥ	Yzeed
Heeyé	Laĥ	Tzeed
Naĥna	Laĥ	Nzeed
Intoo	Laĥ	Tzeedoo
Hinné	Laĥ	Yzeedoo

Command	
Inta	Zeed
Inté	Zeedé
Intoo	Zeedoo
Inta	Ma tzeed
Inté	Ma tzeedé
Intoo	Ma tzeedoo

To inherit

Present	
Ana	Boorat
Inta	Btoorat
Inté	Btooraté
Hoowé	Byoorat
Heeyé	Btoorat
Naĥna	Mnoorat
Intoo	Btooratoo
Hinné	Byooratoo

Present Continuous		
Ana	Ăam	Boorat
Inta	Ăam	Btoorat
Inté	Ăam	Btooraté
Hoowé	Ăam	Byoorat
Heeyé	Ăam	Btoorat
Naĥna	Ăam	Mnoorat
Intoo	Ăam	Btooratoo
Hinné	Ăam	Byooratoo

Past	
Ana	Waratt
Inta	Waratt
Inté	Waratté
Hoowé	Warat
Heeyé	Waratét
Naĥna	Waratna
Intoo	Warattoo
Hinné	Waratoo

Past Continuous		
Ana	Kint Ăam	Boorat
Inta	Kint Ăam	Btoorat
Inté	Kinté Ăam	Btooraté
Hoowé	Kén Ăam	Byoorat
Heeyé	Kénét Ăam	Btoorat
Naĥna	Kinna Ăam	Mnoorat
Intoo	Kintoo Ăam	Btooratoo
Hinné	Kénoo Ăam	Byooratoo

Future		
Ana	Laĥ	'oorat
Inta	Laĥ	Toorat
Inté	Laĥ	tooraté
Hoowé	Laĥ	yoorat
Heeyé	Laĥ	Toorat
Naĥna	Laĥ	noorat
Intoo	Laĥ	tooratoo
Hinné	Laĥ	yooratoo

Command	
Inta	Wrat
Inté	Wraté
Intoo	Wratoo
Inta	Ma toorat
Inté	Ma tooraté
Intoo	Ma tooratoo

Ă= Augh in bought	Ď= a heavy D	É= like A in Bay	G= G in beige	ĥ= like an H with smaller air passage	I= I as in ink	Ķ= like ch in Irish loch
O= O as in home	OO= as in boots	R= roll the rrr	Ť= a heavy T	Ř= like a French R (gargle it)	Ŝ= a heavy S	Ž= a heavy Z

I

I

To insert

Present	
Ana	Bfawwét
Inta	Btfawwét
Inté	Btfawwté
Hoowé	Bifawwét
Heeyé	Btfawwét
Naḣna	Mnfawwét
Intoo	Btfawwtoo
Hinné	Bifawwtoo

Present Continuous		
Ana	Ăam	Bfawwét
Inta	Ăam	Btfawwét
Inté	Ăam	Btfawwté
Hoowé	Ăam	Bifawwét
Heeyé	Ăam	Btfawwét
Naḣna	Ăam	Mnfawwét
Intoo	Ăam	Btfawwtoo
Hinné	Ăam	Bifawwtoo

Past	
Ana	Fawwatt
Inta	Fawwatt
Inté	Fawwatté
Hoowé	Fawwat
Heeyé	Fawwatét
Naḣna	Fawwatna
Intoo	Fawwattoo
Hinné	Fawwatoo

Past Continuous		
Ana	Kint Ăam	Bfawwét
Inta	Kint Ăam	Btfawwét
Inté	Kinté Ăam	Btfawwté
Hoowé	Kén Ăam	Bifawwét
Heeyé	Kénét Ăam	Btfawwét
Naḣna	Kinna Ăam	Mnfawwét
Intoo	Kintoo Ăam	Btfawwtoo
Hinné	Kénoo Ăam	Bifawwtoo

Future		
Ana	Laḣ	Fawwét
Inta	Laḣ	Tfawwét
Inté	Laḣ	Tfawwté
Hoowé	Laḣ	Yfawwét
Heeyé	Laḣ	Tfawwét
Naḣna	Laḣ	Nfawwét
Intoo	Laḣ	Tfawwtoo
Hinné	Laḣ	Yfawwtoo

Command	
Inta	Fawwét
Inté	Fawwté
Intoo	Fawwtoo
Inta	Ma tfawwét
Inté	Ma tfawwté
Intoo	Ma tfawwtoo

To insist

Present	
Ana	bŜirr
Inta	btŜirr
Inté	btŜirré
Hoowé	biŜirr
Heeyé	btŜirr
Naḣna	mnŜirr
Intoo	btŜirroo
Hinné	biŜirroo

Present Continuous		
Ana	Ăam	bŜirr
Inta	Ăam	btŜirr
Inté	Ăam	btŜirré
Hoowé	Ăam	biŜirr
Heeyé	Ăam	btŜirr
Naḣna	Ăam	mnŜirr
Intoo	Ăam	btŜirroo
Hinné	Ăam	biŜirroo

Past	
Ana	aŜarrét
Inta	aŜarrét
Inté	aŜarraité
Hoowé	aŜarr
Heeyé	aŜarrét
Naḣna	aŜarraina
Intoo	aŜarraitoo
Hinné	aŜarroo

Past Continuous		
Ana	Kint Ăam	bŜirr
Inta	Kint Ăam	btŜirr
Inté	Kinté Ăam	btŜirré
Hoowé	Kén Ăam	biŜirr
Heeyé	Kénét Ăam	btŜirr
Naḣna	Kinna Ăam	mnŜirr
Intoo	Kintoo Ăam	btŜirroo
Hinné	Kénoo Ăam	biŜirroo

Future		
Ana	Laḣ	Ŝirr
Inta	Laḣ	tŜirr
Inté	Laḣ	nŜirr
Hoowé	Laḣ	yŜirr
Heeyé	Laḣ	tŜirr
Naḣna	Laḣ	nŜirr
Intoo	Laḣ	tŜirroo
Hinné	Laḣ	yŜirroo

Command	
Inta	Ŝirr
Inté	Ŝirré
Intoo	Ŝirroo
Inta	Ma tŜirr
Inté	Ma tŜirré
Intoo	Ma tŜirroo

Ă= Augh in bought	Ď= a heavy D	É= like A in Bay	G= G in beige	ḣ= like an H with smaller air passage	I= I as in ink	Ќ= like ch in Irish loch
O= O as in home	OO= as in boots	R= roll the rrr	Ť= a heavy T	Ř= like a French R (gargle it)	Ŝ= a heavy S	Ž= a heavy Z

I

I

To insulate

Present

Ana	biĂzol
Inta	btiĂzol
Inté	btiĂzlé
Hoowé	byiĂzol
Heeyé	btiĂzol
Nahna	mniĂzol
Intoo	btiĂzloo
Hinné	byiĂzloo

Present Continuous

Ana	Ăam	biĂzol
Inta	Ăam	btiĂzol
Inté	Ăam	btiĂzlé
Hoowé	Ăam	byiĂzol
Heeyé	Ăam	btiĂzol
Nahna	Ăam	mniĂzol
Intoo	Ăam	btiĂzloo
Hinné	Ăam	byiĂzloo

Past

Ana	Ăazalt
Inta	Ăazalt
Inté	Ăazalté
Hoowé	Ăazal
Heeyé	Ăazalét
Nahna	Ăazalna
Intoo	Ăazaltoo
Hinné	Ăazaloo

Past Continuous

Ana	Kint Ăam	biĂzol
Inta	Kint Ăam	btiĂzol
Inté	Kinté Ăam	btiĂzlé
Hoowé	Kén Ăam	byiĂzol
Heeyé	Kénét Ăam	btiĂzol
Nahna	Kinna Ăam	mniĂzol
Intoo	Kintoo Ăam	btiĂzloo
Hinné	Kénoo Ăam	byiĂzloo

Future

Ana	Laĥ	iĂzol
Inta	Laĥ	tiĂzol
Inté	Laĥ	tiĂzlé
Hoowé	Laĥ	yiĂzol
Heeyé	Laĥ	tiĂzol
Nahna	Laĥ	niĂzol
Intoo	Laĥ	tiĂzloo
Hinné	Laĥ	yiĂzloo

Command

Inta	Ăzol
Inté	Ăzilé
Intoo	Ăziloo
Inta	Ma tĂzol
Inté	Ma tĂzlé
Intoo	Ma tĂzloo

To insult

Present

Ana	Bheen
Inta	Btheen
Inté	Btheené
Hoowé	Biheen
Heeyé	Btheen
Nahna	Mnheen
Intoo	Btheenoo
Hinné	Biheenoo

Present Continuous

Ana	Ăam	Bheen
Inta	Ăam	Btheen
Inté	Ăam	Btheené
Hoowé	Ăam	Biheen
Heeyé	Ăam	Btheen
Nahna	Ăam	Mnheen
Intoo	Ăam	Btheenoo
Hinné	Ăam	Biheenoo

Past

Ana	Hint
Inta	Hint
Inté	Hinté
Hoowé	Hén
Heeyé	Hénét
Nahna	Hinna
Intoo	Hintoo
Hinné	Hinnoo

Past Continuous

Ana	Kint Ăam	Bheen
Inta	Kint Ăam	Btheen
Inté	Kinté Ăam	Btheené
Hoowé	Kén Ăam	Biheen
Heeyé	Kénét Ăam	Btheen
Nahna	Kinna Ăam	Mnheen
Intoo	Kintoo Ăam	Btheenoo
Hinné	Kénoo Ăam	Biheenoo

Future

Ana	Laĥ	Heen
Inta	Laĥ	Theen
Inté	Laĥ	Theené
Hoowé	Laĥ	Yheen
Heeyé	Laĥ	Theen
Nahna	Laĥ	Nheen
Intoo	Laĥ	Theenoo
Hinné	Laĥ	Yheenoo

Command

Inta	Heen
Inté	Heené
Intoo	Heenoo
Inta	Ma theen
Inté	Ma theené
Intoo	Ma theenoo

Ă= Augh in bought	Ď= a heavy D	É= like A in Bay	G= G in beige	ĥ= like an H with smaller air passage	I= I as in ink	Ќ= like ch in Irish loch
O= O as in home	OO= as in boots	R= roll the rrr	Ť= a heavy T	Ř= like a French R (gargle it)	Ŝ= a heavy S	Ž= a heavy Z

I

I

To invent

Present	
Ana	biḰtiriĂ
Inta	btiḰtiriĂ
Inté	btiḰtirĂé
Hoowé	byiḰtiriĂ
Heeyé	btiḰtiriĂ
Naḣna	mniḰtiriĂ
Intoo	btiḰtirĂoo
Hinné	byiḰtirĂoo

Present Continuous		
Ana	Ăam	biḰtiriĂ
Inta	Ăam	btiḰtiriĂ
Inté	Ăam	btiḰtirĂé
Hoowé	Ăam	byiḰtiriĂ
Heeyé	Ăam	btiḰtiriĂ
Naḣna	Ăam	mniḰtiriĂ
Intoo	Ăam	btiḰtirĂoo
Hinné	Ăam	byiḰtirĂoo

Past	
Ana	ḰtaraĂt
Inta	ḰtaraĂt
Inté	ḰtaraĂté
Hoowé	ḰtaraĂ
Heeyé	ḰtaraĂét
Naḣna	ḰtaraĂna
Intoo	ḰtaraĂtoo
Hinné	ḰtaraĂoo

Past Continuous		
Ana	Kint Ăam	biḰtiriĂ
Inta	Kint Ăam	btiḰtiriĂ
Inté	Kinté Ăam	btiḰtirĂé
Hoowé	Kén Ăam	byiḰtiriĂ
Heeyé	Kénét Ăam	btiḰtiriĂ
Naḣna	Kinna Ăam	mniḰtiriĂ
Intoo	Kintoo Ăam	btiḰtirĂoo
Hinné	Kénoo Ăam	byiḰtirĂoo

Future		
Ana	Laḣ	iḰtiriĂ
Inta	Laḣ	tiḰtiriĂ
Inté	Laḣ	tiḰtirĂé
Hoowé	Laḣ	yiḰtiriĂ
Heeyé	Laḣ	tiḰtiriĂ
Naḣna	Laḣ	niḰtiriĂ
Intoo	Laḣ	tiḰtirĂoo
Hinné	Laḣ	yiḰtirĂoo

Command	
Inta	ḰtiriĂ
Inté	ḰtirĂé
Intoo	ḰtirĂoo
Inta	Ma tḰtiriĂ
Inté	Ma tḰtirĂé
Intoo	Ma tḰtirĂoo

To invite

Present	
Ana	biĂzom
Inta	btiĂzom
Inté	btiĂzmé
Hoowé	byiĂzom
Heeyé	btiĂzom
Naḣna	mniĂzom
Intoo	btiĂzmoo
Hinné	byiĂzmoo

Present Continuous			
Ana	Ăam	biĂzom	(Ăézém/Ăézmé)
Inta	Ăam	btiĂzom	(Ăézém)
Inté	Ăam	btiĂzmé	(Ăézmé)
Hoowé	Ăam	byiĂzom	(Ăézém)
Heeyé	Ăam	btiĂzom	(Ăézmé)
Naḣna	Ăam	mniĂzom	(Ăézmeen)
Intoo	Ăam	btiĂzmoo	(Ăézmeen)
Hinné	Ăam	byiĂzmoo	(Ăézmeen)

Past	
Ana	Ăazamt
Inta	Ăazamt
Inté	Ăazamté
Hoowé	Ăazam
Heeyé	Ăazamét
Naḣna	Ăazamna
Intoo	Ăazamtoo
Hinné	Ăazamoo

Past Continuous			
Ana	Kint Ăam	biĂzom	(kint Ăézém/Ăézmé)
Inta	Kint Ăam	btiĂzom	(Kint Ăézém)
Inté	Kinté Ăam	btiĂzmé	(Kinté Ăézmé)
Hoowé	Kén Ăam	byiĂzom	(Kén Ăézém)
Heeyé	Kénét Ăam	btiĂzom	(Kénét Ăézmé)
Naḣna	Kinna Ăam	mniĂzom	(Kinna Ăézmeen)
Intoo	Kintoo Ăam	btiĂzmoo	(Kintoo Ăézmeen)
Hinné	Kénoo Ăam	byiĂzmoo	(Kénoo Ăézmeen)

Future		
Ana	Laḣ	iĂzom
Inta	Laḣ	tiĂzom
Inté	Laḣ	tiĂzmé
Hoowé	Laḣ	yiĂzom
Heeyé	Laḣ	tiĂzom
Naḣna	Laḣ	niĂzom
Intoo	Laḣ	tiĂzmoo
Hinné	Laḣ	yiĂzmoo

Command	
Inta	Ăzom
Inté	Ăzimé
Intoo	Ăzimoo
Inta	Ma tĂzom
Inté	Ma tĂzmé
Intoo	Ma tĂzmoo

Ă= Augh in bought	Ď= a heavy D	É= like A in Bay	G= G in beige	ḣ= like an H with smaller air passage	I= I as in ink	Ḱ= like ch in Irish loch
O= O as in home	OO= as in boots	R= roll the rrr	Ť= a heavy T	Ř= like a French R (gargle it)	Ŝ= a heavy S	Ž= a heavy Z

I

J

To be involved

Present

Ana	bitdaḰKal
Inta	btitdaḰKal
Inté	btitdaḰKalé
Hoowé	byitdaḰKal
Heeyé	btitdaḰKal
Nahna	mnitdaḰKal
Intoo	btitdaḰKaloo
Hinné	btitdaḰKaloo

Present Continuous

Ana	Ăam	bitdaḰKal
Inta	Ăam	btitdaḰKal
Inté	Ăam	btitdaḰKalé
Hoowé	Ăam	byitdaḰKal
Heeyé	Ăam	btitdaḰKal
Nahna	Ăam	mnitdaḰKal
Intoo	Ăam	btitdaḰKaloo
Hinné	Ăam	btitdaḰKaloo

Past

Ana	tdaḰKalt
Inta	tdaḰKalt
Inté	tdaḰKalté
Hoowé	tdaḰKal
Heeyé	tdaḰKalét
Nahna	tdaḰKalna
Intoo	tdaḰKaltoo
Hinné	tdaḰKaloo

Past Continuous

Ana	Kint Ăam	bitdaḰKal
Inta	Kint Ăam	btitdaḰKal
Inté	Kinté Ăam	btitdaḰKalé
Hoowé	Kén Ăam	byitdaḰKal
Heeyé	Kénét Ăam	btitdaḰKal
Nahna	Kinna Ăam	mnitdaḰKal
Intoo	Kintoo Ăam	btitdaḰKaloo
Hinné	Kénoo Ăam	btitdaḰKaloo

Future

Ana	Laĥ	itdaḰKal
Inta	Laĥ	titdaḰKal
Inté	Laĥ	titdaḰKalé
Hoowé	Laĥ	yitdaḰKal
Heeyé	Laĥ	titdaḰKal
Nahna	Laĥ	nitdaḰKal
Intoo	Laĥ	titdaḰKaloo
Hinné	Laĥ	titdaḰKaloo

Command

Inta	tdaḰKal
Inté	tdaḰKalé
Intoo	tdaḰKaloo
Inta	Ma ttdaḰKal
Inté	Ma ttdaḰKalé
Intoo	Ma ttdaḰKaloo

To joke

Present

Ana	Bimzaĥ
Inta	Btimzaĥ
Inté	Btimzaĥé
Hoowé	Byimzaĥ
Heeyé	Btimzaĥ
Nahna	Mnimzaĥ
Intoo	Btimzaĥoo
Hinné	Byimzaĥoo

Present Continuous

Ana	Ăam	Bimzaĥ
Inta	Ăam	Btimzaĥ
Inté	Ăam	Btimzaĥé
Hoowé	Ăam	Byimzaĥ
Heeyé	Ăam	Btimzaĥ
Nahna	Ăam	Mnimzaĥ
Intoo	Ăam	Btimzaĥoo
Hinné	Ăam	Byimzaĥoo

Past

Ana	mazaĥt
Inta	mazaĥt
Inté	Mazaĥté
Hoowé	mazaĥ
Heeyé	mazaĥét
Nahna	Mazaĥna
Intoo	Mazaĥtoo
Hinné	mazaĥoo

Past Continuous

Ana	Kint Ăam	Bimzaĥ
Inta	Kint Ăam	Btimzaĥ
Inté	Kinté Ăam	Btimzaĥé
Hoowé	Kén Ăam	Byimzaĥ
Heeyé	Kénét Ăam	Btimzaĥ
Nahna	Kinna Ăam	Mnimzaĥ
Intoo	Kintoo Ăam	Btimzaĥoo
Hinné	Kénoo Ăam	Byimzaĥoo

Future

Ana	Laĥ	imzaĥ
Inta	Laĥ	timzaĥ
Inté	Laĥ	Timzaĥé
Hoowé	Laĥ	yimzaĥ
Heeyé	Laĥ	timzaĥ
Nahna	Laĥ	nimzaĥ
Intoo	Laĥ	Timzaĥoo
Hinné	Laĥ	yimzaĥoo

Command

Inta	Mzaĥ
Inté	Mzaĥé
Intoo	Mzaĥoo
Inta	Ma timzaĥ
Inté	Ma timzaĥé
Intoo	Ma timzaĥoo

Ă= Augh in bought	**Ď**= a heavy D	**É**= like A in Bay	**G**= G in beige	**ĥ**= like an H with smaller air passage	**I**= I as in ink	**Ḱ**= like ch in Irish loch
O= O as in home	**OO**= as in boots	**R**= roll the rrr	**Ť**= a heavy T	**Ř**= like a French R (gargle it)	**Ŝ**= a heavy S	**Ž**= a heavy Z

J   K

To jump

Present

Ana	bniŤ
Inta	bitniŤ
Inté	bitniŤŤé
Hoowé	biniŤ
Heeyé	bitniŤ
Naĥna	mnniŤ
Intoo	btniŤŤoo
Hinné	biniŤŤoo

Present Continuous

Ana	Ăam	bniŤ
Inta	Ăam	bitniŤ
Inté	Ăam	bitniŤŤé
Hoowé	Ăam	biniŤ
Heeyé	Ăam	bitniŤ
Naĥna	Ăam	mnniŤ
Intoo	Ăam	btniŤŤoo
Hinné	Ăam	biniŤŤoo

Past

Ana	naŤéŤ
Inta	naŤéŤ
Inté	nŤaiŤé
Hoowé	naŤ
Heeyé	NaŤŤéŤ
Naĥna	naŤŤaina
Intoo	naŤŤaiŤoo
Hinné	naŤŤoo

Past Continuous

Ana	Kint Ăam	bniŤ
Inta	Kint Ăam	bitniŤ
Inté	Kinté Ăam	bitniŤŤé
Hoowé	Kén Ăam	biniŤ
Heeyé	Kénét Ăam	bitniŤ
Naĥna	Kinna Ăam	mnniŤ
Intoo	Kintoo Ăam	btniŤŤoo
Hinné	Kénoo Ăam	biniŤŤoo

Future

Ana	Laĥ	niŤ
Inta	Laĥ	tniŤ
Inté	Laĥ	tniŤé
Hoowé	Laĥ	yniŤ
Heeyé	Laĥ	tniŤ
Naĥna	Laĥ	nniŤ
Intoo	Laĥ	tniŤŤoo
Hinné	Laĥ	yniŤŤoo

Command

Inta	niŤ
Inté	niŤé
Intoo	niŤŤoo
Inta	Ma tniŤ
Inté	Ma tniŤé
Intoo	Ma tniŤŤoo

To keep

Present

Ana	bKallé
Inta	btKallé
Inté	btKallé
Hoowé	biKallé
Heeyé	btKallé
Naĥna	mnKallé
Intoo	btKalloo
Hinné	biKalloo

Present Continuous

Ana	Ăam	bKallé	(mKalla/mKilléyé)
Inta	Ăam	btKallé	(mKalla)
Inté	Ăam	btKallé	(mKilléyé)
Hoowé	Ăam	biKallé	(mKalla)
Heeyé	Ăam	btKallé	(mKilléyé)
Naĥna	Ăam	mnKallé	(mKilléyeen)
Intoo	Ăam	btKalloo	(mKilléyeen)
Hinné	Ăam	biKalloo	(mKilléyeen)

Past

Ana	Kallét
Inta	Kallét
Inté	KallAIté
Hoowé	Kalla
Heeyé	Kallét
Naĥna	Kallaina
Intoo	Kallaitoo
Hinné	Kalloo

Past Continuous

Ana	Kint Ăam	bKallé	(kint	(mKalla/mKilléyé)
Inta	Kint Ăam	btKallé	(Kint	(mKalla)
Inté	Kinté Ăam	btKallé	(Kinté	(mKilléyé)
Hoowé	Kén Ăam	biKallé	(Kén	(mKalla)
Heeyé	Kénét Ăam	btKallé	(Kénét	(mKilléyé)
Naĥna	Kinna Ăam	mnKallé	(Kinna	(mKilléyeen)
Intoo	Kintoo Ăam	btKalloo	(Kintoo	(mKilléyeen)
Hinné	Kénoo Ăam	biKalloo	(Kénoo	(mKilléyeen)

Future

Ana	Laĥ	Kallé
Inta	Laĥ	tKallé
Inté	Laĥ	tKallé
Hoowé	Laĥ	yKallé
Heeyé	Laĥ	tKallé
Naĥna	Laĥ	nKallé
Intoo	Laĥ	tKalloo
Hinné	Laĥ	yKalloo

Command

Inta	Kallé
Inté	Kallé
Intoo	Kalloo
Inta	Ma tKallé
Inté	Ma tKallé
Intoo	Ma tKalloo

Ă= Augh in bought	Ď= a heavy D	É= like A in Bay	G= G in beige	ĥ= like an H with smaller air passage	I= I as in ink	Ḱ= like ch in Irish loch
O= O as in home	OO= as in boots	R= roll the rrr	Ť= a heavy T	Ř= like a French R (gargle it)	Ŝ= a heavy S	Ž= a heavy Z

K   K

To kick

Present

Ana	bilboŤ
Inta	btilboŤ
Inté	btilbŤé
Hoowé	byilboŤ
Heeyé	btilboŤ
Nahna	mnilboŤ
Intoo	btilbŤoo
Hinné	byilbŤoo

Present Continuous

Ana	Ăam	bilboŤ
Inta	Ăam	btilboŤ
Inté	Ăam	btilbŤé
Hoowé	Ăam	byilboŤ
Heeyé	Ăam	btilboŤ
Nahna	Ăam	mnilboŤ
Intoo	Ăam	btilbŤoo
Hinné	Ăam	byilbŤoo

Past

Ana	labaŤ
Inta	labaŤ
Inté	labaŤté
Hoowé	labaŤ
Heeyé	labaŤét
Nahna	labaŤna
Intoo	labaŤtoo
Hinné	labaŤoo

Past Continuous

Ana	Kint Ăam	bilboŤ
Inta	Kint Ăam	btilboŤ
Inté	Kinté Ăam	btilbŤé
Hoowé	Kén Ăam	byilboŤ
Heeyé	Kénét Ăam	btilboŤ
Nahna	Kinna Ăam	mnilboŤ
Intoo	Kintoo Ăam	btilbŤoo
Hinné	Kénoo Ăam	byilbŤoo

Future

Ana	Laĥ	ilboŤ
Inta	Laĥ	tilboŤ
Inté	Laĥ	tilbŤé
Hoowé	Laĥ	yilboŤ
Heeyé	Laĥ	tilboŤ
Nahna	Laĥ	nilboŤ
Intoo	Laĥ	tilbŤoo
Hinné	Laĥ	yilbŤoo

Command

Inta	lboŤ
Inté	lbiŤé
Intoo	lbiŤoo
Inta	Ma tlboŤ
Inté	Ma tlbŤé
Intoo	Ma tlbŤoo

To kill

Present

Ana	Bi'tol
Inta	Bti'tol
Inté	Bti'tlé
Hoowé	Byi'tol
Heeyé	Bti'tol
Nahna	mni'tol
Intoo	Bti'tloo
Hinné	Byi'tloo

Present Continuous

Ana	Ăam	Bi'tol
Inta	Ăam	Bti'tol
Inté	Ăam	Bti'tlé
Hoowé	Ăam	Byi'tol
Heeyé	Ăam	Bti'tol
Nahna	Ăam	mni'tol
Intoo	Ăam	Bti'tloo
Hinné	Ăam	Byi'tloo

Past

Ana	atalt
Inta	atalt
Inté	Atalté
Hoowé	Atal
Heeyé	atalét
Nahna	Atalna
Intoo	Ataltoo
Hinné	ataloo

Past Continuous

Ana	Kint Ăam	Bi'tol
Inta	Kint Ăam	Bti'tol
Inté	Kinté Ăam	Bti'tlé
Hoowé	Kén Ăam	Byi'tol
Heeyé	Kénét Ăam	Bti'tol
Nahna	Kinna Ăam	mni'tol
Intoo	Kintoo Ăam	Bti'tloo
Hinné	Kénoo Ăam	Byi'tloo

Future

Ana	Laĥ	'i'tol
Inta	Laĥ	ti'tol
Inté	Laĥ	ti'tlé
Hoowé	Laĥ	yi'tol
Heeyé	Laĥ	ti'tol
Nahna	Laĥ	ni'tol
Intoo	Laĥ	ti'tloo
Hinné	Laĥ	yi'tloo

Command

Inta	'tol
Inté	'tilé
Intoo	'tiloo
Inta	Ma t'tol
Inté	Ma t'tlé
Intoo	Ma t'tloo

Ă= Augh in bought	Ď= a heavy D	É= like A in Bay	G= G in beige	ĥ= like an H with smaller air passage	I= I as in ink	Ḱ= like ch in Irish loch
O= O as in home	OO= as in boots	R= roll the rrr	Ť= a heavy T	Ř= like a French R (gargle it)	Ŝ= a heavy S	Ž= a heavy Z

<u>K</u>   <u>K</u>

To Knock

Present	
Ana	Bdi'
Inta	Btdi'
Inté	Btdi''é
Hoowé	Bidi'
Heeyé	Btdi'
Naĥna	Mndi'
Intoo	Btdi''oo
Hinné	Bidi''oo

Present Continuous		
Ana	Ăam	Bdi'
Inta	Ăam	Btdi'
Inté	Ăam	Btdi''é
Hoowé	Ăam	Bidi'
Heeyé	Ăam	Btdi'
Naĥna	Ăam	Mndi'
Intoo	Ăam	Btdi''oo
Hinné	Ăam	Bidi''oo

Past	
Ana	Da''ét
Inta	Da''ét
Inté	Da''aité
Hoowé	Da'
Heeyé	Da''ét
Naĥna	Da''aina
Intoo	Da''aito
Hinné	Da''oo

Past Continuous		
Ana	Kint Ăam	Bdi'
Inta	Kint Ăam	Btdi'
Inté	Kinté Ăam	Btdi''é
Hoowé	Kén Ăam	Bidi'
Heeyé	Kénét Ăam	Btdi'
Naĥna	Kinna Ăam	Mndi'
Intoo	Kintoo Ăam	Btdi''oo
Hinné	Kénoo Ăam	Bidi''oo

Future		
Ana	Laĥ	di'
Inta	Laĥ	tdi'
Inté	Laĥ	tdi''é
Hoowé	Laĥ	ydi'
Heeyé	Laĥ	tdi'
Naĥna	Laĥ	ndi'
Intoo	Laĥ	tdi''oo
Hinné	Laĥ	ydi''oo

Command	
Inta	Di'
Inté	Di''é
Intoo	Di''oo
Inta	Ma tdi'
Inté	Ma tdi''é
Intoo	Ma tdi''oo

To know

Present	
Ana	BaĂréf
Inta	BtaĂréf
Inté	BtaĂrfé
Hoowé	ByaĂréf
Heeyé	BtaĂréf
Naĥna	MnaĂréf
Intoo	BtaĂrfoo
Hinné	ByaĂrfoo

Present Continuous	
Ana	Ăam BaĂréf (or ana Ăéréf/Ăérfé)
Inta	Ăam BtaĂréf (or Ăéréf)
Inté	Ăam BtaĂrfé (or Ăérfé)
Hoowé	Ăam ByaĂréf (or Ăéréf)
Heeyé	Ăam BtaĂréf (or Ăérfé)
Naĥna	Ăam MnaĂréf (or Ăérfeen)
Intoo	Ăam BtaĂrfoo (or Ăérfeen)
Hinné	Ăam ByaĂrfoo (or Ăérfeen)

Past	
Ana	Ărifit
Inta	Ărifit
Inté	Ărifté
Hoowé	Ăirif
Heeyé	Ăirfét
Naĥna	Ărifna
Intoo	Ăriftoo
Hinné	Ăirfoo

Past Continuous	
Ana	Kint Ăam BaĂréf (or ana Ăéréf/Ăérfé)
Inta	Kint Ăam BtaĂréf (or Ăéréf)
Inté	Kinté Ăam BtaĂrfé (or Ăérfé)
Hoowé	Kén Ăam ByaĂréf (or Ăéréf)
Heeyé	Kénét Ăam BtaĂréf (or Ăérfé)
Naĥna	Kinna Ăam MnaĂréf (or Ăérfeen)
Intoo	Kintoo Ăam BtaĂrfoo (or Ăérfeen)
Hinné	Kénoo Ăam ByaĂrfoo (or Ăérfeen)

Future		
Ana	Laĥ	aĂréf
Inta	Laĥ	taĂréf
Inté	Laĥ	taĂrfé
Hoowé	Laĥ	yaĂréf
Heeyé	Laĥ	taĂréf
Naĥna	Laĥ	naĂréf
Intoo	Laĥ	taĂrfoo
Hinné	Laĥ	yaĂrfoo

Command	
Inta	Ăraf
Inté	Ărafé
Intoo	Ărafoo
Inta	Ma taĂréf
Inté	Ma taĂrfé
Intoo	Ma taĂrfoo

Ă= Augh in bought	Ď= a heavy D	É= like A in Bay	G= G in beige	ĥ= like an H with smaller air passage	I= I as in ink	Ќ= like ch in Irish loch
O= O as in home	OO= as in boots	R= roll the rrr	Ť= a heavy T	Ř= like a French R (gargle it)	Ŝ= a heavy S	Ž= a heavy Z

L   L

To laugh   To lead

Present	
Ana	biĎ̌hak
Inta	btiĎ̌hak
Inté	btiĎ̌haké
Hoowé	byiĎ̌hak
Heeyé	btiĎ̌hak
Naḣna	mniĎ̌hak
Intoo	btiĎ̌hakoo
Hinné	byiĎ̌hakoo

Present Continuous		
Ana	Ăam	biĎ̌hak
Inta	Ăam	btiĎ̌hak
Inté	Ăam	btiĎ̌haké
Hoowé	Ăam	byiĎ̌hak
Heeyé	Ăam	btiĎ̌hak
Naḣna	Ăam	mniĎ̌hak
Intoo	Ăam	btiĎ̌hakoo
Hinné	Ăam	byiĎ̌hakoo

Past	
Ana	Ď̌hakt
Inta	Ď̌hakt
Inté	Ď̌hakté
Hoowé	Ďiḣék
Heeyé	Ďiḣkét
Naḣna	Ď̌hakna
Intoo	Ď̌haktoo
Hinné	Ďiḣkoo

Past Continuous		
Ana	Kint Ăam	biĎ̌hak
Inta	Kint Ăam	btiĎ̌hak
Inté	Kinté Ăam	btiĎ̌haké
Hoowé	Kén Ăam	byiĎ̌hak
Heeyé	Kénét Ăam	btiĎ̌hak
Naḣna	Kinna Ăam	mniĎ̌hak
Intoo	Kintoo Ăam	btiĎ̌hakoo
Hinné	Kénoo Ăam	byiĎ̌hakoo

Future		
Ana	Laḣ	iĎ̌hak
Inta	Laḣ	tiĎ̌hak
Inté	Laḣ	tiĎ̌haké
Hoowé	Laḣ	yiĎ̌hak
Heeyé	Laḣ	tiĎ̌hak
Naḣna	Laḣ	niĎ̌hak
Intoo	Laḣ	tiĎ̌hakoo
Hinné	Laḣ	yiĎ̌hakoo

Command	
Inta	Ď̌hak
Inté	Ď̌haké
Intoo	Ď̌hakoo
Inta	Ma tĎ̌hak
Inté	Ma tĎ̌haké
Intoo	Ma tĎ̌hakoo

Present	
Ana	Bir'as
Inta	Btir'as
Inté	Btir'asé
Hoowé	Byir'as
Heeyé	Btir'as
Naḣna	Mnir'as
Intoo	Btir'asoo
Hinné	Byir'asoo

Present Continuous		
Ana	Ăam	Bir'as
Inta	Ăam	Btir'as
Inté	Ăam	Btir'asé
Hoowé	Ăam	Byir'as
Heeyé	Ăam	Btir'as
Naḣna	Ăam	Mnir'as
Intoo	Ăam	Btir'asoo
Hinné	Ăam	Byir'asoo

Past	
Ana	Ra'ast
Inta	Ra'ast
Inté	Ra'asté
Hoowé	Ra'as
Heeyé	Ra'asét
Naḣna	Ra'asna
Intoo	Ra'astoo
Hinné	Ra'asoo

Past Continuous		
Ana	Kint Ăam	Bir'as
Inta	Kint Ăam	Btir'as
Inté	Kinté Ăam	Btir'asé
Hoowé	Kén Ăam	Byir'as
Heeyé	Kénét Ăam	Btir'as
Naḣna	Kinna Ăam	Mnir'as
Intoo	Kintoo Ăam	Btir'asoo
Hinné	Kénoo Ăam	Byir'asoo

Future		
Ana	Laḣ	ir'as
Inta	Laḣ	tir'as
Inté	Laḣ	tir'asé
Hoowé	Laḣ	yir'as
Heeyé	Laḣ	tir'as
Naḣna	Laḣ	nir'as
Intoo	Laḣ	tir'asoo
Hinné	Laḣ	yir'asoo

Command	
Inta	R'os
Inté	R'isé
Intoo	R'isoo
Inta	Ma tr'os
Inté	Ma tr'sé
Intoo	Ma tr'soo

Ă= Augh in bought	Ď= a heavy D	É= like A in Bay	G= G in beige	ḣ= like an H with smaller air passage	I= I as in ink	Ḱ= like ch in Irish loch
O= O as in home	OO= as in boots	R= roll the rrr	Ť= a heavy T	Ř= like a French R (gargle it)	Ŝ= a heavy S	Ž= a heavy Z

L   L

To lead to   To learn

Present	
Ana	B'addé
Inta	Bt'addé
Inté	Bt'addé
Hoowé	Bi'addé
Heeyé	Bt'addé
Naĥna	Mn'addé
Intoo	Bt'addoo
Hinné	Bi'addoo

Present Continuous		
Ana	Ăam	B'addé
Inta	Ăam	Bt'addé
Inté	Ăam	Bt'addé
Hoowé	Ăam	Bi'addé
Heeyé	Ăam	Bt'addé
Naĥna	Ăam	Mn'addé
Intoo	Ăam	Bt'addoo
Hinné	Ăam	Bi'addoo

Past	
Ana	Addét
Inta	Addét
Inté	Addaité
Hoowé	Adda
Heeyé	Addét
Naĥna	Addaina
Intoo	Addaitoo
Hinné	Addoo

Past Continuous		
Ana	Kint Ăam	B'addé
Inta	Kint Ăam	Bt'addé
Inté	Kinté Ăam	Bt'addé
Hoowé	Kén Ăam	Bi'addé
Heeyé	Kénét Ăam	Bt'addé
Naĥna	Kinna Ăam	Mn'addé
Intoo	Kintoo Ăam	Bt'addoo
Hinné	Kénoo Ăam	Bi'addoo

Future		
Ana	Laĥ	'addé
Inta	Laĥ	T'addé
Inté	Laĥ	T'addé
Hoowé	Laĥ	Y'addé
Heeyé	Laĥ	T'addé
Naĥna	Laĥ	N'addé
Intoo	Laĥ	T'addoo
Hinné	Laĥ	Y'addoo

Command	
Inta	Addé
Inté	Addé
Intoo	Addoo
Inta	Ma t'addé
Inté	Ma t'addé
Intoo	Ma t'addoo

Present	
Ana	bitĂallam
Inta	btitĂallam
Inté	btitĂallamé
Hoowé	byitĂallam
Heeyé	btitĂallam
Naĥna	mnitĂallam
Intoo	btitĂallamoo
Hinné	byitĂallamoo

Present Continuous			
Ana	Ăam	bitĂallam	(mitĂallam/mitĂallamé)
Inta	Ăam	btitĂallam	(mitĂallam)
Inté	Ăam	btitĂallamé	(mitĂallamé)
Hoowé	Ăam	byitĂallam	(mitĂallam)
Heeyé	Ăam	btitĂallam	(mitĂallam)
Naĥna	Ăam	mnitĂallam	(mitĂallameen)
Intoo	Ăam	btitĂallamoo	(mitĂallameen)
Hinné	Ăam	byitĂallamoo	(mitĂallameen)

Past	
Ana	tĂallamt
Inta	tĂallamt
Inté	tĂallamté
Hoowé	tĂallamtoo
Heeyé	tĂallamoo
Naĥna	tĂallamna
Intoo	tĂallamtoo
Hinné	tĂallamoo

Past Continuous			
Ana	Kint Ăam	bitĂallam	(kint mitĂallam/mit Ăallamé)
Inta	Kint Ăam	btitĂallam	(Kint mitĂallam)
Inté	Kinté Ăam	btitĂallamé	(Kinté mitĂallamé)
Hoowé	Kén Ăam	byitĂallam	(Kén mitĂallam)
Heeyé	Kénét Ăam	btitĂallam	(Kénét mitĂallamé)
Naĥna	Kinna Ăam	mnitĂallam	(Kinna mitĂallameen)
Intoo	Kintoo Ăam	btitĂallamoo	(Kintoo mitĂallameen)
Hinné	Kénoo Ăam	byitĂallamoo	(Kénoo mitĂallameen)

Future		
Ana	Laĥ	itĂallam
Inta	Laĥ	titĂallam
Inté	Laĥ	titĂallamé
Hoowé	Laĥ	yitĂallam
Heeyé	Laĥ	titĂallam
Naĥna	Laĥ	nitĂallam
Intoo	Laĥ	titĂallamoo
Hinné	Laĥ	yitĂallamoo

Command	
Inta	tĂallam
Inté	tĂallamé
Intoo	tĂallamoo
Inta	Ma ttĂallam
Inté	Ma ttĂallamé
Intoo	Ma ttĂallamoo

Ă= Augh in bought	Ď= a heavy D	É= like A in Bay	G= G in beige	ĥ= like an H with smaller air passage	I= I as in ink	Ќ= like ch in Irish loch
O= O as in home	OO= as in boots	R= roll the rrr	Ť= a heavy T	Ř= like a French R (gargle it)	Ŝ= a heavy S	Ž= a heavy Z

L

L

To leave

Present	
Ana	Bitrok
Inta	Btitrok
Inté	Btitrké
Hoowé	Byitrok
Heeyé	Btitrok
Nahna	Mnitrok
Intoo	Btitrkoo
Hinné	Byitrkoo

Present Continuous			
Ana	Ăam	Bitrok	(térék/térké)
Inta	Ăam	Btitrok	(térék)
Inté	Ăam	Btitrké	(térké)
Hoowé	Ăam	Byitrok	(térék)
Heeyé	Ăam	Btitrok	(térké)
Nahna	Ăam	Mnitrok	(térkeen)
Intoo	Ăam	Btitrkoo	(térkeen)
Hinné	Ăam	Byitrkoo	(térkeen)

Past	
Ana	Tarakt
Inta	Tarakt
Inté	Tarakté
Hoowé	Tarak
Heeyé	Tarakét
Nahna	Tarakna
Intoo	Taraktoo
Hinné	Tarakoo

Past Continuous			
Ana	Kint Ăam	Bitrok	(kint térék/térké)
Inta	Kint Ăam	Btitrok	(Kint térék)
Inté	Kinté Ăam	Btitrké	(Kinté térké)
Hoowé	Kén Ăam	Byitrok	(Kén térék)
Heeyé	Kénét Ăam	Btitrok	(Kénét térké)
Nahna	Kinna Ăam	Mnitrok	(Kinna térkeen)
Intoo	Kintoo Ăam	Btitrkoo	(Kintoo térkeen)
Hinné	Kénoo Ăam	Byitrkoo	(Kénoo térkeen)

Future		
Ana	Laĥ	Itrok
Inta	Laĥ	Titrok
Inté	Laĥ	Titrké
Hoowé	Laĥ	Yitrok
Heeyé	Laĥ	Titrok
Nahna	Laĥ	Nitrok
Intoo	Laĥ	Titrkoo
Hinné	Laĥ	Yitrkoo

Command	
Inta	Trok
Inté	Triké
Intoo	Trikoo
Inta	Ma ttrok
Inté	Ma ttrké
Intoo	Ma ttrkoo

To let / To allow

Present	
Ana	bḰallé
Inta	btḰallé
Inté	btḰallé
Hoowé	biḰallé
Heeyé	btḰallé
Nahna	mnḰallé
Intoo	btḰalloo
Hinné	biḰalloo

Present Continuous		
Ana	Ăam	bḰallé
Inta	Ăam	btḰallé
Inté	Ăam	btḰallé
Hoowé	Ăam	biḰallé
Heeyé	Ăam	btḰallé
Nahna	Ăam	mnḰallé
Intoo	Ăam	btḰalloo
Hinné	Ăam	biḰalloo

Past	
Ana	Ḱallét
Inta	Ḱallét
Inté	Ḱallaité
Hoowé	Ḱalla
Heeyé	Ḱallét
Nahna	Ḱallaina
Intoo	Ḱallaitoo
Hinné	Ḱalloo

Past Continuous	
Ana	Kint Ăam bḰallé
Inta	Kint Ăam btḰallé
Inté	Kinté Ăam btḰallé
Hoowé	Kén Ăam biḰallé
Heeyé	Kénét Ăam btḰallé
Nahna	Kinna Ăam mnḰallé
Intoo	Kintoo Ăam btḰalloo
Hinné	Kénoo Ăam biḰalloo

Future		
Ana	Laĥ	Ḱallé
Inta	Laĥ	tḰallé
Inté	Laĥ	tḰallé
Hoowé	Laĥ	yḰallé
Heeyé	Laĥ	tḰallé
Nahna	Laĥ	nḰallé
Intoo	Laĥ	tḰalloo
Hinné	Laĥ	yḰalloo

Command	
Inta	Ḱallé
Inté	Ḱallé
Intoo	Ḱalloo
Inta	Ma tḰallé
Inté	Ma tḰallé
Intoo	Ma tḰalloo

Ă= Augh in bought	Ď= a heavy D	É= like A in Bay	G= G in beige	ĥ= like an H with smaller air passage	I= I as in ink	Ḱ= like ch in Irish loch
O= O as in home	OO= as in boots	R= roll the rrr	Ť= a heavy T	Ř= like a French R (gargle it)	Ŝ= a heavy S	Ž= a heavy Z

L   L

To liberate

Present	
Ana	Bĥarrir
Inta	Btĥarrir
Inté	Btĥarriré
Hoowé	Biĥarrir
Heeyé	Btĥarrir
Naĥna	Mnĥarrir
Intoo	Btĥarriroo
Hinné	Biĥarriroo

Present Continuous		
Ana	Ăam	Bĥarrir
Inta	Ăam	Btĥarrir
Inté	Ăam	Btĥarriré
Hoowé	Ăam	Biĥarrir
Heeyé	Ăam	Btĥarrir
Naĥna	Ăam	Mnĥarrir
Intoo	Ăam	Btĥarriroo
Hinné	Ăam	Biĥarriroo

Past	
Ana	Ĥarrart
Inta	Ĥarrart
Inté	Ĥarrarté
Hoowé	Ĥarrar
Heeyé	Ĥarrarét
Naĥna	Ĥarrarna
Intoo	Ĥarrartoo
Hinné	Ĥarraroo

Past Continuous		
Ana	Kint Ăam	Bĥarrir
Inta	Kint Ăam	Btĥarrir
Inté	Kinté Ăam	Btĥarriré
Hoowé	Kén Ăam	Biĥarrir
Heeyé	Kénét Ăam	Btĥarrir
Naĥna	Kinna Ăam	Mnĥarrir
Intoo	Kintoo Ăam	Btĥarriroo
Hinné	Kénoo Ăam	Biĥarriroo

Future		
Ana	Laĥ	Ĥarrir
Inta	Laĥ	Tĥarrir
Inté	Laĥ	Tĥarriré
Hoowé	Laĥ	Yĥarrir
Heeyé	Laĥ	Tĥarrir
Naĥna	Laĥ	Nĥarrir
Intoo	Laĥ	Tĥarriroo
Hinné	Laĥ	Yĥarriroo

Command	
Inta	Ĥarrir
Inté	Ĥarriré
Intoo	Ĥarriroo
Inta	Ma tĥrarrir
Inté	Ma tĥarriré
Intoo	Ma tĥarriroo

To lick

Present	
Ana	Bilĥas
Inta	Btilĥas
Inté	Btilĥasé
Hoowé	Byilĥas
Heeyé	Btilĥas
Naĥna	Mnilĥas
Intoo	Btilĥasoo
Hinné	Byilĥasoo

Present Continuous		
Ana	Ăam	Bilĥas
Inta	Ăam	Btilĥas
Inté	Ăam	Btilĥasé
Hoowé	Ăam	Byilĥas
Heeyé	Ăam	Btilĥas
Naĥna	Ăam	Mnilĥas
Intoo	Ăam	Btilĥasoo
Hinné	Ăam	Byilĥasoo

Past	
Ana	Laĥast
Inta	Laĥast
Inté	Laĥasté
Hoowé	Laĥas
Heeyé	Laĥasét
Naĥna	Laĥasna
Intoo	Laĥastoo
Hinné	Laĥasoo

Past Continuous		
Ana	Kint Ăam	Bilĥas
Inta	Kint Ăam	Btilĥas
Inté	Kinté Ăam	Btilĥasé
Hoowé	Kén Ăam	Byilĥas
Heeyé	Kénét Ăam	Btilĥas
Naĥna	Kinna Ăam	Mnilĥas
Intoo	Kintoo Ăam	Btilĥasoo
Hinné	Kénoo Ăam	Byilĥasoo

Future		
Ana	Laĥ	Ilĥas
Inta	Laĥ	Tilĥas
Inté	Laĥ	Tilĥasé
Hoowé	Laĥ	Yilĥas
Heeyé	Laĥ	Tilĥas
Naĥna	Laĥ	Nilĥas
Intoo	Laĥ	Tilĥasoo
Hinné	Laĥ	Yilĥasoo

Command	
Inta	Lĥas
Inté	Lĥasé
Intoo	Lĥasoo
Inta	Ma tlĥas
Inté	Ma tlĥasé
Intoo	Ma tlĥasoo

Ă= Augh in bought	Đ= a heavy D	É= like A in Bay	G= G in beige	ĥ= like an H with smaller air passage	I= I as in ink	Ќ= like ch in Irish loch
O= O as in home	OO= as in boots	R= roll the rrr	Ŧ= a heavy T	Ř= like a French R (gargle it)	Ŝ= a heavy S	Ž= a heavy Z

L   L

To lie (to tell a lie)

Present

Ana	Bikzob
Inta	Btikzob
Inté	Btikzbé
Hoowé	Byikzob
Heeyé	Btikzob
Naĥna	Mnikzob
Intoo	Btikzboo
Hinné	Byikzboo

Present Continuous

Ana	Ăam	Bikzob
Inta	Ăam	Btikzob
Inté	Ăam	Btikzbé
Hoowé	Ăam	Byikzob
Heeyé	Ăam	Btikzob
Naĥna	Ăam	Mnikzob
Intoo	Ăam	Btikzboo
Hinné	Ăam	Byikzboo

Past

Ana	Kazabt
Inta	Kazabt
Inté	Kazabté
Hoowé	Kazab
Heeyé	Kazabét
Naĥna	Kazabna
Intoo	Kazabtoo
Hinné	Kazaboo

Past Continuous

Ana	Kint Ăam	Bikzob
Inta	Kint Ăam	Btikzob
Inté	Kinté Ăam	Btikzbé
Hoowé	Kén Ăam	Byikzob
Heeyé	Kénét Ăam	Btikzob
Naĥna	Kinna Ăam	Mnikzob
Intoo	Kintoo Ăam	Btikzboo
Hinné	Kénoo Ăam	Byikzboo

Future

Ana	Laĥ	Ikzob
Inta	Laĥ	Tikzob
Inté	Laĥ	Tikzbé
Hoowé	Laĥ	Yikzob
Heeyé	Laĥ	Tikzob
Naĥna	Laĥ	Nikzob
Intoo	Laĥ	Tikzboo
Hinné	Laĥ	Yikzboo

Command

Inta	Kzob
Inté	Kzibé
Intoo	Kziboo
Inta	Ma tkzob
Inté	Ma tkzbé
Intoo	Ma tkzboo

To lie (to lie down)

Present

Ana	Bitmaddad
Inta	Btitmaddad
Inté	Btitmaddadé
Hoowé	Byitmaddad
Heeyé	Btitmaddad
Naĥna	Mnitmaddad
Intoo	Btitmaddadoo
Hinné	Byitmaddadoo

Present Continuous

Ana	Ăam	Bitmaddad	(mitmaddad/mitmaddadé)
Inta	Ăam	Btitmaddad	(mitmaddad)
Inté	Ăam	Btitmaddadé	(mitmaddadé)
Hoowé	Ăam	Byitmaddad	(mitmaddad)
Heeyé	Ăam	Btitmaddad	(mitmaddadé)
Naĥna	Ăam	Mnitmaddad	(mitmaddadeen)
Intoo	Ăam	Btitmaddadoo	(mitmaddadeen)
Hinné	Ăam	Byitmaddadoo	(mitmaddadeen)

Past

Ana	Tmaddadt
Inta	Tmaddadt
Inté	Tmaddadté
Hoowé	Tmaddad
Heeyé	Tmaddadét
Naĥna	Tmaddadna
Intoo	Tmaddadtoo
Hinné	Tmaddadoo

Past Continuous

Ana	Kint Ăam	Bitmaddad	(kint mitmaddad/mitmaddadé)
Inta	Kint Ăam	Btitmaddad	(Kint mitmaddad)
Inté	Kinté Ăam	Btitmaddadé	(Kinté mitmaddadé)
Hoowé	Kén Ăam	Byitmaddad	(Kén mitmaddad)
Heeyé	Kénét Ăam	Btitmaddad	(Kénét mitmaddad)
Naĥna	Kinna Ăam	Mnitmaddad	(Kinna mitmaddadeen)
Intoo	Kintoo Ăam	Btitmaddadoo	(Kintoo mitmaddadeen)
Hinné	Kénoo Ăam	Byitmaddadoo	(Kénoo mitmaddadeen)

Future

Ana	Laĥ	Itmaddad
Inta	Laĥ	Titmaddad
Inté	Laĥ	Titmaddadé
Hoowé	Laĥ	Yitmaddad
Heeyé	Laĥ	Titmaddad
Naĥna	Laĥ	Nitmaddad
Intoo	Laĥ	Titmaddadoo
Hinné	Laĥ	Yitmaddadoo

Command

Inta	Tmaddad
Inté	Tmaddadé
Intoo	Tmaddadoo
Inta	Ma ttmaddad
Inté	Ma ttmaddadé
Intoo	Ma ttmaddadoo

Ă= Augh in bought	Ď= a heavy D	É= like A in Bay	G= G in beige	ĥ= like an H with smaller air passage	I= I as in ink	Ķ= like ch in Irish loch
O= O as in home	OO= as in boots	R= roll the rrr	Ť= a heavy T	Ř= like a French R (gargle it)	Ŝ= a heavy S	Ž= a heavy Z

L

L

To lift

Present	
Ana	birfaĂ
Inta	btirfaĂ
Inté	btirfaĂé
Hoowé	byirfaĂ
Heeyé	btirfaĂ
Nahna	mnirfaĂ
Intoo	btirfaĂoo
Hinné	byirfaĂoo

Present Continuous		
Ana	Ăam	birfaĂ
Inta	Ăam	btirfaĂ
Inté	Ăam	btirfaĂé
Hoowé	Ăam	byirfaĂ
Heeyé	Ăam	btirfaĂ
Nahna	Ăam	mnirfaĂ
Intoo	Ăam	btirfaĂoo
Hinné	Ăam	byirfaĂoo

Past	
Ana	rafaĂt
Inta	rafaĂt
Inté	rafaĂté
Hoowé	rafaĂ
Heeyé	rafaĂét
Nahna	rafaĂna
Intoo	rafaĂtoo
Hinné	rafaĂoo

Past Continuous		
Ana	Kint Ăam	birfaĂ
Inta	Kint Ăam	btirfaĂ
Inté	Kinté Ăam	btirfaĂé
Hoowé	Kén Ăam	byirfaĂ
Heeyé	Kénét Ăam	btirfaĂ
Nahna	Kinna Ăam	mnirfaĂ
Intoo	Kintoo Ăam	btirfaĂoo
Hinné	Kénoo Ăam	byirfaĂoo

Future		
Ana	Laĥ	irfaĂ
Inta	Laĥ	tirfaĂ
Inté	Laĥ	tirfaĂé
Hoowé	Laĥ	yirfaĂ
Heeyé	Laĥ	tirfaĂ
Nahna	Laĥ	nirfaĂ
Intoo	Laĥ	tirfaĂoo
Hinné	Laĥ	yirfaĂoo

Command	
Inta	rfaĂ
Inté	rfaĂé
Intoo	rfaĂoo
Inta	Ma trfaĂ
Inté	Ma trfaĂé
Intoo	Ma trfaĂoo

To limp

Present	
Ana	biĂrog
Inta	btiĂrog
Inté	btiĂrgé
Hoowé	byiĂrog
Heeyé	btiĂrog
Nahna	mniĂrog
Intoo	btiĂrgoo
Hinné	byiĂrgoo

Present Continuous		
Ana	Ăam	biĂrog
Inta	Ăam	btiĂrog
Inté	Ăam	btiĂrgé
Hoowé	Ăam	byiĂrog
Heeyé	Ăam	btiĂrog
Nahna	Ăam	mniĂrog
Intoo	Ăam	btiĂrgoo
Hinné	Ăam	byiĂrgoo

Past	
Ana	Ăaragt
Inta	Ăaragt
Inté	Ăaragté
Hoowé	Ăarag
Heeyé	Ăaragét
Nahna	Ăaragna
Intoo	Ăaragtoo
Hinné	Ăaragoo

Past Continuous		
Ana	Kint Ăam	biĂrog
Inta	Kint Ăam	btiĂrog
Inté	Kinté Ăam	btiĂrgé
Hoowé	Kén Ăam	byiĂrog
Heeyé	Kénét Ăam	btiĂrog
Nahna	Kinna Ăam	mniĂrog
Intoo	Kintoo Ăam	btiĂrgoo
Hinné	Kénoo Ăam	byiĂrgoo

Future		
Ana	Laĥ	iĂrog
Inta	Laĥ	tiĂrog
Inté	Laĥ	tiĂrgé
Hoowé	Laĥ	yiĂrog
Heeyé	Laĥ	tiĂrog
Nahna	Laĥ	niĂrog
Intoo	Laĥ	tiĂrgoo
Hinné	Laĥ	yiĂrgoo

Command	
Inta	Ărog
Inté	Ărigé
Intoo	Ărigoo
Inta	Ma tĂrog
Inté	Ma tĂrgé
Intoo	Ma tĂrgoo

Ă= Augh in bought	Ď= a heavy D	É= like A in Bay	G= G in beige	ĥ= like an H with smaller air passage	I= I as in ink	Ḱ= like ch in Irish loch
O= O as in home	OO= as in boots	R= roll the rrr	Ť= a heavy T	Ř= like a French R (gargle it)	Ŝ= a heavy S	Ž= a heavy Z

L   L

To live

Present

Ana	bĂeesh
Inta	btĂeesh
Inté	btĂeeshé
Hoowé	biĂeesh
Heeyé	btĂeesh
Naḥna	mnĂeesh
Intoo	btĂeeshoo
Hinné	biĂeeshoo

Present Continuous

Ana	Ăam	bĂeesh	(Ăyésh/Ăyshé)
Inta	Ăam	btĂeesh	(Ăyésh)
Inté	Ăam	btĂeeshé	(Ăyshé)
Hoowé	Ăam	biĂeesh	(Ăyésh)
Heeyé	Ăam	btĂeesh	(Ăyshé)
Naḥna	Ăam	mnĂeesh	(Ăysheen)
Intoo	Ăam	btĂeeshoo	(Ăysheen)
Hinné	Ăam	biĂeeshoo	(Ăysheen)

Past

Ana	Ăisht
Inta	Ăisht
Inté	Ăishté
Hoowé	Ăésh
Heeyé	Ăéshét
Naḥna	Ăishna
Intoo	Ăishtoo
Hinné	Ăéshoo

Past Continuous

Ana	Kint Ăam	bĂeesh	(kint	Ăyésh/Ăyshé)
Inta	Kint Ăam	btĂeesh	(Kint	Ăyésh)
Inté	Kinté Ăam	btĂeeshé	(Kinté	Ăyshé)
Hoowé	Kén Ăam	biĂeesh	(Kén	Ăyésh)
Heeyé	Kénét Ăam	btĂeesh	(Kénét	Ăyshé)
Naḥna	Kinna Ăam	mnĂeesh	(Kinna	Ăysheen)
Intoo	Kintoo Ăam	btĂeeshoo	(Kintoo	Ăysheen)
Hinné	Kénoo Ăam	biĂeeshoo	(Kénoo	Ăysheen)

Future

Ana	Laĥ	Ăeesh
Inta	Laĥ	tĂeesh
Inté	Laĥ	tĂeeshé
Hoowé	Laĥ	yĂeesh
Heeyé	Laĥ	tĂeesh
Naḥna	Laĥ	nĂeesh
Intoo	Laĥ	tĂeeshoo
Hinné	Laĥ	yĂeeshoo

Command

Inta	Ăeesh
Inté	Ăeeshé
Intoo	Ăeeshoo
Inta	Ma Ăisht
Inté	Ma Ăishté
Intoo	Ma Ăishtoo

To lock

Present

Ana	Bi'fol
Inta	Bti'fol
Inté	Bti'flé
Hoowé	Byi'fol
Heeyé	Bti'fol
Naḥna	Mni'fol
Intoo	Bti'floo
Hinné	Byi'floo

Present Continuous

Ana	Ăam	Bi'fol	('éfél/'éflé)
Inta	Ăam	Bti'fol	('éfél)
Inté	Ăam	Bti'flé	('éflé)
Hoowé	Ăam	Byi'fol	('éfél)
Heeyé	Ăam	Bti'fol	('éflé)
Naḥna	Ăam	Mni'fol	('éfleen)
Intoo	Ăam	Bti'floo	('éfleen)
Hinné	Ăam	Byi'floo	('éfleen)

Past

Ana	Afalt
Inta	Afalt
Inté	Afalté
Hoowé	Afal
Heeyé	Afalét
Naḥna	Afalna
Intoo	Afaltoo
Hinné	Afaloo

Past Continuous

Ana	Kint Ăam	Bi'fol	(kint	'éfél/'éflé)
Inta	Kint Ăam	Bti'fol	(Kint	'éfél)
Inté	Kinté Ăam	Bti'flé	(Kinté	'éflé)
Hoowé	Kén Ăam	Byi'fol	(Kén	'éfél)
Heeyé	Kénét Ăam	Bti'fol	(Kénét	'éflé)
Naḥna	Kinna Ăam	Mni'fol	(Kinna	'éfleen)
Intoo	Kintoo Ăam	Bti'floo	(Kintoo	'éfleen)
Hinné	Kénoo Ăam	Byi'floo	(Kénoo	'éfleen)

Future

Ana	Laĥ	I'fol
Inta	Laĥ	Ti'fol
Inté	Laĥ	Ti'flé
Hoowé	Laĥ	Yi'fol
Heeyé	Laĥ	Ti'fol
Naḥna	Laĥ	Ni'fol
Intoo	Laĥ	Ti'floo
Hinné	Laĥ	Yi'floo

Command

Inta	'fol
Inté	'filé
Intoo	'filoo
Inta	Ma t'fol
Inté	Ma t'flé
Intoo	Ma t'floo

Ă= Augh in bought	Ď= a heavy D	É= like A in Bay	G= G in beige	ḣ= like an H with smaller air passage	I= I as in ink	Ḱ= like ch in Irish loch
O= O as in home	OO= as in boots	R= roll the rrr	Ť= a heavy T	Ř= like a French R (gargle it)	Ŝ= a heavy S	Ž= a heavy Z

L   L

To lose   To lose weight

Present	
Ana	biꝀŠar
Inta	btiꝀŠar
Inté	btiꝀŠaré
Hoowé	byiꝀŠar
Heeyé	btiꝀŠar
Nahna	mniꝀŠar
Intoo	btiꝀŠaroo
Hinné	byiꝀŠaroo

Present Continuous		
Ana	Ăam biꝀŠar	(ꝀiŠran/ꝀiŠrané)
Inta	Ăam btiꝀŠar	(ꝀiŠran)
Inté	Ăam btiꝀŠaré	(ꝀiŠrané)
Hoowé	Ăam byiꝀŠar	(ꝀiŠran)
Heeyé	Ăam btiꝀŠar	(ꝀiŠrané)
Nahna	Ăam mniꝀŠar	(ꝀiŠraneen)
Intoo	Ăam btiꝀŠaroo	(ꝀiŠraneen)
Hinné	Ăam byiꝀŠaroo	(ꝀiŠraneen)

Past	
Ana	ꝀŠirt
Inta	ꝀŠirt
Inté	ꝀŠirté
Hoowé	ꝀiŠir
Heeyé	ꝀiŠrét
Nahna	ꝀŠirna
Intoo	ꝀŠirtoo
Hinné	ꝀiŠroo

Past Continuous		
Ana	Kint Ăam biꝀŠar	(kint ꝀiŠran/ꝀiŠrané)
Inta	Kint Ăam btiꝀŠar	(Kint ꝀiŠran)
Inté	Kinté Ăam btiꝀŠaré	(Kinté ꝀiŠrané)
Hoowé	Kén Ăam byiꝀŠar	(Kén ꝀiŠran)
Heeyé	Kénét Ăam btiꝀŠar	(Kénét ꝀiŠrané)
Nahna	Kinna Ăam mniꝀŠar	(Kinna ꝀiŠraneen)
Intoo	Kintoo Ăam btiꝀŠaroo	(Kintoo ꝀiŠraneen)
Hinné	Kénoo Ăam byiꝀŠaroo	(Kénoo ꝀiŠraneen)

Future	
Ana	Laĥ iꝀŠaR
Inta	Laĥ tiꝀŠaR
Inté	Laĥ tiꝀŠaRé
Hoowé	Laĥ yiꝀŠaR
Heeyé	Laĥ tiꝀŠaR
Nahna	Laĥ niꝀŠaR
Intoo	Laĥ tiꝀŠaRoo
Hinné	Laĥ yiꝀŠaRoo

Command	
Inta	Ꝁsar
Inté	Ꝁsaré
Intoo	Ꝁsaroo
Inta	Ma tꝀsar
Inté	Ma tꝀsaré
Intoo	Ma tꝀsaroo

Present	
Ana	biĎĂaf
Inta	btiĎĂaf
Inté	btiĎĂafé
Hoowé	byiĎĂaf
Heeyé	btiĎĂaf
Nahna	mniĎĂaf
Intoo	btiĎĂafoo
Hinné	byiĎĂafoo

Present Continuous	
Ana	Ăam biĎĂaf
Inta	Ăam btiĎĂaf
Inté	Ăam btiĎĂafé
Hoowé	Ăam byiĎĂaf
Heeyé	Ăam btiĎĂaf
Nahna	Ăam mniĎĂaf
Intoo	Ăam btiĎĂafoo
Hinné	Ăam byiĎĂafoo

Past	
Ana	ĎĂift
Inta	ĎĂift
Inté	ĎĂifté
Hoowé	ĎiĂf
Heeyé	ĎiĂfét
Nahna	ĎĂifna
Intoo	ĎĂiftoo
Hinné	ĎiĂfoo

Past Continuous	
Ana	Kint Ăam biĎĂaf
Inta	Kint Ăam btiĎĂaf
Inté	Kinté Ăam btiĎĂafé
Hoowé	Kén Ăam byiĎĂaf
Heeyé	Kénét Ăam btiĎĂaf
Nahna	Kinna Ăam mniĎĂaf
Intoo	Kintoo Ăam btiĎĂafoo
Hinné	Kénoo Ăam byiĎĂafoo

Future	
Ana	Laĥ iĎĂaf
Inta	Laĥ tiĎĂaf
Inté	Laĥ tiĎĂafé
Hoowé	Laĥ yiĎĂaf
Heeyé	Laĥ tiĎĂaf
Nahna	Laĥ niĎĂaf
Intoo	Laĥ tiĎĂafoo
Hinné	Laĥ yiĎĂafoo

Command	
Inta	ĎĂaf
Inté	ĎĂafé
Intoo	ĎĂafoo
Inta	Ma tĎĂaf
Inté	Ma tĎĂafé
Intoo	Ma tĎĂafoo

Ă= Augh in bought	Ď= a heavy D	É= like A in Bay	G= G in beige	ĥ= like an H with smaller air passage	I= I as in ink	Ꝁ= like ch in Irish loch
O= O as in home	OO= as in boots	R= roll the rrr	Ť= a heavy T	Ř= like a French R (gargle it)	Š= a heavy S	Ž= a heavy Z

L

L

To love

Present

Ana	Bḣib
Inta	Btḣib
Inté	Btḣibbé
Hoowé	Biḣib
Heeyé	Btḣib
Naḣna	Mnḣib
Intoo	Btḣibboo
Hinné	Biḣibboo

Present Continuous

Ana	Ăam bḣib (or ana Hébéb/Hébbé)
Inta	Ăam btḣib (or ḣébéb)
Inté	Ăam btḣibbé (or ḣébbé)
Hoowé	Ăam biḣib (or ḣébéb)
Heeyé	Ăam btḣib (or ḣébbé)
Naḣna	Ăam mnḣib (or ḣébbeen)
Intoo	Ăam btḣibbo (or ḣébbeen)
Hinné	Ăam biḣibboo (or ḣébbeen)

Past

Ana	Ḣabbét
Inta	Ḣabbét
Inté	Ḣabbaité
Hoowé	Ḣab
Heeyé	Ḣabbét
Naḣna	Ḣabbaina
Intoo	Ḣabbaitoo
Hinné	Ḣabboo

Past Continuous

Ana	Kint Ăam bḣib (or ana kint ḣébéb/ḣébbé)
Inta	Kint Ăam btḣib (or kint ḣébéb)
Inté	Kinté Ăam btḣibbé (or kinté ḣébbé)
Hoowé	Kén Ăam biḣib (or kén ḣébéb)
Heeyé	Kénét Ăam btḣib (or kénét ḣébbé)
Naḣna	Kinna Ăam mnḣib (or kinna ḣébbeen)
Intoo	Kintoo Ăam btḣibboo (kintoo ḣébbeen)
Hinné	Kénoo Ăam biḣibboo (or kénoo ḣébbeen)

Future

Ana	Laḣ ḣib
Inta	Laḣ tḣib
Inté	Laḣ tḣibbé
Hoowé	Laḣ yḣib
Heeyé	Laḣ tḣib
Naḣna	Laḣ nḣib
Intoo	Laḣ tḣibboo
Hinné	Laḣ yḣibboo

Command

Inta	Ḣib
Inté	Ḣibbé
Intoo	Ḣibboo
Inta	Ma tḣib
Inté	Ma tḣibbé
Intoo	Ma tiḣibboo

To lower

Present

Ana	bwaṬṬé
Inta	btwaṬṬé
Inté	btwaṬṬé
Hoowé	biwaṬṬé
Heeyé	btwaṬṬé
Naḣna	mnwaṬṬé
Intoo	btwaṬṬoo
Hinné	biwaṬṬoo

Present Continuous

Ana	Ăam bwaṬṬé
Inta	Ăam btwaṬṬé
Inté	Ăam btwaṬṬé
Hoowé	Ăam biwaṬṬé
Heeyé	Ăam btwaṬṬé
Naḣna	Ăam mnwaṬṬé
Intoo	Ăam btwaṬṬoo
Hinné	Ăam biwaṬṬoo

Past

Ana	waṬṬét
Inta	waṬṬét
Inté	waṬṬaité
Hoowé	waṬṬa
Heeyé	waṬṬét
Naḣna	waṬṬaina
Intoo	waṬṬaitoo
Hinné	waṬṬoo

Past Continuous

Ana	Kint Ăam bwaṬṬé
Inta	Kint Ăam btwaṬṬé
Inté	Kinté Ăam btwaṬṬé
Hoowé	Kén Ăam biwaṬṬé
Heeyé	Kénét Ăam btwaṬṬé
Naḣna	Kinna Ăam mnwaṬṬé
Intoo	Kintoo Ăam btwaṬṬoo
Hinné	Kénoo Ăam biwaṬṬoo

Future

Ana	Laḣ waṬṬé
Inta	Laḣ twaṬṬé
Inté	Laḣ twaṬṬé
Hoowé	Laḣ ywaṬṬé
Heeyé	Laḣ twaṬṬé
Naḣna	Laḣ nwaṬṬé
Intoo	Laḣ twaṬṬoo
Hinné	Laḣ ywaṬṬoo

Command

Inta	waṬṬé
Inté	waṬṬé
Intoo	waṬṬoo
Inta	Ma twaṬṬé
Inté	Ma twaṬṬé
Intoo	Ma twaṬṬoo

Ă= Augh in bought	Ď= a heavy D	É= like A in Bay	G= G in beige	ḣ= like an H with smaller air passage	I= I as in ink	Ḱ= like ch in Irish loch
O= O as in home	OO= as in boots	R= roll the rrr	Ṭ= a heavy T	Ř= like a French R (gargle it)	Ŝ= a heavy S	Ž= a heavy Z

M   M

To maintain

Present

Ana	bḣaféŽ
Inta	btḣaféŽ
Inté	btḣafŽé
Hoowé	biḣaféŽ
Heeyé	btḣaféŽ
Naḣna	mnḣaféŽ
Intoo	btḣafŽoo
Hinné	biḣafŽoo

Present Continuous

Ana	Ăam	bḣaféŽ	(mḣafaŽ/mḣafŽa)
Inta	Ăam	btḣaféŽ	(mḣafaŽ)
Inté	Ăam	btḣafŽé	(mḣafŽa)
Hoowé	Ăam	biḣaféŽ	(mḣafaŽ)
Heeyé	Ăam	btḣaféŽ	(mḣafŽa)
Naḣna	Ăam	mnḣaféŽ	(mḣafŽeen)
Intoo	Ăam	btḣafŽoo	(mḣafŽeen)
Hinné	Ăam	biḣafŽoo	(mḣafŽeen)

Past

Ana	ḣafaŽt
Inta	ḣafaŽt
Inté	ḣafaŽté
Hoowé	ḣafaŽ
Heeyé	ḣafaŽét
Naḣna	ḣafaŽna
Intoo	ḣafaŽtoo
Hinné	ḣafaŽoo

Past Continuous

Ana	Kint Ăam	bḣaféŽ	(kint	mḣafaŽ/mḣafŽa)
Inta	Kint Ăam	btḣaféŽ	(Kint	mḣafaŽ)
Inté	Kinté Ăam	btḣafŽé	(Kinté	mḣafŽa)
Hoowé	Kén Ăam	biḣaféŽ	(Kén	mḣafaŽ)
Heeyé	Kénét Ăam	btḣaféŽ	(Kénét	mḣafŽa)
Naḣna	Kinna Ăam	mnḣaféŽ	(Kinna	mḣafŽeen)
Intoo	Kintoo Ăam	btḣafŽoo	(Kintoo	mḣafŽeen)
Hinné	Kénoo Ăam	biḣafŽoo	(Kénoo	mḣafŽeen)

Future

Ana	Laḣ	ḣaféŽ
Inta	Laḣ	tḣaféŽ
Inté	Laḣ	tḣafŽé
Hoowé	Laḣ	yḣaféŽ
Heeyé	Laḣ	tḣaféŽ
Naḣna	Laḣ	nḣaféŽ
Intoo	Laḣ	tḣafŽoo
Hinné	Laḣ	yḣafŽoo

Command

Inta	ḣaféŽ
Inté	ḣafŽé
Intoo	ḣafŽoo
Inta	Ma tḣaféŽ
Inté	Ma tḣafŽé
Intoo	Ma tḣafŽoo

To make / To do

Present

Ana	biĂmél
Inta	btiĂmél
Inté	btiĂmlé
Hoowé	byiĂmél
Heeyé	btiĂmél
Naḣna	mniĂmél
Intoo	btiĂmloo
Hinné	byiĂmloo

Present Continuous

Ana	Ăam	biĂmél	(Ăémél/Ăémlé)
Inta	Ăam	btiĂmél	(Ăémél)
Inté	Ăam	btiĂmlé	(Ăémlé)
Hoowé	Ăam	byiĂmél	(Ăémél)
Heeyé	Ăam	btiĂmél	(Ăémlé)
Naḣna	Ăam	mniĂmél	(Ăémleen)
Intoo	Ăam	btiĂmloo	(Ăémleen)
Hinné	Ăam	byiĂmloo	(Ăémleen)

Past

Ana	Ămilt
Inta	Ămilt
Inté	Ămilté
Hoowé	Ăimél
Heeyé	Ăimlét
Naḣna	Ămilna
Intoo	Ămiltoo
Hinné	Ăimloo

Past Continuous

Ana	Kint Ăam	biĂmél	(kint	Ăémél/Ăémlé)
Inta	Kint Ăam	btiĂmél	(Kint	Ăémél)
Inté	Kinté Ăam	btiĂmlé	(Kinté	Ăémlé)
Hoowé	Kén Ăam	byiĂmél	(Kén	Ăémél)
Heeyé	Kénét Ăam	btiĂmél	(Kénét	Ăémlé)
Naḣna	Kinna Ăam	mniĂmél	(Kinna	Ăémleen)
Intoo	Kintoo Ăam	btiĂmloo	(Kintoo	Ăémleen)
Hinné	Kénoo Ăam	byiĂmloo	(Kénoo	Ăémleen)

Future

Ana	Laḣ	iĂmél
Inta	Laḣ	tiĂmél
Inté	Laḣ	tiĂmlé
Hoowé	Laḣ	yiĂmél
Heeyé	Laḣ	tiĂmél
Naḣna	Laḣ	niĂmél
Intoo	Laḣ	tiĂmloo
Hinné	Laḣ	yiĂmloo

Command

Inta	Ămél
Inté	Ămilé
Intoo	Ămiloo
Inta	Ma tĂmél
Inté	Ma tĂmle
Intoo	Ma tĂmloo

Ă= Augh in bought	Ď= a heavy D	É= like A in Bay	G= G in beige	ḣ= like an H with smaller air passage	I= I as in ink	Ḱ= like ch in Irish loch
O= O as in home	OO= as in boots	R= roll the rrr	Ť= a heavy T	Ř= like a French R (gargle it)	Ŝ= a heavy S	Ž= a heavy Z

M

M

To marry

Present

Ana	Bitzawwag
Inta	Btitzawwag
Inté	Btitzawwagé
Hoowé	Byitzawwag
Heeyé	Btitzawwag
Nahna	Mnitzawwag
Intoo	Btitzawwagoo
Hinné	Byitzawwagoo

Present Continuous

Ana	Ăam Bitzawwag	(mitzawwag/mitzawwagé)
Inta	Ăam Btitzawwag	(mitzawwag)
Inté	Ăam Btitzawwagé	(mitzawwagé)
Hoowé	Ăam Byitzawwag	(mitzawwag)
Heeyé	Ăam Btitzawwag	(mitzawwagé)
Nahna	Ăam Mnitzawwag	(mitzawwageen)
Intoo	Ăam Btitzawwagoo	(mitzawwageen)
Hinné	Ăam Byitzawwagoo	(mitzawwageen)

Past

Ana	Tzawwagt
Inta	Tzawwagt
Inté	Tzawwagté
Hoowé	Tzawwag
Heeyé	Tzawwagét
Nahna	Tzawwagna
Intoo	Tzawwagtoo
Hinné	Tzawwagoo

Past Continuous

Ana	Kint Ăam	Bitzawwag	(kint mitzawwag/mitzawwagé)
Inta	Kint Ăam	Btitzawwag	(Kint mitzawwag)
Inté	Kinté Ăam	Btitzawwagé	(Kinté mitzawwagé)
Hoowé	Kén Ăam	Byitzawwag	(Kén mitzawwag)
Heeyé	Kénét Ăam	Btitzawwag	(Kénét mitzawwagé)
Nahna	Kinna Ăam	Mnitzawwag	(Kinna mitzawwageen)
Intoo	Kintoo Ăam	Btitzawwagoo	(Kintoo mitzawwageen)
Hinné	Kénoo Ăam	Byitzawwagoo	(Kénoo mitzawwageen)

Future

Ana	Lah	Itzawwag
Inta	Lah	titzawwag
Inté	Lah	titzawwagé
Hoowé	Lah	yitzawwag
Heeyé	Lah	titzawwag
Nahna	Lah	nitzawwag
Intoo	Lah	titzawwagoo
Hinné	Lah	yitzawwagoo

Command

Inta	Tzawwag
Inté	Tzawwagé
Intoo	Tzawwagoo
Inta	Ma ttzawwag
Inté	Ma ttzawwagé
Intoo	Ma ttzawwagoo

To massage

Present

Ana	Bdallék
Inta	Btdallék
Inté	Btdallké
Hoowé	Bidallék
Heeyé	Btdallék
Nahna	Mndallék
Intoo	Btdallkoo
Hinné	Bidallkoo

Present Continuous

Ana	Ăam	Bdallék
Inta	Ăam	Btdallék
Inté	Ăam	Btdallké
Hoowé	Ăam	Bidallék
Heeyé	Ăam	Btdallék
Nahna	Ăam	Mndallék
Intoo	Ăam	Btdallkoo
Hinné	Ăam	Bidallkoo

Past

Ana	Dallakt
Inta	Dallakt
Inté	Dallakté
Hoowé	Dallak
Heeyé	Dallakét
Nahna	Dallakna
Intoo	Dallaktoo
Hinné	Dallakoo

Past Continuous

Ana	Kint Ăam	Bdallék
Inta	Kint Ăam	Btdallék
Inté	Kinté Ăam	Btdallké
Hoowé	Kén Ăam	Bidallék
Heeyé	Kénét Ăam	Btdallék
Nahna	Kinna Ăam	Mndallék
Intoo	Kintoo Ăam	Btdallkoo
Hinné	Kénoo Ăam	Bidallkoo

Future

Ana	Lah	Dallék
Inta	Lah	Tdallék
Inté	Lah	Tdallké
Hoowé	Lah	Ydallék
Heeyé	Lah	Tdallék
Nahna	Lah	Ndallék
Intoo	Lah	Tdallkoo
Hinné	Lah	Ydallkoo

Command

Inta	Dallék
Inté	Dallké
Intoo	Dallkoo
Inta	Ma tdallék
Inté	Ma tdallké
Intoo	Ma tdallkoo

Ă= Augh in bought	Đ= a heavy D	É= like A in Bay	G= G in beige	ĥ= like an H with smaller air passage	I= I as in ink	Ǩ= like ch in Irish loch
O= O as in home	OO= as in boots	R= roll the rrr	Ť= a heavy T	Ř= like a French R (gargle it)	Ŝ= a heavy S	Ž= a heavy Z

M

M

To mean

To melt

Present	
Ana	Bi'Ŝod
Inta	Bti'Ŝod
Inté	Bti'Ŝdé
Hoowé	Byi'Ŝod
Heeyé	Bti'Ŝod
Naĥna	Mni'Ŝod
Intoo	Bti'Ŝdoo
Hinné	Byi'Ŝdoo

Present	
Ana	Bdoob
Inta	Btdoob
Inté	Btdoobé
Hoowé	Bidoob
Heeyé	Btdoob
Naĥna	Mndoob
Intoo	Btdooboo
Hinné	Bidooboo

Present Continuous			
Ana	Ăam	Bi'Ŝod	('aŜéd/'aŜda)
Inta	Ăam	Bti'Ŝod	('aŜéd)
Inté	Ăam	Bti'Ŝdé	('aŜda)
Hoowé	Ăam	Byi'Ŝod	('aŜéd)
Heeyé	Ăam	Bti'Ŝod	('aŜda
Naĥna	Ăam	Mni'Ŝod	('aŜdeen)
Intoo	Ăam	Bti'Ŝdoo	('aŜdeen)
Hinné	Ăam	Byi'Ŝdoo	('aŜdeen)

Present Continuous			
Ana	Ăam	Bdoob	(déyéb/déybé)
Inta	Ăam	Btdoob	(déyéb)
Inté	Ăam	Btdoobé	(déybé)
Hoowé	Ăam	Bidoob	(déyéb)
Heeyé	Ăam	Btdoob	(déybé)
Naĥna	Ăam	Mndoob	(déybeen)
Intoo	Ăam	Btdooboo	(déybeen)
Hinné	Ăam	Bidooboo	(déybeen)

Past	
Ana	aŜadt
Inta	aŜadt
Inté	aŜadté
Hoowé	aŜad
Heeyé	aŜadét
Naĥna	aŜadna
Intoo	aŜadtoo
Hinné	aŜadoo

Past	
Ana	Dibit
Inta	Dibit
Inté	Dibté
Hoowé	Déb
Heeyé	Débét
Naĥna	Dibna
Intoo	Dibtoo
Hinné	Déboo

Past Continuous			
Ana	Kint Ăam	Bi'Ŝod	(kint 'aŜéd/'aŜda)
Inta	Kint Ăam	Bti'Ŝod	(Kint 'aŜéd)
Inté	Kinté Ăam	Bti'Ŝdé	(Kinté 'aŜda)
Hoowé	Kén Ăam	Byi'Ŝod	(Kén 'aŜéd)
Heeyé	Kénét Ăam	Bti'Ŝod	(Kénét 'aŜda
Naĥna	Kinna Ăam	Mni'Ŝod	(Kinna 'aŜdeen)
Intoo	Kintoo Ăam	Bti'Ŝdoo	(Kintoo 'aŜdeen)
Hinné	Kénoo Ăam	Byi'Ŝdoo	(Kénoo 'aŜdeen)

Past Continuous			
Ana	Kint Ăam	Bdoob	(kint déyéb/déybé)
Inta	Kint Ăam	Btdoob	(Kint déyéb)
Inté	Kinté Ăam	Btdoobé	(Kinté déybé)
Hoowé	Kén Ăam	Bidoob	(Kén déyéb)
Heeyé	Kénét Ăam	Btdoob	(Kénét déybé)
Naĥna	Kinna Ăam	Mndoob	(Kinna déybeen)
Intoo	Kintoo Ăam	Btdooboo	(Kintoo déybeen)
Hinné	Kénoo Ăam	Bidooboo	(Kénoo déybeen)

Future		
Ana	Laĥ	i'Ŝod
Inta	Laĥ	ti'Ŝod
Inté	Laĥ	ti'Ŝdé
Hoowé	Laĥ	yi'Ŝod
Heeyé	Laĥ	ti'Ŝod
Naĥna	Laĥ	ni'Ŝod
Intoo	Laĥ	ti'Ŝdoo
Hinné	Laĥ	yi'Ŝdoo

Future		
Ana	Laĥ	Doob
Inta	Laĥ	Tdoob
Inté	Laĥ	Tdoobé
Hoowé	Laĥ	Ydoob
Heeyé	Laĥ	Tdoob
Naĥna	Laĥ	Ndoob
Intoo	Laĥ	Tdooboo
Hinné	Laĥ	Ydooboo

Command	
Inta	'Ŝod
Inté	'Ŝidé
Intoo	'Ŝidoo
Inta	Ma t'Ŝod
Inté	Ma t'Ŝdé
Intoo	Ma t'Ŝdoo

Command	
Inta	Doob
Inté	Doobé
Intoo	Dooboo
Inta	Ma tdoob
Inté	Ma tdoobé
Intoo	Ma tdooboo

Ă= Augh in bought	Ď= a heavy D	É= like A in Bay	G= G in beige	ĥ= like an H with smaller air passage	I= I as in ink	Ķ= like ch in Irish loch
O= O as in home	OO= as in boots	R= roll the rrr	Ť= a heavy T	Ř= like a French R (gargle it)	Ŝ= a heavy S	Ž= a heavy Z

M M

To minimize

Present

Ana	bzaŘŘér
Inta	btzaŘŘér
Inté	btzaŘŘré
Hoowé	bizaŘŘér
Heeyé	btzaŘŘér
Naḥna	mnzaŘŘér
Intoo	btzaŘŘroo
Hinné	bizaŘŘroo

Present Continuous

Ana	Ăam	bzaŘŘér
Inta	Ăam	btzaŘŘér
Inté	Ăam	btzaŘŘré
Hoowé	Ăam	bizaŘŘér
Heeyé	Ăam	btzaŘŘér
Naḥna	Ăam	mnzaŘŘér
Intoo	Ăam	btzaŘŘroo
Hinné	Ăam	bizaŘŘroo

Past

Ana	zaŘŘart
Inta	zaŘŘart
Inté	zaŘŘarté
Hoowé	zaŘŘar
Heeyé	zaŘŘarét
Naḥna	zaŘŘarna
Intoo	zaŘŘartoo
Hinné	zaŘŘaroo

Past Continuous

Ana	Kint Ăam	bzaŘŘér
Inta	Kint Ăam	btzaŘŘér
Inté	Kinté Ăam	btzaŘŘré
Hoowé	Kén Ăam	bizaŘŘér
Heeyé	Kénét Ăam	btzaŘŘér
Naḥna	Kinna Ăam	mnzaŘŘér
Intoo	Kintoo Ăam	btzaŘŘroo
Hinné	Kénoo Ăam	bizaŘŘroo

Future

Ana	Laḥ	zaŘŘér
Inta	Laḥ	tzaŘŘér
Inté	Laḥ	tzaŘŘré
Hoowé	Laḥ	yzaŘŘér
Heeyé	Laḥ	tzaŘŘér
Naḥna	Laḥ	nzaŘŘér
Intoo	Laḥ	tzaŘŘroo
Hinné	Laḥ	yzaŘŘroo

Command

Inta	zaŘŘér
Inté	zaŘŘré
Intoo	zaŘŘroo
Inta	Ma tzaŘŘér
Inté	Ma tzaŘŘré
Intoo	Ma tzaŘŘroo

To miss

Present

Ana	Bishté'
Inta	Btishté'
Inté	Btisht'é
Hoowé	Byishté'
Heeyé	Btishté'
Naḥna	Mnishté'
Intoo	Btishté'oo
Hinné	Byishté'oo

Present Continuous

Ana	Ăam	Bishté'	(mishté'/mishté'a)
Inta	Ăam	Btishté'	(mishté')
Inté	Ăam	Btisht'é	(mishté'a)
Hoowé	Ăam	Byishté'	(mishté')
Heeyé	Ăam	Btishté'	(mishté'a)
Naḥna	Ăam	Mnishté'	(mishté'een)
Intoo	Ăam	Btishté'oo	(mishté'een)
Hinné	Ăam	Byishté'oo	(mishté'een)

Past

Ana	Shta't
Inta	Shta't
Inté	Shta'té
Hoowé	Shté'
Heeyé	Shté'ét
Naḥna	Shta'na
Intoo	Shta'too
Hinné	Shté'oo

Past Continuous

Ana	Kint Ăam	Bishté'	(kint mishté'/mishté'a)
Inta	Kint Ăam	Btishté'	(Kint mishté')
Inté	Kinté Ăam	Btisht'é	(Kinté mishté'a)
Hoowé	Kén Ăam	Byishté'	(Kén mishté')
Heeyé	Kénét Ăam	Btishté'	(Kénét mishté'a)
Naḥna	Kinna Ăam	Mnishté'	(Kinna mishté'een)
Intoo	Kintoo Ăam	Btishté'oo	(Kintoo mishté'een)
Hinné	Kénoo Ăam	Byishté'oo	(Kénoo mishté'een)

Future

Ana	Laḥ	ishté'
Inta	Laḥ	Tishté'
Inté	Laḥ	tisht'é
Hoowé	Laḥ	Yishté'
Heeyé	Laḥ	Tishté'
Naḥna	Laḥ	Nishté'
Intoo	Laḥ	Tishté'oo
Hinné	Laḥ	Yishté'oo

Command

Inta	Shté'
Inté	Shté'é
Intoo	Shté'oo
Inta	Ma tshté'
Inté	Ma tshté'é
Intoo	Ma tshté'oo

Ă= Augh in bought	Ď= a heavy D	É= like A in Bay	G= G in beige	ḥ= like an H with smaller air passage	I= I as in ink	Ќ= like ch in Irish loch
O= O as in home	OO= as in boots	R= roll the rrr	Ť= a heavy T	Ř= like a French R (gargle it)	Ŝ= a heavy S	Ž= a heavy Z

To moisten

Present	
Ana	Bballil
Inta	Btballil
Inté	Btballilé
Hoowé	Biballil
Heeyé	Btballil
Naĥna	Mnballil
Intoo	Btballiloo
Hinné	Biballiloo

Present Continuous			
Ana	Ăam	Bballil	(mballal/mballalé)
Inta	Ăam	Btballil	(mballal)
Inté	Ăam	Btballilé	(mballalé)
Hoowé	Ăam	Biballil	(mballal)
Heeyé	Ăam	Btballil	(mballalé)
Naĥna	Ăam	Mnballil	(mballaleen)
Intoo	Ăam	Btballiloo	(mballaleen)
Hinné	Ăam	Biballiloo	(mballaleen)

Past	
Ana	Ballalt
Inta	Ballalt
Inté	Ballalté
Hoowé	Ballal
Heeyé	Ballalét
Naĥna	Ballalna
Intoo	Ballaltoo
Hinné	Ballaloo

Past Continuous				
Ana	Kint Ăam	Bballil	(kint	mballal/mballalé)
Inta	Kint Ăam	Btballil	(Kint	mballal)
Inté	Kinté Ăam	Btballilé	(Kinté	mballalé)
Hoowé	Kén Ăam	Biballil	(Kén	mballal)
Heeyé	Kénét Ăam	Btballil	(Kénét	mballalé)
Naĥna	Kinna Ăam	Mnballil	(Kinna	mballaleen)
Intoo	Kintoo Ăam	Btballiloo	(Kintoo	mballaleen)
Hinné	Kénoo Ăam	Biballiloo	(Kénoo	mballaleen)

Future		
Ana	Laĥ	ballil
Inta	Laĥ	tballil
Inté	Laĥ	tballilé
Hoowé	Laĥ	yballil
Heeyé	Laĥ	tballil
Naĥna	Laĥ	nballil
Intoo	Laĥ	tballiloo
Hinné	Laĥ	yballiloo

Command	
Inta	Ballil
Inté	Ballilé
Intoo	Balliloo
Inta	Ma tballil
Inté	Ma tballilé
Intoo	Ma tballiloo

To mop

Present	
Ana	Bmasséĥ
Inta	Btmasséĥ
Inté	Btmasshé
Hoowé	Bimasséĥ
Heeyé	Btmasséĥ
Naĥna	Mnmasséĥ
Intoo	Btmasshoo
Hinné	Bimasshoo

Present Continuous		
Ana	Ăam	Bmasséĥ
Inta	Ăam	Btmasséĥ
Inté	Ăam	Btmasshé
Hoowé	Ăam	Bimasséĥ
Heeyé	Ăam	Btmasséĥ
Naĥna	Ăam	Mnmasséĥ
Intoo	Ăam	Btmasshoo
Hinné	Ăam	Bimasshoo

Past	
Ana	Massaĥt
Inta	Massaĥt
Inté	Massaĥté
Hoowé	Massaĥ
Heeyé	Massaĥét
Naĥna	Massaĥna
Intoo	Massaĥtoo
Hinné	Massaĥoo

Past Continuous		
Ana	Kint Ăam	Bmasséĥ
Inta	Kint Ăam	Btmasséĥ
Inté	Kinté Ăam	Btmasshé
Hoowé	Kén Ăam	Bimasséĥ
Heeyé	Kénét Ăam	Btmasséĥ
Naĥna	Kinna Ăam	Mnmasséĥ
Intoo	Kintoo Ăam	Btmasshoo
Hinné	Kénoo Ăam	Bimasshoo

Future		
Ana	Laĥ	Masséĥ
Inta	Laĥ	Tmasséĥ
Inté	Laĥ	Tmasshé
Hoowé	Laĥ	Ymasséĥ
Heeyé	Laĥ	Tmasséĥ
Naĥna	Laĥ	Nmasséĥ
Intoo	Laĥ	Tmasshoo
Hinné	Laĥ	Ymasshoo

Command	
Inta	Masséĥ
Inté	Masshé
Intoo	Masshoo
Inta	Ma tmasséĥ
Inté	Ma tmasshé
Intoo	Ma tmasshoo

Ă= Augh in bought	Ď= a heavy D	É= like A in Bay	G= G in beige	ĥ= like an H with smaller air passage	I= I as in ink	Ќ= like ch in Irish loch
O= O as in home	OO= as in boots	R= roll the rrr	Ť= a heavy T	Ř= like a French R (gargle it)	Ŝ= a heavy S	Ž= a heavy Z

M   M

To mourn/To be sad

Present	
Ana	bizĂal
Inta	btizĂal
Inté	btizĂalé
Hoowé	byizĂal
Heeyé	btizĂal
Nahna	mnizĂal
Intoo	btizĂaloo
Hinné	byizĂaloo

Present Continuous		
Ana	Ăam bizĂal	(ziĂlén/ziĂléné)
Inta	Ăam btizĂal	(ziĂlén)
Inté	Ăam btizĂalé	(ziĂléné)
Hoowé	Ăam byizĂal	(ziĂlén)
Heeyé	Ăam btizĂal	(ziĂléné)
Nahna	Ăam mnizĂal	(ziĂléneen)
Intoo	Ăam btizĂaloo	(ziĂléneen)
Hinné	Ăam byizĂaloo	(ziĂléneen)

Past	
Ana	zĂilt
Inta	zĂilt
Inté	ZĂilté
Hoowé	ziĂil
Heeyé	ziĂlit
Nahna	zĂilna
Intoo	zĂiltoo
Hinné	ziĂloo

Past Continuous		
Ana	Kint Ăam bizĂal	(kint ziĂlén/ziĂléné)
Inta	Kint Ăam btizĂal	(Kint ziĂlén)
Inté	Kinté Ăam btizĂalé	(Kinté ziĂléné)
Hoowé	Kén Ăam byizĂal	(Kén ziĂlén)
Heeyé	Kénét Ăam btizĂal	(Kénét ziĂléné)
Nahna	Kinna Ăam mnizĂal	(Kinna ziĂléneen)
Intoo	Kintoo Ăam btizĂaloo	(Kintoo ziĂléneen)
Hinné	Kénoo Ăam byizĂaloo	(Kénoo ziĂléneen)

Future		
Ana	Laĥ	izĂal
Inta	Laĥ	tizĂal
Inté	Laĥ	tizĂalé
Hoowé	Laĥ	yizĂal
Heeyé	Laĥ	tizĂal
Nahna	Laĥ	nizĂal
Intoo	Laĥ	tizĂaloo
Hinné	Laĥ	yizĂaloo

Command	
Inta	zĂal
Inté	zĂalé
Intoo	zĂaloo
Inta	Ma tzĂal
Inté	Ma tzĂalé
Intoo	Ma tzĂaloo

To move

Present	
Ana	Bitĥarrak
Inta	Btitĥarrak
Inté	Btitĥarraké
Hoowé	Byitĥarrak
Heeyé	Btitĥarrak
Nahna	Mnitĥarrak
Intoo	Btitĥarrakoo
Hinné	Byitĥarrakoo

Present Continuous		
Ana	Ăam	Bitĥarrak
Inta	Ăam	Btitĥarrak
Inté	Ăam	Btitĥarraké
Hoowé	Ăam	Byitĥarrak
Heeyé	Ăam	Btitĥarrak
Nahna	Ăam	Mnitĥarrak
Intoo	Ăam	Btitĥarrakoo
Hinné	Ăam	Byitĥarrakoo

Past	
Ana	Tĥarrakt
Inta	Tĥarrakt
Inté	Tĥarrakté
Hoowé	Tĥarrak
Heeyé	Tĥarrakét
Nahna	Tĥarrakna
Intoo	Tĥarraktoo
Hinné	Tĥarrakoo

Past Continuous		
Ana	Kint Ăam	Bitĥarrak
Inta	Kint Ăam	Btitĥarrak
Inté	Kinté Ăam	Btitĥarraké
Hoowé	Kén Ăam	Byitĥarrak
Heeyé	Kénét Ăam	Btitĥarrak
Nahna	Kinna Ăam	Mnitĥarrak
Intoo	Kintoo Ăam	Btitĥarrakoo
Hinné	Kénoo Ăam	Byitĥarrakoo

Future		
Ana	Laĥ	Itĥarrak
Inta	Laĥ	Titĥarrak
Inté	Laĥ	Titĥarraké
Hoowé	Laĥ	Yitĥarrak
Heeyé	Laĥ	Titĥarrak
Nahna	Laĥ	Nitĥarrak
Intoo	Laĥ	Titĥarrakoo
Hinné	Laĥ	Yitĥarrakoo

Command	
Inta	Tĥarrak
Inté	Tĥarraké
Intoo	Tĥarrakoo
Inta	Ma ttĥarrak
Inté	Ma ttĥarraké
Intoo	Ma ttĥarrakoo

Ă= Augh in bought	Ď= a heavy D	É= like A in Bay	G= G in beige	ĥ= like an H with smaller air passage	I= I as in ink	Ќ= like ch in Irish loch
O= O as in home	OO= as in boots	R= roll the rrr	Ť= a heavy T	Ř= like a French R (gargle it)	Ŝ= a heavy S	Ž= a heavy Z

M

M

To move (house)

Present

Ana	Bin'ol
Inta	BTin'ol
Inté	BTin'lé
Hoowé	BYin'ol
Heeyé	BTin'ol
Naḣna	Mnin'ol
Intoo	Btin'loo
Hinné	Byin'loo

Present Continuous

Ana	Ăam	Bin'ol
Inta	Ăam	BTin'ol
Inté	Ăam	BTin'lé
Hoowé	Ăam	BYin'ol
Heeyé	Ăam	BTin'ol
Naḣna	Ăam	Mnin'ol
Intoo	Ăam	Btin'loo
Hinné	Ăam	Byin'loo

Past

Ana	Na'alt
Inta	Na'alt
Inté	Na'alté
Hoowé	Na'al
Heeyé	Na'alét
Naḣna	Na'alna
Intoo	Na'altoo
Hinné	Na'aloo

Past Continuous

Ana	Kint Ăam	Bin'ol
Inta	Kint Ăam	BTin'ol
Inté	Kinté Ăam	BTin'lé
Hoowé	Kén Ăam	BYin'ol
Heeyé	Kénét Ăam	BTin'ol
Naḣna	Kinna Ăam	Mnin'ol
Intoo	Kintoo Ăam	Btin'loo
Hinné	Kénoo Ăam	Byin'loo

Future

Ana	Laḣ	In'ol
Inta	Laḣ	Tin'ol
Inté	Laḣ	Tin'lé
Hoowé	Laḣ	Yin'ol
Heeyé	Laḣ	Tin'ol
Naḣna	Laḣ	Nin'ol
Intoo	Laḣ	Tin'loo
Hinné	Laḣ	Yin'loo

Command

Inta	N'ol
Inté	N'ilé
Intoo	N'iloo
Inta	Ma tn'ol
Inté	Ma tn'lé
Intoo	Ma tn'loo

To multiply

Present

Ana	biĎrob
Inta	btiĎrob
Inté	btiĎrbé
Hoowé	byiĎrob
Heeyé	btiĎrob
Naḣna	mniĎrob
Intoo	btiĎrboo
Hinné	byiĎrboo

Present Continuous

Ana	Ăam	biĎrob
Inta	Ăam	btiĎrob
Inté	Ăam	btiĎrbé
Hoowé	Ăam	byiĎrob
Heeyé	Ăam	btiĎrob
Naḣna	Ăam	mniĎrob
Intoo	Ăam	btiĎrboo
Hinné	Ăam	byiĎrboo

Past

Ana	Ďarabt
Inta	Ďarabt
Inté	Ďarabté
Hoowé	Ďarab
Heeyé	Ďarbét
Naḣna	Ďarabna
Intoo	Ďarabtoo
Hinné	Ďaraboo

Past Continuous

Ana	Kint Ăam	biĎrob
Inta	Kint Ăam	btiĎrob
Inté	Kinté Ăam	btiĎrbé
Hoowé	Kén Ăam	byiĎrob
Heeyé	Kénét Ăam	btiĎrob
Naḣna	Kinna Ăam	mniĎrob
Intoo	Kintoo Ăam	btiĎrboo
Hinné	Kénoo Ăam	byiĎrboo

Future

Ana	Laḣ	iĎrob
Inta	Laḣ	tiĎrob
Inté	Laḣ	tiĎrbé
Hoowé	Laḣ	yiĎrob
Heeyé	Laḣ	tiĎrob
Naḣna	Laḣ	niĎrob
Intoo	Laḣ	tiĎrboo
Hinné	Laḣ	yiĎrboo

Command

Inta	Ďrob
Inté	Ďribé
Intoo	Ďriboo
Inta	Ma tĎrob
Inté	Ma tiĎrbé
Intoo	Ma tĎrboo

Ă= Augh in bought	**Ď**= a heavy D	**É**= like A in Bay	**G**= G in beige	**ḣ**= like an H with smaller air passage	**I**= I as in ink	**Ќ**= like ch in Irish loch
O= O as in home	**OO**= as in boots	**R**= roll the rrr	**Ť**= a heavy T	**Ř**= like a French R (gargle it)	**Ŝ**= a heavy S	**Ž**= a heavy Z

N

N

To nag

Present

Ana	Bni'
Inta	Btni'
Inté	Btni'é
Hoowé	Bini'
Heeyé	Btni'
Naĥna	Mnni'
Intoo	Btni'oo
Hinné	Bini'oo

Present Continuous

Ana	Ăam	Bni'
Inta	Ăam	Btni'
Inté	Ăam	Btni'é
Hoowé	Ăam	Bini'
Heeyé	Ăam	Btni'
Naĥna	Ăam	Mnni'
Intoo	Ăam	Btni'oo
Hinné	Ăam	Bini'oo

Past

Ana	Na'ét
Inta	Na'ét
Inté	Na'aité
Hoowé	Na'
Heeyé	Na'ét
Naĥna	Na'aina
Intoo	Na'aitoo
Hinné	Na'oo

Past Continuous

Ana	Kint Ăam	Bni'	
Inta	Kint Ăam	Btni'	
Inté	Kinté Ăam	Btni'é	
Hoowé	Kén Ăam	Bini'	
Heeyé	Kénét Ăam	Btni'	
Naĥna	Kinna Ăam	Mnni'	
Intoo	Kintoo Ăam	Btni'oo	
Hinné	Kénoo Ăam	Bini'oo	

Future

Ana	Laĥ	Ni'
Inta	Laĥ	Tni'
Inté	Laĥ	Tni'é
Hoowé	Laĥ	Yni'
Heeyé	Laĥ	Tni'
Naĥna	Laĥ	Nni'
Intoo	Laĥ	Tni'oo
Hinné	Laĥ	Yni'oo

Command

Inta	Ni'
Inté	Ni'é
Intoo	Ni'oo
Inta	Ma tni'
Inté	Ma tni'é
Intoo	Ma tni'oo

To need

Present

Ana	bĂooz
Inta	btĂooz
Inté	btĂoozé
Hoowé	biĂooz
Heeyé	btĂooz
Naĥna	mnĂooz
Intoo	btĂoozoo
Hinné	biĂoozoo

Present Continuous

Ana	Ăam	bĂooz	(Ăéyéz/Ăéyzé)
Inta	Ăam	btĂooz	(Ăéyéz)
Inté	Ăam	btĂoozé	(Ăéyzé)
Hoowé	Ăam	biĂooz	(Ăéyéz)
Heeyé	Ăam	btĂooz	(Ăéyzé)
Naĥna	Ăam	mnĂooz	(Ăéyzeen)
Intoo	Ăam	btĂoozoo	(Ăéyézeen)
Hinné	Ăam	biĂoozoo	(Ăéyézeen)

Past

Ana	Ăizt
Inta	Ăizt
Inté	Ăizté
Hoowé	Ăéz
Heeyé	Ăézét
Naĥna	Ăizna
Intoo	Ăiztoo
Hinné	Ăézoo

Past Continuous

Ana	Kint Ăam	bĂooz	(kint	Ăéyéz/Ăéyzé)
Inta	Kint Ăam	btĂooz	(Kint	Ăéyéz)
Inté	Kinté Ăam	btĂoozé	(Kinté	Ăéyzé)
Hoowé	Kén Ăam	biĂooz	(Kén	Ăéyéz)
Heeyé	Kénét Ăam	btĂooz	(Kénét	Ăéyzé)
Naĥna	Kinna Ăam	mnĂooz	(Kinna	Ăéyzeen)
Intoo	Kintoo Ăam	btĂoozoo	(Kintoo	Ăéyézeen)
Hinné	Kénoo Ăam	biĂoozoo	(Kénoo	Ăéyézeen)

Future

Ana	Laĥ	Ăooz
Inta	Laĥ	tĂooz
Inté	Laĥ	tĂoozé
Hoowé	Laĥ	yĂooz
Heeyé	Laĥ	tĂooz
Naĥna	Laĥ	nĂooz
Intoo	Laĥ	tĂoozoo
Hinné	Laĥ	yĂoozoo

Command

Inta	Ăooz
Inté	Ăoozé
Intoo	Ăoozoo
Inta	Ma tĂooz
Inté	Ma tĂoozé
Intoo	Ma tĂoozoo

Ă= Augh in bought	Ď= a heavy D	É= like A in Bay	G= G in beige	ĥ= an H with smaller air passage	I= I as in ink	Ķ= like ch in Irish loch
O= O as in home	OO= as in boots	R= roll the rrr	Ť= a heavy T	Ř= like a French R (gargle it)	Š= a heavy S	Ž= a heavy Z

N   O

To neglect   To Object / To Oppose

To neglect

Present	
Ana	Bihmél
Inta	Btihmél
Inté	Btihmlé
Hoowé	Byihmél
Heeyé	Btihmél
Naĥna	Mnihmél
Intoo	Btihmloo
Hinné	Byihmloo

Present Continuous			
Ana	Ăam	Bihmél	(hémél/hémlé)
Inta	Ăam	Btihmél	(hémél)
Inté	Ăam	Btihmlé	(hémlé)
Hoowé	Ăam	Byihmél	(hémél)
Heeyé	Ăam	Btihmél	(hémlé)
Naĥna	Ăam	Mnihmél	(hémleen)
Intoo	Ăam	Btihmloo	(hémleen)
Hinné	Ăam	Byihmloo	(hémleen)

Past	
Ana	Hamalt
Inta	Hamalt
Inté	Hamalté
Hoowé	Hamal
Heeyé	Hamalét
Naĥna	Hamalna
Intoo	Hamaltoo
Hinné	Hamaloo

Past Continuous			
Ana	Kint Ăam	Bihmél	(kint hémél/hémlé)
Inta	Kint Ăam	Btihmél	(Kint hémél)
Inté	Kinté Ăam	Btihmlé	(Kinté hémlé)
Hoowé	Kén Ăam	Byihmél	(Kén hémél)
Heeyé	Kénét Ăam	Btihmél	(Kénét hémlé)
Naĥna	Kinna Ăam	Mnihmél	(Kinna hémleen)
Intoo	Kintoo Ăam	Btihmloo	(Kintoo hémleen)
Hinné	Kénoo Ăam	Byihmloo	(Kénoo hémleen)

Future		
Ana	Laĥ	ihmél
Inta	Laĥ	tihmél
Inté	Laĥ	tihmlé
Hoowé	Laĥ	yihmél
Heeyé	Laĥ	tihmél
Naĥna	Laĥ	nihmél
Intoo	Laĥ	tihmloo
Hinné	Laĥ	yihmloo

Command	
Inta	Hmol
Inté	Hmilé
Intoo	Hmiloo
Inta	Ma thmol
Inté	Ma thmlé
Intoo	Ma thmloo

To Object / To Oppose

Present	
Ana	bĂaréĎ
Inta	btĂaréĎ
Inté	btĂarĎé
Hoowé	biĂaréĎ
Heeyé	btĂaréĎ
Naĥna	mnĂaréĎ
Intoo	btĂarĎoo
Hinné	biĂarĎoo

Present Continuous			
Ana	Ăam	bĂaréĎ	(mAaraĎ/mAarĎa)
Inta	Ăam	btĂaréĎ	(mAaraĎ)
Inté	Ăam	btĂarĎé	(mAarĎa)
Hoowé	Ăam	biĂaréĎ	(mAaraĎ)
Heeyé	Ăam	btĂaréĎ	(mAarĎa)
Naĥna	Ăam	mnĂaréĎ	(mAarĎeen)
Intoo	Ăam	btĂarĎoo	(mAarĎeen)
Hinné	Ăam	biĂarĎoo	(mAarĎeen)

Past	
Ana	ĂaraĎt
Inta	ĂaraĎt
Inté	ĂaraĎté
Hoowé	ĂaraĎ
Heeyé	ĂaraĎét
Naĥna	ĂaraĎna
Intoo	ĂaraĎtoo
Hinné	ĂaraĎoo

Past Continuous			
Ana	Kint Ăam	bĂaréĎ	(kint mAaraĎ/mAarĎa)
Inta	Kint Ăam	btĂaréĎ	(Kint mAaraĎ)
Inté	Kinté Ăam	btĂarĎé	(Kinté mAarĎa)
Hoowé	Kén Ăam	biĂaréĎ	(Kén mAaraĎ)
Heeyé	Kénét Ăam	btĂaréĎ	(Kénét mAarĎa)
Naĥna	Kinna Ăam	mnĂaréĎ	(Kinna mAarĎeen)
Intoo	Kintoo Ăam	btĂarĎoo	(Kintoo mAarĎeen)
Hinné	Kénoo Ăam	biĂarĎoo	(Kénoo mAarĎeen)

Future		
Ana	Laĥ	ĂaréĎ
Inta	Laĥ	tĂaréĎ
Inté	Laĥ	tĂarĎé
Hoowé	Laĥ	yĂaréĎ
Heeyé	Laĥ	tĂaréĎ
Naĥna	Laĥ	nĂaréĎ
Intoo	Laĥ	tĂarĎoo
Hinné	Laĥ	yĂarĎoo

Command	
Inta	ĂaréĎ
Inté	ĂarĎé
Intoo	ĂarĎoo
Inta	Ma tĂaréĎ
Inté	Ma tĂarĎé
Intoo	Ma tĂarĎoo

Ă= Augh in bought	Ď= a heavy D	É= like A in Bay	G= G in beige	ĥ= like an H with smaller air passage	I= I as in ink	Ќ= like ch in Irish loch
O= O as in home	OO= as in boots	R= roll the rrr	Ť= a heavy T	Ř= like a French R (gargle it)	Ŝ= a heavy S	Ž= a heavy Z

O

O

To Open

Present

Ana	Biftaĥ
Inta	Btiftaĥ
Inté	Btiftaĥé
Hoowé	Byiftaĥ
Heeyé	Btiftaĥ
Naĥna	Mniftaĥ
Intoo	Btiftaĥoo
Hinné	Byiftaĥoo

Present Continuous

Ana	Ăam	Biftaĥ	(fétéĥ/fétha)
Inta	Ăam	Btiftaĥ	(fétéĥ)
Inté	Ăam	Btiftaĥé	(fétha)
Hoowé	Ăam	Byiftaĥ	(fétéĥ)
Heeyé	Ăam	Btiftaĥ	(fétha)
Naĥna	Ăam	Mniftaĥ	(fétheen)
Intoo	Ăam	Btiftaĥoo	(fétheen)
Hinné	Ăam	Byiftaĥoo	(fétheen)

Past

Ana	Fataĥt
Inta	Fataĥt
Inté	Fataĥté
Hoowé	Fataĥ
Heeyé	Fataĥét
Naĥna	Fataĥna
Intoo	Fataĥtoo
Hinné	Fataĥoo

Past Continuous

Ana	Kint Ăam	Biftaĥ	(kint fétéĥ/fétha)
Inta	Kint Ăam	Btiftaĥ	(Kint fétéĥ)
Inté	Kinté Ăam	Btiftaĥé	(Kinté fétha)
Hoowé	Kén Ăam	Byiftaĥ	(Kén fétéĥ)
Heeyé	Kénét Ăam	Btiftaĥ	(Kénét fétha)
Naĥna	Kinna Ăam	Mniftaĥ	(Kinna fétheen)
Intoo	Kintoo Ăam	Btiftaĥoo	(Kintoo fétheen)
Hinné	Kénoo Ăam	Byiftaĥoo	(Kénoo fétheen)

Future

Ana	Laĥ	Iftaĥ
Inta	Laĥ	Tiftaĥ
Inté	Laĥ	Tiftaĥé
Hoowé	Laĥ	Yiftaĥ
Heeyé	Laĥ	Tiftaĥ
Naĥna	Laĥ	Niftaĥ
Intoo	Laĥ	Tiftaĥoo
Hinné	Laĥ	Yiftaĥoo

Command

Inta	Ftaĥ
Inté	Ftaĥé
Intoo	Ftaĥoo
Inta	Ma tftaĥ
Inté	Ma tftaĥé
Intoo	Ma tftaĥoo

To Organize

Present

Ana	Bnazzém
Inta	Btnazzém
Inté	Btnazzmé
Hoowé	Binazzém
Heeyé	Btnazzém
Naĥna	Mnnazzém
Intoo	Btnazzmoo
Hinné	Binazzmoo

Present Continuous

Ana	Ăam	Bnazzém
Inta	Ăam	Btnazzém
Inté	Ăam	Btnazzmé
Hoowé	Ăam	Binazzém
Heeyé	Ăam	Btnazzém
Naĥna	Ăam	Mnnazzém
Intoo	Ăam	Btnazzmoo
Hinné	Ăam	Binazzmoo

Past

Ana	Nazzamt
Inta	Nazzamt
Inté	Nazzamté
Hoowé	Nazzam
Heeyé	Nazzamét
Naĥna	Nazzamna
Intoo	Nazzamtoo
Hinné	Nazzamoo

Past Continuous

Ana	Kint Ăam	Bnazzém
Inta	Kint Ăam	Btnazzém
Inté	Kinté Ăam	Btnazzmé
Hoowé	Kén Ăam	Binazzém
Heeyé	Kénét Ăam	Btnazzém
Naĥna	Kinna Ăam	Mnnazzém
Intoo	Kintoo Ăam	Btnazzmoo
Hinné	Kénoo Ăam	Binazzmoo

Future

Ana	Laĥ	Nazzém
Inta	Laĥ	Tnazzém
Inté	Laĥ	Tnazzmé
Hoowé	Laĥ	Ynazzém
Heeyé	Laĥ	Tnazzém
Naĥna	Laĥ	Nnazzém
Intoo	Laĥ	Tnazzmoo
Hinné	Laĥ	Ynazzmoo

Command

Inta	Nazzém
Inté	Nazzmé
Intoo	Nazzmoo
Inta	Ma tnazzém
Inté	Ma tnazzmé
Intoo	Ma tnazzmoo

Ă= Augh in bought	Đ= a heavy D	É= like A in Bay	G= G in beige	ĥ= like an H with smaller air passage	I= I as in ink	Ќ= like ch in Irish loch
O= O as in home	OO= as in boots	R= roll the rrr	Ť= a heavy T	Ř= like a French R (gargle it)	Ŝ= a heavy S	Ž= a heavy Z

P   P

To pack

Present	
Ana	bĎibb
Inta	btĎibb
Inté	btĎibbé
Hoowé	biĎi
Heeyé	btĎibb
Nahna	mnĎibb
Intoo	btĎibboo
Hinné	biĎibboo

Present Continuous		
Ana	Ăam	bĎibb
Inta	Ăam	btĎibb
Inté	Ăam	btĎibbé
Hoowé	Ăam	biĎi
Heeyé	Ăam	btĎibb
Nahna	Ăam	mnĎibb
Intoo	Ăam	btĎibboo
Hinné	Ăam	biĎibboo

Past	
Ana	Ďabbét
Inta	Ďabbét
Inté	Ďabbaité
Hoowé	Ďabb
Heeyé	Ďabbét
Nahna	Ďabbaina
Intoo	Ďabbaitoo
Hinné	Ďabboo

Past Continuous			
Ana	Kint Ăam	bĎibb	
Inta	Kint Ăam	btĎibb	
Inté	Kinté Ăam	btĎibbé	
Hoowé	Kén Ăam	biĎi	
Heeyé	Kénét Ăam	btĎibb	
Nahna	Kinna Ăam	mnĎibb	
Intoo	Kintoo Ăam	btĎibboo	
Hinné	Kénoo Ăam	biĎibboo	

Future		
Ana	Laĥ	Ďibb
Inta	Laĥ	tĎibb
Inté	Laĥ	tĎibbé
Hoowé	Laĥ	yĎi
Heeyé	Laĥ	tĎibb
Nahna	Laĥ	nĎibb
Intoo	Laĥ	tĎibboo
Hinné	Laĥ	yĎibboo

Command	
Inta	Ďibb
Inté	Ďibbé
Intoo	Ďibboo
Inta	Ma tĎibb
Inté	Ma tĎibbé
Intoo	Ma tĎibboo

To paddle

Present	
Ana	B'addéf
Inta	Bt'addéf
Inté	Bt'addfé
Hoowé	Bi'addéf
Heeyé	Bt'addéf
Nahna	Mn'addéf
Intoo	Bt'addfoo
Hinné	Bi'addfoo

Present Continuous		
Ana	Ăam	B'addéf
Inta	Ăam	Bt'addéf
Inté	Ăam	Bt'addfé
Hoowé	Ăam	Bi'addéf
Heeyé	Ăam	Bt'addéf
Nahna	Ăam	Mn'addéf
Intoo	Ăam	Bt'addfoo
Hinné	Ăam	Bi'addfoo

Past	
Ana	Addaft
Inta	Addaft
Inté	Addafté
Hoowé	Addaf
Heeyé	Addafét
Nahna	Addafna
Intoo	Addaftoo
Hinné	Addafoo

Past Continuous			
Ana	Kint Ăam	B'addéf	
Inta	Kint Ăam	Bt'addéf	
Inté	Kinté Ăam	Bt'addfé	
Hoowé	Kén Ăam	Bi'addéf	
Heeyé	Kénét Ăam	Bt'addéf	
Nahna	Kinna Ăam	Mn'addéf	
Intoo	Kintoo Ăam	Bt'addfoo	
Hinné	Kénoo Ăam	Bi'addfoo	

Future		
Ana	Laĥ	'addéf
Inta	Laĥ	t'addéf
Inté	Laĥ	t'addfé
Hoowé	Laĥ	Y'addéf
Heeyé	Laĥ	t'addéf
Nahna	Laĥ	n'addéf
Intoo	Laĥ	t'addfoo
Hinné	Laĥ	Y'addfoo

Command	
Inta	Addéf
Inté	Addfé
Intoo	Addfoo
Inta	Ma t'addéf
Inté	Ma t'addfé
Intoo	Ma t'addfoo

Ă= Augh in bought	Ď= a heavy D	É= like A in Bay	G= G in beige	ĥ= like an H with smaller air passage	I= I as in ink	Ќ= like ch in Irish loch
O= O as in home	OO= as in boots	R= roll the rrr	Ŧ= a heavy T	Ř= like a French R (gargle it)	Ŝ= a heavy S	Ž= a heavy Z

<u>P</u>   <u>P</u>

To paint

Present

Ana	Bidhan
Inta	Btidhan
Inté	Btidhané
Hoowé	Byidhan
Heeyé	Btidhan
Naĥna	Mnidhan
Intoo	Btidhanoo
Hinné	Byidhanoo

Present Continuous

Ana	Ăam	Bidhan
Inta	Ăam	Btidhan
Inté	Ăam	Btidhané
Hoowé	Ăam	Byidhan
Heeyé	Ăam	Btidhan
Naĥna	Ăam	Mnidhan
Intoo	Ăam	Btidhanoo
Hinné	Ăam	Byidhanoo

Past

Ana	dahant
Inta	dahant
Inté	Dahanté
Hoowé	Dahan
Heeyé	dahanét
Naĥna	Dahanna
Intoo	Dahantoo
Hinné	dahanoo

Past Continuous

Ana	Kint Ăam	Bidhan
Inta	Kint Ăam	Btidhan
Inté	Kinté Ăam	Btidhané
Hoowé	Kén Ăam	Byidhan
Heeyé	Kénét Ăam	Btidhan
Naĥna	Kinna Ăam	Mnidhan
Intoo	Kintoo Ăam	Btidhanoo
Hinné	Kénoo Ăam	Byidhanoo

Future

Ana	Laĥ	Idhan
Inta	Laĥ	Tidhan
Inté	Laĥ	Tidhané
Hoowé	Laĥ	Yidhan
Heeyé	Laĥ	Tidhan
Naĥna	Laĥ	Nidhan
Intoo	Laĥ	Tidhanoo
Hinné	Laĥ	Yidhanoo

Command

Inta	Dhon
Inté	Dhané
Intoo	Dhanoo
Inta	Ma tdhan
Inté	Ma tdhané
Intoo	Ma tdhanoo

To pant/breathe heavily

Present

Ana	Bilhat
Inta	Btilhat
Inté	Btilhaté
Hoowé	Byilhat
Heeyé	Btilhat
Naĥna	Mnilhat
Intoo	Btilhatoo
Hinné	Byilhatoo

Present Continuous

Ana	Ăam	Bilhat
Inta	Ăam	Btilhat
Inté	Ăam	Btilhaté
Hoowé	Ăam	Byilhat
Heeyé	Ăam	Btilhat
Naĥna	Ăam	Mnilhat
Intoo	Ăam	Btilhatoo
Hinné	Ăam	Byilhatoo

Past

Ana	Lahat
Inta	Lahat
Inté	Lahatté
Hoowé	Lahat
Heeyé	Lahatét
Naĥna	Lahatna
Intoo	Lahattoo
Hinné	Lahatoo

Past Continuous

Ana	Kint Ăam	Bilhat
Inta	Kint Ăam	Btilhat
Inté	Kinté Ăam	Btilhaté
Hoowé	Kén Ăam	Byilhat
Heeyé	Kénét Ăam	Btilhat
Naĥna	Kinna Ăam	Mnilhat
Intoo	Kintoo Ăam	Btilhatoo
Hinné	Kénoo Ăam	Byilhatoo

Future

Ana	Laĥ	Ilhat
Inta	Laĥ	Tilhat
Inté	Laĥ	Tilhaté
Hoowé	Laĥ	Yilhat
Heeyé	Laĥ	Tilhat
Naĥna	Laĥ	Nilhat
Intoo	Laĥ	Tilhatoo
Hinné	Laĥ	Yilhatoo

Command

Inta	Lhot
Inté	Lhité
Intoo	Lhitoo
Inta	Ma tlhot
Inté	Ma tlhté
Intoo	Ma tlhtoo

Ă= Augh in bought	Ď= a heavy D	É= like A in Bay	G= G in beige	ĥ= like an H with smaller air passage	I= I as in ink	Ķ= like ch in Irish loch
O= O as in home	OO= as in boots	R= roll the rrr	Ť= a heavy T	Ř= like a French R (gargle it)	Ŝ= a heavy S	Ž= a heavy Z

<u>P</u>   <u>P</u>

To park

Present

Ana	bŜiff
Inta	btŜiff
Inté	btŜiffé
Hoowé	biŜiff
Heeyé	btŜiff
Naḣna	mnŜiff
Intoo	btŜiffoo
Hinné	biŜiffoo

Present Continuous

Ana	Ăam	bŜiff	(Ŝaféf/Ŝaffé)
Inta	Ăam	btŜiff	(Ŝaféf)
Inté	Ăam	btŜiffé	(Ŝaffé)
Hoowé	Ăam	biŜiff	(Ŝaféf)
Heeyé	Ăam	btŜiff	(Ŝaffé)
Naḣna	Ăam	mnŜiff	(Ŝafeen)
Intoo	Ăam	btŜiffoo	(Ŝafeen)
Hinné	Ăam	biŜiffoo	(Ŝafeen)

Past

Ana	Ŝaffét
Inta	Ŝaffét
Inté	Ŝaffaité
Hoowé	Ŝaff
Heeyé	Ŝaffét
Naḣna	Ŝaffaina
Intoo	Ŝaffaitoo
Hinné	Ŝaffoo

Past Continuous

Ana	Kint Ăam	bŜiff	(kint Ŝaféf/Ŝaffé)
Inta	Kint Ăam	btŜiff	(Kint Ŝaféf)
Inté	Kinté Ăam	btŜiffé	(Kinté Ŝaffé)
Hoowé	Kén Ăam	biŜiff	(Kén Ŝaféf)
Heeyé	Kénét Ăam	btŜiff	(Kénét Ŝaffé)
Naḣna	Kinna Ăam	mnŜiff	(Kinna Ŝafeen)
Intoo	Kintoo Ăam	btŜiffoo	(Kintoo Ŝafeen)
Hinné	Kénoo Ăam	biŜiffoo	(Kénoo Ŝafeen)

Future

Ana	Laḣ	Ŝiff
Inta	Laḣ	tŜiff
Inté	Laḣ	tŜiffé
Hoowé	Laḣ	yŜiff
Heeyé	Laḣ	tŜiff
Naḣna	Laḣ	nŜiff
Intoo	Laḣ	tŜiffoo
Hinné	Laḣ	yŜiffoo

Command

Inta	Ŝiff
Inté	Ŝiffé
Intoo	Ŝiffoo
Inta	Ma tŜiff
Inté	Ma tŜiffé
Intoo	Ma tŜiffoo

To pass

Present

Ana	Bi'ŤaĂ
Inta	Bti'ŤaĂ
Inté	Bti'ŤaĂé
Hoowé	Byi'ŤaĂ
Heeyé	Bti'ŤaĂ
Naḣna	Mni'ŤaĂ
Intoo	Bti'ŤaĂoo
Hinné	Byi'ŤaĂoo

Present Continuous

Ana	Ăam	Bi'ŤaĂ
Inta	Ăam	Bti'ŤaĂ
Inté	Ăam	Bti'ŤaĂé
Hoowé	Ăam	Byi'ŤaĂ
Heeyé	Ăam	Bti'ŤaĂ
Naḣna	Ăam	Mni'ŤaĂ
Intoo	Ăam	Bti'ŤaĂoo
Hinné	Ăam	Byi'ŤaĂoo

Past

Ana	aŤaĂt
Inta	aŤaĂt
Inté	aŤaĂté
Hoowé	aŤaĂ
Heeyé	aŤaĂét
Naḣna	aŤaĂna
Intoo	aŤaĂtoo
Hinné	aŤaĂoo

Past Continuous

Ana	Kint Ăam	Bi'ŤaĂ
Inta	Kint Ăam	Bti'ŤaĂ
Inté	Kinté Ăam	Bti'ŤaĂé
Hoowé	Kén Ăam	Byi'ŤaĂ
Heeyé	Kénét Ăam	Bti'ŤaĂ
Naḣna	Kinna Ăam	Mni'ŤaĂ
Intoo	Kintoo Ăam	Bti'ŤaĂoo
Hinné	Kénoo Ăam	Byi'ŤaĂoo

Future

Ana	Laḣ	I'ŤaĂ
Inta	Laḣ	Ti'ŤaĂ
Inté	Laḣ	Ti'ŤaĂé
Hoowé	Laḣ	Yi'ŤaĂ
Heeyé	Laḣ	Ti'ŤaĂ
Naḣna	Laḣ	Ni'ŤaĂ
Intoo	Laḣ	Ti'ŤaĂoo
Hinné	Laḣ	Yi'ŤaĂoo

Command

Inta	'ŤaĂ
Inté	'ŤaĂé
Intoo	'ŤaĂoo
Inta	Ma t'ŤaĂ
Inté	Ma t'ŤaĂé
Intoo	Ma t'ŤaĂoo

Ă= Augh in bought	**Ď**= a heavy D	**É**= like A in Bay	**G**= G in beige	**ḣ**= like an H with smaller air passage	**I**= I as in ink	**Ḱ**= like ch in Irish loch
O= O as in home	**OO**= as in boots	**R**= roll the rrr	**Ť**= a heavy T	**Ř**= like a French R (gargle it)	**Ŝ**= a heavy S	**Ž**= a heavy Z

<u>P</u>   <u>P</u>

To peel

Present

Ana	B'ashér
Inta	B'ashér
Inté	Bt'ashré
Hoowé	Bi'ashér
Heeyé	Bt'ashér
Naĥna	Mn'ashér
Intoo	Bt'ashroo
Hinné	Bi'ashroo

Present Continuous

Ana	Ăam	B'ashér
Inta	Ăam	B'ashér
Inté	Ăam	Bt'ashré
Hoowé	Ăam	Bi'ashér
Heeyé	Ăam	Bt'ashér
Naĥna	Ăam	Mn'ashér
Intoo	Ăam	Bt'ashroo
Hinné	Ăam	Bi'ashroo

Past

Ana	Ashart
Inta	Ashart
Inté	Asharté
Hoowé	Ashar
Heeyé	Asharét
Naĥna	Asharna
Intoo	Ashartoo
Hinné	Asharoo

Past Continuous

Ana	Kint Ăam	B'ashér
Inta	Kint Ăam	B'ashér
Inté	Kinté Ăam	Bt'ashré
Hoowé	Kén Ăam	Bi'ashér
Heeyé	Kénét Ăam	Bt'ashér
Naĥna	Kinna Ăam	Mn'ashér
Intoo	Kintoo Ăam	Bt'ashroo
Hinné	Kénoo Ăam	Bi'ashroo

Future

Ana	Laĥ	Ashér
Inta	Laĥ	Ashér
Inté	Laĥ	T'ashré
Hoowé	Laĥ	Y'ashér
Heeyé	Laĥ	T'ashér
Naĥna	Laĥ	N'ashér
Intoo	Laĥ	T'ashroo
Hinné	Laĥ	Y'ashroo

Command

Inta	Ashér
Inté	Ashré
Intoo	Ashroo
Inta	Ma t'ashér
Inté	Ma t'ashré
Intoo	Ma t'ashroo

To pet

Present

Ana	bŘannég
Inta	btŘannég
Inté	btŘanngé
Hoowé	biŘannég
Heeyé	btŘannég
Naĥna	mnŘannég
Intoo	btŘanngoo
Hinné	biŘanngoo

Present Continuous

Ana	Ăam	bŘannég
Inta	Ăam	btŘannég
Inté	Ăam	btŘanngé
Hoowé	Ăam	biŘannég
Heeyé	Ăam	btŘannég
Naĥna	Ăam	mnŘannég
Intoo	Ăam	btŘanngoo
Hinné	Ăam	biŘanngoo

Past

Ana	Řannagt
Inta	Řannagt
Inté	Řannagté
Hoowé	Řannag
Heeyé	Řannagét
Naĥna	Řannagna
Intoo	Řannagtoo
Hinné	Řannagoo

Past Continuous

Ana	Kint Ăam	bŘannég
Inta	Kint Ăam	btŘannég
Inté	Kinté Ăam	btŘanngé
Hoowé	Kén Ăam	biŘannég
Heeyé	Kénét Ăam	btŘannég
Naĥna	Kinna Ăam	mnŘannég
Intoo	Kintoo Ăam	btŘanngoo
Hinné	Kénoo Ăam	biŘanngoo

Future

Ana	Laĥ	Řannég
Inta	Laĥ	tŘannég
Inté	Laĥ	tŘanngé
Hoowé	Laĥ	yŘannég
Heeyé	Laĥ	tŘannég
Naĥna	Laĥ	nŘannég
Intoo	Laĥ	tŘanngoo
Hinné	Laĥ	yŘanngoo

Command

Inta	Řannég
Inté	Řanngé
Intoo	Řanngoo
Inta	Ma tŘannég
Inté	Ma tŘanngé
Intoo	Ma tŘanngoo

Ă= Augh in bought	Ď= a heavy D	É= like A in Bay	G= G in beige	ĥ= like an H with smaller air passage	I= I as in ink	Ќ= like ch in Irish loch
O= O as in home	OO= as in boots	R= roll the rrr	Ť= a heavy T	Ř= like a French R (gargle it)	Ŝ= a heavy S	Ž= a heavy Z

<u>P</u>   <u>P</u>

To pick (fruits)

Present	
Ana	Bi'Ťof
Inta	Bti'Ťof
Inté	Bti'Ťfé
Hoowé	Byi'Ťof
Heeyé	Bti'Ťof
Naḥna	Mni'Ťof
Intoo	Bti'Ťfoo
Hinné	Byi'Ťfoo

Present Continuous		
Ana	Ăam	Bi'Ťof
Inta	Ăam	Bti'Ťof
Inté	Ăam	Bti'Ťfé
Hoowé	Ăam	Byi'Ťof
Heeyé	Ăam	Bti'Ťof
Naḥna	Ăam	Mni'Ťof
Intoo	Ăam	Bti'Ťfoo
Hinné	Ăam	Byi'Ťfoo

Past	
Ana	aŤaft
Inta	aŤaft
Inté	aŤafté
Hoowé	aŤaf
Heeyé	aŤafét
Naḥna	aŤafna
Intoo	aŤaftoo
Hinné	aŤafoo

Past Continuous		
Ana	Kint Ăam	Bi'Ťof
Inta	Kint Ăam	Bti'Ťof
Inté	Kinté Ăam	Bti'Ťfé
Hoowé	Kén Ăam	Byi'Ťof
Heeyé	Kénét Ăam	Bti'Ťof
Naḥna	Kinna Ăam	Mni'Ťof
Intoo	Kintoo Ăam	Bti'Ťfoo
Hinné	Kénoo Ăam	Byi'Ťfoo

Future		
Ana	Laĥ	I'Ťof
Inta	Laĥ	Ti'Ťof
Inté	Laĥ	Ti'Ťfé
Hoowé	Laĥ	Yi'Ťof
Heeyé	Laĥ	Ti'Ťof
Naḥna	Laĥ	Ni'Ťof
Intoo	Laĥ	Ti'Ťfoo
Hinné	Laĥ	Yi'Ťfoo

Command	
Inta	'Ťof
Inté	'Ťifé
Intoo	'Ťifoo
Inta	Ma t'Ťof
Inté	Ma t'Ťfé
Intoo	Ma t'Ťfoo

To pinch

Present	
Ana	Bi'roŠ
Inta	Bti'roŠ
Inté	Bti'rŠé
Hoowé	Byi'roŠ
Heeyé	Bti'roŠ
Naḥna	Mni'roŠ
Intoo	Bti'rŠoo
Hinné	Byi'rŠoo

Present Continuous		
Ana	Ăam	Bi'roŠ
Inta	Ăam	Bti'roŠ
Inté	Ăam	Bti'rŠé
Hoowé	Ăam	Byi'roŠ
Heeyé	Ăam	Bti'roŠ
Naḥna	Ăam	Mni'roŠ
Intoo	Ăam	Bti'rŠoo
Hinné	Ăam	Byi'rŠoo

Past	
Ana	araŠt
Inta	araŠt
Inté	araŠté
Hoowé	araŠ
Heeyé	araŠét
Naḥna	araŠna
Intoo	araŠtoo
Hinné	araŠoo

Past Continuous		
Ana	Kint Ăam	Bi'roŠ
Inta	Kint Ăam	Bti'roŠ
Inté	Kinté Ăam	Bti'rŠé
Hoowé	Kén Ăam	Byi'roŠ
Heeyé	Kénét Ăam	Bti'roŠ
Naḥna	Kinna Ăam	Mni'roŠ
Intoo	Kintoo Ăam	Bti'rŠoo
Hinné	Kénoo Ăam	Byi'rŠoo

Future		
Ana	Laĥ	i'roŠ
Inta	Laĥ	ti'roŠ
Inté	Laĥ	ti'rŠé
Hoowé	Laĥ	yi'roŠ
Heeyé	Laĥ	ti'roŠ
Naḥna	Laĥ	ni'roŠ
Intoo	Laĥ	ti'rŠoo
Hinné	Laĥ	yi'rŠoo

Command	
Inta	'roŠ
Inté	'riŠé
Intoo	'riŠoo
Inta	Ma t'roŠ
Inté	Ma t'rŠé
Intoo	Ma t'rŠoo

Ă= Augh in bought	Ď= a heavy D	É= like A in Bay	G= G in beige	ĥ= like an H with smaller air passage	I= I as in ink	Ќ= like ch in Irish loch
O= O as in home	OO= as in boots	R= roll the rrr	Ť= a heavy T	Ř= like a French R (gargle it)	Š= a heavy S	Ž= a heavy Z

P̲   P̲

To plant

Present
Ana	bizraĂ
Inta	btizraĂ
Inté	btizraĂé
Hoowé	byizraĂ
Heeyé	btizraĂ
Nahna	mnizraĂ
Intoo	btizraĂoo
Hinné	bizraĂoo

Present Continuous
Ana	Ăam	bizraĂ
Inta	Ăam	btizraĂ
Inté	Ăam	btizraĂé
Hoowé	Ăam	byizraĂ
Heeyé	Ăam	btizraĂ
Nahna	Ăam	mnizraĂ
Intoo	Ăam	btizraĂoo
Hinné	Ăam	bizraĂoo

Past
Ana	zaraĂt
Inta	zaraĂt
Inté	zaraĂté
Hoowé	zaraĂ
Heeyé	zaraĂét
Nahna	zaraĂna
Intoo	zaraĂtoo
Hinné	zaraĂoo

Past Continuous
Ana	Kint Ăam	bizraĂ
Inta	Kint Ăam	btizraĂ
Inté	Kinté Ăam	btizraĂé
Hoowé	Kén Ăam	byizraĂ
Heeyé	Kénét Ăam	btizraĂ
Nahna	Kinna Ăam	mnizraĂ
Intoo	Kintoo Ăam	btizraĂoo
Hinné	Kénoo Ăam	bizraĂoo

Future
Ana	Laĥ	izraĂ
Inta	Laĥ	tizraĂ
Inté	Laĥ	tizraĂé
Hoowé	Laĥ	yizraĂ
Heeyé	Laĥ	tizraĂ
Nahna	Laĥ	nizraĂ
Intoo	Laĥ	tizraĂoo
Hinné	Laĥ	izraĂoo

Command
Inta	zraĂ
Inté	zraĂé
Intoo	zraĂoo
Inta	Ma tzraĂ
Inté	Ma tzraĂé
Intoo	Ma tzraĂoo

To play

Present
Ana	blĂab
Inta	btlĂab
Inté	btlĂabé
Hoowé	byilĂab
Heeyé	btlĂab
Nahna	mnlĂab
Intoo	btlĂaboo
Hinné	byilĂaboo

Present Continuous
Ana	Ăam	blĂab
Inta	Ăam	btlĂab
Inté	Ăam	btlĂabé
Hoowé	Ăam	byilĂab
Heeyé	Ăam	btlĂab
Nahna	Ăam	mnlĂab
Intoo	Ăam	btlĂaboo
Hinné	Ăam	byilĂaboo

Past
Ana	lĂabt
Inta	lĂabt
Inté	lĂabté
Hoowé	léĂéb
Heeyé	léĂbét
Nahna	lĂibna
Intoo	lĂibtoo
Hinné	lĂiboo

Past Continuous
Ana	Kint Ăam	blĂab
Inta	Kint Ăam	btlĂab
Inté	Kinté Ăam	btlĂabé
Hoowé	Kén Ăam	byilĂab
Heeyé	Kénét Ăam	btlĂab
Nahna	Kinna Ăam	mnlĂab
Intoo	Kintoo Ăam	btlĂaboo
Hinné	Kénoo Ăam	byilĂaboo

Future
Ana	Laĥ	ilĂab
Inta	Laĥ	tilĂab
Inté	Laĥ	tilĂabé
Hoowé	Laĥ	yilĂab
Heeyé	Laĥ	tilĂab
Nahna	Laĥ	nilĂab
Intoo	Laĥ	tilĂaboo
Hinné	Laĥ	yilĂaboo

Command
Inta	lĂab
Inté	lĂabé
Intoo	lĂaboo
Inta	Ma tlĂab
Inté	Ma tlĂabé
Intoo	Ma mtlĂaboo

| Ă= Augh in bought | Ď= a heavy D | É= like A in Bay | G= G in beige | ĥ= like an H with smaller air passage | I= I as in ink | Ḱ= like ch in Irish loch |
| O= O as in home | OO= as in boots | R= roll the rrr | Ť= a heavy T | Ř= like a French R (gargle it) | Ŝ= a heavy S | Ž= a heavy Z |

P   P

To please   To poke

Present	
Ana	bibŠoŤ
Inta	btibŠoŤ
Inté	btibŠŤé
Hoowé	byibŠoŤ
Heeyé	btibŠoŤ
Nahna	mnibŠoŤ
Intoo	btibŠŤoo
Hinné	byibŠŤoo

Present Continuous		
Ana	Ăam	bibŠoŤ
Inta	Ăam	btibŠoŤ
Inté	Ăam	btibŠŤé
Hoowé	Ăam	byibŠoŤ
Heeyé	Ăam	btibŠoŤ
Nahna	Ăam	mnibŠoŤ
Intoo	Ăam	btibŠŤoo
Hinné	Ăam	byibŠŤoo

Past	
Ana	baŠaŤ
Inta	baŠaŤ
Inté	baŠaŤé
Hoowé	baŠaŤ
Heeyé	baŠaŤét
Nahna	baŠaŤna
Intoo	baŠaŤoo
Hinné	baŠaŤoo

Past Continuous		
Ana	Kint Ăam	bibŠoŤ
Inta	Kint Ăam	btibŠoŤ
Inté	Kinté Ăam	btibŠŤé
Hoowé	Kén Ăam	byibŠoŤ
Heeyé	Kénét Ăam	btibŠoŤ
Nahna	Kinna Ăam	mnibŠoŤ
Intoo	Kintoo Ăam	btibŠŤoo
Hinné	Kénoo Ăam	byibŠŤoo

Future		
Ana	Lah	ibŠoŤ
Inta	Lah	tibŠoŤ
Inté	Lah	tibŠŤé
Hoowé	Lah	yibŠoŤ
Heeyé	Lah	tibŠoŤ
Nahna	Lah	nibŠoŤ
Intoo	Lah	tibŠŤoo
Hinné	Lah	yibŠŤoo

Command	
Inta	bŠoŤ
Inté	bŠité
Intoo	bŠiŤoo
Inta	Ma tbŠoŤ
Inté	Ma tbŠté
Intoo	Ma tbŠtoo

Present	
Ana	Binkoz
Inta	Btinkoz
Inté	Btinkzé
Hoowé	Byinkoz
Heeyé	Btinkoz
Nahna	Mninkoz
Intoo	Btinkzoo
Hinné	Byinkzoo

Present Continuous		
Ana	Ăam	Binkoz
Inta	Ăam	Btinkoz
Inté	Ăam	Btinkzé
Hoowé	Ăam	Byinkoz
Heeyé	Ăam	Btinkoz
Nahna	Ăam	Mninkoz
Intoo	Ăam	Btinkzoo
Hinné	Ăam	Byinkzoo

Past	
Ana	Nakazt
Inta	Nakazt
Inté	Nakazté
Hoowé	Nakaz
Heeyé	Nakazét
Nahna	Nakazna
Intoo	Nakaztoo
Hinné	Nakazoo

Past Continuous		
Ana	Kint Ăam	Binkoz
Inta	Kint Ăam	Btinkoz
Inté	Kinté Ăam	Btinkzé
Hoowé	Kén Ăam	Byinkoz
Heeyé	Kénét Ăam	Btinkoz
Nahna	Kinna Ăam	Mninkoz
Intoo	Kintoo Ăam	Btinkzoo
Hinné	Kénoo Ăam	Byinkzoo

Future		
Ana	Lah	Inkoz
Inta	Lah	Tinkoz
Inté	Lah	Tinkzé
Hoowé	Lah	Yinkoz
Heeyé	Lah	Tinkoz
Nahna	Lah	Ninkoz
Intoo	Lah	Tinkzoo
Hinné	Lah	Yinkzoo

Command	
Inta	Nkoz
Inté	Nkizé
Intoo	Nkizoo
Inta	Ma tnkoz
Inté	Ma tnkzé
Intoo	Ma tnkzoo

Ă= Augh in bought	Ď= a heavy D	É= like A in Bay	G= G in beige	ĥ= like an H with smaller air passage	I= I as in ink	Ќ= like ch in Irish loch
O= O as in home	OO= as in boots	R= roll the rrr	Ť= a heavy T	Ř= like a French R (gargle it)	Š= a heavy S	Ž= a heavy Z

P   P

To pour

Present

Ana	Biskob
Inta	Btiskob
Inté	Btiskbé
Hoowé	Byiskob
Heeyé	Btiskob
Nahna	Mniskob
Intoo	Btiskboo
Hinné	Byiskboo

Present Continuous

Ana	Ăam	Biskob
Inta	Ăam	Btiskob
Inté	Ăam	Btiskbé
Hoowé	Ăam	Byiskob
Heeyé	Ăam	Btiskob
Nahna	Ăam	Mniskob
Intoo	Ăam	Btiskboo
Hinné	Ăam	Byiskboo

Past

Ana	Sakabt
Inta	Sakabt
Inté	Sakabté
Hoowé	Sakab
Heeyé	Sakabét
Nahna	Sakabna
Intoo	Sakabtoo
Hinné	Sakaboo

Past Continuous

Ana	Kint Ăam	Biskob
Inta	Kint Ăam	Btiskob
Inté	Kinté Ăam	Btiskbé
Hoowé	Kén Ăam	Byiskob
Heeyé	Kénét Ăam	Btiskob
Nahna	Kinna Ăam	Mniskob
Intoo	Kintoo Ăam	Btiskboo
Hinné	Kénoo Ăam	Byiskboo

Future

Ana	Laĥ	Iskob
Inta	Laĥ	Tiskob
Inté	Laĥ	Tiskbé
Hoowé	Laĥ	Yiskob
Heeyé	Laĥ	Tiskob
Nahna	Laĥ	Niskob
Intoo	Laĥ	Tiskboo
Hinné	Laĥ	Yiskboo

Command

Inta	Skob
Inté	Skibé
Intoo	Skiboo
Inta	Ma tskob
Inté	Ma tskbé
Intoo	Ma tskboo

To practice

Present

Ana	Bmérés
Inta	Btmérés
Inté	Btmérse
Hoowé	Bimérés
Heeyé	Btmérés
Nahna	Mnmérés
Intoo	Btmérsoo
Hinné	Bimérsoo

Present Continuous

Ana	Ăam	Bmérés
Inta	Ăam	Btmérés
Inté	Ăam	Btmérse
Hoowé	Ăam	Bimérés
Heeyé	Ăam	Btmérés
Nahna	Ăam	Mnmérés
Intoo	Ăam	Btmérsoo
Hinné	Ăam	Bimérsoo

Past

Ana	Mérast
Inta	Mérast
Inté	Mérasté
Hoowé	Méras
Heeyé	Mérasét
Nahna	Mérasna
Intoo	Mérastoo
Hinné	Mérasoo

Past Continuous

Ana	Kint Ăam	Bmérés
Inta	Kint Ăam	Btmérés
Inté	Kinté Ăam	Btmérse
Hoowé	Kén Ăam	Bimérés
Heeyé	Kénét Ăam	Btmérés
Nahna	Kinna Ăam	Mnmérés
Intoo	Kintoo Ăam	Btmérsoo
Hinné	Kénoo Ăam	Bimérsoo

Future

Ana	Laĥ	mérés
Inta	Laĥ	tmérés
Inté	Laĥ	tmérse
Hoowé	Laĥ	ymérés
Heeyé	Laĥ	tmérés
Nahna	Laĥ	nmérés
Intoo	Laĥ	tmérsoo
Hinné	Laĥ	ymérsoo

Command

Inta	Mérés
Inté	Mérsé
Intoo	Mérsoo
Inta	Ma tmérés
Inté	Ma tmérsé
Intoo	Ma tmérsoo

Ă= Augh in bought	Đ= a heavy D	É= like A in Bay	G= G in beige	ĥ= like an H with smaller air passage	I= I as in ink	Ќ= like ch in Irish loch
O= O as in home	OO= as in boots	R= roll the rrr	Ť= a heavy T	Ř= like a French R (gargle it)	Š= a heavy S	Ž= a heavy Z

P   P

To pray   To preach

Present	
Ana	bŠallé
Inta	btŠallé
Inté	btŠallé
Hoowé	biŠallé
Heeyé	btŠallé
Naĥna	mnŠallé
Intoo	btŠalloo
Hinné	biŠalloo

Present Continuous		
Ana	Ăam	bŠallé
Inta	Ăam	btŠallé
Inté	Ăam	btŠallé
Hoowé	Ăam	biŠallé
Heeyé	Ăam	btŠallé
Naĥna	Ăam	mnŠallé
Intoo	Ăam	btŠalloo
Hinné	Ăam	biŠalloo

Past	
Ana	Šallét
Inta	Šallét
Inté	Šallaité
Hoowé	Šalla
Heeyé	Šallét
Naĥna	Šallaina
Intoo	Šallaitoo
Hinné	Šalloo

Past Continuous		
Ana	Kint Ăam	bŠallé
Inta	Kint Ăam	btŠallé
Inté	Kinté Ăam	btŠallé
Hoowé	Kén Ăam	biŠallé
Heeyé	Kénét Ăam	btŠallé
Naĥna	Kinna Ăam	mnŠallé
Intoo	Kintoo Ăam	btŠalloo
Hinné	Kénoo Ăam	biŠalloo

Future		
Ana	Laĥ	Šallé
Inta	Laĥ	tŠallé
Inté	Laĥ	tŠallé
Hoowé	Laĥ	yŠallé
Heeyé	Laĥ	tŠallé
Naĥna	Laĥ	nŠallé
Intoo	Laĥ	tŠalloo
Hinné	Laĥ	yŠalloo

Command	
Inta	Šallé
Inté	Šallé
Intoo	Šalloo
Inta	Ma tŠallé
Inté	Ma tŠallé
Intoo	Ma tŠalloo

Present	
Ana	booĂaŽ
Inta	btooĂaŽ
Inté	btooĂaŽé
Hoowé	byooĂaŽ
Heeyé	btooĂaŽ
Naĥna	mnooĂaŽ
Intoo	btooĂaŽoo
Hinné	byooĂaŽoo

Present Continuous		
Ana	Ăam	booĂaŽ
Inta	Ăam	btooĂaŽ
Inté	Ăam	btooĂaŽé
Hoowé	Ăam	byooĂaŽ
Heeyé	Ăam	btooĂaŽ
Naĥna	Ăam	mnooĂaŽ
Intoo	Ăam	btooĂaŽoo
Hinné	Ăam	byooĂaŽoo

Past	
Ana	waĂaŽt
Inta	waĂaŽt
Inté	waĂaŽté
Hoowé	waĂaŽ
Heeyé	waĂaŽét
Naĥna	waĂaŽna
Intoo	waĂaŽtoo
Hinné	waĂaŽoo

Past Continuous		
Ana	Kint Ăam	booĂaŽ
Inta	Kint Ăam	btooĂaŽ
Inté	Kinté Ăam	btooĂaŽé
Hoowé	Kén Ăam	byooĂaŽ
Heeyé	Kénét Ăam	btooĂaŽ
Naĥna	Kinna Ăam	mnooĂaŽ
Intoo	Kintoo Ăam	btooĂaŽoo
Hinné	Kénoo Ăam	byooĂaŽoo

Future		
Ana	Laĥ	'ooĂaŽ
Inta	Laĥ	tooĂaŽ
Inté	Laĥ	tooĂaŽé
Hoowé	Laĥ	yooĂaŽ
Heeyé	Laĥ	tooĂaŽ
Naĥna	Laĥ	nooĂaŽ
Intoo	Laĥ	tooĂaŽoo
Hinné	Laĥ	yooĂaŽoo

Command	
Inta	wĂaŽ
Inté	wĂaŽé
Intoo	wĂaŽoo
Inta	Ma tooĂaŽ
Inté	Ma tooĂaŽé
Intoo	Ma tooĂaŽoo

Ă= Augh in bought	Ď= a heavy D	É= like A in Bay	G= G in beige	ĥ= like an H with smaller air passage	I= I as in ink	Ќ= like ch in Irish loch
O= O as in home	OO= as in boots	R= roll the rrr	Ť= a heavy T	Ř= like a French R (gargle it)	Š= a heavy S	Ž= a heavy Z

<u>P</u>   <u>P</u>

To prefer

Present

Ana	bfaĎĎél
Inta	btfaĎĎél
Inté	btfaĎĎlé
Hoowé	bifaĎĎél
Heeyé	btfaĎĎél
Nahna	mnfaĎĎél
Intoo	btfaĎĎloo
Hinné	bifaĎĎloo

Present Continuous

Ana	Ăam	bfaĎĎél
Inta	Ăam	btfaĎĎél
Inté	Ăam	btfaĎĎlé
Hoowé	Ăam	bifaĎĎél
Heeyé	Ăam	btfaĎĎél
Nahna	Ăam	mnfaĎĎél
Intoo	Ăam	btfaĎĎloo
Hinné	Ăam	bifaĎĎloo

Past

Ana	faĎĎalt
Inta	faĎĎalt
Inté	faĎĎalté
Hoowé	faĎĎal
Heeyé	faĎĎalét
Nahna	faĎĎalna
Intoo	faĎĎaltoo
Hinné	faĎĎaloo

Past Continuous

Ana	Kint Ăam	bfaĎĎél
Inta	Kint Ăam	btfaĎĎél
Inté	Kinté Ăam	btfaĎĎlé
Hoowé	Kén Ăam	bifaĎĎél
Heeyé	Kénét Ăam	btfaĎĎél
Nahna	Kinna Ăam	mnfaĎĎél
Intoo	Kintoo Ăam	btfaĎĎloo
Hinné	Kénoo Ăam	bifaĎĎloo

Future

Ana	Laĥ	faĎĎél
Inta	Laĥ	tfaĎĎél
Inté	Laĥ	tfaĎĎlé
Hoowé	Laĥ	yfaĎĎél
Heeyé	Laĥ	tfaĎĎél
Nahna	Laĥ	nfaĎĎél
Intoo	Laĥ	tfaĎĎloo
Hinné	Laĥ	yfaĎĎloo

Command

Inta	faĎĎél
Inté	faĎĎlé
Intoo	faĎĎloo
Inta	Ma tfaĎĎél
Inté	Ma tfaĎĎlé
Intoo	Ma tfaĎĎloo

To become pregnant

Present

Ana	Biĥbal
Inta	
Inté	Biĥbalé
Hoowé	
Heeyé	Btiĥbal
Nahna	Mniĥbal
Intoo	Btiĥbaloo
Hinné	Byiĥbaloo

Present Continuous

Ana	Ăam	Biĥbal
Inta	Ăam	
Inté	Ăam	Biĥbalé
Hoowé	Ăam	
Heeyé	Ăam	Btiĥbal
Nahna	Ăam	Mniĥbal
Intoo	Ăam	Btiĥbaloo
Hinné	Ăam	Byiĥbaloo

Past

Ana	Ĥbilt
Inta	
Inté	Ĥbilté
Hoowé	
Heeyé	Ĥiblét
Nahna	Ĥbilna
Intoo	Ĥbiltoo
Hinné	Ĥibloo

Past Continuous

Ana	Kint Ăam	Biĥbal
Inta	Kint Ăam	
Inté	Kinté Ăam	Biĥbalé
Hoowé	Kén Ăam	
Heeyé	Kénét Ăam	Btiĥbal
Nahna	Kinna Ăam	Mniĥbal
Intoo	Kintoo Ăam	Btiĥbaloo
Hinné	Kénoo Ăam	Byiĥbaloo

Future

Ana	Laĥ	iĥbal
Inta	Laĥ	
Inté	Laĥ	iĥbalé
Hoowé	Laĥ	
Heeyé	Laĥ	tiĥbal
Nahna	Laĥ	niĥbal
Intoo	Laĥ	tiĥbaloo
Hinné	Laĥ	yiĥbaloo

Command

Inta	
Inté	Ĥbale
Intoo	Ĥbaloo
Inta	Ma
Inté	Ma tĥbalé
Intoo	Ma tĥbaloo

Ă= Augh in bought	Ď= a heavy D	É= like A in Bay	G= G in beige	ĥ= like an H with smaller air passage	I= I as in ink	Ķ= like ch in Irish loch
O= O as in home	OO= as in boots	R= roll the rrr	Ť= a heavy T	Ř= like a French R (gargle it)	Ŝ= a heavy S	Ž= a heavy Z

P   P

To prepare

Present

Ana	bhaĎĎér
Inta	bthaĎĎér
Inté	bthaĎĎré
Hoowé	bihaĎĎér
Heeyé	bthaĎĎér
Naĥna	mnĥaĎĎér
Intoo	bthaĎĎroo
Hinné	bihaĎĎroo

Present Continuous

Ana	Ăam	bhaĎĎér
Inta	Ăam	bthaĎĎér
Inté	Ăam	bthaĎĎré
Hoowé	Ăam	bihaĎĎér
Heeyé	Ăam	bthaĎĎér
Naĥna	Ăam	mnhaĎĎér
Intoo	Ăam	bthaĎĎroo
Hinné	Ăam	bihaĎĎroo

Past

Ana	ĥaĎĎart
Inta	ĥaĎĎart
Inté	ĥaĎĎarté
Hoowé	ĥaĎĎar
Heeyé	ĥaĎĎarét
Naĥna	ĥaĎĎarna
Intoo	ĥaĎĎartoo
Hinné	ĥaĎĎaroo

Past Continuous

Ana	Kint Ăam	bhaĎĎér
Inta	Kint Ăam	bthaĎĎér
Inté	Kinté Ăam	bthaĎĎré
Hoowé	Kén Ăam	bihaĎĎér
Heeyé	Kénét Ăam	bthaĎĎér
Naĥna	Kinna Ăam	mnhaĎĎér
Intoo	Kintoo Ăam	bthaĎĎroo
Hinné	Kénoo Ăam	bihaĎĎroo

Future

Ana	Laĥ	ĥaĎĎér
Inta	Laĥ	thaĎĎér
Inté	Laĥ	thaĎĎré
Hoowé	Laĥ	yĥaĎĎér
Heeyé	Laĥ	thaĎĎér
Naĥna	Laĥ	nhaĎĎér
Intoo	Laĥ	thaĎĎroo
Hinné	Laĥ	yĥaĎĎroo

Command

Inta	ĥaĎĎér
Inté	ĥaĎĎré
Intoo	ĥaĎĎroo
Inta	Ma thaĎĎér
Inté	Ma thaĎĎré
Intoo	Ma thaĎĎroo

To pretend

Present

Ana	biddiĂé
Inta	btiddiĂé
Inté	btiddiĂé
Hoowé	byiddiĂé
Heeyé	btiddiĂé
Naĥna	mniddiĂé
Intoo	btiddiĂoo
Hinné	byiddiĂoo

Present Continuous

Ana	Ăam	biddiĂé
Inta	Ăam	btiddiĂé
Inté	Ăam	btiddiĂé
Hoowé	Ăam	byiddiĂé
Heeyé	Ăam	btiddiĂé
Naĥna	Ăam	mniddiĂé
Intoo	Ăam	btiddiĂoo
Hinné	Ăam	byiddiĂoo

Past

Ana	ddaĂét
Inta	ddaĂét
Inté	ddaĂaité
Hoowé	ddaĂa
Heeyé	ddaĂét
Naĥna	ddaĂaina
Intoo	ddaĂaitoo
Hinné	ddaĂoo

Past Continuous

Ana	Kint Ăam	biddiĂé
Inta	Kint Ăam	btiddiĂé
Inté	Kinté Ăam	btiddiĂé
Hoowé	Kén Ăam	byiddiĂé
Heeyé	Kénét Ăam	btiddiĂé
Naĥna	Kinna Ăam	mniddiĂé
Intoo	Kintoo Ăam	btiddiĂoo
Hinné	Kénoo Ăam	byiddiĂoo

Future

Ana	Laĥ	iddiĂé
Inta	Laĥ	tiddiĂé
Inté	Laĥ	tiddiĂé
Hoowé	Laĥ	yiddiĂé
Heeyé	Laĥ	tiddiĂé
Naĥna	Laĥ	niddiĂé
Intoo	Laĥ	tiddiĂoo
Hinné	Laĥ	yiddiĂoo

Command

Inta	ddiĂé
Inté	ddiĂé
Intoo	ddiĂoo
Inta	Ma tddiĂé
Inté	Ma tddiĂé
Intoo	Ma tddiĂoo

Ă= Augh in bought	**Ď**= a heavy D	**É**= like A in Bay	**G**= G in beige	**ĥ**= like an H with smaller air passage	**I**= I as in ink	**Ḱ**= like ch in Irish loch
O= O as in home	**OO**= as in boots	**R**= roll the rrr	**Ť**= a heavy T	**Ř**= like a French R (gargle it)	**Ŝ**= a heavy S	**Ž**= a heavy Z

P

P

To prey

Present

Ana	Biftiris
Inta	Btiftiris
Inté	Btiftirsé
Hoowé	Byiftiris
Heeyé	Btiftiris
Nahna	Mniftiris
Intoo	Btiftirsoo
Hinné	Byiftirsoo

Present Continuous

Ana	Ăam	Biftiris
Inta	Ăam	Btiftiris
Inté	Ăam	Btiftirsé
Hoowé	Ăam	Byiftiris
Heeyé	Ăam	Btiftiris
Nahna	Ăam	Mniftiris
Intoo	Ăam	Btiftirsoo
Hinné	Ăam	Byiftirsoo

Past

Ana	Ftarast
Inta	Ftarast
Inté	Ftarasté
Hoowé	Ftaras
Heeyé	Ftarasét
Nahna	Ftarasna
Intoo	Ftarastoo
Hinné	Ftarasoo

Past Continuous

Ana	Kint Ăam	Biftiris
Inta	Kint Ăam	Btiftiris
Inté	Kinté Ăam	Btiftirsé
Hoowé	Kén Ăam	Byiftiris
Heeyé	Kénét Ăam	Btiftiris
Nahna	Kinna Ăam	Mniftiris
Intoo	Kintoo Ăam	Btiftirsoo
Hinné	Kénoo Ăam	Byiftirsoo

Future

Ana	Laĥ	Iftiris
Inta	Laĥ	Tiftiris
Inté	Laĥ	Tiftirsé
Hoowé	Laĥ	Yiftiris
Heeyé	Laĥ	Tiftiris
Nahna	Laĥ	Niftiris
Intoo	Laĥ	Tiftirsoo
Hinné	Laĥ	Yiftirsoo

Command

Inta	Ftiris
Inté	Ftirsé
Intoo	Ftirsoo
Inta	Ma tftiris
Inté	Ma tftirsé
Intoo	Ma tftirsoo

To produce

Present

Ana	Bintog
Inta	Btintog
Inté	Btintgé
Hoowé	Byintog
Heeyé	Btintog
Nahna	Mnintog
Intoo	Btintgoo
Hinné	Byintgoo

Present Continuous

Ana	Ăam	Bintog
Inta	Ăam	Btintog
Inté	Ăam	Btintgé
Hoowé	Ăam	Byintog
Heeyé	Ăam	Btintog
Nahna	Ăam	Mnintog
Intoo	Ăam	Btintgoo
Hinné	Ăam	Byintgoo

Past

Ana	Natagt
Inta	Natagt
Inté	Natagté
Hoowé	Natag
Heeyé	Natagét
Nahna	Natagna
Intoo	Natagtoo
Hinné	Natagoo

Past Continuous

Ana	Kint Ăam	Bintog
Inta	Kint Ăam	Btintog
Inté	Kinté Ăam	Btintgé
Hoowé	Kén Ăam	Byintog
Heeyé	Kénét Ăam	Btintog
Nahna	Kinna Ăam	Mnintog
Intoo	Kintoo Ăam	Btintgoo
Hinné	Kénoo Ăam	Byintgoo

Future

Ana	Laĥ	Intog
Inta	Laĥ	Tintog
Inté	Laĥ	Tintgé
Hoowé	Laĥ	Yintog
Heeyé	Laĥ	Tintog
Nahna	Laĥ	Nintog
Intoo	Laĥ	Tintgoo
Hinné	Laĥ	Yintgoo

Command

Inta	Ntog
Inté	Ntigé
Intoo	Ntigoo
Inta	Ma tntog
Inté	Ma tntgé
Intoo	Ma tntgoo

Ă= Augh in bought	Ď= a heavy D	É= like A in Bay	G= G in beige	ĥ= like an H with smaller air passage	I= I as in ink	Ќ= like ch in Irish loch
O= O as in home	OO= as in boots	R= roll the rrr	Ť= a heavy T	Ř= like a French R (gargle it)	Ŝ= a heavy S	Ž= a heavy Z

P   P

To promise

Present

Ana	booĂad
Inta	btooĂad
Inté	btooĂadé
Hoowé	byooĂad
Heeyé	btooĂad
Naĥna	mnooĂad
Intoo	btooĂadoo
Hinné	byooĂadoo

Present Continuous

Ana	Ăam	booĂad
Inta	Ăam	btooĂad
Inté	Ăam	btooĂadé
Hoowé	Ăam	byooĂad
Heeyé	Ăam	btooĂad
Naĥna	Ăam	mnooĂad
Intoo	Ăam	btooĂadoo
Hinné	Ăam	byooĂadoo

Past

Ana	waĂadt
Inta	waĂadt
Inté	waĂadté
Hoowé	waĂad
Heeyé	waĂadét
Naĥna	waĂadna
Intoo	waĂadtoo
Hinné	waĂadoo

Past Continuous

Ana	Kint Ăam	booĂad
Inta	Kint Ăam	btooĂad
Inté	Kinté Ăam	btooĂadé
Hoowé	Kén Ăam	byooĂad
Heeyé	Kénét Ăam	btooĂad
Naĥna	Kinna Ăam	mnooĂad
Intoo	Kintoo Ăam	btooĂadoo
Hinné	Kénoo Ăam byooĂadoo	

Future

Ana	Laĥ	'ooĂad
Inta	Laĥ	TooĂad
Inté	Laĥ	tooĂadé
Hoowé	Laĥ	yooĂad
Heeyé	Laĥ	TooĂad
Naĥna	Laĥ	NooĂad
Intoo	Laĥ	tooĂadoo
Hinné	Laĥ	yooĂadoo

Command

Inta	wĂad
Inté	wĂadé
Intoo	wĂadoo
Inta	Ma tooĂad
Inté	Ma tooĂadé
Intoo	Ma tooĂadoo

To protect

Present

Ana	Biĥmé
Inta	Btiĥmé
Inté	Btiĥmé
Hoowé	Byiĥmé
Heeyé	Btiĥmé
Naĥna	Mniĥmé
Intoo	Btiĥmoo
Hinné	Byiĥmoo

Present Continuous

Ana	Ăam	Biĥmé	(ĥémé/Hemyé)
Inta	Ăam	Btiĥmé	(ĥémé)
Inté	Ăam	Btiĥmé	(ĥémyé)
Hoowé	Ăam	Byiĥmé	(ĥémé)
Heeyé	Ăam	Btiĥmé	(ĥémyé)
Naĥna	Ăam	Mniĥmé	(ĥémyeen)
Intoo	Ăam	Btiĥmoo	(ĥémyeen)
Hinné	Ăam	Byiĥmoo	(ĥémyeen)

Past

Ana	Ĥamét
Inta	Ĥamét
Inté	Ĥamaité
Hoowé	Ĥama
Heeyé	Ĥamét
Naĥna	Ĥamaina
Intoo	Ĥamaitoo
Hinné	Ĥamoo

Past Continuous

Ana	Kint Ăam	Biĥmé	(kint ĥémé/Hemyé
Inta	Kint Ăam	Btiĥmé	(Kint ĥémé)
Inté	Kinté Ăam	Btiĥmé	(Kinté ĥémyé)
Hoowé	Kén Ăam	Byiĥmé	(Kén ĥémé)
Heeyé	Kénét Ăam	Btiĥmé	(Kénét ĥémyé)
Naĥna	Kinna Ăam	Mniĥmé	(Kinna ĥémyeen)
Intoo	Kintoo Ăam	Btiĥmoo	(Kintoo ĥémyeen)
Hinné	Kénoo Ăam	Byiĥmoo	(Kénoo ĥémyeen)

Future

Ana	Laĥ	Iĥmé
Inta	Laĥ	Tiĥmé
Inté	Laĥ	Tiĥmé
Hoowé	Laĥ	Yiĥmé
Heeyé	Laĥ	Tiĥmé
Naĥna	Laĥ	Niĥmé
Intoo	Laĥ	Tiĥmoo
Hinné	Laĥ	Yiĥmoo

Command

Inta	Ĥmee
Inté	Ĥmee
Intoo	Ĥmoo
Inta	Ma tiĥmé
Inté	Ma tiĥmé
Intoo	Ma tiĥmoo

Ă= Augh in bought	**Ď**= a heavy D	**É**= like A in Bay	**G**= G in beige	**ĥ**= like an H with smaller air passage	**I**= I as in ink	**Ḱ**= like ch in Irish loch
O= O as in home	**OO**= as in boots	**R**= roll the rrr	**Ť**= a heavy T	**Ř**= like a French R (gargle it)	**Ŝ**= a heavy S	**Ž**= a heavy Z

R

To be proud of

Present

Ana	biftiḰéR
Inta	btiftiḰéR
Inté	btiftiḰRé
Hoowé	byiftiḰéR
Heeyé	btiftiḰéR
Naḥna	mniftiḰéR
Intoo	btiftiḰRoo
Hinné	byiftiḰRoo

Present Continuous

Ana	Ăam	biftiḰéR	(faḰoor/faḰoora)
Inta	Ăam	btiftiḰéR	(faḰoor)
Inté	Ăam	btiftiḰRé	(faḰoora)
Hoowé	Ăam	byiftiḰéR	(faḰoor)
Heeyé	Ăam	btiftiḰéR	(faḰoora)
Naḥna	Ăam	mniftiḰéR	(faḰooreen)
Intoo	Ăam	btiftiḰRoo	(faḰooreen)
Hinné	Ăam	byiftiḰRoo	(faḰooreen)

Past

Ana	ftaḰart
Inta	ftaḰart
Inté	ftaḰarté
Hoowé	ftaḰar
Heeyé	ftaḰarét
Naḥna	ftaḰarna
Intoo	ftaḰartoo
Hinné	ftaḰaroo

Past Continuous

Ana	Kint Ăam	biftiḰéR	(kint	(faḰoor/faḰoora)
Inta	Kint Ăam	btiftiḰéR	(Kint	(faḰoor)
Inté	Kinté Ăam	btiftiḰRé	(Kinté	(faḰoora)
Hoowé	Kén Ăam	byiftiḰéR	(Kén	(faḰoor)
Heeyé	Kénét Ăam	btiftiḰéR	(Kénét	(faḰoora)
Naḥna	Kinna Ăam	mniftiḰéR	(Kinna	(faḰooreen)
Intoo	Kintoo Ăam	btiftiḰRoo	(Kintoo	(faḰooreen)
Hinné	Kénoo Ăam	byiftiḰRoo	(Kénoo	(faḰooreen)

Future

Ana	Laḥ	iftiḰéR
Inta	Laḥ	tiftiḰéR
Inté	Laḥ	tiftiḰRé
Hoowé	Laḥ	yiftiḰéR
Heeyé	Laḥ	tiftiḰéR
Naḥna	Laḥ	niftiḰéR
Intoo	Laḥ	tiftiḰRoo
Hinné	Laḥ	yiftiḰRoo

Command

Inta	ftiḰér
Inté	ftiḰré
Intoo	ftiḰroo
Inta	Ma tftiḰér
Inté	Ma tftiḰré
Intoo	Ma tftiḰroo

P

To prove

Present

Ana	Bbarhén
Inta	Btbarhén
Inté	Btbarhné
Hoowé	Bibarhén
Heeyé	Btbarhén
Naḥna	Mnbarhén
Intoo	Btbarhnoo
Hinné	Bibarhnoo

Present Continuous

Ana	Ăam	Bbarhén
Inta	Ăam	Btbarhén
Inté	Ăam	Btbarhné
Hoowé	Ăam	Bibarhén
Heeyé	Ăam	Btbarhén
Naḥna	Ăam	Mnbarhén
Intoo	Ăam	Btbarhnoo
Hinné	Ăam	Bibarhnoo

Past

Ana	Barhant
Inta	Barhant
Inté	Barhanté
Hoowé	Barhan
Heeyé	Barhanét
Naḥna	Barhanna
Intoo	Barhantoo
Hinné	Barhanoo

Past Continuous

Ana	Kint Ăam	Bbarhén
Inta	Kint Ăam	Btbarhén
Inté	Kinté Ăam	Btbarhné
Hoowé	Kén Ăam	Bibarhén
Heeyé	Kénét Ăam	Btbarhén
Naḥna	Kinna Ăam	Mnbarhén
Intoo	Kintoo Ăam	Btbarhnoo
Hinné	Kénoo Ăam	Bibarhnoo

Future

Ana	Laḥ	barhén
Inta	Laḥ	tbarhén
Inté	Laḥ	tbarhné
Hoowé	Laḥ	ybarhén
Heeyé	Laḥ	tbarhén
Naḥna	Laḥ	nbarhén
Intoo	Laḥ	tbarhnoo
Hinné	Laḥ	ybarhnoo

Command

Inta	Barhén
Inté	Barhné
Intoo	Barhnoo
Inta	Ma tbarhén
Inté	Ma tbarhné
Intoo	Ma tbarhnoo

Ă= Augh in bought	Ď= a heavy D	É= like A in Bay	G= G in beige	ḥ= like an H with smaller air passage	I= I as in ink	Ḱ= like ch in Irish loch
O= O as in home	OO= as in boots	R= roll the rrr	Ť= a heavy T	Ř= like a French R (gargle it)	Š= a heavy S	Ž= a heavy Z

P̲

P̲

To pull

Present

Ana	Bishab
Inta	Btishab
Inté	Btishabé
Hoowé	Byishab
Heeyé	Btishab
Nahna	Mnishab
Intoo	Btishaboo
Hinné	Byishaboo

Present Continuous

Ana	Ăam	Bishab
Inta	Ăam	Btishab
Inté	Ăam	Btishabé
Hoowé	Ăam	Byishab
Heeyé	Ăam	Btishab
Nahna	Ăam	Mnishab
Intoo	Ăam	Btishaboo
Hinné	Ăam	Byishaboo

Past

Ana	Sahabt
Inta	Sahabt
Inté	Sahabté
Hoowé	Sahab
Heeyé	Sahabét
Nahna	Sahabna
Intoo	Sahabtoo
Hinné	Sahaboo

Past Continuous

Ana	Kint Ăam	Bishab
Inta	Kint Ăam	Btishab
Inté	Kinté Ăam	Btishabé
Hoowé	Kén Ăam	Byishab
Heeyé	Kénét Ăam	Btishab
Nahna	Kinna Ăam	Mnishab
Intoo	Kintoo Ăam	Btishaboo
Hinné	Kénoo Ăam	Byishaboo

Future

Ana	Lah	Ishab
Inta	Lah	Tishab
Inté	Lah	Tishabé
Hoowé	Lah	Yishab
Heeyé	Lah	Tishab
Nahna	Lah	Nishab
Intoo	Lah	Tishaboo
Hinné	Lah	Yishaboo

Command

Inta	Shab
Inté	Shabé
Intoo	Shaboo
Inta	Ma tshab
Inté	Ma tshabé
Intoo	Ma tshaboo

To push

Present

Ana	Bidfosh
Inta	Btidfosh
Inté	Btidfshé
Hoowé	Byidfosh
Heeyé	Btidfosh
Nahna	Mnidfosh
Intoo	Btidfshoo
Hinné	Byidfshoo

Present Continuous

Ana	Ăam	Bidfosh
Inta	Ăam	Btidfosh
Inté	Ăam	Btidfshé
Hoowé	Ăam	Byidfosh
Heeyé	Ăam	Btidfosh
Nahna	Ăam	Mnidfosh
Intoo	Ăam	Btidfshoo
Hinné	Ăam	Byidfshoo

Past

Ana	Dafasht
Inta	Dafasht
Inté	Dafashté
Hoowé	Dafash
Heeyé	Dafashét
Nahna	Dafashna
Intoo	Dafashtoo
Hinné	Dafashoo

Past Continuous

Ana	Kint Ăam	Bidfosh
Inta	Kint Ăam	Btidfosh
Inté	Kinté Ăam	Btidfshé
Hoowé	Kén Ăam	Byidfosh
Heeyé	Kénét Ăam	Btidfosh
Nahna	Kinna Ăam	Mnidfosh
Intoo	Kintoo Ăam	Btidfshoo
Hinné	Kénoo Ăam	Byidfshoo

Future

Ana	Lah	Idfosh
Inta	Lah	Tidfosh
Inté	Lah	Tidfshé
Hoowé	Lah	Yidfosh
Heeyé	Lah	Tidfosh
Nahna	Lah	Nidfosh
Intoo	Lah	Tidfshoo
Hinné	Lah	Yidfshoo

Command

Inta	Dfosh
Inté	Dfishé
Intoo	Dfishoo
Inta	Ma tdfosh
Inté	Ma tdfshé
Intoo	Ma tdfshoo

Ă= Augh in bought	Ď= a heavy D	É= like A in Bay	G= G in beige	ĥ= like an H with smaller air passage	I= I as in ink	Ќ= like ch in Irish loch
O= O as in home	OO= as in boots	R= roll the rrr	Ť= a heavy T	Ř= like a French R (gargle it)	Ŝ= a heavy S	Ž= a heavy Z

P   Q

To put   ## To quit / To resign

Present	
Ana	BĥiṪ
Inta	BthiṪ
Inté	BthiṪé
Hoowé	BiĥiṪ
Heeyé	BthiṪ
Naĥna	MnĥiṪ
Intoo	BthiṪoo
Hinné	BiĥiṪoo

Present Continuous		
Ana	Ăam BĥiṪ	(ĥaṪét/ĥaṪṪa)
Inta	Ăam BthiṪ	(ĥaṪṪa)
Inté	Ăam BthiṪé	(ĥaṪét)
Hoowé	Ăam BiĥiṪ	(ĥaṪét)
Heeyé	Ăam BthiṪ	(ĥaṪṪa)
Naĥna	Ăam MnĥiṪ	(ĥaṪṪeen)
Intoo	Ăam BthiṪoo	(ĥaṪṪeen)
Hinné	Ăam BiĥiṪoo	(ĥaṪṪeen)

Past	
Ana	ĥaṪét
Inta	ĥaṪét
Inté	ĥaṪaité
Hoowé	ĥaṪ
Heeyé	ĥaṪṪét
Naĥna	ĥaṪṪaina
Intoo	ĥaṪṪaitoo
Hinné	ĥaṪṪoo

Past Continuous			
Ana	Kint Ăam	BĥiṪ	(kint ĥaṪét/ĥaṪṪa)
Inta	Kint Ăam	BthiṪ	(Kint ĥaṪét)
Inté	Kinté Ăam	BthiṪé	(Kinté ĥaṪṪa)
Hoowé	Kén Ăam	BiĥiṪ	(Kén ĥaṪét)
Heeyé	Kénét Ăam	BthiṪ	(Kénét ĥaṪṪa)
Naĥna	Kinna Ăam	MnĥiṪ	(Kinna ĥaṪṪeen)
Intoo	Kintoo Ăam	BthiṪoo	(Kintoo ĥaṪṪeen)
Hinné	Kénoo Ăam	BiĥiṪoo	(Kénoo ĥaṪṪeen)

Future		
Ana	Laĥ	ĥiṪ
Inta	Laĥ	thiṪ
Inté	Laĥ	thiṪé
Hoowé	Laĥ	yĥiṪ
Heeyé	Laĥ	thiṪ
Naĥna	Laĥ	nĥiṪ
Intoo	Laĥ	thiṪoo
Hinné	Laĥ	yĥiṪoo

Command	
Inta	ĥiṪ
Inté	ĥiṪé
Intoo	ĥiṪoo
Inta	Ma thiṪ
Inté	Ma thiṪé
Intoo	Ma thiṪoo

Present	
Ana	Bista'eel
Inta	Btista'eel
Inté	Btista'eelé
Hoowé	Byista'eel
Heeyé	Btista'eel
Naĥna	Mnista'eel
Intoo	Btista'eeloo
Hinné	Byista'eeloo

Present Continuous			
Ana	Ăam	Bista'eel	(mista'eel/mista'eelé)
Inta	Ăam	Btista'eel	(mista'eel)
Inté	Ăam	Btista'eelé	(mista'eelé)
Hoowé	Ăam	Byista'eel	(mista'eel)
Heeyé	Ăam	Btista'eel	(mista'eelé)
Naĥna	Ăam	Mnista'eel	(mista'eeleen)
Intoo	Ăam	Btista'eeloo	(mista'eeleen)
Hinné	Ăam	Byista'eeloo	(mista'eeleen)

Past	
Ana	Sta'alt
Inta	Sta'alt
Inté	Sta'alté
Hoowé	Sta'al
Heeyé	Sta'alét
Naĥna	Sta'alna
Intoo	Sta'altoo
Hinné	Sta'aloo

Past Continuous			
Ana	Kint Ăam	Bista'eel	(kint mista'eel/mista'eelé)
Inta	Kint Ăam	Btista'eel	(Kint mista'eel)
Inté	Kinté Ăam	Btista'eelé	(Kinté mista'eelé)
Hoowé	Kén Ăam	Byista'eel	(Kén mista'eel)
Heeyé	Kénét Ăam	Btista'eel	(Kénét mista'eelé)
Naĥna	Kinna Ăam	Mnista'eel	(Kinna mista'eeleen)
Intoo	Kintoo Ăam	Btista'eeloo	(Kintoo mista'eeleen)
Hinné	Kénoo Ăam	Byista'eeloo	(Kénoo mista'eeleen)

Future		
Ana	Laĥ	Ista'eel
Inta	Laĥ	Tista'eel
Inté	Laĥ	Tista'eelé
Hoowé	Laĥ	Yista'eel
Heeyé	Laĥ	Tista'eel
Naĥna	Laĥ	Nista'eel
Intoo	Laĥ	Tista'eeloo
Hinné	Laĥ	Yista'eeloo

Command	
Inta	Sta'eel
Inté	Sta'eelé
Intoo	Sta'eeloo
Inta	Ma tsta'eel
Inté	Ma tsta'eelé
Intoo	Ma tsta'eeloo

Ă= Augh in bought	Ď= a heavy D	É= like A in Bay	G= G in beige	ĥ= like an H with smaller air passage	I= I as in ink	Ḱ= like ch in Irish loch
O= O as in home	OO= as in boots	R= roll the rrr	Ṫ= a heavy T	Ř= like a French R (gargle it)	Š= a heavy S	Ž= a heavy Z

R

R

To raise (kids) (also to discipline)

Present

Ana	Brabbé
Inta	Btrabbé
Inté	Btrabbé
Hoowé	Birabbé
Heeyé	Btrabbé
Naĥna	Mnrabbé
Intoo	Btrabboo
Hinné	Birabboo

Present Continuous

Ana	Ăam	Brabbé
Inta	Ăam	Btrabbé
Inté	Ăam	Btrabbé
Hoowé	Ăam	Birabbé
Heeyé	Ăam	Btrabbé
Naĥna	Ăam	Mnrabbé
Intoo	Ăam	Btrabboo
Hinné	Ăam	Birabboo

Past

Ana	Rabbét
Inta	Rabbét
Inté	Rabbaité
Hoowé	Rabba
Heeyé	Rabbét
Naĥna	Rabbaina
Intoo	Rabbaitoo
Hinné	Rabboo

Past Continuous

Ana	Kint Ăam	Brabbé
Inta	Kint Ăam	Btrabbé
Inté	Kinté Ăam	Btrabbé
Hoowé	Kén Ăam	Birabbé
Heeyé	Kénét Ăam	Btrabbé
Naĥna	Kinna Ăam	Mnrabbé
Intoo	Kintoo Ăam	Btrabboo
Hinné	Kénoo Ăam	Birabboo

Future

Ana	Laĥ	Rabbé
Inta	Laĥ	Trabbé
Inté	Laĥ	Trabbé
Hoowé	Laĥ	Yrabbé
Heeyé	Laĥ	Trabbé
Naĥna	Laĥ	Nrabbé
Intoo	Laĥ	Trabboo
Hinné	Laĥ	Yrabboo

Command

Inta	Rabbé
Inté	Rabbé
Intoo	Rabboo
Inta	Ma trabbé
Inté	Ma trabbé
Intoo	Ma trabboo

To raise

Present

Ana	bĂallé
Inta	btĂallé
Inté	btĂallé
Hoowé	biĂallé
Heeyé	btĂallé
Naĥna	mnĂallé
Intoo	btĂalloo
Hinné	biĂalloo

Present Continuous

Ana	Ăam	bĂallé
Inta	Ăam	btĂallé
Inté	Ăam	btĂallé
Hoowé	Ăam	biĂallé
Heeyé	Ăam	btĂallé
Naĥna	Ăam	mnĂallé
Intoo	Ăam	btĂalloo
Hinné	Ăam	biĂalloo

Past

Ana	Ăallét
Inta	Ăallét
Inté	Ăallaité
Hoowé	Ăalla
Heeyé	Ăallét
Naĥna	Ăallaina
Intoo	Ăallaitoo
Hinné	Ăalloo

Past Continuous

Ana	Kint Ăam	bĂallé
Inta	Kint Ăam	btĂallé
Inté	Kinté Ăam	btĂallé
Hoowé	Kén Ăam	biĂallé
Heeyé	Kénét Ăam	btĂallé
Naĥna	Kinna Ăam	mnĂallé
Intoo	Kintoo Ăam	btĂalloo
Hinné	Kénoo Ăam	biĂalloo

Future

Ana	Laĥ	Ăallé
Inta	Laĥ	tĂallé
Inté	Laĥ	tĂallé
Hoowé	Laĥ	yĂallé
Heeyé	Laĥ	tĂallé
Naĥna	Laĥ	nĂallé
Intoo	Laĥ	tĂalloo
Hinné	Laĥ	yĂalloo

Command

Inta	Ăallé
Inté	Ăallé
Intoo	Ăalloo
Inta	Ma tĂallé
Inté	Ma tĂallé
Intoo	Ma tĂalloo

Ă= Augh in bought	Ď= a heavy D	É= like A in Bay	G= G in beige	ĥ= like an H with smaller air passage	I= I as in ink	Ḱ= like ch in Irish loch
O= O as in home	OO= as in boots	R= roll the rrr	Ť= a heavy T	Ř= like a French R (gargle it)	Ŝ= a heavy S	Ž= a heavy Z

<u>R</u>   # <u>R</u>

To rain

Present	
Ana	
Inta	
Inté	
Hoowé	
Heeyé	Btshatté
Naḣna	
Intoo	
Hinné	

Present Continuous		
Ana	Ăam	
Inta	Ăam	
Inté	Ăam	
Hoowé	Ăam	
Heeyé	Ăam	Btshatté
Naḣna	Ăam	
Intoo	Ăam	
Hinné	Ăam	

Past	
Ana	
Inta	
Inté	
Hoowé	
Heeyé	Shattét
Naḣna	
Intoo	
Hinné	

Past Continuous		
Ana	Kint Ăam	
Inta	Kint Ăam	
Inté	Kinté Ăam	
Hoowé	Kén Ăam	
Heeyé	Kénét Ăam	Btshatté
Naḣna	Kinna Ăam	
Intoo	Kintoo Ăam	
Hinné	Kénoo Ăam	

Future		
Ana	Laḣ	
Inta	Laḣ	
Inté	Laḣ	
Hoowé	Laḣ	
Heeyé	Laḣ	tshatté
Naḣna	Laḣ	
Intoo	Laḣ	
Hinné	Laḣ	

Command	
Inta	
Inté	Shatté
Intoo	
Inta	
Inté	Ma tshatté
Intoo	

To reach

Present	
Ana	booŜal
Inta	btooŜal
Inté	btooŜalé
Hoowé	byooŜal
Heeyé	btooŜal
Naḣna	mnooŜal
Intoo	btooŜaloo
Hinné	byooŜaloo

Present Continuous			
Ana	Ăam	booŜal	(waŜél/waŜlé)
Inta	Ăam	btooŜal	(waŜél)
Inté	Ăam	btooŜalé	(waŜlé)
Hoowé	Ăam	byooŜal	(waŜél)
Heeyé	Ăam	btooŜal	(waŜlé)
Naḣna	Ăam	mnooŜal	(waŜleen)
Intoo	Ăam	btooŜaloo	(waŜleen)
Hinné	Ăam	byooŜaloo	(waŜleen)

Past	
Ana	waŜalt
Inta	waŜalt
Inté	waŜalté
Hoowé	waŜal
Heeyé	waŜalét
Naḣna	waŜalna
Intoo	waŜaltoo
Hinné	waŜaloo

Past Continuous				
Ana	Kint Ăam	booŜal	(kint	(waŜél/waŜlé)
Inta	Kint Ăam	btooŜal	(Kint	(waŜél)
Inté	Kinté Ăam	btooŜalé	(Kinté	(waŜlé)
Hoowé	Kén Ăam	byooŜal	(Kén	(waŜél)
Heeyé	Kénét Ăam	btooŜal	(Kénét	(waŜlé)
Naḣna	Kinna Ăam	mnooŜal	(Kinna	(waŜleen)
Intoo	Kintoo Ăam	btooŜaloo	(Kintoo	(waŜleen)
Hinné	Kénoo Ăam	byooŜaloo	(Kénoo	(waŜleen)

Future		
Ana	Laḣ	'ooŜal
Inta	Laḣ	tooŜal
Inté	Laḣ	tooŜalé
Hoowé	Laḣ	yooŜal
Heeyé	Laḣ	tooŜal
Naḣna	Laḣ	nooŜal
Intoo	Laḣ	tooŜaloo
Hinné	Laḣ	yooŜaloo

Command	
Inta	wŜal
Inté	wŜalé
Intoo	wŜaloo
Inta	Ma tooŜal
Inté	Ma tooŜalé
Intoo	Ma tooŜaloo

Ă= Augh in bought	Ď= a heavy D	É= like A in Bay	G= G in beige	ḣ= like an H with smaller air passage	I= I as in ink	Ḱ= like ch in Irish loch
O= O as in home	OO= as in boots	R= roll the rrr	Ť= a heavy T	Ř= like a French R (gargle it)	Ŝ= a heavy S	Ž= a heavy Z

R   R

To read

Present

Ana	Bi'ra
Inta	Bti'ra
Inté	Bti'ré
Hoowé	Byi'ra
Heeyé	Bti'ra
Nahna	Mni'ra
Intoo	Bti'roo
Hinné	Byi'roo

Present Continuous

Ana	Ăam	Bi'ra
Inta	Ăam	Bti'ra
Inté	Ăam	Bti'ré
Hoowé	Ăam	Byi'ra
Heeyé	Ăam	Bti'ra
Nahna	Ăam	Mni'ra
Intoo	Ăam	Bti'roo
Hinné	Ăam	Byi'roo

Past

Ana	'reet
Inta	'reet
Inté	'reeté
Hoowé	'iré
Heeyé	'iryét
Nahna	'reena
Intoo	'reetoo
Hinné	'iryoo

Past Continuous

Ana	Kint Ăam	Bi'ra
Inta	Kint Ăam	Bti'ra
Inté	Kinté Ăam	Bti'ré
Hoowé	Kén Ăam	Byi'ra
Heeyé	Kénét Ăam	Bti'ra
Nahna	Kinna Ăam	Mni'ra
Intoo	Kintoo Ăam	Bti'roo
Hinné	Kénoo Ăam	Byi'roo

Future

Ana	Laĥ	'i'ra
Inta	Laĥ	ti'ra
Inté	Laĥ	ti'ré
Hoowé	Laĥ	yi'ra
Heeyé	Laĥ	ti'ra
Nahna	Laĥ	ni'ra
Intoo	Laĥ	ti'roo
Hinné	Laĥ	yi'roo

Command

Inta	'ra
Inté	'ree
Intoo	'roo
Inta	Ma t'ra
Inté	Ma t'ré
Intoo	Ma t'roo

To record

Present

Ana	Bsaggél
Inta	Btsaggél
Inté	Btsagglé
Hoowé	Bisaggél
Heeyé	Btsaggél
Nahna	Mnsaggél
Intoo	Btsaggloo
Hinné	Bisaggloo

Present Continuous

Ana	Ăam	Bsaggél
Inta	Ăam	Btsaggél
Inté	Ăam	Btsagglé
Hoowé	Ăam	Bisaggél
Heeyé	Ăam	Btsaggél
Nahna	Ăam	Mnsaggél
Intoo	Ăam	Btsaggloo
Hinné	Ăam	Bisaggloo

Past

Ana	Saggalt
Inta	Saggalt
Inté	Saggalté
Hoowé	Saggal
Heeyé	Saggalét
Nahna	Saggalna
Intoo	Saggaltoo
Hinné	Saggaloo

Past Continuous

Ana	Kint Ăam	Bsaggél
Inta	Kint Ăam	Btsaggél
Inté	Kinté Ăam	Btsagglé
Hoowé	Kén Ăam	Bisaggél
Heeyé	Kénét Ăam	Btsaggél
Nahna	Kinna Ăam	Mnsaggél
Intoo	Kintoo Ăam	Btsaggloo
Hinné	Kénoo Ăam	Bisaggloo

Future

Ana	Laĥ	Saggél
Inta	Laĥ	Tsaggél
Inté	Laĥ	Tsagglé
Hoowé	Laĥ	Ysaggél
Heeyé	Laĥ	Tsaggél
Nahna	Laĥ	Nsaggél
Intoo	Laĥ	Tsaggloo
Hinné	Laĥ	Ysaggloo

Command

Inta	Saggél
Inté	Sagglé
Intoo	Saggloo
Inta	Ma tsaggél
Inté	Ma tsagglé
Intoo	Ma tsaggloo

Ă= Augh in bought	Ď= a heavy D	É= like A in Bay	G= G in beige	ĥ= like an H with smaller air passage	I= I as in ink	Ḱ= like ch in Irish loch
O= O as in home	OO= as in boots	R= roll the rrr	Ť= a heavy T	Ř= like a French R (gargle it)	Ŝ= a heavy S	Ž= a heavy Z

R   R

To recover

Present

Ana	bŜaĥĥ
Inta	btŜaĥĥ
Inté	btŜaĥĥé
Hoowé	biŜaĥĥ
Heeyé	btŜaĥĥ
Naĥna	mnŜaĥĥ
Intoo	btŜaĥĥoo
Hinné	biŜaĥĥoo

Present Continuous

Ana	Ăam	bŜaĥĥ
Inta	Ăam	btŜaĥĥ
Inté	Ăam	btŜaĥĥé
Hoowé	Ăam	biŜaĥĥ
Heeyé	Ăam	btŜaĥĥ
Naĥna	Ăam	mnŜaĥĥ
Intoo	Ăam	btŜaĥĥoo
Hinné	Ăam	biŜaĥĥoo

Past

Ana	Ŝaĥĥét
Inta	Ŝaĥĥét
Inté	Ŝaĥĥaité
Hoowé	Ŝaĥĥ
Heeyé	Ŝaĥĥét
Naĥna	Ŝaĥĥaina
Intoo	Ŝaĥĥaitoo
Hinné	Ŝaĥĥoo

Past Continuous

Ana	Kint Ăam	bŜaĥĥ
Inta	Kint Ăam	btŜaĥĥ
Inté	Kinté Ăam	btŜaĥĥé
Hoowé	Kén Ăam	biŜaĥĥ
Heeyé	Kénét Ăam	btŜaĥĥ
Naĥna	Kinna Ăam	mnŜaĥĥ
Intoo	Kintoo Ăam	btŜaĥĥoo
Hinné	Kénoo Ăam	biŜaĥĥoo

Future

Ana	Laĥ	Ŝaĥĥ
Inta	Laĥ	tŜaĥĥ
Inté	Laĥ	tŜaĥĥé
Hoowé	Laĥ	yŜaĥĥ
Heeyé	Laĥ	tŜaĥĥ
Naĥna	Laĥ	nŜaĥĥ
Intoo	Laĥ	tŜaĥĥoo
Hinné	Laĥ	yŜaĥĥoo

Command

Inta	Ŝaĥĥ
Inté	Ŝaĥĥé
Intoo	Ŝaĥĥoo
Inta	Ma tŜaĥĥ
Inté	Ma tŜaĥĥé
Intoo	Ma tŜaĥĥoo

To refuse

Present

Ana	birfoĎ
Inta	btirfoĎ
Inté	btirfĎé
Hoowé	byirfoĎ
Heeyé	btirfoĎ
Naĥna	mnirfoĎ
Intoo	btirfĎoo
Hinné	byirfĎoo

Present Continuous

Ana	Ăam	birfoĎ	(raféĎ/rafĎa)
Inta	Ăam	btirfoĎ	(raféĎ)
Inté	Ăam	btirfĎé	(rafĎa)
Hoowé	Ăam	byirfoĎ	(raféĎ)
Heeyé	Ăam	btirfoĎ	(rafĎa)
Naĥna	Ăam	mnirfoĎ	(rafĎeen)
Intoo	Ăam	btirfĎoo	(rafĎeen)
Hinné	Ăam	byirfĎoo	(rafĎeen)

Past

Ana	rafaĎt
Inta	rafaĎt
Inté	rafaĎté
Hoowé	rafaĎ
Heeyé	rafaĎét
Naĥna	rafaĎna
Intoo	rafaĎtoo
Hinné	rafaĎoo

Past Continuous

Ana	Kint Ăam	birfoĎ	(kint raféĎ/rafĎa)
Inta	Kint Ăam	btirfoĎ	(Kint raféĎ)
Inté	Kinté Ăam	btirfĎé	(Kinté rafĎa)
Hoowé	Kén Ăam	byirfoĎ	(Kén raféĎ)
Heeyé	Kénét Ăam	btirfoĎ	(Kénét rafĎa)
Naĥna	Kinna Ăam	mnirfoĎ	(Kinna rafĎeen)
Intoo	Kintoo Ăam	btirfĎoo	(Kintoo rafĎeen)
Hinné	Kénoo Ăam	byirfĎoo	(Kénoo rafĎeen)

Future

Ana	Laĥ	irfoĎ
Inta	Laĥ	tirfoĎ
Inté	Laĥ	tirfĎé
Hoowé	Laĥ	yirfoĎ
Heeyé	Laĥ	tirfoĎ
Naĥna	Laĥ	nirfoĎ
Intoo	Laĥ	tirfĎoo
Hinné	Laĥ	yirfĎoo

Command

Inta	rfoĎ
Inté	rfiĎé
Intoo	rfiĎoo
Inta	Ma trfoĎ
Inté	Ma trfĎé
Intoo	Ma trfĎoo

Ă= Augh in bought	Ď= a heavy D	É= like A in Bay	G= G in beige	ĥ= like an H with smaller air passage	I= I as in ink	Ќ= like ch in Irish loch
O= O as in home	OO= as in boots	R= roll the rrr	Ť= a heavy T	Ř= like a French R (gargle it)		Ŝ= a heavy S	Ž= a heavy Z

R

R

To regret

Present

Ana	Bindam
Inta	Btindam
Inté	Btindamé
Hoowé	Byindam
Heeyé	Btindam
Nahna	Mnindam
Intoo	Btindamoo
Hinné	Byindamoo

Present Continuous

Ana	Ăam	Bindam	(nidmén/nidméné)
Inta	Ăam	Btindam	(nidmén)
Inté	Ăam	Btindamé	(nidméné)
Hoowé	Ăam	Byindam	(nidmén)
Heeyé	Ăam	Btindam	(nidméné)
Nahna	Ăam	Mnindam	(nidméneen)
Intoo	Ăam	Btindamoo	(nidméneen)
Hinné	Ăam	Byindamoo	(nidméneen)

Past

Ana	Ndimt
Inta	Ndimt
Inté	Ndimté
Hoowé	Nidim
Heeyé	Nidmét
Nahna	Ndimna
Intoo	Ndimtoo
Hinné	Nidmoo

Past Continuous

Ana	Kint Ăam	Bindam	(kint	(nidmén/nidméné)
Inta	Kint Ăam	Btindam	(Kint	(nidmén)
Inté	Kinté Ăam	Btindamé	(Kinté	(nidméné)
Hoowé	Kén Ăam	Byindam	(Kén	(nidmén)
Heeyé	Kénét Ăam	Btindam	(Kénét	(nidméné)
Nahna	Kinna Ăam	Mnindam	(Kinna	(nidméneen)
Intoo	Kintoo Ăam	Btindamoo	(Kintoo	(nidméneen)
Hinné	Kénoo Ăam	Byindamoo	(Kénoo	(nidméneen)

Future

Ana	Laĥ	Indam
Inta	Laĥ	Tindam
Inté	Laĥ	Tindamé
Hoowé	Laĥ	Yindam
Heeyé	Laĥ	Tindam
Nahna	Laĥ	Nindam
Intoo	Laĥ	Tindamoo
Hinné	Laĥ	Yindamoo

Command

Inta	Ndam
Inté	Ndamé
Intoo	Ndamoo
Inta	Ma tndam
Inté	Ma tndamé
Intoo	Ma tndamoo

To remember

Present

Ana	Bizkor
Inta	Btizkor
Inté	Btizkré
Hoowé	Byizkor
Heeyé	Btizkor
Nahna	Mnizkor
Intoo	Btizkroo
Hinné	Byizkroo

Present Continuous

Ana	Ăam	Bizkor
Inta	Ăam	Btizkor
Inté	Ăam	Btizkré
Hoowé	Ăam	Byizkor
Heeyé	Ăam	Btizkor
Nahna	Ăam	Mnizkor
Intoo	Ăam	Btizkroo
Hinné	Ăam	Byizkroo

Past

Ana	Tzakkart
Inta	Tzakkart
Inté	Tzakkarté
Hoowé	Tzakkar
Heeyé	Tzakkarét
Nahna	Tzakkarna
Intoo	Tzakkartoo
Hinné	Tzakkaroo

Past Continuous

Ana	Kint Ăam	Bizkor
Inta	Kint Ăam	Btizkor
Inté	Kinté Ăam	Btizkré
Hoowé	Kén Ăam	Byizkor
Heeyé	Kénét Ăam	Btizkor
Nahna	Kinna Ăam	Mnizkor
Intoo	Kintoo Ăam	Btizkroo
Hinné	Kénoo Ăam	Byizkroo

Future

Ana	Laĥ	Izkor
Inta	Laĥ	Tizkor
Inté	Laĥ	Tizkré
Hoowé	Laĥ	Yizkor
Heeyé	Laĥ	Tizkor
Nahna	Laĥ	Nizkor
Intoo	Laĥ	Tizkroo
Hinné	Laĥ	Yizkroo

Command

Inta	Tzakkar
Inté	Tzakkaré
Intoo	Tzakkaroo
Inta	Ma ttzakkar
Inté	Ma ttzakkaré
Intoo	Ma ttzakkaroo

Ă= Augh in bought	Ď= a heavy D	É= like A in Bay	G= G in beige	ĥ= like an H with smaller air passage	I= I as in ink	Ќ= like ch in Irish loch
O= O as in home	OO= as in boots	R= roll the rrr	Ť= a heavy T	Ř= like a French R (gargle it)	Š= a heavy S	Ž= a heavy Z

R   R

To remind   To remove

Present	
Ana	Bzakkér
Inta	Btzakkér
Inté	Btzakkré
Hoowé	Bizakkér
Heeyé	Btzakkér
Naḣna	Mnzakkér
Intoo	Btzakkroo
Hinné	Bizakkroo

Present Continuous		
Ana	Ăam	Bzakkér
Inta	Ăam	Btzakkér
Inté	Ăam	Btzakkré
Hoowé	Ăam	Bizakkér
Heeyé	Ăam	Btzakkér
Naḣna	Ăam	Mnzakkér
Intoo	Ăam	Btzakkroo
Hinné	Ăam	Bizakkroo

Past	
Ana	Zakkart
Inta	Zakkart
Inté	Zakkarté
Hoowé	Zakkar
Heeyé	Zakkarét
Naḣna	Zakkarna
Intoo	Zakkartoo
Hinné	Zakkaroo

Past Continuous		
Ana	Kint Ăam	Bzakkér
Inta	Kint Ăam	Btzakkér
Inté	Kinté Ăam	Btzakkré
Hoowé	Kén Ăam	Bizakkér
Heeyé	Kénét Ăam	Btzakkér
Naḣna	Kinna Ăam	Mnzakkér
Intoo	Kintoo Ăam	Btzakkroo
Hinné	Kénoo Ăam	Bizakkroo

Future		
Ana	Laḣ	Zakkér
Inta	Laḣ	Tzakkér
Inté	Laḣ	Tzakkré
Hoowé	Laḣ	Yzakkér
Heeyé	Laḣ	Tzakkér
Naḣna	Laḣ	Nzakkér
Intoo	Laḣ	Tzakkroo
Hinné	Laḣ	Yzakkroo

Command	
Inta	Zakkér
Inté	Zakkré
Intoo	Zakkroo
Inta	Ma tzakkér
Inté	Ma tzakkré
Intoo	Ma tzakkroo

To remove

Present	
Ana	Bsheel
Inta	Btsheel
Inté	Btsheelé
Hoowé	Bisheel
Heeyé	Btsheel
Naḣna	Mnsheel
Intoo	Btsheeloo
Hinné	Bisheeloo

Present Continuous		
Ana	Ăam	Bsheel
Inta	Ăam	Btsheel
Inté	Ăam	Btsheelé
Hoowé	Ăam	Bisheel
Heeyé	Ăam	Btsheel
Naḣna	Ăam	Mnsheel
Intoo	Ăam	Btsheeloo
Hinné	Ăam	Bisheeloo

Past	
Ana	Shilt
Inta	Shilt
Inté	Shilté
Hoowé	Shél
Heeyé	Shélét
Naḣna	Shilna
Intoo	Shiltoo
Hinné	Shéloo

Past Continuous		
Ana	Kint Ăam	Bsheel
Inta	Kint Ăam	Btsheel
Inté	Kinté Ăam	Btsheelé
Hoowé	Kén Ăam	Bisheel
Heeyé	Kénét Ăam	Btsheel
Naḣna	Kinna Ăam	Mnsheel
Intoo	Kintoo Ăam	Btsheeloo
Hinné	Kénoo Ăam	Bisheeloo

Future		
Ana	Laḣ	Sheel
Inta	Laḣ	Tsheel
Inté	Laḣ	Tsheelé
Hoowé	Laḣ	Ysheel
Heeyé	Laḣ	Tsheel
Naḣna	Laḣ	Nsheel
Intoo	Laḣ	Tsheeloo
Hinné	Laḣ	Ysheeloo

Command	
Inta	Sheel
Inté	Sheelé
Intoo	Sheeloo
Inta	Ma tsheel
Inté	Ma tsheelé
Intoo	Ma tsheeloo

Ă= Augh in bought	**Ď**= a heavy D	**É**= like A in Bay	**G**= G in beige	**ḣ**= like an H with smaller air passage	**I**= I as in ink	**Ќ**= like ch in Irish loch
O= O as in home	**OO**= as in boots	**R**= roll the rrr	**Ť**= a heavy T	**Ř**= like a French R (gargle it)	**Ŝ**= a heavy S	**Ž**= a heavy Z

R

R

To repair

Present

Ana	bŽabbéŤ
Inta	btŽabbéŤ
Inté	btŽabbŤé
Hoowé	biŽabbéŤ
Heeyé	btŽabbéŤ
Nahna	mnŽabbéŤ
Intoo	btŽabbŤoo
Hinné	biŽabbŤoo

Present Continuous

Ana	Ăam	bŽabbéŤ
Inta	Ăam	btŽabbéŤ
Inté	Ăam	btŽabbŤé
Hoowé	Ăam	biŽabbéŤ
Heeyé	Ăam	btŽabbéŤ
Nahna	Ăam	mnŽabbéŤ
Intoo	Ăam	btŽabbŤoo
Hinné	Ăam	biŽabbŤoo

Past

Ana	ŽabbaŤt
Inta	ŽabbaŤt
Inté	ŽabbaŤté
Hoowé	ŽabbaŤ
Heeyé	ŽabbaŤét
Nahna	ŽabbaŤna
Intoo	ŽabbaŤtoo
Hinné	ŽabbaŤoo

Past Continuous

Ana	Kint Ăam	bŽabbéŤ
Inta	Kint Ăam	btŽabbéŤ
Inté	Kinté Ăam	btŽabbŤé
Hoowé	Kén Ăam	biŽabbéŤ
Heeyé	Kénét Ăam	btŽabbéŤ
Nahna	Kinna Ăam	mnŽabbéŤ
Intoo	Kintoo Ăam	btŽabbŤoo
Hinné	Kénoo Ăam	biŽabbŤoo

Future

Ana	Laĥ	ŽabbéŤ
Inta	Laĥ	tŽabbéŤ
Inté	Laĥ	tŽabbŤé
Hoowé	Laĥ	yŽabbéŤ
Heeyé	Laĥ	tŽabbéŤ
Nahna	Laĥ	nŽabbéŤ
Intoo	Laĥ	tŽabbŤoo
Hinné	Laĥ	yŽabbŤoo

Command

Inta	ŽabbéŤ
Inté	ŽabbŤé
Intoo	ŽabbŤoo
Inta	Ma tŽabbéŤ
Inté	Ma tŽabbŤé
Intoo	Ma tŽabbŤoo

To repeat

Present

Ana	bĂeed
Inta	btĂeed
Inté	btĂeedé
Hoowé	biĂeed
Heeyé	btĂeed
Nahna	mnĂeed
Intoo	btĂeedoo
Hinné	biĂeedoo

Present Continuous

Ana	Ăam	bĂeed
Inta	Ăam	btĂeed
Inté	Ăam	btĂeedé
Hoowé	Ăam	biĂeed
Heeyé	Ăam	btĂeed
Nahna	Ăam	mnĂeed
Intoo	Ăam	btĂeedoo
Hinné	Ăam	biĂeedoo

Past

Ana	Ăidt
Inta	Ăidt
Inté	Ăidté
Hoowé	Ăéd
Heeyé	Ăédét
Nahna	Ăidna
Intoo	Ăidtoo
Hinné	Ăédoo

Past Continuous

Ana	Kint Ăam	bĂeed
Inta	Kint Ăam	btĂeed
Inté	Kinté Ăam	btĂeedé
Hoowé	Kén Ăam	biĂeed
Heeyé	Kénét Ăam	btĂeed
Nahna	Kinna Ăam	mnĂeed
Intoo	Kintoo Ăam	btĂeedoo
Hinné	Kénoo Ăam	biĂeedoo

Future

Ana	Laĥ	Ăeed
Inta	Laĥ	tĂeed
Inté	Laĥ	tĂeedé
Hoowé	Laĥ	yĂeed
Heeyé	Laĥ	tĂeed
Nahna	Laĥ	nĂeed
Intoo	Laĥ	tĂeedoo
Hinné	Laĥ	yĂeedoo

Command

Inta	Ăeed
Inté	Ăeedé
Intoo	Ăeedoo
Inta	Ma tĂeed
Inté	Ma tĂeedé
Intoo	Ma tĂeedoo

Ă= Augh in bought	Ď= a heavy D	É= like A in Bay	G= G in beige	ĥ= like an H with smaller air passage	I= I as in ink	Ķ= like ch in Irish loch
O= O as in home	OO= as in boots	R= roll the rrr	Ť= a heavy T	Ř= like a French R (gargle it)	Š= a heavy S	Ž= a heavy Z

<u>R</u>   <u>R</u>

To reward   To ring

Present	
Ana	Bgézé
Inta	Btgézé
Inté	Btgézé
Hoowé	Bigézé
Heeyé	Btgézé
Nahna	Mngézé
Intoo	Btgézoo
Hinné	Bigézoo

Present Continuous		
Ana	Ăam	Bgézé
Inta	Ăam	Btgézé
Inté	Ăam	Btgézé
Hoowé	Ăam	Bigézé
Heeyé	Ăam	Btgézé
Nahna	Ăam	Mngézé
Intoo	Ăam	Btgézoo
Hinné	Ăam	Bigézoo

Past	
Ana	Gézét
Inta	Gézét
Inté	Gézaité
Hoowé	Géza
Heeyé	Gézét
Nahna	Gézaina
Intoo	Gézaitoo
Hinné	Gézoo

Past Continuous		
Ana	Kint Ăam	Bgézé
Inta	Kint Ăam	Btgézé
Inté	Kinté Ăam	Btgézé
Hoowé	Kén Ăam	Bigézé
Heeyé	Kénét Ăam	Btgézé
Nahna	Kinna Ăam	Mngézé
Intoo	Kintoo Ăam	Btgézoo
Hinné	Kénoo Ăam	Bigézoo

Future		
Ana	Lah	Gézé
Inta	Lah	Tgézé
Inté	Lah	Tgézé
Hoowé	Lah	Ygézé
Heeyé	Lah	Tgézé
Nahna	Lah	Ngézé
Intoo	Lah	Tgézoo
Hinné	Lah	Ygézoo

Command	
Inta	Gézé
Inté	Gézé
Intoo	Gézoo
Inta	Ma tgézé
Inté	Ma tgézé
Intoo	Ma tgézoo

Present	
Ana	Brinn
Inta	Btrinn
Inté	Btrinné
Hoowé	Birinn
Heeyé	Btrinn
Nahna	Mnrinn
Intoo	Btrinnoo
Hinné	Birinnoo

Present Continuous			
Ana	Ăam	Brinn	(rénén/rénné)
Inta	Ăam	Btrinn	(rénén)
Inté	Ăam	Btrinné	(rénné)
Hoowé	Ăam	Birinn	(rénén)
Heeyé	Ăam	Btrinn	(rénné)
Nahna	Ăam	Mnrinn	(rénneen)
Intoo	Ăam	Btrinnoo	(rénneen)
Hinné	Ăam	Birinnoo	(rénneen)

Past	
Ana	Rannét
Inta	Rannét
Inté	Rannaité
Hoowé	Rann
Heeyé	Rannét
Nahna	Rannaina
Intoo	Rannaitoo
Hinné	Rannoo

Past Continuous			
Ana	Kint Ăam	Brinn	(kint rénén/rénné)
Inta	Kint Ăam	Btrinn	(Kint rénén)
Inté	Kinté Ăam	Btrinné	(Kinté rénné)
Hoowé	Kén Ăam	Birinn	(Kén rénén)
Heeyé	Kénét Ăam	Btrinn	(Kénét rénné)
Nahna	Kinna Ăam	Mnrinn	(Kinna rénneen)
Intoo	Kintoo Ăam	Btrinnoo	(Kintoo rénneen)
Hinné	Kénoo Ăam	Birinnoo	(Kénoo rénneen)

Future		
Ana	Lah	Rinn
Inta	Lah	Trinn
Inté	Lah	Trinné
Hoowé	Lah	Yrinn
Heeyé	Lah	Trinn
Nahna	Lah	Nrinn
Intoo	Lah	Trinnoo
Hinné	Lah	Yrinnoo

Command	
Inta	Rinn
Inté	Rinné
Intoo	Rinnoo
Inta	Ma trinn
Inté	Ma trinné
Intoo	Ma trinnoo

Ă= Augh in bought	Ď= a heavy D	É= like A in Bay	G= G in beige	h= like an H with smaller air passage	I= I as in ink	Ќ= like ch in Irish loch
O= O as in home	OO= as in boots	R= roll the rrr	Ť= a heavy T	Ř= like a French R (gargle it)	Ŝ= a heavy S	Ž= a heavy Z

R

R

To rinse

Present

Ana	bshaT̂T̂éf
Inta	btshaT̂T̂éf
Inté	btshaT̂T̂fé
Hoowé	bishaT̂T̂éf
Heeyé	btshaT̂T̂éf
Nahna	mnshaT̂T̂éf
Intoo	btshaT̂T̂foo
Hinné	bishaT̂T̂foo

Present Continuous

Ana	Ăam	bshaT̂T̂éf
Inta	Ăam	btshaT̂T̂éf
Inté	Ăam	btshaT̂T̂fé
Hoowé	Ăam	bishaT̂T̂éf
Heeyé	Ăam	btshaT̂T̂éf
Nahna	Ăam	mnshaT̂T̂éf
Intoo	Ăam	btshaT̂T̂foo
Hinné	Ăam	bishaT̂T̂foo

Past

Ana	shaT̂T̂aft
Inta	shaT̂T̂aft
Inté	shaT̂T̂afté
Hoowé	shaT̂T̂af
Heeyé	shaT̂T̂afét
Nahna	shaT̂T̂afna
Intoo	shaT̂T̂aftoo
Hinné	shaT̂T̂afoo

Past Continuous

Ana	Kint Ăam	bshaT̂T̂éf
Inta	Kint Ăam	btshaT̂T̂éf
Inté	Kinté Ăam	btshaT̂T̂fé
Hoowé	Kén Ăam	bishaT̂T̂éf
Heeyé	Kénét Ăam	btshaT̂T̂éf
Nahna	Kinna Ăam	mnshaT̂T̂éf
Intoo	Kintoo Ăam	btshaT̂T̂foo
Hinné	Kénoo Ăam	bishaT̂T̂foo

Future

Ana	Laĥ	shaT̂T̂éf
Inta	Laĥ	tshaT̂T̂éf
Inté	Laĥ	tshaT̂T̂fé
Hoowé	Laĥ	yshaT̂T̂éf
Heeyé	Laĥ	tshaT̂T̂éf
Nahna	Laĥ	nshaT̂T̂éf
Intoo	Laĥ	tshaT̂T̂foo
Hinné	Laĥ	yshaT̂T̂foo

Command

Inta	shaT̂T̂éf
Inté	shaT̂T̂fé
Intoo	shaT̂T̂foo
Inta	Ma tshaT̂T̂éf
Inté	Ma tshaT̂T̂fé
Intoo	Ma tshaT̂T̂foo

To roll (to make a roll)

Present

Ana	Bliff
Inta	Btliff
Inté	Btliffé
Hoowé	Biliff
Heeyé	Btliff
Nahna	Mnliff
Intoo	Btliffoo
Hinné	Biliffoo

Present Continuous

Ana	Ăam	Bliff
Inta	Ăam	Btliff
Inté	Ăam	Btliffé
Hoowé	Ăam	Biliff
Heeyé	Ăam	Btliff
Nahna	Ăam	Mnliff
Intoo	Ăam	Btliffoo
Hinné	Ăam	Biliffoo

Past

Ana	Laffét
Inta	Laffét
Inté	Laffaité
Hoowé	Laff
Heeyé	Laffét
Nahna	Laffaina
Intoo	Laffaitoo
Hinné	Laffoo

Past Continuous

Ana	Kint Ăam	Bliff
Inta	Kint Ăam	Btliff
Inté	Kinté Ăam	Btliffé
Hoowé	Kén Ăam	Biliff
Heeyé	Kénét Ăam	Btliff
Nahna	Kinna Ăam	Mnliff
Intoo	Kintoo Ăam	Btliffoo
Hinné	Kénoo Ăam	Biliffoo

Future

Ana	Laĥ	Liff
Inta	Laĥ	Tliff
Inté	Laĥ	Tliffé
Hoowé	Laĥ	Yliff
Heeyé	Laĥ	Tliff
Nahna	Laĥ	Nliff
Intoo	Laĥ	Tliffoo
Hinné	Laĥ	Yliffoo

Command

Inta	Liff
Inté	Liffé
Intoo	Liffoo
Inta	Ma tliff
Inté	Ma tliffé
Intoo	Ma tliffoo

Ă= Augh in bought	Ď= a heavy D	É= like A in Bay	G= G in beige	ĥ= like an H with smaller air passage	I= I as in ink	Ķ= like ch in Irish loch
O= O as in home	OO= as in boots	R= roll the rrr	T̂= a heavy T	Ř= like a French R (gargle it)	Ŝ= a heavy S	Ž= a heavy Z

R   R

To run

Present	
Ana	Birkod
Inta	Btirkod
Inté	Btirkdé
Hoowé	Byirkod
Heeyé	Btorkod
Naĥna	Mnirkod
Intoo	Btirkdoo
Hinné	Byirkdoo

Present Continuous		
Ana	Ăam	Birkod
Inta	Ăam	Btirkod
Inté	Ăam	Btirkdé
Hoowé	Ăam	Byirkod
Heeyé	Ăam	Btorkod
Naĥna	Ăam	Mnirkod
Intoo	Ăam	Btirkdoo
Hinné	Ăam	Byirkdoo

Past	
Ana	Rakadit
Inta	Rakadit
Inté	Rakadté
Hoowé	Rakad
Heeyé	Rakdit
Naĥna	Rakadna
Intoo	Rakadtoo
Hinné	Rakdoo

Past Continuous		
Ana	Kint Ăam	Birkod
Inta	Kint Ăam	Btirkod
Inté	Kinté Ăam	Btirkdé
Hoowé	Kén Ăam	Byirkod
Heeyé	Kénét Ăam	Btorkod
Naĥna	Kinna Ăam	Mnirkod
Intoo	Kintoo Ăam	Btirkdoo
Hinné	Kénoo Ăam	Byirkdoo

Future		
Ana	Laĥ	Irkod
Inta	Laĥ	Tirkod
Inté	Laĥ	Tirkdé
Hoowé	Laĥ	Yirkod
Heeyé	Laĥ	Tirkod
Naĥna	Laĥ	Nirkod
Intoo	Laĥ	Tirkdoo
Hinné	Laĥ	Yirkdoo

Command	
Inta	Rkod
Inté	Rkidé
Intoo	Rkidoo
Inta	Ma tirkod
Inté	Ma tirkdé
Intoo	Ma tirkdoo

To rub

Present	
Ana	Bifrok
Inta	Btifrok
Inté	Btifrké
Hoowé	Byifrok
Heeyé	Btifrok
Naĥna	Mnifrok
Intoo	Btifrkoo
Hinné	Byifrkoo

Present Continuous		
Ana	Ăam	Bifrok
Inta	Ăam	Btifrok
Inté	Ăam	Btifrké
Hoowé	Ăam	Byifrok
Heeyé	Ăam	Btifrok
Naĥna	Ăam	Mnifrok
Intoo	Ăam	Btifrkoo
Hinné	Ăam	Byifrkoo

Past	
Ana	Farakt
Inta	Farakt
Inté	Farakté
Hoowé	Farak
Heeyé	Farakét
Naĥna	Farakna
Intoo	Faraktoo
Hinné	Farakoo

Past Continuous		
Ana	Kint Ăam	Bifrok
Inta	Kint Ăam	Btifrok
Inté	Kinté Ăam	Btifrké
Hoowé	Kén Ăam	Byifrok
Heeyé	Kénét Ăam	Btifrok
Naĥna	Kinna Ăam	Mnifrok
Intoo	Kintoo Ăam	Btifrkoo
Hinné	Kénoo Ăam	Byifrkoo

Future		
Ana	Laĥ	Ifrok
Inta	Laĥ	Tifrok
Inté	Laĥ	Tifrké
Hoowé	Laĥ	Yifrok
Heeyé	Laĥ	Tifrok
Naĥna	Laĥ	Nifrok
Intoo	Laĥ	Tifrkoo
Hinné	Laĥ	Yifrkoo

Command	
Inta	Frok
Inté	Friké
Intoo	Frikoo
Inta	Ma tfrok
Inté	Ma tfrké
Intoo	Ma tfrkoo

Ă= Augh in bought	Ď= a heavy D	É= like A in Bay	G= G in beige	ĥ= like an H with smaller air passage	I= I as in ink	Ḱ= like ch in Irish loch
O= O as in home	OO= as in boots	R= roll the rrr	Ť= a heavy T	Ř= like a French R (gargle it)	Ŝ= a heavy S	Ž= a heavy Z

S̲   S̲

To sail

Present	
Ana	Bibh̄ér
Inta	Btibh̄ér
Inté	Btibh̄ré
Hoowé	Byibh̄ér
Heeyé	Btibh̄ér
Nah̄na	Mnibh̄ér
Intoo	Btibh̄roo
Hinné	Btibh̄roo

Present Continuous		
Ana	Ăam	Bibh̄ér
Inta	Ăam	Btibh̄ér
Inté	Ăam	Btibh̄ré
Hoowé	Ăam	Byibh̄ér
Heeyé	Ăam	Btibh̄ér
Nah̄na	Ăam	Mnibh̄ér
Intoo	Ăam	Btibh̄roo
Hinné	Ăam	Btibh̄roo

Past	
Ana	Abh̄art
Inta	Abh̄art
Inté	Abh̄arét
Hoowé	Abh̄ar
Heeyé	Abh̄arét
Nah̄na	Abh̄arna
Intoo	Abh̄artoo
Hinné	Abh̄aroo

Past Continuous		
Ana	Kint Ăam	Bibh̄ér
Inta	Kint Ăam	Btibh̄ér
Inté	Kinté Ăam	Btibh̄ré
Hoowé	Kén Ăam	Byibh̄ér
Heeyé	Kénét Ăam	Btibh̄ér
Nah̄na	Kinna Ăam	Mnibh̄ér
Intoo	Kintoo Ăam	Btibh̄roo
Hinné	Kénoo Ăam	Btibh̄roo

Future		
Ana	Lah̄	ibh̄ér
Inta	Lah̄	tibh̄ér
Inté	Lah̄	tibh̄ré
Hoowé	Lah̄	yibh̄ér
Heeyé	Lah̄	tibh̄ér
Nah̄na	Lah̄	nibh̄ér
Intoo	Lah̄	tibh̄roo
Hinné	Lah̄	tibh̄roo

Command	
Inta	n/a
Inté	n/a
Intoo	n/a
Inta	n/a
Inté	n/a
Intoo	n/a

To save (same as to finish)

Present	
Ana	bḰalléŠ
Inta	btḰalléŠ
Inté	btḰallSé
Hoowé	biḰalléŠ
Heeyé	btḰalléŠ
Nah̄na	mnḰalléŠ
Intoo	btḰallŠoo
Hinné	biḰallŠoo

Present Continuous		
Ana	Ăam	bḰalléŠ (mḰallaŠ/mḰallŠa)
Inta	Ăam	btḰalléŠ (mḰallaŠ)
Inté	Ăam	btḰallSé (mḰallŠa)
Hoowé	Ăam	biḰalléŠ (mḰallaŠ)
Heeyé	Ăam	btḰalléŠ (mḰallŠa)
Nah̄na	Ăam	mnḰalléŠ (mḰallŠeen)
Intoo	Ăam	btḰallŠoo (mḰallŠeen)
Hinné	Ăam	biḰallŠoo (mḰallŠeen)

Past	
Ana	ḰallaŠt
Inta	ḰallaŠt
Inté	ḰallaŠté
Hoowé	ḰallaŠ
Heeyé	ḰallaŠét
Nah̄na	ḰallaŠna
Intoo	ḰallaŠtoo
Hinné	ḰallaŠoo

Past Continuous		
Ana	Kint Ăam	bḰalléŠ (kint mḰallaŠ/mḰallŠa)
Inta	Kint Ăam	btḰalléŠ (Kint mḰallaŠ)
Inté	Kinté Ăam	btḰallSé (Kinté mḰallŠa)
Hoowé	Kén Ăam	biḰalléŠ (Kén mḰallaŠ)
Heeyé	Kénét Ăam	btḰalléŠ (Kénét mḰallŠa)
Nah̄na	Kinna Ăam	mnḰalléŠ (Kinna mḰallŠeen)
Intoo	Kintoo Ăam	btḰallŠoo (Kintoo mḰallŠeen)
Hinné	Kénoo Ăam	biḰallŠoo (Kénoo mḰallŠeen)

Future		
Ana	Lah̄	ḰalléŠ
Inta	Lah̄	tḰalléŠ
Inté	Lah̄	tḰallŠé
Hoowé	Lah̄	yḰalléŠ
Heeyé	Lah̄	tḰalléŠ
Nah̄na	Lah̄	nḰalléŠ
Intoo	Lah̄	tḰallŠoo
Hinné	Lah̄	ḰallaŠoo

Command	
Inta	ḰalléŠ
Inté	ḰallaŠté
Intoo	ḰallaŠtoo
Inta	Ma tḰalleŠ
Inté	Ma tḰallŠé
Intoo	Ma tḰallŠoo

Ă= Augh in bought	Ď= a heavy D	É= like A in Bay	G= G in beige	h̄= like an H with smaller air passage	I= I as in ink	Ḱ= like ch in Irish loch
O= O as in home	OO= as in boots	R= roll the rrr	Ť= a heavy T	Ř= like a French R (gargle it)		Š= a heavy S	Ž= a heavy Z

<u>S</u> <u>S</u>

To say

Present

Ana	B'ool
Inta	Bt'ool
Inté	Bt'oolé
Hoowé	Bi'ool
Heeyé	Bt'ool
Naḣna	Mn'ool
Intoo	Bt'ooloo
Hinné	Bi'ooloo

Present Continuous

Ana	Ăam	B'ool
Inta	Ăam	Bt'ool
Inté	Ăam	Bt'oolé
Hoowé	Ăam	Bi'ool
Heeyé	Ăam	Bt'ool
Naḣna	Ăam	Mn'ool
Intoo	Ăam	Bt'ooloo
Hinné	Ăam	Bi'ooloo

Past

Ana	ilt
Inta	ilt
Inté	ilté
Hoowé	'all
Heeyé	'alét
Naḣna	Ilna
Intoo	Iltoo
Hinné	'aloo

Past Continuous

Ana	Kint Ăam	B'ool
Inta	Kint Ăam	Bt'ool
Inté	Kinté Ăam	Bt'oolé
Hoowé	Kén Ăam	Bi'ool
Heeyé	Kénét Ăam	Bt'ool
Naḣna	Kinna Ăam	Mn'ool
Intoo	Kintoo Ăam	Bt'ooloo
Hinné	Kénoo Ăam	Bi'ooloo

Future

Ana	Laḣ	'ool
Inta	Laḣ	T'ool
Inté	Laḣ	T'oolé
Hoowé	Laḣ	Y'ool
Heeyé	Laḣ	T'ool
Naḣna	Laḣ	N'ool
Intoo	Laḣ	T'ooloo
Hinné	Laḣ	Y'ooloo

Command

Inta	'ool
Inté	'oolé
Intoo	'ooloo
Inta	Ma t'ool
Inté	Ma t'oolé
Intoo	Ma t'ooloo

To scare

Present

Ana	bḰawwéf
Inta	btḰawwéf
Inté	btḰawwfé
Hoowé	biḰawwéf
Heeyé	btḰawwéf
Naḣna	mnḰawwéf
Intoo	btḰawwfoo
Hinné	biḰawwfoo

Present Continuous

Ana	Ăam	bḰawwéf
Inta	Ăam	btḰawwéf
Inté	Ăam	btḰawwfé
Hoowé	Ăam	biḰawwéf
Heeyé	Ăam	btḰawwéf
Naḣna	Ăam	mnḰawwéf
Intoo	Ăam	btḰawwfoo
Hinné	Ăam	biḰawwfoo

Past

Ana	Ḱawwaft
Inta	Ḱawwaft
Inté	Ḱawwafté
Hoowé	Ḱawwaf
Heeyé	Ḱawwafét
Naḣna	Ḱawwafna
Intoo	Ḱawwaftoo
Hinné	Ḱawwafoo

Past Continuous

Ana	Kint Ăam	bḰawwéf
Inta	Kint Ăam	btḰawwéf
Inté	Kinté Ăam	btḰawwfé
Hoowé	Kén Ăam	biḰawwéf
Heeyé	Kénét Ăam	btḰawwéf
Naḣna	Kinna Ăam	mnḰawwéf
Intoo	Kintoo Ăam	btḰawwfoo
Hinné	Kénoo Ăam	biḰawwfoo

Future

Ana	Laḣ	Ḱawwéf
Inta	Laḣ	tḰawwéf
Inté	Laḣ	tḰawwfé
Hoowé	Laḣ	yḰawwéf
Heeyé	Laḣ	tḰawwéf
Naḣna	Laḣ	nḰawwéf
Intoo	Laḣ	tḰawwfoo
Hinné	Laḣ	yḰawwfoo

Command

Inta	Ḱawwéf
Inté	Ḱawwfé
Intoo	Ḱawwfoo
Inta	Ma tḰawwéf
Inté	Ma tḰawwfé
Intoo	Ma tḰawwfoo

Ă= Augh in bought	Ď= a heavy D	É= like A in Bay	G= G in beige	ḣ= like an H with smaller air passage	I= I as in ink	Ḱ= like ch in Irish loch
O= O as in home	OO= as in boots	R= roll the rrr	Ť= a heavy T	Ř= like a French R (gargle it)	Ŝ= a heavy S	Ž= a heavy Z

S̲ & S̲

To scratch

Present

Ana	bŘarmésh
Inta	btŘarmésh
Inté	btŘarmshé
Hoowé	biŘarmésh
Heeyé	btŘarmésh
Naḥna	mnŘarmésh
Intoo	btŘarmshoo
Hinné	biŘarmshoo

Present Continuous

Ana	Ăam	bŘarmésh
Inta	Ăam	btŘarmésh
Inté	Ăam	btŘarmshé
Hoowé	Ăam	biŘarmésh
Heeyé	Ăam	btŘarmésh
Naḥna	Ăam	mnŘarmésh
Intoo	Ăam	btŘarmshoo
Hinné	Ăam	biŘarmshoo

Past

Ana	Řarmasht
Inta	Řarmasht
Inté	Řarmashté
Hoowé	Řarmash
Heeyé	Řarmashét
Naḥna	Řarmashna
Intoo	Řarmashtoo
Hinné	Řarmashoo

Past Continuous

Ana	Kint Ăam	bŘarmésh
Inta	Kint Ăam	btŘarmésh
Inté	Kinté Ăam	btŘarmshé
Hoowé	Kén Ăam	biŘarmésh
Heeyé	Kénét Ăam	btŘarmésh
Naḥna	Kinna Ăam	mnŘarmésh
Intoo	Kintoo Ăam	btŘarmshoo
Hinné	Kénoo Ăam	biŘarmshoo

Future

Ana	Laḥ	Řarmésh
Inta	Laḥ	tŘarmésh
Inté	Laḥ	tŘarmshé
Hoowé	Laḥ	yŘarmésh
Heeyé	Laḥ	tŘarmésh
Naḥna	Laḥ	nŘarmésh
Intoo	Laḥ	tŘarmshoo
Hinné	Laḥ	yŘarmshoo

Command

Inta	Řarmésh
Inté	Řarmshé
Intoo	Řarmshoo
Inta	Ma tŘarmésh
Inté	Ma tŘarmshé
Intoo	Ma tŘarmshoo

To scream

Present

Ana	bŜarréḰ
Inta	btŜarréḰ
Inté	btŜarrḰé
Hoowé	biŜarréḰ
Heeyé	btŜarréḰ
Naḥna	mnŜarréḰ
Intoo	btŜarrḰoo
Hinné	biŜarrḰoo

Present Continuous

Ana	Ăam	bŜarréḰ
Inta	Ăam	btŜarréḰ
Inté	Ăam	btŜarrḰé
Hoowé	Ăam	biŜarréḰ
Heeyé	Ăam	btŜarréḰ
Naḥna	Ăam	mnŜarréḰ
Intoo	Ăam	btŜarrḰoo
Hinné	Ăam	biŜarrḰoo

Past

Ana	ŜarraḰt
Inta	ŜarraḰt
Inté	ŜarraḰté
Hoowé	ŜarraḰ
Heeyé	ŜarraḰét
Naḥna	ŜarraḰna
Intoo	ŜarraḰtoo
Hinné	ŜarraḰoo

Past Continuous

Ana	Kint Ăam	bŜarréḰ
Inta	Kint Ăam	btŜarréḰ
Inté	Kinté Ăam	btŜarrḰé
Hoowé	Kén Ăam	biŜarréḰ
Heeyé	Kénét Ăam	btŜarréḰ
Naḥna	Kinna Ăam	mnŜarréḰ
Intoo	Kintoo Ăam	btŜarrḰoo
Hinné	Kénoo Ăam	biŜarrḰoo

Future

Ana	Laḥ	ŜarréḰ
Inta	Laḥ	tŜarréḰ
Inté	Laḥ	tŜarrḰé
Hoowé	Laḥ	yŜarréḰ
Heeyé	Laḥ	tŜarréḰ
Naḥna	Laḥ	nŜarréḰ
Intoo	Laḥ	tŜarrḰoo
Hinné	Laḥ	yŜarrḰoo

Command

Inta	ŜarréḰ
Inté	ŜarrḰé
Intoo	ŜarrḰoo
Inta	Ma tŜarréḰ
Inté	Ma tŜarrḰé
Intoo	Ma tŜarrḰoo

Ă= Augh in bought	Ď= a heavy D	É= like A in Bay	G= G in beige	ḥ= like an H with smaller air passage	I= I as in ink	Ḱ= like ch in Irish loch
O= O as in home	OO= as in boots	R= roll the rrr	Ť= a heavy T	Ř= like a French R (gargle it)	Ŝ= a heavy S	Ž= a heavy Z

<u>S</u>   # <u>S</u>

To screw   ## To scribble / To doodle

Present	
Ana	bbarŘé
Inta	btbarŘé
Inté	btbarŘé
Hoowé	bibarŘé
Heeyé	btbarŘé
Nahna	mnbarŘé
Intoo	btbarŘoo
Hinné	bibarŘoo

Present	
Ana	bḰarbésh
Inta	btḰarbésh
Inté	btḰarbshé
Hoowé	biḰarbésh
Heeyé	btḰarbésh
Nahna	mnḰarbésh
Intoo	btḰarbshoo
Hinné	biḰarbshoo

Present Continuous		
Ana	Ăam	bbarŘé
Inta	Ăam	btbarŘé
Inté	Ăam	btbarŘé
Hoowé	Ăam	bibarŘé
Heeyé	Ăam	btbarŘé
Nahna	Ăam	mnbarŘé
Intoo	Ăam	btbarŘoo
Hinné	Ăam	bibarŘoo

Present Continuous		
Ana	Ăam	bḰarbésh
Inta	Ăam	btḰarbésh
Inté	Ăam	btḰarbshé
Hoowé	Ăam	biḰarbésh
Heeyé	Ăam	btḰarbésh
Nahna	Ăam	mnḰarbésh
Intoo	Ăam	btḰarbshoo
Hinné	Ăam	biḰarbshoo

Past	
Ana	barŘét
Inta	barŘét
Inté	barŘaité
Hoowé	barŘa
Heeyé	barŘét
Nahna	barŘaina
Intoo	barŘaitoo
Hinné	barŘoo

Past	
Ana	Ḱarbasht
Inta	Ḱarbasht
Inté	Ḱarbashté
Hoowé	Ḱarbash
Heeyé	Ḱarbashét
Nahna	Ḱarbashna
Intoo	Ḱarbashtoo
Hinné	Ḱarbashoo

Past Continuous		
Ana	Kint Ăam	bbarŘé
Inta	Kint Ăam	btbarŘé
Inté	Kinté Ăam	btbarŘé
Hoowé	Kén Ăam	bibarŘé
Heeyé	Kénét Ăam	btbarŘé
Nahna	Kinna Ăam	mnbarŘé
Intoo	Kintoo Ăam	btbarŘoo
Hinné	Kénoo Ăam	bibarŘoo

Past Continuous		
Ana	Kint Ăam	bḰarbésh
Inta	Kint Ăam	btḰarbésh
Inté	Kinté Ăam	btḰarbshé
Hoowé	Kén Ăam	biḰarbésh
Heeyé	Kénét Ăam	btḰarbésh
Nahna	Kinna Ăam	mnḰarbésh
Intoo	Kintoo Ăam	btḰarbshoo
Hinné	Kénoo Ăam	biḰarbshoo

Future		
Ana	Lah	barŘé
Inta	Lah	tbarŘé
Inté	Lah	tbarŘé
Hoowé	Lah	ybarŘé
Heeyé	Lah	tbarŘé
Nahna	Lah	nbarŘé
Intoo	Lah	tbarŘoo
Hinné	Lah	ybarŘoo

Future		
Ana	Lah	Ḱarbésh
Inta	Lah	tḰarbésh
Inté	Lah	tḰarbshé
Hoowé	Lah	yḰarbésh
Heeyé	Lah	tḰarbésh
Nahna	Lah	nḰarbésh
Intoo	Lah	tḰarbshoo
Hinné	Lah	yḰarbshoo

Command	
Inta	barŘé
Inté	barŘé
Intoo	barŘoo
Inta	Ma tbarŘé
Inté	Ma tbarŘé
Intoo	Ma tbarŘoo

Command	
Inta	Ḱarbésh
Inté	Ḱarbshé
Intoo	Ḱarbshoo
Inta	Ma tḰarbésh
Inté	Ma tḰarbshé
Intoo	Ma tḰarbshoo

Ă= Augh in bought	Ď= a heavy D	É= like A in Bay	G= G in beige	ĥ= like an H with smaller air passage	I= I as in ink	Ḱ= like ch in Irish loch
O= O as in home	OO= as in boots	R= roll the rrr	Ť= a heavy T	Ř= like a French R (gargle it)	Ŝ= a heavy S	Ž= a heavy Z

<u>S</u>   <u>S</u>

To search

Present

Ana	Bfattésh
Inta	Btfattésh
Inté	Btfattshé
Hoowé	bifattésh
Heeyé	btfattésh
Nahna	mnfattésh
Intoo	Btfattshoo
Hinné	Bifattshoo

Present Continuous

Ana	Ăam	Bfattésh
Inta	Ăam	Btfattésh
Inté	Ăam	Btfattshé
Hoowé	Ăam	bifattésh
Heeyé	Ăam	btfattésh
Nahna	Ăam	mnfattésh
Intoo	Ăam	Btfattshoo
Hinné	Ăam	Bifattshoo

Past

Ana	Fattasht
Inta	Fattasht
Inté	Fattashté
Hoowé	Fattash
Heeyé	Fattashét
Nahna	Fattashna
Intoo	Fattashtoo
Hinné	Fattashoo

Past Continuous

Ana	Kint Ăam	Bfattésh
Inta	Kint Ăam	Btfattésh
Inté	Kinté Ăam	Btfattshé
Hoowé	Kén Ăam	bifattésh
Heeyé	Kénét Ăam	btfattésh
Nahna	Kinna Ăam	mnfattésh
Intoo	Kintoo Ăam	Btfattshoo
Hinné	Kénoo Ăam	Bifattshoo

Future

Ana	Lah	fattésh
Inta	Lah	tfattésh
Inté	Lah	tfattésh
Hoowé	Lah	yfattésh
Heeyé	Lah	tfattésh
Nahna	Lah	nfattésh
Intoo	Lah	Tfattshoo
Hinné	Lah	yfattshoo

Command

Inta	Fattésh
Inté	Fattshé
Intoo	Fattshoo
Inta	Ma tfattésh
Inté	Ma tfattshé
Intoo	Ma tfattshoo

To see

Present

Ana	Bshoof
Inta	Btshoof
Inté	Btshoofé
Hoowé	Bishoof
Heeyé	Btshoof
Nahna	Mnshoof
Intoo	BTshoofoo
Hinné	Bishoofoo

Present Continuous

Ana	Ăam	Bshoof	(shéyéf/shéyfé)
Inta	Ăam	Btshoof	(shéyéf)
Inté	Ăam	Btshoofé	(shéyfé)
Hoowé	Ăam	Bishoof	(shéyéf)
Heeyé	Ăam	Btshoof	(shéyfé)
Nahna	Ăam	Mnshoof	(shéyfeen)
Intoo	Ăam	BTshoofoo	(shéyfeen)
Hinné	Ăam	Bishoofoo	(shéyfeen)

Past

Ana	Shift
Inta	Shift
Inté	Shifté
Hoowé	Shéf
Heeyé	Shéfét
Nahna	Shifna
Intoo	Shiftoo
Hinné	Shéfoo

Past Continuous

Ana	Kint Ăam	Bshoof	(kint shéyéf/shéyfé)
Inta	Kint Ăam	Btshoof	(Kint shéyéf)
Inté	Kinté Ăam	Btshoofé	(Kinté shéyfé)
Hoowé	Kén Ăam	Bishoof	(Kén shéyéf)
Heeyé	Kénét Ăam	Btshoof	(Kénét shéyfé)
Nahna	Kinna Ăam	Mnshoof	(Kinna shéyfeen)
Intoo	Kintoo Ăam	BTshoofoo	(Kintoo shéyfeen)
Hinné	Kénoo Ăam	Bishoofoo	(Kénoo shéyfeen)

Future

Ana	Lah	Shoof
Inta	Lah	Tshoof
Inté	Lah	Tshoofé
Hoowé	Lah	Yshoof
Heeyé	Lah	Tshoof
Nahna	Lah	Nshoof
Intoo	Lah	Tshoofoo
Hinné	Lah	Yshoofoo

Command

Inta	Shoof
Inté	Shoofé
Intoo	Shoofoo
Inta	Ma tshhof
Inté	Ma tshoofé
Intoo	Ma tshoofoo

Ă= Augh in bought	Ď= a heavy D	É= like A in Bay	G= G in beige	ĥ= like an H with smaller air passage	I= I as in ink	Ќ= like ch in Irish loch
O= O as in home	OO= as in boots	R= roll the rrr	Ť= a heavy T	Ř= like a French R (gargle it)	Ŝ= a heavy S	Ž= a heavy Z

<u>S</u>
(see below)
To select / To chose

Present	
Ana	Bna''é
Inta	Btna''é
Inté	Btna''é
Hoowé	Bina''é
Heeyé	Btna''é
Naħna	mnna''é
Intoo	Btna''oo
Hinné	Bina''oo

Present Continuous		
Ana	Ăam	Bna''é
Inta	Ăam	Btna''é
Inté	Ăam	Btna''é
Hoowé	Ăam	Bina''é
Heeyé	Ăam	Btna''é
Naħna	Ăam	mnna''é
Intoo	Ăam	Btna''oo
Hinné	Ăam	Bina''oo

Past	
Ana	Na''ét
Inta	Na''ét
Inté	Na''aité
Hoowé	Na''a
Heeyé	Na''ét
Naħna	Na''aina
Intoo	Na''aitoo
Hinné	Na''oo

Past Continuous		
Ana	Kint Ăam	Bna''é
Inta	Kint Ăam	Btna''é
Inté	Kinté Ăam	Btna''é
Hoowé	Kén Ăam	Bina''é
Heeyé	Kénét Ăam	Btna''é
Naħna	Kinna Ăam	mnna''é
Intoo	Kintoo Ăam	Btna''oo
Hinné	Kénoo Ăam	Bina''oo

Future		
Ana	Laħ	Na''é
Inta	Laħ	Tna''é
Inté	Laħ	Tna''é
Hoowé	Laħ	yna''é
Heeyé	Laħ	Tna''é
Naħna	Laħ	nna''é
Intoo	Laħ	Tna''oo
Hinné	Laħ	yna''oo

Command	
Inta	Na''é
Inté	Na''é
Intoo	Na''oo
Inta	Ma tna''é
Inté	Ma tna''é
Intoo	Ma tna''oo

<u>S</u>
(see above)
To select/ To chose

Present	
Ana	biǨtar
Inta	btiǨtar
Inté	btiǨtaré
Hoowé	byiǨtar
Heeyé	btiǨtar
Naħna	mniǨtar
Intoo	btiǨtaroo
Hinné	byiǨtaroo

Present Continuous		
Ana	Ăam	biǨtar
Inta	Ăam	btiǨtar
Inté	Ăam	btiǨtaré
Hoowé	Ăam	byiǨtar
Heeyé	Ăam	btiǨtar
Naħna	Ăam	mniǨtar
Intoo	Ăam	btiǨtaroo
Hinné	Ăam	byiǨtaroo

Past	
Ana	Ǩtart
Inta	Ǩtart
Inté	Ǩtarté
Hoowé	Ǩtar
Heeyé	Ǩtarét
Naħna	Ǩtarna
Intoo	Ǩtartoo
Hinné	Ǩtaroo

Past Continuous		
Ana	Kint Ăam	biǨtar
Inta	Kint Ăam	btiǨtar
Inté	Kinté Ăam	btiǨtaré
Hoowé	Kén Ăam	byiǨtar
Heeyé	Kénét Ăam	btiǨtar
Naħna	Kinna Ăam	mniǨtar
Intoo	Kintoo Ăam	btiǨtaroo
Hinné	Kénoo Ăam	byiǨtaroo

Future		
Ana	Laħ	iǨtar
Inta	Laħ	tiǨtar
Inté	Laħ	tiǨtaré
Hoowé	Laħ	yiǨtar
Heeyé	Laħ	tiǨtar
Naħna	Laħ	niǨtar
Intoo	Laħ	tiǨtaroo
Hinné	Laħ	yiǨtaroo

Command	
Inta	Ǩtar
Inté	Ǩtaré
Intoo	Ǩtaroo
Inta	Ma tǨtar
Inté	Ma tǨtaré
Intoo	Ma tǨtaroo

Ă= Augh in bought	Ď= a heavy D	É= like A in Bay	G= G in beige	ħ= like an H with smaller air passage	I= I as in ink	Ǩ= like ch in Irish loch
O= O as in home	OO= as in boots	R= roll the rrr	Ť= a heavy T	Ř= like a French R (gargle it)	Š= a heavy S	Ž= a heavy Z

<u>S</u>   <u>S</u>

To sell   ## To send

Present	
Ana	bbeeĂ
Inta	btbeeĂ
Inté	btbeeĂé
Hoowé	bibeeĂ
Heeyé	btbeeĂ
Naĥna	mnbeeĂ
Intoo	btbeeĂoo
Hinné	bibeeĂoo

Present	
Ana	bibĂat
Inta	btibĂat
Inté	btibĂaté
Hoowé	byibĂat
Heeyé	btibĂat
Naĥna	mnibĂat
Intoo	btibĂatoo
Hinné	byibĂatoo

Present Continuous		
Ana	Ăam	bbeeĂ
Inta	Ăam	btbeeĂ
Inté	Ăam	btbeeĂé
Hoowé	Ăam	bibeeĂ
Heeyé	Ăam	btbeeĂ
Naĥna	Ăam	mnbeeĂ
Intoo	Ăam	btbeeĂoo
Hinné	Ăam	bibeeĂoo

Present Continuous			
Ana	Ăam	bibĂat	(béĂét/béĂté)
Inta	Ăam	btibĂat	(béĂét)
Inté	Ăam	btibĂaté	(béĂté)
Hoowé	Ăam	byibĂat	(béĂét)
Heeyé	Ăam	btibĂat	(béĂté)
Naĥna	Ăam	mnibĂat	(béĂteen)
Intoo	Ăam	btibĂatoo	(béĂteen)
Hinné	Ăam	byibĂatoo	(béĂteen)

Past	
Ana	biĂt
Inta	biĂt
Inté	biĂté
Hoowé	béĂ
Heeyé	béĂét
Naĥna	biĂna
Intoo	biĂtoo
Hinné	biĂoo

Past	
Ana	baĂatt
Inta	baĂatt
Inté	baĂatté
Hoowé	baĂatt
Heeyé	baĂtét
Naĥna	baĂattna
Intoo	baĂattoo
Hinné	baĂatoo

Past Continuous		
Ana	Kint Ăam	bbeeĂ
Inta	Kint Ăam	btbeeĂ
Inté	Kinté Ăam	btbeeĂé
Hoowé	Kén Ăam	bibeeĂ
Heeyé	Kénét Ăam	btbeeĂ
Naĥna	Kinna Ăam	mnbeeĂ
Intoo	Kintoo Ăam	btbeeĂoo
Hinné	Kénoo Ăam	bibeeĂoo

Past Continuous			
Ana	Kint Ăam	bibĂat	(kint béĂét/béĂté)
Inta	Kint Ăam	btibĂat	(Kint béĂét)
Inté	Kinté Ăam	btibĂaté	(Kinté béĂté)
Hoowé	Kén Ăam	byibĂat	(Kén béĂét)
Heeyé	Kénét Ăam	btibĂat	(Kénét béĂté)
Naĥna	Kinna Ăam	mnibĂat	(Kinna béĂteen)
Intoo	Kintoo Ăam	btibĂatoo	(Kintoo béĂteen)
Hinné	Kénoo Ăam	byibĂatoo	(Kénoo béĂteen)

Future		
Ana	Laĥ	beeĂ
Inta	Laĥ	tbeeĂ
Inté	Laĥ	tbeeĂé
Hoowé	Laĥ	ybeeĂ
Heeyé	Laĥ	tbeeĂ
Naĥna	Laĥ	nbeeĂ
Intoo	Laĥ	tbeeĂoo
Hinné	Laĥ	ybeeĂoo

Future		
Ana	Laĥ	ibĂat
Inta	Laĥ	tibĂat
Inté	Laĥ	tibĂaté
Hoowé	Laĥ	yibĂat
Heeyé	Laĥ	tibĂat
Naĥna	Laĥ	nibĂat
Intoo	Laĥ	tibĂatoo
Hinné	Laĥ	yibĂatoo

Command	
Inta	beeĂ
Inté	beeĂé
Intoo	beeĂoo
Inta	Ma tbeeĂ
Inté	Ma tbeeĂé
Intoo	Ma tbeeĂoo

Command	
Inta	bĂat
Inté	bĂaté
Intoo	bĂatoo
Inta	Ma tbĂat
Inté	Ma tbĂaté
Intoo	Ma tbĂatoo

Ă= Augh in bought	Ď= a heavy D	É= like A in Bay	G= G in beige	ĥ= like an H with smaller air passage	I= I as in ink	Ќ= like ch in Irish loch
O= O as in home	OO= as in boots	R= roll the rrr	Ť= a heavy T	Ř= like a French R (gargle it)	Š= a heavy S	Ž= a heavy Z

<u>S</u>   <u>S</u>

To seperate   To serve

Present	
Ana	Bfarré'
Inta	Btfarré'
Inté	Btfarr'é
Hoowé	Bifarré'
Heeyé	Btfarré'
Naĥna	mnfarré'
Intoo	Btfarr'oo
Hinné	Bifarr'oo

Present Continuous		
Ana	Ăam	Bfarré'
Inta	Ăam	Btfarré'
Inté	Ăam	Btfarr'é
Hoowé	Ăam	Bifarré'
Heeyé	Ăam	Btfarré'
Naĥna	Ăam	mnfarré'
Intoo	Ăam	Btfarr'oo
Hinné	Ăam	Bifarr'oo

Past	
Ana	Farra't
Inta	Farra't
Inté	Farra'té
Hoowé	Farra'
Heeyé	Farra'ét
Naĥna	Farra'na
Intoo	Farra'too
Hinné	Farra'oo

Past Continuous		
Ana	Kint Ăam	Bfarré'
Inta	Kint Ăam	Btfarré'
Inté	Kinté Ăam	Btfarr'é
Hoowé	Kén Ăam	Bifarré'
Heeyé	Kénét Ăam	Btfarré'
Naĥna	Kinna Ăam	mnfarré'
Intoo	Kintoo Ăam	Btfarr'oo
Hinné	Kénoo Ăam	Bifarr'oo

Future		
Ana	Laĥ	farré'
Inta	Laĥ	tfarré'
Inté	Laĥ	tfarr'é
Hoowé	Laĥ	yfarré'
Heeyé	Laĥ	tfarré'
Naĥna	Laĥ	nfarré'
Intoo	Laĥ	tfarr'oo
Hinné	Laĥ	yfarr'oo

Command	
Inta	Farré'
Inté	Farr'é
Intoo	Far'oo
Inta	Ma tfarré'
Inté	Ma tfarr'é
Intoo	Ma tfar'oo

Present	
Ana	biḰdom
Inta	btiḰdom
Inté	btiḰdmé
Hoowé	byiḰdom
Heeyé	btiḰdom
Naĥna	mniḰdom
Intoo	btiḰdmoo
Hinné	byiḰdmoo

Present Continuous		
Ana	Ăam	biḰdom
Inta	Ăam	btiḰdom
Inté	Ăam	btiḰdmé
Hoowé	Ăam	byiḰdom
Heeyé	Ăam	btiḰdom
Naĥna	Ăam	mniḰdom
Intoo	Ăam	btiḰdmoo
Hinné	Ăam	byiḰdmoo

Past	
Ana	Ḱadamt
Inta	Ḱadamt
Inté	Ḱadamté
Hoowé	Ḱadam
Heeyé	Ḱadamét
Naĥna	Ḱadamna
Intoo	Ḱadamtoo
Hinné	Ḱadamoo

Past Continuous		
Ana	Kint Ăam	biḰdom
Inta	Kint Ăam	btiḰdom
Inté	Kinté Ăam	btiḰdmé
Hoowé	Kén Ăam	byiḰdom
Heeyé	Kénét Ăam	btiḰdom
Naĥna	Kinna Ăam	mniḰdom
Intoo	Kintoo Ăam	btiḰdmoo
Hinné	Kénoo Ăam	byiḰdmoo

Future		
Ana	Laĥ	iḰdom
Inta	Laĥ	tiḰdom
Inté	Laĥ	tiḰdmé
Hoowé	Laĥ	yiḰdom
Heeyé	Laĥ	tiḰdom
Naĥna	Laĥ	niḰdom
Intoo	Laĥ	tiḰdmoo
Hinné	Laĥ	yiḰdmoo

Command	
Inta	Ḱdom
Inté	Ḱdimé
Intoo	Ḱdimoo
Inta	Ma tḰdom
Inté	Ma tḰdmé
Intoo	Ma tḰdmoo

Ă= Augh in bought	Ď= a heavy D	É= like A in Bay	G= G in beige	ĥ= like an H with smaller air passage	I= I as in ink	Ḱ= like ch in Irish loch
O= O as in home	OO= as in boots	R= roll the rrr	Ť= a heavy T	Ř= like a French R (gargle it)	Ŝ= a heavy S	Ž= a heavy Z

S̲
(see below)
To shake

Present	
Ana	Bhizz
Inta	Bthizz
Inté	Bthizzé
Hoowé	Bihizz
Heeyé	Bthizz
Naĥna	Mnhizz
Intoo	Bthizzoo
Hinné	Bihizzoo

Present Continuous		
Ana	Ăam	Bhizz
Inta	Ăam	Bthizz
Inté	Ăam	Bthizzé
Hoowé	Ăam	Bihizz
Heeyé	Ăam	Bthizz
Naĥna	Ăam	Mnhizz
Intoo	Ăam	Bthizzoo
Hinné	Ăam	Bihizzoo

Past	
Ana	Hazzét
Inta	Hazzét
Inté	Hazzaité
Hoowé	Hazz
Heeyé	Hazzét
Naĥna	Hazzaina
Intoo	Hazzaitoo
Hinné	Hazzoo

Past Continuous		
Ana	Kint Ăam	Bhizz
Inta	Kint Ăam	Bthizz
Inté	Kinté Ăam	Bthizzé
Hoowé	Kén Ăam	Bihizz
Heeyé	Kénét Ăam	Bthizz
Naĥna	Kinna Ăam	Mnhizz
Intoo	Kintoo Ăam	Bthizzoo
Hinné	Kénoo Ăam	Bihizzoo

Future		
Ana	Laĥ	Hizz
Inta	Laĥ	Thizz
Inté	Laĥ	Thizzé
Hoowé	Laĥ	Yhizz
Heeyé	Laĥ	Thizz
Naĥna	Laĥ	Nhizz
Intoo	Laĥ	Thizzoo
Hinné	Laĥ	Yhizzoo

Command	
Inta	Hizz
Inté	Hizzé
Intoo	Hizzoo
Inta	Ma thizz
Inté	Ma thizzé
Intoo	Ma thizzoo

S̲
(see above)
To shake

Present	
Ana	bḰiĎ
Inta	btḰiĎ
Inté	btḰiĎé
Hoowé	biḰiĎ
Heeyé	btḰiĎ
Naĥna	mnḰiĎ
Intoo	btḰiĎoo
Hinné	biḰiĎoo

Present Continuous		
Ana	Ăam	bḰiĎ
Inta	Ăam	btḰiĎ
Inté	Ăam	btḰiĎé
Hoowé	Ăam	biḰiĎ
Heeyé	Ăam	btḰiĎ
Naĥna	Ăam	mnḰiĎ
Intoo	Ăam	btḰiĎoo
Hinné	Ăam	biḰiĎoo

Past	
Ana	ḰiĎĎét
Inta	ḰiĎĎét
Inté	ḰiĎĎaité
Hoowé	ḰaĎĎ
Heeyé	ḰaĎĎét
Naĥna	ḰaĎĎaina
Intoo	ḰaĎĎaitoo
Hinné	ḰaĎĎoo

Past Continuous		
Ana	Kint Ăam	bḰiĎ
Inta	Kint Ăam	btḰiĎ
Inté	Kinté Ăam	btḰiĎé
Hoowé	Kén Ăam	biḰiĎ
Heeyé	Kénét Ăam	btḰiĎ
Naĥna	Kinna Ăam	mnḰiĎ
Intoo	Kintoo Ăam	btḰiĎoo
Hinné	Kénoo Ăam	biḰiĎoo

Future		
Ana	Laĥ	ḰiĎ
Inta	Laĥ	tḰiĎ
Inté	Laĥ	tḰiĎé
Hoowé	Laĥ	yḰiĎ
Heeyé	Laĥ	tḰiĎ
Naĥna	Laĥ	nḰiĎ
Intoo	Laĥ	tḰiĎoo
Hinné	Laĥ	yiḰiĎoo

Command	
Inta	ḰiĎ
Inté	ḰiĎé
Intoo	ḰiĎoo
Inta	Ma tḰiĎ
Inté	Ma tḰiĎé
Intoo	Ma tḰiĎoo

Ă= Augh in bought	Ď= a heavy D	É= like A in Bay	G= G in beige	ĥ= like an H with smaller air passage		I= I as in ink	Ḱ= like ch in Irish loch
O= O as in home	OO= as in boots	R= roll the rrr	Ť= a heavy T	Ř= like a French R (gargle it)		S̱= a heavy S	Ž= a heavy Z

S̲
(see below)
To share

S̲
(see above)
To share / To partner

Present	
Ana	Bit'aŜam
Inta	Btit'aŜam
Inté	Btit'aŜamé
Hoowé	Byit'aŜam
Heeyé	Btit'aŜam
Naḣna	Mnit'aŜam
Intoo	Btit'aŜamoo
Hinné	Byit'aŜamoo

Present	
Ana	Bshérék
Inta	Btshérék
Inté	Btshérké
Hoowé	Bishérék
Heeyé	Btshérék
Naḣna	Mnshérék
Intoo	Btshérkoo
Hinné	Bishérkoo

Present Continuous		
Ana	Ăam	Bit'aŜam
Inta	Ăam	Btit'aŜam
Inté	Ăam	Btit'aŜamé
Hoowé	Ăam	Byit'aŜam
Heeyé	Ăam	Dtit'aŜam
Naḣna	Ăam	Mnit'aŜam
Intoo	Ăam	Btit'aŜamoo
Hinné	Ăam	Byit'aŜamoo

Present Continuous			
Ana	Ăam	Bshérék	(mahérak/mshérké)
Inta	Ăam	Btshérék	(mahérak)
Inté	Ăam	Btshérké	(mshérké)
Hoowé	Ăam	Bishérék	(mahérak)
Heeyé	Ăam	Btshérék	(mshérké)
Naḣna	Ăam	mnshérék	(mshérkeen)
Intoo	Ăam	Btshérkoo	(mshérkeen)
Hinné	Ăam	Bishérkoo	(mshérkeen)

Past	
Ana	T'aŜamt
Inta	T'aŜamt
Inté	T'aŜamté
Hoowé	T'aŜam
Heeyé	T'aŜamét
Naḣna	T'aŜamna
Intoo	T'aŜamtoo
Hinné	T'aŜamoo

Past	
Ana	Shérakt
Inta	Shérakt
Inté	Shérakté
Hoowé	Shérak
Heeyé	Shérakét
Naḣna	Shérakna
Intoo	Shéraktoo
Hinné	Shérakoo

Past Continuous		
Ana	Kint Ăam	Bit'aŜam
Inta	Kint Ăam	Btit'aŜam
Inté	Kinté Ăam	Btit'aŜamé
Hoowé	Kén Ăam	Byit'aŜam
Heeyé	Kénét Ăam	Btit'aŜam
Naḣna	Kinna Ăam	Mnit'aŜam
Intoo	Kintoo Ăam	Btit'aŜamoo
Hinné	Kénoo Ăam	Byit'aŜamoo

Past Continuous				
Ana	Kint Ăam	Bshérék	(kint	mahérak/mshérké)
Inta	Kint Ăam	Btshérék	(Kint	Mahérak)
Inté	Kinté Ăam	Btshérké	(Kinté	mshérké)
Hoowé	Kén Ăam	Bishérék	(Kén	Mahérak)
Heeyé	Kénét Ăam	Btshérék	(Kénét	mshérké)
Naḣna	Kinna Ăam	Mnshérék	(Kinna	mshérkeen)
Intoo	Kintoo Ăam	Btshérkoo	(Kintoo	mshérkeen)
Hinné	Kénoo Ăam	Bishérkoo	(Kénoo	mshérkeen)

Future		
Ana	Laḣ	it'aŜam
Inta	Laḣ	tit'aŜam
Inté	Laḣ	tit'aŜamé
Hoowé	Laḣ	yit'aŜam
Heeyé	Laḣ	tit'aŜam
Naḣna	Laḣ	nit'aŜam
Intoo	Laḣ	tit'aŜamoo
Hinné	Laḣ	yit'aŜamoo

Future		
Ana	Laḣ	Shérék
Inta	Laḣ	Tshérék
Inté	Laḣ	Tshérké
Hoowé	Laḣ	Yshérék
Heeyé	Laḣ	Tshérék
Naḣna	Laḣ	Nshérék
Intoo	Laḣ	Tshérkoo
Hinné	Laḣ	Yshérkoo

Command	
Inta	T'aŜam
Inté	T'aŜamé
Intoo	T'aŜamoo
Inta	Ma tT'aŜam
Inté	Ma tT'aŜmé
Intoo	Ma tT'aŜmoo

Command	
Inta	Shérék
Inté	Shérké
Intoo	Shérkoo
Inta	Ma tshérék
Inté	Ma tshérké
Intoo	Ma tshérkoo

Ă= Augh in bought	Ď= a heavy D	É= like A in Bay	G= G in beige	ḣ= like an H with smaller air passage	I= I as in ink	Ḱ= like ch in Irish loch
O= O as in home	OO= as in boots	R= roll the rrr	Ť= a heavy T	Ř= like a French R (gargle it)	Ŝ= a heavy S	Ž= a heavy Z

<u>S</u>   <u>S</u>

To shine   ## To shoot

Present	
Ana	bilmaĂ
Inta	btilmaĂ
Inté	btilmaĂé
Hoowé	byilmaĂ
Heeyé	btilmaĂ
Naĥna	mnilmaĂ
Intoo	btilmaĂoo
Hinné	byilmaĂoo

Present Continuous		
Ana	Ăam	bilmaĂ
Inta	Ăam	btilmaĂ
Inté	Ăam	btilmaĂé
Hoowé	Ăam	byilmaĂ
Heeyé	Ăam	btilmaĂ
Naĥna	Ăam	mnilmaĂ
Intoo	Ăam	btilmaĂoo
Hinné	Ăam	byilmaĂoo

Past	
Ana	lamaĂt
Inta	lamaĂt
Inté	lamaĂté
Hoowé	lamaĂ
Heeyé	lamaĂét
Naĥna	lamaĂna
Intoo	lamaĂtoo
Hinné	lamaĂoo

Past Continuous		
Ana	Kint Ăam	bilmaĂ
Inta	Kint Ăam	btilmaĂ
Inté	Kinté Ăam	btilmaĂé
Hoowé	Kén Ăam	byilmaĂ
Heeyé	Kénét Ăam	btilmaĂ
Naĥna	Kinna Ăam	mnilmaĂ
Intoo	Kintoo Ăam	btilmaĂoo
Hinné	Kénoo Ăam	byilmaĂoo

Future		
Ana	Laĥ	ilmaĂ
Inta	Laĥ	tilmaĂ
Inté	Laĥ	tilmaĂé
Hoowé	Laĥ	yilmaĂ
Heeyé	Laĥ	tilmaĂ
Naĥna	Laĥ	nilmaĂ
Intoo	Laĥ	tilmaĂoo
Hinné	Laĥ	yilmaĂoo

Command	
Inta	lmaĂ
Inté	laĂé
Intoo	lmaĂoo
Inta	Ma tlmaĂ
Inté	Ma tlmaĂé
Intoo	Ma tlmaĂoo

Present	
Ana	B'awwéŜ
Inta	Bt'awwéŜ
Inté	Bt'awwéŜé
Hoowé	Bi'awwéŜ
Heeyé	Bt'awwéŜ
Naĥna	Mn'awwéŜ
Intoo	Bt'awwŜoo
Hinné	Bi'awwŜoo

Present Continuous		
Ana	Ăam	B'awwéŜ
Inta	Ăam	Bt'awwéŜ
Inté	Ăam	Bt'awwŜé
Hoowé	Ăam	Bi'awwéŜ
Heeyé	Ăam	Bt'awwéŜ
Naĥna	Ăam	Mn'awwéŜ
Intoo	Ăam	Bt'awwŜoo
Hinné	Ăam	Bi'awwŜoo

Past	
Ana	awwaŜt
Inta	awwaŜt
Inté	awwaŜté
Hoowé	awwaŜ
Heeyé	awwaŜét
Naĥna	awwaŜna
Intoo	awwaŜtoo
Hinné	awwaŜoo

Past Continuous		
Ana	Kint Ăam	B'awwéŜ
Inta	Kint Ăam	Bt'awwéŜ
Inté	Kinté Ăam	Bt'awwŜé
Hoowé	Kén Ăam	Bi'awwéŜ
Heeyé	Kénét Ăam	Bt'awwéŜ
Naĥna	Kinna Ăam	Mn'awwéŜ
Intoo	Kintoo Ăam	Bt'awwŜoo
Hinné	Kénoo Ăam	Bi'awwŜoo

Future		
Ana	Laĥ	'awwéŜ
Inta	Laĥ	T'awwéŜ
Inté	Laĥ	T'awwŜé
Hoowé	Laĥ	Y'awwéŜ
Heeyé	Laĥ	T'awwéŜ
Naĥna	Laĥ	N'awwéŜ
Intoo	Laĥ	T'awwŜoo
Hinné	Laĥ	Y'awwŜoo

Command	
Inta	awwéŜ
Inté	awwŜé
Intoo	awwŜoo
Inta	Ma t'awwéŜ
Inté	Ma t'awwŜé
Intoo	Ma t'awwŜoo

Ă= Augh in bought	Đ= a heavy D	É= like A in Bay	G= G in beige	ĥ= like an H with smaller air passage	I= I as in ink	Ќ= like ch in Irish loch
O= O as in home	OO= as in boots	R= roll the rrr	Ŧ= a heavy T	Ř= like a French R (gargle it)	Ŝ= a heavy S	Ž= a heavy Z

S̲

S̲

To show

Present	
Ana	Bfargé
Inta	Btfargé
Inté	Btfargé
Hoowé	Bifargé
Heeyé	Btfargé
Nahna	Mnfargé
Intoo	Btfargoo
Hinné	Bifargoo

Present Continuous		
Ana	Ăam	Bfargé
Inta	Ăam	Btfargé
Inté	Ăam	Btfargé
Hoowé	Ăam	Bifargé
Heeyé	Ăam	Btfargé
Nahna	Ăam	Mnfargé
Intoo	Ăam	Btfargoo
Hinné	Ăam	Bifargoo

Past	
Ana	fargét
Inta	fargét
Inté	Fargaité
Hoowé	Farga
Heeyé	fargét
Nahna	Fargaina
Intoo	Fargaitoo
Hinné	Fargoo

Past Continuous		
Ana	Kint Ăam	Bfargé
Inta	Kint Ăam	Btfargé
Inté	Kinté Ăam	Btfargé
Hoowé	Kén Ăam	Bifargé
Heeyé	Kénét Ăam	Btfargé
Nahna	Kinna Ăam	Mnfargé
Intoo	Kintoo Ăam	Btfargoo
Hinné	Kénoo Ăam	Bifargoo

Future		
Ana	Laĥ	fargé
Inta	Laĥ	tfargé
Inté	Laĥ	tfargé
Hoowé	Laĥ	yfargé
Heeyé	Laĥ	tfargé
Nahna	Laĥ	nfargé
Intoo	Laĥ	tfargoo
Hinné	Laĥ	yfargoo

Command	
Inta	Fargé
Inté	Fargé
Intoo	Fargoo
Inta	Ma tfargé
Inté	Ma tfargé
Intoo	Ma tfargoo

To shower

Present	
Ana	Bitĥammam
Inta	Btitĥammam
Inté	Btitĥammamé
Hoowé	Byitĥammam
Heeyé	Btitĥammam
Nahna	Mnitĥammam
Intoo	Btitĥammamoo
Hinné	Byitĥammamoo

Present Continuous		
Ana	Ăam	Bitĥammam
Inta	Ăam	Btitĥammam
Inté	Ăam	Btitĥammamé
Hoowé	Ăam	Byitĥammam
Heeyé	Ăam	Btitĥammam
Nahna	Ăam	Mnitĥammam
Intoo	Ăam	Btitĥammamoo
Hinné	Ăam	Byitĥammamoo

Past	
Ana	tĥammamt
Inta	tĥammamt
Inté	Tĥammamté
Hoowé	Tĥammam
Heeyé	tĥammamét
Nahna	Tĥammamna
Intoo	Tĥammamtoo
Hinné	Tĥammamoo

Past Continuous		
Ana	Kint Ăam	Bitĥammam
Inta	Kint Ăam	Btitĥammam
Inté	Kinté Ăam	Btitĥammamé
Hoowé	Kén Ăam	Byitĥammam
Heeyé	Kénét Ăam	Btitĥammam
Nahna	Kinna Ăam	Mnitĥammam
Intoo	Kintoo Ăam	Btitĥammamoo
Hinné	Kénoo Ăam	Byitĥammamoo

Future		
Ana	Laĥ	itĥammam
Inta	Laĥ	titĥammam
Inté	Laĥ	titĥammamé
Hoowé	Laĥ	yitĥammam
Heeyé	Laĥ	titĥammam
Nahna	Laĥ	nitĥammam
Intoo	Laĥ	titĥammamoo
Hinné	Laĥ	yitĥammamoo

Command	
Inta	tĥammam
Inté	Tĥammamé
Intoo	Tĥammamoo
Inta	Ma ttĥammam
Inté	Ma ttĥammamé
Intoo	Ma ttĥammamoo

Ă= Augh in bought	Ď= a heavy D	É= like A in Bay	G= G in beige	ĥ= like an H with smaller air passage	I= I as in ink	Ḱ= like ch in Irish loch
O= O as in home	OO= as in boots	R= roll the rrr	Ť= a heavy T	Ř= like a French R (gargle it)	Š= a heavy S	Ž= a heavy Z

<u>S</u>   <u>S</u>

To shrink

Present

Ana	Bzimm
Inta	Btzimm
Inté	Btzimmé
Hoowé	Bizimm
Heeyé	Btzimm
Nahna	Mnzimm
Intoo	Btzimmoo
Hinné	Bizimmoo

Present Continuous

Ana	Ăam	Bzimm	(zémém/zémmé)
Inta	Ăam	Btzimm	(zémém)
Inté	Ăam	Btzimmé	(zémmé)
Hoowé	Ăam	Bizimm	(zémém)
Heeyé	Ăam	Btzimm	(zémmé)
Nahna	Ăam	Mnzimm	(zémmeen)
Intoo	Ăam	Btzimmoo	(zémmeen)
Hinné	Ăam	Bizimmoo	(zémmeen)

Past

Ana	Zammét
Inta	Zammét
Inté	Zammaité
Hoowé	Zamm
Heeyé	Zammét
Nahna	Zammaina
Intoo	Zammaitoo
Hinné	Zammoo

Past Continuous

Ana	Kint Ăam	Bzimm	(kint	zémém/zémmé)
Inta	Kint Ăam	Btzimm	(Kint	zémém)
Inté	Kinté Ăam	Btzimmé	(Kinté	zémmé)
Hoowé	Kén Ăam	Bizimm	(Kén	zémém)
Heeyé	Kénét Ăam	Btzimm	(Kénét zémmé)	
Nahna	Kinna Ăam	Mnzimm	(Kinna zémmeen)	
Intoo	Kintoo Ăam	Btzimmoo	(Kintoo zémmeen)	
Hinné	Kénoo Ăam	Bizimmoo	(Kénoo zémmeen)	

Future

Ana	Lah	Zimm
Inta	Lah	Tzimm
Inté	Lah	Tzimmé
Hoowé	Lah	Yzimm
Heeyé	Lah	Tzimm
Nahna	Lah	Nzimm
Intoo	Lah	tzimmoo
Hinné	Lah	yzimmoo

Command

Inta	Zimm
Inté	Zimmé
Intoo	Zimmoo
Inta	Ma tzimm
Inté	Ma tzimmé
Intoo	Ma tzimmoo

To sit

Present

Ana	B'Ăod
Inta	Bt'Ăod
Inté	Bt'Ădé
Hoowé	Bi'Ăod
Heeyé	Bt'Ăod
Nahna	Mn'Ăod
Intoo	bt'Ădoo
Hinné	Bi'Ădoo

Present Continuous

Ana	Ăam	B'Ăod	('aĂéd/'aĂdé)
Inta	Ăam	Bt'Ăod	('aĂéd)
Inté	Ăam	Bt'Ădé	('aĂdé)
Hoowé	Ăam	Bi'Ăod	('aĂéd)
Heeyé	Ăam	Bt'Ăod	('aĂdé)
Nahna	Ăam	Mn'Ăod	('aĂdeen)
Intoo	Ăam	bt'Ădoo	('aĂdeen)
Hinné	Ăam	Bi'Ădoo	('aĂdeen)

Past

Ana	aĂadit
Inta	aĂadit
Inté	aĂadté
Hoowé	aĂad
Heeyé	aĂadét
Nahna	aĂadna
Intoo	aĂadtoo
Hinné	aĂadoo

Past Continuous

Ana	Kint Ăam	B'Ăod	(kint	'aĂéd/'aĂdé)
Inta	Kint Ăam	Bt'Ăod	(Kint	'aĂéd)
Inté	Kinté Ăam	Bt'Ădé	(Kinté	'aĂdé)
Hoowé	Kén Ăam	Bi'Ăod	(Kén	'aĂéd)
Heeyé	Kénét Ăam	Bt'Ăod	(Kénét	'aĂdé)
Nahna	Kinna Ăam	Mn'Ăod	(Kinna 'aĂdeen)	
Intoo	Kintoo Ăam	bt'Ădoo	(Kintoo 'aĂdeen)	
Hinné	Kénoo Ăam	Bi'Ădoo	(Kénoo 'aĂdeen)	

Future

Ana	Lah	I'Ăod
Inta	Lah	Ti'Ăod
Inté	Lah	Ti'Ăadé
Hoowé	Lah	Yi'Ăod
Heeyé	Lah	Ti'Ăod
Nahna	Lah	Ni'Ăod
Intoo	Lah	Ti'Ăadoo
Hinné	Lah	Yi'Ăadoo

Command

Inta	'Ăod
Inté	'Ăadé
Intoo	'Ăadoo
Inta	Ma t'Ăod
Inté	Ma t'Ăadé
Intoo	Ma t'Ăadoo

Ă= Augh in bought	Ď= a heavy D	É= like A in Bay	G= G in beige	ĥ= like an H with smaller air passage	I= I as in ink	Ќ= like ch in Irish loch
O= O as in home	OO= as in boots	R= roll the rrr	Ť= a heavy T	Ř= like a French R (gargle it)	Ŝ= a heavy S	Ž= a heavy Z

S̲   S̲

To sin / To err

Present

Ana	biK̓ṱé
Inta	btiK̓ṱé
Inté	btiK̓ṱé
Hoowé	byiK̓ṱé
Heeyé	btiK̓ṱé
Naẖna	mniK̓ṱé
Intoo	btiK̓ṱoo
Hinné	byiK̓ṱoo

Present Continuous

Ana	Ăam	biK̓ṱé	(K̓aṱé/K̓aṱyé)
Inta	Ăam	btiK̓ṱé	(K̓aṱé)
Inté	Ăam	btiK̓ṱé	(K̓aṱyé)
Hoowé	Ăam	byiK̓ṱé	(K̓aṱé)
Heeyé	Ăam	btiK̓ṱé	(K̓aṱyé)
Naẖna	Ăam	mniK̓ṱé	(K̓aṱyeen)
Intoo	Ăam	btiK̓ṱoo	(K̓aṱyeen)
Hinné	Ăam	byiK̓ṱoo	(K̓aṱyeen)

Past

Ana	K̓ṱeet
Inta	K̓ṱeet
Inté	K̓ṱeeté
Hoowé	K̓iṱé
Heeyé	K̓iṱyét
Naẖna	K̓ṱeena
Intoo	K̓ṱeetoo
Hinné	K̓iṱyoo

Past Continuous

Ana	Kint Ăam	biK̓ṱé	(kint K̓aṱé/K̓aṱyé)
Inta	Kint Ăam	btiK̓ṱé	(Kint K̓aṱé)
Inté	Kinté Ăam	btiK̓ṱé	(Kinté K̓aṱyé)
Hoowé	Kén Ăam	byiK̓ṱé	(Kén K̓aṱé)
Heeyé	Kénét Ăam	btiK̓ṱé	(Kénét K̓aṱyé)
Naẖna	Kinna Ăam	mniK̓ṱé	(Kinna K̓aṱyeen)
Intoo	Kintoo Ăam	btiK̓ṱoo	(Kintoo K̓aṱyeen)
Hinné	Kénoo Ăam	byiK̓ṱoo	(Kénoo K̓aṱyeen)

Future

Ana	Laẖ	iK̓ṱé
Inta	Laẖ	tiK̓ṱé
Inté	Laẖ	tiK̓ṱé
Hoowé	Laẖ	yiK̓ṱé
Heeyé	Laẖ	tiK̓ṱé
Naẖna	Laẖ	niK̓ṱé
Intoo	Laẖ	tiK̓ṱoo
Hinné	Laẖ	yiK̓ṱoo

Command

Inta	K̓ṱee
Inté	K̓ṱee
Intoo	K̓ṱoo
Inta	Ma tK̓ṱé
Inté	Ma tK̓ṱé
Intoo	Ma tK̓ṱoo

To skate / To ski

Present

Ana	bitzallag
Inta	btitzallag
Inté	Btitzallagé
Hoowé	byitzallag
Heeyé	btitzallag
Naẖna	mnitzallag
Intoo	Btitzallagoo
Hinné	byitzallagoo

Present Continuous

Ana	Ăam	bitzallag
Inta	Ăam	btitzallag
Inté	Ăam	Btitzallagé
Hoowé	Ăam	byitzallag
Heeyé	Ăam	btitzallag
Naẖna	Ăam	mnitzallag
Intoo	Ăam	Btitzallagoo
Hinné	Ăam	byitzallagoo

Past

Ana	Tzallagt
Inta	Tzallagt
Inté	Tzallagté
Hoowé	Tzallag
Heeyé	Tzallagét
Naẖna	Tzallagna
Intoo	Tzallagtoo
Hinné	Tzallagoo

Past Continuous

Ana	Kint Ăam	bitzallag
Inta	Kint Ăam	btitzallag
Inté	Kinté Ăam	Btitzallagé
Hoowé	Kén Ăam	byitzallag
Heeyé	Kénét Ăam	btitzallag
Naẖna	Kinna Ăam	mnitzallag
Intoo	Kintoo Ăam	Btitzallagoo
Hinné	Kénoo Ăam	byitzallagoo

Future

Ana	Laẖ	itzallag
Inta	Laẖ	titzallag
Inté	Laẖ	titzallagé
Hoowé	Laẖ	yitzallag
Heeyé	Laẖ	titzallag
Naẖna	Laẖ	nitzallag
Intoo	Laẖ	titzallagoo
Hinné	Laẖ	yitzallagoo

Command

Inta	Tzallag
Inté	Tzallagé
Intoo	Tzallagoo
Inta	Ma ttzallag
Inté	Ma ttzallagé
Intoo	Ma ttzallagoo

Ă= Augh in bought	Ď= a heavy D	É= like A in Bay	G= G in beige	ẖ= like an H with smaller air passage	I= I as in ink	K̓= like ch in Irish loch
O= O as in home	OO= as in boots	R= roll the rrr	Ṱ= a heavy T	Ř= like a French R (gargle it)	Ŝ= a heavy S	Ž= a heavy Z

S̲   S̲

To skip   To slam

Present	
Ana	B'affé
Inta	Bt'affé
Inté	Bt'affé
Hoowé	Bi'affé
Heeyé	Bt'affé
Nahna	Mn'affé
Intoo	Bt'affoo
Hinné	Bi'affoo

Present	
Ana	biK̇boṪ
Inta	btiK̇boṪ
Inté	btiK̇bṪé
Hoowé	byiK̇boṪ
Heeyé	btiK̇boṪ
Nahna	mniK̇boṪ
Intoo	btiK̇bṪoo
Hinné	byiK̇bṪoo

Present Continuous		
Ana	Ăam	B'affé
Inta	Ăam	Bt'affé
Inté	Ăam	Bt'affé
Hoowé	Ăam	Bi'affé
Heeyé	Ăam	Bt'affé
Nahna	Ăam	Mn'affé
Intoo	Ăam	Bt'affoo
Hinné	Ăam	Bi'affoo

Present Continuous		
Ana	Ăam	biK̇boṪ
Inta	Ăam	btiK̇boṪ
Inté	Ăam	btiK̇bṪé
Hoowé	Ăam	byiK̇boṪ
Heeyé	Ăam	btiK̇boṪ
Nahna	Ăam	mniK̇boṪ
Intoo	Ăam	btiK̇bṪoo
Hinné	Ăam	byiK̇bṪoo

Past	
Ana	'affét
Inta	'affét
Inté	'affaité
Hoowé	'affa
Heeyé	'affét
Nahna	'affaina
Intoo	'affaitoo
Hinné	'affoo

Past	
Ana	K̇abaṪét
Inta	K̇abaṪét
Inté	K̇abaṪté
Hoowé	K̇abaṪ
Heeyé	K̇abaṪét
Nahna	K̇abaṪna
Intoo	K̇abaṪtoo
Hinné	K̇abaṪtoo

Past Continuous		
Ana	Kint Ăam	B'affé
Inta	Kint Ăam	Bt'affé
Inté	Kinté Ăam	Bt'affé
Hoowé	Kén Ăam	Bi'affé
Heeyé	Kénét Ăam	Bt'affé
Nahna	Kinna Ăam	Mn'affé
Intoo	Kintoo Ăam	Bt'affoo
Hinné	Kénoo Ăam	Bi'affoo

Past Continuous		
Ana	Kint Ăam	biK̇boṪ
Inta	Kint Ăam	btiK̇boṪ
Inté	Kinté Ăam	btiK̇bṪé
Hoowé	Kén Ăam	byiK̇boṪ
Heeyé	Kénét Ăam	btiK̇boṪ
Nahna	Kinna Ăam	mniK̇boṪ
Intoo	Kintoo Ăam	btiK̇bṪoo
Hinné	Kénoo Ăam	byiK̇bṪoo

Future		
Ana	Laĥ	'affé
Inta	Laĥ	t'affé
Inté	Laĥ	t'affé
Hoowé	Laĥ	Y'affé
Heeyé	Laĥ	t'affé
Nahna	Laĥ	n'affé
Intoo	Laĥ	t'affoo
Hinné	Laĥ	y'affoo

Future		
Ana	Laĥ	iK̇boṪ
Inta	Laĥ	tiK̇boṪ
Inté	Laĥ	tiK̇bṪé
Hoowé	Laĥ	yiK̇boṪ
Heeyé	Laĥ	tiK̇boṪ
Nahna	Laĥ	niK̇boṪ
Intoo	Laĥ	tiK̇bṪoo
Hinné	Laĥ	yiK̇bṪoo

Command	
Inta	affé
Inté	Affé
Intoo	Affoo
Inta	Ma t'affé
Inté	Ma t'affé
Intoo	Ma t'affoo

Command	
Inta	K̇boṪ
Inté	K̇biṪé
Intoo	K̇biṪoo
Inta	Ma tK̇boṪ
Inté	Ma tK̇bṪé
Intoo	Ma tK̇bṪoo

Ă= Augh in bought	Ď= a heavy D	É= like A in Bay	G= G in beige	ĥ= like an H with smaller air passage	I= I as in ink	K̇= like ch in Irish loch
O= O as in home	OO= as in boots	R= roll the rrr	Ṫ= a heavy T	Ř= like a French R (gargle it)	Š= a heavy S	Ž= a heavy Z

S̲

S̲

To slap

Present

Ana	biŜfaĂ
Inta	btiŜfaĂ
Inté	btiŜfaĂé
Hoowé	byiŜfaĂ
Heeyé	btiŜfaĂ
Naĥna	mniŜfaĂ
Intoo	btiŜfaĂoo
Hinné	byiŜfaĂoo

Present Continuous

Ana	Ăam	biŜfaĂ
Inta	Ăam	btiŜfaĂ
Inté	Ăam	btiŜfaĂé
Hoowé	Ăam	byiŜfaĂ
Heeyé	Ăam	btiŜfaĂ
Naĥna	Ăam	mniŜfaĂ
Intoo	Ăam	btiŜfaĂoo
Hinné	Ăam	byiŜfaĂoo

Past

Ana	ŜafaĂt
Inta	ŜafaĂt
Inté	ŜafaĂté
Hoowé	ŜafaĂ
Heeyé	ŜafaĂét
Naĥna	ŜafaĂna
Intoo	ŜafaĂtoo
Hinné	ŜafaĂoo

Past Continuous

Ana	Kint Ăam	biŜfaĂ	
Inta	Kint Ăam	btiŜfaĂ	
Inté	Kinté Ăam	btiŜfaĂé	
Hoowé	Kén Ăam	byiŜfaĂ	
Heeyé	Kénét Ăam	btiŜfaĂ	
Naĥna	Kinna Ăam	mniŜfaĂ	
Intoo	Kintoo Ăam	btiŜfaĂoo	
Hinné	Kénoo Ăam	byiŜfaĂoo	

Future

Ana	Laĥ	iŜfaĂ
Inta	Laĥ	tiŜfaĂ
Inté	Laĥ	tiŜfaĂé
Hoowé	Laĥ	yiŜfaĂ
Heeyé	Laĥ	tiŜfaĂ
Naĥna	Laĥ	niŜfaĂ
Intoo	Laĥ	tiŜfaĂoo
Hinné	Laĥ	yiŜfaĂoo

Command

Inta	SfaĂ
Inté	SfaĂé
Intoo	SfaĂoo
Inta	Ma tSfaĂ
Inté	Ma tSfaĂé
Intoo	Ma tSfaĂoo

To sleep

Present

Ana	Bném
Inta	Btném
Inté	Btnémé
Hoowé	Biném
Heeyé	Btném
Naĥna	Mnném
Intoo	Btnémoo
Hinné	Binémoo

Present Continuous

Ana	Ăam	Bném	(néyém/néymé)
Inta	Ăam	Btném	(néyém)
Inté	Ăam	Btnémé	(néymé)
Hoowé	Ăam	Biném	(néyém)
Heeyé	Ăam	Btném	(néymé)
Naĥna	Ăam	Mnném	(néymeen)
Intoo	Ăam	Btnémoo	(néymeen)
Hinné	Ăam	Binémoo	(néymeen)

Past

Ana	Nimt
Inta	Nimt
Inté	Nimté
Hoowé	Ném
Heeyé	Némét
Naĥna	Nimna
Intoo	Nimtoo
Hinné	Némoo

Past Continuous

Ana	Kint Ăam	Bném	(kint	(néyém/néymé)
Inta	Kint Ăam	Btném	(Kint	(néyém)
Inté	Kinté Ăam	Btnémé	(Kinté	(néymé)
Hoowé	Kén Ăam	Biném	(Kén	(néyém)
Heeyé	Kénét Ăam	Btném	(Kénét	(néymé)
Naĥna	Kinna Ăam	Mnném	(Kinna	(néymeen)
Intoo	Kintoo Ăam	Btnémoo	(Kintoo	(néymeen)
Hinné	Kénoo Ăam	Binémoo	(Kénoo	(néymeen)

Future

Ana	Laĥ	Ném
Inta	Laĥ	Tném
Inté	Laĥ	Tnémé
Hoowé	Laĥ	Yném
Heeyé	Laĥ	Tném
Naĥna	Laĥ	Nném
Intoo	Laĥ	Tnémoo
Hinné	Laĥ	Ynémoo

Command

Inta	Ném
Inté	Némé
Intoo	Némoo
Inta	Ma tném
Inté	Ma tnémé
Intoo	Ma tnémoo

Ă= Augh in bought	Ď= a heavy D	É= like A in Bay	G= G in beige	ĥ= like an H with smaller air passage	I= I as in ink	Ḱ= like ch in Irish loch
O= O as in home	OO= as in boots	R= roll the rrr	Ť= a heavy T	Ř= like a French R (gargle it)	Ŝ= a heavy S	Ž= a heavy Z

S̲   S̲

To slice

Present	
Ana	Bsharréh
Inta	Btsharréh
Inté	Btsharrĥé
Hoowé	Bisharréh
Heeyé	Btsharréh
Naĥna	Mnsharréh
Intoo	Btsharrĥoo
Hinné	Bisharrĥoo

Present Continuous		
Ana	Ăam	Bsharréh
Inta	Ăam	Btsharréh
Inté	Ăam	Btsharrĥé
Hoowé	Ăam	Bisharréh
Heeyé	Ăam	Btsharréh
Naĥna	Ăam	Mnsharréh
Intoo	Ăam	Btsharrĥoo
Hinné	Ăam	Bisharrĥoo

Past	
Ana	sharraĥt
Inta	sharraĥt
Inté	Sharraĥté
Hoowé	Sharraĥ
Heeyé	sharraĥét
Naĥna	Sharraĥna
Intoo	Sharraĥtoo
Hinné	sharraĥoo

Past Continuous		
Ana	Kint Ăam	Bsharréh
Inta	Kint Ăam	Btsharréh
Inté	Kinté Ăam	Btsharrĥé
Hoowé	Kén Ăam	Bisharréh
Heeyé	Kénét Ăam	Btsharréh
Naĥna	Kinna Ăam	Mnsharréh
Intoo	Kintoo Ăam	Btsharrĥoo
Hinné	Kénoo Ăam	Bisharrĥoo

Future		
Ana	Laĥ	sharréh
Inta	Laĥ	tsharréh
Inté	Laĥ	tsharrĥé
Hoowé	Laĥ	ysharréh
Heeyé	Laĥ	tsharréh
Naĥna	Laĥ	nsharréh
Intoo	Laĥ	tsharrĥoo
Hinné	Laĥ	ysharrĥoo

Command	
Inta	sharréh
Inté	Sharrĥé
Intoo	Sharĥoo
Inta	Ma tsharréh
Inté	Ma tsharrĥé
Intoo	Ma tsharĥoo

To smell

Present	
Ana	Bshim
Inta	Btshim
Inté	Btshimmé
Hoowé	Bishim
Heeyé	Btshim
Naĥna	Mnshim
Intoo	Btshimmoo
Hinné	Bishimmoo

Present Continuous	
Ana	Ăam Bshim
Inta	Ăam Btshim
Inté	Ăam Btshimmé
Hoowé	Ăam Bishim
Heeyé	Ăam Btshim
Naĥna	Ăam Mnshim
Intoo	Ăam Btshimmoo
Hinné	Ăam Bishimmoo

Past	
Ana	Shammét
Inta	Shammét
Inté	Shamméité
Hoowé	Sham
Heeyé	Shammét
Naĥna	Shammayna
Intoo	Shammaytoo
Hinné	Shammoo

Past Continuous	
Ana	Kint Ăam shim
Inta	Kint Ăam btshim
Inté	Kinté Ăam Btshimmé
Hoowé	Kén Ăam bishim
Heeyé	Kénét Ăam Btshim
Naĥna	Kinna Ăam Mnshim
Intoo	Kintoo Ăam btshimmoo
Hinné	Kénoo Ăam bishimmoo

Future	
Ana	Laĥ shim
Inta	Laĥ tshim
Inté	Laĥ tshimme
Hoowé	Laĥ yshim
Heeyé	Laĥ tshim
Naĥna	Laĥ nshim
Intoo	Laĥ tshimmoo
Hinné	Laĥ yshimmoo

Command	
Inta	Shim
Inté	Shimmé
Intoo	Shimmoo
Inta	Ma tshim
Inté	Ma tshimmé
Intoo	Ma tshimmoo

Ă= Augh in bought	Ď= a heavy D	É= like A in Bay	G= G in beige	ĥ= like an H with smaller air passage	I= I as in ink	Ќ= like ch in Irish loch
O= O as in home	OO= as in boots	R= roll the rrr	Ť= a heavy T	Ř= like a French R (gargle it)	Š= a heavy S	Ž= a heavy Z

S̲   S̲

To smile

Present

Ana	Bibtisém
Inta	Btibtisém
Inté	Btibtismé
Hoowé	Byibtisém
Heeyé	Btibtisém
Naḣna	Mnibtisém
Intoo	Btibtismoo
Hinné	Byibtismoo

Present Continuous

Ana	Ăam	Bibtisém	(mibtisém/ mibtismé)
Inta	Ăam	Btibtisém	(mibtisém)
Inté	Ăam	Btibtismé	(mibtismé)
Hoowé	Ăam	Byibtisém	(mibtisém)
Heeyé	Ăam	Btibtisém	(mibtismé)
Naḣna	Ăam	Mnibtisém	(mibtismeen)
Intoo	Ăam	Btibtismoo	(mibtismeen)
Hinné	Ăam	Byibtismoo	(mibtismeen)

Past

Ana	Btasamt
Inta	Btasamt
Inté	Btasamté
Hoowé	Btasam
Heeyé	Btasamét
Naḣna	Btasamna
Intoo	Btasamtoo
Hinné	Btasamoo

Past Continuous

Ana	Kint Ăam	Bibtisém	(kint mibtisém/ mibtismé)
Inta	Kint Ăam	Btibtisém	(Kint Mibtisém)
Inté	Kinté Ăam	Btibtismé	(Kinté mibtismé)
Hoowé	Kén Ăam	Byibtisém	(Kén mibtisém)
Heeyé	Kénét Ăam	Btibtisém	(Kénét mibtismé)
Naḣna	Kinna Ăam	Mnibtisém	(Kinna mibtismeen)
Intoo	Kintoo Ăam	Btibtismoo	(Kintoo mibtismeen)
Hinné	Kénoo Ăam	Byibtismoo	(Kénoo mibtismeen)

Future

Ana	Laḣ	Ibtisém
Inta	Laḣ	Tibtisém
Inté	Laḣ	Tibtismé
Hoowé	Laḣ	Yibtisém
Heeyé	Laḣ	Tibtisém
Naḣna	Laḣ	Nibtisém
Intoo	Laḣ	Tibtismoo
Hinné	Laḣ	Yibtismoo

Command

Inta	Btisém
Inté	Btismé
Intoo	Btismoo
Inta	Ma tbtisém
Inté	Ma tbtismé
Intoo	Ma tbtismoo

To smooth

Present

Ana	bnaĂĂém
Inta	btnaĂĂém
Inté	btnaĂĂmé
Hoowé	binaĂĂém
Heeyé	btnaĂĂém
Naḣna	mnnaĂĂém
Intoo	btnaĂĂmoo
Hinné	binaĂĂmoo

Present Continuous

Ana	Ăam	bnaĂĂém
Inta	Ăam	btnaĂĂém
Inté	Ăam	btnaĂĂmé
Hoowé	Ăam	binaĂĂém
Heeyé	Ăam	btnaĂĂém
Naḣna	Ăam	mnnaĂĂém
Intoo	Ăam	btnaĂĂmoo
Hinné	Ăam	binaĂĂmoo

Past

Ana	naĂĂamt
Inta	naĂĂamt
Inté	naĂĂamté
Hoowé	naĂĂam
Heeyé	naĂĂamét
Naḣna	naĂĂamna
Intoo	naĂĂamtoo
Hinné	naĂĂamoo

Past Continuous

Ana	Kint Ăam	bnaĂĂém
Inta	Kint Ăam	btnaĂĂém
Inté	Kinté Ăam	btnaĂĂmé
Hoowé	Kén Ăam	binaĂĂém
Heeyé	Kénét Ăam	btnaĂĂém
Naḣna	Kinna Ăam	mnnaĂĂém
Intoo	Kintoo Ăam	btnaĂĂmoo
Hinné	Kénoo Ăam	binaĂĂmoo

Future

Ana	Laḣ	naĂĂém
Inta	Laḣ	tnaĂĂém
Inté	Laḣ	tnaĂĂmé
Hoowé	Laḣ	ynaĂĂém
Heeyé	Laḣ	tnaĂĂém
Naḣna	Laḣ	nnaĂĂém
Intoo	Laḣ	tnaĂĂmoo
Hinné	Laḣ	ynaĂĂmoo

Command

Inta	naĂĂém
Inté	naĂĂmé
Intoo	naĂĂmoo
Inta	Ma tnaĂĂém
Inté	Ma tnaĂĂmé
Intoo	Ma tnaĂĂmoo

Ă= Augh in bought	Ď= a heavy D	É= like A in Bay	G= G in beige	ḣ= like an H with smaller air passage	I= I as in ink	Ḱ= like ch in Irish loch
O= O as in home	OO= as in boots	R= roll the rrr	Ť= a heavy T	Ř= like a French R (gargle it)	Š= a heavy S	Ž= a heavy Z

<u>S</u>   <u>S</u>

To speed-up

Present	
Ana	bĂaggél
Inta	btĂaggél
Inté	btĂagglé
Hoowé	biĂaggél
Heeyé	btĂaggél
Nahna	mnĂaggél
Intoo	btĂaggloo
Hinné	biĂaggloo

Present Continuous			
Ana	Ăam	bĂaggél	(mĂaggal/mĂagglé)
Inta	Ăam	btĂaggél	(mĂaggal)
Inté	Ăam	btĂagglé	(mĂagglé)
Hoowé	Ăam	biĂaggél	(mĂaggal)
Heeyé	Ăam	btĂaggél	(mĂagglé)
Nahna	Ăam	mnĂaggél	(mĂaggleen)
Intoo	Ăam	btĂaggloo	(mĂaggleen)
Hinné	Ăam	biĂaggloo	(mĂaggleen)

Past	
Ana	Ăaggalt
Inta	Ăaggalt
Inté	Ăaggalté
Hoowé	Ăaggal
Heeyé	Ăaggalét
Nahna	Ăaggalna
Intoo	Ăaggaltoo
Hinné	Ăaggaloo

Past Continuous				
Ana	Kint Ăam	bĂaggél	(kint	mĂaggal/mĂagglé)
Inta	Kint Ăam	btĂaggél	(Kint	mĂaggal)
Inté	Kinté Ăam	btĂagglé	(Kinté	mĂagglé)
Hoowé	Kén Ăam	biĂaggél	(Kén	mĂaggal)
Heeyé	Kénét Ăam	btĂaggél	(Kénét	mĂagglé)
Nahna	Kinna Ăam	mnĂaggél	(Kinna	mĂaggleen)
Intoo	Kintoo Ăam	btĂaggloo	(Kintoo	mĂaggleen)
Hinné	Kénoo Ăam	biĂaggloo	(Kénoo	mĂaggleen)

Future		
Ana	Lah	Ăaggél
Inta	Lah	tĂaggél
Inté	Lah	tĂagglé
Hoowé	Lah	yĂaggél
Heeyé	Lah	tĂaggél
Nahna	Lah	nĂaggél
Intoo	Lah	tĂaggloo
Hinné	Lah	yĂaggloo

Command	
Inta	Ăaggél
Inté	Ăagglé
Intoo	Ăaggloo
Inta	Ma tĂaggél
Inté	Ma tĂagglé
Intoo	Ma tĂaggloo

To spend

Present	
Ana	biŜrof
Inta	btiŜrof
Inté	btiŜrfé
Hoowé	byiŜrof
Heeyé	btiŜrof
Nahna	mniŜrof
Intoo	btiŜrfoo
Hinné	byiŜrfoo

Present Continuous		
Ana	Ăam	biŜrof
Inta	Ăam	btiŜrof
Inté	Ăam	btiŜrfé
Hoowé	Ăam	byiŜrof
Heeyé	Ăam	btiŜrof
Nahna	Ăam	mniŜrof
Intoo	Ăam	btiŜrfoo
Hinné	Ăam	byiŜrfoo

Past	
Ana	Ŝaraft
Inta	Ŝaraft
Inté	Ŝarafté
Hoowé	Ŝaraf
Heeyé	Ŝarafét
Nahna	Ŝarafna
Intoo	Ŝaraftoo
Hinné	Ŝarafoo

Past Continuous		
Ana	Kint Ăam	biŜrof
Inta	Kint Ăam	btiŜrof
Inté	Kinté Ăam	btiŜrfé
Hoowé	Kén Ăam	byiŜrof
Heeyé	Kénét Ăam	btiŜrof
Nahna	Kinna Ăam	mniŜrof
Intoo	Kintoo Ăam	btiŜrfoo
Hinné	Kénoo Ăam	byiŜrfoo

Future		
Ana	Lah	iŜrof
Inta	Lah	tiŜrof
Inté	Lah	tiŜrfé
Hoowé	Lah	yiŜrof
Heeyé	Lah	tiŜrof
Nahna	Lah	niŜrof
Intoo	Lah	tiŜrfoo
Hinné	Lah	yiŜrfoo

Command	
Inta	Ŝrof
Inté	Ŝrifé
Intoo	Ŝrifoo
Inta	Ma tŜrof
Inté	Ma tŜrfé
Intoo	Ma tŜrfoo

Ă= Augh in bought	Ď= a heavy D	É= like A in Bay	G= G in beige	ĥ= like an H with smaller air passage	I= I as in ink	Ќ= like ch in Irish loch
O= O as in home	OO= as in boots	R= roll the rrr	Ť= a heavy T	Ř= like a French R (gargle it)	Ŝ= a heavy S	Ž= a heavy Z

S̲

S̲

To spill

Present

Ana	Bshirr (a variation of this verb is bsharshér)
Inta	btshirr
Inté	Btshirré
Hoowé	Bishirr
Heeyé	Btshirr
Nahna	Mnshirr
Intoo	Btshirroo
Hinné	bishirroo

Present Continuous

Ana	Ăam	bshirr
Inta	Ăam	btshirr
Inté	Ăam	Btshirré
Hoowé	Ăam	bishirr
Heeyé	Ăam	btshirr
Nahna	Ăam	mnshirr
Intoo	Ăam	Btshirroo
Hinné	Ăam	bishirroo

Past

Ana	Sharrét
Inta	Sharrét
Inté	Sharraité
Hoowé	Sharr
Heeyé	Sharrét
Nahna	Sharraina
Intoo	Sharraitoo
Hinné	Sharroo

Past Continuous

Ana	Kint Ăam	bshirr
Inta	Kint Ăam	btshirr
Inté	Kinté Ăam	Btshirré
Hoowé	Kén Ăam	bishirr
Heeyé	Kénét Ăam	btshirr
Nahna	Kinna Ăam	mnshirr
Intoo	Kintoo Ăam	Btshirroo
Hinné	Kénoo Ăam	bishirroo

Future

Ana	Laĥ	shirr
Inta	Laĥ	tshirr
Inté	Laĥ	tshirré
Hoowé	Laĥ	yshirr
Heeyé	Laĥ	tshirr
Nahna	Laĥ	nshirr
Intoo	Laĥ	tshirroo
Hinné	Laĥ	yshirroo

Command

Inta	Shirr
Inté	Shirré
Intoo	Shirroo
Inta	Ma tshirr
Inté	Ma tshirré
Intoo	Ma tshirroo

To spit

Present

Ana	Bibzo'
Inta	Btibzo'
Inté	Btibz'é
Hoowé	Byibzo'
Heeyé	Btibzo'
Nahna	mnibzo'
Intoo	Btibz'oo
Hinné	Byibz'oo

Present Continuous

Ana	Ăam	Bibzo'
Inta	Ăam	Btibzo'
Inté	Ăam	Btibz'é
Hoowé	Ăam	Byibzo'
Heeyé	Ăam	Btibzo'
Nahna	Ăam	mnibzo'
Intoo	Ăam	Btibz'oo
Hinné	Ăam	Byibz'oo

Past

Ana	Baza't
Inta	Baza't
Inté	Baza'té
Hoowé	Baza'
Heeyé	Baza'ét
Nahna	Baza'na
Intoo	Baza'to
Hinné	Baza'oo

Past Continuous

Ana	Kint Ăam	Bibzo'
Inta	Kint Ăam	Btibzo'
Inté	Kinté Ăam	Btibz'é
Hoowé	Kén Ăam	Byibzo'
Heeyé	Kénét Ăam	Btibzo'
Nahna	Kinna Ăam	mnibzo'
Intoo	Kintoo Ăam	Btibz'oo
Hinné	Kénoo Ăam	Byibz'oo

Future

Ana	Laĥ	ibzo'
Inta	Laĥ	tibzo'
Inté	Laĥ	tibz'é
Hoowé	Laĥ	yibzo'
Heeyé	Laĥ	tibzo'
Nahna	Laĥ	nibzo'
Intoo	Laĥ	tibz'oo
Hinné	Laĥ	yibz'oo

Command

Inta	Bzo'
Inté	Bzi'é
Intoo	Bzi'oo
Inta	Ma tbzo'
Inté	Ma tbz'é
Intoo	Ma tbz'oo

Ă= Augh in bought	Ď= a heavy D	É= like A in Bay	G= G in beige	ĥ= like an H with smaller air passage	I= I as in ink	Ќ= like ch in Irish loch
O= O as in home	OO= as in boots	R= roll the rrr	Ť= a heavy T	Ř= like a French R (gargle it)	Ŝ= a heavy S	Ž= a heavy Z

<u>S</u>   <u>S</u>

To splash   To split / To divide

To splash

Present	
Ana	bŤarrésh
Inta	btŤarrésh
Inté	btŤarrshé
Hoowé	biŤarrésh
Heeyé	btŤarrésh
Naĥna	mnŤarrésh
Intoo	btŤarrshoo
Hinné	biŤarrshoo

Present Continuous		
Ana	Ăam	bŤarrésh
Inta	Ăam	btŤarrésh
Inté	Ăam	btŤarrshé
Hoowé	Ăam	biŤarrésh
Heeyé	Ăam	btŤarrésh
Naĥna	Ăam	mnŤarrésh
Intoo	Ăam	btŤarrshoo
Hinné	Ăam	biŤarrshoo

Past	
Ana	Ťarrasht
Inta	Ťarrasht
Inté	Ťarrashté
Hoowé	Ťarrash
Heeyé	Ťarrashét
Naĥna	Ťarrashna
Intoo	Ťarrashtoo
Hinné	Ťarrashoo

Past Continuous		
Ana	Kint Ăam	bŤarrésh
Inta	Kint Ăam	btŤarrésh
Inté	Kinté Ăam	btŤarrshé
Hoowé	Kén Ăam	biŤarrésh
Heeyé	Kénét Ăam	btŤarrésh
Naĥna	Kinna Ăam	mnŤarrésh
Intoo	Kintoo Ăam	btŤarrshoo
Hinné	Kénoo Ăam	biŤarrshoo

Future		
Ana	Laĥ	Ťarrésh
Inta	Laĥ	tŤarrésh
Inté	Laĥ	tŤarrshé
Hoowé	Laĥ	yŤarrésh
Heeyé	Laĥ	tŤarrésh
Naĥna	Laĥ	nŤarrésh
Intoo	Laĥ	tŤarrshoo
Hinné	Laĥ	yŤarrshoo

Command	
Inta	Ťarresh
Inté	Ťarrshé
Intoo	Ťarrshoo
Inta	Ma tŤarrésh
Inté	Ma tŤarshé
Intoo	Ma tŤarshoo

To split / To divide

Present	
Ana	Bi'Šom
Inta	Bti'Šom
Inté	Bti'Šmé
Hoowé	Byi'Šom
Heeyé	Bti'Šom
Naĥna	mni'Šom
Intoo	Bti'Šmoo
Hinné	Byi'Šmoo

Present Continuous			
Ana	Ăam	Bi'Šom	('aŠém/aŠmé)
Inta	Ăam	Bti'Šom	('aŠém)
Inté	Ăam	Bti'Šmé	('aŠmé)
Hoowé	Ăam	Byi'Šom	('aŠém)
Heeyé	Ăam	Bti'Šom	('aŠmé)
Naĥna	Ăam	mni'Šom	('aŠmeen)
Intoo	Ăam	Bti'Šmoo	('aŠmeen)
Hinné	Ăam	Byi'Šmoo	('aŠmeen)

Past	
Ana	aŠamt
Inta	aŠamt
Inté	aŠamté
Hoowé	aŠam
Heeyé	aŠamét
Naĥna	aŠamna
Intoo	aŠamtoo
Hinné	aŠamoo

Past Continuous			
Ana	Kint Ăam	Bi'Šom	(kint 'aŠém/aŠmé)
Inta	Kint Ăam	Bti'Šom	(Kint 'aŠém)
Inté	Kinté Ăam	Bti'Šmé	(Kinté 'aŠmé)
Hoowé	Kén Ăam	Byi'Šom	(Kén 'aŠém)
Heeyé	Kénét Ăam	Bti'Šom	(Kénét 'aŠmé)
Naĥna	Kinna Ăam	mni'Šom	(Kinna 'aŠmeen)
Intoo	Kintoo Ăam	Bti'Šmoo	(Kintoo 'aŠmeen)
Hinné	Kénoo Ăam	Byi'Šmoo	(Kénoo 'aŠmeen)

Future		
Ana	Laĥ	i'Šom
Inta	Laĥ	ti'Šom
Inté	Laĥ	ti'Šmé
Hoowé	Laĥ	yi'Šom
Heeyé	Laĥ	ti'Šom
Naĥna	Laĥ	ni'Šom
Intoo	Laĥ	ti'Šmoo
Hinné	Laĥ	yi'Šmoo

Command	
Inta	'Šom
Inté	'Šimé
Intoo	'Šimoo
Inta	Ma t'Šom
Inté	Ma t'Šmé
Intoo	Ma t'Šmoo

Ă= Augh in bought	Ď= a heavy D	É= like A in Bay	G= G in beige	ĥ= like an H with smaller air passage	I= I as in ink	Ќ= like ch in Irish loch
O= O as in home	OO= as in boots	R= roll the rrr	Ť= a heavy T	Ř= like a French R (gargle it)	Š= a heavy S	Ž= a heavy Z

<u>S</u>   <u>S</u>

To spray

Present	
Ana	Brish
Inta	Btrish
Inté	Btrishé
Hoowé	Birish
Heeyé	Btrish
Naĥna	Mnrish
Intoo	Btrishoo
Hinné	Birishoo

Present Continuous		
Ana	Ăam	Brish
Inta	Ăam	Btrish
Inté	Ăam	Btrishé
Hoowé	Ăam	Birish
Heeyé	Ăam	Btrish
Naĥna	Ăam	Mnrish
Intoo	Ăam	Btrishoo
Hinné	Ăam	Birishoo

Past	
Ana	Rashét
Inta	Rashét
Inté	Rashaité
Hoowé	Rash
Heeyé	Rashét
Naĥna	Rashaina
Intoo	Rashaitoo
Hinné	Rashoo

Past Continuous		
Ana	Kint Ăam	Brish
Inta	Kint Ăam	Btrish
Inté	Kinté Ăam	Btrishé
Hoowé	Kén Ăam	Birish
Heeyé	Kénét Ăam	Btrish
Naĥna	Kinna Ăam	Mnrish
Intoo	Kintoo Ăam	Btrishoo
Hinné	Kénoo Ăam	Birishoo

Future		
Ana	Laĥ	Rish
Inta	Laĥ	Trish
Inté	Laĥ	Trishé
Hoowé	Laĥ	Yrish
Heeyé	Laĥ	Trish
Naĥna	Laĥ	Nrish
Intoo	Laĥ	trishoo
Hinné	Laĥ	yrishoo

Command	
Inta	Rish
Inté	Rishé
Intoo	Rishoo
Inta	Ma trish
Inté	Ma trishé
Intoo	Ma trisho

To spread

Present	
Ana	binshor
Inta	btinshor
Inté	Btinshré
Hoowé	byinshor
Heeyé	btinshor
Naĥna	mninshor
Intoo	Btinshroo
Hinné	byinshroo

Present Continuous		
Ana	Ăam	binshor
Inta	Ăam	btinshor
Inté	Ăam	Btinshré
Hoowé	Ăam	byinshor
Heeyé	Ăam	btinshor
Naĥna	Ăam	mninshor
Intoo	Ăam	Btinshroo
Hinné	Ăam	byinshroo

Past	
Ana	Nashart
Inta	Nashart
Inté	Nasharté
Hoowé	Nashar
Heeyé	Nasharét
Naĥna	Nasharna
Intoo	Nashartoo
Hinné	Nasharoo

Past Continuous		
Ana	Kint Ăam	binshor
Inta	Kint Ăam	btinshor
Inté	Kinté Ăam	Btinshré
Hoowé	Kén Ăam	byinshor
Heeyé	Kénét Ăam	btinshor
Naĥna	Kinna Ăam	mninshor
Intoo	Kintoo Ăam	Btinshroo
Hinné	Kénoo Ăam	byinshroo

Future		
Ana	Laĥ	inshor
Inta	Laĥ	tinshor
Inté	Laĥ	tinshré
Hoowé	Laĥ	yinshor
Heeyé	Laĥ	tinshor
Naĥna	Laĥ	ninshor
Intoo	Laĥ	tinshroo
Hinné	Laĥ	yinshroo

Command	
Inta	Nshor
Inté	Nshiré
Intoo	Nshiroo
Inta	Ma tnshor
Inté	Ma tnshré
Intoo	Ma tnshroo

Ă= Augh in bought	Ď= a heavy D	É= like A in Bay	G= G in beige	ĥ= like an H with smaller air passage	I= I as in ink	Ќ= like ch in Irish loch
O= O as in home	OO= as in boots	R= roll the rrr	Ť= a heavy T	Ř= like a French R (gargle it)	Ŝ= a heavy S	Ž= a heavy Z

S̲   S̲

To squeeze

Present

Ana	biĂŠor
Inta	btiĂŠor
Inté	btiĂŠré
Hoowé	byiĂŠor
Heeyé	btiĂŠor
Nahna	mniĂŠor
Intoo	btiĂŠroo
Hinné	byiĂŠroo

Present Continuous

Ana	Ăam	biĂŠor
Inta	Ăam	btiĂŠor
Inté	Ăam	btiĂŠré
Hoowé	Ăam	byiĂŠor
Heeyé	Ăam	btiĂŠor
Nahna	Ăam	mniĂŠor
Intoo	Ăam	btiĂŠroo
Hinné	Ăam	byiĂŠroo

Past

Ana	ĂaSart
Inta	ĂaSart
Inté	ĂaSarté
Hoowé	ĂaSar
Heeyé	ĂaSarét
Nahna	ĂaSarna
Intoo	ĂaSartoo
Hinné	ĂaSaroo

Past Continuous

Ana	Kint Ăam	biĂŠor
Inta	Kint Ăam	btiĂŠor
Inté	Kinté Ăam	btiĂŠré
Hoowé	Kén Ăam	byiĂŠor
Heeyé	Kénét Ăam	btiĂŠor
Nahna	Kinna Ăam	mniĂŠor
Intoo	Kintoo Ăam	btiĂŠroo
Hinné	Kénoo Ăam	byiĂŠroo

Future

Ana	Laĥ	iĂŠor
Inta	Laĥ	tiĂŠor
Inté	Laĥ	tiĂŠré
Hoowé	Laĥ	yiĂŠor
Heeyé	Laĥ	tiĂŠor
Nahna	Laĥ	niĂŠor
Intoo	Laĥ	tiĂŠroo
Hinné	Laĥ	yiĂŠroo

Command

Inta	ĂŠor
Inté	ĂŠiré
Intoo	ĂŠiroo
Inta	Ma tĂŠor
Inté	Ma tĂŠré
Intoo	Ma tĂŠroo

To stab

Present

Ana	biŤĂan
Inta	btiŤĂan
Inté	btiŤĂané
Hoowé	byiŤĂan
Heeyé	btiŤĂan
Nahna	mniŤĂan
Intoo	btiŤĂanoo
Hinné	byiŤĂanoo

Present Continuous

Ana	Ăam	biŤĂan
Inta	Ăam	btiŤĂan
Inté	Ăam	btiŤĂané
Hoowé	Ăam	byiŤĂan
Heeyé	Ăam	btiŤĂan
Nahna	Ăam	mniŤĂan
Intoo	Ăam	btiŤĂanoo
Hinné	Ăam	byiŤĂanoo

Past

Ana	ŤaĂant
Inta	ŤaĂant
Inté	ŤaĂanté
Hoowé	ŤaĂan
Heeyé	ŤaĂanét
Nahna	ŤaĂanna
Intoo	ŤaĂantoo
Hinné	ŤaĂanoo

Past Continuous

Ana	Kint Ăam	biŤĂan
Inta	Kint Ăam	btiŤĂan
Inté	Kinté Ăam	btiŤĂané
Hoowé	Kén Ăam	byiŤĂan
Heeyé	Kénét Ăam	btiŤĂan
Nahna	Kinna Ăam	mniŤĂan
Intoo	Kintoo Ăam	btiŤĂanoo
Hinné	Kénoo Ăam	byiŤĂanoo

Future

Ana	Laĥ	iŤĂan
Inta	Laĥ	tiŤĂan
Inté	Laĥ	tiŤĂané
Hoowé	Laĥ	yiŤĂan
Heeyé	Laĥ	tiŤĂan
Nahna	Laĥ	niŤĂan
Intoo	Laĥ	tiŤĂanoo
Hinné	Laĥ	yiŤĂanoo

Command

Inta	ŤĂan
Inté	ŤĂané
Intoo	ŤĂanoo
Inta	Ma tŤĂan
Inté	Ma tŤĂané
Intoo	Ma tŤĂanoo

S̲   S̲

To stain   To stare

Present	
Ana	bdabbéŘ
Inta	btdabbéŘ
Inté	btdabbŘé
Hoowé	bidabbéŘ
Heeyé	btdabbéŘ
Nahna	mndabbéŘ
Intoo	btdabbŘoo
Hinné	bidabbŘoo

Present Continuous		
Ana	Ăam bdabbéŘ	(mdabbaŘ/mdabbŘa)
Inta	Ăam btdabbéŘ	(mdabbaŘ)
Inté	Ăam btdabbŘé	(mdabbŘa)
Hoowé	Ăam bidabbéŘ	(mdabbaŘ)
Heeyé	Ăam btdabbéŘ	(mdabbŘa)
Nahna	Ăam mndabbéŘ	(mdabReen)
Intoo	Ăam btdabbŘoo	(mdabReen)
Hinné	Ăam bidabbŘoo	(mdabReen)

Past	
Ana	dabbaŘt
Inta	dabbaŘt
Inté	dabbaŘté
Hoowé	dabbaŘ
Heeyé	dabbaŘét
Nahna	dabbaŘna
Intoo	dabbaŘtoo
Hinné	dabbaŘoo

Past Continuous		
Ana	Kint Ăam bdabbéŘ	(kint mdabbaŘ/mdabbŘa)
Inta	Kint Ăam btdabbéŘ	(Kint mdabbaŘ)
Inté	Kinté Ăam btdabbŘé	(Kinté mdabbŘa)
Hoowé	Kén Ăam bidabbéŘ	(Kén mdabbaŘ)
Heeyé	Kénét Ăam btdabbéŘ	(Kénét mdabbŘa)
Nahna	Kinna Ăam mndabbéŘ	(Kinna mdabReen)
Intoo	Kintoo Ăam btdabbŘoo	(Kintoo mdabReen)
Hinné	Kénoo Ăam bidabbŘoo	(Kénoo mdabReen)

Future		
Ana	Lah	dabbéŘ
Inta	Lah	tdabbéŘ
Inté	Lah	tdabbŘé
Hoowé	Lah	ydabbéŘ
Heeyé	Lah	tdabbéŘ
Nahna	Lah	ndabbéŘ
Intoo	Lah	tdabbŘoo
Hinné	Lah	ydabbŘoo

Command	
Inta	dabbéŘ
Inté	dabbŘé
Intoo	dabbŘoo
Inta	Ma tdabbéŘ
Inté	Ma tdabbŘé
Intoo	Ma tdabbŘoo

Present	
Ana	Bbaĥlé'
Inta	Btbaĥlé'
Inté	Btbaĥl'é
Hoowé	Bibaĥlé'
Heeyé	Btbaĥlé'
Nahna	Mnbaĥlé'
Intoo	Btbaĥl'oo
Hinné	Bibaĥl'oo

Present Continuous		
Ana	Ăam	Bbaĥlé'
Inta	Ăam	Btbaĥlé'
Inté	Ăam	Btbaĥl'é
Hoowé	Ăam	Bibaĥlé'
Heeyé	Ăam	Btbaĥlé'
Nahna	Ăam	Mnbaĥlé'
Intoo	Ăam	Btbaĥl'oo
Hinné	Ăam	Bibaĥl'oo

Past	
Ana	Baĥla't
Inta	Baĥla't
Inté	Baĥla'té
Hoowé	Baĥla'
Heeyé	Baĥla'ét
Nahna	Baĥla'na
Intoo	Baĥla'too
Hinné	Baĥla'oo

Past Continuous		
Ana	Kint Ăam	Bbaĥlé'
Inta	Kint Ăam	Btbaĥlé'
Inté	Kinté Ăam	Btbaĥl'é
Hoowé	Kén Ăam	Bibaĥlé'
Heeyé	Kénét Ăam	Btbaĥlé'
Nahna	Kinna Ăam	Mnbaĥlé'
Intoo	Kintoo Ăam	Btbaĥl'oo
Hinné	Kénoo Ăam	Bibaĥl'oo

Future		
Ana	Lah	Baĥlé'
Inta	Lah	Tbaĥlé'
Inté	Lah	Tbaĥl'é
Hoowé	Lah	Ybaĥlé'
Heeyé	Lah	Tbaĥlé'
Nahna	Lah	Nbaĥlé'
Intoo	Lah	Tbaĥl'oo
Hinné	Lah	Ybaĥl'oo

Command	
Inta	Baĥlé'
Inté	Baĥl'é
Intoo	Baĥl'oo
Inta	Ma tbaĥlé'
Inté	Ma tbaĥl'é
Intoo	Ma tbaĥl'oo

Ă= Augh in bought	Ď= a heavy D	É= like A in Bay	G= G in beige	ĥ= like an H with smaller air passage	I= I as in ink	Ř= like ch in Irish loch
O= O as in home	OO= as in boots	R= roll the rrr	Ť= a heavy T	Ř= like a French R (gargle it)	Ŝ= a heavy S	Ž= a heavy Z

<u>S</u>   <u>S</u>

To start

Present	
Ana	Bballésh
Inta	Btballésh
Inté	Btballshé
Hoowé	Biballésh
Heeyé	Btballésh
Naḣna	Mnballésh
Intoo	Btballshoo
Hinné	Biballshoo

Present Continuous			
Ana	Ăam	Bballésh	(mballash/mballshé)
Inta	Ăam	Btballésh	(mballash)
Inté	Ăam	Btballshé	(mballshé)
Hoowé	Ăam	Biballésh	(mballash)
Heeyé	Ăam	Btballésh	(mballshé)
Naḣna	Ăam	Mnballésh	(mballsheen)
Intoo	Ăam	Btballshoo	(mballsheen)
Hinné	Ăam	Biballshoo	(mballsheen)

Past	
Ana	Ballasht
Inta	Ballasht
Inté	Ballashté
Hoowé	Ballash
Heeyé	Ballashét
Naḣna	Ballashna
Intoo	Ballashtoo
Hinné	Ballashoo

Past Continuous			
Ana	Kint Ăam	Bballésh	(kint mballash/mballshé)
Inta	Kint Ăam	Btballésh	(Kint mballash)
Inté	Kinté Ăam	Btballshé	(Kinté mballshé)
Hoowé	Kén Ăam	Biballésh	(Kén mballash)
Heeyé	Kénét Ăam	Btballésh	(Kénét mballshé)
Naḣna	Kinna Ăam	Mnballésh	(Kinna mballsheen)
Intoo	Kintoo Ăam	Btballshoo	(Kintoo mballsheen)
Hinné	Kénoo Ăam	Biballshoo	(Kénoo mballsheen)

Future		
Ana	Laḣ	Ballésh
Inta	Laḣ	Tballésh
Inté	Laḣ	Tballshé
Hoowé	Laḣ	Yballésh
Heeyé	Laḣ	Tballésh
Naḣna	Laḣ	Nballésh
Intoo	Laḣ	Tballshoo
Hinné	Laḣ	Yballshoo

Command	
Inta	Ballésh
Inté	Ballshé
Intoo	Ballshoo
Inta	Ma tballésh
Inté	Ma tballshé
Intoo	Ma tballshoo

To steal

Present	
Ana	Bisro'
Inta	Btisro'
Inté	Btisr'é
Hoowé	Byisro'
Heeyé	Btisro'
Naḣna	mnisro'
Intoo	Btisr'oo
Hinné	Byisr'oo

Present Continuous		
Ana	Ăam	Bisro'
Inta	Ăam	Btisro'
Inté	Ăam	Btisr'é
Hoowé	Ăam	Byisro'
Heeyé	Ăam	Btisro'
Naḣna	Ăam	mnisro'
Intoo	Ăam	Btisr'oo
Hinné	Ăam	Byisr'oo

Past	
Ana	Sara't
Inta	Sara't
Inté	Sara'té
Hoowé	Sara'
Heeyé	Sara'ét
Naḣna	Sara'na
Intoo	Sara'too
Hinné	Sara'oo

Past Continuous		
Ana	Kint Ăam	Bisro'
Inta	Kint Ăam	Btisro'
Inté	Kinté Ăam	Btisr'é
Hoowé	Kén Ăam	Byisro'
Heeyé	Kénét Ăam	Btisro'
Naḣna	Kinna Ăam	mnisro'
Intoo	Kintoo Ăam	Btisr'oo
Hinné	Kénoo Ăam	Byisr'oo

Future		
Ana	Laḣ	isro'
Inta	Laḣ	tisro'
Inté	Laḣ	tisr'é
Hoowé	Laḣ	yisro'
Heeyé	Laḣ	tisro'
Naḣna	Laḣ	nisro'
Intoo	Laḣ	tisr'oo
Hinné	Laḣ	yisr'oo

Command	
Inta	Sro'
Inté	Sri'é
Intoo	Sri'oo
Inta	Ma tsro'
Inté	Ma tsr'é
Intoo	Ma ts'oo

Ă= Augh in bought	Ď= a heavy D	É= like A in Bay	G= G in beige	ḣ= like an H with smaller air passage	I= I as in ink	Ḱ= like ch in Irish loch
O= O as in home	OO= as in boots	R= roll the rrr	Ť= a heavy T	Ř= like a French R (gargle it)	Ŝ= a heavy S	Ž= a heavy Z

<u>S</u> <u>S</u>

To stick / To glue

Present

Ana	Blazzé'
Inta	Btlazzé'
Inté	Btlazz'é
Hoowé	Bilazzé'
Heeyé	Btlazzé'
Naĥna	mnlazzé'
Intoo	Btlazz'oo
Hinné	Bilazz'oo

Present Continuous

Ana	Ăam	Blazzé'
Inta	Ăam	Btlazzé'
Inté	Ăam	Btlazz'é
Hoowé	Ăam	Bilazzé'
Heeyé	Ăam	Btlazzé'
Naĥna	Ăam	mnlazzé'
Intoo	Ăam	Btlazz'oo
Hinné	Ăam	Bilazz'oo

Past

Ana	Lazza't
Inta	Lazza't
Inté	Lazza'té
Hoowé	Lazza'
Heeyé	Lazza'ét
Naĥna	Lazza'na
Intoo	Lazza'too
Hinné	Lazza'oo

Past Continuous

Ana	Kint Ăam	Blazzé'
Inta	Kint Ăam	Btlazzé'
Inté	Kinté Ăam	Btlazz'é
Hoowé	Kén Ăam	Bilazzé'
Heeyé	Kénét Ăam	Btlazzé'
Naĥna	Kinna Ăam	mnlazzé'
Intoo	Kintoo Ăam	Btlazz'oo
Hinné	Kénoo Ăam	Bilazz'oo

Future

Ana	Laĥ	lazzé'
Inta	Laĥ	Tlazzé'
Inté	Laĥ	tlazz'é
Hoowé	Laĥ	ylazzé'
Heeyé	Laĥ	Tlazzé'
Naĥna	Laĥ	nlazzé'
Intoo	Laĥ	tlazz'oo
Hinné	Laĥ	Ylazz'oo

Command

Inta	Lazzé'
Inté	Lazz'é
Intoo	Lazz'oo
Inta	Ma tlazzé'
Inté	Ma tlazz'é
Intoo	Ma tlazz'oo

To sting

Present

Ana	biĂ'oŜ
Inta	btiĂ'oŜ
Inté	btiĂ'Ŝé
Hoowé	byiĂ'oŜ
Heeyé	btiĂ'oŜ
Naĥna	mniĂ'oŜ
Intoo	btiĂ'Ŝoo
Hinné	byiĂ'Ŝoo

Present Continuous

Ana	Ăam	biĂ'oŜ
Inta	Ăam	btiĂ'oŜ
Inté	Ăam	btiĂ'Ŝé
Hoowé	Ăam	byiĂ'oŜ
Heeyé	Ăam	btiĂ'oŜ
Naĥna	Ăam	mniĂ'oŜ
Intoo	Ăam	btiĂ'Ŝoo
Hinné	Ăam	byiĂ'Ŝoo

Past

Ana	Ăa'aŜt
Inta	Ăa'aŜt
Inté	Ăa'aŜté
Hoowé	Ăa'aŜ
Heeyé	Ăa'aŜét
Naĥna	Ăa'aŜna
Intoo	Ăa'aŜtoo
Hinné	Ăa'aŜoo

Past Continuous

Ana	Kint Ăam	biĂ'oŜ
Inta	Kint Ăam	btiĂ'oŜ
Inté	Kinté Ăam	btiĂ'Ŝé
Hoowé	Kén Ăam	byiĂ'oŜ
Heeyé	Kénét Ăam	btiĂ'oŜ
Naĥna	Kinna Ăam	mniĂ'oŜ
Intoo	Kintoo Ăam	btiĂ'Ŝoo
Hinné	Kénoo Ăam	byiĂ'Ŝoo

Future

Ana	Laĥ	iĂ'oŜ
Inta	Laĥ	tiĂ'oŜ
Inté	Laĥ	tiĂ'Ŝé
Hoowé	Laĥ	yiĂ'oŜ
Heeyé	Laĥ	tiĂ'oŜ
Naĥna	Laĥ	niĂ'oŜ
Intoo	Laĥ	tiĂ'Ŝoo
Hinné	Laĥ	yiĂ'Ŝoo

Command

Inta	Ă'oŜ
Inté	Ă'iŜé
Intoo	Ă'iŜoo
Inta	Ma tĂ'oŜ
Inté	Ma tĂ'sé
Intoo	Ma tĂ'soo

| Ă= Augh in bought | Ď= a heavy D | É= like A in Bay | G= G in beige | ĥ= like an H with smaller air passage | I= I as in ink | Ǩ= like ch in Irish loch |
| O= O as in home | OO= as in boots | R= roll the rrr | Ť= a heavy T | Ř= like a French R (gargle it) | Ŝ= a heavy S | Ž= a heavy Z |

<u>S</u>   <u>S</u>

To stop

Present	
Ana	Boo'af
Inta	Btoo'af
Inté	Btoo'afé
Hoowé	Byoo'af
Heeyé	Btoo'af
Nahna	mnoo'af
Intoo	Btoo'afoo
Hinné	Byoo'afoo

Present Continuous			
Ana	Ăam	Boo'af	(wé'éf/wé'fé)
Inta	Ăam	Btoo'af	(wé'éf)
Inté	Ăam	Btoo'afé	(wé'fé)
Hoowé	Ăam	Byoo'af	(wé'éf)
Heeyé	Ăam	Btoo'af	(wé'fé)
Nahna	Ăam	Mnoo'af	(wé'feen)
Intoo	Ăam	Btoo'afoo	(wé'feen)
Hinné	Ăam	Byoo'afoo	(wé'feen)

Past	
Ana	W'aft
Inta	W'aft
Inté	W'afté
Hoowé	Wi'éf
Heeyé	Wi'fét
Nahna	W'ifna
Intoo	W'iftoo
Hinné	Wi'foo

Past Continuous			
Ana	Kint Ăam	Boo'af	(kint wé'éf/wé'fé)
Inta	Kint Ăam	Btoo'af	(Kint wé'éf)
Inté	Kinté Ăam	Btoo'afé	(Kinté wé'fé)
Hoowé	Kén Ăam	Byoo'af	(Kén wé'éf)
Heeyé	Kénét Ăam	Btoo'af	(Kénét wé'fé)
Nahna	Kinna Ăam	mnoo'af	(Kinna wé'feen)
Intoo	Kintoo Ăam	Btoo'afoo	(Kintoo wé'feen)
Hinné	Kénoo Ăam	Byoo'afoo	(Kénoo wé'feen)

Future		
Ana	Laĥ	'oo'af
Inta	Laĥ	Too'af
Inté	Laĥ	Too'afé
Hoowé	Laĥ	Yoo'af
Heeyé	Laĥ	Too'af
Nahna	Laĥ	Noo'af
Intoo	Laĥ	Too'afoo
Hinné	Laĥ	Yoo'afoo

Command	
Inta	W'af
Inté	W'afé
Intoo	W'afoo
Inta	Ma too'af
Inté	Ma too'afé
Intoo	Ma too'afoo

To store

Present	
Ana	bKazzén
Inta	btKazzén
Inté	btKazzné
Hoowé	biKazzén
Heeyé	btKazzén
Nahna	mnKazzén
Intoo	btKazznoo
Hinné	biKazznoo

Present Continuous			
Ana	Ăam	bKazzén	(mKazzan/mKazzné)
Inta	Ăam	btKazzén	(mKazzan)
Inté	Ăam	btKazzné	(mKazzné)
Hoowé	Ăam	biKazzén	(mKazzan)
Heeyé	Ăam	btKazzén	(mKazzné)
Nahna	Ăam	mnKazzén	(mKazzneen)
Intoo	Ăam	btKazznoo	(mKazzneen)
Hinné	Ăam	biKazznoo	(mKazzneen)

Past	
Ana	Kazzant
Inta	Kazzant
Inté	Kazzanté
Hoowé	Kazzan
Heeyé	Kazzanét
Nahna	Kazzanna
Intoo	Kazzantoo
Hinné	Kazzanoo

Past Continuous			
Ana	Kint Ăam	bKazzén	(kint mKazzan/mKazzné)
Inta	Kint Ăam	btKazzén	(Kint mKazzan)
Inté	Kinté Ăam	btKazzné	(Kinté mKazzné)
Hoowé	Kén Ăam	biKazzén	(Kén mKazzan)
Heeyé	Kénét Ăam	btKazzén	(Kénét mKazzné)
Nahna	Kinna Ăam	mnKazzén	(Kinna mKazzneen)
Intoo	Kintoo Ăam	btKazznoo	(Kintoo mKazzneen)
Hinné	Kénoo Ăam	biKazznoo	(Kénoo mKazzneen)

Future		
Ana	Laĥ	Kazzén
Inta	Laĥ	tKazzén
Inté	Laĥ	tKazzné
Hoowé	Laĥ	yKazzén
Heeyé	Laĥ	tKazzén
Nahna	Laĥ	nKazzén
Intoo	Laĥ	tKazznoo
Hinné	Laĥ	yKazznoo

Command	
Inta	Kazzant
Inté	Kazzanté
Intoo	Kazzantoo
Inta	Ma tKazzén
Inté	Ma tKazzné
Intoo	Ma tKazznoo

Ă= Augh in bought	Đ= a heavy D	É= like A in Bay	G= G in beige	ĥ= like an H with smaller air passage	I= I as in ink	K= like ch in Irish loch
O= O as in home	OO= as in boots	R= roll the rrr	Ť= a heavy T	Ř= like a French R (gargle it)	Ŝ= a heavy S	Ž= a heavy Z

S

S

To struggle

To study

Present

Ana	bĂané
Inta	btĂané
Inté	btĂané
Hoowé	biĂané
Heeyé	btĂané
Nahna	mnĂané
Intoo	btĂanoo
Hinné	biĂanoo

Present

Ana	Bidros
Inta	Btidros
Inté	Btidrsé
Hoowé	Byidros
Heeyé	Btidros
Nahna	Mnidros
Intoo	Btidrsoo
Hinné	Byidrsoo

Present Continuous

Ana	Ăam	bĂané
Inta	Ăam	btĂané
Inté	Ăam	btĂané
Hoowé	Ăam	biĂané
Heeyé	Ăam	btĂané
Nahna	Ăam	mnĂané
Intoo	Ăam	btĂanoo
Hinné	Ăam	biĂanoo

Present Continuous

Ana	Ăam	Bidros	(dérés/dérsé)
Inta	Ăam	Btidros	(dérés)
Inté	Ăam	Btidrsé	(dérsé)
Hoowé	Ăam	Byidros	(dérés)
Heeyé	Ăam	Btidros	(dérsé)
Nahna	Ăam	Mnidros	(dérseen)
Intoo	Ăam	Btidrsoo	(dérseen)
Hinné	Ăam	Byidrsoo	(dérseen)

Past

Ana	Ăanét
Inta	Ăanét
Inté	Ăanaité
Hoowé	Ăana
Heeyé	Ăanét
Nahna	Ăanaina
Intoo	Ăanaitoo
Hinné	Ăanoo

Past

Ana	Darast
Inta	Darast
Inté	Darasté
Hoowé	Daras
Heeyé	Darasét
Nahna	Darasna
Intoo	Darastoo
Hinné	Darasoo

Past Continuous

Ana	Kint Ăam	bĂané	
Inta	Kint Ăam	btĂané	
Inté	Kinté Ăam	btĂané	
Hoowé	Kén Ăam	biĂané	
Heeyé	Kénét Ăam	btĂané	
Nahna	Kinna Ăam	mnĂané	
Intoo	Kintoo Ăam	btĂanoo	
Hinné	Kénoo Ăam	biĂanoo	

Past Continuous

Ana	Kint Ăam	Bidros	(kint Dérés/dérsé)
Inta	Kint Ăam	Btidros	(Kint dérés)
Inté	Kinté Ăam	Btidrsé	(Kinté dérsé)
Hoowé	Kén Ăam	Byidros	(Kén dérés)
Heeyé	Kénét Ăam	Btidros	(Kénét dérsé)
Nahna	Kinna Ăam	Mnidros	(Kinna dérseen)
Intoo	Kintoo Ăam	Btidrsoo	(Kintoo dérseen)
Hinné	Kénoo Ăam	Byidrsoo	(Kénoo dérseen)

Future

Ana	Laĥ	Ăané
Inta	Laĥ	tĂané
Inté	Laĥ	tĂané
Hoowé	Laĥ	yĂané
Heeyé	Laĥ	tĂané
Nahna	Laĥ	nĂané
Intoo	Laĥ	tĂanoo
Hinné	Laĥ	yĂanoo

Future

Ana	Laĥ	idros
Inta	Laĥ	tidros
Inté	Laĥ	tidrsé
Hoowé	Laĥ	yidros
Heeyé	Laĥ	tidros
Nahna	Laĥ	nidros
Intoo	Laĥ	tidrsoo
Hinné	Laĥ	yidrsoo

Command

Inta	Ăané
Inté	Ăané
Intoo	Ăanoo
Inta	Ma tĂané
Inté	Ma tĂané
Intoo	Ma tĂanoo

Command

Inta	Dros
Inté	Drisé
Intoo	Drisoo
Inta	Ma tdros
Inté	Ma tdrsé
Intoo	Ma tdrsoo

Ă= Augh in bought	Đ= a heavy D	É= like A in Bay	G= G in beige	ĥ= like an H with smaller air passage	I= I as in ink	Ǩ= like ch in Irish loch
O= O as in home	OO= as in boots	R= roll the rrr	Ť= a heavy T	Ř= like a French R (gargle it)	Ŝ= a heavy S	Ž= a heavy Z

<u>S</u>   <u>S</u>

To subtract   To succeed

Present	
Ana	biṪraȟ
Inta	btiṪraȟ
Inté	btiṪrahé
Hoowé	byiṪraȟ
Heeyé	btiṪraȟ
Nahna	mniṪrah
Intoo	btiṪrahoo
Hinné	byiṪrahoo

Present	
Ana	Bingaȟ
Inta	Btingaȟ
Inté	Btingahé
Hoowé	Byingaȟ
Heeyé	Btingahé
Nahna	Mningaȟ
Intoo	Btingahoo
Hinné	Byingahoo

Present Continuous		
Ana	Ăam	biṪraȟ
Inta	Ăam	btiṪrah
Inté	Ăam	btiṪrahé
Hoowé	Ăam	byiṪrah
Heeyé	Ăam	btiṪrah
Nahna	Ăam	mniṪrah
Intoo	Ăam	btiṪrahoo
Hinné	Ăam	byiṪrahoo

Present Continuous			
Ana	Ăam	Bingaȟ	(négéȟ/négȟa)
Inta	Ăam	Btingaȟ	(négéȟ)
Inté	Ăam	Btingahé	(négȟa)
Hoowé	Ăam	Byingaȟ	(négéȟ)
Heeyé	Ăam	Btingahé	(négȟa)
Nahna	Ăam	Mningaȟ	(négȟeen)
Intoo	Ăam	Btingahoo	(négȟeen)
Hinné	Ăam	Byingahoo	(négheen)

Past	
Ana	Ṫaraȟt
Inta	Ṫaraȟt
Inté	Ṫarahté
Hoowé	Ṫaraȟ
Heeyé	Ṫarahét
Nahna	Ṫarahna
Intoo	Ṫarahtoo
Hinné	Ṫarahoo

Past	
Ana	Nagaȟt
Inta	Nagaȟt
Inté	Nagahté
Hoowé	Nagaȟ
Heeyé	Nagahét
Nahna	Nagahna
Intoo	Nagahtoo
Hinné	Nagahoo

Past Continuous		
Ana	Kint Ăam	biṪraȟ
Inta	Kint Ăam	btiṪrah
Inté	Kinté Ăam	btiṪrahé
Hoowé	Kén Ăam	byiṪrah
Heeyé	Kénét Ăam	btiṪrah
Nahna	Kinna Ăam	mniṪrah
Intoo	Kintoo Ăam	btiṪrahoo
Hinné	Kénoo Ăam	byiṪrahoo

Past Continuous			
Ana	Kint Ăam	Bingaȟ	(kint Négéȟ/négȟa)
Inta	Kint Ăam	Btingaȟ	(Kint négéȟ)
Inté	Kinté Ăam	Btingahé	(Kinté négȟa)
Hoowé	Kén Ăam	Byingaȟ	(Kén négéȟ)
Heeyé	Kénét Ăam	Btingahé	(Kénét négȟa)
Nahna	Kinna Ăam	Mningaȟ	(Kinna négȟeen)
Intoo	Kintoo Ăam	Btingahoo	(Kintoo négȟeen)
Hinné	Kénoo Ăam	Byingahoo	(Kénoo négȟeen)

Future		
Ana	Laȟ	iṪraȟ
Inta	Laȟ	tiṪraȟ
Inté	Laȟ	tiṪrahé
Hoowé	Laȟ	yiṪrah
Heeyé	Laȟ	tiṪrah
Nahna	Laȟ	niṪrah
Intoo	Laȟ	tiṪrahoo
Hinné	Laȟ	yiṪrahoo

Future		
Ana	Laȟ	Ingaȟ
Inta	Laȟ	Tingaȟ
Inté	Laȟ	Tingahé
Hoowé	Laȟ	Yingaȟ
Heeyé	Laȟ	Tingahé
Nahna	Laȟ	Ningaȟ
Intoo	Laȟ	Tingahoo
Hinné	Laȟ	Yingahoo

Command	
Inta	Ṫraȟ
Inté	Ṫrahé
Intoo	ṪraHoo
Inta	Ma tṪrah
Inté	Ma tṪrahé
Intoo	Ma tṪrahoo

Command	
Inta	Ngaȟ
Inté	Ngahé
Intoo	Ngahoo
Inta	Ma tngaȟ
Inté	Ma tngahé
Intoo	Ma tngahoo

Ă= Augh in bought	Ď= a heavy D	É= like A in Bay	G= G in beige	ȟ= like an H with smaller air passage	I= I as in ink	Ǩ= like ch in Irish loch
O= O as in home	OO= as in boots	R= roll the rrr	Ṫ= a heavy T	Ř= like a French R (gargle it)	Ŝ= a heavy S	Ž= a heavy Z

<u>S</u>   # <u>S</u>

To suck   ## To supply

Present	
Ana	bmiŜŜ
Inta	btmiŜŜ
Inté	btmiŜŜé
Hoowé	bimiŜŜ
Heeyé	btmiŜŜ
Nahna	mnmiŜŜ
Intoo	btmiŜŜoo
Hinné	bimiŜŜoo

Present Continuous		
Ana	Ăam	bmiŜŜ
Inta	Ăam	btmiŜŜ
Inté	Ăam	btmiŜŜé
Hoowé	Ăam	bimiŜŜ
Heeyé	Ăam	btmiŜŜ
Nahna	Ăam	mnmiŜŜ
Intoo	Ăam	btmiŜŜoo
Hinné	Ăam	bimiŜŜoo

Past	
Ana	maŜŜét
Inta	maŜŜét
Inté	maŜŜaité
Hoowé	maŜŜ
Heeyé	maŜŜét
Nahna	maŜŜaina
Intoo	maŜŜaitoo
Hinné	maŜŜoo

Past Continuous		
Ana	Kint Ăam	bmiŜŜ
Inta	Kint Ăam	btmiŜŜ
Inté	Kinté Ăam	btmiŜŜé
Hoowé	Kén Ăam	bimiŜŜ
Heeyé	Kénét Ăam	btmiŜŜ
Nahna	Kinna Ăam	mnmiŜŜ
Intoo	Kintoo Ăam	btmiŜŜoo
Hinné	Kénoo Ăam	bimiŜŜoo

Future		
Ana	Laĥ	miŜŜ
Inta	Laĥ	tmiŜŜ
Inté	Laĥ	tmiŜŜé
Hoowé	Laĥ	ymiŜŜ
Heeyé	Laĥ	tmiŜŜ
Nahna	Laĥ	nmiŜŜ
Intoo	Laĥ	tmiŜŜoo
Hinné	Laĥ	ymiŜŜoo

Command	
Inta	miŜŜ
Inté	miŜŜé
Intoo	miŜŜoo
Inta	Ma tmiŜŜ
Inté	Ma tmiŜŜé
Intoo	Ma tmiŜŜoo

Present	
Ana	Bmawwén
Inta	Btmawwén
Inté	Btmawwné
Hoowé	Bimawwén
Heeyé	Btmawwén
Nahna	Mnmawwén
Intoo	Btmawwnoo
Hinné	Bimawwnoo

Present Continuous		
Ana	Ăam	Bmawwén
Inta	Ăam	Btmawwén
Inté	Ăam	Btmawwné
Hoowé	Ăam	Bimawwén
Heeyé	Ăam	Btmawwén
Nahna	Ăam	Mnmawwén
Intoo	Ăam	Btmawwnoo
Hinné	Ăam	Bimawwnoo

Past	
Ana	Mawwant
Inta	Mawwant
Inté	Mawwanté
Hoowé	Mawwan
Heeyé	Mawwanét
Nahna	Mawwanna
Intoo	Mawwantoo
Hinné	mawwanoo

Past Continuous		
Ana	Kint Ăam	Bmawwén
Inta	Kint Ăam	Btmawwén
Inté	Kinté Ăam	Btmawwné
Hoowé	Kén Ăam	Bimawwén
Heeyé	Kénét Ăam	Btmawwén
Nahna	Kinna Ăam	Mnmawwén
Intoo	Kintoo Ăam	Btmawwnoo
Hinné	Kénoo Ăam	Bimawwnoo

Future		
Ana	Laĥ	Mawwén
Inta	Laĥ	Tmawwén
Inté	Laĥ	Tmawwné
Hoowé	Laĥ	Ymawwén
Heeyé	Laĥ	Tmawwén
Nahna	Laĥ	Nmawwén
Intoo	Laĥ	Tmawwnoo
Hinné	Laĥ	Ymawwnoo

Command	
Inta	Mawwén
Inté	Mawwné
Intoo	Mawnoo
Inta	Ma tmawwén
Inté	Ma tmawwné
Intoo	Ma tmawnoo

Ă= Augh in bought	Ď= a heavy D	É= like A in Bay	G= G in beige	ĥ= like an H with smaller air passage	I= I as in ink	Ќ= like ch in Irish loch
O= O as in home	OO= as in boots	R= roll the rrr	Ť= a heavy T	Ř= like a French R (gargle it)	Ŝ= a heavy S	Ž= a heavy Z

<u>S</u>   <u>S</u>

To support   To surround

Present	
Ana	bidĂam
Inta	btidĂam
Inté	btidĂamé
Hoowé	byidĂam
Heeyé	btidĂam
Nahna	mnidĂam
Intoo	btidĂamoo
Hinné	byidĂamoo

Present Continuous		
Ana	Ăam	bidĂam
Inta	Ăam	btidĂam
Inté	Ăam	btidĂamé
Hoowé	Ăam	byidĂam
Heeyé	Ăam	btidĂam
Nahna	Ăam	mnidĂam
Intoo	Ăam	btidĂamoo
Hinné	Ăam	byidĂamoo

Past	
Ana	daĂamt
Inta	daĂamt
Inté	daĂamté
Hoowé	daĂam
Heeyé	daĂamét
Nahna	daĂamna
Intoo	daĂamtoo
Hinné	daĂamoo

Past Continuous		
Ana	Kint Ăam	bidĂam
Inta	Kint Ăam	btidĂam
Inté	Kinté Ăam	btidĂamé
Hoowé	Kén Ăam	byidĂam
Heeyé	Kénét Ăam	btidĂam
Nahna	Kinna Ăam	mnidĂam
Intoo	Kintoo Ăam	btidĂamoo
Hinné	Kénoo Ăam	byidĂamoo

Future		
Ana	Laĥ	idĂam
Inta	Laĥ	tidĂam
Inté	Laĥ	tidĂamé
Hoowé	Laĥ	yidĂam
Heeyé	Laĥ	tidĂam
Nahna	Laĥ	nidĂam
Intoo	Laĥ	tidĂamoo
Hinné	Laĥ	yidĂamoo

Command	
Inta	dĂam
Inté	dĂamé
Intoo	dĂamoo
Inta	Ma tdAam
Inté	Ma tdAamé
Intoo	Ma tdAamoo

Present	
Ana	BĥawéŤ
Inta	BtĥawéŤ
Inté	BtĥawŤé
Hoowé	BiĥawéŤ
Heeyé	BtĥawéŤ
Nahna	MnĥawéŤ
Intoo	BtĥawŤoo
Hinné	BiĥawŤoo

Present Continuous			
Ana	Ăam	BĥawéŤ	(mĥawaŤ/mĥawaŤa)
Inta	Ăam	BtĥawéŤ	(mĥawaŤ)
Inté	Ăam	BtĥawŤé	(mĥawaŤa)
Hoowé	Ăam	BiĥawéŤ	(mĥawaŤ)
Heeyé	Ăam	BtĥawéŤ	(mĥawaŤa)
Nahna	Ăam	MnĥawéŤ	(mĥawaŤeen)
Intoo	Ăam	BtĥawŤoo	(mĥawaŤeen)
Hinné	Ăam	BiĥawŤoo	(mĥawaŤeen)

Past	
Ana	ĥawaŤt
Inta	ĥawaŤt
Inté	ĥawaŤté
Hoowé	ĥawaŤ
Heeyé	ĥawaŤét
Nahna	ĥawaŤna
Intoo	ĥawaŤtoo
Hinné	ĥawaŤoo

Past Continuous			
Ana	Kint Ăam	BĥawéŤ	(kint mĥawaŤ/mĥawaŤa)
Inta	Kint Ăam	BtĥawéŤ	(Kint mĥawaŤ)
Inté	Kinté Ăam	BtĥawŤé	(Kinté mĥawaŤa)
Hoowé	Kén Ăam	BiĥawéŤ	(Kén mĥawaŤ)
Heeyé	Kénét Ăam	BtĥawéŤ	(Kénét mĥawaŤa)
Nahna	Kinna Ăam	MnĥawéŤ	(Kinna mĥawaŤeen)
Intoo	Kintoo Ăam	BtĥawŤoo	(Kintoo mĥawaŤeen)
Hinné	Kénoo Ăam	BiĥawŤoo	(Kénoo mĥawaŤeen)

Future		
Ana	Laĥ	ĥawéŤ
Inta	Laĥ	tĥawéŤ
Inté	Laĥ	tĥawŤé
Hoowé	Laĥ	yĥawéŤ
Heeyé	Laĥ	tĥawéŤ
Nahna	Laĥ	nĥawéŤ
Intoo	Laĥ	tĥawŤoo
Hinné	Laĥ	yĥawŤoo

Command	
Inta	ĥawéŤ
Inté	ĥawŤé
Intoo	ĥawŤoo
Inta	Ma tĥawéŤ
Inté	Ma tĥawŤé
Intoo	Ma tĥawŤoo

Ă= Augh in bought	Ď= a heavy D	É= like A in Bay	G= G in beige	ĥ= like an H with smaller air passage		I= I as in ink	Ḱ= like ch in Irish loch
O= O as in home	OO= as in boots	R= roll the rrr	Ť= a heavy T	Ř= like a French R (gargle it)		Š= a heavy S	Ž= a heavy Z

S̱

S̱

To surround/ besiege

Present

Ana	BḣaS̱ér
Inta	BthaS̱ér
Inté	BthaS̱ré
Hoowé	BihaS̱ér
Heeyé	BthaS̱ér
Naḣna	mnḣaS̱ér
Intoo	BthaS̱roo
Hinné	BihaS̱roo

Present Continuous

Ana	Ăam	BḣaS̱ér	(mḣaS̱ar/mḣaS̱ar)
Inta	Ăam	BthaS̱ér	(mḣaS̱ar)
Inté	Ăam	BthaS̱ré	(mḣaS̱ra)
Hoowé	Ăam	BihaS̱ér	(mḣaS̱ar)
Heeyé	Ăam	BthaS̱ér	(mḣaS̱ra)
Naḣna	Ăam	mnḣaS̱ér	(mḣaS̱reen)
Intoo	Ăam	BthaS̱roo	(mḣaS̱reen)
Hinné	Ăam	BihaS̱roo	(mḣaS̱reen)

Past

Ana	ḣaS̱art
Inta	ḣaS̱art
Inté	ḣaS̱arté
Hoowé	ḣaS̱ar
Heeyé	ḣaS̱arét
Naḣna	ḣaS̱arna
Intoo	ḣaS̱artoo
Hinné	ḣaS̱aroo

Past Continuous

Ana	Kint Ăam	BḣaS̱ér	(kint	mḣaS̱ar / mḣaS̱ra)
Inta	Kint Ăam	BthaS̱ér	(Kint	mḣaS̱ar)
Inté	Kinté Ăam	BthaS̱ré	(Kinté	mḣaS̱ra)
Hoowé	Kén Ăam	BihaS̱ér	(Kén	mḣaS̱ar)
Heeyé	Kénét Ăam	BthaS̱ér	(Kénét	mḣaS̱ra)
Naḣna	Kinna Ăam	mnḣaS̱ér	(Kinna	mḣaS̱reen)
Intoo	Kintoo Ăam	BthaS̱roo	(Kintoo	mḣaS̱reen)
Hinné	Kénoo Ăam	BihaS̱roo	(Kénoo	mḣaS̱reen)

Future

Ana	Laḣ	ḣaS̱ér
Inta	Laḣ	thaS̱ér
Inté	Laḣ	thaS̱ré
Hoowé	Laḣ	yhaS̱ér
Heeyé	Laḣ	thaS̱ér
Naḣna	Laḣ	nhaS̱ér
Intoo	Laḣ	thaS̱roo
Hinné	Laḣ	yhaS̱roo

Command

Inta	ḣaS̱ér
Inté	ḣaS̱ré
Intoo	ḣaS̱roo
Inta	Ma thaS̱ér
Inté	Ma thaS̱ré
Intoo	Ma thaS̱roo

To suspect

Present

Ana	Bshikk
Inta	Btshikk
Inté	Btshikké
Hoowé	Bishikk
Heeyé	Bsthikk
Naḣna	Mnshikk
Intoo	Btshikkoo
Hinné	Bishikkoo

Present Continuous

Ana	Ăam	Bshikk	(shékék/shékké)
Inta	Ăam	Btshikk	(shékék)
Inté	Ăam	Btshikké	(shékké)
Hoowé	Ăam	Bishikk	(shékék)
Heeyé	Ăam	Bsthikk	(shékké)
Naḣna	Ăam	mnshikk	(shékkeen)
Intoo	Ăam	Btshikkoo	(shékkeen)
Hinné	Ăam	Bishikkoo	(shékkeen)

Past

Ana	Shakkét
Inta	Shakkét
Inté	Shakkaité
Hoowé	Shakk
Heeyé	Shakkét
Naḣna	Shakkaina
Intoo	Shakkaitoo
Hinné	Shakkoo

Past Continuous

Ana	Kint Ăam	Bshikk	(kint	(shékék/shék ké)
Inta	Kint Ăam	Btshikk	(Kint	(shékék)
Inté	Kinté Ăam	Btshikké	(Kinté	(shékké)
Hoowé	Kén Ăam	Bishikk	(Kén	(shékék)
Heeyé	Kénét Ăam	Bsthikk	(Kénét	(shékké)
Naḣna	Kinna Ăam	mnshikk	(Kinna	(shékkeen)
Intoo	Kintoo Ăam	Btshikkoo	(Kintoo	(shékkeen)
Hinné	Kénoo Ăam	Bishikkoo	(Kénoo	(shékkeen)

Future

Ana	Laḣ	shikk
Inta	Laḣ	tshikk
Inté	Laḣ	tshikké
Hoowé	Laḣ	yshikk
Heeyé	Laḣ	sthikk
Naḣna	Laḣ	nshikk
Intoo	Laḣ	tshikkoo
Hinné	Laḣ	yshikkoo

Command

Inta	Shikk
Inté	Shikké
Intoo	Shikkoo
Inta	Ma tshikk
Inté	Ma tshikké
Intoo	Ma tshikkoo

Ă= Augh in bought	Ď= a heavy D	É= like A in Bay	G= G in beige	ḣ= like an H with smaller air passage	I= I as in ink	Ḱ= like ch in Irish loch
O= O as in home	OO= as in boots	R= roll the rrr	Ť= a heavy T	Ř= like a French R (gargle it)	S̱= a heavy S	Ž= a heavy Z

<u>S</u>   <u>S</u>

To swallow   To swear / To vow

Present	
Ana	biblaĂ
Inta	btiblaĂ
Inté	btiblaĂé
Hoowé	byiblaĂ
Heeyé	btiblaĂ
Nahna	mniblaĂ
Intoo	btiblaĂoo
Hinné	byiblaĂoo

Present Continuous		
Ana	Ăam	biblaĂ
Inta	Ăam	btiblaĂ
Inté	Ăam	btiblaĂé
Hoowé	Ăam	byiblaĂ
Heeyé	Ăam	btiblaĂ
Nahna	Ăam	mniblaĂ
Intoo	Ăam	btiblaĂoo
Hinné	Ăam	byiblaĂoo

Past	
Ana	balaĂt
Inta	balaĂt
Inté	balaĂté
Hoowé	balaĂ
Heeyé	balaĂét
Nahna	balaĂna
Intoo	balaĂtoo
Hinné	balaĂoo

Past Continuous		
Ana	Kint Ăam	biblaĂ
Inta	Kint Ăam	btiblaĂ
Inté	Kinté Ăam	btiblaĂé
Hoowé	Kén Ăam	byiblaĂ
Heeyé	Kénét Ăam	btiblaĂ
Nahna	Kinna Ăam	mniblaĂ
Intoo	Kintoo Ăam	btiblaĂoo
Hinné	Kénoo Ăam	byiblaĂoo

Future		
Ana	Laĥ	iblaĂ
Inta	Laĥ	tiblaĂ
Inté	Laĥ	tiblaĂé
Hoowé	Laĥ	yiblaĂ
Heeyé	Laĥ	tiblaĂ
Nahna	Laĥ	niblaĂ
Intoo	Laĥ	tiblaĂoo
Hinné	Laĥ	yiblaĂoo

Command	
Inta	blaĂ
Inté	blaĂé
Intoo	blaĂoo
Inta	Ma tblaĂ
Inté	Ma tblaĂé
Intoo	Ma tblaĂoo

To swear / To vow

Present		
Ana	Biĥléf	(also biĥlof)
Inta	Btiĥléf	
Inté	Btiĥlfé	
Hoowé	Byiĥléf	
Heeyé	Btiĥléf	
Nahna	Mniĥléf	
Intoo	Btiĥlfoo	
Hinné	Byiĥlfoo	

Present Continuous		
Ana	Ăam	Biĥléf
Inta	Ăam	Btiĥléf
Inté	Ăam	Btiĥlfé
Hoowé	Ăam	Byiĥléf
Heeyé	Ăam	Btiĥléf
Nahna	Ăam	Mniĥléf
Intoo	Ăam	Btiĥlfoo
Hinné	Ăam	Byiĥlfoo

Past	
Ana	Ĥlift
Inta	Ĥlift
Inté	Ĥlifté
Hoowé	Ĥiléf
Heeyé	Ĥilfét
Nahna	Ĥlifna
Intoo	Ĥliftoo
Hinné	Ĥilfoo

Past Continuous		
Ana	Kint Ăam	Biĥléf
Inta	Kint Ăam	Btiĥléf
Inté	Kinté Ăam	Btiĥlfé
Hoowé	Kén Ăam	Byiĥléf
Heeyé	Kénét Ăam	Btiĥléf
Nahna	Kinna Ăam	Mniĥléf
Intoo	Kintoo Ăam	Btiĥlfoo
Hinné	Kénoo Ăam	Byiĥlfoo

Future		
Ana	Laĥ	Iĥléf	(also iĥlof)
Inta	Laĥ	Tiĥléf	
Inté	Laĥ	Tiĥlfé	
Hoowé	Laĥ	Yiĥléf	
Heeyé	Laĥ	Tiĥléf	
Nahna	Laĥ	Niĥléf	
Intoo	Laĥ	Tiĥlfoo	
Hinné	Laĥ	Tiĥlfoo	

Command		
Inta	Ĥléf	(also ĥlof)
Inté	Ĥlifé	
Intoo	Ĥlifoo	
Inta	Ma tĥléf	
Inté	Ma tĥlfé	
Intoo	Ma tĥlfoo	

Ă= Augh in bought	Ď= a heavy D	É= like A in Bay	G= G in beige	ĥ= like an H with smaller air passage	I= I as in ink	Ќ= like ch in Irish loch
O= O as in home	OO= as in boots	R= roll the rrr	Ť= a heavy T	Ř= like a French R (gargle it)	Ŝ= a heavy S	Ž= a heavy Z

S̲   S̲

To swear / To curse   ## To sweat

Present	
Ana	bsibb
Inta	btsibb
Inté	Btsibbé
Hoowé	bisibb
Heeyé	btsibb
Nahna	Mnsibb
Intoo	Btsibbo
Hinné	Bisibboo

Present Continuous		
Ana	Ăam	bsibb
Inta	Ăam	btsibb
Inté	Ăam	Btsibbé
Hoowé	Ăam	bisibb
Heeyé	Ăam	btsibb
Nahna	Ăam	Mnsibb
Intoo	Ăam	Btsibbo
Hinné	Ăam	Bisibboo

Past	
Ana	sabbét
Inta	sabbét
Inté	sabaité
Hoowé	Sabb
Heeyé	Sabbét
Nahna	Sabbaina
Intoo	Sabbaitoo
Hinné	Sabboo

Past Continuous		
Ana	Kint Ăam	bsibb
Inta	Kint Ăam	btsibb
Inté	Kinté Ăam	Btsibbé
Hoowé	Kén Ăam	bisibb
Heeyé	Kénét Ăam	btsibb
Nahna	Kinna Ăam	Mnsibb
Intoo	Kintoo Ăam	Btsibbo
Hinné	Kénoo Ăam	Bisibboo

Future		
Ana	Laĥ	sibb
Inta	Laĥ	tsibb
Inté	Laĥ	Tsibbé
Hoowé	Laĥ	ysibb
Heeyé	Laĥ	Tsibb
Nahna	Laĥ	nsibb
Intoo	Laĥ	Tsibboo
Hinné	Laĥ	Ysibboo

Command	
Inta	sibb
Inté	Sibbé
Intoo	Sibboo
Inta	Ma tsibb
Inté	Ma tsibbé
Intoo	Ma tsibboo

Present	
Ana	biĂra'
Inta	btiĂra'
Inté	btiĂra'é
Hoowé	byiĂra'
Heeyé	btiĂra'
Nahna	mniĂra'
Intoo	btiĂra'oo
Hinné	byiĂra'oo

Present Continuous			
Ana	Ăam	biĂra'	(Ăir'an/Ăir'ané)
Inta	Ăam	btiĂra'	(Ăir'an)
Inté	Ăam	btiĂra'é	(Ăir'ané)
Hoowé	Ăam	byiĂra'	(Ăir'an)
Heeyé	Ăam	btiĂra'	(Ăir'ané)
Nahna	Ăam	mniĂra'	(Ăir'aneen)
Intoo	Ăam	btiĂra'oo	(Ăir'aneen)
Hinné	Ăam	byiĂra'oo	(Ăir'aneen)

Past	
Ana	Ări't
Inta	Ări't
Inté	Ări'té
Hoowé	Ăiri'
Heeyé	Ăir'ét
Nahna	Ări'na
Intoo	Ări'too
Hinné	Ări'oo

Past Continuous			
Ana	Kint Ăam	biĂra'	(kint Ăir'an/Ăir'ané)
Inta	Kint Ăam	btiĂra'	(Kint Ăir'an)
Inté	Kinté Ăam	btiĂra'é	(Kinté Ăir'ané)
Hoowé	Kén Ăam	byiĂra'	(Kén Ăi'an)
Heeyé	Kénét Ăam	btiĂra'	(Kénét Ăir'ané)
Nahna	Kinna Ăam	mniĂra'	(Kinna Ăir'aneen)
Intoo	Kintoo Ăam	btiĂra'oo	(Kintoo Ăir'aneen)
Hinné	Kénoo Ăam	byiĂra'oo	(Kénoo Ăir'aneen)

Future		
Ana	Laĥ	iĂra'
Inta	Laĥ	tiĂra'
Inté	Laĥ	tiĂra'é
Hoowé	Laĥ	yiĂra'
Heeyé	Laĥ	tiĂra'
Nahna	Laĥ	niĂra'
Intoo	Laĥ	tiĂra'oo
Hinné	Laĥ	yiĂra'oo

Command	
Inta	Ăra'
Inté	Ăra'é
Intoo	Ăra'oo
Inta	Ma tĂra'
Inté	Ma tĂra'é
Intoo	Ma tĂra'oo

Ă= Augh in bought	Ď= a heavy D	É= like A in Bay	G= G in beige	ĥ= like an H with smaller air passage	I= I as in ink	Ǩ= like ch in Irish loch
O= O as in home	OO= as in boots	R= roll the rrr	Ť= a heavy T	Ř= like a French R (gargle it)	Ŝ= a heavy S	Ž= a heavy Z

<u>S</u>   <u>S</u>

To swell

Present

Ana	bwarrém
Inta	btwarrém
Inté	Btwarrmé
Hoowé	biwarrém
Heeyé	btwarrém
Naḣna	mnwarrém
Intoo	Btwarrmoo
Hinné	Biwarrmoo

Present Continuous

Ana	Ăam	Bwarrém	(mwarram/mwarramé)
Inta	Ăam	Btwarrém	(mwarram)
Inté	Ăam	Btwarrmé	(mwarramé)
Hoowé	Ăam	Biwarrém	(mwarram)
Heeyé	Ăam	Btwarrém	(mwarramé)
Naḣna	Ăam	Mnwarrém	(mwarrameen)
Intoo	Ăam	Btwarrmoo	(mwarrameen)
Hinné	Ăam	Biwarrmoo	(mwarrameen)

Past

Ana	Warramt
Inta	Warramt
Inté	Warramté
Hoowé	Warram
Heeyé	Warramét
Naḣna	Warramna
Intoo	Warramtoo
Hinné	Warramoo

Past Continuous

Ana	Kint Ăam	bwarrém	(kint	Mwarram/mw arramé)
Inta	Kint Ăam	btwarrém	(Kint	mwarram)
Inté	Kinté Ăam	Btwarrmé	(Kinté	mwarramé)
Hoowé	Kén Ăam	biwarrém	(Kén	mwarram)
Heeyé	Kénét Ăam	btwarrém	(Kénét	mwarramé)
Naḣna	Kinna Ăam	mnwarrém	(Kinna	mwarrameen)
Intoo	Kintoo Ăam	Btwarrmoo	(Kintoo	mwarrameen)
Hinné	Kénoo Ăam	Biwarrmoo	(Kénoo	mwarrameen)

Future

Ana	Laḣ	warrém
Inta	Laḣ	twarrém
Inté	Laḣ	twarrmé
Hoowé	Laḣ	ywarrém
Heeyé	Laḣ	twarrém
Naḣna	Laḣ	nwarrém
Intoo	Laḣ	twarrmoo
Hinné	Laḣ	ywarrmoo

Command

Inta	Warrém
Inté	Warrmé
Intoo	warrmoo
Inta	Ma twarrém
Inté	Ma twarrmé
Intoo	Ma twarrmoo

To sweep

Present

Ana	Bkannés
Inta	Btkannés
Inté	Btkannsé
Hoowé	Bikannés
Heeyé	Btkannés
Naḣna	Mnkannés
Intoo	Btkannsoo
Hinné	Bikannsoo

Present Continuous

Ana	Ăam	Bkannés
Inta	Ăam	Btkannés
Inté	Ăam	Btkannsé
Hoowé	Ăam	Bikannés
Heeyé	Ăam	Btkannés
Naḣna	Ăam	Mnkannés
Intoo	Ăam	Btkannsoo
Hinné	Ăam	Bikannsoo

Past

Ana	Kannast
Inta	Kannast
Inté	Kannste
Hoowé	Kannas
Heeyé	Kannasét
Naḣna	Kannasna
Intoo	Kannastoo
Hinné	Kannasoo

Past Continuous

Ana	Kint Ăam	Bkannés
Inta	Kint Ăam	Btkannés
Inté	Kinté Ăam	Btkannsé
Hoowé	Kén Ăam	Bikannés
Heeyé	Kénét Ăam	Btkannés
Naḣna	Kinna Ăam	Mnkannés
Intoo	Kintoo Ăam	Btkannsoo
Hinné	Kénoo Ăam	Bikannsoo

Future

Ana	Laḣ	kannés
Inta	Laḣ	tkannés
Inté	Laḣ	tkannsé
Hoowé	Laḣ	ykannés
Heeyé	Laḣ	tkannés
Naḣna	Laḣ	nkannés
Intoo	Laḣ	tkannsoo
Hinné	Laḣ	ykannsoo

Command

Inta	Kannés
Inté	Kannsé
Intoo	Kannsoo
Inta	Ma tkannés
Inté	Ma tkannsé
Intoo	Ma tkansoo

Ă= Augh in bought	Ď= a heavy D	É= like A in Bay	G= G in beige	ḣ= like an H with smaller air passage	I= I as in ink	Ḱ= like ch in Irish loch
O= O as in home	OO= as in boots	R= roll the rrr	Ť= a heavy T	Ř= like a French R (gargle it)	Ŝ= a heavy S	Ž= a heavy Z

S̲   S̲

To swim

Present

Ana	Bisbaĥ
Inta	Btisbaĥ
Inté	Btisbaĥé
Hoowé	Byisbah
Heeyé	Btisbaĥ
Naĥna	Mnisbaĥ
Intoo	Btisbahoo
Hinné	Byisbahoo

Present Continuous

Ana	Ăam	Bisbaĥ
Inta	Ăam	Btisbaĥ
Inté	Ăam	Btisbaĥé
Hoowé	Ăam	Byisbah
Heeyé	Ăam	Btisbaĥ
Naĥna	Ăam	Mnisbaĥ
Intoo	Ăam	Btisbahoo
Hinné	Ăam	Byisbahoo

Past

Ana	sabaĥt
Inta	sabaĥt
Inté	Sabaĥté
Hoowé	Sabaĥ
Heeyé	sabaĥét
Naĥna	Sabaĥna
Intoo	Sabaĥtoo
Hinné	Sabaĥoo

Past Continuous

Ana	Kint Ăam	Bisbaĥ
Inta	Kint Ăam	Btisbaĥ
Inté	Kinté Ăam	Btisbaĥé
Hoowé	Kén Ăam	Byisbah
Heeyé	Kénét Ăam	Btisbaĥ
Naĥna	Kinna Ăam	Mnisbaĥ
Intoo	Kintoo Ăam	Btisbahoo
Hinné	Kénoo Ăam	Byisbahoo

Future

Ana	Laĥ	isbaĥ
Inta	Laĥ	tisbah
Inté	Laĥ	tisbaĥé
Hoowé	Laĥ	yisbaĥ
Heeyé	Laĥ	tisbah
Naĥna	Laĥ	nisbah
Intoo	Laĥ	tisbahoo
Hinné	Laĥ	yisbahoo

Command

Inta	Sbaĥ
Inté	Sbaĥé
Intoo	sbahoo
Inta	Ma tsbaĥ
Inté	Ma tsbaĥé
Intoo	Ma tsbahoo

To switch / To trade

Present

Ana	bbaddél
Inta	btbaddél
Inté	Btbaddlé
Hoowé	bibaddél
Heeyé	btbaddél
Naĥna	mnbaddél
Intoo	Btbaddloo
Hinné	bibaddloo

Present Continuous

Ana	Ăam	bbaddél
Inta	Ăam	btbaddél
Inté	Ăam	Btbaddlé
Hoowé	Ăam	bibaddél
Heeyé	Ăam	btbaddél
Naĥna	Ăam	mnbaddél
Intoo	Ăam	Btbaddloo
Hinné	Ăam	bibaddloo

Past

Ana	Baddalt
Inta	Baddalt
Inté	Baddalté
Hoowé	Baddal
Heeyé	Baddalét
Naĥna	Baddalna
Intoo	Baddaltoo
Hinné	Baddaloo

Past Continuous

Ana	Kint Ăam	bbaddél
Inta	Kint Ăam	btbaddél
Inté	Kinté Ăam	Btbaddlé
Hoowé	Kén Ăam	bibaddél
Heeyé	Kénét Ăam	btbaddél
Naĥna	Kinna Ăam	mnbaddél
Intoo	Kintoo Ăam	Btbaddloo
Hinné	Kénoo Ăam	bibaddloo

Future

Ana	Laĥ	baddél
Inta	Laĥ	tbaddél
Inté	Laĥ	tbaddlé
Hoowé	Laĥ	ybaddél
Heeyé	Laĥ	tbaddél
Naĥna	Laĥ	nbaddél
Intoo	Laĥ	tbaddloo
Hinné	Laĥ	ybaddloo

Command

Inta	Baddél
Inté	Baddlé
Intoo	Badloo
Inta	Ma tbaddél
Inté	Ma tbaddlé
Intoo	Ma tbadloo

Ă= Augh in bought	Đ= a heavy D	É= like A in Bay	G= G in beige	ĥ= like an H with smaller air passage	I= I as in ink	Ḱ= like ch in Irish loch
O= O as in home	OO= as in boots	R= roll the rrr	Ť= a heavy T	Ř= like a French R (gargle it)	Ŝ= a heavy S	Ž= a heavy Z

T   T

To take   To taste

To take

Present	
Ana	béK̇od
Inta	btéK̇od
Inté	btéK̇dé
Hoowé	byéK̇od
Heeyé	btéK̇od
Naḣna	mnéK̇od
Intoo	btéK̇doo
Hinné	byéK̇doo

Present Continuous		
Ana	Ăam béK̇od	(éK̇éd/éK̇dé)
Inta	Ăam btéK̇od	(éK̇éd)
Inté	Ăam btéK̇dé	(éK̇dé)
Hoowé	Ăam byéK̇od	(éK̇éd)
Heeyé	Ăam btéK̇od	(éK̇dé)
Naḣna	Ăam mnéK̇od	(éK̇deen)
Intoo	Ăam btéK̇doo	(éK̇deen)
Hinné	Ăam byéK̇doo	(éK̇deen)

Past	
Ana	aK̇adt
Inta	aK̇adt
Inté	aK̇adté
Hoowé	aK̇ad
Heeyé	aK̇adét
Naḣna	aK̇adna
Intoo	aK̇adtoo
Hinné	aK̇adoo

Past Continuous		
Ana	Kint Ăam béK̇od	(kint éK̇éd/éK̇dé)
Inta	Kint Ăam btéK̇od	(Kint éK̇éd)
Inté	Kinté Ăam btéK̇dé	(Kinté éK̇éd)
Hoowé	Kén Ăam byéK̇od	(Kén éK̇éd)
Heeyé	Kénét Ăam btéK̇od	(Kénét éK̇dé)
Naḣna	Kinna Ăam mnéK̇od	(Kinna éK̇deen)
Intoo	Kintoo Ăam btéK̇doo	(Kintoo éK̇deen)
Hinné	Kénoo Ăam byéK̇doo	(Kénoo éK̇deen)

Future		
Ana	Laḣ	éK̇od
Inta	Laḣ	téK̇od
Inté	Laḣ	téK̇dé
Hoowé	Laḣ	yéK̇od
Heeyé	Laḣ	téK̇od
Naḣna	Laḣ	néK̇od
Intoo	Laḣ	téK̇doo
Hinné	Laḣ	yéK̇doo

Command	
Inta	K̇od
Inté	K̇idé
Intoo	K̇idoo
Inta	Ma téK̇od
Inté	Ma téK̇dé
Intoo	Ma téK̇doo

To taste

Present	
Ana	Bdoo'
Inta	Btdoo'
Inté	Btdoo'é
Hoowé	Bidoo'
Heeyé	Btdoo'
Naḣna	Mndoo'
Intoo	Btdoo'oo
Hinné	Bidoo'oo

Present Continuous	
Ana	Ăam Bdoo'
Inta	Ăam Btdoo'
Inté	Ăam Btdoo'é
Hoowé	Ăam Bidoo'
Heeyé	Ăam Btdoo'
Naḣna	Ăam Mndoo'
Intoo	Ăam Btdoo'oo
Hinné	Ăam Bidoo'oo

Past	
Ana	Di't
Inta	Di't
Inté	Di'té
Hoowé	Dé'
Heeyé	Dé'ét
Naḣna	Di'na
Intoo	Di'too
Hinné	Dé'oo

Past Continuous	
Ana	Kint Ăam Bdoo'
Inta	Kint Ăam btdoo'
Inté	Kinté Ăam Btdoo'é
Hoowé	Kén Ăam Bidoo'
Heeyé	Kénét Ăam Btdoo'
Naḣna	Kinna Ăam Mndoo'
Intoo	Kintoo Ăam Btdoo'oo
Hinné	Kénoo Ăam Bidoo'oo

Future	
Ana	Laḣ doo'
Inta	Laḣ tdoo'
Inté	Laḣ tdoo'é
Hoowé	Laḣ ydoo'
Heeyé	Laḣ tdoo'
Naḣna	Laḣ ndoo'
Intoo	Laḣ tdoo'oo
Hinné	Laḣ ydoo'oo

Command	
Inta	Doo'
Inté	Doo'é
Intoo	Doo'oo
Inta	Ma tdoo'
Inté	Ma tdoo'é
Intoo	Ma tdoo'oo

Ă= Augh in bought	Ď= a heavy D	É= like A in Bay	G= G in beige	ḣ= like an H with smaller air passage	I= I as in ink	K̇= like ch in Irish loch
O= O as in home	OO= as in boots	R= roll the rrr	Ť= a heavy T	Ř= like a French R (gargle it)	Ŝ= a heavy S	Ž= a heavy Z

T   T

To teach   To tear

To teach

Present	
Ana	bĂallém
Inta	btĂallém
Inté	btĂallmé
Hoowé	biĂallém
Heeyé	btĂallém
Nahna	mnĂallém
Intoo	btĂallmoo
Hinné	biĂallmoo

Present Continuous		
Ana	Ăam	bĂallém
Inta	Ăam	btĂallém
Inté	Ăam	btĂallmé
Hoowé	Ăam	biĂallém
Heeyé	Ăam	btĂallém
Nahna	Ăam	mnĂallém
Intoo	Ăam	btĂallmoo
Hinné	Ăam	biĂallmoo

Past	
Ana	Ăallamt
Inta	Ăallamt
Inté	Ăallamté
Hoowé	Ăallam
Heeyé	Ăallamét
Nahna	Ăallamna
Intoo	Ăallamtoo
Hinné	Ăallamoo

Past Continuous		
Ana	Kint Ăam	bĂallém
Inta	Kint Ăam	btĂallém
Inté	Kinté Ăam	btĂallmé
Hoowé	Kén Ăam	biĂallém
Heeyé	Kénét Ăam	btĂallém
Nahna	Kinna Ăam	mnĂallém
Intoo	Kintoo Ăam	btĂallmoo
Hinné	Kénoo Ăam	biĂallmoo

Future		
Ana	Lah	Ăallém
Inta	Lah	tĂallém
Inté	Lah	tĂallmé
Hoowé	Lah	yĂallém
Heeyé	Lah	tĂallém
Nahna	Lah	nĂallém
Intoo	Lah	tĂallmoo
Hinné	Lah	yĂallmoo

Command	
Inta	Ăallém
Inté	Ăallmé
Intoo	Ăallmoo
Inta	Ma tĂallém
Inté	Ma tĂallmé
Intoo	Ma tĂallmoo

To tear

Present	
Ana	bĶazzé'
Inta	btĶazzé'
Inté	btĶazz'é
Hoowé	biĶazzé'
Heeyé	btĶazzé'
Nahna	mnĶazzé'
Intoo	btĶazz'oo
Hinné	biĶazz'oo

Present Continuous		
Ana	Ăam	bĶazzé'
Inta	Ăam	btĶazzé'
Inté	Ăam	btĶazz'é
Hoowé	Ăam	biĶazzé'
Heeyé	Ăam	btĶazzé'
Nahna	Ăam	mnĶazzé'
Intoo	Ăam	btĶazz'oo
Hinné	Ăam	biĶazz'oo

Past	
Ana	Ķazza't
Inta	Ķazza't
Inté	Ķazza'té
Hoowé	Ķazza'
Heeyé	Ķazza'ét
Nahna	Ķazza'na
Intoo	Ķazza'too
Hinné	Ķazza'oo

Past Continuous		
Ana	Kint Ăam	bĶazzé'
Inta	Kint Ăam	btĶazzé'
Inté	Kinté Ăam	btĶazz'é
Hoowé	Kén Ăam	biĶazzé'
Heeyé	Kénét Ăam	btĶazzé'
Nahna	Kinna Ăam	mnĶazzé'
Intoo	Kintoo Ăam	btĶazz'oo
Hinné	Kénoo Ăam	biĶazz'oo

Future		
Ana	Lah	Ķazzé'
Inta	Lah	tĶazzé'
Inté	Lah	tĶazz'é
Hoowé	Lah	yĶazzé'
Heeyé	Lah	tĶazzé'
Nahna	Lah	nĶazzé'
Intoo	Lah	tĶazz'oo
Hinné	Lah	yĶazz'oo

Command	
Inta	Ķazzé'
Inté	Ķazz'é
Intoo	Ķazz'oo
Inta	Ma tĶazzé'
Inté	Ma tĶazz'é
Intoo	Ma tĶazz'oo

Ă= Augh in bought	Ď= a heavy D	É= like A in Bay	G= G in beige	ĥ= like an H with smaller air passage	I= I as in ink	Ķ= like ch in Irish loch
O= O as in home	OO= as in boots	R= roll the rrr	Ť= a heavy T	Ř= like a French R (gargle it)	Ŝ= a heavy S	Ž= a heavy Z

T   T

To tease

Present	
Ana	Bĥar'éŜ
Inta	Btĥar'éŜ
Inté	Btĥar'Ŝé
Hoowé	Biĥar'éŜ
Heeyé	Btĥar'éŜ
Nahna	Mnĥar'éŜ
Intoo	Btĥar'Ŝoo
Hinné	Biĥar'Ŝoo

Present Continuous		
Ana	Ăam	Bĥar'éŜ
Inta	Ăam	Btĥar'éŜ
Inté	Ăam	Btĥar'Ŝé
Hoowé	Ăam	Biĥar'éŜ
Heeyé	Ăam	Btĥar'éŜ
Nahna	Ăam	Mnĥar'éŜ
Intoo	Ăam	Btĥar'Ŝoo
Hinné	Ăam	Biĥar'Ŝoo

Past	
Ana	Ĥar'aŜt
Inta	Ĥar'aŜt
Inté	Ĥar'aŜté
Hoowé	Ĥar'aŜ
Heeyé	Ĥar'aŜét
Nahna	Ĥar'aŜna
Intoo	Ĥar'aŜtoo
Hinné	Ĥar'aŜoo

Past Continuous		
Ana	Kint Ăam	Bĥar'éŜ
Inta	Kint Ăam	Btĥar'éŜ
Inté	Kinté Ăam	Btĥar'Ŝé
Hoowé	Kén Ăam	Biĥar'éŜ
Heeyé	Kénét Ăam	Btĥar'éŜ
Nahna	Kinna Ăam	Mnĥar'éŜ
Intoo	Kintoo Ăam	Btĥar'Ŝoo
Hinné	Kénoo Ăam	Biĥar'Ŝoo

Future		
Ana	Laĥ	Ĥar'éŜ
Inta	Laĥ	Tĥar'éŜ
Inté	Laĥ	Tĥar'Ŝé
Hoowé	Laĥ	Yĥar'éŜ
Heeyé	Laĥ	Tĥar'éŜ
Nahna	Laĥ	Nĥar'éŜ
Intoo	Laĥ	Tĥar'Ŝoo
Hinné	Laĥ	Yar'Ŝoo

Command	
Inta	Ĥar'éŜ
Inté	Ĥar'Ŝé
Intoo	Ĥar'Ŝoo
Inta	Ma tĥar'éŜ
Inté	Ma tĥar'Ŝé
Intoo	Ma tĥar'Ŝoo

To tell

Present	
Ana	bĶabbér
Inta	btĶabbér
Inté	btĶabbér
Hoowé	biĶabbér
Heeyé	btĶabbér
Nahna	mnĶabbér
Intoo	btĶabbroo
Hinné	biĶabbroo

Present Continuous		
Ana	Ăam	bĶabbér
Inta	Ăam	btĶabbér
Inté	Ăam	btĶabbér
Hoowé	Ăam	biĶabbér
Heeyé	Ăam	btĶabbér
Nahna	Ăam	mnĶabbér
Intoo	Ăam	btĶabbroo
Hinné	Ăam	biĶabbroo

Past	
Ana	Ķabbart
Inta	Ķabbart
Inté	Ķabbarté
Hoowé	Ķabbar
Heeyé	Ķabbarét
Nahna	Ķabbarna
Intoo	Ķabbartoo
Hinné	Ķabbaroo

Past Continuous		
Ana	Kint Ăam	bĶabbér
Inta	Kint Ăam	btĶabbér
Inté	Kinté Ăam	btĶabbér
Hoowé	Kén Ăam	biĶabbér
Heeyé	Kénét Ăam	btĶabbér
Nahna	Kinna Ăam	mnĶabbér
Intoo	Kintoo Ăam	btĶabbroo
Hinné	Kénoo Ăam	biĶabbroo

Future		
Ana	Laĥ	Ķabbér
Inta	Laĥ	tĶabbér
Inté	Laĥ	tĶabbré
Hoowé	Laĥ	yĶabbér
Heeyé	Laĥ	tĶabbér
Nahna	Laĥ	nĶabbér
Intoo	Laĥ	tĶabbroo
Hinné	Laĥ	yĶabbroo

Command	
Inta	Ķabber
Inté	Ķabbre
Intoo	Kabbroo
Inta	Ma tĶabber
Inté	Ma tĶabbré
Intoo	Ma tĶabroo

Ă= Augh in bought	Ď= a heavy D	É= like A in Bay	G= G in beige	ĥ= like an H with smaller air passage	I= I as in ink	Ķ= like ch in Irish loch
O= O as in home	OO= as in boots	R= roll the rrr	Ť= a heavy T	Ř= like a French R (gargle it)	Ŝ= a heavy S	Ž= a heavy Z

T

T

To tend /To incline

Present

Ana	Bmeel
Inta	Btmeel
Inté	Btmeelé
Hoowé	Bimeel
Heeyé	Btmeel
Naĥna	Mnmeel
Intoo	Btmeeloo
Hinné	Bimeeloo

Present Continuous

Ana	Ăam	Bmeel	(méyél/méylé)
Inta	Ăam	Btmeel	(méyél)
Inté	Ăam	Btmeelé	(méyle)
Hoowé	Ăam	Bimeel	(méyél)
Heeyé	Ăam	Btmeel	(méylé)
Naĥna	Ăam	Mnmeel	(méyleen)
Intoo	Ăam	Btmeeloo	(méyleen)
Hinné	Ăam	Bimeeloo	(méyleen)

Past

Ana	Milt
Inta	Milt
Inté	Milté
Hoowé	Mél
Heeyé	Mélét
Naĥna	Milna
Intoo	Miltoo
Hinné	Méloo

Past Continuous

Ana	Kint Ăam	Bmeel	(kint méyél/méylé)
Inta	Kint Ăam	Btmeel	(Kint méyél)
Inté	Kinté Ăam	Btmeelé	(Kinté méyle)
Hoowé	Kén Ăam	Bimeel	(Kén méyél)
Heeyé	Kénét Ăam	Btmeel	(Kénét méylé)
Naĥna	Kinna Ăam	Mnmeel	(Kinna méyleen)
Intoo	Kintoo Ăam	Btmeeloo	(Kintoo méyleen)
Hinné	Kénoo Ăam	Bimeeloo	(Kénoo méyleen)

Future

Ana	Laĥ	Meel
Inta	Laĥ	Tmeel
Inté	Laĥ	Tmeelé
Hoowé	Laĥ	Ymeel
Heeyé	Laĥ	Tmeel
Naĥna	Laĥ	Nmeel
Intoo	Laĥ	Tmeeloo
Hinné	Laĥ	Ymeeloo

Command

Inta	Meel
Inté	Meelé
Intoo	Meeloo
Inta	Ma tmeel
Inté	Ma tmeelé
Intoo	Ma tmeeloo

To test

Present

Ana	bifĥaŜ
Inta	btifĥaŜ
Inté	btifĥaŜé
Hoowé	byifĥaŜ
Heeyé	btifĥaŜ
Naĥna	mnifĥaŜ
Intoo	btifĥaŜoo
Hinné	byifĥaŜoo

Present Continuous

Ana	Ăam	bifĥaŜ
Inta	Ăam	btifĥaŜ
Inté	Ăam	btifĥaŜé
Hoowé	Ăam	byifĥaŜ
Heeyé	Ăam	btifĥaŜ
Naĥna	Ăam	mnifĥaŜ
Intoo	Ăam	btifĥaŜoo
Hinné	Ăam	byifĥaŜoo

Past

Ana	faĥaŜt
Inta	faĥaŜt
Inté	faĥaŜté
Hoowé	faĥaŜ
Heeyé	faĥaŜét
Naĥna	faĥaŜna
Intoo	faĥaŜtoo
Hinné	faĥaŜoo

Past Continuous

Ana	Kint Ăam	bifĥaŜ
Inta	Kint Ăam	btifĥaŜ
Inté	Kinté Ăam	btifĥaŜé
Hoowé	Kén Ăam	byifĥaŜ
Heeyé	Kénét Ăam	btifĥaŜ
Naĥna	Kinna Ăam	mnifĥaŜ
Intoo	Kintoo Ăam	btifĥaŜoo
Hinné	Kénoo Ăam	byifĥaŜoo

Future

Ana	Laĥ	ifĥaŜ
Inta	Laĥ	tifĥaŜ
Inté	Laĥ	tifĥaŜé
Hoowé	Laĥ	yifĥaŜ
Heeyé	Laĥ	tifĥaŜ
Naĥna	Laĥ	nifĥaŜ
Intoo	Laĥ	tifĥaŜoo
Hinné	Laĥ	yifĥaŜoo

Command

Inta	fĥaŜ
Inté	fĥaŜé
Intoo	fĥaŜoo
Inta	Ma tfĥaŜ
Inté	Ma tfĥaŜé
Intoo	Ma tfĥaŜoo

Ă= Augh in bought	Ď= a heavy D	É= like A in Bay	G= G in beige	ĥ= like an H with smaller air passage	I= I as in ink	Ḱ= like ch in Irish loch
O= O as in home	OO= as in boots	R= roll the rrr	Ť= a heavy T	Ř= like a French R (gargle it)	Ŝ= a heavy S	Ž= a heavy Z

T   T

To think

Present	
Ana	Bfakkér
Inta	Btfakkér
Inté	Btfakkré
Hoowé	Bifakkér
Heeyé	Btfakkér
Nahna	Mnfakkér
Intoo	Btfakkroo
Hinné	Bifakkroo

Present Continuous		
Ana	Ăam Bfakkér	(mfakkar/mfakkra)
Inta	Ăam Btfakkér	(mfakkar)
Inté	Ăam Btfakkré	(mfakkra)
Hoowé	Ăam Bifakkér	(mfakkar)
Heeyé	Ăam Btfakkér	(mfakkra)
Nahna	Ăam mnfakkér	(mfakkreen)
Intoo	Ăam Btfakkroo	(mfakkreen)
Hinné	Ăam Bifakkroo	(mfakkreen)

Past	
Ana	Fakkart
Inta	Fakkart
Inté	Fakkarté
Hoowé	Fakkar
Heeyé	Fakkarét
Nahna	Fakkarna
Intoo	Fakkartoo
Hinné	Fakkaroo

Past Continuous			
Ana	Kint Ăam	Bfakkér	(kint mfakkar/mfakkra)
Inta	Kint Ăam	Btfakkér	(Kint mfakkar)
Inté	Kinté Ăam	Btfakkré	(Kinté mfakkra)
Hoowé	Kén Ăam	Bifakkér	(Kén mfakkar)
Heeyé	Kénét Ăam	Btfakkér	(Kénét mfakkra)
Nahna	Kinna Ăam	mnfakkér	(Kinna mfakkreen)
Intoo	Kintoo Ăam	Btfakkroo	(Kintoo mfakkreen)
Hinné	Kénoo Ăam	Bifakkroo	(Kénoo mfakkreen)

Future		
Ana	Laĥ	Fakkér
Inta	Laĥ	Tfakkér
Inté	Laĥ	Tfakkré
Hoowé	Laĥ	Yfakkér
Heeyé	Laĥ	Tfakkér
Nahna	Laĥ	Nfakkér
Intoo	Laĥ	Tfakkroo
Hinné	Laĥ	Yfakkroo

Command	
Inta	Fakkér
Inté	Fakkré
Intoo	Fakkroo
Inta	Ma tfakkér
Inté	Ma tfakkré
Intoo	Ma tfakkroo

To throw

Present	
Ana	Bkibb
Inta	Btkibb
Inté	Btkibbé
Hoowé	Bikibb
Heeyé	Btkibb
Nahna	Mnkibb
Intoo	Btkibboo
Hinné	Bikibboo

Present Continuous	
Ana	Ăam Bkibb
Inta	Ăam Btkibb
Inté	Ăam Btkibbé
Hoowé	Ăam Bikibb
Heeyé	Ăam Btkibb
Nahna	Ăam Mnkibb
Intoo	Ăam Btkibboo
Hinné	Ăam Bikibboo

Past	
Ana	kabbét
Inta	kabbét
Inté	kabbait
Hoowé	Kabb
Heeyé	kabbét
Nahna	Kabbaina
Intoo	Kabbaitoo
Hinné	Kabboo

Past Continuous		
Ana	Kint Ăam	Bkibb
Inta	Kint Ăam	Btkibb
Inté	Kinté Ăam	Btkibbé
Hoowé	Kén Ăam	Bikibb
Heeyé	Kénét Ăam	Btkibb
Nahna	Kinna Ăam	Mnkibb
Intoo	Kintoo Ăam	Btkibboo
Hinné	Kénoo Ăam	Bikibboo

Future		
Ana	Laĥ	Kibb
Inta	Laĥ	Tkibb
Inté	Laĥ	Tkibbé
Hoowé	Laĥ	Ykibb
Heeyé	Laĥ	Tkibb
Nahna	Laĥ	Nkibb
Intoo	Laĥ	Tkibboo
Hinné	Laĥ	Ykibboo

Command	
Inta	Kibb
Inté	Kibbé
Intoo	Kibboo
Inta	Ma tkibb
Inté	Ma tkibbé
Intoo	Ma tkibboo

Ă= Augh in bought	Ď= a heavy D	É= like A in Bay	G= G in beige	ĥ= like an H with smaller air passage	I= I as in ink	Ќ= like ch in Irish loch
O= O as in home	OO= as in boots	R= roll the rrr	Ť= a heavy T	Ř= like a French R (gargle it)	Š= a heavy S	Ž= a heavy Z

T T

To tie

Present

Ana	Birboṯ
Inta	Btirboṯ
Inté	Btirbṯé
Hoowé	Byirboṯ
Heeyé	Btirboṯ
Naḥna	Mnirboṯ
Intoo	Btirbṯoo
Hinné	Byirbṯoo

Present Continuous

Ana	Ăam	Birboṯ	(rabéṯ/rabṯa)
Inta	Ăam	Btirboṯ	(rabéṯ)
Inté	Ăam	Btirbṯé	(rabṯa)
Hoowé	Ăam	Byirboṯ	(rabéṯ)
Heeyé	Ăam	Btirboṯ	(rabṯa)
Naḥna	Ăam	Mnirboṯ	(rabṯeen)
Intoo	Ăam	Btirbṯoo	(rabṯeen)
Hinné	Ăam	Byirbṯoo	(rabṯeen)

Past

Ana	Rabaṯt
Inta	Rabaṯt
Inté	Rabaṯté
Hoowé	Rabaṯ
Heeyé	Rabaṯét
Naḥna	Rabaṯna
Intoo	Rabaṯtoo
Hinné	Rabaṯoo

Past Continuous

Ana	Kint Ăam	Birboṯ	(kint rabéṯ/rabṯa)
Inta	Kint Ăam	Btirboṯ	(Kint rabéṯ)
Inté	Kinté Ăam	Btirbṯé	(Kinté rabṯa)
Hoowé	Kén Ăam	Byirboṯ	(Kén rabéṯ)
Heeyé	Kénét Ăam	Btirboṯ	(Kénét rabṯa)
Naḥna	Kinna Ăam	Mnirboṯ	(Kinna rabṯeen)
Intoo	Kintoo Ăam	Btirbṯoo	(Kintoo rabṯeen)
Hinné	Kénoo Ăam	Byirbṯoo	(Kénoo rabṯeen)

Future

Ana	Laḥ	irboṯ
Inta	Laḥ	tirboṯ
Inté	Laḥ	tirbṯé
Hoowé	Laḥ	yirboṯ
Heeyé	Laḥ	tirboṯ
Naḥna	Laḥ	nirboṯ
Intoo	Laḥ	tirbṯoo
Hinné	Laḥ	yirbṯoo

Command

Inta	rboṯ
Inté	rbiṯé
Intoo	rbiṯoo
Inta	Ma trboṯ
Inté	Ma trbṯé
Intoo	Ma trbṯoo

To time

Present

Ana	Bwa''ét
Inta	Btwa''ét
Inté	Btwa''té
Hoowé	Biwa''ét
Heeyé	Btwa''ét
Naḥna	Mnwa''ét
Intoo	Btwa''too
Hinné	Biwa''too

Present Continuous

Ana	Ăam	Bwa''ét
Inta	Ăam	Btwa''ét
Inté	Ăam	Btwa''té
Hoowé	Ăam	Biwa''ét
Ilceyé	Ăam	Btwa''ét
Naḥna	Ăam	Mnwa''ét
Intoo	Ăam	Btwa''too
Hinné	Ăam	Biwa''too

Past

Ana	Wa''att
Inta	Wa''att
Inté	Wa''atté
Hoowé	Wa''att
Heeyé	Wa''atét
Naḥna	Wa''attna
Intoo	Wa''attoo
Hinné	Wa''atoo

Past Continuous

Ana	Kint Ăam	Bwa''ét
Inta	Kint Ăam	Btwa''ét
Inté	Kinté Ăam	Btwa''té
Hoowé	Kén Ăam	Biwa''ét
Heeyé	Kénét Ăam	Btwa''ét
Naḥna	Kinna Ăam	Mnwa''ét
Intoo	Kintoo Ăam	Btwa''too
Hinné	Kénoo Ăam	Biwa''too

Future

Ana	Laḥ	Wa''ét
Inta	Laḥ	Twa''ét
Inté	Laḥ	Twa''té
Hoowé	Laḥ	Ywa''ét
Heeyé	Laḥ	Twa''ét
Naḥna	Laḥ	Nwa''ét
Intoo	Laḥ	Twa''too
Hinné	Laḥ	Ywa''too

Command

Inta	Wa''ét
Inté	Wa''té
Intoo	Wa''too
Inta	Ma twa''ét
Inté	Ma twa''té
Intoo	Ma twa''too

Ă= Augh in bought	Ď= a heavy D	É= like A in Bay	G= G in beige	ḥ= like an H with smaller air passage	I= I as in ink	Ķ= like ch in Irish loch
O= O as in home	OO= as in boots	R= roll the rrr	Ṯ= a heavy T	Ř= like a French R (gargle it)	Ŝ= a heavy S	Ž= a heavy Z

T   T

To touch

Present		
Ana	Bd$_i$'	(Bilmos)
Inta	Btd$_i$'	(Btilmos)
Inté	Btd$_i$'é	(Btilimsé)
Hoowé	Bid$_i$'	(Biyilmos)
Heeyé	Btd$_i$'	(Btilmos)
Nahna	Mnd$_i$'	(Mnilmos)
Intoo	Btd$_i$'oo	(Btilimsoo)
Hinné	Bid$_i$'oo	(Biyilimsoo)

Present Continuous		
Ana	Ăam Bd$_i$'	(Ăam Bilmos)
Inta	Ăam Btd$_i$'	(Ăam Btilmos)
Inté	Ăam Btd$_i$'é	(Ăam Btilimsé)
Hoowé	Ăam Bid$_i$'	(Ăam Biyilmos)
Heeyé	Ăam Btd$_i$'	(Ăam Btilmos)
Nahna	Ăam Mnd$_i$'	(Ăam Mnilmos)
Intoo	Ăam Btd$_i$'oo	(Ăam Btilimsoo)
Hinné	Ăam Bid$_i$'oo	(Ăam Biyilimsoo)

Past		
Ana	Da''ét	(Lmast)
Inta	Da''ét	(Lmast)
Inté	Da''aité	(Lmasté)
Hoowé	D$_a$''	(Lamas)
Heeyé	D$_a$''ét	(Lamsét)
Nahna	D$_a$''aina	(Lmasna)
Intoo	D$_a$''aitoo	(Lmastoo)
Hinné	D$_a$''oo	(Lamsoo)

Past Continuous		
Ana	Kint Ăam Bd$_i$'	(Kint Ăam Bilmos)
Inta	Kint Ăam btKallé	(Kint Ăam Btilmos)
Inté	Kinté Ăam Btd$_i$'é	(Kinté Ăam Btilimsé)
Hoowé	Kén Ăam Bid$_i$'	(Kén Ăam Biyilmos)
Heeyé	Kénét Ăam Btd$_i$'	(Kénét Ăam Btilmos)
Nahna	Kinna Ăam Mnd$_i$'	(Kinna Ăam Mnilmos)
Intoo	Kintoo Ăam Btd$_i$'oo	(Kintoo Ăam Btilimsoo)
Hinné	Kénoo Ăam Bid$_i$'oo	(Kénoo Ăam Biyilimsoo)

Future		
Ana	Lah d$_i$'	(Lah ilmos)
Inta	Lah td$_i$'	(Lah tilmos)
Inté	Lah td$_i$''é	(Lah tilimsé)
Hoowé	Lah yd$_i$'	(Lah yilmos)
Heeyé	Lah td$_i$'	(Lah tilmos)
Nahna	Lah nd$_i$'	(Lah nilmos)
Intoo	Lah td$_i$'oo	(Lah tilimsoo)
Hinné	Lah yd$_i$'oo	(Lah yilimsoo)

Command		
Inta	d$_i$'	(Lmos)
Inté	d$_i$''é	(Lmisé)
Intoo	d$_i$''oo	(Lmisoo)
Inta	Ma t d$_i$'	(Ma tilmos)
Inté	Ma t d$_i$''é	(Ma tilmsé)
Intoo	Ma t d$_i$''oo	(Ma tilimsoo)

To trade (in commerce)

Present	
Ana	Btégér
Inta	Bttégér
Inté	Bttégré
Hoowé	Bitégér
Heeyé	Bttégér
Nahna	Mntégér
Intoo	Bttégroo
Hinné	Bitégroo

Present Continuous		
Ana	Ăam	Btégér
Inta	Ăam	Bttégér
Inté	Ăam	Bttégré
Hoowé	Ăam	Bitégér
Heeyé	Ăam	Bttégér
Nahna	Ăam	Mntégér
Intoo	Ăam	Bttégroo
Hinné	Ăam	Bitégroo

Past	
Ana	tégart
Inta	tégart
Inté	Tégarté
Hoowé	Tégar
Heeyé	tégarét
Nahna	Tégarna
Intoo	Tégartoo
Hinné	tégaroo

Past Continuous		
Ana	Kint Ăam	Btégér
Inta	Kint Ăam	Bttégér
Inté	Kinté Ăam	Bttégré
Hoowé	Kén Ăam	Bitégér
Heeyé	Kénét Ăam	Bttégér
Nahna	Kinna Ăam	Mntégér
Intoo	Kintoo Ăam	Bttégroo
Hinné	Kénoo Ăam	Bitégroo

Future		
Ana	Lah	Tégér
Inta	Lah	Ttégér
Inté	Lah	Ttégré
Hoowé	Lah	Ytégér
Heeyé	Lah	Ttégér
Nahna	Lah	Ntégér
Intoo	Lah	Ttégroo
Hinné	Lah	Ytégroo

Command	
Inta	Tégér
Inté	Tégré
Intoo	Tégroo
Inta	Ma ttégér
Inté	Ma ttégré
Intoo	Ma ttégroo

Ă= Augh in bought	Ď= a heavy D	É= like A in Bay	G= G in beige	ĥ= like an H with smaller air passage	I= I as in ink	Ķ= like ch in Irish loch
O= O as in home	OO= as in boots	R= roll the rrr	Ť= a heavy T	Ř= like a French R (gargle it)	Ŝ= a heavy S	Ž= a heavy Z

T   T

To train

Present	
Ana	Bmarrin
Inta	Btmarrin
Inté	Btmarrné
Hoowé	Bimarrin
Heeyé	Btmarrin
Nahna	Mnmarrin
Intoo	Btmarrnoo
Hinné	Bimarrnoo

Present Continuous		
Ana	Ăam	Bmarrin
Inta	Ăam	Btmarrin
Inté	Ăam	Btmarrné
Hoowé	Ăam	Bimarrin
Heeyé	Ăam	Btmarrin
Nahna	Ăam	Mnmarrin
Intoo	Ăam	Btmarrnoo
Hinné	Ăam	Bimarrnoo

Past	
Ana	Marrant
Inta	Marrant
Inté	Marranté
Hoowé	Marran
Heeyé	Marranét
Nahna	Marranna
Intoo	Marrantoo
Hinné	Marranoo

Past Continuous		
Ana	Kint Ăam	Bmarrin
Inta	Kint Ăam	Btmarrin
Inté	Kinté Ăam	Btmarrné
Hoowé	Kén Ăam	Bimarrin
Heeyé	Kénét Ăam	Btmarrin
Nahna	Kinna Ăam	Mnmarrin
Intoo	Kintoo Ăam	Btmarrnoo
Hinné	Kénoo Ăam	Bimarrnoo

Future		
Ana	Lah	Marrin
Inta	Lah	Tmarrin
Inté	Lah	Tmarrné
Hoowé	Lah	Ymarrin
Heeyé	Lah	Tmarrin
Nahna	Lah	Nmarrin
Intoo	Lah	Tmarrnoo
Hinné	Lah	Ymarrnoo

Command	
Inta	Marrin
Inté	Marrné
Intoo	Marrnoo
Inta	Ma tmarrin
Inté	Ma tmarrné
Intoo	Ma tmarrnoo

To travel

Present	
Ana	Bséfér
Inta	Btséfér
Inté	Btséfré
Hoowé	Biséfér
Heeyé	Btséfér
Nahna	Mnséfér
Intoo	Btséfroo
Hinné	Biséfroo

Present Continuous			
Ana	Ăam	Bséfér	(mséfar/mséfra)
Inta	Ăam	Btséfér	(mséfar)
Inté	Ăam	Btséfré	(mséfra)
Hoowé	Ăam	Biséfér	(mséfar)
Heeyé	Ăam	Btséfér	(mséfra)
Nahna	Ăam	Mnséfér	(mséfreen)
Intoo	Ăam	Btséfroo	(mséfreen)
Hinné	Ăam	Biséfroo	(mséfreen)

Past	
Ana	Séfart
Inta	Séfart
Inté	Séfarté
Hoowé	Séfar
Heeyé	Séfarét
Nahna	Séfarna
Intoo	Séfartoo
Hinné	Séfaroo

Past Continuous			
Ana	Kint Ăam	Bséfér	(kint mséfar/mséfra)
Inta	Kint Ăam	Btséfér	(Kint mséfar)
Inté	Kinté Ăam	Btséfré	(Kinté mséfra)
Hoowé	Kén Ăam	Biséfér	(Kén mséfar)
Heeyé	Kénét Ăam	Btséfér	(Kénét mséfra)
Nahna	Kinna Ăam	Mnséfér	(Kinna mséfreen)
Intoo	Kintoo Ăam	Btséfroo	(Kintoo mséfreen)
Hinné	Kénoo Ăam	Biséfroo	(Kénoo mséfreen)

Future		
Ana	Lah	Séfér
Inta	Lah	Tséfér
Inté	Lah	Tséfré
Hoowé	Lah	Yséfér
Heeyé	Lah	Tséfér
Nahna	Lah	Nséfér
Intoo	Lah	Tséfroo
Hinné	Lah	Yséfroo

Command	
Inta	Séfér
Inté	Séfré
Intoo	Séfroo
Inta	Ma tséfér
Inté	Ma tséfré
Intoo	Ma tsefroo

Ă= Augh in bought	Ď= a heavy D	É= like A in Bay	G= G in beige	h̉= like an H with smaller air passage	I= I as in ink	Ḱ= like ch in Irish loch
O= O as in home	OO= as in boots	R= roll the rrr	Ť= a heavy T	Ř= like a French R (gargle it)	Ŝ= a heavy S	Ž= a heavy Z

T   T

To treat   ## To treat (medically)

Present	
Ana	bĂamél
Inta	btĂamél
Inté	btĂamlé
Hoowé	biĂamél
Heeyé	btĂamél
Nahna	mnĂamél
Intoo	btĂamloo
Hinné	biĂamloo

Present Continuous		
Ana	Ăam	bĂamél
Inta	Ăam	btĂamél
Inté	Ăam	btĂamlé
Hoowé	Ăam	biĂamél
Heeyé	Ăam	btĂamél
Nahna	Ăam	mnĂamél
Intoo	Ăam	btĂamloo
Hinné	Ăam	biĂamloo

Past	
Ana	Ăamalt
Inta	Ăamalt
Inté	Ăamalté
Hoowé	Ăamal
Heeyé	Ăamalét
Nahna	Ăamalna
Intoo	Ăamaltoo
Hinné	Ăamaloo

Past Continuous		
Ana	Kint Ăam	bĂamél
Inta	Kint Ăam	btĂamél
Inté	Kinté Ăam	btĂamlé
Hoowé	Kén Ăam	biĂamél
Heeyé	Kénét Ăam	btĂamél
Nahna	Kinna Ăam	mnĂamél
Intoo	Kintoo Ăam	btĂamloo
Hinné	Kénoo Ăam	biĂamloo

Future		
Ana	Laĥ	Ăamél
Inta	Laĥ	tĂamél
Inté	Laĥ	tĂamlé
Hoowé	Laĥ	yĂamél
Heeyé	Laĥ	tĂamél
Nahna	Laĥ	nĂamél
Intoo	Laĥ	tĂamloo
Hinné	Laĥ	yĂamloo

Command	
Inta	Ăamél
Inté	Ăamlé
Intoo	Ăamloo
Inta	Ma tĂamél
Inté	Ma tAamlé
Intoo	Ma tĂamloo

Present	
Ana	bĂalég
Inta	btĂalég
Inté	btĂalgé
Hoowé	biĂalég
Heeyé	btĂalég
Nahna	mnĂalég
Intoo	btĂalgoo
Hinné	biĂalgoo

Present Continuous		
Ana	Ăam	bĂalég
Inta	Ăam	btĂalég
Inté	Ăam	btĂalgé
Hoowé	Ăam	biĂalég
Heeyé	Ăam	btĂalég
Nahna	Ăam	mnĂalég
Intoo	Ăam	btĂalgoo
Hinné	Ăam	biĂalgoo

Past	
Ana	Ăalagt
Inta	Ăalagt
Inté	Ăalagté
Hoowé	Ăalag
Heeyé	Ăalagét
Nahna	Ăalagna
Intoo	Ăalagtoo
Hinné	Ăalagoo

Past Continuous		
Ana	Kint Ăam	bĂalég
Inta	Kint Ăam	btĂalég
Inté	Kinté Ăam	btĂalgé
Hoowé	Kén Ăam	biĂalég
Heeyé	Kénét Ăam	btĂalég
Nahna	Kinna Ăam	mnĂalég
Intoo	Kintoo Ăam	btĂalgoo
Hinné	Kénoo Ăam	biĂalgoo

Future		
Ana	Laĥ	Ăalég
Inta	Laĥ	tĂalég
Inté	Laĥ	tĂalgé
Hoowé	Laĥ	yĂalég
Heeyé	Laĥ	tĂalég
Nahna	Laĥ	nĂalég
Intoo	Laĥ	tĂalgoo
Hinné	Laĥ	yĂalgoo

Command	
Inta	Ăalég
Inté	Ăalgé
Intoo	Ăalgoo
Inta	Ma tĂalég
Inté	Ma tĂalgé
Intoo	Ma tĂalgoo

Ă= Augh in bought	Ď= a heavy D	É= like A in Bay	G= G in beige	ĥ= like an H with smaller air passage	I= I as in ink	Ḱ= like ch in Irish loch
O= O as in home	OO= as in boots	R= roll the rrr	Ť= a heavy T	Ř= like a French R (gargle it)	Ŝ= a heavy S	Ž= a heavy Z

T   T

To trip

Present

Ana	Bitfashkal
Inta	Btitfashkal
Inté	Btitfashkalé
Hoowé	Byitfashkal
Heeyé	Btitfashkal
Naĥna	Mnitfashkal
Intoo	Btitfashkaloo
Hinné	Byitfashkaloo

Present Continuous

Ana	Ăam	Bitfashkal
Inta	Ăam	Btitfashkal
Inté	Ăam	Btitfashkalé
Hoowé	Ăam	Byitfashkal
Heeyé	Ăam	Btitfashkal
Naĥna	Ăam	Mnitfashkal
Intoo	Ăam	Btitfashkaloo
Hinné	Ăam	Byitfashkaloo

Past

Ana	Tfashkalt
Inta	Tfashkalt
Inté	Tfashkalté
Hoowé	Tfashkal
Heeyé	Tfashkalét
Naĥna	Tfashkalna
Intoo	Tfashkaltoo
Hinné	Tfashkaloo

Past Continuous

Ana	Kint Ăam	Bitfashkal
Inta	Kint Ăam	Btitfashkal
Inté	Kinté Ăam	Btitfashkalé
Hoowé	Kén Ăam	Byitfashkal
Heeyé	Kénét Ăam	Btitfashkal
Naĥna	Kinna Ăam	Mnitfashkal
Intoo	Kintoo Ăam	Btitfashkaloo
Hinné	Kénoo Ăam	Byitfashkaloo

Future

Ana	Laĥ	Itfashkal
Inta	Laĥ	Titfashkal
Inté	Laĥ	Titfashkalé
Hoowé	Laĥ	Yitfashkal
Heeyé	Laĥ	Titfashkal
Naĥna	Laĥ	Nitfashkal
Intoo	Laĥ	Titfashkaloo
Hinné	Laĥ	Yitfashkaloo

Command

Inta	Tfashkal
Inté	Tfashklé
Intoo	Tfashkloo
Inta	Ma ttfashkal
Inté	Ma ttfashklé
Intoo	Ma ttfashkloo

To trust

Present

Ana	Boosa'
Inta	Btoosa'
Inté	Btoosa'é
Hoowé	Byoosa'
Heeyé	Btoosa'
Naĥna	mnoosa'
Intoo	Btoosa'oo
Hinné	Byoosa'oo

Present Continuous

Ana	Ăam	Boosa'	(wésé'/wés'a)
Inta	Ăam	Btoosa'	(wésé')
Inté	Ăam	Btoosa'é	(wés'a)
Hoowé	Ăam	Byoosa'	(wésé')
Heeyé	Ăam	Btoosa'	(wés'a)
Naĥna	Ăam	mnoosa'	(wés'een)
Intoo	Ăam	Btoosa'oo	(wés'een)
Hinné	Ăam	Byoosa'oo	(wés'een)

Past

Ana	Wasa't
Inta	Wasa't
Inté	Wasa'té
Hoowé	Wasa'
Heeyé	Wasa'ét
Naĥna	Wasa'na
Intoo	Wasa'too
Hinné	Wasa'oo

Past Continuous

Ana	Kint Ăam	Boosa'	(kint wésé'/wés'a)
Inta	Kint Ăam	Btoosa'	(Kint wésé')
Inté	Kinté Ăam	Btoosa'é	(Kinté wés'a)
Hoowé	Kén Ăam	Byoosa'	(Kén wésé')
Heeyé	Kénét Ăam	Btoosa'	(Kénét wés'a)
Naĥna	Kinna Ăam	mnoosa'	(Kinna wés'een)
Intoo	Kintoo Ăam	Btoosa'oo	(Kintoo wés'een)
Hinné	Kénoo Ăam	Byoosa'oo	(Kénoo wés'een)

Future

Ana	Laĥ	'oosa'
Inta	Laĥ	Toosa'
Inté	Laĥ	Toosa'é
Hoowé	Laĥ	Yoosa'
Heeyé	Laĥ	Toosa'
Naĥna	Laĥ	Noosa'
Intoo	Laĥ	Toosa'oo
Hinné	Laĥ	Yoosa'oo

Command

Inta	Wsa'
Inté	Wsa'é
Intoo	Wsa'oo
Inta	Ma toosa'
Inté	Ma toosa'é
Intoo	Ma toosa'

Ă= Augh in bought	Ď= a heavy D	É= like A in Bay	G= G in beige	ĥ= like an H with smaller air passage	I= I as in ink	Ќ= like ch in Irish loch
O= O as in home	OO= as in boots	R= roll the rrr	Ť= a heavy T	Ř= like a French R (gargle it)	Ŝ= a heavy S	Ž= a heavy Z

T   T

To try / To tempt

Present	
Ana	Bgarréb
Inta	Btgarréb
Inté	Btgarrbé
Hoowé	Bigarréb
Heeyé	Btgarréb
Nahna	Mngarréb
Intoo	Btgarrboo
Hinné	Bigarrboo

Present Continuous		
Ana	Ăam Bgarréb	(mgarrab/mgarrbé)
Inta	Ăam btgarréb	(mgarrab)
Inté	Ăam Btgarrbé	(mgarrbé)
Hoowé	Ăam Bigarréb	(mgarrab)
Heeyé	Ăam Btgarréb	(mgarrbé)
Nahna	Ăam Mngarréb	(mgarrbeen)
Intoo	Ăam Btgarrboo	(mgarrbeen)
Hinné	Ăam Bigarrboo	(mgarrbeen)

Past	
Ana	Garrabt
Inta	Garrabt
Inté	Garrabté
Hoowé	Garrab
Heeyé	Garrabét
Nahna	Garrabna
Intoo	Garrabtoo
Hinné	Garraboo

Past Continuous			
Ana	Kint Ăam	bgarréb	(kint mgarrab/mgarrbé)
Inta	Kint Ăam	btgarréb	(Kint mgarrab)
Inté	Kinté Ăam	btgarrbé	(Kinté mgarrbé)
Hoowé	Kén Ăam	bigarréb	(Kén mgarrab)
Heeyé	Kénét Ăam	btgarréb	(Kénét mgarrbé)
Nahna	Kinna Ăam	mngarréb	(Kinna mgarrbeen)
Intoo	Kintoo Ăam	Btgarrboo	(Kintoo mgarrbeen)
Hinné	Kénoo Ăam	Bigarrboo	(Kénoo mgarrbeen)

Future		
Ana	Laĥ	Garréb
Inta	Laĥ	tgarréb
Inté	Laĥ	tgarrbé
Hoowé	Laĥ	ygarréb
Heeyé	Laĥ	tgarréb
Nahna	Laĥ	ngarréb
Intoo	Laĥ	Tgarrboo
Hinné	Laĥ	ygarréboo

Command	
Inta	Garréb
Inté	Garrbé
Intoo	Garrboo
Inta	Ma tgarréb
Inté	Ma tgarrbé
Intoo	Ma tgarrboo

To turn

Present	
Ana	Bibrom
Inta	Btibrom
Inté	Btibrmé
Hoowé	Byibrom
Heeyé	Btibrom
Nahna	Mnibrom
Intoo	Btibrmoo
Hinné	Byibrmoo

Present Continuous	
Ana	Ăam Bibrom
Inta	Ăam Btibrom
Inté	Ăam Btibrmé
Hoowé	Ăam Byibrom
Heeyé	Ăam Btibrom
Nahna	Ăam Mnibrom
Intoo	Ăam Btibrmoo
Hinné	Ăam Byibrmoo

Past	
Ana	Baramt
Inta	Baramt
Inté	Baramté
Hoowé	Baram
Heeyé	Baramét
Nahna	Baramna
Intoo	Baramtoo
Hinné	Baramoo

Past Continuous		
Ana	Kint Ăam	Bibrom
Inta	Kint Ăam	Btibrom
Inté	Kinté Ăam	Btibrmé
Hoowé	Kén Ăam	Byibrom
Heeyé	Kénét Ăam	Btibrom
Nahna	Kinna Ăam	Mnibrom
Intoo	Kintoo Ăam	Btibrmoo
Hinné	Kénoo Ăam	Byibrmoo

Future		
Ana	Laĥ	Ibrom
Inta	Laĥ	Tibrom
Inté	Laĥ	Tibrmé
Hoowé	Laĥ	Yibrom
Heeyé	Laĥ	Tibrom
Nahna	Laĥ	Nibrom
Intoo	Laĥ	Tibrmoo
Hinné	Laĥ	Yibrmoo

Command	
Inta	Brom
Inté	Brimé
Intoo	Brimoo
Inta	Ma tbrom
Inté	Ma tbrmé
Intoo	Ma tbrmoo

Ă= Augh in bought	Ď= a heavy D	É= like A in Bay	G= G in beige	ĥ= like an H with smaller air passage	I= I as in ink	Ḱ= like ch in Irish loch
O= O as in home	OO= as in boots	R= roll the rrr	Ť= a heavy T	Ř= like a French R (gargle it)	Ŝ= a heavy S	Ž= a heavy Z

T   T

To turn on (something)

Present

Ana	Bdawwér
Inta	Btdawwér
Inté	Btdawwré
Hoowé	Bidawwér
Heeyé	Btdawwér
Nahna	Mndawwér
Intoo	Btdawwroo
Hinné	Bidawwroo

Present Continuous

Ana	Ăam	Bdawwér
Inta	Ăam	Btdawwér
Inté	Ăam	Btdawwré
Hoowé	Ăam	Bidawwér
Heeyé	Ăam	Btdawwér
Nahna	Ăam	Mndawwér
Intoo	Ăam	Btdawwroo
Hinné	Ăam	Bidawwroo

Past

Ana	Dawwart
Inta	Dawwart
Inté	Dawwarté
Hoowé	Dawwar
Heeyé	Dawwarét
Nahna	Dawwarna
Intoo	Dawwartoo
Hinné	Dawwaroo

Past Continuous

Ana	Kint Ăam	Bdawwér
Inta	Kint Ăam	Btdawwér
Inté	Kinté Ăam	Btdawwré
Hoowé	Kén Ăam	Bidawwér
Heeyé	Kénét Ăam	Btdawwér
Nahna	Kinna Ăam	Mndawwér
Intoo	Kintoo Ăam	Btdawwroo
Hinné	Kénoo Ăam	Bidawwroo

Future

Ana	Laĥ	Dawwér
Inta	Laĥ	Tdawwér
Inté	Laĥ	Tdawwré
Hoowé	Laĥ	Ydawwér
Heeyé	Laĥ	Tdawwér
Nahna	Laĥ	Ndawwér
Intoo	Laĥ	Tdawwroo
Hinné	Laĥ	Ydawwroo

Command

Inta	Dawwér
Inté	Dawwré
Intoo	Dawwroo
Inta	Ma tdawwér
Inté	Ma tdawwré
Intoo	Ma tdawwroo

To turn off (something)

Present

Ana	BiŤfé
Inta	BtiŤfé
Inté	BtiŤfé
Hoowé	ByiŤfé
Heeyé	BtiŤfé
Nahna	MniŤfé
Intoo	BtiŤfoo
Hinné	ByiŤfoo

Present Continuous

Ana	Ăam	BiŤfé
Inta	Ăam	BtiŤfé
Inté	Ăam	BtiŤfé
Hoowé	Ăam	ByiŤfé
Heeyé	Ăam	BtiŤfé
Nahna	Ăam	MniŤfé
Intoo	Ăam	BtiŤfoo
Hinné	Ăam	ByiŤfoo

Past

Ana	Ťfeet
Inta	Ťfeet
Inté	Ťfeeté
Hoowé	Ťifé
Heeyé	Ťifyét
Nahna	Ťfeena
Intoo	Ťfeetoo
Hinné	Ťifyoo

Past Continuous

Ana	Kint Ăam	BiŤfé
Inta	Kint Ăam	BtiŤfé
Inté	Kinté Ăam	BtiŤfé
Hoowé	Kén Ăam	ByiŤfé
Heeyé	Kénét Ăam	BtiŤfé
Nahna	Kinna Ăam	MniŤfé
Intoo	Kintoo Ăam	BtiŤfoo
Hinné	Kénoo Ăam	ByiŤfoo

Future

Ana	Laĥ	iŤfé
Inta	Laĥ	tiŤfé
Inté	Laĥ	tiŤfé
Hoowé	Laĥ	yiŤfé
Heeyé	Laĥ	tiŤfé
Nahna	Laĥ	niŤfé
Intoo	Laĥ	tiŤfoo
Hinné	Laĥ	yiŤfoo

Command

Inta	Ťfee
Inté	Ťfee
Intoo	Ťfoo
Inta	Ma tŤfé
Inté	Ma tŤfé
Intoo	Ma tŤfoo

Ă= Augh in bought	Ď= a heavy D	É= like A in Bay	G= G in beige	ĥ= like an H with smaller air passage	I= I as in ink	Ķ= like ch in Irish loch
O= O as in home	OO= as in boots	R= roll the rrr	Ť= a heavy T	Ř= like a French R (gargle it)	Š= a heavy S	Ž= a heavy Z

T   T

To turn on (the light)

Present

Ana	BĎawwé
Inta	BtĎawwé
Inté	BtĎawwé
Hoowé	BiĎawwé
Heeyé	BtĎawwé
Naẖna	MnĎawwé
Intoo	BtĎawwoo
Hinné	BiĎawwoo

Present Continuous

Ana	Ăam	BĎawwé
Inta	Ăam	BtĎawwé
Inté	Ăam	BtĎawwé
Hoowé	Ăam	BiĎawwé
Heeyé	Ăam	BtĎawwé
Naẖna	Ăam	MnĎawwé
Intoo	Ăam	BtĎawwoo
Hinné	Ăam	BiĎawwoo

Past

Ana	Ďawwét
Inta	Ďawwét
Inté	Ďawwaité
Hoowé	Ďawwa
Heeyé	Ďawwét
Naẖna	Ďawwaina
Intoo	Ďawwaitoo
Hinné	Ďawwoo

Past Continuous

Ana	Kint Ăam	BĎawwé
Inta	Kint Ăam	BtĎawwé
Inté	Kinté Ăam	BtĎawwé
Hoowé	Kén Ăam	BiĎawwé
Heeyé	Kénét Ăam	BtĎawwé
Naẖna	Kinna Ăam	MnĎawwé
Intoo	Kintoo Ăam	BtĎawwoo
Hinné	Kénoo Ăam	BiĎawwoo

Future

Ana	Laẖ	Ďawwé
Inta	Laẖ	tĎawwé
Inté	Laẖ	tĎawwé
Hoowé	Laẖ	yĎawwé
Heeyé	Laẖ	tĎawwé
Naẖna	Laẖ	nĎawwé
Intoo	Laẖ	tĎawwoo
Hinné	Laẖ	Ďawwoo

Command

Inta	Ďawwé
Inté	Ďawwé
Intoo	Ďawwoo
Inta	Ma tĎawwé
Inté	Ma tĎawwé
Intoo	Ma tĎawwoo

To turn off (the light)

Present

Ana	BŤaffé
Inta	BtŤaffé
Inté	BtŤaffé
Hoowé	BiŤaffé
Heeyé	BtŤaffé
Naẖna	MnŤaffé
Intoo	BtŤaffoo
Hinné	BiŤaffoo

Present Continuous

Ana	Ăam	BŤaffé
Inta	Ăam	BtŤaffé
Inté	Ăam	BtŤaffé
Hoowé	Ăam	BiŤaffé
Heeyé	Ăam	BtŤaffé
Naẖna	Ăam	MnŤaffé
Intoo	Ăam	BtŤaffoo
Hinné	Ăam	BiŤaffoo

Past

Ana	Ťaffét
Inta	Ťaffét
Inté	Ťaffaité
Hoowé	Ťaffa
Heeyé	Ťaffét
Naẖna	Ťaffaina
Intoo	Ťaffaitoo
Hinné	Ťaffoo

Past Continuous

Ana	Kint Ăam	BŤaffé
Inta	Kint Ăam	BtŤaffé
Inté	Kinté Ăam	BtŤaffé
Hoowé	Kén Ăam	BiŤaffé
Heeyé	Kénét Ăam	BtŤaffé
Naẖna	Kinna Ăam	MnŤaffé
Intoo	Kintoo Ăam	BtŤaffoo
Hinné	Kénoo Ăam	BiŤaffoo

Future

Ana	Laẖ	Ťaffé
Inta	Laẖ	tŤaffé
Inté	Laẖ	tŤaffé
Hoowé	Laẖ	yŤaffé
Heeyé	Laẖ	tŤaffé
Naẖna	Laẖ	nŤaffé
Intoo	Laẖ	tŤaffoo
Hinné	Laẖ	yŤaffoo

Command

Inta	Ťaffé
Inté	Ťaffé
Intoo	Ťaffoo
Inta	Ma tŤaffé
Inté	Ma tŤaffé
Intoo	Ma tŤaffoo

Ă= Augh in bought	Ď= a heavy D	É= like A in Bay	G= G in beige	ẖ= like an H with smaller air passage	I= I as in ink	Ḱ= like ch in Irish loch
O= O as in home	OO= as in boots	R= roll the rrr	Ť= a heavy T	Ř= like a French R (gargle it)	Š= a heavy S	Ž= a heavy Z

U   U

To understand   ## To use

Present	
Ana	Bifham
Inta	Btifham
Inté	Btifhamé
Hoowé	Byifham
Heeyé	Btifham
Naĥna	Mnifham
Intoo	Btifhamoo
Hinné	byifhamoo

Present Continuous		
Ana	Ăam Bifham	(féhém/féhmé)
Inta	Ăam Btifham	(féhém)
Inté	Ăam Btifhamé	(féhmé)
Hoowé	Ăam Byifham	(féhmé)
Heeyé	Ăam Btifham	(féhmé)
Naĥna	Ăam Mnifham	(féhmeen)
Intoo	Ăam Btifhamoo	(féhmeen)
Hinné	Ăam byifhamoo	(féhmeen)

Past	
Ana	Fhimt
Inta	Fhimt
Inté	Fhimté
Hoowé	Fihém
Heeyé	Fihmét
Naĥna	Fhimna
Intoo	Fhimtoo
Hinné	Fihmoo

Past Continuous		
Ana	Kint Ăam Bifham	(kint féhém/féhmé)
Inta	Kint Ăam Btifham	(Kint féhém)
Inté	Kinté Ăam Btifhamé	(Kinté féhmé)
Hoowé	Kén Ăam Byifham	(Kén féhmé)
Heeyé	Kénét Ăam Btifham	(Kénét féhmé)
Naĥna	Kinna Ăam Mnifham	(Kinna féhmeen)
Intoo	Kintoo Ăam Btifhamoo	(Kintoo féhmeen)
Hinné	Kénoo Ăam byifhamoo	(Kénoo féhmeen)

Future		
Ana	Laĥ	Ifham
Inta	Laĥ	Tifham
Inté	Laĥ	Tifhamé
Hoowé	Laĥ	Yifham
Heeyé	Laĥ	Tifham
Naĥna	Laĥ	Nifham
Intoo	Laĥ	Tifhamoo
Hinné	Laĥ	Yifhamoo

Command	
Inta	Fhém / fham
Inté	Fhamé
Intoo	Fhamoo
Inta	Ma tifham
Inté	Ma tifhamé
Intoo	Ma tifhamoo

Present	
Ana	bistaĂmél
Inta	btistaĂmél
Inté	btistaĂmlé
Hoowé	byistaĂmél
Heeyé	btistaĂmél
Naĥna	mnistaĂmél
Intoo	btistaĂmloo
Hinné	byistaĂmloo

Present Continuous		
Ana	Ăam	bistaĂmél
Inta	Ăam	btistaĂmél
Inté	Ăam	btistaĂmlé
Hoowé	Ăam	byistaĂmél
Heeyé	Ăam	btistaĂmél
Naĥna	Ăam	mnistaĂmél
Intoo	Ăam	btistaĂmloo
Hinné	Ăam	byistaĂmloo

Past	
Ana	staĂmalt
Inta	staĂmalt
Inté	staĂmalté
Hoowé	staĂmal
Heeyé	staĂmalét
Naĥna	staĂmalna
Intoo	staĂmaltoo
Hinné	staĂmaloo

Past Continuous		
Ana	Kint Ăam	bistaĂmél
Inta	Kint Ăam	btistaĂmél
Inté	Kinté Ăam	btistaĂmlé
Hoowé	Kén Ăam	byistaĂmél
Heeyé	Kénét Ăam	btistaĂmél
Naĥna	Kinna Ăam	mnistaĂmél
Intoo	Kintoo Ăam	btistaĂmloo
Hinné	Kénoo Ăam	byistaĂmloo

Future		
Ana	Laĥ	istaĂmél
Inta	Laĥ	tistaĂmél
Inté	Laĥ	tistaĂmlé
Hoowé	Laĥ	yistaĂmél
Heeyé	Laĥ	tistaĂmél
Naĥna	Laĥ	nistaĂmél
Intoo	Laĥ	tistaĂmloo
Hinné	Laĥ	yistaĂmloo

Command	
Inta	staĂmél
Inté	staĂmlé
Intoo	staĂmloo
Inta	Ma tstaĂmél
Inté	Ma tstaĂmlé
Intoo	Ma tstaĂmloo

Ă= Augh in bought	Ď= a heavy D	É= like A in Bay	G= G in beige	ĥ= like an H with smaller air passage	I= I in ink	Ķ= like ch in Irish loch
O= O as in home	OO= as in boots	R= roll the rrr	Ť= a heavy T	Ř= like a French R (gargle it)	Š= a heavy S	Ž= a heavy Z

U

V

used to

To vandalize

Present	
Ana	n/a
Inta	n/a
Inté	n/a
Hoowé	n/a
Heeyé	n/a
Naẖna	n/a
Intoo	n/a
Hinné	n/a

Present	
Ana	bḰarréb
Inta	btḰarréb
Inté	btḰarrbé
Hoowé	biḰarréb
Heeyé	btḰarréb
Naẖna	mnḰarréb
Intoo	btḰarrboo
Hinné	biḰarrboo

Present Continuous	
Ana	Ăam bitĂawwad (mitĂawwad/mitĂawwdé)
Inta	Ăam btitĂawwad (mitĂawwad)
Inté	Ăam btitĂawdé (mitĂawwdé)
Hoowé	Ăam byitĂawwad (mitĂawwad)
Heeyé	Ăam btitĂawwad (mitĂawwdé)
Naẖna	Ăam mnitĂawwad (mitĂawdeen)
Intoo	Ăam btitĂawdoo (mitĂawdeen)
Hinné	Ăam byitĂawdoo (mitĂawdeen)

Present Continuous		
Ana	Ăam	bḰarréb
Inta	Ăam	btḰarréb
Inté	Ăam	btḰarrbé
Hoowé	Ăam	biḰarréb
Heeyé	Ăam	btḰarréb
Naẖna	Ăam	mnḰarréb
Intoo	Ăam	btḰarrboo
Hinné	Ăam	biḰarrboo

Past	
Ana	tĂawwadit
Inta	tĂawwadit
Inté	tĂawwadté
Hoowé	tĂawwad
Heeyé	tĂawwₐdᵢt
Naẖna	tĂawwadna
Intoo	tĂawwadtoo
Hinné	tĂawwadoo

Past	
Ana	Ḱarrabt
Inta	Ḱarrabt
Inté	Ḱarrabté
Hoowé	Ḱarrab
Heeyé	Ḱarrabét
Naẖna	Ḱarrabna
Intoo	Ḱarrabtoo
Hinné	Ḱarraboo

Past Continuous	
Ana	Kint Ăam bitĂawwad (kint mitĂawwad/mitĂawwdé)
Inta	Kint Ăam btitĂawwad (kint mitĂawwad)
Inté	Kinté Ăam btitĂawdé (kinté mitĂawwdé)
Hoowé	Kén Ăam byitĂawwad (kén mitĂawwad)
Heeyé	Kénét Ăam btitĂawwad (kénét mitĂawwdé)
Naẖna	Kinna Ăam mnitĂawwad (kinna mitĂawdeen)
Intoo	Kintoo Ăam btitĂawdoo (kintoo mitĂawdeen)
Hinné	Kénoo Ăam byitĂawdoo

Past Continuous		
Ana	Kint Ăam	bḰarréb
Inta	Kint Ăam	btḰarréb
Inté	Kinté Ăam	btḰarrbé
Hoowé	Kén Ăam	biḰarréb
Heeyé	Kénét Ăam	btḰarréb
Naẖna	Kinna Ăam	mnḰarréb
Intoo	Kintoo Ăam	btḰarrboo
Hinné	Kénoo Ăam	biḰarrboo

Future	
Ana	Laẖ itĂawwad
Inta	Laẖ titĂawwad
Inté	Laẖ titĂawdé
Hoowé	Laẖ yitĂawwad
Heeyé	Laẖ titĂawwad
Naẖna	Laẖ nitĂawwad
Intoo	Laẖ titĂawdoo
Hinné	Laẖ yitĂawwdoo

Future		
Ana	Laẖ	Ḱarréb
Inta	Laẖ	tḰarréb
Inté	Laẖ	tḰarrbé
Hoowé	Laẖ	yḰarréb
Heeyé	Laẖ	tḰarréb
Naẖna	Laẖ	nḰarréb
Intoo	Laẖ	tḰarrboo
Hinné	Laẖ	yḰarrboo

Command	
Inta	tĂawwad
Inté	tĂawdé
Intoo	tĂawdoo
Inta	Ma titĂawwad
Inté	Ma ttĂawdé
Intoo	Ma titĂawdoo

Command	
Inta	Ḱarréb
Inté	Ḱarrbé
Intoo	Karrboo
Inta	Ma tḰarréb
Inté	Ma tḰarrbé
Intoo	Ma tḰarrboo

Ă= Augh in bought	**Ď**= a heavy D	**É**= like A in Bay	**G**= G in beige	**ẖ**= like an H with smaller air passage	**I**= I as in ink	**Ḱ**= like ch in Irish loch
O= O as in home	**OO**= as in boots	**R**= roll the rrr	**Ť**= a heavy T	**Ř**= like a French R (gargle it)	**Ŝ**= a heavy S	**Ž**= a heavy Z

V

W

To vibrate

Present

Ana	Brigg
Inta	Btrigg
Inté	Btriggé
Hoowé	Birigg
Heeyé	Btrigg
Nahna	Mnrigg
Intoo	Btriggoo
Hinné	Biriggoo

Present Continuous

Ana	Ăam	Brigg
Inta	Ăam	Btrigg
Inté	Ăam	Btriggé
Hoowé	Ăam	Birigg
Heeyé	Ăam	Btrigg
Nahna	Ăam	Mnrigg
Intoo	Ăam	Btriggoo
Hinné	Ăam	Biriggoo

Past

Ana	Raggét
Inta	Raggét
Inté	Raggaité
Hoowé	Ragg
Heeyé	Raggét
Nahna	Raggaina
Intoo	Raggaitoo
Hinné	Raggoo

Past Continuous

Ana	Kint Ăam	Brigg
Inta	Kint Ăam	Btrigg
Inté	Kinté Ăam	Btriggé
Hoowé	Kén Ăam	Birigg
Heeyé	Kénét Ăam	Btrigg
Nahna	Kinna Ăam	Mnrigg
Intoo	Kintoo Ăam	Btriggoo
Hinné	Kénoo Ăam	Biriggoo

Future

Ana	Laĥ	Rigg
Inta	Laĥ	Trigg
Inté	Laĥ	triggé
Hoowé	Laĥ	Yrigg
Heeyé	Laĥ	Trigg
Nahna	Laĥ	Nrigg
Intoo	Laĥ	triggoo
Hinné	Laĥ	yriggoo

Command

Inta	Rigg
Inté	Riggé
Intoo	Riggoo
Inta	Ma trigg
Inté	Ma triggé
Intoo	Ma triggoo

To wait

Present

Ana	binŤor
Inta	btinŤor
Inté	btinŤré
Hoowé	byinŤor
Heeyé	btinŤor
Nahna	mninŤor
Intoo	btinŤroo
Hinné	byinŤroo

Present Continuous

Ana	Ăam	binŤor	(naŤér/naŤra)
Inta	Ăam	btinŤor	(naŤér)
Inté	Ăam	btinŤré	(naŤra)
Hoowé	Ăam	byinŤor	(naŤér)
Heeyé	Ăam	btinŤor	(naŤra)
Nahna	Ăam	mninŤor	(naŤreen)
Intoo	Ăam	btinŤroo	(naŤreen)
Hinné	Ăam	byinŤroo	(naŤreen)

Past

Ana	naŤart
Inta	naŤart
Inté	naŤarté
Hoowé	naŤar
Heeyé	naŤarét
Nahna	naŤarna
Intoo	naŤartoo
Hinné	naŤaroo

Past Continuous

Ana	Kint Ăam	binŤor	(kint naŤér/naŤra)
Inta	Kint Ăam	btinŤor	(Kint naŤér)
Inté	Kinté Ăam	btinŤré	(Kinté naŤra)
Hoowé	Kén Ăam	byinŤor	(Kén naŤér)
Heeyé	Kénét Ăam	btinŤor	(Kénét naŤra)
Nahna	Kinna Ăam	mninŤor	(Kinna naŤreen)
Intoo	Kintoo Ăam	btinŤroo	(Kintoo naŤreen)
Hinné	Kénoo Ăam	byinŤroo	(Kénoo naŤreen)

Future

Ana	Laĥ	inŤor
Inta	Laĥ	tinŤor
Inté	Laĥ	tinŤré
Hoowé	Laĥ	yinŤor
Heeyé	Laĥ	tinŤor
Nahna	Laĥ	ninŤor
Intoo	Laĥ	tinŤroo
Hinné	Laĥ	yinŤroo

Command

Inta	nŤor
Inté	nŤiré
Intoo	nŤiroo
Inta	Ma tnŤor
Inté	Ma tnŤré
Intoo	Ma tnŤroo

Ă= Augh in bought	Ď= a heavy D	É= like A in Bay	G= G in beige	ĥ= like an H with smaller air passage	I= I as in ink	Ḱ= like ch in Irish loch
O= O as in home	OO= as in boots	R= roll the rrr	Ť= a heavy T	Ř= like a French R (gargle it)	Š= a heavy S	Ž= a heavy Z

To wake (one's self)

Present

Ana	Bfee'
Inta	Btfee'
Inté	Btfee'é
Hoowé	Bifee'
Heeyé	Btfee'
Nahna	Mnfee'
Intoo	Btfee'oo
Hinné	Bifee'oo

Present Continuous

Ana	Ăam	Bfee'	(féyé'/féy'a)
Inta	Ăam	Btfee'	(féyé')
Inté	Ăam	Btfee'é	(féy'a)
Hoowé	Ăam	Bifee'	(féyé')
Heeyé	Ăam	Btfee'	(féy'a)
Nahna	Ăam	Mnfee'	(féy'een)
Intoo	Ăam	Btfee'oo	(féy'een)
Hinné	Ăam	Bifee'oo	(féy'een)

Past

Ana	Fi't
Inta	Fi't
Inté	Fi'té
Hoowé	Fé'
Heeyé	Fé'ét
Nahna	Fi'na
Intoo	Fi'too
Hinné	Fé'oo

Past Continuous

Ana	Kint Ăam	Bfee'	(kint féyé'/féy'a)
Inta	Kint Ăam	Btfee'	(Kint féyé')
Inté	Kinté Ăam	Btfee'é	(Kinté féy'a)
Hoowé	Kén Ăam	Bifee'	(Kén féyé')
Heeyé	Kénét Ăam	Btfee'	(Kénét féy'a)
Nahna	Kinna Ăam	Mnfee'	(Kinna féy'een)
Intoo	Kintoo Ăam	Btfee'oo	(Kintoo féy'een)
Hinné	Kénoo Ăam	Bifee'oo	(Kénoo féy'een)

Future

Ana	Lah	Fee'
Inta	Lah	Tfee'
Inté	Lah	Tfee'é
Hoowé	Lah	Yfee'
Heeyé	Lah	Tfee'
Nahna	Lah	Nfee'
Intoo	Lah	Tfee'oo
Hinné	Lah	Yfee'oo

Command

Inta	Fee'
Inté	Fee'é
Intoo	Fee'oo
Inta	Ma tfee'
Inté	Ma tfee'é
Intoo	Ma tfee'oo

To wake (someone)

Present

Ana	Bfayé'
Inta	Btfayé'
Inté	Btfay'é
Hoowé	Bifayé'
Heeyé	Btfayé'
Nahna	Mnfayé'
Intoo	Btfay'oo
Hinné	Bifay'oo

Present Continuous

Ana	Ăam	Bfayé'
Inta	Ăam	Btfayé'
Inté	Ăam	Btfay'é
Hoowé	Ăam	Bifayé'
Heeyé	Ăam	Btfayé'
Nahna	Ăam	Mnfayé'
Intoo	Ăam	Btfay'oo
Hinné	Ăam	Bifay'oo

Past

Ana	Faya't
Inta	Faya't
Inté	Faya'té
Hoowé	Faya'
Heeyé	Faya'ét
Nahna	Faya'na
Intoo	Faya'too
Hinné	Faya'oo

Past Continuous

Ana	Kint Ăam	Bfayé'
Inta	Kint Ăam	Btfayé'
Inté	Kinté Ăam	Btfay'é
Hoowé	Kén Ăam	Bifayé'
Heeyé	Kénét Ăam	Btfayé'
Nahna	Kinna Ăam	Mnfayé'
Intoo	Kintoo Ăam	Btfay'oo
Hinné	Kénoo Ăam	Bifay'oo

Future

Ana	Lah	Fayé'
Inta	Lah	Tfayé'
Inté	Lah	Tfay'é
Hoowé	Lah	Yfayé'
Heeyé	Lah	Tfayé'
Nahna	Lah	Nfayé'
Intoo	Lah	Tfay'oo
Hinné	Lah	Yfay'oo

Command

Inta	Fayé'
Inté	Fay'é
Intoo	Fay'oo
Inta	Ma tfayé'
Inté	Ma tfay'é
Intoo	Ma tfay'oo

Ă= Augh in bought	Ď= a heavy D	É= like A in Bay	G= G in beige	ĥ= like an H with smaller air passage	I= I as in ink	Ḱ= like ch in Irish loch
O= O as in home	OO= as in boots	R= roll the rrr	Ť= a heavy T	Ř= like a French R (gargle it)	Ŝ= a heavy S	Ž= a heavy Z

To walk

Present	
Ana	Bimshé
Inta	Btimshé
Inté	Btimshé
Hoowé	Byimshé
Heeyé	Btiumshé
Nahna	Mnimshé
Intoo	Btimshoo
Hinné	Byimshoo

Present Continuous	
Ana	Ăam Bimshé (méshé/méshyé)
Inta	Ăam Btimshé (méshé)
Inté	Ăam Btimshé (méshyé)
Hoowé	Ăam Byimshé (méshé)
Heeyé	Ăam Btiumshé (mésyhé)
Nahna	Ăam Mnimshé (méshyeen)
Intoo	Ăam Btimshoo (méshyeen)
Hinné	Ăam Byimshoo (méshyeen)

Past	
Ana	Mashét
Inta	Mashét
Inté	Mashaité
Hoowé	Masha
Heeyé	Mashyét
Nahna	Mashaina
Intoo	Mashaitoo
Hinné	Mashyoo

Past Continuous	
Ana	Kint Ăam Bimshé (kint méshé/méshyé)
Inta	Kint Ăam Btimshé (kint méshé)
Inté	Kinté Ăam Btimshé (kinté méshyé)
Hoowé	Kén Ăam Byimshé (kén méshé)
Heeyé	Kénét Ăam Btimshé (kénét mésyhé)
Nahna	Kinna Ăam Mnimshé (kinna méshyeen)
Intoo	Kintoo Ăam Btimshoo (kintoo méshyeen)
Hinné	Kénoo Ăam Byimshoo (kénoo méshyeen)

Future	
Ana	Laĥ imshé
Inta	Laĥ timshé
Inté	Laĥ timshé
Hoowé	Laĥ yimshé
Heeyé	Laĥ timshé
Nahna	Laĥ nimshé
Intoo	Laĥ timshoo
Hinné	Laĥ yimshoo

Command	
Inta	Mshee
Inté	Mshee
Intoo	Mshoo
Inta	Ma timshé
Inté	Ma timshé
Intoo	Ma timshoo

To want

Present	
Ana	Baddé
Inta	Baddak
Inté	Baddik
Hoowé	Baddoo
Heeyé	Badda
Nahna	Baddna
Intoo	Baddkon
Hinné	Baddon

Present Continuous	
Ana	Baddé
Inta	Baddak
Inté	Baddik
Hoowé	Baddoo
Heeyé	Badda
Nahna	Baddna
Intoo	Baddkon
Hinné	Baddon

Past	
Ana	
Inta	
Inté	
Hoowé	
Heeyé	
Nahna	
Intoo	
Hinné	

Past Continuous		
Ana	Kint	Baddé
Inta	Kint	Baddak
Inté	Kinté	Baddik
Hoowé	Kén	Baddoo
Heeyé	Kénét	Badda
Nahna	Kinna	Baddna
Intoo	Kintoo	Baddkon
Hinné	Kénoo	Baddon

Future		
Ana	Laĥ	Ykoon Baddé
Inta	Laĥ	Ykoon Baddak
Inté	Laĥ	Ykoon Baddik
Hoowé	Laĥ	Ykoon Badoo
Heeyé	Laĥ	Ykoon Badda
Nahna	Laĥ	Ykoon Baddna
Intoo	Laĥ	Ykoon Baddkon
Hinné	Laĥ	Ykoon Baddon

Command	
Inta	n/a
Inté	n/a
Intoo	n/a
Inta	n/a
Inté	n/a
Intoo	n/a

Ă= Augh in bought	Ď= a heavy D	É= like A in Bay	G= G in beige	ĥ= like an H with smaller air passage	I= I as in ink	Ḱ= like ch in Irish loch
O= O as in home	OO= as in boots	R= roll the rrr	Ť= a heavy T	Ř= like a French R (gargle it)	Š= a heavy S	Ž= a heavy Z

To warm

Present	
Ana	bdaffé
Inta	btdaffé
Inté	btdaffé
Hoowé	bidaffé
Heeyé	btdaffé
Nahna	mndaffé
Intoo	Btdaffoo
Hinné	bidaffoo

Present Continuous		
Ana	Ăam	bdaffé
Inta	Ăam	btdaffé
Inté	Ăam	btdaffé
Hoowé	Ăam	bidaffé
Heeyé	Ăam	btdaffé
Nahna	Ăam	mndaffé
Intoo	Ăam	Btdaffoo
Hinné	Ăam	bidaffoo

Past	
Ana	Daffét
Inta	Daffét
Inté	Daffaité
Hoowé	Daffa
Heeyé	Daffét
Nahna	Daffaina
Intoo	Daffaitoo
Hinné	Daffoo

Past Continuous		
Ana	Kint Ăam	bdaffé
Inta	Kint Ăam	btdaffé
Inté	Kinté Ăam	btdaffé
Hoowé	Kén Ăam	bidaffé
Heeyé	Kénét Ăam	btdaffé
Nahna	Kinna Ăam	mndaffé
Intoo	Kintoo Ăam	Btdaffoo
Hinné	Kénoo Ăam	bidaffoo

Future		
Ana	Laĥ	Daffé
Inta	Laĥ	Tdaffé
Inté	Laĥ	Tdaffé
Hoowé	Laĥ	Ydaffé
Heeyé	Laĥ	Tdaffé
Nahna	Laĥ	Ndaffé
Intoo	Laĥ	Tdaffoo
Hinné	Laĥ	Ydaffoo

Command	
Inta	Daffé
Inté	Daffé
Intoo	Daffoo
Inta	Ma tdaffé
Inté	Ma tdaffé
Intoo	Ma tdaffoo

To wash

Present	
Ana	bŘassél
Inta	btŘassél
Inté	btŘasslé
Hoowé	biŘassél
Heeyé	btŘassél
Nahna	mnŘassél
Intoo	btŘassloo
Hinné	biŘassloo

Present Continuous		
Ana	Ăam	bŘassél
Inta	Ăam	btŘassél
Inté	Ăam	btŘasslé
Hoowé	Ăam	biŘassél
Heeyé	Ăam	btŘassél
Nahna	Ăam	mnŘassél
Intoo	Ăam	btŘassloo
Hinné	Ăam	biŘassloo

Past	
Ana	Řassalt
Inta	Řassalt
Inté	Řassalté
Hoowé	Řassal
Heeyé	Řassalét
Nahna	Řassalna
Intoo	Řassaltoo
Hinné	Řassaloo

Past Continuous		
Ana	Kint Ăam	bŘassél
Inta	Kint Ăam	btŘassél
Inté	Kinté Ăam	btŘasslé
Hoowé	Kén Ăam	biŘassél
Heeyé	Kénét Ăam	btŘassél
Nahna	Kinna Ăam	mnŘassél
Intoo	Kintoo Ăam	btŘassloo
Hinné	Kénoo Ăam	biŘassloo

Future		
Ana	Laĥ	Řassél
Inta	Laĥ	tŘassél
Inté	Laĥ	tŘasslé
Hoowé	Laĥ	yŘassél
Heeyé	Laĥ	tŘassél
Nahna	Laĥ	nŘassél
Intoo	Laĥ	tŘassloo
Hinné	Laĥ	yŘassloo

Command	
Inta	Řassél
Inté	Řasslé
Intoo	Řassloo
Inta	Ma tŘassél
Inté	Ma tŘasslé
Intoo	Ma tŘassloo

Ă= Augh in bought	Ď= a heavy D	É= like A in Bay	G= G in beige	ĥ= like an H with smaller air passage	I= I as in ink	Ќ= like ch in Irish loch
O= O as in home	OO= as in boots	R= roll the rrr	Ť= a heavy T	Ř= like a French R (gargle it)	Š= a heavy S	Ž= a heavy Z

To watch

Present

Ana	bihĎar
Inta	btihĎar
Inté	btihĎaré
Hoowé	byihĎar
Heeyé	btihĎar
Nahna	mnihĎar
Intoo	btihĎaroo
Hinné	byihĎaroo

Present Continuous

Ana	Ăam	bihĎar
Inta	Ăam	btihĎar
Inté	Ăam	btihĎaré
Hoowé	Ăam	byihĎar
Heeyé	Ăam	btihĎar
Nahna	Ăam	mnihĎar
Intoo	Ăam	btihĎaroo
Hinné	Ăam	byihĎaroo

Past

Ana	hĎirt
Inta	hĎirt
Inté	hĎirté
Hoowé	hiĎér
Heeyé	hiĎrét
Nahna	hĎirna
Intoo	hĎirtoo
Hinné	hiĎroo

Past Continuous

Ana	Kint Ăam	bihĎar
Inta	Kint Ăam	btihĎar
Inté	Kinté Ăam	btihĎaré
Hoowé	Kén Ăam	byihĎar
Heeyé	Kénét Ăam	btihĎar
Nahna	Kinna Ăam	mnihĎar
Intoo	Kintoo Ăam	btihĎaroo
Hinné	Kénoo Ăam	byihĎaroo

Future

Ana	Laĥ	ihĎar
Inta	Laĥ	tihĎar
Inté	Laĥ	tihĎaré
Hoowé	Laĥ	yihĎar
Heeyé	Laĥ	tihĎar
Nahna	Laĥ	nihĎar
Intoo	Laĥ	tihĎaroo
Hinné	Laĥ	yihĎaroo

Command

Inta	hĎar
Inté	hĎaré
Intoo	hĎaroo
Inta	Ma thĎar
Inté	Ma thĎaré
Intoo	Ma thĎaroo

To water

Present

Ana	Bis'é
Inta	Btis'é
Inté	Btis'é
Hoowé	Byis'é
Heeyé	Btis'é
Nahna	Mnis'é
Intoo	Btis'oo
Hinné	Byis'oo

Present Continuous

Ana	Ăam	Bis'é
Inta	Ăam	Btis'é
Inté	Ăam	Btis'é
Hoowé	Ăam	Byis'é
Heeyé	Ăam	Btis'é
Nahna	Ăam	Mnis'é
Intoo	Ăam	Btis'oo
Hinné	Ăam	Byis'oo

Past

Ana	S'eet
Inta	S'eet
Inté	S'eeté
Hoowé	Si'é
Heeyé	Si'yét
Nahna	S'eena
Intoo	S'eetoo
Hinné	Si'yoo

Past Continuous

Ana	Kint Ăam	Bis'é
Inta	Kint Ăam	Btis'é
Inté	Kinté Ăam	Btis'é
Hoowé	Kén Ăam	Byis'é
Heeyé	Kénét Ăam	Btis'é
Nahna	Kinna Ăam	Mnis'é
Intoo	Kintoo Ăam	Btis'oo
Hinné	Kénoo Ăam	Byis'oo

Future

Ana	Laĥ	Is'é
Inta	Laĥ	Tis'é
Inté	Laĥ	Tis'é
Hoowé	Laĥ	Yis'é
Heeyé	Laĥ	Tis'é
Nahna	Laĥ	Nis'é
Intoo	Laĥ	Tis'oo
Hinné	Laĥ	Yis'oo

Command

Inta	S'ee
Inté	S'ee
Intoo	S'oo
Inta	Ma ts'é
Inté	Ma ts'é
Intoo	Ma ts'oo

Ă= Augh in bought	Ď= a heavy D	É= like A in Bay	G= G in beige	ĥ= like an H with smaller air passage	I= I as in ink	Ḱ= like ch in Irish loch
O= O as in home	OO= as in boots	R= roll the rrr	Ť= a heavy T	Ř= like a French R (gargle it)	Ŝ= a heavy S	Ž= a heavy Z

To weaken

Present

Ana	bĎaĂĂéf
Inta	btĎaĂĂéf
Inté	btĎaĂĂfé
Hoowé	biĎaĂĂéf
Heeyé	btĎaĂĂéf
Nahna	mnĎaĂĂéf
Intoo	btĎaĂĂfoo
Hinné	biĎaĂĂfoo

Present Continuous

Ana	Ăam	bĎaĂĂéf
Inta	Ăam	btĎaĂĂéf
Inté	Ăam	btĎaĂĂfé
Hoowé	Ăam	biĎaĂĂéf
Heeyé	Ăam	btĎaĂĂéf
Nahna	Ăam	mnĎaĂĂéf
Intoo	Ăam	btĎaĂĂfoo
Hinné	Ăam	biĎaĂĂfoo

Past

Ana	ĎaĂĂaft
Inta	ĎaĂĂaft
Inté	ĎaĂĂafté
Hoowé	ĎaĂĂaf
Heeyé	ĎaĂĂafét
Nahna	ĎaĂĂafna
Intoo	ĎaĂĂaftoo
Hinné	ĎaĂĂafoo

Past Continuous

Ana	Kint Ăam	bĎaĂĂéf
Inta	Kint Ăam	btĎaĂĂéf
Inté	Kinté Ăam	btĎaĂĂfé
Hoowé	Kén Ăam	biĎaĂĂéf
Heeyé	Kénét Ăam	btĎaĂĂéf
Nahna	Kinna Ăam	mnĎaĂĂéf
Intoo	Kintoo Ăam	btĎaĂĂfoo
Hinné	Kénoo Ăam	biĎaĂĂfoo

Future

Ana	Laĥ	ĎaĂĂéf
Inta	Laĥ	tĎaĂĂéf
Inté	Laĥ	tĎaĂĂfé
Hoowé	Laĥ	yĎaĂĂéf
Heeyé	Laĥ	tĎaĂĂéf
Nahna	Laĥ	nĎaĂĂéf
Intoo	Laĥ	tĎaĂĂfoo
Hinné	Laĥ	yĎaĂĂfoo

Command

Inta	ĎaĂĂéf
Inté	ĎaĂĂfé
Intoo	ĎaĂĂfoo
Inta	Ma tĎaĂĂéf
Inté	Ma tĎaĂĂfé
Intoo	Ma tĎaĂĂfoo

To wear

Present

Ana	Bilbés
Inta	Btilbés
Inté	Btilbsé
Hoowé	Byilbés
Heeyé	Btilbés
Nahna	Mnilbés
Intoo	Btilbsoo
Hinné	Byilbsoo

Present Continuous

Ana	Ăam	Bilbés	(lébés/lébsé)
Inta	Ăam	Btilbés	(lébés)
Inté	Ăam	Btilbsé	(lébsé)
Hoowé	Ăam	Byilbés	(lébés)
Heeyé	Ăam	Btilbés	(lébsé)
Nahna	Ăam	Mnilbés	(lébseen)
Intoo	Ăam	Btilbsoo	(lébseen)
Hinné	Ăam	Byilbsoo	(lébseen)

Past

Ana	Lbist
Inta	Lbist
Inté	Lbisté
Hoowé	Libés
Heeyé	Libsét
Nahna	Lbisna
Intoo	Lbistoo
Hinné	Libsoo

Past Continuous

Ana	Kint Ăam	Bilbés	(kint lébés/lébsé)
Inta	Kint Ăam	Btilbés	(Kint lébés)
Inté	Kinté Ăam	Btilbsé	(Kinté lébsé)
Hoowé	Kén Ăam	Byilbés	(Kén lébés)
Heeyé	Kénét Ăam	Btilbés	(Kénét lébsé)
Nahna	Kinna Ăam	Mnilbés	(Kinna lébseen)
Intoo	Kintoo Ăam	Btilbsoo	(Kintoo lébseen)
Hinné	Kénoo Ăam	Byilbsoo	(Kénoo lébseen)

Future

Ana	Laĥ	Ilbés
Inta	Laĥ	Tilbés
Inté	Laĥ	Tilbsé
Hoowé	Laĥ	Yilbés
Heeyé	Laĥ	Tilbés
Nahna	Laĥ	Nilbés
Intoo	Laĥ	Tilbsoo
Hinné	Laĥ	Yilbsoo

Command

Inta	Lbés
Inté	Lbisé
Intoo	Lbisoo
Inta	Ma tlbés
Inté	Ma tlbsé
Intoo	Ma tlbsoo

Ă= Augh in bought	Ď= a heavy D	É= like A in Bay	G= G in beige	ĥ= like an H with smaller air passage	I= I as in ink	Ķ= like ch in Irish loch
O= O as in home	OO= as in boots	R= roll the rrr	Ť= a heavy T	Ř= like a French R (gargle it)	Š= a heavy S	Ž= a heavy Z

W

W

To whisper

Present

Ana	bŜawfér
Inta	btŜawfér
Inté	btŜawfré
Hoowé	biŜawfér
Heeyé	btŜawfér
Naĥna	mnŜawfér
Intoo	btŜawfroo
Hinné	biŜawfroo

Present Continuous

Ana	Ăam	bŜawfér
Inta	Ăam	btŜawfér
Inté	Ăam	btŜawfré
Hoowé	Ăam	biŜawfér
Heeyé	Ăam	btŜawfér
Naĥna	Ăam	mnŜawfér
Intoo	Ăam	btŜawfroo
Hinné	Ăam	biŜawfroo

Past

Ana	Ŝawfart
Inta	Ŝawfart
Inté	Ŝawfarté
Hoowé	Ŝawfar
Heeyé	Ŝawfarét
Naĥna	Ŝawfarna
Intoo	Ŝawfartoo
Hinné	Ŝawfaroo

Past Continuous

Ana	Kint Ăam	bŜawfér
Inta	Kint Ăam	btŜawfér
Inté	Kinté Ăam	btŜawfré
Hoowé	Kén Ăam	biŜawfér
Heeyé	Kénét Ăam	btŜawfér
Naĥna	Kinna Ăam	mnŜawfér
Intoo	Kintoo Ăam	btŜawfroo
Hinné	Kénoo Ăam	biŜawfroo

Future

Ana	Laĥ	Ŝawfér
Inta	Laĥ	tŜawfér
Inté	Laĥ	tŜawfré
Hoowé	Laĥ	yŜawfér
Heeyé	Laĥ	tŜawfér
Naĥna	Laĥ	nŜawfér
Intoo	Laĥ	tŜawfroo
Hinné	Laĥ	yŜawfroo

Command

Inta	Ŝawfér
Inté	Ŝafré
Intoo	Ŝawfroo
Inta	Ma tŜawfér
Inté	Ma tŜawfré
Intoo	Ma tŜawfroo

To win

Present

Ana	Birbaĥ
Inta	Btirbaĥ
Inté	Btirbahé
Hoowé	Byirbaĥ
Heeyé	Btirbaĥ
Naĥna	Mnirbaĥ
Intoo	Btirbaĥoo
Hinné	Byirbaĥoo

Present Continuous

Ana	Ăam	Birbaĥ	(ribĥan/ribĥané)
Inta	Ăam	Btirbaĥ	(ribĥan)
Inté	Ăam	Btirbahé	(ribĥané)
Hoowé	Ăam	Byirbaĥ	(ribĥan)
Heeyé	Ăam	Btirbaĥ	(ribĥaneen)
Naĥna	Ăam	Mnirbaĥ	(ribĥaneen)
Intoo	Ăam	Btirbaĥoo	(ribĥaneen)
Hinné	Ăam	Byirbaĥoo	(ribĥaneen)

Past

Ana	Rbiĥt
Inta	Rbiĥt
Inté	Rbiĥté
Hoowé	Ribéĥ
Heeyé	Ribĥét
Naĥna	Rbiĥna
Intoo	Rbiĥtoo
Hinné	Ribĥoo

Past Continuous

Ana	Kint Ăam	Birbaĥ	(kint ribĥan/ribĥané)
Inta	Kint Ăam	Btirbaĥ	(Kint ribĥan)
Inté	Kinté Ăam	Btirbahé	(Kinté Ribĥané)
Hoowé	Kén Ăam	Byirbaĥ	(Kén ribĥan)
Heeyé	Kénét Ăam	Btirbaĥ	(Kénét ribĥané)
Naĥna	Kinna Ăam	Mnirbaĥ	(Kinna ribĥaneen)
Intoo	Kintoo Ăam	Btirbaĥoo	(Kintoo ribĥaneen)
Hinné	Kénoo Ăam	Byirbaĥoo	(Kénoo ribĥaneen)

Future

Ana	Laĥ	irbaĥ
Inta	Laĥ	tirbaĥ
Inté	Laĥ	Tirbahé
Hoowé	Laĥ	yirbaĥ
Heeyé	Laĥ	tirbaĥ
Naĥna	Laĥ	nirbaĥ
Intoo	Laĥ	Tirbaĥoo
Hinné	Laĥ	Yirbaĥoo

Command

Inta	Rbaĥ
Inté	Rbahé
Intoo	Rbaĥoo
Inta	Ma trbaĥ
Inté	Ma trbahé
Intoo	Ma trbaĥoo

Ă= Augh in bought	Đ= a heavy D	É= like A in Bay	G= G in beige	ĥ= like an H with smaller air passage	I= I as in ink	Ķ= like ch in Irish loch
O= O as in home	OO= as in boots	R= roll the rrr	Ť= a heavy T	Ř= like a French R (gargle it)	Ŝ= a heavy S	Ž= a heavy Z

To wink

Present	
Ana	biŘmoz
Inta	biŘmoz
Inté	btiŘmzé
Hoowé	byiŘmoz
Heeyé	btiŘmoz
Nahna	mniŘmoz
Intoo	btiŘmzoo
Hinné	byiŘmzoo

Present Continuous		
Ana	Ăam	biŘmoz
Inta	Ăam	biŘmoz
Inté	Ăam	btiŘmzé
Hoowé	Ăam	byiŘmoz
Heeyé	Ăam	btiŘmoz
Nahna	Ăam	mniŘmoz
Intoo	Ăam	btiŘmzoo
Hinné	Ăam	byiŘmzoo

Past	
Ana	Řamazt
Inta	Řamazt
Inté	Řamazté
Hoowé	Řamaz
Heeyé	Řamazét
Nahna	Řamazna
Intoo	Řamaztoo
Hinné	Řamazoo

Past Continuous		
Ana	Kint Ăam	biŘmoz
Inta	Kint Ăam	biŘmoz
Inté	Kinté Ăam	btiŘmzé
Hoowé	Kén Ăam	byiŘmoz
Heeyé	Kénét Ăam	btiŘmoz
Nahna	Kinna Ăam	mniŘmoz
Intoo	Kintoo Ăam	btiŘmzoo
Hinné	Kénoo Ăam	byiŘmzoo

Future		
Ana	Laĥ	iŘmoz
Inta	Laĥ	iŘmoz
Inté	Laĥ	tiŘmzé
Hoowé	Laĥ	yiŘmoz
Heeyé	Laĥ	tiŘmoz
Nahna	Laĥ	niŘmoz
Intoo	Laĥ	tiŘmzoo
Hinné	Laĥ	yiŘmzoo

Command	
Inta	Řmoz
Inté	Řmizé
Intoo	Řmizoo
Inta	Ma tŘmoz
Inté	Ma tŘmzé
Intoo	Ma tŘmzoo

To wipe

Present	
Ana	Bimsaĥ
Inta	Btimsaĥ
Inté	Btimsaĥé
Hoowé	Byimsaĥ
Heeyé	Btimsaĥ
Nahna	Mnimsaĥ
Intoo	Btimsaĥoo
Hinné	Byimsaĥoo

Present Continuous		
Ana	Ăam	Bimsaĥ
Inta	Ăam	Btimsaĥ
Inté	Ăam	Btimsaĥé
Hoowé	Ăam	Byimsaĥ
Heeyé	Ăam	Btimsaĥ
Nahna	Ăam	Mnimsaĥ
Intoo	Ăam	Btimsaĥoo
Hinné	Ăam	Byimsaĥoo

Past	
Ana	Masaĥt
Inta	Masaĥt
Inté	Masaĥté
Hoowé	Masaĥ
Heeyé	Masaĥét
Nahna	Masaĥna
Intoo	Masaĥtoo
Hinné	Masaĥoo

Past Continuous		
Ana	Kint Ăam	Bimsaĥ
Inta	Kint Ăam	Btimsaĥ
Inté	Kinté Ăam	Btimsaĥé
Hoowé	Kén Ăam	Byimsaĥ
Heeyé	Kénét Ăam	Btimsaĥ
Nahna	Kinna Ăam	Mnimsaĥ
Intoo	Kintoo Ăam	Btimsaĥoo
Hinné	Kénoo Ăam	Byimsaĥoo

Future		
Ana	Laĥ	Imsaĥ
Inta	Laĥ	Timsaĥ
Inté	Laĥ	Timsaĥé
Hoowé	Laĥ	Yimsaĥ
Heeyé	Laĥ	Timsaĥ
Nahna	Laĥ	Nimsaĥ
Intoo	Laĥ	Timsaĥoo
Hinné	Laĥ	Yimsaĥoo

Command	
Inta	Msaĥ
Inté	Msaĥé
Intoo	Msaĥoo
Inta	Ma tmsaĥ
Inté	Ma tmsaĥe
Intoo	Ma tmsaĥoo

Ă= Augh in bought	Ď= a heavy D	É= like A in Bay	G= G in beige	ĥ= like an H with smaller air passage	I= I as in ink	Ķ= like ch in Irish loch
O= O as in home	OO= as in boots	R= roll the rrr	Ť= a heavy T	Ř= like a French R (gargle it)	Ŝ= a heavy S	Ž= a heavy Z

To wonder

Present

Ana	bitĂaggab
Inta	btitĂaggab
Inté	btitĂaggabé
Hoowé	byitĂaggab
Heeyé	btitĂaggab
Nahna	mnitĂaggab
Intoo	btitĂaggaboo
Hinné	byitĂaggaboo

Present Continuous

Ana	Ăam	bitĂaggab	(mitĂaggab/mitĂaggbé)
Inta	Ăam	btitĂaggab	(mitĂaggab)
Inté	Ăam	btitĂaggabé	(mitĂaggbé)
Hoowé	Ăam	byitĂaggab	(mitĂaggab)
Heeyé	Ăam	btitĂaggab	(mitĂaggbé)
Nahna	Ăam	mnitĂaggab	(mitĂaggben)
Intoo	Ăam	btitĂaggaboo	(mitĂaggben)
Hinné	Ăam	byitĂaggaboo	(mitĂaggben)

Past

Ana	tĂaggabt
Inta	tĂaggabt
Inté	tĂaggabté
Hoowé	tĂaggab
Heeyé	tĂaggabét
Nahna	tĂaggabna
Intoo	tĂaggabtoo
Hinné	tĂaggaboo

Past Continuous

Ana	Kint Ăam	bitĂaggab	(kint mitĂaggab)
Inta	Kint Ăam	btitĂaggab	(Kint mitĂaggab)
Inté	Kinté Ăam	btitĂaggabé	(Kinté mitĂaggbé)
Hoowé	Kén Ăam	byitĂaggab	(Kén mitĂaggab)
Heeyé	Kénét Ăam	btitĂaggab	(Kénét mitĂaggbé)
Nahna	Kinna Ăam	mnitĂaggab	(Kinna mitĂaggbeen)
Intoo	Kintoo Ăam	btitĂaggaboo	(Kintoo mitĂaggbeen)
Hinné	Kénoo Ăam	byitĂaggaboo	(Kénoo mitĂaggbeen)

Future

Ana	Lah	itĂaggab
Inta	Lah	titĂaggab
Inté	Lah	titĂaggabé
Hoowé	Lah	yitĂaggab
Heeyé	Lah	titĂaggab
Nahna	Lah	nitĂaggab
Intoo	Lah	titĂaggaboo
Hinné	Lah	yitĂaggaboo

Command

Inta	tĂaggab
Inté	tĂaggbé
Intoo	tĂaggboo
Inta	Ma titĂaggab
Inté	Ma titĂggbé
Intoo	Ma titĂaggboo

To work

Present

Ana	bishtiŘél
Inta	btishtiŘél
Inté	btishtiŘlé
Hoowé	byishtiŘél
Heeyé	btishtiŘél
Nahna	mnishtiŘél
Intoo	btishtiŘloo
Hinné	byishtiŘloo

Present Continuous

Ana	Ăam	bishtiŘél
Inta	Ăam	btishtiŘél
Inté	Ăam	btishtiŘlé
Hoowé	Ăam	byishtiŘél
Heeyé	Ăam	btishtiŘél
Nahna	Ăam	mnishtiŘél
Intoo	Ăam	btishtiŘloo
Hinné	Ăam	byishtiŘloo

Past

Ana	shtaŘalt
Inta	shtaŘalt
Inté	shtaŘalté
Hoowé	shtaŘal
Heeyé	shtaŘalét
Nahna	shtaŘalna
Intoo	shtaŘaltoo
Hinné	shtaŘaloo

Past Continuous

Ana	Kint Ăam	bishtiŘél
Inta	Kint Ăam	btishtiŘél
Inté	Kinté Ăam	btishtiŘlé
Hoowé	Kén Ăam	byishtiŘél
Heeyé	Kénét Ăam	btishtiŘél
Nahna	Kinna Ăam	mnishtiŘél
Intoo	Kintoo Ăam	btishtiŘloo
Hinné	Kénoo Ăam	byishtiŘloo

Future

Ana	Lah	ishtiŘél
Inta	Lah	tishtiŘél
Inté	Lah	tishtiŘlé
Hoowé	Lah	yishtiŘél
Heeyé	Lah	tishtiŘél
Nahna	Lah	nishtiŘél
Intoo	Lah	tishtiŘloo
Hinné	Lah	yishtiŘloo

Command

Inta	shtiŘél
Inté	shtiŘlé
Intoo	shtiŘloo
Inta	Ma tshtiŘél
Inté	Ma tshtiŘlé
Intoo	Ma tshtiŘloo

Ă= Augh in bought	Đ= a heavy D	É= like A in Bay	G= G in beige	ĥ= like an H with smaller air passage	I= I as in ink	Ḱ= like ch in Irish loch
O= O as in home	OO= as in boots	R= roll the rrr	Ť= a heavy T	Ř= like a French R (gargle it)	Ŝ= a heavy S	Ž= a heavy Z

To worry

Present

Ana	biĂtil hamm
Inta	btiĂtil hamm
Inté	btiĂtlé hamm
Hoowé	byiĂtil hamm
Heeyé	btiĂtil hamm
Naĥna	mniĂtil hamm
Intoo	btiĂtloo hamm
Hinné	byiĂtloo hamm

Present Continuous

Ana	Ăam biĂtil hamm	(Ăitlén/Ăitléné hamm)
Inta	Ăam btiĂtil hamm	(Ăitlén hamm)
Inté	Ăam btiĂtlé hamm	(Ăitléné hamm)
Hoowé	Ăam byiĂtil hamm	(Ăitlén hamm)
Heeyé	Ăam btiĂtil hamm	(Ăitléné hamm)
Naĥna	Ăam mniĂtil hamm	(Ăitléneen hamm)
Intoo	Ăam btiĂtloo hamm	(Ăitléneen hamm)
Hinné	Ăam byiĂtloo hamm	(Ăitléneen hamm)

Past

Ana	Ăatalt hamm
Inta	Ăatalt hamm
Inté	Ăatalté hamm
Hoowé	Ăatal hamm
Heeyé	Ăatalét hamm
Naĥna	Ăatalna hamm
Intoo	Ăataltoo hamm
Hinné	Ăataloo hamm

Past Continuous

Ana	Kint Ăam	biĂtil hamm	(kint Ăitlén/Ăitléné hamm)
Inta	Kint Ăam	btiĂtil hamm	(Kint Ăitlén hamm)
Inté	Kinté Ăam	btiĂtlé hamm	(Kinté Ăitléné hamm)
Hoowé	Kén Ăam	byiĂtil hamm	(Kén Ăitlén hamm)
Heeyé	Kénét Ăam	btiĂtil hamm	(Kénét Ăitléné hamm)
Naĥna	Kinna Ăam	mniĂtil hamm	(Kinna Ăitléneen hamm)
Intoo	Kintoo Ăam	btiĂtloo hamm	(Kintoo Ăitléneen hamm)
Hinné	Kénoo Ăam	byiĂtloo hamm	(Kénoo Ăitléneen hamm)

Future

Ana	Laĥ	iĂtil hamm
Inta	Laĥ	tiĂtil hamm
Inté	Laĥ	tiĂtlé hamm
Hoowé	Laĥ	yiĂtil hamm
Heeyé	Laĥ	tiĂtil hamm
Naĥna	Laĥ	niĂtil hamm
Intoo	Laĥ	tiĂtloo hamm
Hinné	Laĥ	yiĂtloo hamm

Command

Inta	Ătal hamm
Inté	Ătalé hamm
Intoo	Ătaloo hamm
Inta	Ma tĂtal hamm
Inté	Ma tĂtalé hamm
Intoo	Ma tĂtaloo hamm

To wrap

Present

Ana	Bliff
Inta	Btliff
Inté	Btliffé
Hoowé	Biliff
Heeyé	Btliff
Naĥna	Mnliff
Intoo	Btliffoo
Hinné	Biliffoo

Present Continuous

Ana	Ăam	Bliff
Inta	Ăam	Btliff
Inté	Ăam	Btliffé
Hoowé	Ăam	Biliff
Heeyé	Ăam	Btliff
Naĥna	Ăam	Mnliff
Intoo	Ăam	Btliffoo
Hinné	Ăam	Biliffoo

Past

Ana	Laffét
Inta	Laffét
Inté	Laffaité
Hoowé	Laff
Heeyé	Laffét
Naĥna	Laffaina
Intoo	Laffaitoo
Hinné	Laffoo

Past Continuous

Ana	Kint Ăam	Bliff
Inta	Kint Ăam	Btliff
Inté	Kinté Ăam	Btliffé
Hoowé	Kén Ăam	Biliff
Heeyé	Kénét Ăam	Btliff
Naĥna	Kinna Ăam	Mnliff
Intoo	Kintoo Ăam	Btliffoo
Hinné	Kénoo Ăam	Biliffoo

Future

Ana	Laĥ	Liff
Inta	Laĥ	Tliff
Inté	Laĥ	Tliffé
Hoowé	Laĥ	Yliff
Heeyé	Laĥ	Tliff
Naĥna	Laĥ	Nliff
Intoo	Laĥ	Tliffoo
Hinné	Laĥ	Yliffoo

Command

Inta	Liff
Inté	Liffé
Intoo	Liffoo
Inta	Ma tliff
Inté	Ma tliffé
Intoo	Ma tliffoo

Ă= Augh in bought	Ď= a heavy D	É= like A in Bay	G= G in beige	ĥ= like an H with smaller air passage	I= I as in ink	Ќ= like ch in Irish loch
O= O as in home	OO= as in boots	R= roll the rrr	Ť= a heavy T	Ř= like a French R (gargle it)	Ŝ= a heavy S	Ž= a heavy Z

W

Y

To write

Present

Ana	Biktob
Inta	Btiktob
Inté	Btiktbé
Hoowé	Btiktob
Heeyé	Btiktob
Naḣna	Mniktob
Intoo	Btiktboo
Hinné	Byikoboo

Present Continuous

Ana	Ăam	Biktob
Inta	Ăam	Btiktob
Inté	Ăam	Btiktbé
Hoowé	Ăam	Btiktob
Heeyé	Ăam	Btiktob
Naḣna	Ăam	Mniktob
Intoo	Ăam	Btiktboo
Hinné	Ăam	Byikoboo

Past

Ana	Katabt
Inta	Katabt
Inté	Katabté
Hoowé	Katab
Heeyé	Katabét
Naḣna	Katabna
Intoo	Katabtoo
Hinné	Kataboo

Past Continuous

Ana	Kint Ăam	Biktob
Inta	Kint Ăam	Btiktob
Inté	Kinté Ăam	Btiktbé
Hoowé	Kén Ăam	Btiktob
Heeyé	Kénét Ăam	Btiktob
Naḣna	Kinna Ăam	Mniktob
Intoo	Kintoo Ăam	Btiktboo
Hinné	Kénoo Ăam	Byikoboo

Future

Ana	Laḣ	Iktob
Inta	Laḣ	Tiktob
Inté	Laḣ	Tiktbé
Hoowé	Laḣ	Yiktob
Heeyé	Laḣ	Tiktob
Naḣna	Laḣ	Niktob
Intoo	Laḣ	Tiktboo
Hinné	Laḣ	Yiktboo

Command

Inta	Ktob
Inté	Ktibé
Intoo	Ktiboo
Inta	Ma tktib
Inté	Ma tiktbé
Intoo	Ma tiktboo

To yell / To shout

Present

Ana	bĂayéṪ
Inta	btĂayéṪ
Inté	btĂayṪé
Hoowé	biĂayéṪ
Heeyé	btĂayéṪ
Naḣna	mnĂayéṪ
Intoo	btĂayṪoo
Hinné	biĂayṪoo

Present Continuous

Ana	Ăam	bĂayéṪ
Inta	Ăam	btĂayéṪ
Inté	Ăam	btĂayṪé
Hoowé	Ăam	biĂayéṪ
Heeyé	Ăam	btĂayéṪ
Naḣna	Ăam	mnĂayéṪ
Intoo	Ăam	btĂayṪoo
Hinné	Ăam	biĂayṪoo

Past

Ana	ĂayaṪit
Inta	ĂayaṪit
Inté	ĂayaṪté
Hoowé	ĂayaṪ
Heeyé	ĂayaṪ_it
Naḣna	ĂayaṪna
Intoo	ĂayaṪtoo
Hinné	ĂayaṪoo

Past Continuous

Ana	Kint Ăam	bĂayéṪ
Inta	Kint Ăam	btĂayéṪ
Inté	Kinté Ăam	btĂayṪé
Hoowé	Kén Ăam	biĂayéṪ
Heeyé	Kénét Ăam	btĂayéṪ
Naḣna	Kinna Ăam	mnĂayéṪ
Intoo	Kintoo Ăam	btĂayṪoo
Hinné	Kénoo Ăam	biĂayṪoo

Future

Ana	Laḣ	ĂayéṪ
Inta	Laḣ	tĂayéṪ
Inté	Laḣ	tĂayṪé
Hoowé	Laḣ	yĂayéṪ
Heeyé	Laḣ	tĂayéṪ
Naḣna	Laḣ	nĂayéṪ
Intoo	Laḣ	tĂayṪoo
Hinné	Laḣ	yĂayṪoo

Command

Inta	ĂayéṪ
Inté	ĂayṪé
Intoo	ĂayṪoo
Inta	Ma tĂayéṪ
Inté	Ma tĂayṪé
Intoo	Ma tĂayṪoo

Ă= Augh in bought	Ď= a heavy D	É= like A in Bay	G= G in beige	ḣ= like an H with smaller air passage	I= I as in ink	Ḱ= like ch in Irish loch
O= O as in home	OO= as in boots	R= roll the rrr	Ṫ= a heavy T	Ř= like a French R (gargle it)	Ŝ= a heavy S	Ž= a heavy Z

DICTIONARY

In Lebanese, there is a special form for pairs. This dictionary is showing the singular and the plural forms skipping the pair-form. You may use the plural for pairs and preceed it by "a pair of" which is in Lebanese: "goz".

A

a (doesn't exist in Lebanese)

abandoned mahgoor

abbreviation mouḰtaŜar

abduction ḰaŤf

ability 'idra(s-f) idrat(p)

abnormal Řair ŤabeeĂé

abortion trweeĥ – ighaĎ(s-m) ighaĎat(p)

about ĥawl - Ăan

above fo'

abroad Řirbé(s-f) Řirbét(p) – mooŘtarab(s-m) mooŘtarabét(p) – mahgar(s-m) mahégér(p)

absence Řyéb(s-m) Řyébét(p)

absent (adj.) Řayéb(m) Raybé(f) Řaybeen(p)

absolute(adj.) moogarrad(m) moogarradé(f) moogarradeen(p)

absorption imtiŜaŜ(s-m) imtiŜaŜat(p)

abstaining from imtinéĂ Ăan

abstract(adj.) tagreedé(m) tagreedyyé(f) tagreedyyeen(p)

absurd(adj.) saḰeef(m) saḰeefé(f) saḰeefeen(p) – téféh(m) téfha(f) téfheen(p)

abundant(adj.) mtwaffar(m) mitwaffra(f) mitwaffreen(p) - kteer

abuse isé'ét L-mĂamalé

academy akadémyé(s-f) akadémyét(p)

acceleration sirĂa(s-f) sirĂat(p)

accent (in speech) lahgé(s-f) lahgét(p)

acceptance 'oobool (s-p)– mwéfa'a(s-f) mwéfa'at(p)

access ĥa' LwooŜool

accessory(adj.) sanawé(m) sanawyyé(f) sanawyyeen(p)

accident ĥadés(s-m) ĥawédés(p)

by accident bi ŜŜiĎfé

accommodation(n.) iskén(s-m)

accompaniment moorafa'a(s-f) moorafa'at(p)

accomplishment tiĥ'ee'(s-m) tiĥ'ee'at(p)

account ĥséb(s) ĥsébét(p)

accumulation trakoom(s-m) trakoomét(p)

accuracy di''a(s-p)(f)

accurate (adj.) da'ee'(m) da'ee'a(f) da'ee'een(p)

accusation tilĥmé(s-f) tiham(p)

ache wagaĂ(s-m) awgéĂ(p)

achieving tiĥ'ee'(s-m) tiĥ'ee'at(p)

acquaintance maĂrifé(s-f) maĂaréf(p)

acquiring iktiséb(s-m) iktisébét(p)

across L-gihha ttényé min

act/action Ăamal(s-m) aĂmél(p) – fiĂl(s-m) afĂal(p)

acting tamseel(s-p)(m)

active (adj) ĥirék(m) ĥirké(f) ĥirkeen(p) – nasheeŤ(m) nasheeŤa(f) nasheeŤeen(p)

activity nashaŤ(s-m) nashaŤat(p)

actor/actress moomassél(m) moomaslé(f) moomassileen(p)

actual(adj.) wé'Ăé(m) wé'Ăyyé(f) wé'Ăyeen(p)

actually bi L-wé'éĂ

acute(adj.) ĥad(m) ĥaddé(f) ĥaddeen(p)

adaptation ta'aklom(s-m) ta'akloomét(p)

addict(n.) moodmén(m) moodminé(f) moodmineen(p)

addiction idmén(s-m) idménét(p)

addition gamĂ(s-p)(m)

address Ăinwén(s-m) Aanéween(p)

adequate (adj.) kéfé(m) kéfyé(f) kéfyeen(p)

adjective Ŝifa(s-f) Ŝifét(p)

adhesive(n.) lézé'(m) léz'a(f) léz'een(p)

adjoining gamĂ(s-p)(m) – waŜl(s-p)(m)

administration idara(s-f) idarat(p)

admiration iĥtiram(s-m) iĥtiramét(p)

admission 'oobool(s-m) 'ooboolét(p)

adoption tabanné(s-m) tabannyyét(p)

adult(n.) béléŘ(m) bélŘa(f) bélŘeen(p)

in advance moosba'an

advantage(n.) manfaĂa(s-f) manéféĂ(p) – féydé(s-f) fawéyéd(p)

adventure mooŘamara(s-f) mooŘamarat(p)

adverb(n.) Źarf(s-m) Źooroof(p)

advertisement diĂayé(s-f) diĂayét(p) – iĂlén(s-m) iĂlénét(p)

advice naŜeeĥa(s-f) naŜayéĥ(p)

affected(adj.) mit'assar(m) mit'assra(f) mit'assreen(p)

affection Hanén(s-p)(m)

affectionate(adj.) ĥanoon(m) ĥanooné(f) ĥanooneen(p)

affluence(n.) raféha(s-f) – Řina(s-m)

afraid(adj.) Ḱayéf(m) Ḱayfé(f) Ḱayfeen(p)

African afree'é(m) afree'yyé(f) afér'a(p)

after baĂd

afternoon baĂd ĎĎihir

afterwards baĂdén

again Ăan gdeed – marra tényé

against Ďidd

age Ăimr(s-m) aĂmar(p)

agent(n.) Ăameel(m) Ăameelé(f) Ăoomala(p)

ago sébi'an – bi L-maĎé

five years ago min Ḱams sneen

agreement ittifé'(s-m) ittifé'at(p)

aggressive(adj.) Ăaneef(m) Ăaneefé(f) Aaneefeen(p)

agricultural(adj.) ziraĂé(m) ziraĂyyé(f) ziraĂyyeen(p)

Ă= Augh in bought	Ď= a heavy D	É= like A in Bay	G= G in beige	ĥ= like an H with smaller air passage	I= I as in ink	Ḱ= like ch in Irish loch
O= O as in home	OO= as in boots	R= roll the rrr	Ť= a heavy T	Ř= like a French R (gargle it)	Ŝ= a heavy S	Ź= a heavy Z

agriculture Ăilm L-ziraĂa

ahead iddém

aid mooséAadé(s-f) mooséĂadét(p)

air hawa

air conditioner mookayif(s) mookayifét(p)

air mail bareed gawwé

airplane Ťiyara(s-f) Ťiyarat(p)

aisle(n.) mamarr(s-m) mamarrat(p)

alike mitl - shabah

alive(adj.) ĥay(m) ĥayé(f) aĥyé'(p)

all kill

alliance ĥilf(s-m) aĥléf(p) – tĥalof(s-m) tĥaloofét(p)

alright Ťayéb

allergy Hasésyé(s-p)(f)

alley zéroob(s-m) zwéreeb(p)

ally(n.) ĥaleef(m) ĥaleefé(f) ĥoolafa(p)

almost Ăa shway

alone waĥdoo(m) waĥda(f) waĥdon(p)

also kamén

alternately bi ttanéwob

although maĂ innoo

altitude irtiféĂ(s-m) irtiféĂat(p)

always déyman

amazed(adj.) mindihésh(m) mindihshé(f) mindihsheen(p)

amazement dahshé(s-f) dahshét(p)

amazing(adj.) midhésh(m) midhshé(f) midhsheen(p)ĥ

ambassador safeer(m) safeera(f) soofara(p)

ambition Ťoomooĥ(s-m) Ťoomooĥat(p)

ambitious(adj.) Ťamooĥ(m) Ťamooĥa(f) Ťamooĥeen(p)

American(n.) amrkéné(m) amrkényé(f) amrkén(p)

among bén

amount kammyé(s-f) kammyét(p)

ample(adj.) ĥirzén(m) ĥirzéné(f) ĥirzéneen(p)

amusement taslyé(s) tasélé(p) – lahoo(s-p)

amusing(adj.) moosallé(m) moosallyé(f) moosallyeen(p)

analysis tiĥleel(s-m) taĥaleel(p)

anchor(n.) mirsét(s-f) marasé(p)

ancient(adj.) Ăatee'(m) Ăatee'a(f) Ăté'(p) – adeem(m) adeemé(f) 'dém(p)

anecdote 'iŜŜa 'aŜeeré(s-f) iŜaŜ iŜar(p)

anaesthetic bing(s-p) – mooḰaddir(s-m) mooḰaddirat(p)

angel malék(s-m) malé'iké(p)

anger ŘaĎab(s-p)(m) – tiĂŜeeb(s-p)(m)

angry(adj.) mĂaŜŜab(m) mĂaŜŜbé(f) mĂaŜŜbeen(p)

animal(n.) ĥayawén(m) ĥayawéné(f) ĥayawénét(p)

animation roosoom mootaĥarrika

annex moolĥa'(s-m) maléĥé'(p)

anniversary zzikra ssanawyé(s-f)

announcement iĂlén(s-m) iĂlénét(p) – tŜreeĥ(s-m) taŜareeĥ(p) – bayén(s-m) bayénét(p)

annoying(adj.) mizĂég(m) mizĂgé(f) mizĂgeen(p)

annual(adj.) sanawé(m) sanawwyé(f)

anonymous(adj.) maghool(m) maghoolé(f) maghooleen(p)

another (others) téné(m) tényé(f) tényeen(p)

answer gawéb(s-m) agwibé(p)

ant namlé(s-f) naml(p)

anterior(adj.) amémé(m) amémyé(f) amémyeen(p)

anticipation tawa'oĂ(s-m) tawa'oĂat(p)

anxiety(n.) ala'(s-m) – lahfé(s-f) lahfét(p)

anxious(n.) il'an(m) il'ané(f) il'aneen(p)

any ayya

anybody ayya shaḰŜ

anyone ayya wéĥéd(m) ayya wiĥdé(f)

anything ayya shee

anyway Ăa kil ĥal – bi kil L aĥwél

anywhere ayya makén

apart bĂeed

apartment shi''a(s-f) shi'a'(p)

apology iĂtizar(s-m) iĂtizarat(p)

apparent(adj.) Źahér(m) Źahra(f) Źahreen(p)

apparently ŹŹahér

appearance maŹhar(s-m) maŹahér(p)

appendix moolĥa'(s-m) maléĥé'(p)

appetite shahyyé(s-f) shahyyét(p)

applause tiz'eef(s-p)(m)

apple tifféĥa(s-f) tifféĥ(p)

application(use)(n.) istiĂmél(s-m) istiĂmélét(p)

application(form)(n.) Ťalab(s-m) Ťalabét(p)

appointment mawĂad(s-m) mwéĂeed(p)

appreciation ta'deer(s-p)(m)

appropriate(adj.) mnéséb(m) mnésbé(f) mnésbeen(p)

approval mwéfa'a(s-f) mwéfa'at(p)

April nisén

Apron maryool(s-m) mrarweel(p)

arbitrary(adj.) Ăashwé'é(m) Ăashwé'yé(f) Ăashwé'yeen(p)

area maséĥa(s-f) maséĥat(p)

argument mooné'ashé(s-f) mooné'ashét(p)

arm draĂ(s-m) draĂat(p)

arms (weapons) sléĥ(s-m) asliĥa(p)

fire arms alĂab naryé(p)

army gésh(s-m) gyoosh(p)

around ĥawl

arrangement(n.) tirteeb - tinsee' - tinŹeem

arrest iĂti'al(s-m) iĂti'alét(p)

arrival wooŜool(s-p)(m)

Ă= Augh in bought	Ď= a heavy D	É= like A in Bay	G= G in beige	ĥ= like an H with smaller air passage	I= I as in ink	Ḱ= like ch in Irish loch
O= O as in home	OO= as in boots	R= roll the rrr	Ť= a heavy T	Ř= like a French R (gargle it)	Ŝ= a heavy S	Ź= a heavy Z

art fan(s-m) fnoon(p)

article ma'alé(s-f) ma'alét(p)

artificial(adj.) iŜtinéĂé(m) iŜtinéĂyé(f) iŜtinéĂyeen(p)

artist(n.) finnén(m) finnéné(f) finnéneen(p)

artistic(adj.) fanné(m) fannyé(f) fanyeen(p)

as (like) mitl - ad

as much – as long – as little etc... add

ash rméd(p)

aside ĥadd

asleep(adj.) néyém(m) néymé(f) néymeen(p)

aspiration waĥé(s-p)(m)

assault taĂaddé(s-m) taĂaddyét(p)

assembly tagammoĂ(s-m) tagammoĂat(p)

assistance mooséĂadé(s-f) mooséĂadét(p)

assistant(n.) mooséĂéd(m) mooséĂdé(f) mooséĂdeen(p)

assumption iĂti'ad(s-m) iĂti'adét(p)

assurance tiŤmeen(s-m) tiŤmeenét(p)

astonishing midhésh(m) midhshé(f) midhsheen(p)

at first awwalan – bi L awwal

at last aḰeeran – bi L 'éḰér

at once diŘré

at the home of Ăand

at the place of business of Ăand

athletic ryaĎé(m) ryaĎyé(f) ryaĎyeen(p)

atmosphere gaw

atomic bomb 'inblé zirryé

attack hoogoom(s-p)

attempt mooĥawalé(s-f) mooĥawalét(p)

attention intibéh

attic takana

attitude(n.) soolook(s-m)

attorney mĥamé(m) mĥamyé(f) mĥameen(p)

attraction gézbyé

audience goomhoor – moostamiĂ(m) moostamiĂa(f) moostamiĂeen(p)

august 'éb

aunt Ăammé - Ḱalé

author(n.) moo'allif(m) moo'allifé(f) moo'allifeen(p)

authority ŜoolŤa(s-f) ŜoolŤat(p)

automobile syyara(s-f) syyarat(p)

autumn Ḱareef

avenue shéréĂ(s-m) shwéreĂ(p)

average mĂaddal(s-m) mĂaddlét(p)

avoiding tafédé(s-m) tafédyyét(p)

award gé'izé(s-f) gawé'éz(p)

away(adj.) bĂeed(m) bĂeedé(f) bĂad(p)

awful(adj.) faŹeeĂ(m) faŹeeĂa(f) faŹeeĂeen(p) – shaneeĂ(m) shaneeĂa(f) shaneeĂeen(p)

awkward(adj.) mirbék(m) mirbké(f) mirbkeen(p)

B

baby(n.) Ťifl(m) Ťiflé(f) aŤfal(p)

back (behind) wara

back (body) Ďahr

background Ḱalfyé(s-f) Ḱalfyét(p)

backwards rgooĂ

bad(adj.) ĂaŤél(m) ĂaŤlé(f) ĂaŤleen(p) – mish mneeĥ(m) mish mneeĥa(f) mish mnéĥ(p)

badge(n.) shiĂar(s-m) shiĂarat(p) – wisém(s-m) awsimé(p)

bag kees(s-m) kyés(p) – shanta(s-f) shanat(p)

baker(n.) firran(m) firrané(f) firrané(p)

bakery firn(s-m) afran(p)

balance meezén(s-m) mwézeen(p) – tawezon (body balance)

bald(adj.) aŜlaĂ(m) ŜalĂa(f) ŜilĂ(p)

ball Ťabé(s-f) Ťabét(p)

ball-point pen alam ĥibr(s-m) 'lém ĥibr(p)

balloon balloon(s-m) balonét(p) – balon(s-m) balonét(p)

banana mowzé(s-f) moz(p)

band (music) fir'a(s-f) fira'(p)

bandage(n.) Ďamédé(s-f) Ďamédét(p)

banister(n.) drabzeen(s-p-m)

bank bank(s-m) bnooké(p)

bankrupt(adj.) mfallas(m) mfallsé(f) mfallseen(p)

bankruptcy iflés(s-m) iflését(p)

banquet(n.) waleemé(s-f) waléyém(p)

bar bar(s-m) barat(p)

barber ĥillé'(m) ĥillé'een(p)

bare(adj.) Ăaré(m) Ăaryé(f) Aaryeen(p) – mŹallaŤ(m) mŹallŤa(f) mŹallŤeen(p)

bargaining mséwamé(s-f) mséwamét(p)

barn zreebé(s-f) zarayéb(p)

barrel barmeel(s-m) brameel(p)

base aĂde(s-f) awéĂéd(p)

basin maŘslé(s-f) maŘésél(p)

basis asés(s-m) isos(p)

basket sallé(s-f) sallét(p)

bath ĥimmém(s-f) ĥimmémét(p)

battery biŤŤaryé(s-f) biŤŤaryét(p)

battle maĂrké(s-f) maĂarék(p)

beach shaŤ(s-m) shŤoot(p)

beam shooĂaĂ(s-m) ashiĂĂa(p)

bean faŜoolya(s-p)(f)

bear (the animal - also adj.) dibb(m) dibbé(f) dibab(p)
beat wa'Ă(s-p)(m) – naŘmé(s-f) naŘmét(p)

beautiful(adj.) ĥiloo(m) ĥilwé(f) ĥilween(p)
beauty gamél(s-p)(m)

Ă= Augh in bought	Ď= a heavy D	É= like A in Bay	G= G in beige	ĥ= like an H with smaller air passage	I= I as in ink	Ḱ= like ch in Irish loch
O= O as in home	OO= as in boots	R= roll the rrr	Ť= a heavy T	Ř= like a French R (gargle it)	Ŝ= a heavy S	Ž= a heavy Z

because li'anno

because of bisabab

bed taḰt(s-m) tḰooté(p) – sreer(s-m) asirra(p)

bed clothes sharshaf ttaḰt(s-m) shrashéf ttaḰt(p)

bedroom Řirfét nnom(s-f) Řiraf nnom(p) – 'ooĎét nnom(s-f) 'ooaĎ nnom(p)

beef laĥm ba'ar(s-p)(m)

beer beera(s-p)(f)

beet shmandar

before abl

beggar(n.) shiĥĥad(m) shiĥĥadé(f) shiĥĥadeen(p)

beginning bidéyé(s-f) bidéyét(p)

behavior taŜarrof(s-p)(m)

behind wara - Ḱalf

belgian(n.) bélgeeké(m) bélgeekyé(f) bélgeekyeen(p)

belief 'eemén(s-p)(m) – 'iǍti'ad(s-m) 'iǍti'adét(p)

bell garaŜ(s-m) agraŜ(p)

below taĥt

belt 'shaŤ(s-m) 'shaŤat(p)

bench(n.) ma'Ǎad(s-m) ma'aǍéd(p)

bending ŤaǍg(s-p)(m) – Ťawé(s-p)(m) - lawé(s-p)(m)

beneath taĥt

benefit manfaǍa(s-f) manéféǍ(p) – féydé(s-f) fawéyéd(p)

beside ĥad

besides bil'iĎafé

best L'afĎal – L'aĥsan

bet sharŤ(s-m) shrooŤ(p)

betrayal Ḱiyéné(s-m) Ḱiyénét(p)

better afĎal - aĥsan

between bén

beyond(prep.) ma wara'

bid ǍarĎ(s-m) ǍrooĎat(p)

big(adj.) kbeer(m) kbeeré(f) kbar(p)

bill fétoora(s-f) fwéteer(p)

billion miliar

biology Ǎilm L'aĥyé'

bird ǍaŜfoor(s) ǍŜafeer(p) – Ťayr(s) Ťyoor(p)

birth(n.) mawléd(s-m) – meeléd(s-m)

birthday Ǎeed meeléd(s-m) aǍyéd meeléd(p)

biscuit (same)

bishop miŤran(s-m) mŤareen(p)

bit nitfé(s-f) nitaf(p)– shway(f)

bite ǍaĎĎa(s-f) ǍaĎĎat(p)

bitter(adj.) mirr(m) mirra(f) mirreen(p)

bitterness mroora

black(adj.) aswad(m) sawda(f) sood(p)

blade shafra(s-f) shafrat(p)

blame lom(s-p)

blank(adj.) faĎé(m) faĎyé(f) faĎyeen(p)

blanket ĥrém(s-f) ĥrémét(p)

bleed nazeef(s-p)

bless baraké(s-f) barakét(p)

blessing moobéraké(s-f) moobérakét(p)

blind(adj.) aǍma(m) Ǎamya(f) Ǎimyén(p)

block(n.) 'aléb(s-m) 'awéléb(p)

blond(adj.) ash'ar(m) sha'ra(f) shi'r(f)

blood damm(s-p)

blouse ameeŜ(s-f) imŜan(p) – blooz(s-f) blooaz(p)

blow nafḰa(s-f) nafḰat(p)

blue(adj.) azra'(m) zar'a(f) zir'(p)

blushing Ḱagal

board loĥ(s-m) lwéĥ(p)

boat shaḰtoor(s) shḰateer(p) – zawra'(s) zawéré'(p)

body gism(s-m) agsém(p) – gasad(s-m) agséd(p)

boiling Řalayén(s-p)(m)

boldness wa'aĥa (s-f) wa'aĥat(p) – gir'a(s-f) gir'at(p)

bond(n.) rabéŤ(s-m) rawabéŤ(p)

bone ǍaĎmé(s-f) ǍĎam(p)

book ktéb(s-m) kitob(p)

booking ĥagz(s-m) ĥgoozét(p)

booklet(n.) kotayyéb(s-m) kotayyibét(p)

bookstore maktabé(s-f) maktabét(p)

border ĥdood(s-p)

boredom Ďagar(s-p)(m) - malal(s-p)(m)

boring(adj.) mooĎgér(m) mooĎgra(f) mooDgreen(p) – moomill(m) moomillé(f) moomilleen(p)

borough manŤ'a(s-f) manaTé'(p)

both Ltnén - tnaynéton

bothering izǍag(s-p)(m)

bottle anneené(s-f) anéné(p)

bottom kaǍb(s-m) kǍab(p)

bounce(jump) naŤŤa(s-f) naŤŤat(p)

bounce(ball bounce) Ťaggé(s-f) Ťaggét(p)

boundary ĥdood(s-p)

boundless bala Hdood – bdoon ĥdood

bowl gaŤ(s-m) gaŤat(p)

box Ŝandoo'(s-m) Ŝnadee'(p)

box office Ŝandoo' Lbareed(s) Ŝnadee' Lbareed(p)

boy Ŝabé(s-m) Sibyén(p)

bracelet Ǎa'd(s-m) Ǎ'ood(p)

braid gaddoolé(s-f) gdédeel(p)

braided(adj.) mgaddal(m) mgaddlé(f) mgaddleen(p)

brain dméŘ(s-m) admiŘa(p) – Ǎa'l(s-m) Ǎ'ool(p)

brake(n.) frém(s-m) frémét(p)

branch farǍ(s-m) frooǍ(p)

brave(adj.) shoogéǍ(m) shoogéǍa(f) shigǍan(p) – garee'(m) garee'a(f) garee'een(p)

Ǎ= Augh in bought	Ď= a heavy D	É= like A in Bay	G= G in beige	ĥ= like an H with smaller air passage	I= I as in ink	Ḱ= like ch in Irish loch
O= O as in home	OO= as in boots	R= roll the rrr	Ť= a heavy T	Ř= like a French R (gargle it)	Ŝ= a heavy S	Ž= a heavy Z

bread Ќibz(s-p)

breadth ĂarĎ - wisĂ

break down inhiyar(s-m) inhiyarat(p)
(*nervous break down*) inhyar ĂaŜabé

breakfast tirwee'a(s-f) tirwee'at(;p)

breath lahat(s-p)(m) – nafas(s)(m)
anfés(p)

breeze nasmé(s-f) nasmét(p)

bribe barŤeel(s-p)(m)

brick(n.) Ťaboo'(s-m)

bride Ăaroos(s-f) Ăarayés(p)

bridge gisr(s-m) gsoora(p)

brief(adj.) mooЌtaŜar(m) mooЌtaŜara(f)
mooЌtaŜareen(p)

bright(smart) (adj.) zaké(m) zakyyé(f)
azkya(p)

brilliant(adj.) zaké(m) zakyyé(f)
azkya(p)

bringing up tarbyé(s-f) tarbyét(p)

British(n.) breeTané(m) breeŤanyyé(f)
breeŤanyyeen(p)

Broad(adj.) ĂareeĎ(m) ĂareeĎa(f)
ĂraĎ(p) – wéséĂ(m) wésĂa(f)
wésĂeen(p) – shéséĂ(m) shésĂa(m)
shésĂeen(p)

Broken(adj.) maksoor(m) maksoora(f)
maksooreen(p)

Bronze (same)

Brook(n.) gadwal(s-m) gadéwél(p) –
sé'yé(s-f) sawe'é(p)

broom miknsé(s-f) mkénés(p)

brother Ќay(s-m) iЌwé(p)

brother in law (see "family" in
LeboLand)

brown(adj.) binne(m) binneeyé(f)
bineeyeen(p)

bruise ŘaĎĎa(s-f) raĎĎat(p)

brush firshéyé(s-f) firshéyét(p)

bubble foo'éĂa(s-f) f'é'eeĂ(p)

buckle biklé(s-f) bikal(p)
bud birĂom(s-m) baraĂém(p)

budget meezényyé(s-f) meezényyét(p)

buffet (same)

building binéyé(s-f) binéyét(p) –
Ăimara(s-f) Ăimarat(p)

bulletin(n.) nashra(s-f) nashrat(p)

bundle rizmé(s-f) rizam(p)

burden ĥiml(s-m) ĥmoolé(p)

bureau maktab(s-m) makétéb(p)

burn ĥir'(s-m) ĥroo'(p)

bus (same)

bush gim(s-m) gmém(p)

business (same) - shiŘl(s-m) ashŘal(p)

businessman (same) – ragol aĂmél(s-m)
rigél aĂmél(p)

businesswoman (same)

bust(adj.) mĂaŤŤal(m) mĂaŤŤlé(f)
mĂaŤŤleen(p)

busy(adj.) mashŘool(m) mashŘoolé(f)
mashgooleen)(p)

but bass - lékén

butcher(n.) liĥĥam(m) liĥĥamé(f)
liĥĥameen(p)

butcher shop malĥamé(s-m) malĥamét(p)

butter zibdé(s-p-f)

button zirr(s-m) zrar(p)

buyer(n.) sharra(m) shirréyé(f)
shirréyeen(p)

buzzing(adj.) ĥayawé(m) Hayawyyé(f)
ĥayawyyeen(p)

C

cab taxi

cabbage malfoofé(s-f) malfoof(p)

cabin (same)

cabinet Ќzéné(s-f) Ќzénét(p)

cable (same)

cage afaŜ(s-m) 'faŜ(p)

cake (same)

calendar riznéma(s-f) rianémét(p)

calf baŤŤa(s-f) baŤTat(p)
- baŤTit L igir(s-f) baŤTat L igrén(p)

calm(adj.) rayé'(m) ray'a(f) ray'een(p) –
hédé(m) hédyé(f) hédyeen(p)

camera (same)

camp (same) – mooЌayyam(s-m)
mooЌayyamét(p)

can tanké(s-f) tanak(p)

Canadian(n.) kanadé(m) kanadyyé(f)
canadyyeen(p)

candidate mrashaĥ(m) mrashĥa(f)
mrashĥeen(p)

candle shamĂa(s-f) shamĂ(p)

canvas laowĥa(s-f) laowĥat(p) – Ŝoora(s-
f) soowar(p) – rasmé(s-f) rasmét(p)

cap (lid) ŘaŤa(s-m) iŘŤyé(p)

cap (limit) sa'f(s-m) s'oof(p) – ĥadd(s-m)
ĥdood(p)

capacity Ťa'a(s-f) Ťa'at(p) – 'idra(s-f)
'idrat(p)

capital (city) ĂaŜmé(s-f) AawaŜém(p)

capital (money) ras mél(s-m) roo'oos
amwél(p)

capricious(adj.) mazégé(m) mazégyyé(f)
mazegyyeen(p)

captain (same) – 'ibŤan(s-m) abaŤné(p)

captive(n.) aseer(m) aseera(f) asra(p) –
mooĂta'al(m) mooĂta'alé(f)
mooĂta'aleen(p)

captivity asr(s-p-m) – iĂti'al(s-m)

captured(adj.) mooĂta'al(m)
mooĂta'alé(f) mooĂta'aleen(p) –
ma'soor(m) ma'soora(f) ma'sooreen(p)

car seeyara(s-f) seeyarat(p)

card kart(s-m) kroot(p) – biŤa'a(s-f)
biŤa'at(p)

care Ăinéyé(s-f) Ăinéyét(p)

career mihné(s-f) mihan(p)

carefullness intibéh(s-p-m)

careless(adj.) mihmél(m) mihmlé(f)
mihmleen(p)

carpenter(n.) niggar(m) niggara(f)
niggareen(p)

Ă= Augh in bought	Ď= a heavy D	Ė= like A in Bay	G= G in beige	ĥ= like an H with smaller air passage	I= I as in ink	Ќ= like ch in Irish loch
O= O as in home	OO= as in boots	R= roll the rrr	Ť= a heavy T	Ř= like a French R (gargle it)	Ŝ= a heavy S	Ž= a heavy Z

carpet siggédé(s-f) siggédét(p) / siggéd(p)

cartoon roosoom mootaȟarrika(p)

case (box) ŜanĎoo'(m) SanĎoo'a(f) ŜnaĎee'(p)

cash na'dé(s-p-m)

cash register (same)

cashier (same)

cask(n.) barmeel(s-m) brameel(p) – dinn(s-m) dnén(p)

cassette (same) – shreeŤ(s-m) ishriTa(p)

castle aŜr(s-m) 'Ŝoor(p)

cat bsén(m) bséyné(f) bséynét(p) – biss(m) bissé(f) bissass(p)

catastrophe kérsé(s-f) kawérés(p)

category(n.) fi'a(s-f) fi'ét(p) – Ŝinf(s-m) aŜnéf(p)

Catholic(n.) katoliké(m) katolikyyé(f) kwetlé(p)

Cattle(n.) meshyé(s-f) mawéshé(p)

cause sabab)s-m) asbéb(p)

cavalry fooroosyyé(s-f)

cavity(n.) fagwé(s-f) fagwét(p) – ȟifra(s-f) ȟifar(p) – tagweef(s-m) tagéweef(p)

ceiling sa'f(s-m) s'oof(p)

celebration iȟtifél(s-m) iȟtifélét(p)

cellar(n.) aboo(s-m)

cement (same)

cemetery ma'bra(s-f) m'abér(p)

censorship moora'abé(s-f) moora'abét(p)

cent 'irsh(s-m) 'roosh(p)

centre (same) – waŜat(s-m) awŜat(p) – niŜŜ(s-m) nŜaŜ(p)

centimeter (same)

central(adj.) markazé(m) markazyyé(f) markazyyeen(p)

century arn(s-m) 'ooroon(p)

cereal (same)

ceremony (same) – Ťa'Ŝ(s-m) Ťoo'ooŜ(p) - iȟtifél(s-m) iȟtifélét(p)

certain(adj.) akeed(m) akeedé(f) akeedeen(p)

certainty(n.) ya'een(s-p-m)

certificate shhédé(s-f) shhédét(p)

chain silslé(s-f) salésél(p)

chair kirsé(s-f) krasé(p)

chairman(n.) ra'ees(m) ra'eesé(f) roo'asa(p)

chalk Ťabshoora(s-f) Tbasheer(p)

challenge taȟaddé(s-m) taȟaddyét(p)

champion(n.) baŤal(m) baŤalé(f) abŤal(p)

chance ȟaŹ(s-m) ȟŹooŹ(p)

change tiŘyeer(s-m) tiŘyeerat(p)

chapel kneesé(s-f) kanéyés(p) – maĂbad(s-m) maĂébéd(p)

chapter faŜl(s-m) fooŜool(p)

character shaḰŜye(s-f) shaḰŜyét(p)

characteristic Ŝifa(s-f) Ŝifét(p) – meezé(s-f) meezét(p)

charitable(adj.) Ḱayré(m) Ḱayryé(f) Ḱayryé(p)

charity Ăamal Ḱayré(s-m) aĂmal Kayryé(p)

charm gezbye(s-p-f) – rawĂa(s-f) rawAat(p)

charming(adj.) gizzéb(m) gizzébé(f) gizzébeen(p) – ra'éĂ(m) ra'Ăa(f) ra'Ăeen(p)

charter shirĂa(s-f) shirĂat(p)

chat dardashé(s-f) dardashét(p)

cheap(adj.) rḰeeŜ(m) rḰeeŜa(f) rḰaŜ(p)

cheater(n.) Řishésh(m) Řishéshé(f) Řishésheen(p)

cheering tihyeeŜ(s-p-m) - hayŜa(s-f) hayŜat(p) - baŜŤ

cheerful(adj.) mabŜooŤ(m) mabŜooŤa(f) mabŜooŤeen(p)

cheese gibné(s-f) agbén(p)

chemical(n.) keeméwé(m) keeméwyé(f) keeméwyeen(p)

chemist(n.) (chemistry scientist) Ăalém keemya(m) Ăalmét keemya(f) Ăoolama keemya(p)

chemistry keemya(s-p-m)

cherry karzé(s-f) karaz(p)

chest (body part) ŜiĎr(s-m) ŜĎoor(p)

chest (box) ŜanĎoo'(s-m) ŜnaDee'(p)

chestnut(n.) kastana(s-p-f)

chicken dgégé(s-f) dgég(p)

chief(n.) ra'ees(m) ra'eesé(f) roo'asa(p) – zaĂeem(m) zaĂeeme(f) zooĂama(p)

child walad(m) wléd(p)

chimney déḰoon(s-m) /also/ déḰooné(s-f) dwéḰeen(p)

chin da'n(s-f) d'oon(p)

china(n.) Ḱazaf(p)

China ŜŜeen

Chinese(n.) Ŝeené(m) Ŝeenyyé(f) Ŝinyyeen(p)

chip sha'fé(s-f) shi'af(p)

chocolate (same) - shokola

chocolate bar daff shokola(s-m) dfoof shokola(p)

choice Ḱeeyar(s-m) Ḱeeyarat(p)

choir kawras(s-p-m)

Christian(n.) maseeȟé(m) maseeȟyyé(f) maseeȟyyeen(p)

Christmas meeléd – Ăeed Lmeeléd

church kneesé(s-f) knéyés(p)

cigar (same)

cigarette seekara(s-f) swékeer(p)

cinema (same)

circle doowayra(s-f) doowayrat(p) – da'ira(s-f) dawéyér(p)

circular(adj.) mdawwar(m) mdawwra(f) mdawwreen(p)

circulation dawra(s-f) dawrat(p)

circumstances Źarf(s-m) Źooroof(p)

citizen(n.) moowaŤén(m)moowaTné(f)moowaŤneen(p)

Ă= Augh in bought	Ď= a heavy D	É= like A in Bay	G= G in beige	ȟ= like an H with smaller air passage	I= I as in ink	Ḱ= like ch in Irish loch
O= O as in home	OO= as in boots	R= roll the rrr	Ť= a heavy T	Ř= like a French R (gargle it)	Ŝ= a heavy S	Ź= a heavy Z

city madeené(s-f) midon(p)

city hall saray(s-f) /also/ saraya(s-f) saraya(p)

civil(adj.) madané(m) madanyyé(f) madanyyeen(p)

civilization ĥaĎara(s-f) ĥaĎarat(p)

civilized(adj.) mitĥaĎĎér(m) mitĥaĎĎra(f) mitĥaĎĎreen(p)

claim iddiĂa'(s-m) iddiĂa'ét(p)

clarinet (same)

class Ŝaff(s-m) Ŝfoof(p)

classified(adj.) mŜannaf(m) mŜannafé(f) mŜannafeen(p)

clause band(s-m) boonood(p)

clean(adj.) nĎeef(m) nĎeefé(f) nĎaf(p)

cleaning tinĎeef(s-m) tinĎeefét(p)

cleanliness naĎafé(s-p-f)

clear(adj.) waĎéĥ(m) waĎĥa(f) waĎĥeen(p)

clearly bi wooĎooĥ – bi shakl waĎéĥ

clerk(n.) mwaŹŹaf(m) mwaŹŹfé(f) mwaŹŹfeen(p)

clever(adj.) zaké(m) zakyyé(f) azkyya(p)

climate Ťa'Ŝ(s-m) Ťoo'ooŜ(p) – manéḰ(s-m) manéḰat(p)

clip(n.) mashbak(s-m) mashébék(p)

clippers m'aŜŜ(m) m'aŜŜat(p) – iŤŤaĂa(s-f) iŤŤaĂat(p)

cloak(n.) Ăbéyé(s-f) Ăabéyét(p)

clock séĂa(s-f) séĂat(p)

close(adj.) areeb(m) areebé(f) 'rab(p)

closed(adj.) msakkar(m) msakkra(f) msakkreen(p)

closet Ḱzéné(s-f) Ḱzénét(p)

cloth 'mésh(s-m) a'mishé(p)

clothes tyéb(p)

clothe hanger tiĂlee'it ttyéb(s-f) tĂalee' ttyéb(p)

cloud Řayme(s-f) Řyoom(p) – saĥabé(s-f) saĥab(p)

cloudy mŘaymé

club (same) - nédé(s-m) andiyé(p)

coach(n.) mdarréb(m) mdarrbé(f) mdarrbeen(p)

coal faĥmé(s-f) faĥm(p)

coarse(adj.) Ḱishin(m) Ḱishné(f) Ḱishneen(p) – 'asé(m) 'asyé(f) 'asyeen(p)

coast shaŤ(s-m) shŤooŤ(p)

coat kabboot(s-m) kbébeet(p) – gakét(s-f) gakétét(p)

cocoa kakaw

code (same) – sheefra(s-f) sheefrat(p)

coffee ahwé

coffee(coffee place) ahwé(s-f) ahéwé(p)

coffee pot rakwé(s-f) rakéwé(p)

coffin kafan(s-m) akfén(p)

coin niklé(s-f) nikil(p)

cold bard

coldness bard

collar abbé(s-f) abbét(p)

collection magmooĂa(s-f) magmooĂat(p)

college (same) – gémAa(s-f) gémAat(p)

colony gélyé(s-f) gélyét(p) – moostaĂmara(s-f) moostaĂmarat(p)

color lon(s-m) alwén(p)

column Ăamood(s-m) Ăwémeed(p)

comb mishŤ(s-m) amshaŤ(p)

combination(n.) ra'm sirré(s-m) ar'am sirryyé(p)

comedy (same)

comet nayzak(s-m) nayézék(p)

comfort raĥa(s-f) raĥat(p)

comfortable(adj.) mooreeĥ(m) mooreeĥa(f) mooreeĥeen(p)

comma faŜlé(s-f) fawaŜél(p)

command amr(s-m) awémér(p)

commander(n.) ra'ees(m) ra'eesé(f) roo'asa(p)

commerce tigara(s-f) tigarat(p)

commercial(adj.) tigaré(m) tigaryyé(f) tigaryyé(p)

commission (same)

commitment(n.) taĂahhod(s-m) taĂahhodét(p)

common ma'loof(s-m) ma'loofeen(p)

communication (same)

community moogtamaĂ(s-m) moogtamaĂat(p)

compact disk (same) - CD

companion(adj.) moorafé'(m) mooraf'a(f) mooraf'een(p)

company (corporation) shirké(s-f) shirkét(p)

company (companionship) rif'a(s-f) rif'at(p)

comparison moo'arané(s-f) moo'aranét(p)

competition moonéfasé(s-f) moonéfasét(p)

complaint shakwa(s-f) shakéwé(p)

complete(adj.) kémél(m) kémlé(f) kémleen(p)

complexion (skin color) lon Lgild

complicated(adj.) mĂa''ad(m) mĂa''dé(f) mĂa''deen(p)
compliment

composer (n.) moolaĥĥén(m) moolaĥĥné(f) moolaĥĥneen(p)

composition ta'leef(s-p-m)

compromise(n.) tasweeyé(s-f) tasweeyét(p)

computer (same)

concentration tarkeez(s-m)

concern hamm(s-m) hmoom(p)

concert ĥaflé(s-f) ĥaflét(p)

concierge(n.) boowéb(m) boowébé(f) boowébeen(p)

condition ĥalé(s-f) ĥalét(p) – waĎĂ(s-m) awĎaĂ(p)

condom kabboot(s-m) kbébeet(p)

conduct taŜŜarrof(s-m) taŜŜaroofét(p)

conductor(n.) Ďabét 'eekaĂ(s-m)

Ă= Augh in bought	Ď= a heavy D	É= like A in Bay	G= G in beige	ĥ= like an H with smaller air passage	I= I as in ink	Ḱ= like ch in Irish loch
O= O as in home	OO= as in boots	R= roll the rrr	Ť= a heavy T	Ř= like a French R (gargle it)	Ŝ= a heavy S	Ź= a heavy Z

confession iĂtiraf(s-m) iĂtirafét(p)

confidence si'a(s-f) si'at(p)

confident(adj.) wésé' binafsoo(m) wés'a binafsa(f) wés'een binafson(p)

confidential(adj.) sirré(m) sirryé(f) siryeen(p)

confirmation ta'keed(s-m) ta'keedét(p)

confused(adj.) ĎayéĂ(m) ĎayĂa(f) ĎayĂeen(p)

confusing(adj.) bi ĎayyéĂ(m) bit ĎayyéĂ(f) bi ĎayyĂoo(p)

confusion ĎayéĂ(s-p-m)

congratulations mabrouk(s-p-f)

connection(n.) irtibaŤ(s-m)irtibaŤat(p) – Ăalé'a(s-f) Ăalé'at(p)

conquered(adj.) miĥtall(m) miĥtallé(f) miĥtalleen(p) – mahzoom(m) mahzoomé(f) mahzoomeen(p)

conquest iĥtilél(s-m) iĥtilélét(p) – hazeemé(s-f) hazéyém(p)

conscience Ďameer(s-m) Ďamayér(p)

conscientious(adj.) Ŝaĥéb Ďameer(m) Ŝaĥbét Ďameer(f) aŜĥab Ďameer(p)

conscious waĂé(s-p-m)

consent izn(s-m) 'ézén(p)– moowéfa'a(s-f) moowéfa'at(p)

conservation mooĥafaŹa(s-p-f)

conservative(adj.) mooĥaféŹ(m) mooĥafŹa(f) mooĥafŹeen(p)

considerable(adj.) ĥirzén(m) ĥirzéné(f) ĥirzéneen(p)

consideration iĂtibar(s-m) iĂtibarat(p)

consistent(adj.) mitŤabé'(m) mitŤab'a(f) mitŤab'een(p)

constant(adj.) sébét(m) sébté(f) sébteen(p)

constantly bi istimrar

constitution doostoor(s-m) daséteer(p)

constitutional(adj.) doostooré(m) doostooryé(f) doostooryeen(p)

consul(adj.) 'oonŜol(m) 'oonŜlé(f) anaŜél(p)

consumer(n.) mistahlék(m) mistahlké(f) mistahlkeen(p)

contagious(adj.) mooĂdé(m) mooĂdyé(f) mooĂdyeen(p)

container(n.) wiĂé(s-m) awĂyyé(p)

contemporary(adj.) mooĂaŜér(m) mooĂaŜra(f) mooĂaŜreen(p)

contempt(n.) iĥti'ar(s-p-m)

content mooĥtawa(s-m) mooĥtawayét(p)

continent arra(s-f) arrat(p)

continual(adj.) mitwaŜél(m) mitwaŜlé(f) mitwaŜleen(p)

contract Ăa'd(s-m) Ăoo'ood(p)

contractor mitlazzém(m) mitlazzmé(f) mitlazzmeen (p)

contradiction tana'oĎ(s-m) tana'ooĎat(p)

contradicting(adj.) moona'éĎ(m) moona'Ďa(f) moona'Ďeen(p)

contrary Ăaks(s-p-m)

contrast(n.) moféra'a(s-f) mooféra'at(p)

contribution(n.) tabarroĂ(s-m) tabarroAat(p)

control taĥakkom(s-p-m)

controversy(n.) Ḱiléf(s-m) Ḱiléfét(p) – gadal(s-p-m)

convenient(adj.) moonéséb(m) moonésbé(f) moonésbeen(p)

convention (same)

conversation ĥadees(s-m) aĥadees(p)

convict(n.) migrém(m) migrmé(f) migrmeen(p)

conviction(n.) idéné(s-f) idénét(p)

convincing 'i'néĂ(s-p-m)

cook(n.) Ťibbéḱ(m) Ťibbéḱa(f) Ťibbéḱeen(p)

cooked(adj.) maŤbooḱ(m) maŤbooḱa(f) maŤbooḱeen(p)

cool(adj.) béréd(m) bérdé(f) bérdeen(p)

copy nasḱa(s-f) nasḱat(p) – Ŝoora(s-f) Ŝoowar(p)

cork falleené(s-f) falleen(p)

corn dara(s-p)

corner zéwyé(s-f) zawéya(p)

corporation shirké(s-f) shirak(p)

correct(adj.) Ŝaĥeeĥ(m) Ŝaĥeeĥa(f) Ŝaĥeeĥeen(p)

correction taŜĥeeĥ(s-m) taŜĥeeĥat(p)

correspondence moorasalé(s-f) moorasalét(p)

correspondent(adj.) moorasél(m) mooraslé(f) moorasleen(p)

corruption faséd(s-p-m)

cost siĂr(s-m) asĂar(p) – kilfé(s-f) kilfét(p)

costly(adj.) Řalé(m) Řalyé(f) Řalyeen(p)

costume zay(s-m) azyé'(p)

couch kanabéyé(s-f) kanabéyét(p)

cough saĂlé(s-f) saĂlét(p)

counter Ťawlé(s-f) Ťawlét(p)

country balad(s-m) bildén(p) /also/ bléd(p)

couple zog(s-m) azwég(p)

courage shagéĂa(s-f) shagéĂat(p)

course Ťaree'(s-m) Ťir'at(p) – darb(s-m) droob(p)

court maĥkamé(s-f) maĥkamét(p)

courteous(adj.) mhazzab(m) mhazzbé(f) mhazbeen(p)

courtesy tahzeeb(s-p-m) – aḰlé'(s-p-f)

courtyard(n.) séĥa(s-f) séĥat(p)

cousin (see family in leboland)

cover Řata(s-m) iŘŤyé(p)

cow ba'ra(s-f) ba'ar(p)

crack shi'(s-m) sh'oo'(p)

cradle(n.) mahd(s-m) moohood(p)

craft ĥirfé(s-f) ĥiraf(p)

crazy(adj.) magnoon(m) magnooné(f) mgéneen(p)

cream (same)

creation Ḱal'(s-p-m)

creature(n.) maḰloo'(m) maḰloo'a(f) maḰelee'(p)

Ă= Augh in bought	Ď= a heavy D	É= like A in Bay	G= G in beige	ĥ= like an H with smaller air passage	I= I as in ink	Ḱ= like ch in Irish loch
O= O as in home	OO= as in boots	R= roll the rrr	Ť= a heavy T	Ř= like a French R (gargle it)	Ŝ= a heavy S	Ź= a heavy Z

credit (same)

creed(n.) Ăa'eedé(s-f) Aa'éyéd(p) – 'eemén(s-p-m)

cricket(n.) ŜarŜoor(s-m) ŜraŜeer(p)

crime gareemé(s-f) garayém(p)

criminal(n.) migrém(m) migrmé(f) migrmeen(p)

crisis Ťawaré'(s-p-f)

critic(n.) na'iĎ(m) na'iĎa(f) ni''aĎ(p)

crooked(adj.) féséd(m) fésdé(f) fésdeen(p)

crop ĥaŜad(s-p-m)

cross(mad at)(adj.) ziĂlén(m) ziĂléné(f) ziĂléneen(p)

cross(n.) Ŝaleeb(s-m) Ŝilbén(p)

crossing Ăooboor(s-m)

cross-roads t'aŤoĂ Ťooro'(s-m)

crossword puzzle kilmét mit'aŤĂa

crow Řoorab(s-m) Řirbén(p) – 'a'(s-m) 'ee'an(p)

crowd gamĂ(s-m) – ĥashd(s-m)

crowded Ăégé'(m) Ăég'a(f) Ăég'een(p)

crown tég(s-m) teegén(p)

cruel(adj.) igramé(m) igramyé(f) igramyeen(p)

cruelty igram

crumb ftét(p) – ftéfeet(p)

crumbling thirhor - tafattot

crutch(n.) Ăikkéz(s-m) Ăikkézét(p)

cuff (hand cuff) kalabsha(s-f) kalabshét(p)

cuff (shirt cuff) kimm(s-m) kmém(p)

cult fi'a deenyyé(s-f) fi'ét deenyyé(p)

cunning(adj.) zaké(m) zakyé(f) azkyya(p)

cup fingén(s-m) fnégeen(p)

cure Ăilég(s-m) Ăilégét(p)

curiosity ĥishryé(s-p-f)

curious(adj.) ĥishré(m) ĥishryyé(f) ĥishryyeen(p)

curly(adj.) giĂdé(m) giĂdyyé(f) giĂdyyeen(p) – mgaĂĂad(m) mgaĂdé(f) mgaĂdeen(p)

current(adj.) ĥalé(m) ĥalyyé(f) ĥalyyeen(p) – ĥadees(m) ĥadeesé(f) ĥadeseen(p)

current (electrical) tayyar(s-m) tayyarat(p)

curtain birdéyé(s-f) baradé(p)

curve kooĂ(s-m) kwéĂ(p)

cushion(n.) mĶaddé(s-f) mĶaddét(p) – tikkéyé(s-f) tikkéyét(p)

custom ta'leed(s-m) ta'éleed(p)

customary(adj.) ta'leedé(m) ta'leedyyé(f) ta'leedyyeen(p)

customer(n.) zboon(m) zbooné(f) zabéyén(p)

customs gamérék – amn Ăam

cut girĥ(s-m) grooĥ(p) – aŜŜa(s-f) aŜŜat(p)

D

dagger Ķangar(s-m) Ķanégér(p)

daily(adj.) yaowmé(m) yaomyyé(f) yaowmyyeen(p) –

daily basis yaowmyyan

dairy mooshta''at Lĥaleeb

dam sadd(s-m) soodood(p)

damage Ďarar(s-m) aĎrar(p)

damp(adj.) riŤéb(m) riŤbé(f) riŤbeen(p) – mraŤTab(m) mraŤŤbé(f) mraŤŤbeen(p) – mballal(m) mballalé(f) mballaleen(p)

dance ra'Ŝa(s-f) ra'Ŝat(p)

danger ĶaŤar(s-m) aĶŤar(p)

dangerous(adj.) ĶaŤeer(m) ĶaŤeera(f) ĶaŤeereen(p)

Danish(n.) danimarké(m) danimarkyyé(f) danimarkyyeen(p)

dark(adj.) Řamé'(m) Řam'a(f) Řam'een(p) – mĂattam(m) mĂattmé(f) mĂattmeen(p)

darkness Ăatmé(s-f) Ăatmét(p)

data (information) maĂloomét(p)

date(with a person) mawĂad(s-b) mwéĂeed(p) – Ďahra(s-f) Ďahrat(p)

date (of a day) téreeĶ(s-m) twéreeĶ(p)

daughter bint(s-f) banét(p)

dawn shooroo'(s-m) – fagr(s-m)

day yom(s-m) 'yyém(p)

day after tomorrow baĂd bookra (s-m)

day before (yesterday) mbéréĥ(s-m)
day before yesterday awwilt mbéréĥ(s-m) – awwal mbéréĥ(s-m)

dead(adj.) mayyét(m) mayyté(f) mayteen(p)

deaf(adj.) aŤrash(m) Ťarsha(f) Ťirshén(p)

deal Ŝaf'a(s-f) Ŝaf'at(p)

dealer(n.) wakeel(m) wakeelé(f) wookala(p)

dear(adj.) Ăazeez(m) Ăazeezé(f) Aazeezeen(p)

death mot(s-m)

debate ni'ash(s-m) ni'ashét(p)

debris ĥooŤam(s-m)

debt déyn(s-m) dyoon(p)

decay taĥallol – tafakkok - iĎmiĥlél

decayed(adj.) mfakkak(m) mfakkaké(f) mfakkakeen(p) – mitĥallal(m) mitĥallalé(f) mitĥallaleen(p)

deceased(adj.) mayyét(m) mayté(f) mayteen(p) – mitwaffa(m) mitwifféyé(f) mitwifféyeen(p)

December kénoon Lawwal

decent(adj.) mooĥtaram(m) mooĥtaramé(f) mooĥtarameen(p)

decision arar(s-m) ararat(p)

decisive(adj.) ĥasém(m) ĥasmé(f) Hasmeen(p)

deck maŜtbé(s-f) maŜatéb(p)

declaration(n.) ŤaŜreeĥ(s-m) ŤaŜareeĥ(p)

decoration (same) – tizyeen

decrease inĶifaĎ(s-m) inĶifaĎat(p) – hoobooŤ(s-m) hoobooŤat(p)

decree(n.) marsoom(s-m) maraseem(p)

Ă= Augh in bought	Ď= a heavy D	É= like A in Bay	G= G in beige	ĥ= like an H with smaller air passage	I= I as in ink	Ķ= like ch in Irish loch
O= O as in home	OO= as in boots	R= roll the rrr	Ť= a heavy T	Ř= like a French R (gargle it)	Ŝ= a heavy S	Ž= a heavy Z

dedicated(adj.) mkarrass(m) mkarrassé(f) mkarrasseen(p)

deed Aamal(s-m) aĂmél(p) – fiĂl(s-m) afĂal(p)

deep(adj.) Řamee'(m) Řamee'a(f) Řamee'een(p)

deeply bi Ăim'

deer Řazél(s-m) Rizlén(p)

defeat Ḱsara(s-f) Ḱsarat(p) – hazeemé(s-f) hazéyém(p)

defect (same) - na'Ŝ(s-m) nawa'éŜ(p)

defence diféĂ(s-m) diféĂat(p)

defiance(n.) tamarrod(s-m) tamsrrodét(p)

definite(adj.) m'akkad(m) m'akkadé(f) m'akkadeen(p)

definitely akeed - ŤabĂan

degree(like in temperature) daragé(s-f) daragét(p)

delay ta'Ḱeer(s-m) ta'Ḱeerat(p)

delegate(n.) mandoob(m) mandoobé(f) mandoobeen(p)

deliberate(adj.) ma'Ŝood(m) ma'Ŝooda(f) ma'Ŝoodeen(p)

deliberately aŜdan – Ăan aŜd

delicacy ri''a(s-f) – di''a

delicate(adj.) da'ee'(m) da'ee'a(f) da'ee'een(p) – r'ee'(m) r'ee'a(f) r'a'(p) – ĥissés(m) ĥissésé(f) ĥisséseen(p)

delight faraĥ(s-m) – saAadé(s-f) – bahgé(s-f) - baŜt

delighted(adj.) mabŜoot(m) mabŜoota(f) mabŜooteen(p)

deliverance(n.) nagét(s-p-f) – ḰalaŜ(s-p-f)

delivery(giving birth) wilédé(s-f) wilédét(p) – Ḱilfé(s-f) Ḱilfét(p)

delivery(item) toowŜeel

demand Ťalab(s-m) Talabét(p) – maŤlab(s-m) maŤaléb(p)

demonstration(n.) istiĂraḒ(s-m) istiĂraḒat(p)

denial rafḒ(s-m)

dense(adj.) Ăabé(m) Aabyyé(f) Ăbéya(p) – kaseef(m) kaseefé(f) kaseefeen(p)

density kaséfé(s-f)

dentist(n.) ĥakeem snén(m) ĥakeemit snén(f) ĥikama snén(p) – Ťabeeb snén(m) Ťabeebét snén(f) aŤibba snén(p)

deodorant (same)

department iŜm(s-m) a'Ŝém(p)

departure i'léĂ(s-m)

dependence iĂtiméd(s-p-m) ittikél(s-p-m)

dependent(adj.) moodmén(m) moodmin(m) moodmoneen(p)

deposit(n.) wadeeĂa(s-f) wadéyéĂ(p)

depot maḰzan(s-m) maḰazén(p)

depressed(adj.) minhar nafsyyan(m) minhara nafsyyan (f) minhareen nafsyyan (p)

depression inhiyar nafsé(s-m) inhyarat nafsyyé(p)

deprived(adj.) maĥroom(m) maĥroome(f) maĥroomeen(p)

depth Řim'(s-m) - Ăim'(s-m)

deputy(n.) néyéb(m) néybé(f) noowéb(p)

derived(adj.) mishta'(m) mishta''a(f) mishta''een(p)

descendant(adj.) saleel(m) saleelé(f)

descent sleelé(s-f) saléyél(p)

described(adj.) maowŜoof(m) maoŜoofé(f) maowŜoofeen(p)

describing waŜf

description waŜf(s-m) awŜaf(p)

desert Ŝaĥra(s-f) Ŝaĥara(p)

design taŜmeem(s-m) taŜameem(p)

designed(adj.) mŜammam(m) mŜammamé(f) mŜammameen(p)

desirable(adj.) marŘoob(m) marŘoobé(f) marŘoobeen(p)

desire raŘbé(s-f) raŘbét(p)

desk maktab(s-m) makétéb(p)

despair(n.) ya's(s-p-m)

desperate(adj.) yé'és(m) yé'sé(f) yé'seen(p)

despite bi rriŘim min

dessert (same)

destination(n.) wigha(s-f) wighat(p)

destiny adar(s-m) a'dar(p)

destroyed(adj.) mḰarrab(m) mḰarrabé(f) mḰarrabeen(p)

destruction tiḰreeb(s-m) – tidmeer(s-m)

detached(adj.) minfiŜél(m) mifiŜlé(f) min fiŜleen(p)

detail tafŜeel(s-m) tafaŜeel(p)

detailed(adj.) mfaŜŜal(m) mfaŜŜalé(f) mfaŜŜaleen(p)

detained(adj.) maow'oof(m) maow'oofé(f) maow'oofeen(p)

determination iŜrar(s-m)

detriment Ďarar(s-m) aḒrar(p) – ĂiŤl(s-m) aĂTal(p)

developed(adj.) mitŤawwar(m) mitŤawwra(f) mitŤawreen(p) – mit'addam(m) mit'addmé(f) mit'addmeen(p)

development taTawwor(s-m) taŤawworat(p) – ta'addom(s-m)

device 'élé(s-f) 'élét(p)

devil(n.) shirreer(m) shirreera(f) ashrar(p) – shaiŤan(m) shaiŤané(f) shiaŤeen(p)

devoted(adj.) mkarras(m) mkarrasé(f) mkarraseen(p)

devouring iltihém(s-m)

dew(n.) nidé(s-p-m)

dialect lahgé(s-m) lahgét

dialogue(n.) ĥiwar(s-m) ĥiwarat(p)

diameter 'iŤr(s-m) a'Ťar(p)

diamond ilmésé(s-f) ilmés(p)

diary moozakkarat(p)

dictating tin'eel(s-m)

dictionary 'amooŜ(s-m) awameeŜ(p) -

diet (same) - ĥimyé(s-f) ĥimyét(p)

difference far'(s-m) froo'at(p) – iḰiléf(s-m) iḰiléfét(p)

different(adj.) miḰiléf(m) miḰilfé(f) miḰilfeen(p)

Ă= Augh in bought	Ď= a heavy D	É= like A in Bay	G= G in beige	ĥ= like an H with smaller air passage	I= I as in ink	Ḱ= like ch in Irish loch
O= O as in home	OO= as in boots	R= roll the rrr	Ť= a heavy T	Ř= like a French R (gargle it)	Ŝ= a heavy S	Ž= a heavy Z

difficult(adj.) SaĂb(m) ŜaĂbé(f) ŜaĂbeen(p)

difficulty ŜĂoobé(s-f) ŜĂoobét(p)

digging ĥafr(s-m)

digesting haĎm(s-m)

dignity karamé(s-f) karamét(p) – sharaf(s--pm)

dim(adj.) Ḱafeef(m) Ḱafeefé(f) Ḱféf(p) – miĂtém(m) miĂtmé(f) miAtmeen(p)

dimension(n.) biĂd(s-m) abĂad(p) – ĥagm(s-m) aĥgém(p)

dinner Ăasha(s-m)

dip (same)

diploma shhédé(s-f) shhédét(p)

diplomacy diblomécyyé(s-f) diblomécyyét(p)

diplomat(n.) diblomécé(m) diblomécyyé(f) diblomécyyeen(p)

direct diŘré(s-p-m)

directed(adj.) mwaggah(m) mwaggha(f) mwaggheen(p)

directing taowgeeh

direction taĂlimét(p) – taowgeeh(s-m) taowgeehat(p) – irshéd(s-m) irshédét(p)

director(n.) moodeer(m) moodeera(f) moodara(p)

directory fahras

dirt wasaḰ(s-m) awséḰ(p) – gayyé(s-p-f)

dirty(adj.) migwé(m) migwyyé(f) migwyyeen(p)

disabled(adj.) mooĂa'(m) mooĂa'a(f) moooĂa'een(p)

disability 'iĂa'a(s-f) 'iĂa'at(p)

disadvantage sayyi'a(s-f) sayyi'at(p)

disagreement iḰtiléf(s-m) iḰtiléfét(p)

disappearance iḰtifé'(s-m) iḰtifé'at(p)

disappointment(n.) Ḱaybét amal(s-f) Ḱaybét Lamal(p)

disapproval rafĎ(s-p-m)

disaster kérse(s-f) kawérés(p)

disastrous(adj.) fédéĥ(m) fédĥa(f) fédĥeen(p)

discipline tahzeeb(s-p-m)

disclosure(n.) faĎĥ(s-p-m)

discomfort inziĂag

discontent zaĂal - ĥizn

discontented(adj.) ziĂlén(m) ziĂléné(f) ziĂléneen(p) – ĥazeen(m) ĥazeené(f) ĥazeeneen(p)

discord(n.) Ḱiléf(s-m) Ḱiléfét(p)

discount ḰaŜm(s-m) ḰŜoomét(p)

discouragement(n.) fi'dén shagéĂa – fi'dén L ĥamés

discovered(adj.) mooktashaf(m) mooktashafé(f) mooktashafeen(p)

discovery iktishéf(s-m) iktishéfét(p)

discreet(adj.) sirré(m) sirryyé(f) sirryyeen(p)

discretion sirryyé(s-p-f)

discussion ni'ash(s-m) ni'ashét(p) – baĥs(s-m) abĥas(p)

disdain(n.) istiḰféf(s-p-m)

disease maraĎ(s-m) amraĎ(p) – Ăillé(s-m) Ăilal(p)

disgrace Ăar(s-p-m)

disguise tanakkor(s-p-m)

disgust araf(s-p-m)

disgusted(adj.) irfén(m) irféné(f) irféneen(p)

disgusting(adj.) mi'réf(m) mi'irfé(f) mi'irfeen(p)

dish Ŝaĥn(s-m) Ŝĥoon(p)

dishonest(adj.) kizzéb(m) kizzébé(f) kizzébeen(p)

disk (same) – irŜ(s-m) 'raŜ(p)

dismissal Ŝarf(s-p-m)

disorder fawĎa(s-p-f)

disposal(n.) taḰalloŜ(s-p-m)

dispute Ḱiléf (s-m) Ḱiléfét(p)

distance maséfé(s-f) maséfét(p)

distant(adj.) bĂeed(m) bĂeedé(f) bĂad(p)

distinct(adj.) moomayyaz(m) moomayyazé(f) moomayyazeen(p)

distinction tamyyeez(s-m) – tafri'a(s-f)

distress mĂanét - Ăazéb

distributed(adj.) mwazzaĂ(m) mwazzĂa(f) mwazzAeen(p)

distribution tawzeeĂ(s-m)

district moo'aŤaĂa(s-f) moo'aŤaAat(p)

distrust Ăadam si'a

disturbance izĂag(s-p-m)

ditch sé'yé(s-f) sawé'é(p)

divine(adj.) m'addas(m) m'ddasé(f) m'addaseen(p) – saméwé(m) saméwyyé(f) saméwyyeen(p) – iléhé(m) iléĥyyé(f) iléĥyyeen(p)

division iŜmé(s-m) iŜmét(p)

divorce Ťalé'(s-p-m)

dizziness daowḰa(s-f) daowḰat(p)

dizzy(adj.) déyéḰ(m) déyḰa(f) déyḰeen(p)

dock(n.) raŜeef L mina

doctor(n.) ĥakeem(m) ĥakeemé(f) ĥookama(p) – Ťabeeb(m) Tabeebé(f) aŤibba(p)

doctrine mabda'(s-m) mabédé'(p) – Ăa'eedé(s-f) Ăa'ayéd(p)

document(n.) wasee'a(s-f) waséyé'(p)

dog(n.) kalb(m) kalbé(f) kléb(p)

dollar (same)

dome ibbé(s-f) ibbét(p)

domestic(adj.) maĥallé(m) maĥallyyé(f) maĥallyyeen(p)

domination ŜaiŤara(s-p-f)

door béb(s-m) bwéb(p)

doorkeeper(n.) boowwéb(m) boowwébé(f) boowwébeen(p)

dose (same)

dot ni'Ťa(s-f) ni'aŤ(p)

double (same)

doubt shakk(s-m) shkook(p)

Ă= Augh in bought	Ď= a heavy D	É= like A in Bay	G= G in beige	ĥ= like an H with smaller air passage	I= I as in ink	Ḱ= like ch in Irish loch
O= O as in home	OO= as in boots	R= roll the rrr	Ť= a heavy T	Ř= like a French R (gargle it)	Ŝ= a heavy S	Ž= a heavy Z

doubtful shikkék(m) shikkéké(f) shikkékeen(p)

doubtless bi doon shak

dough Ăageené(s-f) Ăageen(p)

down taĥt

downwards nzool

dozen (same) - dazzeené(s-f) dzézeen(p)

draft ḰarŤoosh(s-p-m)

drain mizréb(s0m) mzéreeb(p)

drama (same)

dramatic (same)

drawback sayyi'a(s-f) sayyi'at(p)

drawer girrar(s-m) gwéreer(p)

drawing rasm(s-m)

dread Ḱof(s-m) rahbé(s-f)

dreaded(adj.) marhoob(s-m) marhoobé(f) marhoobeen(p)

dream ĥilm(s-m) aĥlém(p)

dress fisŤan(s-m) fsaŤeen(p)

drink mashroob(s-m) mashroobét(p)

drinking shirb(s-m)

driver(n.) soowwé'(m) soowwé'a(f) soowwé'een(p)

drought(n.) gaféf(s-p-m)

drowning Řara'(s-m)

drug dawa(s-m) adwiyé

drugstore Ŝaydalyyé(s-f) Ŝaydalyyét(p)

drum Ťabl(s-m) Ťablé(s-f) Ťbool(p)

drunk(n.) sikran(m) sikrané(f) sikraneen(p)

dry(adj.) néshéf(m) néshfé(f) néshfeen(p)

dryness nashéf(s-m)

due(n.) mistĥa'(m) mistĥa''a(f) mistĥa''at(p)

duke (same)

dumb(adj.) Řabé(m) Řabyyé(f) aŘbiya(p)

during Ḱilél – asné'

dust Řabra(s-p-f)

dusty(adj.) mŘabbar(m) mŘabbra(f) mŘabbreen(p)

duty waŹeefé(s-f) wazayéf(p) – shaŘlé(s-f) shaŘlét(p)

dwelling sakan(s-p-m) – maskan(s-m) masékén(p)

dye ŜabŘa(s-f) ŜabŘat(p) -

E

each kill

each one kill wéĥéd(m) kill wwiĥdé(f)

each other baĂĎ

each time kill marra

eager(adj.) mitĥammas(m) mitĥammasé(f) mitĥammaseen(p)

eagle nisr(s-m) nsoor(p)

ear idin(s-f) – dayné(s-f) deenén(p)

early bakkeer

earnings madḰool(s-m) madaḰeel(p)

Earth arĎ

earth(soil) trab

ease s-hoolé

east shar'(s-m) shooroo'(p)

Easter fiŜĥ

eastern(adj.) shar'é(m) shar'yyé(f) shar'yyeen(p)

easy(adj.) sahl(m) sahlé(f) sahleen(p)

eating akl

echo Ŝada

economical(adj.) i'tiŜadé(m) i'tiŜadyyé(f) i'tiŜadyyeen(p)

economy i'tiŜad

edge ĥarf(s-m) ĥroof(p)

edition nasḰa(s-f) nasḰat(p) – ŤabĂa(s-f) ŤabĂat(p)

editor(n.) moĥarrir(m) mooĥarrira(f) mooĥarrireen(p)

editorial(adj.) taĥreeré(m) taĥreeryyé(f) taĥreeryyé(p)

education tarbiyé(s-p-f) – taĂleem(s-p-m)

effect ta'seer(s-m) ta'seerat(p)

effective(adj.) faĂĂal(m) faĂĂalé(f) faĂĂaleen(p)

efficiency faĂalyyé(s-f) faĂalyyét(p)

effort maghood(s-m)

egg bayĎa(s-f) béĎ(p) – bayĎat(p)

egoism anényyé(s-f)

eight (look numbers on Leboland)

either(-or) ya

either one ayya wéhéd(s-m) ayya wiĥdé(s-f)

elastic miŘŘéŤ(s-p-f-m)

elbow kooĂ(s-m) kwéĂ(p)

elder(n.) akbar(s-p-m-f)

elderly(n.) Ḱityar(m) Ḱityara(f) kityéryyé(p)

eldest L akbar

election intiḰab(s-m) intiḰabét(p)

elector(adj.) nékéb(m) neḰbé(f) neḰbeen(p)

electric-al(adj.) kahrabé'é(m) kahrabé'yyé(f) kahrabé'yyé(p)

electricity kahraba(s-p-f)

elegant(adj.) (same) - libé'(m) lib'a(f) lib'een(p)

element(adj.) ĂoĎoo(m) ĂoĎwé(f) aĂĎa'(p)

elementary(adj.) ibtidé'é(m) ibtidé'yyé(f) ibtidé'yyé(p)

elephant feel(s-m) fiyalé(p) – fyoolé(p)

elevator (same)

eleven(see numbers in Leoland)

elimination(n.) ĥazf(s-p-m)

eloquence(n.) baléŘa(s-f) baléŘat(p) – faŜaĥa(s-f) faŜaĥat(p)

eloquent(n.) faŜeeĥ(m) faŜeeĥa(f) faŜeeĥeen(p) – baleeŘ(m) baleeŘa(f) baleeŘeen(p)

else Řér

Ă= Augh in bought	Ď= a heavy D	É= like A in Bay	G= G in beige	ĥ= like an H with smaller air passage	I= I as in ink	Ḱ= like ch in Irish loch
O= O as in home	OO= as in boots	R= roll the rrr	Ť= a heavy T	Ř= like a French R (gargle it)	Ŝ= a heavy S	Ž= a heavy Z

elsewhere maḣal téné – maŤraḣ téné

embarkation(n.) rookoob - shaḣn

embarrassing(adj.) mooḰgél(m) mooḰghilé(f) mooḰgileen(p)

embarrassment Ḱagal(s-p-m)

embassy safara (s-f) safarat(p)

embroidery(n.) tiŤreez(s-m) taŤareez(p)

emerging(n.) Źohoor(s-m) Źoohoorat(p)

emergency Ťawaré'

eminent(adj.) béréz(m) berzé(f) berzeen(p)

emotion shooĂoor(s-m) mashéĂér(p)

emperor(n.) imbaraŤor(m) imbaraŤora(f) abaŤra(p)

emphasis tishdeed

emphatic(n.) ta'keedé(m) ta'keedyyé(f) ta'keedyyeen(p)

empire imbaraŤoryyé(s-f) imbaraŤoryyét(p)

employee(n.) mwaŹŹaf(m) mwaŹŹafé(f) mwaŹŹafeen(p)

employer rabb L-Ăamal(s-m) arbéb L aĂmél(p)

employment waŹeefé(s-f) waŹayéf(p)

empty(adj.) faĎé(m) faĎyé(f) fadyeen(p)

enamel(n.) mina(s-p-m)

enclosed(adj.) msayyag(m) msayyagé(f) msayyageen(p)

encouragement tishgeeĂ(s-p-m) – tiḣmees(s-p-m)

end nihéyé(s-f) nihéyét(p)

endeavour(n.) mooḣéwalé(s-f) mooḣewalét(p) – masĂa(s-m) maséĂé(p)

endurance(n.) tahammol(s-p-m) - Ŝabr(s-p-m) – galad(s-p-m)

enemy(n.) Ăadoo(m) Ăadoowé(f) aĂdé'(p)

energetic(adj.) nasheeŤ(m) nasheeŤa(f) nasheeŤeen(p)

energy Ťa'a(s-f) Ta'at(p)

enforcement(n.) ilzém(s-p-m) – tanfeez(s-p-m)

engaged(adj.) maḰŤoob(m) maḰŤoobé(f) maḰŤoobeen(p)

engagement(n.) ḰiŤbé(s-f) ḰiŤbét(p)

engine(n.) (same)

engineer(n.) mhandés(m) mhandsé(f) mhandseen(p)

England(n.) (same)

English(adj.) inkleeze(m) inkleezyyé(f) inkleez(p)

engraving(n.) naḣt(s-p-m) – ḣafr(s-p-m)

enjoyment(n.) saĂadé(s-p-f) – lizzé(s-f) lizzét(p) – faraḣ(s-m) afraḣ(p)

enlargement(n.) tikbeer(s-p-m)

enlistment(n.) tagneed(s-p-m) – inḰiraŤ(s-p-m)

enormous(adj.) hé'él(m) hé'ilé(f) hé'ileen(p)

enough(adj.) kféyé - bi zyédé – kéfé(m) kéfyé(f) kéfyeen(p)

enriching(n.) iřné'(s-p-m) – ishbéĂ(s-p-m)

entertaining(adj.) moosallé(m) mossalyyé(f) moosallyyeen(p)

entertainment(n.) taslyé(s-f) taselé(p)

enthusiasm(n.) Hamés(s-p-m) – shařaf(s-p-m)

enthusiastic(adj.) mḣammas(m) mḣammasé(f) mḣammaseen(p)

entire kill

entitlement(n.) ḣa'(s-m) ḣ'oo'(p)

entrance(n.) madḰal(s-m) madéḰél(p)

envelope(n.) Źarf(s-m) Źroof(p) - mřallaf(s-m) mřallafét(p)

envious(adj.) ḣasood(m) ḣasoodé(f) ḣasoodeen(p)
envy(n.) ḣasad(s-p-m)

episode(n.) ḣal'a(s-f) ḣal'at(p)

equal(adj.) mooséwé(m) mooséwyé(f) mooséwyeen(p)

equality(n.) mooséwét(s-p-f)

equilibrium(n.) tawézon(s-m) tawézonét(p)

equipment(n.) Ăiddé(s-f) Ăiddét(p)

equity(n.) Ăadl(s-p-m)

era(n.) ĂaŜr(s-m) ĂooŜoor(p) – zaman(s-m) azminé(p)

eraser(n.) miḣḣayé(s-f) miḣḣayét(p)

erect(adj.) minŤiŜéb(m) minŤiŜbé(f) minŤiŜbeen(p)

errand(n.) shařlé(s-f) shařlét(p) – mahammé(s-f) mahammét(p)

error(n.) ḰaŤa'(s-m) aḰTa'(p) – řalaŤ(s-m) ařlaŤ(p)

escalator(n.) (same)

escape(n.) hooroob(s-p-m)

especially ḰaŜŜatan - ḰooŜŜooSan

essay(n.) ma'alé(s-f) ma'alét(p) – naŜŜ(s-m) nooŜooŜ(p)

essence(n.) rooḣ(s-p-f)

essential(adj.) asésé(m) asésyyé(f) asésyyeen(p)

establishment(n.) moo'assassé(s-f) mo'assasét(p)

estate(n.) arĎ(s-f) araĎé(p)

esteem(n.) iḣtiram(s-m) - ta'deer(s-m)

(self esteem) Ăizzét nafs

esthetic/aesthetic (same)

estimate(n.) ta'deer(s-m) ta'deerat(p)

estimation (see estimate)

eternal(n.) abadé(m) abadyyé(f) abadyyeen(p)

eternity(n.) abad(s-p-m)

ether(n.) faĎa(s-p-m)

Europe(n.) (same) – 'oroppa

European(adj.) 'oroppé(m) 'oroppyyé(f) 'oropyyeen(p)

Evasion(n.) tafédé(s-p-m)

even(in numbers)(n.) migwez(m) migowzé(f) migozeen(p)

even ḣatta

evening(n.) masa(s-m) - Ăashyyé(s-p-f) – lél(s-m) layélé(p)

event(n.) ḣadas(s-m) aḣdés(p)

ever(n.) déyém(m) déymé(f) déymeen(p)

Ă= Augh in bought	Ď= a heavy D	É= like A in Bay	G= G in beige	ḣ= like an H with smaller air passage	I= I as in ink	Ḱ= like ch in Irish loch
O= O as in home	OO= as in boots	R= roll the rrr	Ť= a heavy T	ř= like a French R (gargle it)	Ŝ= a heavy S	Ž= a heavy Z

every kill

everybody kill nnés – kill wéĥéd

everything kill shee

everywhere kill Lamékén – wén ma kén

evidence(n.) daleel(s-m) adillé(p)

evident(adj.) waĎéĥ(m) waĎĥa(f) waĎĥeen(p) – moosbat(m) moosbaté(f) mossbateen(p)

evil(n.) sharr

evil(adj.) shirreer(m) shirreera(f) shirreereen(p)

evoking(n.) isarét ĂawaŤéf – isarét mashéĂér

evolving(n.) taŤawwor(s-m) taŤawwoorat(p)

exact(adj.) da'ee'(m) da'ee'a(f) da'ee'een(p)

exactly taméman – Ăal add

exaggeration(n.) moobélaŘa(s-f) moobélaŘat(p)

exalting(n.) madĥ(s-p-m)

examination(n.) faĥŜ(s-m) fĥoŜat(p) – imtiĥan(s-m) imtiĥanét(p)

example(n.) matal(s-m) amtél(p) - masal(s-m) amsél(p)

exceeding(adj.) mitḰaŤŤa(m) mitḰaŤŤye(f) mitḰaŤŤyeen(p) – mitĂadda(m) mitĂaddéyé(f) mitĂaddéyeen(p)

excellence(n.) imtyyéz(s-p-m)

excellent(adj.) moomtéz(m) moomtézé(f) moomtézeen(p)

except bi istisné' – ma Ăada

exception(n.) istisné'

exceptional(adj./adv.) istisné'é(m) istisné'yyé(f) istisné'yyeen(p)

excess(n.) ziyédé

excessive(adj.) fayéĎ(m) fayĎa(f) fayĎeen(p) – aktar min Llzoom

exchanging(n.) tiŠreef(s-p-m)

excitement(n.) ĥamas(s-m-p) – hayagén(s-p-m)

exclamation(n.) ŠarḰa(s-f) ŠarḰat(p) – ĂayŤa(s-f) ĂayŤat(p)

exclamation mark(n.) Ăalémét taĂggob(s-f) Ăalémét taĂaggob(p)

exclusion(n.) istisné'(s-m) istisné'at(p)

exclusive right(n.) ĥa' ĥaŜré

excursion(n.) riĥlé istikshéfyyé(s-f) riĥlét istikshéfyyé(p)

excuse(n.) Ăizr(m) aĂzar(p)

execution(n.) taŤbee'(s-p-m) – tanfeez(s-p-m)

exempt(adj.) miĂfé(m) miĂfyé(f) miĂfyyeen(p)

exercise(n.) (same) - ryyaĎa

exertion(n.) majhood(s-m) majéheed(p)

exhausted(adj.) manhook(m) manhooké(f) manhookeen(p)

exhaustion(n.) ijhéd(s-p-m)

exhibition(n.) maĂraĎ(s-m) maĂaréĎ(p)

exile(n.) manfa(s-m) manéfé(p)

existence(n.) woogood(s-p-m)

exit(n.) maḰrag(s-m) maḰérég

expansion(n.) tawwassoĂ(m) tawassoĂat(p) nomooo(s-p-m)

expansive(adj.) kareem(m) kareemé(f) koorama(p) – miĂŤa'(m) miĂŤa'a(p) miĂŤa'een(p)

expectation(n.) tawwa'oĂ(s-m) taww'oĂat(p)

expedition(n.) riĥlé(s-f) riĥlét(p) – riĥlé istikshéfyyé(s-f) riĥlét istikshéfyyé(p)

expelling(n.) Ťard(s-p-m)

expense(n.) kilfé(s-f) kilfét(p)

expensive(adj.) Řalé(m) Řalyé(f) Řalyeen(p)

experience(n.) Ḱibra(s-f) Ḱibrat(p)

experiment(n.) tagribé(s-f) tagéréb(p)

expert(n.) Ḱabeer(m) Ḱabeera(f) Ḱabeereen(p) – iḰtiŜaŜé(m) iḰtiŜaŜyyé(f) iḰtiŜaŜyyeen(p)

expiration(n.) intihé' L faĂalyyé – middét L intihé'

explained(adj.) mashrooĥ(m) mashrooĥa(f) mashrooĥeen(p) – mfassar(m) mfassra(f) mfassreen(p)

explanation(n.) sharĥ(s-m) shrooĥat(p) – tafseer(s-m) tafseerat(p)

explanatory(adj.) tafseeré(m) tafseeryyé(f) tafseeryyeen(p)

explorer(n.) raĥĥalé(s-p-m-f)

explosion(n.) infigar(s-m) infigarat(p)

export(n.) taŜdeer(s-p-m)

exposed(adj.) makshoof(m) makshoofé(f) makshoofeen(p) – mĂarraĎ(m) mĂarraĎa(f) mAarraĎeen(p)

exposure(n.) taĂarroĎ(s-p-m)

expression(n.) taĂbeer(s-m) taĂabeer(p)

expressive(adj.) mooĂabbér(m) mooĂabbra(f) mooĂabbreen(p)

expulsion(n.) zat (s-p-m) - tiŤleeĂ(s-p-m) - ramé'(s-p-m)

exquisite(adj.) ra'éĂ(m) ra'iĂa(f) ra'iĂeen(p)

extension(n.) imtidéd(s-m) imtidédét(p) - zawdé(s-f) zawdét(p)

extensive(adj.) shémél(m) shémlé(f) shémleen(p) - shéséĂ(m) shésĂa(f) shésĂeen(p)

extent(n.) daragé(s-f) daragét(p) – ĥadd(s-m) ĥdood(p;)

exterior(n.) Ḱarég(s-p-m) – barra(s-m-p)

exterior(adj.) Ḱargé(m) Ḱargyyé(f) Ḱargyyeen(p)

extermination(n.) fané'(s-p-m)

external(adj.) Ḱargé(m) Ḱargyyé(f) Ḱargyyeen(p)

extinct(adj.) féné(m) fényé(f) fényeen(p)

extinction(n.) fané'(s-p-m)

extinguishing(n.) tamyeez(s-m) tamyeezét(p) – tafree'(s-m) tafri'a(p)

extra(n.) fayéĎ(m) fayĎa(f) fawayéĎ(p) – zawdé(s-f) zawdét(p)

extraction(n.) istiḰrag(s-m) istiḰragét(p)

extraordinary(adj.) fo' ŤŤabeeĂé (s-p-m-f)

extravagance(n.) ifraŤ(s-p-m) – tkibkob(s-p-m)

extravagant(adj.) Ŝarreef(m) Ŝarreefé(f) Ŝarreefeen(p) – mifréŤ(m) mifirŤa(f) mifirŤeen(p)

Ă= Augh in bought	**Ď**= a heavy D	**É**= like A in Bay	**G**= G in beige	**ĥ**= like an H with smaller air passage	**I**= I as in ink	**Ḱ**= like ch in Irish loch
O= O as in home	**OO**= as in boots	**R**= roll the rrr	**Ť**= a heavy T	**Ř**= like a French R (gargle it)	**Ŝ**= a heavy S	**Ž**= a heavy Z

extreme(n.) (same) – Lĥad L'a'Ŝa

extremely(adv.) kteer

extremity(n.) Ťaraf(s-m) aŤraf(p)

eye(n.) Ăén(s-f) Ăyoon(p)

eyebrow(n.) ĥagéb(s-m) ĥwégéb(p)

eyeglasses(n.) Ăwaynét(s-p-f)

eyelash(n.) rimsh(s-m) rmoosh(p)

eyelid gifn(s-m) gfoon(p)

F

fable(n.) 'iŜŜa(s-f) 'iŜSaŜ(p) – ĥkéyé(s-f) ĥkéyét(p)

fabric(n.) 'mésh(s-p-m)

face(n.) wigg(s-m) wgéĥ(p)

facsimile(n.) fax(s-m.) faxét(p)

fact(n.) wé'éĂ(s-m) wa'ayéĂ(p)

factory(n.) maĂmal(s-m) maĂamél(p) – maŜnaĂ(s-m) maŜanéĂ(p)

faculty(n.) 'iŜm(s-m) a'Ŝém(p) – farĂ(s-m) frooĂ(p)

faded(adj.) béhét(m) béhté(f) béhteen(p)

failure(n.) fashal(s-p-m)

faint(adj.) ĎĂeef(m) ĎĂeefé(f) ĎĂaf(p)

fair(adj.) ash'ar(m) sha'ra(f) shi'r(p)

faith(n.) 'eemén(s-p-m)

faithful(adj.) mo'min(m) mo'miné(f) mo'mineen(p)

fall(n.) wa'Aa(s-f) wa'Ăat(p)

fall(autumn)(n.) Ḱareef(s-p-m)

false(adj.) ŘalaŤ(s-p-m-f) - ḰaŤa'(s-p-m-f)

fame(n.) shihra(s-f) shihrat(p)

familiar(adj.) ma'loof(m) ma'loofé(f) ma'loofeen(p)

family(n.) Ăaylé(s-f) Ăiyal(p)

famine(n.) magéĂa(s-f) magéĂat(p)

famous(adj.) mash-hoor(m) mash-hoora(f) mash-hooreen(p)

fan(airfan)(n.) marwaĥa(s-f) maraweĥ(p)

fan(sports fan)(n.) moshaggéĂ(m) moshaggĂa(f) moshaggĂeen(p)

fanatic(adj.) mitĂaŜéb(m) mitĂaŜbé(f) mitĂaŜbeen(p)

fantastic(adj.) ra'éĂ(m) ra'iĂa(f) ra'iĂeen(p) – raheeb(m) raheebé(f) raheebeen(p)

far(adj.) bĂeed(m) bĂeedé(f) bAad(p)

farce(n.) mahzalé(s-f) mahézél(p)

fare(n.) siĂr(s-m) asĂar(p) – kilfé(s-f) kilfét(p)

farm(n.) mazrĂa(s-f) mazéréĂ(p)

farmer(n.) moozéréĂ(m) moozérĂa(f) moozérĂeen(p) – filléĥ(m) filléĥa(f) filléĥeen(p)

farming(n.) ziraĂa(s-p-f) – fléĥa(s-p-f)

farther abĂad

farthest L abĂad

fashion(n.) mooĎa(s-f) mooĎat(p)

fashionable(adj.) Ăal mooĎa (s-p-m-f)

fast(adj.) sareeĂ(m) sareeĂa(f) sareeĂeen(p)

fat(grease)(n.) shaĥm(s-m) shĥoom(p) – dihn(s-m) dhoon(p)

fat(adj.) naŜéĥ(m) naŜĥa(f) naŜĥeen(p)

fatal(adj.) 'étoolé(m) 'étoolyyé(f) 'étoolyyeen(p)

fate(n.) maŜeer(s-m) maŜayér(p)

father(n.) bay(s-m) bayyét(p)

faucet(n.) ĥanaffyyé(s-f) ĥanaffyyét(p)

fault(n.) ḰaŤa'(s-m) aḰŤa'(p) – ŘalaŤ(m) aŘlaŤ(p)

favour(n.) Ḱidmé(s-f) Ḱidmét(p)

favourable(adj.) molé'ém(m) molé'mé(f) molé'meen(p)

favourite(adj.) mofaĎĎal(m) mofaĎĎalé(f) mofaĎĎaleen(p)

fear(n.) Ḱof

fearless(adj.) garee'(m) garee'a(f) garee'een(p)

feather(n.) reeshé(s-f) reesh(p)

feature(n.) maléméĥ(p)

February(n.) shbaŤ

Federal(n.) fédéralé(m) fédéralyé(f) fédéralyeen(p)

Fee(n.) igra(f) igrat(p)

Feeble(adj.) ĎĂeef(m) ĎĂeefé(f) ĎĂaf(p)

Feeling(n.) shoĂoor(s-m) mashéĂér(p)

Fellow(n.) rfee'(m) rfee'a(f) rfé'(p) – zameel(m) zameelé(f) zoomala(p)

Fellowship(n.) zamélé(f) zamélét(p) – rabŤa(f) rabŤat(p)

Female(n.) inta(f) anéta(p)

Feminine(adj.) m'annté(f) m'annat(m) m'annteen(p)

Fence(n.) soor(s-m) aswar(p)

Fencing(n.) tiŜween(s-m-p) tsweer(s-m-p)

Ferocious(adj.) shirés(m) shirsé(f) shirseen(p) – waĥshé(m) waĥshyyé(f) waĥshyyeen(p)

fertile(adj.) ḰiŜb(m) ḰiŜbé(f) ḰiŜbeen(p)

fertilized(n.) mḰaŜŜab(m) mḰaŜŜbé(f) mḰaŜŜbeen(p)

fertilizer(n.) sméd(s-m) asmidé(p)

fervent(adj.) mitĥammas(m) mitĥammsé(f) mitĥamseen(p)

fervour(n.) ĥamésé(s-f-p)

festival(n.) mahragén(s-m) mahragénét(p)

fetching(adj.) gizzéb(m) gizzébé(f) gizzébeen(p)

fetus(n.) Ťifl(s-m) aŤfél(p)

fever(n.) ĥarara(s-p-f)

few shway – aleel(m) aleelé(f) 'lél(p)

fiancé(n.) ḰaŤeeb(m) ḰaŤeebé(f) ḰŤab(p)

fibre(n.) leefé(s-f) alyéf(p)

fiction(n.) Ḱoorafé(s-f) Ḱoorafét(p)

fidelity(n.) walé'(s-m) walé'at(p) – améné(s-f) aménét(p)

field(n.) ĥa'l(s-m) ĥa'lé(s-f) ĥ'ool(p)

Ă= Augh in bought	Ď= a heavy D	É= like A in Bay	G= G in beige	ĥ= like an H with smaller air passage	I= I as in ink	Ḱ= like ch in Irish loch
O= O as in home	OO= as in boots	R= roll the rrr	Ť= a heavy T	Ř= like a French R (gargle it)	Ŝ= a heavy S	Ž= a heavy Z

fierce(adj.) mitwaĥésh(m) mitwaĥshé(f) mitwaĥsheen(p) – shirés(m) shirsé(f) shirseen(p)

fiery(adj.) miltihéb(m) miltihbé(f) miltihbeen(p)

fifteen (see numbers in LeboLand)

fig(n.) teené(s-f) teen(p)

figure(number)(n.) ra'm(s-m) ar'am(p)

figure(picture)(n.) shakl(s-m) ashkél(p)

file(n.) malaff(s-m) malaffét(p)

film(n.) (same)

filthy(adj.) migwé(m) migwyé(f) migwyeen(p)

final(adj.) aḰeer(m) aḰeera(f) aḰeereen(p)

finance(n.) mél(s-p-m)

financial(adj.) mélé(m) mélyyé(f) mélyyé(p)

fine(good)(adj.) mneeĥ(m) mneeĥa(f) mnéĥ(p)

fine(thin)(adj.) da'ee'(m) da'ee'a(f) da'ee'een(p)

fine(penalty)(n.) Řaramé(s-f) Řaramét(p)

finger(n.) iŜbaĂ(s-m) aŜabéĂ(p) – ŜabeeĂ(p)

fingernail(n.) Ďifr(s-m) aĎafér(p) – Ďafeer(p)

finish(n.) nihéyé(s-f) nihéyét(p)

fire(n.) nar(s-f) niran(p)

fireplace(n.) (same)

firm(adj.) 'asé(m) 'asyé(f) 'asyeen(p) – jaddé(m) jaddyyé(f) jadyyeen(p)

firm(n.) shirké(s-f) shirkét(p)

first(adj.) awwal(m) awlé(f) awé'él(p)

fish(n.) samké(s-f) samak(p)

fisherman(n.) Ŝyyéd(m) Ŝyyédé(f) Ŝyyédé(p) – Ŝyyédeen(p)

fist(n.) abĎa(s-f) abDat(p)

fit(nervous)(n.) nawbé(s-f) nawbét(p)

fitness(n.) layé'a badanyyé(s-p-f)

fixing(n.) tiŜleeĥ(s-m) tiŜleeĥat(p) – tiŹbeet(s-m) tiŹbeeŤat(p)

flag(n.) Ăalam(s-m) aĂlém(p) – rayé(s-f) rayét(p)

flame(n.) lihbé(s-f) lihbét(p) – shiĂlé(f) shiĂlét(p)

flank(n) ganb(s-m) gnéb(p) – ḰaŜra(s-f) kwaŜér(p)

flash(n.) lamĂ(s-m) lamĂat(p) – wamĎ(s-m) wamĎat(p)

flat(adj.) msaŤŤaĥ(s-m) msaŤŤĥa(f) msaŤŤĥeen(p)

flat(tire)(adj.) mnaffas(m) mnaffsé(f) mnaffseen(p)

flattery(n.) tamallo'(s-p-m) tazallof(s-p-m)

flavour(n.) nakha(s-f) nakhat(p)

flea(n.) barŘoot(s-m) braŘeet(p)

flea market(n.) soo' L bélé(s-p-f)

fleet(n.) 'oosŤool(s-m) 'sŤeel(p)

flesh(n.) laĥm(s-p-m)

flexibility(n.) looyooné(s-f) looyoonét(p) – moorooné(s-f) mooroonét

flexible(adj.) layyén(m) layyné(f) layyneen(p) – mirén(m) mirné(f) mirneen(p)

flight(n.) riĥlé(s-f) riĥlét(p)

flint(n.) Ŝoowwén(s-p-m) – ĥagar L willéĂa – ĥagar L 'iddéĥa

flood(n.) fayaĎan(s-m) fayaĎanét(p)

floor(n.) arĎ(s-f) araĎé(p)

flow(n.) magra(s-m) magéré(p) - insyéb(s-m) insyébét(p)

flower(n.) zahra(s-f) zahrat(p) – azhar(p)

fluent(adj.) faŜeeĥ(m) faŜeeĥa(f) faŜeeĥeen(p)

fluid(n.) sé'él(s-m) sawé'él(p)

flute(n.) (same) -

fly(n.) dibbéné(s-f) dibbén(p)

flying(n.) Ťayaran(s-p-m)

foam(n.) raŘwé(s-f) raŘwét(p)

fog(n.) ŘŤayŤa(s-p-f) – Ďabéb(s-p-m)

fold(n.) Ťawyé(s-f) Ťawyét(p) – ŤaĂgé(s-f) aĂgét(p)

folding(n.) Ťawé(s-p-m) ŤaĂg(s-p-m)

foliage(n.) wra' sh-shagar(p)

follower(adj.) tébéĂ(m) tébĂa(f) tébĂeen(p)

following(n.) léĥé'(m) léĥ'a(f) léĥ'een(p)

fond(adj.) Ăandoo shaŘaf(m) Ăanda shaŘaf(f) Ăandon shaŘaf(p)

fondness(n.) shaŘaf(s-p-m)

food(n.) akl(p)

fool(n.) Řabé(m) Řabyyé(f) aŘbya(p) – bahlé(m) bahlé(f) bihlén(p)

foolish(adj.) Řabé(m) Řabyyé(f) aŘbya(p) – bahlé(m) bahlé(f) bihlén(p)

foot(n.) igr(s-f) igrén(p)

football(n.) gol – koorit adam

footstep(n.) ḰoŤwé(s-f) ḰoŤwét(p)

forbidden(adj.) mamnooĂ(m) mamnooĂa(f) mamnooĂeen(p)

force(n.) 'oowwé(s-f) 'oowwét(p)

forcing(n.) gabr – igbar - ilzém

forehead(n.) gbeen(s-m) gabéyén(p) – gabha(s-f) gabhat(p) – Ŝandeeĥa(s-f) Ŝandeeĥat

foreign(adj.) agnabé(m) agnabyyé(f) agénéb(p)

foreigner(adj.) agnabé(m) agnabyyé(f) agénéb(p)

foreseeing(n.) tanabbo'(s-m) tannabbo'at(p-)

forest(n.) Řabé(s-f) Řabét(p)

forgetfulness(n.) nisyén(s-p-m)

forgiveness(n.) Řifran(s-p-m) – maŘfira(s-p-f)

fork(n.) shawké(s-f) shawkét(p)

form(n.) bshakl(s-m) ashkél(p)

forming(n.) tishkeel(s-m) tishkeelét(p) – tikween(s-m) tikweenét(p)

formal(adj.) rasmé(m) rasmyyé(f) rasmyyeen(p)

formality(n.) rasmyyé(s-p-f)

formation(n.) tishkeel(s-m) tishkeelét(p) – tikween(s-m) tikweenét(p)

Ă= Augh in bought	Ď= a heavy D	É= like A in Bay	G= G in beige	ĥ= like an H with smaller air passage	I= I as in ink	Ḱ= like ch in Irish loch
O= O as in home	OO= as in boots	R= roll the rrr	Ť= a heavy T	Ř= like a French R (gargle it)	Ŝ= a heavy S	Ź= a heavy Z

former(adj.) sébé'(m) séb'a(f) séb'een(p)

formerly(n.) sébi'an

formula(n.) (same)

fort(n.) alĂa(s-f) 'léĂ(p)

fortunate(adj.) mahŹooŹ(m) mahŹooŹa(f) mahŹooŹa(p)

fortunately(n.) la ĥosn L ĥaŹ

fortune(n.) sarwé(s-f) sarwét(p)

forward(n.) amamé(m) amamyyé(f) amayyé(p)

forwarding(n.) irsél(s-p-m)

foster(n.) ĥaĎané

foul(adj.) wiséḰ(m) wisḰa(f) wisḰeen(p) – migwé(m) migwyyé(f) migwyyeen(p)

foundation(n.) asés(s-m) isos(p)

founder(n.) moo'assés(m) moo'assisé(f) moo'assiseen(p)

founding(n.) ta'sees(s-p-m)

fountain(n.) (same) – nefoora(s-f) nwéfeer(p)

fowl(n.) Tayr mé'é(s-m) Ťyoor mé'yyé(p)

fox(n.) saĂlab(s-m) saAaléb(p)

foyer(n.) 'aĂa(s-f) 'aĂat(p)

fraction(n.) giz'(s-m) agzé'(p)

fragile(adj.) hash(m) hashé(f) hasheen(p)

fragment(n.) sha'fé(s-f) shi'af(p)

fragrance(n.) ĂiŤr(s-m) ĂooToor(p)

fragrant(adj.) mAaŤTar(m) mĂaŤTra(f) mĂaŤTreen(p)

frail(adj.) hazeel(m) hazeelé(f) hazeeleen(p)

frame(n.) birwéŹ(s-m) braweez(p)

frank(adj.) Sareeĥ(m) Ŝareeĥa(f) Ŝareeĥeen(p)

frankness(n.) Saraĥa(s-p-f)

free(adj.) ĥir(m) ĥirra(f) aĥrar(p)

free(costless)(n.) maggéné(m) maggényyé(f) maggényyé(p) – balésh(s-p-f-m)

freedom(n.) ĥirryyé(s-f) ĥirryyét(p)

freeing(n.) tiHreer(s-p-m)

freezing(n.) tigmeed(s-p-m)

freight(n.) ĥmoolé(s-f) ĥmoolét(p) – shahn(s-p-m)

French(n.) faransé(m) faransyyé(f) faransyyeen(p)

french fries(n.) naŤaTa mi'lyyé(s-p-f)

frequency(n.) zabzabé(s-f) zabzabet(p)

frequent(adj.) mkarrar(m) mkarrara(f) mkarrareen(p)

frequently(n.) takarror(s-p-m)

fresh(adj.) Ťaza(m-f-s-p)

friction(n.) iĥtikék(s-m) iĥtikékét(p)

Friday(n.) gimĂa

friend(n.) Ŝaĥéb(m) Ŝaĥbé(f) aŜĥab(p) – Ŝadee'(m) ŜaĎee'a(f) aŜdika'(p)

friendly(adj.) wadood(m) wadoodé(f) wadoodeen(p)

friendship(n.) Ŝada'a(s-f) Ŝada'at(p)

frightened(adj.) Ḱayéf(m) Ḱayfé(f) Kayfeen(p)

frightening(adj.) mooḰeef(m) mooḰeefé(f) mooḰeefeen(p)

frivolity(n.) Ťaysh(s-p-m)

frivolous(adj.) Ťayésh(m) Tayshé(f) Ťaysheen(p)

frog(n.) ĎifdaĂ(m) ĎifdĂa(f) ĎfadéĂ(p)

from min

front(n.) iddém(s-p-m-f)

frontier(n.) ĥad(s-m) ĥdood(p)

fruit(n.) fawéké(s-p)

frying(n.) alé

frying pan(n.) ma'lé(s-f) – mi'léyé(f) mi'léyét(s-f)

fuel(n.) (same)

fugitive(n.) héréb(m) hérbé(f) hérbeen(p) – Ťareed(m) Ťareeda(f) Ťareedeen(p)

fulfillment(n.) tiĥ'ee'(s-m) tiĥ'ee'at(p) – tinfeez(s-m) tinfeezét(p)

fully(n.) koollyan

fun(n.) maraĥ(s-p-m) – liĂb(s-p-m) – lahoo(s-p-m)

function(n.) mahammé(s-f) mahammét(p) – waŹeefé(s-f) waŹayéf(p)

fund(n.) raŜeed(s-m) arŜida(p)

fundamental(adj.) asésé(m) asésyyé(f) asésyyeen(p) – gawharé(m) gawharyye(f) gawharyyeen(p)

funny(adj.) mahĎoom(m) mahĎoome(f) mahĎoomeen(p)

fur(n.) faroo(s-p-m-f)

furious(adj.) miĥtad(m) miĥtaddé(f) miĥtadeen(p)

furnace(n.) firn (s-m) afran(p) – tannour(s-m)

furniture(n.) mafrooshét(s-p-f)

furrow(n.) tilm(s-m) tlém(p)

further(adj) abĂad(s-p-m-f)

future(n.) mista'bal(s-m-)

future(adj.) mista'balé(m) mista'balyyé(f) mista'balyyeen(p)

G

gadget(n.) shaŘlé(s-f) shaŘlét(p)

gaiety(n.) saĂadé(s-f)

gain(n.) ribĥ(s-m) arbéĥ(p)

gallant(adj.) shahm(s-m) shoohama(p)

gallery(n.) same

gambling(n.) liĂb L 'mar

game(n.) liĂbé(s-f) alĂab(p)

garage(n.) same

garden(n.) gnayné(s-f) gnaynét(p)

gardener(n.) gnaynété(m) gnaynétyyé(f) gnaynétyyé(p)

garlic(n.) toom(s-p-m)

garment(n.) mashlaĥ(s-m) mashéléĥ(p) – Ăabéyé(s-f) Ăabéyét(p)

gas(n.) Řaz(s-p-m)

gasoline(n.) benzeen(s-p-m)

gate(n.) boowébé(s-f) boowébét(p)

Ă= Augh in bought	Ď= a heavy D	É= like A in Bay	G= G in beige	ĥ= like an H with smaller air passage	I= I as in ink	Ḱ= like ch in Irish loch
O= O as in home	OO= as in boots	R= roll the rrr	Ť= a heavy T	Ř= like a French R (gargle it)	Ŝ= a heavy S	Ž= a heavy Z

gathering(n.) tagammoĂ(s-m) tagammoĂat(p0

gay(happy)(adj.) mabŜoot(m) mabŜoota(f) mabŜooteen(p)

gay(homosexual)(adj) Ťibgé(s-m) Ťabagné(p) – looté(s-m) looŤyyé(p)

gem(n.) ĥagar kareem(s-m) aĥgar karemé(p)

gender(n.) gins(s-m) agnés(p)

general Ăam(m) Ăammé(f) Ăammyyé(p)

general(the rank) same

generalizing(n.) taĂmeem

generation(n.) geel(s-m) agyél(p)

generosity(n.) karam(s-p-m)

generous(adj.) kareem(m) kareemé(f) koorama(p)

genius(adj.) nébŘa(m) nébŘa(f) nawébéŘ(p)

gentle(adj.) laŤeeĥ(m) laŤeefé(f) looŤafa(p) – néĂém(m) néĂmé(f) néĂmeen(p)

gentleman same

gentleness(n.) nooĂoomé(s-p-f) – laŤafé(s-p-f)

genuine(adj.) aŜlé(m) aŜlyyé(f) aŜlyyé(p)

geographical(adj.) giŘrafé(m) giŘrafyyé(f) giŘrafyyé(p)

geography(n.) giŘrafya(s-f) giŘrafyet(p)

germ(n.) girsoomé(s-f) graseem(p)

German(n.) ilmané(m) ilmanyyé(f) ilman(p)

gesture(n.) ishara(s-f) isharat(p)

ghastly(adv.) mirĂéb(m) mirĂbé(f) mirĂbeen(p)

giant(n.) Ăimlé'(m) Ăimlé'a(f) Ăamélee'(p)

gift(n.) haddyé(s-f) hadéya(p)

gifted(adj.) mawhoob(m) mawhoobé(f) mawhoobeen(p)

girl(n.) bint(s-f) banét(p)

giving(n.) wahb – manĥ - ĂaŤé

glad(adj.) mabŜoot(m) mabŜoota(f) mabŜooteen(p)

glance(n.) lamĥa(s-f) lamĥat(p)

glancing(n.) lamĥ

glass(n.) izéz(s-p-m)

gleam(n.) wamĎ(s-p-m)

glittering(n.) tli'lo'(s-p-m)

global(adj.) Ăalamé(m) Ăalamyyé(f) Ăalamyyé(p)

globe(world)(n.) Ăalam

gloomy(adj.) Řamé'(m) Řam'a(f) Řam'een(p)

glorious(adj.) mageed(m) mageedé(f) mageedé(p)

glory(n.) magd(s-m) amgéd(p)

glove(n.) kaff(s-m) kfoof(p)

goalkeeper(n.) ĥarés marma(m) ĥarsét marma(f) ĥirras marma(p)

gold(n.) dahab(s-p-m)

golden(adj.) dahabé(m) dahabyyé(f) dahabyyé(p)

golf(n.) same

good(adj.) mneeĥ(m) mneeĥa(f) mnéĥ(p)

goods(n.) bĎaĂa(s-f) baĎayéĂ(p)

goodwill(n.) nyyé ĥasané(s-f) nyyét ĥasané(p)

goose(n.) wazzé(s-f) wazz(p)

gorgeous(adj.) raheeb(m) raheebé(f) raheebeen(p) – ra'éĂ(m) ra'iĂa(f) ra'Ăeen(p)

gossip(n.) sarsara(s-p-f)

government(n.) ĥokoomé(s-f) ĥokoomét(p)

governor(n.) ĥakém(m) ĥakmé(f) ĥikkém(p)

grace(n.) rashé'a(s-p-f)

graceful(adj.) rashee'(m) rashee'a(f) rashee'een(p)

grade(n.) daragé(s-f) daragét(p)

grain(n.) ĥabbé(s-f) ĥboob(p)

grammar(n.) awéĂéd(s-p-f)

grand(adj.) kbeer(m) kbeeré(f) kbar(p) -

grandchild(n.) ĥafeed(m) ĥafeedé(f) aĥféd(p)

granddaughter(n.) ĥafeedé(s-f) ĥafeedét(p)

grandeur(n.) Ăazamé (s-p-f)– galél(s-p-m)

grandfather(n.) gid(s-m) gdood(p)

grandmother(n.) sit(s-f) sittét(p)

grandson(n) ĥafeed(s-m) aĥféd(p)

grant(n.) minĥa(s-f) minaĥ(p)

granting(n.) manĥ

grape(n.) Ăinab(s-p-m)

grapefruit(n.) same

grass(n.) ĥasheesh(s-p-m)

grasshopper(n.) abbooŤ(s-m) 'babeeŤ(p)

grateful(adj.)mamnoon(m) mamnooné(f) mamnooneen(p)

gratitude(n.) shikr(s-p-m) – imtinén(s-p-m)

grave(n.) abr(s-m) aboor(p)

grave(n.) gaddé(m) gaddyyé(f) gadyyé(p)

gravel(n.) baĥŜa(f) baĥSat(p) also baĥŜ(p)

gray(n.) rmédé(m) rmédyyé(f) rmédyyé(p)

grease(n.) shaĥm(s-p-m)

greasing(n) tishĥeem(p)

great(adj.) Ăazeem(m) Ăazeemé(f) Ăazeemeen(p)

greatness(n.) Ăazamé(s-f) Ăazamét(p)

greed(n.) ŤamaĂ(s-m) aŤmaĂ(p)

greedy(adj.) ŤammeeĂ(m) ŤammeeĂa(f) ŤammeeĂeen(p)

Greek(n.) yoonéné(m) yoonényyé(f) yoonén(p)

green(n.) aḰĎar(m) ḰaĎra(f) ḰiĎr(p)

greeting(n.) salém(m) salémét(p)

greif(n.) ĥizn(s-m) aĥzén(p)

grinder(n.) maŤĥané(s-f) maŤahéN(P)

Ă= Augh in bought	Ď= a heavy D	É= like A in Bay	G= G in beige	ĥ= like an H with smaller air passage	I= I as in ink	Ḱ= like ch in Irish loch
O= O as in home	OO= as in boots	R= roll the rrr	Ť= a heavy T	Ř= like a French R (gargle it)	Ŝ= a heavy S	Ž= a heavy Z

grinding(n.) Ťaĥn

groaning(n.) Ăann

grocer(n.) simmén(m) simméné(f) simméné(p)

grocery store(n.) maĥal sméné(s-m) maĥallét sméné(p) – dikkén(s-m) dkékeen(p)

gross(adj.) mi'réf(m) mi'irfé(f) mi'irfeen(p)

ground(n.) arĎ(s-f) araĎé(p)

group(n.) magmooĂa(s-f) magmooĂat(p) – (same)

grouping(n.) tigmeeĂ

growing(plants)(n.) zarĂ(s-p-m) – ziraĂa(s-p-f)

growth(n.) noomoo(s-p-m)

grudge(n.) ĥi'd(s-m) aĥ'ad(p)

guard(n.) ĥarés(m) ĥarsé(f) ĥirras(p)

guardian(n.) ĥarés(m) ĥarsé(f) ĥirras(p)

guarding(n.) ĥirasé(s-p-f)

guessing(n.) tiĥzeer

guide(n.) daleel(m) daleelé(f) adillé(p)

guiding(n.) dall(s-p-m) – irshéd(s-p-m)

guilt(n.) zanb(s-m) znoob(p)

gulf(n.) Ḱaleeg(s-m) Ḱilgén(p)

gullible(adj.) baŜeeŤ(m) baŜeeŤa(f) booŜaŤa

gum(n.) Ăilké

gun(n.) fard(s-m) froodé(p) – baroodé(s-f) bwéreed(p)

H

habit(n.) Ăadé(s-f) Ăadét(p)

habitual(adj.) Ăadé(m) Ăadyyé(f) Ăadyyé(p)

hail(n.) barad(s-p-m)

hair(n.) shaĂr(s-p-m)

hair clippers(n.) same

hair dresser(n.) ĥalla'(m) ĥalla'a(f) ĥalla'een(p)

hair dryer(n.) same

hairy(adj.) mishiĂrané(m) mishiĂranyye(f) mishiĂranyyé(p)

half(n.) niŜŜ(s-m) nŜŜaŜ(p)

half hour(n.) niŜŜ ŜéĂa(s-m)

hall(n.) 'aĂa(s-f) 'aĂat(p)

ham(n.) laĥm Ḱanzeer(s-p-m)

hammer(n.) shékoosh(s-m) shwékeesh(p) – maŤra'a(s-f) maŤaré'(p)

hand(n.) 'eed(s-f) 'eedén(p) also ayédé(p)

handbag(n.) gizdén(s-m) gzédeen(p)

handful(n.) kamshé(s-f) kamshét(p)

handkerchief(n.) mandeel(s-m) mnédeel(p)

handle(n.) maské(s-f) maskét(p)

handling(n.) mooĂémalé(s-f) mooĂélagé(p)

handsome(n.) ĥiloo(m) ĥilwé(f) ĥilween(p)

hanger(n.) taĂlee'a(s-f) tĂalee'(p)

hanging(n) taĂlee'

happiness(n.) baŜŤ(s-p-m) – saĂadé(s-p-f) – faraĥ(s-m) afraĥ(p)

happy(adj.) mabŜooŤ(m) mabŜooŤa(f) mabŜooŤeen(p)

harbour(n.) Ḱaleeg(s-m) Ḱilgén(p) – goon(s-m) gwén(p)

hard(difficult)(adj.) SaĂb(m) ŜaĂbé(f) ŜaĂbeen(p)

hard(stiff)(adj.) asé(m) asyé(f) asyeen(p)

hardly(n.) B ŜooĂoobé

hardness(n.) aséwé(s-p-f)

hare(n.) arnab(m) arnabé(f) aranéb(p)

harm(n.) Ďarar(s-m) aĎrar(p) – aza(s-p-m)

harmful(adj.) mi'zé(m) mi'zyyé(f) mi'zyyeen(p)

harmonious(adj.) mitnéŘém(m) mitnéŘmé(f) mitnéŘmeen(p)

harmony(n.) tanéŘom(s-p-m)

harsh(adj.) Ḱishén(m) Ḱishné(f) kishneen(p)

harvest(n.) maĥŜool(s-m) maĥaŜeel(p)

haste(n.) sirĂa(s-f) sirĂat(p)

hat(n.) same - birnayŤa(s-f) braneeŤ(p) – abboŎa(s-f) abébeeĂ(p)

hateful(adj.) ĥa'ood(m) ĥa'oodé(f) ĥa'oodeen(p)

hatred(n.) kirh(s-p-m) – ĥi'd(s-p-m)

haughty(adj.) mitkabbér(m) mitkabbra(f) mitkabreen(p)

haven(n.) malga'(s-m) malégé'(p)

hay(n.) ash-sh(s-p-m)

head(n.) ras(s-m) roos(p)

headache(n.) wagaĂ ras(s-p-m)

heading(n.) tawaggoh

headphones(n.) same

healing(n.) shifé'(s-p-m)

health(n.) Ŝaĥĥa(s-p-m)

healthy(n.) Ŝiĥĥé(m) Ŝiĥĥyyé(f) Ŝiĥĥyyé(p)

heap(n.) kawmé(s-f) kawmét(p)

hearing(n.) samaĂ(s-m)

heart(n.) alb(s-m) aloob(p)

heat(n.) shob(s-p-m) – hibb(s-p-m) – ĥarara(s-p-f)

heaven(n.) ganné(s-f) gannét(p)

heavy(adj.) t'eel(m) t'eelé(f) t'al(p)

heel(n.) kaĂb L igr(s-m) kĂab L igrén(p)

height(n.) irtiféĂ(s-m) irtiféĂat(p) – Ăloo(s-p-m)

heir(n.) Kalaf(s-p-m-f) – warees(m) wareesé(f) woorasa(p)

hello marĥaba

help(n.) mooséĂadé(s-f) mooséĂadét(p)

helper(n) mooséĂéd(m) mooséĂdé(f) mooséĂdeen(p)

helpful(adj.) Ḱadoom(m) Ḱadoomé(f) Ḱadoomeen(p)

helping(n.) mooséĂadé(s-f) mooséĂadét(p)

hem(of pants)(n.) zéf(s-p-m)

Ă= Augh in bought	Ď= a heavy D	É= like A in Bay	G= G in beige	ĥ= like an H with smaller air passage	I= I as in ink	Ḱ= like ch in Irish loch
O= O as in home	OO= as in boots	R= roll the rrr	Ť= a heavy T	Ř= like a French R (gargle it)	Ŝ= a heavy S	Ž= a heavy Z

hen(n.) dgégé(s-f) dgég(p)

hence(n.) fa'izan

herb(n.) Ăishb(s-m) aĂshéb(p) – ĥasheesh(s-m) ĥashéyésh(p)

herd(n.) aŤeeĂ(s-m) iŤĂan(p)

here hon

hermit(n.) ĥabees(m) ĥabeesé(f) ĥoobasa(p)

hero(n.) baŤal(m) abŤal(p)

heroic(adj.) booŤoolé(m) booŤoolyyé(f) booŤoolyyé(p)

heroine(n.) baŤalé(f) baŤalét(p)

herself(n.) nafsa(s-f) nafson(p)

hesitation(n.) taraddod(s-m) taraddodét(p)

hideous(adj.) abeeĥ(m) abeeĥa(f) abeeĥeen(p)

hiding(n.) tiḰbéyé(s-p-f)

high(adj.) Ăélé(m) Ăélyé(f) Ăélyeen(p)

higher(superlative) aĂla(s-p-m-f)

hill(n.) tallé(s-f) tlél(p)

himself(n.) nafsoo(s-m) nafsa(p)

hind(adj.) Ḱalfé(m) Ḱalfyyé(f) Ḱalfyyé(p)

hindering(n.) 'iĂa'a(s-p-f)

hinge(n.) mfaŜŜlé(s-f) mfaŜŜlét(p)

hint(n.) daleel(s-m) adillé(p) – lamĥa(s-f) lamĥat(p)

hinting(n.) tilmeeĥ(s-m) tilmeeĥat(p)

hip(n.) wirk(s-m) wrak(p)

hiring(n.) tawzeef(s-m) tawzeefét(p)

hissing(n.) washwashé(s-f) washwashét(p)

historian(n.) moo'arriḰ(m) moo'arriḰa(f) moo'arrḰeen(p)

historic(adj.) téreeḰé(m) téreeḰyyé(f) téreeḰyyé(p)

history(n.) téreeḰ(s-m) twéreeḰ(p)

hoarse(adj.) Ḱishén(m) Ḱishné(f) Ḱishneen(p) – mabĥooĥ(m) mabĥooĥa(f) mabĥooĥeen(p)

holding(n.) mask(s-p-m)

hole(n.) goora(s-f) goowar(p)

holiday(n.) Ăeed(s-m) aĂyéd(p)

holiness(n.) adésé(s-f) adését(p)

hollow(adj.) faĎé(m) faĎyé(f) faĎyeen(p)

holy(adj.) m'addas(m) m'addsé(f) m'addseen(p)

home(n.) beit(s-m) byoot(p)

homework(n.) farĎ(s-m) frooĎ(p)

homosexual(adj.) Ťibgé(m) Ťibgyyé(f) Ťabagné(p) – looŤé(m) looŤyyé(f) looŤyeen(p)

homosexuality(n.) Ťabgané(s-p-f) – lawaŤ(s-p-m)

honest(adj.) Ŝadé'(m) Ŝad'a(f) Ŝad'een(p)

honesty(n.) Ŝid'(s-p-m)

honey(n.) Ăasal(s-p-m)

honeymoon(n.) shahr L Ăasal(s-p-m)

honour(n.) sharaf(s-p-m)

honourable(adj.) shareef(m) shareefé(f) shoorafa(p)

honouring(n.) tishreef(s-p-m)

hood(n.) ŘaŤa(s-m) aŘŤyé(p)

hoof(n.) Ḱiff(s-m) Ḱféf(p)

hook(n.) shankal(s-m) shanékél(p)

hope(n.) amal(s-m) amél(p)

hoping(n.) ta'ammol(s-p-m)

horizon(n.) 'oofo'(s-m) 'éfé'(p)

horizontal(adj.) 'oofoo'é(m) 'oofoo'yyé(f) 'oofoo'yyé(p)

horn(n.) zammoor(s-m) zmémeer(p)

horrible(adj.) mooreeĂ(m) mooreeĂa(f) mooreeĂeen(p)

horror(n.) riĂb(s-p-m)

horse(n.) ĥŜan(s-m) iĥŜné(p) – faras(s-f) Ḱél(p)

hospitable(adj.) miĎyéf(m) miĎyéfé(f) miĎyéfeen(p)

hospital(n.) mistashfa(s-f) mistashféyét(p)

host(n.) mooĎeef(s-m) mooĎeefeen(p)

hostess(n.) mooĎeefé(s-f) mooĎeefét(p)

hostile(adj.) Ăidé'é(m) Ăidé'yyé(f) Ăidé'yyeen(p)

hot(adj.) ŜiḰn(m) ŜiḰné(f) ŜiḰneen(p)

hot(weather)(n.) shob

hotel(n.) same

hour(n.) séĂa(s-f) séĂat(p)

house(n.) beit(s-m) byoot(p)

how? keef?

however(n.) Ăa kill ĥal

human(n.) insén(s-m) nés(p)

humane(adj.) inséné(m) insényyé(f) insényyé(p)

humanity(n.) basharyyé(s-p-f)

humble(adj.) mitwaĎaĂ(m) mitwaĎĂa(f) mitwaĎĂeen(p)

humid(adj.) riŤéb(m) riŤbé(f) riŤbeen(p)

humidity(n.) rŤoobé(s-p-f)

humiliation(n.) ihéné(s-f) ihénét(p)

humiliating(n.) ihéné(s-p-f)

humming(n.) thimdor(s-p-f)

humour(n.) haĎamé(s-p-f)

hunger(n.) gooĂ(s-p-m)

hungry(adj.) gooĂan(m) gooĂané(f) gooĂaneen(p)

hunter(n.) Ŝiyyd(m) Ŝiyyédé(f) Ŝiyyédé(p)

hunting(n.) Séd(s-p-m)

hurry(n.) Ăagalé

husband(n.) zog(s-m) azwég(p)

hyphen(n.) shiĥŤa(s-f) shiĥaŤ(p)

hypocrisy(n.) malaané(s-f) malAanét(p) – Ḱabsané(s-f) Kabsanét(p) – sharr(s-m) shroor(p)

hyprocrite(adj.) Ḱabees(m) Ḱabeesé(f) Ḱoobasa(p) – malĂoon(m) malĂooné(f) mléĂeen(p) – shreer(m) shreera(f) ashrar(p)

Ă= Augh in bought	Ď= a heavy D	É= like A in Bay	G= G in beige	ĥ= like an H with smaller air passage	I= I as in ink	Ḱ= like ch in Irish loch
O= O as in home	OO= as in boots	R= roll the rrr	Ť= a heavy T	Ř= like a French R (gargle it)	Ŝ= a heavy S	Ž= a heavy Z

hypothesis(n.) nazaryye(s-f)
nazarryyét(p)

I

Ice(n.) galeed(s-p-m)

Ice cubes(n.) talg(s-p-m)

Icy(adj.) galidé(m) galidyyé(f)
galidyyé(p)

Idea(n.) fikra(s-f) afkar(p)

Ideal(adj.) misélé(m) misélyyé(f)
misélyyeen(p)

Idealism(n.) misélyyé(s-p-f)

Idealist(adj.) misélé(m) misélyyé(f)
misélyyeen(p)

Identical(adj.) mitshébéh(m)
mitshébha(f) mitshébheen(p)

identification paper(n.) hawwyé(s-f)
hawwyét(p) – biŤa'a shaḰŜyyé(s-f)
biŤa'at shaḰŜyyé(p)

idiot(adj.) Řabé(m) Řabyyé(f) aŘbiya(p)

idle(adj.) wé'éf(m) wé'fé(f) wé'feen(p) –
géméd(m) gémdé(f) gémdeen(p)

idleness(n.) misélyyé(s-f) -

if iza

ignoble(adj.) bala aḰlé' (s-p-m-f)

ignorance(n.) gahl(s-p-m)

ignorant(adj.) géhél(m) géhlé(f)
gahalé(p)

ill(adsj.) mareeĎ(m) mareeĎa(f)
marĎa(p)

illness(n.) maraĎ(s-m) amraĎ(p)

illusion(n.) wahm(s-m) awhém(p) –
tahayyo'(s-m) tahayyo'at(p)

illustration(n.) moolaḰḰaŜ(s-m)
moolaḰKaŜat(p)

image(n.) Ŝoora(s-f) Ŝoowar(p)

imaginary(adj.) Ḱayélé(m) Ḱayélyyé(f)
Ḱayélyyé(p)

imagination(n.) mooḰayyilé(s-f)
mooḰayyilét(p)

immitation(n.) ta'leed(s-p-m)

immediate(adj.) ḧalé(m) ḧalyyé(f) ḧalyyé

immediatly ḧalan

immigration(n.) higra(s-f) higrat(p)

imminent(adj.) L géyé(m) L géyé(f)
Lgéyeen(p)

immobility(n.) Ăadam L ḧaraké(s-p-m-f)
-

immoral(adj.) bala aḰlé'(s-p-m-f)

immorality(n.) inĂidém L aḰlé'

immortal(adj.) Ḱaléd(m) Ḱaldé(f)
Ḱaldeen(p)

immortality(n.) Ḱolood(s-p-m)

impartial(adj.) Řér minḧaz(m) Řér
minḧazé(f) Řér minḧazeen(p)

impatient(adj.) Ăadeem ŜŜabr(m)
Ăadeemét ŜŜabr(f) Ăadeemy ŜŜabr(p)

impatience(n.) Ăadam ŜŜabr(s-p-m)

imperfect(adj.) Řér kémél(m) Řér
kémlé(f) Řér kémleen(p)

impious(adj.) Ḱaté(m) Ḱatyé(f)
Ḱatyeen(p) – shirreer(m) shirreera(f)
ashrar(p)

importance(n.) ahammyyé(s-f)
ahammyyét(p)

important(adj.) mhim(m) mhimmé(f)
mhimmeen(P)

impossible(adj.) moostaḧeel(m)
moostaḧeelé(f) moostaḧeelé(p)

impression(n.) inŤibéĂ(s-m)
inŤibéĂat(p)

impressionist(adj.) mo'alléd(m)
mo'allidé(f) mo'allideen(p)

impressive(adj.) mo'assér(m)
mo'assira(f) (plural not used)

improvement(n.) taḧseenét(s-p-f)

imprudence(n.) Ťaish(s-p-m)

imprudent(adj.) Ťayésh(m) Ťayshé(f)
Ťaysheen(p)

impulse(n.) déféĂ(s-m) dawéféĂ(p)

impure(adj.) mish Ŝafé(m) mish Ŝafyé(f)
mish Ŝafyeen(p)

inadequate(adj.) Řér kéfé(m) Řér
kéfyé(f) Řér kefyeen(p)

incapable(adj.) mish 'adér(m) mish
'adra(f) mish 'adreen(p)

inch same

incident(n.) ḧadas(s-m) aḧdés(p)

included(n.) Ďimn

including(adj.) Ďimnoo(m) Ďimna(m)
Ďimnon(p)

income(n.) madḰool(s-m) mmadaḰeel(p)

incomplete(adj.) na'éŜ(m) na'Ŝa(f)
na'Ŝeen(p)

incomprehensible(adj.) mish
mafhoom(m) mish mafhoomé(f) mish
mafhoomeen(p)

inconvenient(adj.) mish Ăamalé(m) mish
Aamalyyé(f) mish Aamalyyé(p)

incorrect(adj.) ŘalaŤ(s-m-f) aŘlaŤ(p)

incredible(adj.) mish maĂ'ool(m) mish
maĂ'oolé(f) mish maĂ'ooleen(p)

indebted(adj.) madyoon(m) madyooné(f)
madyooneen(p)

indeed(n.) la shak -

independence(n.) isti'lél(s-p-m)

independent(adj.) mista'ill(m)
mista'illé(f) mista'illeen(p)

index(n.) fahras(s-p-m)

indirect(adj.) Řér moobéshar(m) Řér
moobéshra(f) Řér moobeshreen(p)

indirectly(adv.) shakl Řer moobéshar

indispensable(adj.) Ďarooré(m)
Ďarooryyé(f) Ďarooryyé(p)

individual(n.) shaḰŜ(s-m-f) ashḰaŜ(p)

indivisible(adj.) ma byin'iŜém(m) ma
btin'iŜém(f) ma byin'iŜmoo(p)

indoors(adj.) déḰlé(m) déḰlyyé(f)
déḰlyyé(p)

industrial(adj.) ŜinéĂé(m) ŜinéĂyyé(f)
ŜinéĂyyé(p)

industry(n.) ŜinaĂa(s-f) ŜinaĂat(p)

inexplicable(adj.) ŘameĎ(m) ŘamĎa(f)
ŘamĎeen(p)

inexpressible(adj.) ma byinwaŜaf(m) ma
btinwaŜaf(f) ma byinwaŜfoo(p)

infancy(n.) Ťofoolé(s-f) Ťofoolét(p)

infant(n.) Ťifl(m) Ťiflé(f) aŤfél(p)

| Ă= Augh in bought | Ď= a heavy D | É= like A in Bay | G= G in beige | ḧ= like an H with smaller air passage | I= I as in ink | Ḱ= like ch in Irish loch |
| O= O as in home | OO= as in boots | R= roll the rrr | Ť= a heavy T | Ř= like a French R (gargle it) | Ŝ= a heavy S | Ž= a heavy Z |

infantry(n.) mooshét(m-f-s-p)

infection(n.) iltihéb(s-m) iltihébét(p)

inferior(adj) waŤé(m) waŤyé(f) waŤyeen(p)

infinite(n.) bala nihéyé

infinity(n.) la nihéyé

influence(n.) ta'seer(s-m) ta'seerat(p)

information(n.) maĂloomét(s-p-m)

ingenious(adj.) nébŘa(m) nébŘa(f) nawébéŘ(p)

ingenuity(n.) noobooŘ(s-p-m)

inheritance(n.) wirté(s-p-f)

inhuman(adj.) mitwaĥĥésh(m) mitwaĥĥshé(f) mitwaĥĥsheen(f)

initial(adj.) awwal(s-p-m-f)

initiative(n.) moobédara(s-f) moobédarat(p)

injury(n.) Ďarar(s-m) aĎrar(p) – girĥ(s-m) grooĥ(p)

injustice(n.) Źilm(s-m) maŹalém(p)

ink(n.) ĥibr(s-p-m-f)

inn(n.) nazl(s-m)

innocence(n.) bara'a(s-f) bara'at(p)

innocent(adj.) baree'(m) baree'a(f) abrya(p)

inquiry(n.) tiĥ'ee'(s-m) tiĥ'ee'at(p)

inscribed(adj.) manŜooŜ(m) manŜooŜa(f) manŜooŜeen(p)

insect(n.) ĥashara(s-f) ĥasharat(p)

insensible(adj.) bala iĥsés(s-p-m-f)

inside(n.) goowwa(s-p-m-f)

insight(n.) baŜeera(s-f) baŜayér(p)

insignificant(adj.) mish mhimm(m) mish mhimmé(f) mish mhimmeen(p)

insincere(adj.) kizzéb(m) kizzébé(f) kizzébeen(p)

instantly(n.) diŘré

insistence(n.) iŜrar

inspection(n.) kashf(s-p-m-f)

inspiration(n.) waĥé(s-p-m-f)

installment(n.) dafĂa(s-m) dafĂat(p)

instance(n.) laĥŹa(s-f) laĥŹat(p)

instant(adj.) ĥalé(m) ĥalyyé(f) Halyyé(p)

instantaneous(adj.) sareeĂ(m) sareeĂa(f) sareeĂeen(p)

instantly(n.) bsirĂa

instead of(n.) badal

instinct(n.) ĥads(s-p-m)

institute(n) maĂhad(s-m) maĂahéd(p)

institution(n.) mo'assasé(s-f) mo'assassét(p)

instruction(n.) taĂleemét(s-p-m)

instructor(n.) istéz(m) mĂallmé(f) asétzé(p)

instrument(n.) Ăiddé(s-p-f)

insufficient(adj.) mish kéfé(m) mish kéfyé(f) mish kéfyeen(p)

insult(n.) ihéné(s-f) ihénét(p)

insurance(n.) ta'meen(s-p-m)

intellect(n.) zaka(s-p-m) – sa'afé(s-f) sa'afét(p)

intellectual(n.) zaké(m) zakyyé(f) azkya(p) – msa''af(m) msa'fé(f) msa'feen(p)

intelligence(n.) zaka(s-p-m)

intelligence(agency)(n.) istiĶbarat(s-p-f) – mooĶabarat(s-p-f)

intelligent(adj.) zaké(m) zakyyé(f) azkya(p)

intense(adj.) awé(m) awyyé(f) 'wéya(p)

intensity(n.) 'oowwé(s-f) 'oowwét(p)

intention(n.) neeyé(s-f) neeyét(p)

interest(n.) ihtimém(s-m) ihtimémét(p)

interest(loan)(n.) féydé(s-f) fawéyéd(p)

interesting(adj.) (calls for interest) byidĂé lal ihtimém(m) btidĂé lal ihtimém(f) byidĂoo lal ihtimém(p)

interference(n.) tadaĶĶol(s-m) tadaĶĶolét(p)

interior(adj.) déĶlé(m) déĶlyyé(f) déĶlyyé(p)

intermediate(adj.) mitwaŜŜéŤ(m) mitwaŜŜŤa(f) mitwaŜŜŤeen(p)

intermission(n.) firŜa(s-f) firaŜ(p)

international(adj.) Ăalamé(m) Ăalamyyé(f) Ăalamyyé(p)

interpretation(n.) targamé(s-f) targamét(p)

interpreter(n.) tirgmén(m) tirgméné(f) tirgményyé(p) – mitargém(m) mitargmé(f) mitargmeen(p)

interruption(n.) m'aŤĂa(s-f) m'aŤĂat(p)

intersection(n.) ta'aŤoĂ(s-m) ta'aŤoĂat(p)

interval(n.) middé(s-f) middét(p) – marĥalé(s-f) maraĥél(p)

interview(n.) moo'abalé(s-f) moo'abalét(p)

intimidation(n.) tirheeb(s-p-m)

intolerable(adj.) ma byinĥamal(m) ma btinĥamal(f) ma byinĥamaloo(p)

intolerance(n.) Ăadam taĥammol(s-p-m-f)

intolerant(adj.) ma byitĥammal(m) ma btitĥammal(f) ma byitĥammaloo(p)

introduction(n.) taĂarof(s-m) taĂarofét(p)

intuition(n.) ĥads(s-p-m)

invariable(adj.) sébét(m) sébté(f) sébteen(p)

invasion(n.) Řazoo(s-m) Řazwét(p)

invention(n.) iĶtiraĂ(s-m) iĶtiraĂaat(p)

inventor(n.) mooĶtaréĂ(m) mooĶtariĂa(f) mooĶtariĂeen(p)

investment(n.) istismar(s-m) istismarat(p)

invisible(adj.) Ķafé(m) Ķafyyé(f) Ķafyyé(p)

invitation(n.) daĂwé(s-f) daAwét(p) – Ăazeemé(s-f) Ăazéyém(p;)

invoice(n.) fétoora(s-f) fwéteer(p)

iron(n.) ĥadeed(s-p-m-f)

irony(n.) sooĶryé(s-f) sooĶryét(p)

irregular(adj.) mish mitséwé(m) mish mitséwyé(f) mish mitséween(p)

Ă= Augh in bought	Ď= a heavy D	É= like A in Bay	G= G in beige	ĥ= like an H with smaller air passage	I= I as in ink	Ķ= like ch in Irish loch
O= O as in home	OO= as in boots	Ř= roll the rrr	Ť= a heavy T	Ř= like a French R (gargle it)	Ŝ= a heavy S	Ž= a heavy Z

irreparable(adj.) ma byitŜallaḣ(m) ma btitŜallaḣ(f) ma byitŜallaḣo(p)

irresistable(adj.) ma byit'awam(m) ma btit'awam(f) ma byit'awamo(p)

irritation(n.) inziĂag(s-p-m)

islamic(adj.) islémé(m) islémyyé(f) islémyyé(p)

island(n.) gazeeré(s-f) gizor(p)

isolation(n.) Ăizlé(s-f) Ăizlét(p)

issue(n.) mas'alé(s-f) masé'él(p)

Italian(adj.) Ťilyéné(m) Ťilyényyé(f)Ťilyén(p) – 'iŤalé(m) 'iŤalyyé(f) 'iŤalyyé(p)

item(n.) shaŘlé(s-f) shaŘlét(p)

itinerary(n.) birnémég(s-m) baramég(p)

itself(n.) (doesn't exist in Lebanese as things are either masculin or feminin)

ivory(n.) Ăag(s-p-m)

J

jacket(n.) (same)

jam(n.) mrabba(s-m) mrabbayét(p)

jam(traffic)(n.) ḣashra(s-f) ḣashrat(p)

January(n.) Kénoon tténé

Japanese(adj.) yabané(m) yabanyyé(f) yaban(p)

jar(n.) jarra(s-f) jrar(p)

jaw(n.) fakk(s-m) fkook(p) – ḣanak(s-m) ḣnék(p)

jealous(adj.) Řayyoor(m) Řayyoora(f) Rayyooreen(p)

jealousy(n.) Řeeré(s-p-f)

jewel(n.) moogawhara(s-f) moogawharat(p)

Jewish(adj.) yéhoodé(m) yéhoodyyé(f) yehood(p)

job(n.) waŹeefé(s-f) waŹayéf(p)

joint(n.) mafŜal(s-m) mafaŜél(p)

joke(n.) nikté(s-f) nikat(p)

jolly(n.) kteer

journal(n.) magallé(s-f) magallét(p)

journalism(n.) Ŝaḣafé(s-p-f)

journalist(adj.) Ŝaḣafé(m.) Ŝaḣafyyé(f) Ŝaḣafyeen(p)

journey(n.) riḣlé(s-f) riḣlét(p)

joy(n.) saĂadé(s-f) saĂadét(p) – faraḣ(s-m) afraḣ(p)

joyous(n.) mifréḣ(m) mifirḣa(f) mifrḣeen(p)

judge(n.) 'aĎé(m) 'aĎyé(f) 'ooĎat(p)

judgment(n.) ḣikm(s-m) aḣkém(p)

judicial(adj.) aĎa'é(m) 'aDa'yyé(f) 'aĎa'yyé(p)

juice(n.) ĂaŜeer(s-p-m)

July(n.) tammooz

jump(n.) naŤŤa(s-f) naŤŤat(p)

June(n.) ḣzairan

just(adj.) Ăadél(m) Ăadlé(f) Ădleen(p)

just(only) bass

justice(n.) Ăadl(s-p-m)

K

keen(adj.) mḣammas(m) mḣammasé(f) mḣammaseen(p)

keeper(adj.) ḣarés(m) ḣarsé(f) ḣirras(p)

kernel(n.) ḣabbé(s-f) ḣboob(p)

kettle(n.) bree'(s-m) bir'an(p) – also 'ibir'a(p)

key(n.) miftéḣ(s-m) mféteeḣ(p)

keyboard(n.) (same)

kick(n.) labŤa(s-f) labŤat(p)

kid(n.) Ťifl(m) Ťiflé(f) aŤfél(p)

kilometer(n.) (same)

kind(n.) noĂ(s-m) anwéĂ(p)

kind(adj.) laŤeef(m) laŤeefé(f) laŤeefeen(p)

kindergarten(n.) (same)

kindly(n.) looŤfan

kindness(n.) looŤf(s-p-m)

king(n.) malak(s-m) mlook(p)

kingdom(n.) mamlaké(s-f) mamélék(p;)

kiss(n.) bawsé(s-f) bawsét(p)

kitchen(n.) maŤbaḰ(s-m) maŤabéḰ(p)

knee(n.) rikbé(s-f) rikab(p)

kneeling(n.) rkooĂ(s-p-m)

knife(n) sikkeen(s-f) skékeen(p)

knight(n.) ferés(s-m) firsén(p)

knock(n) da''a(s-f) da''at(p)

knocking(n.) da'(s-p-m)

knot(n.) Ăi'dé(s-f) Ăi'ad(p)

knowledge(n.) maĂrfé(s-f) maĂaréf(p)

L

labor(n.) Ăamal(s-p-m)

laboratory(n.) mooḰtabar(s-m) mooḰtabarat(p)

lace(n.) shreeŤ(s-m) shrayéŤ(p)

lady(n.) sitt(s-f) sittét(p)

lake(n.) booḣaira(s-f) booḣairat(p)

lamp(n.) (same) – Ďaw(s-m) iĎwyé(p)

land(n.) arĎ(s-f) araĎé(p)

landing(n.) hoobooŤ(s-p-m)

language(n.) liŘŘa(s-f) liŘŘat(p)

lap(n.) ḣiĎn(s-m) aḣĎan(p)

laptop(n.) (same)

large(adj.) kbeer(m) kbeeré(f) kbar(p)

laser(n.) (same)

last(adj.) 'éḰér(m-f-s-p) – aḰeer(m) aḰeera(f) aḰeereen(p)

latch(n.) shankal(s-m) shanékél(p)

late(adj.) m'aḰḰar(m) m'aḰḰra(f) m'aḰḰreen(p)

lately(n.) moo'aḰḰaran(p)

lateral(adj.) génibé(m) génibyyé(f) génibyyeen(p)

Latin(adj.) létiné(m) létinyyé(f) lateen(p)

Ă= Augh in bought	Ď= a heavy D	É= like A in Bay	G= G in beige	ḣ= like an H with smaller air passage	I= I as in ink	Ḱ= like ch in Irish loch
O= O as in home	OO= as in boots	R= roll the rrr	Ť= a heavy T	Ř= like a French R (gargle it)	Ŝ= a heavy S	Ź= a heavy Z

latter(adj.) aǨeer(m) aǨeera(f)
aǨeereen(p)

laugh(n.) Ďiñké(s-f) Ďiñkét(p)

laughter(n.) Ďiñk
laundering(n.) Řaseel(s-p-m)

laundry(n.) Řaseel(s-p-m)

lavish(adj.) fayéĎ(m) fayĎa(f)
fayDeen(p)

law(n.) 'anoon(s-m) 'wéneen(p)

lawful(adj.) 'anooné(m) 'anoonyyé(f)
'anoonyeen(p)

lawn(n.) ĥasheesh(s-p-m)

layer(n.) Ťab'a(s-f) Ťab'at(p)

lazy(adj.) kislén(m) kisléné(f)
kisléneen(p)

lead(mineral)(n.) rŜas(s-p-m)

lead(n.) mo'addimé(s-f) mo'addimét(p)

leader(adj.) ra'ees(m) ra'eesé(f)
roo'asa(p) – zaĂeem(m) zaĂeemé(f)
zooAama(p)

leadership(n.) ri'ésé(s-f) ri'ését(p) –
zaĂamé(s-f) zaAamét(p)

leaf(n.) war'a(s-f) wara'(p)

lean(adj.) Ťaré(m) Ťaryyé(f) Ťraya(p)

leap(n.) naŤTa(s-f) naŤTat(p)

least(adj.) 'a'all

leather(n.) gild(s-m) glood(p)

lecture(n.) mooĥaĎara(s-f)
mooĥaĎarat(p)

left(n.) shmél

leg(n.) igir(s-f) igrén(p)

legal(adj.) sharĂé(m) sharĂyyé(f)
sharĂyyé(p) – 'anooné(m) 'anoonyyé(f)
'anoonyyé(p)

legend(n.) isŤoora(s-f) asaŤeer(p)

legitimate(adj.) sharĂé(m) sharĂyyé(f)
sharĂyyé(p) – 'anooné(m) 'anoonyyé(f)
'anoonyyé(p)

leisure(n.) wa't L faraŘ(s-m) aw'at L
faraŘ(p)

lemon(n.) laymoon(s-p-m)

lemonade(n.) (same)

length(n.) Ťool(s-m) aŤwél(p)

lens(n.) Ăadasé(s-f) Ăadsét(p)

lesbian(adj.) (same)

less(n.) 'a'all

lesson(n.) dars(s-m) droos(p)

letter(n.) risélé(s-f) raséyél(p)

level(n.) daragé(s-f) daragét(p)

liable(adj.) mas'ool(m) mas'oolé(f)
mas'ooleen(p)

liar(adj.) kizzéb(m) kizzébé(f)
kizzébeen(p)

liberal(adj.) libéralé(m) libéralyyé(f)
libéralyyeen(p) – ĥirr(m) ĥirra(f) aĥrar(p)

liberty(n.) ĥirryyé(s-f) ĥirryyét(p)

library(n.) maktabé(s-f) maktabét(p)

license(n.) riǨŜa(s-f) riǨaŜ(p)

lieutenant(n.) (same)

life(n.) ĥayét(s-p-f)

lift(n.) (same)

light(n.) Ďaw(s-m) iĎwyé(p)

light(adj.) Ǩafeef(m) Ǩafeefé(f) Ǩféf(p)

lighthouse(n.) manara(s-f) manarat(p)

lighting(n.) iDa'a(s-p-f)

lightning(n.) lamĂ(s-p-m)

likable(adj.) byinĥabb(m) btinĥabb(f)
byinĥabboo(p)

like(n.) mitl

likely(n.) Ăal argaĥ

likeness(n.) shabah(s-p-m)

limb(n.) Ťaraf(s-m) aŤraf(p)

limit(n.) ĥad(s-m) ĥdood(p)

line(n.) ǨaŤ(s-m) ǨŤoot(p)

linen(n.) 'mésh(s-m) a'mishé(p)

lining(n.) tilbeesé(s-f) tilbeesét(p)

link(n.) rabéŤ(s-m) rawabéŤ(p)

lion(n.) asad(s-m) asood(p)

lip(n.) shiffé(s-f) shféf(p)

liquid(n.) sé'él(s-m) sawé'él(p)

liquor(n.) mashroob(s-m) mashroobét(p)
– (same)

list(n.) leesta(s-f) leestét(p)
listening(n.) samaĂ

liter(n.) (same)

literary(adj.) adabé(m) adabyyé(f)
adabyyé(p)

literature(n.) adab(s-m) 'édéb(p)

little(adj.) ŜŘeer(m) ŜŘeeré(f) ŜŘar(p)

live(adj.) ĥay(m) ĥayyé(f) aĥyé'(p)

liver(n.) kibd(s-m) akbéd(p)

load(n.) ĥiml(s-m) aĥmél(p)

loan(n.) arĎ(s-m) 'oorooĎ(p)

local(adj.) maĥallé(m) maĥallyyé(f)
maĥallyyeen(p)

location(n.) maw'aĂ(s-m) mawé'éĂ(p)

lock(n.) 'ifil(s-m) 'foolé(p)

log(n.) sigill(s-m) sigillét(p)

logic(n.) manŤé'(s-p-m)

logical(adj.) manŤi'é(m) manŤi'yyé(f)
manŤi'yyé(p)

loneliness(n.) wiĥdé(s-p-f)

lonely(adj.) waĥeed(m) waĥeedé(f)
waĥeedeen(p)

long(adj.) Ťaweel(m) Ťaweelé(f) Ťwal(p)

longing(n.) sho'

look(n.) naŹra(s-f) naŹrat(p)

loose(adj.) raǨoo(m) raǨwé(f)
raǨween(p)

lord(n.) rabb – iléh

loss(n.) Ǩsara(s-f) Ǩaséyér(p) (also
Ǩsarat-p)

lost(adj.) ĎayéĂ(m) ĎayĂa(f)
ĎayĂeen(p)

lot(n.) séĥa(s-f) séĥat(p)

lotion(n.) (same)

loud(adj.) Ăélé(m) Ăélyé(f) Ăélyeen(p)

love(n.) ĥibb(s-p-m)

low(adj.) waŤé(m) waŤyé(f) waŤyeen(p)

Ă= Augh in bought	Ď= a heavy D	É= like A in Bay	G= G in beige	ĥ= like an H with smaller air passage	I= I as in ink	Ǩ= like ch in Irish loch
O= O as in home	OO= as in boots	R= roll the rrr	Ť= a heavy T	Ř= like a French R (gargle it)	Ŝ= a heavy S	Ž= a heavy Z

loyal(adj.) ameen(m)ameené(f) ameeneen(p) – walé(m) walyyé(f) awlya(p)

loyalty(n.) walé'(s-m) walé'at(p)

lubrication(n) tizyeet(s-p-m)

luck(n.) ḣaŹ(s-m) ḣŹooŹ(p)

lucky(adj.) maḣŹooŹ(s-m) maḣŹooŹa(f) maḣŹooŹeen(p)

luggage(n.) shanta(s-f) shanat(p)

luminous(adj.) mnawwar(m) mnawra(f) mnawreen(p)

lump(n.) waram(s-m) awram(p)

lung(n.) reeyé(s-f) rwéya(p)

luxurious(adj.) faḰm(m.) faḰmé(f) faḰmeen(p) – raḰm(m) raḰmé(f) raḰmeen(p)

luxury(n.) faḰamé(s-p-f) – raḰamé(s-p-f)

M

machine(n.) makana(s-f) makanét(p)

mad(adj.) magnoon(m) magnooné(f) mgéneen(p)

madam(n.) (same)

madness(n.) gnoon(s-p-m)

magazine(n.) magallé(s-f) magallét(p)

magnetic(adj.) maŘnaŤeesé(m) maŘnaŤeesyyé(f) maŘnaŤeesyyé(p)

magnificent(adj.) ra'iĂ(m) ra'iĂa(f) ra'iĂeen(p)

maid(n.) ŜanĂa(s-f) ŜanĂat(p)

mail(n.) bareed(s-p-m)

main(adj.) asésé(s-m) asésyyé(f) asésyyé(p)

mainatenance(n.) Ŝiyéné(s-f) Ŝiyénét(p)

majesty(n.) faḰamé(s-f) faḰamét(p)

majority(n.) aktaryyé(s-p-f)

male(n.) dakar(s-m) dkoora(p)

man(n.) riggél(s-m) rgél(p)

management(n.) 'idara(s-f) 'idarat(p)

manager(n.) moodeer(m) moodeera(f) moodara(p)

manicure(n.) (same)

mankind(n.) bashar(s-p-m)

manner(n.) Ťaree'a(s-f) Ťoro'(p)

manners(n.) aḰlé'(s-p-f)

manufacturer(n.) maŜnaĂ(s-m) maŜanéĂ(p) – mŜannéĂ(m) mŜannĂa(f) mŜannĂeen(p)

manuscript(n.) maḰŤooŤa(s-m) maḰŤooŤat(p)

many(n.) kteer

map(n.) ḰareeŤa(s-f) ḰarayéŤ(p)

March(n.) adar(s-m)

march(n.) maseera(s-f) maseerat(p)

margin(n.) ḣadd(s-m) ḣdood(p) – Ťaraf(s-m) aŤraf(p)

mark(n.) Ăalémé(s-f) Ăalémét(p)

market(n.) soo'(s-m) aswé'(p)

marketing(n.) taswee'(s-p-m)

marriage(n.) zawég(s-m) zawégét(p)

marvelous(adj.) ra'iĂ(m) ra'iĂa(f) ra'iĂeen(p)

masculine(adj.) mozakkar(s-p-m)

mask(n.) (same)

mason(adj.) binné'(m) binné'a(f) binné'een(p)

mass(n.) kitlé(s-f) kital(p)

mast(n.) séryé(s-f) sawéré(p)

master(n.) sayyéd(s-m) asyéd(p)

material(n.) méddé(s-f) mawéd(p)

maternal(adj.) 'moomé(s-p-f)

mathematics(n.) ḣséb(s-p-m) – (same)

matter(n.) méddé(s-f) mawéd(p)

mattress(n.) farshé(s-f) farshét(p)

mature(adj.) béléŘ(m) bélŘa(f) bélŘeen(p)

maximum(n.) (same)

May(n) ayyar(m)

mayor(n.) miḰtar(s-m) mḰéteer(p)

meal(n.) wa'Ăa(s-f) wa'Ăat(p)

mean(adj.) la'eem(m) la'eemé(f) loo'ama(p)

meaning(n.) maĂna(s-m) maĂané(p)

means(n.) waseelé(s-f) waséyél(p)

meanwhile(n.) bi hal asné'

meat(n.) laḣm(s-p-m)

mechanic(adj.) mikaneeké(m) mikaneekyyé(f) mikaneekyyé(p)

mechanical(adj.) mikaneeké(m) mikaneekyyé(f) mikaneekyyé(p)

medal(n.) meedélyyé(s-f) meedélyyét(p) – wisam(s-m) awsimé(p)

medical(adj.) Ťibbé(s-m) Ťibbyyé(f) Ťibbyyé(p)

medicine(n.) Ťibb(s-p-m)

mediocre(adj.) mitwaĎéĂ(m) mitwaĎĂa(f) mitwaĎĂeen(p)

mediocrity(n.) tawaĎoĂ(s-p-m)

mediation(n.) tawassoŤ(s-m) tawassoŤat(p)

medium(n.) wasaŤ(s-m) wasaŤ(p)

meeting(n.) igtiméĂ(s-m) igtiméĂat(p)

member(n.) ĂḋOo(m) ĂooĎwé(f) aĂĎa'(p)

memory(n.) zékra(s-f) zékrat(p)

mental(adj.) fikré(m) fikryyé(f) fikryyé(p)

menu(n.) (same)

merchandise(n.) bĎaĂa(s-p-f)

merchant(n.) byyéĂ(m) byyéĂa(f) byyéĂeen(p)

merciful(adj.) raḣoom(m) raḣoomé(f) raḣoomeen(p)

merciless(adj.) bala raḣmé(s-p-m-f)

mercury(n.) zaiba'(s-p-m)

mercy(n.) raḣmé(s-f) raḣmét(p)

merry(adj.) mabsooŤ(m) mabsooŤa(f) mabsooŤeen(p) – saĂeed(m) saĂeedé(f) saŜeedeen(p)

message(n.) risélé(s-f) raséyél(p)

messenger(n.) rasool(s-m) risol(p)

metal(n.) maĂdan(s-m) maĂadén(p;)

Ă= Augh in bought	Ď= a heavy D	É= like A in Bay	G= G in beige	ḣ= like an H with smaller air passage	I= I as in ink	Ḱ= like ch in Irish loch
O= O as in home	OO= as in boots	R= roll the rrr	Ť= a heavy T	Ř= like a French R (gargle it)	Ŝ= a heavy S	Ź= a heavy Z

metallic(adj.) maĂdané(m) maĂdanyyé(f) maĂdanyyé(p)

meter(n.) Ăiddéd(s-m) Ăiddédét(p)

method(n.) Ťaree'a(s-f) Ťiro'(p)

metropolis(n.) madeené(s-f) midon(p) – manŤa'a(s-f) manaŤé'(p)

microphone(n.) (same)

microwave(n.) (same)

middle(n.) waŜat(s-m) awŜat(p) – niŜŜ(s-p-m)

midnight(n.) niŜŜ L lél(s-m) nŜaŜ L lyélé(p)

might(n.) 'idra(s-f) 'idrat(p) – 'oowwé(s-f) 'oowwét(p)

mighty(adj.) adeer(m) adeera(f) adeereen(p) – awé(m) awyyé(f) 'wéya(p)

mild(adj.) Ќafeef(m) Ќafeefé(f) Ќféf(p)

military(n.) Ăaskaryyé(s-p-f)

milk(n.) ĥaleeb(s-p-m)

mill(n.) Ťaĥooné(s-f) Ťawaĥeen(p)

million(n.) (same)

millionaire(adj.) (same)

mind(n.) Ăa'l(s-m) Ă'ool(p) – dméŘ(s-m) admiŘa(p)

mine(n.) manjam(s-m) manéjém(p)

mineral(n.) amléĥ(s-p-f)

minimum(adj.) (same)

minister(n.) wazeer(m) wazeera(f) woozara(p)

ministry(n.) wizara(s-f) wizarat(p)

minor(adj.) 'aŜér(m) 'aŜra(f) 'aŜreen(p)

minority(n.) 'a'allyyé(s-f) 'a'allyyet(p)

minute(n.) da'ee'a(s-f) da'ayé'(p)

minute(adj.) ŜŘeer(m) ŜŘeeré(f) ŜŘar(p)

miracle(n.) Ăageebé(s-f) Ăagéyéb(p)

mirror(n.) mréyé(s-f) mréyét(p)

miser(adj.) baЌeel(m) baЌeelé(f) booЌala(p)

miserable(adj.) yé'és(m) yé'sé(f) yé'seen(p) – ĥazeen(m) ĥazeené(f) ĥazeeneen(p)

misery(n.) ĥizn(s-m) aĥzén(p) – ya's(s-p-m)

misfortune(n.) soo' L ĥaŹ(s-m)

misprint(n.) ЌaŤa' maŤbaĂé(s-m) aЌŤa' maŤbaĂyyé(p)

Miss(n.) (same)

mission(n.) mahammé(s-f) mahammét(p)

missionary(n.) irsélyyé(s-f) irsélyyét(p)

mist(n.) Ďabéb(s-p-m) – ŘťayŤa(s-p-f)

mistake(n.) ŘalaŤ(s-m) aŘlaŤ(p) – Ќaťa'(s-m) aЌTa'(p)

Mister(n.) (same) – sayyéd(s-m) sédé(p)

mistrust(n.) shakk(s-m) shkook(p)

mistrustful(adj.) shikkék(m) shikkéké(f) shikkékeen(p)

misunderstanding(n.) soo' tafahom(s-p-m)

misuse(n.) isé'ét istiĂmél(s-p-f)

mix(n.) KaleeŤ(s-p-m)

mixture(n.) KaleeŤ(s-p-m)

mob(n.) ĂiŜabé(s-f) ĂiŜabét(p)

mobile(adj.) mitHarrék(m) mitĥarrké(f) mitĥarkeen(p)

mobility(n.) ĥaraké(s-p-f)

mobilization(n.) tiĥreek(s-p-m)

mockery(n.) siЌryé(s-f) siЌryét(p)

mode(n.) (same)

model(n.) (same) – noĂ(s-m) anwéĂ(p)

moderate(adj.) miĂtidél(m) miĂtidlé(f) miĂtidleen(p)

moderation(n.) iĂtidél(s-m)

modern(adj.) mitŤawwar(m) mitŤawra(f) mitŤawreen(p) – (same)

modest(adj.) mitwaĎaĂ(m) mitwaĎĂa(f) mitwaĎĂeen(p)

modesty(n.) tawaĎoĂ(s-p-m)

modification(n.) taĂdeel(s-m) taĂdeelét(p)

moist(adj.) mraŤŤab(m) mraŤŤabé(f) mraŤŤabeen(p)

moment(n.) laĥŹa(s-f) laĥŹat(p)

monarchy(n.) malakyyé(s-f) malakyyét(p)

monastery(n.) dér(s-m) adyira(p)

Monday(n.) tanén

money(n.) maŜaré(s-p-f) – floos(s-p-f) – Ăimlé(s-p-f)

monk(n.) rahéb(s-m) rihbén(p)

monkey(n.) siĂdén(m) siĂdéné(f) sĂédeen(p)

monologue(n.) (same)

monopoly(n.) (same) – iĥtikar(s-m) iĥtikarat(p)

monotonous(adj.) (same)

monotony(n.) (same) – tikrar momill(s-p-m)

monster(n.) waĥsh(m) waĥshé(f) wĥoosh(p)

monstrosity(n.) waĥshyyé(s-f) waĥshyyét(p)

monstrous(adj.) waĥshé(m) waĥshyyé(f) waĥshyyé(p)

month(n.) shahr(s-m) ash-hor(p)

monthly(adj.) shahré(m) shahryyé(f) shahryyé(p)

monument(n.) timsél(s-m) tméseel(p) – na'sh(s-m) no'oosh(p)

monumental(adj.) ĎaЌm(m) ĎaЌmé(f) ĎaЌmeen(p)

mood(n.) (same)

moody(adj.) mit'alléb(m) mit'allbé(f) mit'allbeen(p)

moon(n.) 'amar(s-m) 'a'mar(p)

moonlight(n.) Ďaw L 'amar(s-m)

mop(n.) mamsaĥa(s-f) maméséĥ(p)

moral(adj.) aЌlé'é(m) aЌlé'yyé(f) aЌlé'yyé(p)

morality(n.) aЌlé'(s-p-f)

morals(n.) aЌlé'(s-p-f)

more(n.) aktar

morning(n.) Ŝibĥ(s-m)

mortal(adj.) féné(m) fényé(f) fényeen(p)

Ă= Augh in bought	Ď= a heavy D	É= like A in Bay	G= G in beige	ĥ= like an H with smaller air passage	I= I as in ink	Ќ= like ch in Irish loch
O= O as in home	OO= as in boots	R= roll the rrr	Ť= a heavy T	Ř= like a French R (gargle it)	Ŝ= a heavy S	Ź= a heavy Z

mortal(lethal)(adj.) ʻatél(m) ʻatlé(f) ʻatleen(p)

mortgage(n.) iŜŤ(s-m) ʻaʼŜaŤ(p)

mosque(n.) géméĂ(s-m) gawéméĂ(p) – masgéd(s-m) maségéd(p)

mosquito(n.) barŘashé(s-f) barŘash(p)

moth(n.) Ăit(s-p-m)

mother(n.) imm(s-f) immét(p)

mother in law(n.) ĥama(s-f) ĥamawét(p)

motion(n.) ĥaraké(s-f) ĥarakét(p)

motive(n.) déféĂ(s-m) dawéféĂ(p)

motor(n.) (same)

mountain(n.) gabal(s-m) gbél(p)

mourning(n.) naĥeeb(s-p-m)

mouse(n.) far(m) fara(f) feeran(p)

mouth(n.) timm(s-m) tmém(p)

movable(adj.) mitĥarrék(m) mitĥarrké(f) mitĥarkeen(p)

move(n.) naʼlé(s-f) naʼlét(p)

movement(n.) ĥaraké(s-f) ĥarakét(p)

movies(n.) (same) – cinema(s-f) cinamét(p)

mud(n.) waĥl(s-m) wĥool(p)

muddy(adj.) mwaĥĥal(m) mwaĥĥlé(f) mwaĥHleen(p)

mule(n.) baŘl(s-m) bŘal(p)

multiple(n.) Ăiddé

multitude(n.) kammyyé kbeeré(s-f) kammyyét kbeeré(p)

municipal(adj.) baladé(m) baladyyé(f) baladyyé(p)

municipality(n.) baladyyé(s-f) baladyyét(p)

munitions(n.) sléĥ(s-p-m) – Ăitéd(s-p-m)

murmur(n.) (same) – hamdara(s-p-f)

muscle(n.) ĂaĎalé(s-f) ĂaĎalét(p)

museum(n.) matĥaf(s-m) matéĥéf(p)

mushroom(n.) fiŤr(s-p-m) – (same)

music(n.) moosiʼa(s-p-f)

musical(adj.) moosiʼé(m) moosiʼyyé(f) moosiʼyyeen(p)

musician(adj.) moosiʼar(m-f) moosiʼaryyé(P)

must lézém

mustard(n.) (same)

mute(adj.) aḰras(m) Ḱarsa(f) Ḱirsén(p)

myself(n.) ĥalé(m-f) – nafsé(m-f)

mysterious(adj.) ŘaméĎ(m) ŘamĎa(f) ŘamĎeen(p)

mystery(n.) laŘz(s-m) alŘaz(p) – ĥazzoora(s-f) ĥzézeer(p)

N

nail(n.) mismar(s-m) msémeer(p)

naïve(adj.) sézég(m) sézgé(f) sézgeen(p)

naked(adj.) mŹallaŤ(m) mŹallaŤa(f) mŹallaŤeen(p) – Ăiryén(m) Ăiryéné(f) Ăiryéneen(p)

Name(n.) ism(s-m) asmé'(p)

nap(n.) (same) - ŘaŤŤa(s-f) ŘaŤŤat(p) –

napkin(n.) maĥramé(s-f) maĥarém(p)

narrow(adj.) dayyé'(m) day'a(f) day'een(p)

nasty(adj.) wiséḰ(m) wisḰa(f) wisḰeen(p)

nation(n.) immé(s-f) imₐm(p)

national(adj.) Ăalamé(m) Ăalamyyé(f) Ăalamyyé(p)

nationality(n.) ginsyyé(s-f) ginsyyét(p)

nationalization(n.) Ăawlamé(s-p-f)

natural(adj.) ŤabeeĂé(m) ŤabeeĂyyé(f) ŤabeeĂyyé(p)

nature(n.) ŤabeeAa(s-f) Ťaba'éĂ(p)

naughty(adj.) azĂar(m) zaĂra(f) ziĂran(p)

nautical(adj.) baĥré(m) baĥryyé(f) baĥryyé(p)

naval(adj.) baĥré(m) baĥryyé(f) baĥryyé(p)

navy(n.) baĥryyé(s-p-f)

near ĥad

neat(adj.) nĎeef(m) nĎeefé(f) nĎaf(p)

neatness(n.) naĎafé(s-p-f)

necessary(adj.) Ďarooré(m) Ďarooryyé(f) Ďarooryyé(p)

necessity(n.) Ďaroora(s-f) Daroorat(p)

neck(n.) ra'bé(s-f) ra'bét(p)

necklace(n.) Ăa'd(s-m) Ă'ood(p)

necktie(n.) (same) - krafat

need(n.) ĥagé(s-f) ĥagét(p)

needle(n.) ibré(s-f) ibar(p)

needy(adj.) miĥtég(m) miĥtégé(f) miĥtégeen(p)

negative(adj.) salbé(m) salbyyé(f) salbyyé(p)

negotiation(n.) mséwamé(s-f) mséwamét(p)

neighbour(n) gar(m) gara(f) geeran(p)

neighbourhood(n.) geeré(s-p-f)

neon(n.) (same)

nephew(n.) look family in Leboland conversation

nerve(n.) ĂaŜab(s-m) aĂŜab(p)

nervous(adj.) ĂaSabé(m) ĂaŜabyyé(f) ĂaŜabyyé(p)

nest(n.) Ăish(s-m) Ăshésh(p)

net(n.) Ḱaimé(s-f) Ḱeeyam(p)

network(n.) shabaké(s-f) shabakét(p)

neutered(adj.) ḰaŜé(s-m) ḰiŜyén(p;)

never abadan

new(adj.) gdeed(m) gdeedé(f) gdéd(p)

news(n.) aḰbar(s-p-f)

newspaper(n.) gareedé(s-f) garayéd(p) – Ŝaĥeefé(s-f) Ŝoĥof(p)

next téné(m) tényé(f) tényeen(p)

nice(adj.) lateef(m) lateefé(f) lateefeen(p)

nickname(n) la'ab

niece(n) bint Ḱay (brother's daughter) bint iḰt (sister's daughter)

night(n) lél

Ă= Augh in bought	Ď= a heavy D	É= like A in Bay	G= G in beige	ĥ= like an H with smaller air passage	I= I as in ink	Ḱ= like ch in Irish loch
O= O as in home	OO= as in boots	R= roll the rrr	Ť= a heavy T	Ř= like a French R (gargle it)	Ŝ= a heavy S	Ž= a heavy Z

nightgown(n.) (same)

nightingale(n.) Ăandaleeb

nightmare(n.) kéboos

no l$_a$A

noble (same)

nobody(adj.) ma ĥada

noise(n.) Ď$_a$GGé, Ă$_a$G'a

noisy(adj.) ĂéGé'(m) ĂéG'a(f)
ĂéG'een(p)

nomination(n.) tirsheeĥ

nonsense(adj.) ma fee manté' (there's no
logic), or (same)

noon(n.) ĎuHr

normal(adj.) ŤabeeĂé(m) ŤabeeĂyé(f)
ŤabeeĂyé(p)

north(n.) shmél

northern(adj.) shmélé(m) shmélyé(f)
shmélyé(p)

northwest(n.) shmél Ř$_a$rb

nose(n.) minĶar

note(n.) (same), mulaĥaza(f)

notebook(n.) (same)

nothing(n.) ma shee

notion(n.) fikra(f), mabda'(m)

noun(n.) Aisim(m) AsméA(p)

nourishment(n.) ŘiZa(m)(p)

novel(adj.) Gdeed(m) Gdeedé(f) Gdéd(p)

November(n.) Tishreen tténé

now Hall$_a$'

nowadays Hal iyyém

nowhere wala maĥal

nuclear(adj.) nawawé

nude(n.) Ă$_i$ré(s-m)

numb(adj.) mnamm$_a$l(m) mnamlé(f)
mnamleen(p)

number(n.) r$_a$'m(m) Ar'am(p)

numbered(adj.) mr$_a$'am(m) mr$_a$'mé(f)
mr$_a$'meen(p)

nun(n.) raHbé(f) raHbét(p)

nurse(n.) mmarréĎ(m) mmarrĎa(f)
mmarrĎeen(p)

nursery(n.) ĥ$_a$Ďané(s-f)

O

oak(n.) ballooŤa(f) ballooŤ (p)

oath(n.) k$_a$Ŝ$_a$m

obedience(n.) ŤaĂ$_a$

obedient(adj.) m$_u$teeĂ(m) m$_u$teeĂa(f)
m$_u$teeĂeen(p)

objection(n.) iĂt$_i$raĎ(s-m)

objective(n.) Hadaf(m) Ahdéf(p)

obligatory(adj.) ilzémé(m) ilzémiyé(f)
ilzémiyé(p)

oblique(adj.) (same)

obscure(adj.) Řam$_e$Ď(m) ŘamĎ$_a$(f)
ŘamĎ$_a$(p)

obscurity(n.) ŘumooĎ(s-m)

observatory(n.) (same)

observer(n.) m$_u$ra'$_e$b(m) m$_u$ra'b$_é$(f)
m$_u$ra'been(p)

obstacle(n.) Ă$_a$'$_a$b$_é$(f) Ă$_a$'$_a$bét(f)

obvious(adj.) waĎ$_é$ĥ(m) waĎĥ$_a$(f)
waĎĥeen(p)

obviously(n.) Ť$_a$bĂ$_a$n

occasion(n.) m$_u$nés$_a$b$_é$(f) m$_u$nés$_a$bét(f)

occasionally Aĥyén$_a$n, Aw'at

occupation(n.) waŽeefé(f) waŽayéf(p)

ocean(n.) muĥeeŤ(s-m)

October(n.) Tishreen lAwwal

odd(adj.) m$_u$fr$_a$d(m) m$_u$fr$_a$dé (p)

odds(n.) ĥuŽooŽ(p)

odor(n.) reeĥa(f) rawéyéĥ(p)

offense(n.) G$_i$rm(m) Garayém(p)

offensive(adj.) Ă$_i$dé'$_é$(m) Ă$_i$dé'y$_é$(f)
Ă$_i$dé'y$_é$(p)

offer(n.) Ă$_a$rĎ(m) ĂrooĎ(p)

office(n.) makt$_a$b(m) makét$_e$b(p)

official(adj.) r$_a$sm$_é$(m) r$_a$smy$_é$(f) r$_a$smy$_é$(p)

oil(n.) zét(m) zyoot(p)

old(adj. for things) Ă$_a$tee'(m) Ă$_a$tee'$_a$(f)
Ă$_a$tee'$_a$(p)

old(adj. for people/anaimals) Ķ$_i$tyar(m)
Ķ$_i$tyar$_a$(f) Ķ$_i$tyéry$_é$ (p)

olive(n.) zaitoon(m-p)

once(n.) marr$_a$(s-f)

one(n.) wéĥéd(m) wiĥdé(f)

onion(n.) b$_a$Ŝ$_a$l

only b$_a$ss

open(adj.) m$_a$ftooĥ(m) m$_a$ftooĥ$_a$(f)
m$_a$ftooĥeen(p)

opening(n.) fatĥ$_a$(f) fatĥat(p)

opera(n.) (same)

operation(n.) Ăamaly$_é$(f) Ăamalyét(p)

opinion(n.) r$_a$'$_é$(m) 'éra'(p)

opponent(n.) Ķ$_a$Ŝm(m) ĶŜoom(p)

opportunity(n.) f$_i$rŜ$_a$(f) f$_i$r$_a$Ŝ(p)

opposite(n.) Ă$_a$ks

opposition(n.) mĂarĎ$_a$(s-f)

oppression(n.) k$_a$bt

optimism(n.) 'eegébyé

optimistic(adj.) m$_i$tshé'ém(m)
m$_i$tshé'mé(f) m$_i$tshé'meen(f)

or aou

orange (same)

orchestra (same)

order(command - n.) amr

ordinary(adj.) Ăadé(m) Ăadyyé(f)
Ăadyyé(p)
organ(n.) Ă$_i$Ďoo(m) AĂĎa'(p)

organization(n.) m$_u$'assasé(f)
m$_u$'assasét(p)

organized(adj.) mnaŽŽam(m)
mnaŽŽamé(m) mnaŽŽameen(p)

orient(n.) shar'

oriental(adj.) shar'é(m) shar'yyé(f)
shar'yyé(p)

origin(n.) aŜl

Ă= Augh in bought	Ď= a heavy D	É= like A in Bay	G= G in beige	ĥ= like an H with smaller air passage	I= I as in ink	Ķ= like ch in Irish loch
O= O as in home	OO= as in boots	R= roll the rrr	Ť= a heavy T	Ř= like a French R (gargle it)	Ŝ= a heavy S	Ž= a heavy Z

original(adj.) aŜlé(m) aŜlyyé(f) aŜlyyé(p)

ornament (same)

orphan(adj.) yₐteem(m) yateemé(f) aytém(p)

other Řér

ought lézém

ounce (same)

out barra

outcome(n.) nateegé(f) natéyég(p)

outline (same)

outrage(n.) ŘaĎab

outside(n.) Barrₐ

oval(adj.) bₐyĎawₑ(m) bₐyĎawyyₑ(f) bₐyĎawyyₑ(p)

oven(n.) fᵢrn(m) afran(p)

over fo'

overflow(n.) fayeĎ

owner(eg. Realestate) (n.) Ŝaĥᵢb lmilk

ox(n.) tor

oxygen(n.) (same)

P

pacific ocean(n.) lmooĥeeŤ lhédₑ'

page(n.) Ŝafĥₐ(s) Ŝafĥat(p)

paint(n.) dhén(s-m)

pair(adj.) goz(s-m) agwéz(p)

paper(n.) war'ₐ(s-f) wra'(p)

paragraph(n.) (same)

park(n.) (same)

part(n.) gᵢz'(s-m) agzé'(p)

party(n.) ĥₐflₑ(s-f) ĥₐflét(p)

past(adj.) maĎé(s-m)

pattern(n.) nₐmₐŤ(s-m) anmaŤ(p)

people(n.) Ăalₐm(p)

prhaps yimkén
period(n.) middé(s-f)

person(n.) shaḰŜ(s-m) ashḰaŜ(p)

phrase(n.) gᵢmlé(s-f) gᵢmal(p)

picture(n.) Ŝoorₐ(s-f) Ŝoowₐr(p)

piece(n.) aŤĂₐ(s-f) 'iŤaĂ(p)

place(n.) mₐkén(s-m) amékₑn(p), mₐĥₐl(s-m) mₐĥₐllét(p)

plan(n.) ḰiŤŤₐ(s-f) ḰiŤŤₐŤ(p)

plane(n.) Ťyyarₐ(s-f) Ťyyarat(p)

plant(n.) nabté(s-f) nabét(p)

please (same)

plural(adj.) gₐmĂ

poem(n.) shᵢĂr(s-m) ashĂar(p)

point(n.) ni'Ťₐ(s-f) nᵢ'aŤ(p)

pole(n.) Ăₐmood(s-m) Ăwémed(p)

poor(n.) fa'eer(m) fa'eerₐ(f) fo'ₐrₐ(p)

position(n.) markaz(s-m) marakₑz(p)

possible(adj.) momkén, maĂ'ool

power(n.) 'oowé(s-f)

practice(n.) timreen(s-m) tamareen(p)

prepared(adj.) mĥaĎar(m) mĥaĎrₐ(f) mĥaĎreen(p)

president(n.) ra'ees(m) ra'eesé(f) roo'asa(p)

pretty(adj.) ĥᵢlo(m) ĥilwₑ(f) ĥilween(p)

probably Ăal argaĥ

problem(n.) mashkₐl(s-m) mashékₑl(p)

product(n.) mₒₒntag(s-m) mₒₒntagét(p)

property(n.) milkyé(s-f) amlék(p)

Q

quarry(n.) mₐ'lₐĂ(s-m) ma'éléĂ(p)

quality(n.) (same)

quantity(n.) kammiyₑ(s-f) kammiyét(p)

quarter(n.) ribĂ(s-m) arbéĂ(p)

queen(n.) malké(s-f) malkét(p)

question(n.) soo'él(s-m) as'ilₑ(p)

quickly(adv.) bsirĂₐ

quiet(adj.) rayé'(m) ray'ₐ(f) ray'een(p)

R

race(n.) Ăᵢr'(s-m) Ăₒₒroo'(p)

radio(n.) (same)

rain(n.) shité(s-m)

ready(adj.) géhₑz(m) géhzₑ(f) géhzeen(p)

really gₐd

reason(n.) sₐbₐb(s-m) asbéb(p)

record(n.) sigill(s-m) sigillét(p)

red(n.) aĥmₐr(m) ĥamrₐ(f) ĥᵢmᵢr(p)

region(n.) mₐnŤₐ'ₐ(s-f) mₐnaŤé'(p)

repeated(adj.) mkarrₐr(m) mkarrₐrₐ(f) mkarrₐreen(p)

report(n.) ti'reer(s-m) tₐ'areer(p)

resentment(n.) 'istiyé'(s-m)

rest(n.) raĥₐ(s-f)

result(n.) nₐteegₑ(s-f) natéyég(p)

rhythm(n.) 'iḰaĂ(s-m)

rich(adj.) Řané(m) Řanyyé(f) aŘnya(p)

right *(vs. left)* yameen

ring(n.) Ḱatₑm(s-m) Ḱawétₑm(p)

river(n.) nₐhr(s-m) anhar(p)

road(n.) Ťaree'(s-m) Ťₒrₒ'(p)

rock(n.) ŜₐḰrₐ(s-f) ŜḰoor(p)

room(n.) Řᵢrfé(s-f) Řᵢrₐf(p)

root(n.) shilsh(s-m) shloosh(p)

rope(n.) ĥabl(s-m) ĥbél(p)

rose(n.) wₐrdé(s-f) wrood(p)

round(adj.) mdₐwwₐr(m) mdₐuwrₐ(f) mdₐwreen(p)

row(n.) Ŝₐf(s-m) Ŝfoof(p)

rule(n.) 'aĂdₑ(s-f) 'awéĂₑd(p)

S

safe(adj.) 'émén(m) 'émné(f) 'émneen(p)

Ă= Augh in bought	Ď= a heavy D	É= like A in Bay	G= G in beige	ĥ= like an H with smaller air passage	I= I as in ink	Ḱ= like ch in Irish loch
O= O as in home	OO= as in boots	R= roll the rrr	Ť= a heavy T	Ř= like a French R (gargle it)	Ŝ= a heavy S	Ž= a heavy Z

sail(n.) sh$_i$raĂ(s-m) ahr$_i$Ă$_a$(p)

same(adj.) nafs

sand(n.) raml(s-m) rmél(p)

saw(n.) m$_i$nshar(s-m) mnésheer(p)

scale(n.) mi'yés(s-m) m$_a$'éyees(p)

school(n.) madras$_e$(s-f) madérés(p)

science(n.) Ă$_i$lm(s-m) Ă$_{oo}$loom(p)

scientist(n.) Ăal$_e$m(m) Ăalm$_e$(f) Ă$_{oo}$l$_a$m$_a$(p)

sea(n.) baĥr(s-m) bĥoor(p)

seat(n.) m$_a$'Ă$_a$d(m) m'aĂéd(p)

second(n.) téné(m) tényé(f)

section(n.) '$_i$Ŝm(s-m) '$_a$'Ŝ am(p)

seed(n.) b$_i$zr$_e$(s-f) b$_{oo}$zoor(p)

sense(n.) ĥéss$_e$(s-f) ĥawés(p)

sentence(n.) g$_i$mlé(s-f) g$_i$m$_a$l(p)

set(n.) Ť$_a$'m(s-m)

seven(n.) s$_a$bĂ$_a$

shape(n.) shakl(s-m) ashkél(p)

sharp(adj.) ĥ$_a$dd(m) ĥ$_a$dd$_e$(f) ĥ$_a$ddeen(p)

ship(n.) béĶr$_a$(s-f) b$_a$wéĶér(p)

shoe(n.) ĥizé'(s-m) aĥzyi$_e$(p)

shop(n.) m$_a$ĥ$_a$l(s-m) m$_a$ĥ$_a$llét(p), d$_i$kkén(s-m) dkékeen(p)

short(adj.) aŜeer(m) aŜeer$_a$(f) 'Ŝar(p)

shoulder(n.) k$_i$t$_i$f(s-m) ktéf(p)

show(n.) Ă$_a$rĎ(s-m) ĂrooĎ(p)

side(n.) Ťaraf(s-m) aŤraf(p)

sight(n.) naŽar(s-m)

sign(n.) Ă$_a$lém$_e$(s-f) Ăalémét(p)

signal(n.) '$_i$shara(s-f) '$_i$sharat(p)

silent(adj.) Ŝam$_e$t(m) Ŝamt$_a$(f) Ŝamteen(p)

similar(adj.) m$_i$t$_i$l

simple(adj.) b$_a$ŜeeŤ(m) b$_a$ŜeeŤ$_a$(f) b$_a$Ŝeeteen(p)

sir(n.) (same)

sister(n.) '$_i$Ķt(s-f) '$_i$Ķwét(p)

six(n.) sitté

size(n.) ĥagm(s-m) aĥgém(p)

skin(n.) g$_i$ld(s-m) glood(p)

sky(n.) s$_a$m$_a$(s-f) s$_a$m$_a$wét(p)

sleep(n.) nom(s-m)

slowly(adv.) Ă$_a$l h$_a$d$_a$, shw$_a$y shw$_a$y

small(adj.) ŜŘeer(m) ŜŘeer$_e$(f) ŜŘar(p)

smell(n.) reeĥ$_a$(s-f) rawéy$_e$ĥ(p)

smile(n.) b$_a$sm$_e$(s-f) b$_a$smét(p)

snow(n.) t$_a$lg(s-m) tloog(p)

so l$_a$k$_a$n

soft(adj.) néĂ$_e$m(m) néĂm$_e$(f) néĂmeen(p)

soil(n.) trab(s-m) atr$_i$b$_e$(p)

soldier(n.) g$_i$ndé(m) g$_i$ndyyé(f) gnood(p)

solution(n.) ĥ$_a$l(s-m) ĥlool(p)

some b$_a$ĂĎ

someone(n.) ĥ$_a$d$_a$(s-m)

something(n.) shee(s-m) '$_i$shya(p)

sometimes(n.) auw'at

son(n.) '$_i$bn(s-m) abné'(p)

song(n.) Řinnyyé(s-f) aŘané(p)

soon areeb$_a$n

sound(n.) ŜauwŤ(s-m) aŜwat(p)

south(n.) gnoob(s-m)

southern(adj.) gnoobé(m) gnoobyyé(f)(p)

space(n.) faĎa(s-m)

special(adj.) ĶaŜ(m) ĶaŜŜ$_a$(f) ĶaŜŜeen(p)

speed(n.) sirĂ$_a$(s-f) sirĂat(p)

spring *(season)* **(n.)** rabeeĂ(s-m)

square(n.) m$_{oo}$r$_a$bbaĂ(s-m) m$_{oo}$r$_a$bb$_a$Ăat(p)

star(n.) nigmé(s-f) ngoom(p)

start(n.) b$_i$déyé(s-f) b$_i$déyét(p)

state(n.) w$_i$léy$_e$(s-f) w$_i$léyét(p)

step(n.) Ķ$_i$Ťw$_e$(s-f) Ķ$_i$twét(p)

stone(n.) ĥagar(s-m) ĥgar(p)

stop (same)

store(n.) *(see shop)*

story(n.) 'iŜŜ$_a$(s-f) 'iŜaŜ(p)

straight(adj.) gél$_e$s(m) gél$_e$(f) gélseen(p)

strange(adj.) Ř$_a$reeb(m) Ř$_a$reebé(f) Ř$_a$reebeen(p)

stream(n.) m$_a$gr$_a$(s-m)

street(n.) Ť$_a$ree'(s-m) Ť$_o$ro'(p)

string(n.) ĶéŤ(s-m) ĶyooŤ(p)

strong(adj.) awé(m) awyyé(f) 'wéya(p)

student(n.) tilmeez(m) tilmeezé(f) tlémeez(p)

subject(n.) mauwĎooĂ(m) mwaĎeeĂ(p)

substance(n.) médd$_e$(s-f) mawéd(p)

suddenly(adv.) f$_a$g'$_a$

sugar(n.) sikkar(s-m)

sum(n.) magmooĂ(s-m)

summer(n.) Ŝéf(s-m)

sun(n.) shams(s-f) shmoos(p)

sure akeed

surface(n.) S$_a$Ťĥ(s-m) ŜŤooĥ(p)

surprise(n.) mfég'$_a$(s-f) mfég'at(p)

symbol(n.) r$_a$mz(s-m) rmooz(p)

system(n.) n$_i$Žam(s-m) anŽ$_i$m$_e$(p)

T

table(n.) Ťawl$_a$(s-f) Tawlét(p)

tail(n.) danab(s-m) adnéb(p)

tall(adj.) Ť$_a$weel(m) Ť$_a$weel$_e$(f) Twal(p)

teacher(n.) istéz(m) asétz$_e$(p-m) mĂalm$_e$(f) mĂlmét(p-f)

team(n.) f$_a$ree'(s-m) f$_i$r$_a$'(p)

temperature(n.) ĥ$_a$rar$_a$(s-f)

ten(n.) Ă$_a$shra

test(n.) faĥŜ(s-m), '$_i$mt$_i$ĥan(s-m) '$_i$mt$_i$ĥanét(p)

Ă= Augh in bought	**Ď**= a heavy D	**É**= like A in Bay	**G**= G in beige	**ĥ**= like an H with smaller air passage		**I**= I as in ink	**Ķ**= like ch in Irish loch
O= O as in home	**OO**= as in boots	**R**= roll the rrr	**Ť**= a heavy T	**Ř**= like a French R (gargle it)		**Ŝ**= a heavy S	**Ž**= a heavy Z

that haydék(m) haydeeké(f) hauwdeek(p)

there hauwneek

these hauwdé(p)

thick(adj.) smeek(m) smeeké(f) smék(p)

thin(adj.) r$_a$feeĂ(m) r$_a$feeĂ$_a$(f) rféĂ(p)

thing(n.) shee(s-m) '$_i$shy$_a$(p)

third(adj.) tél$_é$t(m) télt$_e$(f) télteen(p)

this(n.) hayda(m) haydé(f)

those(n.) hauwdeek(p)

thousand(n.) alf(s-m) 'loof(p)

three(n.) tlét$_é$

tied(adj.) marbooŤ(m) marbooŤ$_a$(f) marbooteen(p)

time(n.) wa't(s-m) aw'at(p)

tiny(adj.) ŜŘeer(m) ŜŘeer$_e$(f) ŜŘar(p)

today(n.) l-yom

together(n.) m$_a$Ă b$_a$ĂĎ

tone *(of voice)*(n.) n$_a$br$_a$(s-f) n$_a$brat(p)

too k$_a$mén

tool(n.) 'élé(s-f) 'élét(p)

total(n.) magmooĂ(s-m)

toward(adj.) Ŝob, naĥ$_{oo}$

town(n.) Ďay Ă$_a$ (s-f) Ďiy$_a$Ă(p)

trade(n.) m$_i$hné(s-f) m$_i$h$_a$n(p)

train(n.) (same)

tree(n.) sh$_a$gr$_a$(s-m) ashgar(p)

triangle(n.) mtallat(p)

trip(n.) r$_i$ĥl$_e$(s-f) r$_i$ĥlét(p)

truck(n.) (same)

true(adj.) Saĥ

tube(n.) '$_i$nboob(s-m) anabeeb(p)

turn(n.) kooĂ(s-m)

two(n.) tnén

type(n.) noĂ(s-m) anwéĂ(p)

U

Uncle *(from the father's side)*(n.) Ă$_a$m(s-m) Ămoom(p)

Uncle *(from the mother's side)*(n.) Ḱal(s-m) Ḱwél(p)

under taĥt

understood(adj.) m$_a$fhoom(m) m$_a$fhoomé(f) m$_a$fhoomeen(p)

unit(n.) (same)

until ĥatt$_a$

up f$_o$'

use(n.) '$_i$st$_i$Ămél(s=m) 'istiĂmélét(p)

usually Ăad$_a$t$_a$n

V

valley(n.) wédé(s-m) widyén(p)

value(n.) 'eem$_e$(s-f) 'eemét(p)

verb(n.) fiĂl(s-m) afĂal(p)

very kteer

victory(n.) naŜr(s-m), '$_i$nt$_i$Ŝar(s-m) '$_i$nt$_i$Ŝarat(p)

view(n.) m$_a$nŽ$_a$r(s-m) manaŽ$_é$r(p)

village(n.) Ďay Ă$_a$(s-f) Ďyy$_a$Ă(p)

visit(n.) ziar$_a$(s-f) ziarat(p)

voice(n.) ŜoŤ(s-m) aŜwaŤ(p)

W

wait(n.) N$_a$Ťr$_a$(s-f) n$_a$ŤraŤ(p)

wall(n.) ĥéŤ(s-m) ĥeeŤan(p)

war(n.) ĥarb(s-m) ĥroob(p)

warm(adj.) defé(m) défyé(f) défyeen(p)

watch(n.) séĂ$_a$(s-f) séAat(p)

water(n.) may(s-f)

wave(n.) mauwgé(s-f) mauwgét(p)

way(n.) *(as in road)*Taree'(s-m) Ť$_o$r$_o$'(p), *(as in method)* Taree'$_a$(s-f) Toro'(p)

weather(n.) Ťa'Ŝ(s-m)

week(n.) '$_i$sbooĂ(s-m) asabeeĂ(p)

weight(n.) wazn(s-m) awzén(p)

well(adj.) mneeĥ(m) mneeĥa(f) mnéĥ(p)

well(n.) beer(s-m) byara(p)

west(n.) Ř$_a$rb

western(adj.) Ř$_a$rbé(m) Ř$_a$rbyyé(f) Ř$_a$rbyyeen(p)

wheel(n.) d$_{oo}$léb(s-m) dwéleeb(p)

when 'émta

where wén

whether '$_i$za

which ayya

while b$_a$yn$_a$m$_a$

white(n.) abi$_a$Ď(m) b$_a$yĎ$_a$(f) beeĎ(p)

who meen

why lésh

wide(adj.) Ă$_a$reeĎ(m) Ă$_a$reeĎ$_a$(f) ĂraĎ(p)

wife(n.) m$_a$r$_a$(s-f), n$_i$swén(p)

wild(n.) barré(m) barryyé(f)(p)

will(n.) '$_i$radé(s-f) '$_i$radét(p), waŜyyé(s-f) waŜaya(p)

wind(n.) hawa(s-m)

window(n.) sh$_i$bbék(s-m) shbébeek(p)

wing(n.) gén$_é$ĥ(s-m) gwén$_é$ĥ(p)

winter(n.) sh$_a$twyyé(s-f)

wire(n.) shreeŤ(s-m) shray$_é$Ť(p)

wish(n.) '$_{oo}$mnyé(s-f) améné(p)

with m$_a$Ă

without bidoon

woman(n.) m$_a$r$_a$(s-f) n$_i$swén(p)

wood(n.) Ḱ$_a$sh$_a$b(s=m) aḰshéb(p)

word(n.) k$_i$lmé(s-f) k$_i$lmét(p)

work(n.) shiŘl(s-m) ashŘal(p)

worker(n.) Ă$_a$mél(m) Ăam$_i$lé(f) Ăamlét(p)

world(n.) Aal$_a$m

written(adj.) m$_a$ktoob(m) m$_a$ktoobé(f) m$_a$tktoobeen(p)

wrong(adj.) ŘalaŤ

Ă= Augh in bought	Ď= a heavy D	É= like A in Bay	G= G in beige	ĥ= like an H with smaller air passage	I= I as in ink	Ḱ= like ch in Irish loch
O= O as in home	OO= as in boots	R= roll the rrr	Ť= a heavy T	Ř= like a French R (gargle it)	Ŝ= a heavy S	Ž= a heavy Z

X

Y

year(n.) sin$_é$(s-f) sneen(p)

yellow(n.) aŜf$_a$r(m) S$_a$fr$_a$(f) Ŝ$_i$fr(p)

yes n$_a$Ă$_a$m(p)

yet ʼissa

young(adj.) sh$_a$bb(m) sh$_a$bbé(f) sh$_a$béb(p)

Z

zero(n.) Ŝifr

zone(n.) m$_a$nŤʼ$_a$(s-f) manat$_é$ʼ(p)

zoo(n.) (same)

Ă= Augh in bought	Đ= a heavy D	É= like A in Bay	G= G in beige	ħ= like an H with smaller air passage	I= I as in ink	Ќ= like ch in Irish loch
O= O as in home	OO= as in boots	R= roll the rrr	Ť= a heavy T	Ř= like a French R (gargle it)	Ŝ= a heavy S	Ž= a heavy Z

Printed in the USA
CPSIA information can be obtained
at www.ICGtesting.com
LVHW061930190124
769037LV00016B/21